Patty,
love you.

DOROTHY DAY

Dorothy Day

A BIOGRAPHY

William D. Miller

1817

Harper & Row, Publishers, San Francisco

Cambridge, Hagerstown, New York, Philadelphia
London, Mexico City, São Paulo, Sydney

FIRST EDITION

Designer: Jim Mennick

Library of Congress Cataloging in Publication Data

Miller, William D., 1916–
  DOROTHY DAY : A BIOGRAPHY.

  Includes index.
  1. Day, Dorothy, 1897–   . 2. Catholics—United States—Biography. 3. Catholic Worker Movement. I. Title.
BX4705.D283M54 1982   267'.182'0924 [B]   81-47428
ISBN 0-06-065752-8   AACR2

---

82 83 84 85 86 10 9 8 7 6 5 4 3 2 1

To my mother,
Verna Sharp Miller,
and to the memory of her mother and father,
Clara and Dell Sharp,
and the memory of her brother and sister,
Uncle Bill and Aunt Carol

Contents

Preface

THIS CAN hardly be called an authorized biography—not authorized by Dorothy Day or by anyone in her family. I began to think of this book in 1970 as I was finishing *A Harsh and Dreadful Love,* a history of the Catholic Worker movement. The book had a strong biographical line in it, but then, as I saw it, how could anyone write a history of the Worker movement without having Dorothy at the center of it? Otherwise, this book said what the Worker movement was and gave an account of its life. But there was another story, the story of Dorothy, and as I got some understanding of its character I began to think that it had the elements of an epic tale, unmatched by any other in recent times.

So I wrote to Dorothy and asked her if I could do her biography. She responded promptly. Yes, she said. Somebody would do it, and she preferred that it be I, that I was a convert and that I understood her. I was, of course, delighted, and began to think of getting to work on the subject. Within two weeks the flame of my delight, as someone with a poetic fancy might say, was reduced to ashes. Dorothy did not want a biography. She would have no biography, and I should assure her that I would conform to her wishes. Well, Dorothy was Dorothy and I had my own point of view, and because I was under no vow of obedience to her, I did not give the requested assurance—then or ever.

Dorothy's resistance to a biography came, as I saw it, from two factors. She said that she was afraid that the errant conduct of her youthful years might be cited by some as an excuse for others to do likewise. "If Dorothy Day did it, why not I?" This did not make sense to me. The whole of Dorothy's life does not suggest to anyone that she or he should go and sin for a while in order to be good. It powerfully suggests the contrary.

The other reason, it seems to me, that Dorothy resisted the thought of a biography was that it represented a placing of her life into someone else's hands—and that she could not abide. She justified her attitude by saying that she had written all that was necessary to be said about herself. Besides, she may have thought, who could ever tell her story? But for reasons I shall mention shortly, I wonder if, while still protesting, she may not have accepted the idea and even collaborated with it?

And then there have been others, expressing a solicitude for her interest, who said that it would be better if certain episodes in her life were left untold—or at least not told for another quarter century or so. This would be true if anyone now living were to be hurt by their telling. But even on this point, it seems to me that the whole story is better than any of its parts.

In one of her last letters to me, Dorothy said that she hoped that nothing would be written about her until after she had died. Now she is history, and Dorothy is not the issue. The issue is history, and because she confronted history, history will want to deal with her. As for the proposition that it would be better to wait twenty-five years before the story is told, my reaction is that to wait twenty-five years now is like a wait of several centuries if the subject had come up fifty years ago. The process of history is accelerating so rapidly that waiting ten years is like dropping it off the tailgate of time where it is lost and forgotten.

Why should it be I who writes about her? Because I believe I have the substance. I do not think the meaning of Dorothy can be found in any of the current fads of personal analysis that are popular in some instances in biographical writing. She cannot be made to fit into the generalizations of the social historians and, most of all, she cannot be psychologically dissected so that all of her psychic components add up to anything but a flat plain view of her.

Her passion was a primal one. It was to end time because her longing was for eternity, to cast off mortality for immortality, and to tear down all the walls that separated person from person. Her passion was God. And because I have been associated with the profession of history too long to be anything but skeptical about the succession of interpretive "truths" that have passed in the flow of historical thought and writing during my days, I consider myself free from a kind of blinding intellectual vassalage. Ideas such as "eternity" and "God" do not appall me because of their nonobjective character; yet I do believe that the dogma of our age that "out there" in time and space there is some objective reality, to which the truth can be made to conform, is nonsense. Truth, finally, is not an object. It is *the* subject.

Still, it is through the object that we come to apprehend the subject, and I believe that in this sense I have more of the basic raw material of Dorothy's life than most have—or ever will have, for that matter. In 1965, while teaching history at Marquette University, I wrote to Dorothy to ask her if I might have her approval and cooperation to do a history of the Catholic Worker movement. She said yes, she liked the idea. In fact, she said, she was in the process of sending all of the Catholic Worker papers to the Marquette library. Will Ready, the librarian, had had the foresight to get in his request for these papers before anyone else and because of this, and because Dorothy liked Marquette, its Gesu Church, and the little Abbottcrest Hotel across the street from Gesu, she sent on to Marquette all that she had in the Worker files. It was, on the whole, a considerable amount of material—so much so that it took me over a year to examine it and note it.

In the meantime, I met Dorothy. It was in the spring of 1965. She gave a talk in the large lecture hall of the Marquette Science Building, but because her talk was at a time when I had to teach a class I did not hear it. After my class, though, I met her emerging from the building onto Wisconsin Avenue. I knew immediately who among the crowd was Dorothy Day. She was plainly dressed but her appearance was striking—a large woman with braided, graying hair wound around her head and a white face set off by the long line of her jaw and her slanting eyes.

After this, I saw Dorothy from time to time. She visited our family twice when we lived in the country in Wisconsin. In 1969 we moved to Lloyd, Florida, a country cross-roads settlement whose inhabitants remembered the past and who thought that the present was deformed. From there I commuted twenty miles to Tallahassee, where I taught at Florida State University. In the meanwhile, our family got to know Dorothy better. We visited Tivoli a number of times and then, when I happened to be in New York, I would go to see her at the First Street Worker house.

The Catholic Worker history, *A Harsh and Dreadful Love,* was published by Liveright in 1970. On the whole, Dorothy accepted it very well, though she complained about its subtitle, *Dorothy Day and the Catholic Worker Movement.* Why was her name in the title? This was to be a history of the movement, and so on. I do not know if she ever read it. She said that she did not, but once in a while I would get a letter from her referring to something I had said in it. I weathered that storm in good shape, then ran into another squall over the issue of the biography. I should do a biography of Peter Maurin, she insisted.

For a while I thought I might—that I could placate Dorothy and perhaps tell her story through Maurin. I told Dorothy I would try. But the more I thought about it the more the approach seemed to be too much of a contrivance. The logical way was to tell the Maurin story through Dorothy.

I was confirmed in this view (so I believe) by Dorothy herself in May 1975. She was spending the spring in the Catholic Worker beach cottage. Would I drive up and help her dispose of a lot of papers she had? She had been tempted many times to throw them all in the garbage, to burn them, but she could not bring herself to do it. I could take them and decide myself what to do with them.

I went, of course, setting out from Lloyd one day at noon and driving all night through a rain, reaching Washington the following night. It was still raining. I got to New York the next day at mid-morning and went to the First Street Worker house to get complicated instructions on how to reach Dorothy on the Island. Frank Donovan, the dedicated and obliging manager of Worker affairs, drew a map and gave me the mail to take to Dorothy.

I got to the place shortly after noon. The word shacks would be too mean to label the two houses there, but to call them "beach cottages" would be a little grand. The first place was a small structure on a 30- by 40-feet plot of land. Next to it, poised atop a high embankment that overlooked the bay, was the second house in which Marge Hughes and her son Johnny lived. The embankment, and the house too, looked precariously fragile, for down below the waves from the bay came rolling in over stones and debris to wash away at its base. But the day was bright and mild and if the little shack was going to tumble into the bay it would be a while.

When knocking on the front door of the first house—which I presumed was Dorothy's—brought no response, I walked around to the back yard and there I met her. Her greeting was warm, and shortly we were sitting in Marge Hughes' place, talking as Marge fixed lunch.

That afternoon Dorothy said she wanted to take a ride. She would be the navigator and I, the pilot. First we drove down Hyland Boulevard to the location of St. Joseph's Home, the place

where she had met Sister Aloysia that morning in the spring of
1926 when she was out wheeling her baby daughter in her carriage. Then we drove to Tottenville, several miles away. It was in
the church there that she had been baptized on December 28,
1927. When we got there Dorothy said that she wanted to go in for
a moment—alone—and that I should not take a picture of her. So
she got out of the car and with the help of her cane hobbled across
the street and into the church. The picture, nevertheless, is still in
my mind.

After that, we went to the site of the old Peter Maurin farm.
Then it was to the beach where her first cottage had been and had
burned. She talked about the poem that she, Max Bodenheim, and
Eugene O'Neill had written one night back in 1918 in Jimmy Wallace's saloon. It had burned with the house.

The next afternoon I, as Dorothy had asked, met her in the
small living room of her cottage. There was no sociable conversation to start things. She went straight to the business. First, she led
me into a small adjoining room. On the floor was a wooden chest
with a hasp lock on its top. On the floor beside it were some cardboard cartons. The box contained the journal she had kept over
the years and many family letters. I should take them and do with
them what I thought best, she said.

We moved into the living room. I sat down but Dorothy continued to stand. Walking over to the table, she picked up several
books and turned to me. She held out one book and asked, "what
should I do about this?" I knew the book. It was *The Eleventh Virgin,* her autobiographical novel. "It's all true," she said. It was a
book I knew that she hated and would have rejoiced if every copy
could have been consumed in flames and then be forever put out
of her mind. But now she stood there, holding out to me one of
the few copies left.

I said nothing. Dorothy was controlled, but I could tell by the
pale, taut look in her face that the business of turning all of this
material over to me was a moment of great stress and pain for her.
She was, in a way, confronting history. I spent a year going though
this material. In 1976 I returned to Marquette to teach, placing at
the same time, all of Dorothy's personal material in the Marquette
archives.

Dorothy's published books, the Catholic Worker papers, and
the material I got from her in April 1975 have been my main
sources. There are, to be sure, many other sources that I have

used. Because I have mentioned the principal ones in the text as I used material from them, I see no point in a formal repetition of them here. There is no one left to grade me down for taking liberties with the *Turabian Manual of Style.* The Marquette University Archives has a full bibliographical listing of Dorothy's writings, compiled by Alex Avitabile. Anyone interested in this can, for the cost of postage and duplication, get it from the archives. I understand too, that Anne Klejment, who teaches in the history department at the New York State University at Plattsburgh, will shortly have published a complete bibliographical guide to Dorothy Day and the Worker movement.

I have received generous help from many people who, in one way or another, have contributed to this book. If I mentioned everyone to whom I have talked about Dorothy, especially those people who have been a part of the Catholic Worker movement, it would take another book to contain their names. After all, this study has been going on for fifteen years. Many of their names, though, show up in the book.

Archivists have had a vital part in getting information that I, myself, was unable to find. Mrs. Lee Majors, archivist for the Chicago *Tribune,* somehow or other found material on Lionel Moise that otherwise would have completely escaped me. Maynard Brichford, archivist at the University of Illinois, spent several days getting up material for me that helped immensely to give a picture of Dorothy's student days at the University. Reverend Daniel Berrigan gave me permission to use the extensive depository of his papers in the Cornell University archives. James Tyler, of the Cornell University special collections, searched out the material that was applicable to my subject.

Charles Elston, Marquette University Library archivist, and Phil Runkel, whose special work is the Catholic Worker–Dorothy Day papers, gave me much help. While abiding by every condition placed on the use of these papers, Phil has nonetheless provided me with almost instantaneous information on certain facts that I needed to have to give substance to the story. Whenever someone came to town bearing the credential of a Catholic Worker past, Phil's mother, Mrs. Lydia Runkel, prepared a beatific meal in honor of the guest and invited my wife and me. So I thank her, too.

There are many special aspects of the Catholic Worker story that I have only mentioned. The Marquette University archives can provide anyone interested in working on any part of Worker history a statement of materials available for research.

I have had, in the researching of this work, grants from Marquette University and the Rockefeller Foundation, and I hope this book is worthy of their investment and goodwill.

At a more personal level, I thank Sarah Witte for her dedication to this project. What she did in the way of typing the manuscript was far beyond the ordinary call of duty. But it was not just her typing I appreciate. Sarah is a strong and good person who, in addition to being intelligent, possesses the added grace of having a sense of humor.

I thank Rhea, my wife, and I would like to put something into this statement beyond the customary remarks that constitute the obeisance one makes to one's spouse after completing a book. Rhea and I were married in 1944, one month after I met her. But then why tarry when confronted by beauty, intelligence, and old-fashioned goodness? Besides, she was Southern. She has borne us eight absolutely outstanding children who in turn have had eight of their own, equally good. With Rhea, family has been everything, worth every sacrifice.

So much for hasty marriages. Dorothy once wrote about Rhea in *The Catholic Worker*. She said that Rhea was a "brilliant woman," that Rhea recognized and knew good books, and that she had introduced her to much good reading. She said, further, that because of Rhea our household had an atmosphere of peace about it. So I should be grateful for all of this—as I surely am. Rhea is now an assistant professor at Marquette who sits up until late hours grading English papers. After performing this task, she has, for the past year, been straightening out my own meandering style and putting participles, helplessly dangling, back on safe ground. I thank her for this work, but mostly for our peaceful household, where first things come first.

✹ 1

The Daughter

IN HER extensive autobiographical writing Dorothy Day usually avoided assigning dates to the main events of her life. In her autobiography, *The Long Loneliness,* she does say that she was born at Bath Beach, Brooklyn, on November 8, 1897. She arrived, according to her birth certificate, at 6:50 in the evening in the Day home at 71 Pineapple Street. The location was just a few blocks from the Brooklyn Bridge, the bridge towers surely visible from the house. The dramatic change of her exist ence from the somnolent and all-sufficient life of the womb to a world in which she would have to make her own way took place without complications, although one can hardly doubt that she registered her indignation over the altered state of affairs with a loud bawl. Perhaps she bawled again when she heard that her middle name was "May," because how could anyone ever think that "Dorothy May Day" could sound anything but slightly silly?

If one is to judge from the few times that Dorothy men tioned her father in her books and journals, he appeared not to have entered the concerns of her life at all, although, of course, the opposite may be just as true. She does give him a paragraph in *The Long Loneliness* in which she describes him in a detached manner. "We children did not know him very well, so we stood in awe of him, only learning to talk to him after we had left home and he began to treat us as friends—casual friends it is true, since he was always impatient with our ideas and hated the radical movement in which both my sister and I were involved later.... Probably his greatest unhappiness came from us whose ideas he did not understand and which he thought were subversive and dangerous to the peace of the country."

Although he was described as a "clerk" at the time of Dorothy's birth, his universe was horse-racing, and throughout his subsequent career as a journalist, horse-racing was his subject. In his prime years he wrote a column, "On and Off the Turf," for the old New York *Morning Telegraph*. Later, he was a steward and partner at Hialeah, the first racetrack in Florida, and before his death he served as an inspector for the New York State Commission.

John Day was Scotch-Irish, big-boned and tall, with sandy hair. He was born in Cleveland, Tennessee, in 1870. Some years after his death, one of his Southern nephews, Robert Hunt of Chattanooga, wrote to Dorothy, offering to tell her "what I know of your kinspeople." As a warm-up he gave her some preliminary information. Her grandmother had been a Mary Mee, whose direct family background included the McElwee family. "Your great-great-grandfather was James McElwee," Hunt said. "He fought in the Revolutionary War as a soldier participating in the Battles of King's Mountain, Musgrove's Mill and Guilford Courthouse." Great-great-grandfather McElwee was a kinsman of Daniel Boone and had "accompanied him on either the first or second trip to Tennessee and the first settlement west of the Alleghenys and had helped to survey and lay out the city of Knoxville." Hunt explained his relationship to Dorothy: "Mary Mee and my grandmother, Elizabeth Mee, were sisters." Concluding, Hunt said that he would bet that Dorothy did not know that she was "a D.A.R." (Daughters of the American Revolution). He was correct— or at least if Dorothy knew it, she never mentioned it. Hunt told Dorothy that he would send more family information to her if "you are interested." Apparently she was not, for as Hunt said later, she never answered his letter.

Shortly, though, Hunt was sending a letter to Mrs. Della Spier, Dorothy's sister, "to tell you a few stories for your grandchildren." Hunt could remember Dorothy's grandmother, who was his "Aunt Mary" by virtue of the fact that she and his mother were first cousins. After the death of her husband, Aunt Mary had moved from Cleveland, Tennessee, to Chattanooga and would frequently visit the Hunt household. "She would come to spend the day ... riding a streetcar and walking up the long back steps. She would always announce herself, out of breath, at the ... door, 'It is I, be not afraid.' " Then, continued Hunt, she would "sit down and have me unlace her high-topped shoes. She was a little stocky and had a most pleasant personality."

Soon after the end of the Civil War, this Aunt Mary, who was then Mary Mee, had married Sam Houston Day, a doctor in Cleveland. Born on a farm in Bradley County, Tennessee, on September 10, 1839, he graduated in medicine from "the New York University" in 1861, just as the Civil War was breaking out. Returning home, he enlisted in the Confederate army and served throughout the war as a surgeon in Joe Wheeler's army. In the last year of that conflict, he was wounded three times and spent the last forty days of the war in a prison camp. So Dorothy was not only a "D.A.R.," she was preeminently a "U.D.C."—United Daughters of the Confederacy—but she never laid claim to this latter title either.

Even so, the Days and the Mees represented a family background of which Dorothy should have been proud. Her great-great-grandfather, Isaac Day, had moved into the Cleveland area in 1835 and had been involved in the organization of churches and schools there. For the memory of her grandfather, Samuel Houston Day, she might have had a special reverence, because she shared with him a sensitivity to the claims of the dispossessed for their right to life. The account in the Cleveland newspaper of Dr. Day's life and death depicts him as a good man. "He had a larger acquaintance than any person in the county," the article read, "and wherever known he was honored, respected and loved. To the poor and humble he was equally as ready to attend as the rich and prosperous. He rode around day and night."

The funeral services were held at the Cumberland Presbyterian Church, and every business house was closed that day from ten in the morning until noon. "Thousands of persons" followed the procession to the cemetery, the paper said, adding that "one touching gesture of the exercises were 300 children of the colored schools of the city marching to and past the residence with uncovered heads, as a tribute to one who had done much for the upbuilding of their schools."

The obituary noted that the funeral services had been delayed a day or so to provide time for a son, John I. Day, to travel from New York to attend the funeral. Whatever reflections son John had on his father's death, as the train bore him southward, are, of course, not known. But it is likely that he knew better than to expect a bequest from his father because there was little to bequeath. "He died a much loved but poor man," Hunt wrote. "When I knew Aunt Mary she was penniless." But there was money on the Mee side of the family, Hunt said, and it was the disposition of some of this wealth at the death of one Columbus Mee that caused a rupture in the family. When Columbus died "he divided the estate between certain members of the family and the Campbellite Church, infuriating other members of the Mee family. Dorothy's side was left out."

Perhaps it was hearing her father lash out at some of her Southern relatives that caused Dorothy in the course of her lifetime not to seek them out and affirm the bonds of her family. Once, in a piece she wrote for the magazine *Jubilee,* her comments concerning her father and his Southern kinsmen were most ungenerous. "My own father was ... intemperate in his remarks about the 'foreigner' and about the Negro, coming from Tennessee as he did, and there were my Georgia cracker cousins, hardshelled Baptists, fundamentalists, Campbellites, religious bigots and racists undoubtedly."

The degree to which "Uncle Clum's" selective disposition of his estate lacerated the feelings of John Day is shown in a letter he wrote to one of his Southern relatives on October 7, 1937. Day wrote the letter on the occasion of the death of his sister, but rather than being consumed with grief over her passing, he used these words to damn his Uncle Columbus.

When I arrived back from the race track last night I got the telegram from Clem, telling me of Margaret's passing. I won't say that I was shocked, for I don't believe anything would shock me. Time has made me even tougher than your Uncle Clum . . . (you are welcome to all my share of the kinship, and I certainly don't hope he's resting easily beyond the alleged pearly gates), but I still am satisfied that I'm more of a human and even more of a Christian than he ever was, even if I am an atheist. However, to hell with him, if there is such a place.

This opening paragraph in a letter purporting to comment on the passing of one's sister is startling, but then it is very much in character with John Day, and to explain the letter one must try to explain him. He was, certainly, an oddity, an eccentric. When Hunt was asked to characterize Day, he responded immediately: "He was gruff, surly, smart, respected. Just about everybody referred to him as 'Judge Day.' He had the confidence of the people like the New York Giant's manager, John McGraw, and Al Smith. He also drank."

Day, as everyone is to some degree, was a role-player. That he played his roles so inflexibly might indicate how strongly certain images of himself attracted him. His type was recognizable in the rural South—the frontier atheist who scoffed at the sometimes ludicrous excesses of the revival meeting and who recognized the hypocrisy of sharp-dealing, money-grabbing types that cloaked their grasping in public declamations of piety. He doubtless thought of his Uncle Columbus in this respect. The extravagance of speech was likewise a role—that of the "character" who sat in the barber's chair on a Saturday morning and amused the countrymen in town for a haircut with his verbal assaults on the super-pious.

Why these poses? Why did he declare himself an atheist and remain a stranger to his children? One suspects that he suffered from a basic spiritual short-circuitry—that he was paralyzed and turned inside out by a demon, the Great Fear. There were no answers; so to avoid being trapped and deluded, one stood away from it all and affirmed nothing. So he was the scoffer, the denier.

But something one must affirm. He affirmed the racetrack and the bottle, and, above all, the woman he married. Otherwise his character was composed of the frontier and Calvin. He would do his duty to his children and fulfill his commitments to the end. He may have declared himself an atheist for its shock effect on the overly credulous, as well as to preserve himself against the intrusion of affecting and debilitating sentiments, but as Dorothy wrote toward the end of her own life, "My father carried a Bible with him always." With him, it may have been a talisman, to stand at last between him and those great questions that were still there, even though he denied that there were answers. When his life was over, he could at least present to his creator, if there were one, this evidence of his fidelity to that bedrock of truth affirmed by his Presbyterian ancestors.

Grace Day, Dorothy's mother, is a familiar figure in Dorothy's writings. "Mother Grace" (as she was actually called) is central in Dorothy's wholly autobiographical novel, *The Eleventh Virgin,* and she also appears with some frequency in Dorothy's journals as well as her other published writing. Dorothy was close to her mother, and during those years of young womanhood when Dorothy was pursuing a tortured and willful course, her mother was as close to her as her father was distant.

"Mother Grace" was born Grace Satterlee in Marlboro, New York, in 1870. Dorothy once characterized her mother as having great natural virtues and a delightful temperament that helped her through much hardship and uncertainty. She refused to worry when things were going badly, or when the family had its periods of poverty. There were days when she had to do the family washing, the sheets, blankets, and all, and after a day in the basement laundry, she used to bathe and dress as though she were going to a "dinner party." And a dinner party it was, for "she reigned over the supper table as a queen, powdered, perfumed, daintily clothed. . . ." She loved life "and all the gayeties and frivolities of life, but when through poverty she was deprived of 'good times' she made them for herself and got enjoyment from little things."

Once, after a visit with her mother's sister, Alice, Dorothy noted in her journal some of the things her aunt had told her about the Satterlee family. Great-great-grandfather Satterlee had come from England as the captain of a whaler, settling in Wappinger Falls, New York. Captain Satterlee, some time in the course of his fortunes and misfortunes, married Charity Hummel Washburn, a widow, presumably. Satterlee had sailed up the Hudson with a cargo of whale oil and "had fallen from a mast and cracked his head and was never quite right after that, running down Delafield Street in his night shirt and finally drowning in a brook." "Cracked" head notwithstanding, Captain Satterlee begat a son, Napoleon Bonaparte. With a name like that, how could he not join the forces of the Union when Lincoln made his first call for volunteers?

At the age of eighty, Dorothy provided a continuation of this story in her "On Pilgrimage" column in the *Catholic Worker*. "I remember my mother telling us children at the supper table when she was a little girl and lived in Poughkeepsie [how] the river froze over solid so that you could walk to the other shore. And how her father [Napoleon Bonaparte] had been wounded in the Civil War and a gash in his throat kept him from speaking above a whisper." Napoleon was captured during the war, and when it was over and he could come home, he had gotten tuberculosis in the larnyx, presumably from his wound. Never strong afterwards, he became a chairmaker, married "Anna," and with the consolations of a good wife and six children, he enjoyed the additional felicity of an occasional eggnog made "strengthening" with whiskey. It was the duty of his little daughter, Grace, to fetch him his medicine, which she did, sipping it as she carried it to him. If this were not recompense enough, her father would designate her a Lady and call her "Graceful."

These light touches in Napoleon's life were few. He suffered much and died in 1879 when "Graceful" was nine. When she was twelve, she had to go to work in a shirt factory. Then an aunt thought that the family of seven might be due something from the government because of Napoleon's service, and after inquiries were made and forms filled out, a pension was obtained. Grace left the shirt factory, returned to school, and then went to Eastman's Business School in New York City. It was there in New York, apparently, that she met John Day. They married at the old Episcopal church on Perry Street in Greenwich Village.

It seems that the new couple did not give favorable consideration to the idea of "family planning" because the first three children came at ten-month intervals: Donald in 1895, Sam Houston in 1896, and then Dorothy. These two brothers were never close to Dorothy, and in all of her writings she infrequently mentioned Donald and never mentioned Sam. Yet both had reputable careers as journalists. Of all the Day children, and there were five of them, Sam appears as the one who achieved the goal of middle-class security and suburban respectability that John Day took as the measure of success for his children. He even made it into *Who's Who,* a recognition of his long years and managerial record in the field of journalism. Born on September 2, 1896, in Brooklyn, he went to Waller High School after the family moved to Chicago. When the First World War came, he joined the navy. Sometime in this period, during his two years in the service or just after, he married a Chicago high school sweetheart. The son they had, once described by John Day as a promising boy, died of polio. The sad denouement of this tragedy was divorce. Sam Day married again and advanced as a newspaperman. In 1928, he went with the New York *Journal American* and, in 1942, became its managing editor, a position he held until his retirement in 1961.

Like his father, Sam believed in hard work and the American Way, and like his father, too, he enjoyed sports and the outdoors, although he was preeminently a fisherman rather than a devotee of the racetrack. He wrote occasional fiction for magazines under the name of Houston Day, which, it must be admitted, sounds more literary than Sam Day. Dorothy's radicalism must have disturbed him, and, as Dorothy later confessed, so did her disposition to "bare the soul of the family," in her autobiographical writing.

As long as John Day was alive it was his feeling that his son, Donald, would be the success story in the Day family, and for a while it looked as if he would be right. Donald, born in 1895, grew to be a large, strapping youth with a taste for adventure. The first of the three Day children to graduate from Chicago's Waller High

School, he got into newspaper work even before he graduated. Personable and intelligent, he advanced quickly. By the age of twenty-three, he was sports editor of the New York *Journal American*. But then there was the war, and young Day, seeking a more glamorous and daring branch of the service, joined the naval air force. His machine never dove on the enemy. His service was that of an observer in a plane that patrolled the coastal waters off New England, looking for submarines. It was a boring business, except for the three times his craft fell into the sea, although each time he escaped unscathed. In World War II, when Donald, as a *Chicago Tribune* foreign correspondent, took a strong anti-Soviet position, his journalistic career ended. Fired by the *Tribune,* he lived out his remaining days in Europe.

Beyond the years of their youth, there was little that Donald and Dorothy shared in the way of family closeness. When it is all summed up, though, they were alike in one respect: both were bound to follow their courses, no matter what.

Two years after Dorothy was born, her sister Della arrived, and the two, quite different in temperament, had an unusual sisterly closeness that was lifelong. Their difference was that Dorothy was a seeker, while Della, kind and agreeable, was content to live with life as she found it. She probably never understood Dorothy's need for a religious answer to the problem of existence, nor cared much about it, yet neither did Della try to change her or do anything but try to moderate the tempests in Dorothy's life by her own calming and good-natured presence.

These were the four Day children born in Brooklyn, all except Della crowding on one another and making a lot of work for Mother Grace. So the family got help, a servant, and for John Day, at least, what better indication was there of the upward-bound character of his life than to have an Irish girl, who "lived in," to attend the family? She was known to the children in their Brooklyn years as "the girl," but her name was Mary Manley and she slept in Dorothy's room. Years later, Dorothy got in touch with Miss Manley, who probably was surprised to know that her onetime charge had become a Catholic. She told Dorothy that she had taken her to Mass one Sunday and that the child had revealed no special signs of piety; rather, she had stood in the pew and gawked at the people around her. That was the last of Dorothy's church-going for a while.

What registered in the experiences and sense impressions of

the child in this period of dawning consciousness that she would later remember? For when one is old, what remains always new and timeless but the memories of early childhood? In her later years Dorothy would return to these memories with pleasure again and again. There was playing on the beach (there was a beach then, a block or so from the house) and running away with a younger cousin to an abandoned shack near Fort Hamilton. One sunny afternoon she adventured off alone, walking down sidewalks, hearing sounds from afar which, in the stillness of the summer heat, pierced her senses, to indelibly stamp themselves into her consciousness. It was an experience of serene pleasure until suddenly the anonymity of the outside world took on the dark character of evil, and she turned and ran home. She remembered an experience from the first grade in Brooklyn: how in the morning all in the class would recite the Our Father. She remembered the smell of the varnish on the desk as she bent low her head, and the circle of moisture her breath made on the desk. She recalled no feeling of piety attached to this action, but it is easy to see her sensing the ritual of the moment, bowing her head profoundly and quickly.

Aside from that primitive sense of the polarities of good and evil that confront existence, the child had no religious sense of the order of things, nor was she instructed in any. To be sure, all the Day children had been taught their "Now I lay me down to sleep," but beyond that, their parents had ignored the subject. John Day had been reared a Congregationalist, and Grace, an Episcopalian, but both seemed to feel that talking about religion was, as Dorothy said later, "like baring your soul." Neither parent ever went to church, and none of the children were baptized. John Day, the professional skeptic, would have nothing to do with such matters, and Grace, ever disposed to accept his view of things, took no action on her own.

In 1904, John Day, who was never loath to take a venture, and who, likely, had always wanted to write, moved the family to California where he had gotten a newspaper job reporting racetrack news. The first stop was Berkeley, where a furnished house was rented until the family furniture could be brought around the Horn. It was in this house that Dorothy had her first sense of a religious feeling. One rainy Sunday afternoon she went up to the attic, finding a Bible there, "the first Bible I had ever seen," she later recounted. That she spent several hours reading it is not surprising, since she had been reading since she was four years old.

Later, she could remember nothing of what she had read, but she did have a "sense of holiness in holding the book in my hands. I did not know then that the Word in the Book and Word in the flesh of Christ's humanity were the same, but I felt I was handling something holy."

When the furniture arrived, the Days moved into a bungalow in Oakland that was close to Idora Park and near a racetrack. Life must have seemed good then to John Day. He was young and vigorous, and over at the track he would have been regarded as one of the chief "characters" at a place where the type abounded. He liked the fellowship of those who lived by racing, even the down-and-outers who hung on, hoping for that golden moment when they could recoup not only all of what had been lost, but a kingdom to boot. To them, the crusty and profane Day, pulling at his bottle occasionally, could deliver oracular pronouncements with allusions to Shakespeare and the Bible, that made them feel that "the judge" could put them on to something. Perhaps they were right. John Day studied his craft; he knew horselore. At the Oakland track he kept his own horse stabled, and no doubt he took Donald and Sam there frequently. But if he ever took Dorothy, she never mentioned it. Besides, she was afraid of animals.

There were, to be sure, other things that interested her—reading books. When she was seven, she read Martha Finley's *Elsie Dinsmore,* the story of a little Southern girl, born into the high style of plantation life. At the age of four, little Elsie had been converted by her slave "mammy," and thereafter the story ranged over Elsie's various sufferings incurred from the insensitivity and unsaved character of her father, young and imperious Horace Dinsmore. The crisis came when father Horace ordered Elsie to play the piano for guests one Sunday afternoon, but Elsie, mindful that it was the Sabbath, refused to play anything but hymns. It was, in effect, a trial laid upon this saintly creature as to whether she would obey the will of her Heavenly father or that of her earthly father, and though the tears dropped ceaselessly from her long dark lashes, she refused to play. At last, she toppled from the piano stool in a faint and contracted "brain fever." Horace, in the agony of wondering whether his daughter would survive, saw the error of his way and repented. Elsie, of course, pulled through—for volumes more, in fact.

Dorothy may have admired Elsie's sanctity, but she was no Elsie.

Elsie eventually did get around to the subject of boys, but Dorothy got to it very early. Even before leaving Brooklyn she knew that between girls and boys there was a difference, and therein lay something exciting and attractive, ending in what, she did not know. She talked about it with her brothers, and together they laughed at their naughtiness in discussing it. The subject had two aspects, one lofty and the other immediate and physical. At the age of eight she confronted both. "I remember," she wrote years later, "passing a note to a little boy in school saying 'I love you' and the teacher keeping us both after school and probing us both to find the wickedness that my simple words were not meant to convey. I had merely thought he was beautiful."

On the other hand, she remembered children "who talked dirty and one little boy especially. We had been making tunnels through a field of thistles (we ate the semi-hard core in the center of the prickley green and purple flower). Sometimes we found what we liked to consider rooms in those sheltered recesses among the weeds. It was like living in a green sea, a shallow sea with sunlight sifting through, with the odor of the earth, and the hum of insects and the drowsy heat all around us. In one of these rooms this one boy, he might have been ten or so, wanted to 'play house, mama and papa,' but this was an intrusion on my happy mind, and I rejected him."

In another account of this episode, she says that the boy "wanted to caress me, but I avoided him, sensing something 'not right,' but not deeply concerned about it, nor shocked." This same story is related in her novel, *The Eleventh Virgin*. The boy this time was fourteen rather than ten, and he did more than just suggest some mamma-papa-type public caressing. He "took her in his arms and kissed her, pressing himself up against her." One suspects, though, that this latter account was written to help sell the book, and that she wrote her later journal accounts to give a more accurate statement of what actually happened.

She remembered another occasion in California when she was made aware of sex. "Once when our parents went on a vacation we were left to the care of a young woman who lived in a slum not so far but that she could run home in the afternoon, taking me and my sister with her. I only knew it as a slum because the rooms were tiny and papered with comic strips and full page pictures of handsome youths and beauties of the nineties . . . with bulging bosoms and protuberant buttocks and bustles to accentuate them. This was no pious household and the girl and her friends indulged in lewd remarks and gestures."

Such encounters with sex were unremarkable, the usual incidents in the development of a normal child and probably a lot healthier in the long run, and certainly more interesting, than had Grace Day explained to her daughter "where little girls come from." Mother Grace was not of a generation nor of a disposition to have comfy little discourses with her children on this subject.

An occasion of thievery and deception wrenched little Dorothy's conscience considerably. Once she took a nickel from her mother's purse, and on another occasion she sold a schoolbook for a dime—all to buy candy. Immersed in the deepest gloom over this wrongdoing, she finally confessed it to her mother.

It seems that this child could at times be a hellion. When teased by her brothers, she would strike back with a cold, white-lipped fury, biting and kicking with an exercise of name-calling that made tough little boys glow with admiration. Grace, aghast at one performance, washed out her daughter's mouth with soap and water, a folk-approved remedy for this problem.

Yet Dorothy, now eight years old, could put on a show of great piety, perhaps affected to some degree. Next door to the Day house lived the Reed family, a widowed mother and her children who kept a grocery store that had a small apartment in the rear. One of the girls, Naomi, was Dorothy's age, and soon Dorothy was going to church and Sunday school with the family. The Reeds were Methodists, and in the fashion of Methodists, hymns like "In the Garden" and "The Old Rugged Cross" were sung with feeling, while "Beulah Land" could be rendered with great force. Dorothy loved the singing and loved the Reeds, and shortly she was trying to emulate them in those ways that seemed to make them so special to her as a family. She knelt by her bed at night to say her prayers and sung hymns too, but she never felt that she was one of them. She was of her own family, and not one of her own family ever went to church or invoked the name of God with reverence. She asked her mother why they did not pray and sing hymns, and got no answer that satisfied her. What could her mother say—that John Day thought that churches and hymn singing were a lot of bunk and that the end of existence was nothing? Scarcely.

Like father, like daughter. The nothingness was there for Dorothy, too. "My childhood fears were concerned with the awfulness of God and I often had a nightmare of a monstrous being beating a batter in a huge bowl, a noise which got louder and louder until I woke up to find my mother sitting beside me, holding my hand, for I had cried out." In *The Long Loneliness,* she says that it was at the time of her association with the Reeds that she "began to be afraid of God, of death, of eternity. As soon as I closed my eyes at night the blackness of death surrounded me. I believed and yet was afraid of nothingness. . . . If I fell asleep God became in my ears a great noise. . . ." God, she thought, was a "tremendous Force, a frightening impersonal God." She wondered later if her mother had associated these nightmares with her newfound piety. If so, she said nothing about it.

Whatever the case, the association with the Reeds was short-lived. Little Naomi stopped playing with little Dorothy because the latter had been heard calling her brother a "bad name." It was during a dispute as to who owned some guinea pigs, one that culminated with Dorothy's throwing handy objects at her brother. Mother Reed forbade her daughter to play with the bad Day girl and extended no more invitations to Dorothy to attend church. What matter? "I took refuge with a tough gang of kids who ran to Idora Park, who stayed out after dark and didn' t mind their mothers; and I had a very good time indeed." As for being "saved," the thought ceased to bother her. She did not want to be saved, anyway, unless her family could be included.

The family, on the whole, was doing all right. Grace had four healthy and intelligent children, none of whom had any problems, with perhaps the exception of Dorothy, who was a little "impressionable," as they used to say. They lived in a comfortable house, across the street from a vacant lot, and the air was scented with the odor of smoke from brush fires beyond the hills.

One evening, Mother Grace, on the way to the bathroom, fainted on the floor of Dorothy's room, and John Day carried her back to bed. One can only speculate on what ailed her, but it could have been one of the miscarriages that seemed to have frequently occurred with her. Several evenings later, a sultry one, people recalled, John Day went to the track to see about his horse. He noticed that the horses were nervous, stamping about, tossing their heads and snorting. Something was wrong, he thought. The next morning, April 18 at 5:13, there occurred a monstrous shuddering of the earth that lasted for more than a full minute. Dorothy remembered the windmill in back of the house, with a water tank up in its framework, rocking back and forth, spilling water on the rooftop over her head. John took the two boys out of the house, and Grace carried Della to the yard. Because her mother was still ill, Dorothy later wondered how she had had the strength to carry her sister.

Who carried out Dorothy? No one. Her brass bed rolled back and forth across the floor, chandeliers fell, and the walls cracked, but she was not frightened. When the ruckus subsided, she walked out to join the family.

In Oakland things were not so bad, but in San Francisco half the city lay in ruins, and fires raged uncontrollably because the water mains had been ruptured. Fifty thousand people left San Francisco and many came by ferry across the bay to camp at Idora Park and the racetrack. So far as John Day was concerned, his life in California was over. The plant that printed his newspaper had burned, and abruptly he decided to go East. Selling their furniture for cash, within days the family was on the train for Chicago.

Over a half-century later, Dorothy, on a visit to Chicago, was riding with a friend, Nina Polcyn, and with Nina driving, they decided to go along Cottage Avenue to Thirty-seventh Street, the location of the flat the Day family lived in when they first came to Chicago. It was still there, "that long block of flats, three stories high, and there is still the apartment with one window looking out to the lake, where my sister and I used to draw pictures, and write stories and dress our dolls." The place was so drab that after Dorothy started to school and made friends, some of whom lived on the more prestigeous Ellis Avenue, she would, when walking home, turn into the doorway of an apartment house, pretending that it was where she lived rather than in a flat over a saloon. "We had our first taste of poverty there," she recalled.

There was poverty, and it was Mother Grace that led the fight against it. For lunch, the family ate potato soup and for supper, it was bread, bananas, tea, and jelly. Dorothy shopped for the bananas. "Get dead ripe ones," her mother would say. "They ought to be only ten cents a dozen." And if she could not get them for ten cents at one place, she must try another.

Her mother got cast-off remnants, made dining room and living room curtains out of them, and hung them over fishing rods. She made bookcases out of orange crates and kitchen stools out of nail kegs. Without a sewing machine, she made shirts for the men in the family and dresses for the girls. "I can still see the sheen of our ginghams," Dorothy related years later, "pale blue and pink, and feel the flowered challis. Linen, wool and cotton were the only things in 'good taste' for little girls, and all our clothes were beautifully made and laundered no matter how poor we were."

Grace worked at projects to relieve for her daughters the drabness of living in a row tenement. Behind each flat was a large porch, each of which had a gate that led to a passageway running behind the row. Walking along this passageway, Dorothy could see other porches with their boxes of flowers and, sometimes, playthings for some children Dorothy knew. Grace noticed this, too, and she saw that these little girls were having afternoon tea parties on their porches and not inviting anyone to them. She scrubbed the porch, put out a rug, table, and chairs, and heaped the table with oatmeal cookies and molasses candy. Not only invited were the two girls, so exclusive about their parties, but six other children as well. When Dorothy wanted a doll, her mother took some clothespins and scraps and made several of them, all having buttonhole mouths and faces of different characters created by an adept use of crayons.

Still, after a difficult day of scrubbing floors and laundering in the common laundry in the basement of the tenement, she would dress up for the evening. It was a ritual in which Dorothy was privileged to assist. The girl would draw the bath, put a drop of cologne in it, and then lay out the towels and her mother's treasured silk kimono with the storks and flowers embroidered on it. After the bath, her mother would rest for fifteen minutes while Dorothy took charge of Della, playing on the back porch. Then came the dressing: brushing the hair, as her mother lamented through teeth that clenched hairpins: "Oh, dear, oh dear, won't it *ever* get all gray?" In her late thirties, Grace was proud of her hair, which, when done up, made a white circle around her face. Her hair done, she would powder her neck and shoulders and dab a little rouge on her cheeks. The toilet was completed with a touch of perfume to her eyebrows and behind her ears, with a final touch of it bestowed on the front of Dorothy's frock.

One day, though, Grace broke. Perhaps there had been an unpleasant scene with a bill collector threatening to take away their furniture. Shameful though it had been for all of them, John Day had had to buy furniture "on time," and sometimes they were late with their payments. It was after supper, while doing dishes, that Grace broke into hysterics and, one by one, slammed the dishes on the floor. Coming up behind her, John Day tried to hold her, saying "Grace, now Grace dear." But the slamming and screaming continued, and brother Sam herded all the children into the bedroom and told them to get down on their knees and pray. They did, except Donald, who sat grim-faced and pretended to continue his reading.

Finally it ended, with Grace lying on the bed, shaking and weak. Trying to revive the spirits of his children, John Day sent out for ice cream, but Dorothy could eat none. She sat and wept—wept for her mother and for her father, wept for her father especially, because he did not know what to do; he did not understand, and his attempt to restore good feeling in the household by getting ice cream had been so clumsy.

The next morning Grace was calm, and all she said was that she had lost her nerve. Part of the problem was poverty, but not all of it. John Day must have been a good deal of it. He was the "head" of the family, a role which he inflexibly affirmed for himself, but he was like a general who removes himself from the scene of battle to better plan the advance that only his vision can comprehend. It was Grace who executed the orders, who stood between him and the children, who probably met the bill collector at the door, and who still, at the end of the day, would bathe and perfume herself to keep up appearances for the children and be attractive to her husband.

When the family got to Chicago, there was no job for John Day. So he decided that, until he could get back into the newspaper business, he would write a novel of "adventure," one which he hoped, and apparently so assured the family, would be a "bestseller." He would recast misfortune into fortune. Daily he sat in a Morris chair in the living room and worked at a typewriter on a table leaf positioned over the arm of the chair. Beside the typewriter was a package of cigarettes and a dish that was quickly filled with stubbed-out butts. Likely as not, a glass with whiskey in it was there, too, for as Dorothy observed, "Father usually has the smell of whiskey about him." The novel, if it was ever finished, was not published, although John did seem to manage some small income for the family by selling short pieces, probably stories or articles about racing and the racetrack.

His presence at home meant tension, and it was Grace's job to keep the children away from him and herself at hand. "He always wanted to be alone with her, "Dorothy wrote in *The Eleventh Virgin*. When he was home, Grace seemed to become "infected by his formal attitude towards his offspring; or perhaps she was afraid of incurring his wrath against her and them, by her usual show of affection." There was, for example, the time when Dorothy and Della, having finished the Sunday dishes, decided to make some fudge. They decided not to ask their mother, since "she can't say yes in front of father. He'd just begin to talk about pampering." Thinking that they were safe, since their mother and father were two rooms removed, they began the operation. "After it had boiled for a few minutes, and the smell began to permeate the house and fill the girls with apprehension, Mother Grace came out, clad in the loose negligee which she affected around the house, and asked them what they were doing." When told, she ordered them to desist and then "sailed away, leaving a faint odor of lavender and violets behind her."

For John Day, Grace was not only wife, but courtesan and handmaid as well. It was a heavy load for her, yet there is no indication she bore any resentment toward him. There was no bickering or nagging and no appealing to the children for support in a grievance against him. She had erupted the one time the pressure had become too much. She had "lost her nerve." The fault was hers.

In *The Long Loneliness*, Dorothy says that her childhood "was a happy time." Happy?—living in a row tenement above a saloon, unable to bring friends home because it interfered with her father's privacy? Yes, her father's peculiarities notwithstanding, there was, she said, some underlying sense of security in the family relationship. She and Della were close, exchanging confidences, especially at night before they went to sleep in the double bed they shared. By the time she was ten, she and Della were regularly helping their mother with housework. Yet it seemed to her, she wrote later, that she and her sister had much time to themselves. For Dorothy the child, as for Dorothy the adult, time was never oppressive. It was used for imagining, for knowing herself, and for reading. It must have been while the family was still living on Thirty-seventh Street that she read Elizabeth Wetherell's *The Wide, Wide World* and *Queechy*, both of which had been first published during the Civil War. Years later, she recalled how she had loved these books "for their religious feeling," and the dignity with which they had endowed work.

On Thirty-seventh Street, Dorothy's religious feeling surfaced again. In the evenings, after the dishes were done, she would visit one of the "porch children," as she called her acquaintances who lived in the row tenements. This girl, little Lenore Clancey, was several years older than Dorothy and was a Catholic. The oldest in a family of nine children, she spent most of her time helping with the housework, but in the evening she was allowed time to play. Too tired to play, she and Dorothy would lie on the open back porch, and Lenore would tell Dorothy about her religion. Lying there, looking at the gleaming stars, and breathing the warm air laden with the dusky odor of the alley below, Dorothy was caught in a spell through which moved saints, angels, and the Virgin Mary. Lenore also gave Dorothy the story of a saint to read, "Saint Pelagia," Dorothy's birthday saint. So every time that Dorothy was threatened with a whipping, which she seemed to have gotten with fair regularity, she prayed to Saint Pelagia to avert the catastrophe. But of course it was not averted, especially whenever she was caught swimming with her brothers in Lake Michigan.

Nonetheless, the mood of piety was heavy upon her, and one hot night, "when the hurdy-gurdies were playing in the street and the call of the 'hot tamale' man and the voices of the passersby kept the night alive," Dorothy decreed that she and Della should sleep on the floor to emulate the austerities of those saints who ate bread and water, and slept on the bare stone floor of their cells. "And every night the smell of beer and whiskey came up in waves from the saloon below, and the Drunken Lady who lived in the flat above fell into bed and snorted and groaned with the heat all night."

One day, though, the subject of religion was brought before the whole family in a more formal way. A "Doctor Wilson," pastor of an Episcopalian Church on Cottage Grove Avenue and Thirty-seventh Street, had heard that Grace Day had been reared as an Episcopalian. He called on the family, thinking to have a conference with John that might result in the whole family's being brought into the fold. John, busy with his novel and with a highball on his typing board, found himself at a disadvantage and was slow to counter with appropriate quotations from Tom Paine and Colonel Bob Ingersoll. Possibly in this vulnerable condition he agreed to permit his children to attend services. So the four children did attend, and Donald and Sam sang in the choir. As Dorothy observed with pleasure, they wore surplices. She also noted that she was "much attracted to a blond boy soprano soloist." But it was not just to admire the boy soprano that she went to church. She came to love the Psalms and the prayers. "I had never heard anything as beautiful as the *Benedictus* and the *Te Deum*. The words have remained with me ever since." The Psalms, as they would in her later years, spoke to the depths of those feelings that could stir her—"whenever I felt the beauty of the world ... in the material universe around me, or glimpsed it in human love, I wanted to cry out with joy." This cry that she wanted to give, in joy or in grief, she found uttered in the Psalms.

When Dorothy was ten, her father got a job as the sports editor of a Chicago newspaper, *The Inter Ocean*. Shortly the family moved into a better neighborhood, first on Oakwood Boulevard and then to a house on the North Side. In the years that Dorothy lived with the family in Chicago, the Days moved four times. In each of the two moves after Thirty-seventh Street, the stay must have been of short duration, because neither residence seemed to have left a significant impression on Dorothy's memory. When she was thirteen, though, the family moved to a large house on Webster Avenue near Lincoln Park, and in *The Long Loneliness,* Dorothy draws an idyllic picture of life there. In addition to a sufficient number of bedrooms, the house had a library, in the center of which was a large table illuminated by a gas lamp. There in the evening, Donald, Sam, Dorothy, Della, and Grace would sit in five chairs, with their backs to the table so the light would shine over their shoulders. "Often we made hot cocoa over the fire before we went to bed. We burned huge lumps of soft coal that hissed and sputtered and sent out blue and rose flames. To draw the curtains at night on a street where people bent against the wind, and where a steady whirl of snowflakes blurred the outlines of trees and shrubs ... and to turn to a room where a fire glowed in the basket grate and a smell of fresh bread filled the house—this was comfort, security, peace—community."

The mood, though, to which Dorothy seems to give the most emphasis in these years of her early teens is one of introspection and some loneliness. Questions of existence began to form, although hitherto it had seemed to her that her life found its fullness in the community of her family. She was saddened by the fleeting character of joy and wondered what it meant—what an ennobling passion of any kind meant when all came to that final eternity of death. Her mother no longer called her a "comfort" but began to wonder what had gotten into her.

She was, of course, experiencing adolescence. She found little to do except read, go to school, and help with the housework.

Generally, she read good books prescribed for her by her father—Scott, Hugo, Dickens, Stevenson, and Poe—although occasionally she did sneak a "romance" or a Rider Haggard book into the house. And every Sunday afternoon she and Della went to the movies.

Otherwise, Sunday was the gloomiest day of the week. It was John Day's time with the family. Working at night, he was little seen by his children. When he ate, he insisted on eating alone with Grace—every meal except Sunday dinner. Donald and Sam, now fourteen and fifteen respectively, and employed as telegraphers, also worked at night, and Sunday dinner was the one time that the elder Day would have the family together. No matter what, everyone had to be there. In *The Eleventh Virgin*, Dorothy gives what is probably an accurate account of the Sunday meal. "None spoke; all ate in gloomy silence. They could hear each other swallow and the strain to eat quietly was so great that by the time the dessert was brought on, appetites had fled."

On these occasions Dorothy would sit and look at her father—the family eating in this curious way—and feel sorry for him. "Did he feel as shy and embarrassed and miserable as they did? She was sure of it, and her self-consciousness and resultant anger relaxed and she gulped less. At moments like these she felt a . . . sympathy for him. She suddenly realized that she and her father looked very much alike—their eyes and the shape of their mouths. The same blood ran in their veins and probably the same feelings in their hearts."

John Day was not, however, invariably distant from his children and their tribulations, although a tribulation had to be obvious and dramatic for him to respond. One Saturday night, after the family had moved to the Lincoln Park area, Dorothy broke her arm. Grace was icing a cake, the doorbell rang, and Dorothy, wanting to be the first to answer the door, tripped over her brother's foot. Years later, Dorothy remembered the incident and wrote about it in the *Catholic Worker*. "Our dear Dr. Lunn, a horse and buggy doctor, was telephoned for and came at once. I was laid out on the kitchen table. My mother administered chloroform and Dr. Lunn set the arm. My father . . . came home . . . bringing an Oz book in one pocket, and in the other, a little white poodle." As she was never a dog fancier, the poodle is singularly absent from Dorothy's biographical narrations, but her recollection does suggest the existence of a glow of affectionate warmth that John Day should be able to rustle up an Oz book and a poodle in the late hours of a Saturday night.

Still, one wonders at the quirk in the makeup of this man who seldom demonstrated his affection for his children. Dorothy's reflection that she and her father shared "the same feelings in their hearts" was an accurate intuition. Grace Day would say in later years that her daughter always had a "presence." And that "presence" was the surrounding of her person with a no-man's-land of distance that shielded her from a too-ready vulnerability of feeling. Again, she was like her father.

Religion continued to preoccupy Dorothy. After the family moved to the North Side, she went to the Episcopal Church of Our Savior on Fullerton Avenue. There she began confirmation classes, going every Monday afternoon with a "playmate," who is called "Henrietta" in her autobiographical novel. In due course, Dorothy was baptized and confirmed, but in later years she could remember little of these occasions, only that her godparents were a mother and son picked from the congregation and that when she was baptized she was very self-conscious. She had grown tall and skinny. She felt out of place.

Nonetheless, her zeal for religion increased. She read the sermons of John Wesley and greatly admired his piety. She read lives of the early Christian saints, *The Imitation of Christ,* and essays on Jonathan Edwards. Again, she sought to emulate the rigors of saintly life, and surely at this age nothing would have delighted her more than to be given to swooning and trancelike states. At night before going to bed, she and Della, who was dragooned into emulating Dorothy's enthusiasms, would try to outdo each other in seeing who could pray the longest. Usually, though, their spirits failed, and even as they knelt beside the bed, sleep engulfed them. Of course, Dorothy attended church regularly, even going to Wednesday evening services, coercing the reluctant Della to go, too.

If John Day noticed any of this, nothing was said, although Grace had thoughts on the subject. The Sunday morning churchgoing, in her view, could well have been a way of avoiding the extensive preparations involved in the Sunday meal. It was all a pose, she thought, and of all her children was not Dorothy the one most given to that sort of thing? So, resignedly, Grace took on the work of preparing the dinner and did not say too much.

It was in this period that Dorothy began to put to paper her moods and feelings, some parts of which, it appears, she sent to her friend, Henrietta, who was also religious and whom Dorothy elevated to the status of companion-saint. She quotes several pages of her adolescent outpourings, in *The Long Loneliness*. There is a series of pious reflections in her "letter" to Henrietta, written on a gloomy Sunday. "Yesterday afternoon I rode home on the lake boat from downtown. . . . The trees were rustling and the sun flickered on my book. I was happy, but not in the right way. I did not have the spiritual happiness that I crave, only a wicked thrilly feeling at my heart." She reflected on the matter of her and Della's going to the movies on Sunday afternoon. They had "been following an exciting serial . . . and father usually lets us go on Sunday afternoon, but not any other time during the week. . . . I have learned that it is rather hypocritical to be so strict on the Sabbath and not on every other day. Every day belongs to God and every day we are to serve Him, doing His pleasure. And as 'every good thing is prepared for them that love God' and my moving pictures are a good thing, if you stop to think of the educational advantages of them, therefore I can see no wrong in going to the show and pleasing . . . [Della] (for she cannot go alone) and incidentally myself."

Sexual desires? Yes, she supposed she and Henrietta were prone to have them at their age. "But I think that they are impure. It is sensual and God is spiritual. We must harden ourselves to these feelings, for God is love and God is all, so that the only love is of God and is spiritual without taint of earthliness. I am afraid I have never really experienced this love or I would never desire the sensual love or the thrill that comes with the meeting of lips."

This letter-writing and diary-keeping made choice reading for Donald and Sam, and Dorothy became aware that they were doing this when they began casually to quote bits of it in her presence. Again, the reaction was violent. She chased them around the house with a bread knife, and they, affecting to believe that she would do them harm, raised an outcry. Still, they persisted with their sport and Dorothy began locking the door of her bedroom and putting her journal under the mattress. To no avail. They climbed on the roof of the shed behind the kitchen and went through the window to Dorothy's room. Finally, Dorothy found a hiding place under the backstairs carpet, and there the diary was safe.

The practice of keeping a journal and sending Henrietta parts of it Dorothy put down to "introspection," a word that she had come across and immediately savored. Introspection it was, no doubt, but it was a practice she would continue for the rest of her life.

Henrietta was by no means a special soul-mate. Years later Dorothy would write deprecatingly of this girl. She was, as Dorothy saw her later, a sexually precocious, chubby, blue-eyed, blond-haired girl, who hung around the Day household because of the presence of Donald and Sam. She was, in fact, "a most unwholesome companion but none of our elders suspected it because her manners were very pretty and she was always most respectful to them." A distasteful trait of Henrietta's, Dorothy recalled, was that she was forever hugging and kissing everyone with affectionate abandonment. "I was repelled by her soft arms and growing breasts pressed against me. There was never any kissing in my family, and never a close embrace."

With men it was different, and whether her feelings were centered on the fair-haired child in Miss Davis' room in the second grade at Oakland or the blond choir boy in Chicago, there were few times in these years when they were not centered on somebody. Except for the presumed fondling that occurred in the "caves" in the weeds across the street from the house in Oakland, there had been nothing that she recognized as physical about her association with boys. In May, 1912, she fell in love, and this love plummeted her into feelings of physical longing that were new to her.

She remembered it very well. The day before, Grace had gone to the hospital to have a baby. A housekeeper had been employed. That morning Dorothy got word from her father that she had a little brother and that he hoped she was glad. Yes, she was glad, mainly because she wanted to see her mother back to a normal routine and into some sensible clothes. After lunch she went to the front porch to do some crocheting, and a strange mood came over her, one that had nothing to do with the arrival of her baby brother. The afternoon sun glanced through the new leaves on the trees and shimmered on the pavement. From the adjoining yard came the sweet odor of blooming lilacs. An ecstasy of life and beauty fell upon her. Hearing steps on the porch next door, she looked up to see a male figure, young, tall, looking at her. She knew who he was—Armand Hand, who played the violin and who had just moved into the house. Meeting his gaze, she "shuddered."

Well, maybe she did. In *The Eleventh Virgin,* she said she did.

Actually, there was not much to shudder about. Mr. Hand's life was already tightly arranged. He was married to a singer, and she, having given up her career for family, had a year-old child and another one on the way. No matter. Their eyes had met, and Dorothy, flushing hotly, had to put down her crocheting because of her trembling hands. Perhaps she was already composing her letter to Henrietta—a letter that would be spattered with washes of pale blue ink, made by the tears that came because of the sweet hopelessness of it all.

Going into the house, Dorothy put her crocheting on the dining room table and got her hat. She would walk and try to fathom her mood. As she left, Della followed along, but Dorothy was running, heading for the lakeshore. When Della reached her, Dorothy was gasping for breath, but her mood was more considered. She passed off her agitation as coming from a concern over the burdens that the new baby would place on Della and her.

At the moment, though, they were free, and scrambling over the rocks that made the breakwater, they went far out to the very end and lay on the last rock. All was silence except for small waves washing against a piling. They stayed a long time, Dorothy savoring the emotion that stirred within her and Della reading a copy of *Jane Eyre* that she had pulled from her blouse. It was nearly dark when they got home. What must the housekeeper have thought about the long absence of her charges, perched afar out in Lake Michigan? She apparently was unconcerned.

There was another adventure about which the housekeeper seemed unconcerned. On Sunday afternoons and Wednesday nights, Armand Hand led the band in Lincoln Park. Living just a block away, Dorothy had, during the previous summer, lain abed at night and listened to the occasional swell of sound from the concert through the window. Though she had begged to go, Grace said no, Dorothy was too young. But now with her mother in the hospital and her father working at night, she put the matter up to Della. Della, always more conscientious than Dorothy, was reluctant. The boys would tell on them. No, said Dorothy, they would not; she had too much on them. She knew that Sam had broken out a window somewhere and had had to confront the police. Donald had been participating in "prizefights" in the backroom of a saloon on Emery Street and had broken his thumb. The girls were safe.

So that evening they went early to the park. There had been a shower that afternoon. When they sat in the second row of benches, Dorothy on the aisle, everything was damp, but the air was cool and the sky sparkled. After an eternity, Hand, with muscular lightness, strode toward the conductor's platform, brushing Dorothy as he passed. For the remainder of the evening she sat almost immobile, thinking that by staring intently at his back, as he sinuously swayed with the arcing and stabbing of his baton, she could impress her presence upon his consciousness.

Her passion rose with the heat of summer, but she never got beyond an exchange of glances—hers adoring and his brief and casual. But he *knew,* she thought. She dreamed of ways of showing her love for him. Since automobiles were beginning to chug along the streets, she envisioned the Hand baby toddling in front of a car and her running to snatch it from beneath the wheels, herself crushed, but with strength enough to place the child in Hand's arms just as she died. Or, Mrs. Hand, having decamped with a tenor, she, Dorothy, would nurse the child through a near-fatal illness.

Such were the dreams of a girl in her early teens in 1912. The dreams did not persist. When the leaves turned, the concerts in the park ended. Dorothy returned to school, and her baby brother John moved into her life. The radiance around Hand faded until, finally, he was just a person next door. For the next two years, John was almost her singular preoccupation and, to a degree beyond the usual limits assigned to a teenage sister, her responsibility.

When Grace at last came home from the hospital, the baby with her, she seemed tired. She sat at the window all day, looking vacantly into the street. She refused to go to bed at night. Dorothy was concerned and asked her mother if having the baby had been a bad time. Her mother looked at her hard and asked her what she had been reading—"who's been saying things to you?" Irritably, she changed the subject. Had the dishes been washed yet? Grace's illness made more work for Della and Dorothy, and sometimes at night, when they went to bed, they wept because their home life had become so unnatural.

For the next two years, baby John took over most of Dorothy's life. Home from school by three, she would frequently put the infant in his carriage and take long walks through Lincoln Park. The changes of fall in the color of leaves and of the lake itself fascinated her. Sometimes, though, she walked south to North

Avenue and then west for blocks, past taverns and rows of unkempt houses whose first floors were below street level. She would walk "through slum districts, and watch the slatternly women and unkempt children and ponder over the poverty of the homes as contrasted with the wealth along the shore drive. I wanted even then to play my part. . . . I wanted to do something toward making a 'new earth wherein justice dwelleth.'" These were heavy thoughts for a fifteen-year-old girl.

Della, now in the sixth grade, sometimes went on these walks, holding on to the side of the carriage as they made their way down the streets. Home again, Della would help get supper ready and Dorothy would put the baby to bed, but frequently he seemed more inclined toward sociability than sleep, and she would have to rock him for long periods, exhausting her repertory of songs from the Episcopal hymnal before he finally gave up the struggle.

After the dishes were done, she had the rest of the evening to herself, and it was her greatest pleasure to sit by the fireplace and read, an occupation that took her far into the night, long after the others had gone to bed. It was usually after midnight when she retired. In fact, as a fifteen-year-old schoolgirl who was supposed to get eight hours of sleep a night, she did well to get four. Baby John, it seems, was put to bed in a crib in his mother's room, but when he first awakened, around four in the morning, Grace would carry him into Dorothy's room and deposit him in a crib there. She did this because father John, having just returned from his nightly work at the newspaper, did not want the silence of his chamber disturbed by a crying infant, nor did he want to forego the warm presence of Grace. After all, he needed his sleep.

So baby John continued his clamor each morning in the crib in Dorothy's room, awakened her, and she, moving upward through layers of sleep, was at last able to swing her legs out from under the covers. Grabbing her clothes under one arm and the baby under another, she hurried downstairs, hoping that there were live coals in the fireplace. With a fire going, she changed the baby, laid him on a blanket in front of the fire, and went into the kitchen to heat his bottle and to make coffee. Then, for two hours, she did her homework for the day, mainly studying Latin and Greek. Sometime after six, she would awaken Della and the boys, the latter two already out and working. As they prepared to face the day, she made their breakfast. It was eight o'clock when she set out for school.

She went to Robert Waller High School where, as might be expected, she liked English, Latin, and Greek. In *The Long Loneliness,* she writes of a "Mr. Matheson" who was "so good" that he voluntarily taught Greek after school to a group of interested students. It was, of course, a time when the "serious" students aspired to classical excellence. Dorothy, doubtless infected by the enthusiasm of Mr. Matheson for this ideal, spent hours working on Latin and Greek. In the after-school sessions she went through the Georgics and Bucolics of Virgil, and from a second-hand bookstore she bought, for a dime, a hundred-and-fifty-year-old New Testament written in Greek, which she thereupon studiously translated.

But what of the joys of close companionships, of parties, and of having a "sweetheart"—those marks of rich sociability that graced the lives of young people of that era and to which in later years they invariably harked back with loving memory? There was for Dorothy none at all. Later she would say that she remembered little of school except from the lunch period and two study halls—the latter because she could suck on a piece of hard candy as she read a "romance." She observed that "it occasionally surprised her when she realized how little she knew of her school fellows who sat together at lunch and giggled and gossiped, or passed notes during other periods." Well, there was "Henrietta," but she was now going to business school, and the role of bosom friend that Dorothy had assigned to her was artificial anyway.

Why did she live such a barren social life? She was not inarticulate—anything but. She conversed well, she liked people, and she could share their concerns and interests. But how could any high school girl who was involved so completely in family matters have time for anything else? She might have made time, but the fact was that she preferred her life as it was. She probably thought of herself as unattractive, since she had grown tall, with a large, bare-boned frame and little to recommend her appearance except her unusual eyes. But the substance of the matter was that the gossiping, giggling, note-passing, and all those things that seem so electric and crucial to high school students did not interest her at all. Her interest, almost solely, was in reading.

By the time she was fifteen years old she was taking on material that today would make the average graduate student look for a handy condensation of the author's thoughts. In reading Jack London's *Martin Eden,* she came across references to Herbert Spencer and she tried to wade through the insufferable ponderosities of his

First Principles, a work that would reduce cosmic questions to elementary physics. Along the same line, she read in Darwin and Huxley, whom she found understandable. She even tried to read Kant and Spinoza. Apparently none of these works contributed any significant components to her thinking. Spencer's evolutionary idea, abstractly considered, did not excite her, but Jack London's essays on the class struggle did seize her imagination. It was reading Upton Sinclair's *The Jungle* that, she said, prompted her to take the long winter walks into Chicago's western tenement area, attracted there by a curiosity to see for herself how immigrant families lived. She read Peter Kropotkin and Vera Figner on anarchism and absorbed their descriptions of the plight of the poor. When she was fifteen, her brother Donald began his newspaper career on a paper called *The Day Book,* described by Dorothy as "the size of the dime novels we used to read, but it was lurid in another way. It told of the struggles in the labor movement and especially in Chicago."

Her interest in this kind of reading produced a growing social consciousness on her part, and her concern with religion waned. When she was sixteen, she dabbled briefly in Christian Science. Her mother had initiated this interest when she herself had started reading Christian Science during the depressed period she suffered after Donald's birth. So when Dorothy, in her last year in high school, began to suffer blinding headaches, Grace invoked the assistance of a practitioner for Dorothy. Reading *Science and Health,* Dorothy decided that it sounded about as reasonable as what she had professed to believe in the Episcopal church. But neither mother nor daughter ever attended the Christian Science church.

In *The Eleventh Virgin,* she gives a somewhat fictionalized version of her decision to stop going to church—fictionalized in its appearance, but perhaps closer to her real feelings than that she would write later. What she now believed, she wrote, "was that it was really better for the soul to bask in the sun on a warm spring day, or walk in a snowy park when the twilight made deep blue shadows behind the trees, or to read beautiful poetry than to go to church." And when she thought of poetry, she thought of Swinburne's "Tristram," which she had been reading and which was hidden in back of the bookcase. Yes, she "would like to lie on the grass in the woods with a lover all night just like Tristram and Iseult."

This new mood of emancipation from religion and churches

came upon her on the gloomy Sunday afternoon that she and Della had gotten caught making fudge. If the confrontation with their mother had depressed their spirits, Dorothy's were revived by her new sense of freedom. Turning to Della, she proclaimed that she was "sick and tired of religion," and further, she would cease lecturing her sister on the subject. They would go to no more Wednesday night prayer meetings. To ratify this pronouncement, Dorothy proposed that they sneak off to the movies by climbing out of her window and down the roof of the shed. She had gotten some money from Donald.

In response to this proposal the cautious Della hesitated only a moment. "Then she came over and hugged Dorothy tightly. 'I'm glad you're through with it. If you really mean it, it would have been all right, but you were playing a game and it made me so mad. . . . Come on. Let's go. What do we care if we get a scolding when we get back?' "

Dorothy's lapse from religion did not go unquestioned. The pastor of the Fullerton Avenue Episcopal church, having taken note of his once-devoted parishioner's absence from services, and no doubt having "heard things," went to the Day residence on Webster Avenue to see what the trouble was. As Dorothy relates the episode, he talked to her all one afternoon, "but I was obdurate in my refusal to return to church. I was in a 'free' mood and my reading at the time made me skeptical. My belief in God remained firm and I continued to read the New Testament regularly, but I felt it was no longer necessary to go to church. I distrusted all churches after reading the books of London and Sinclair."

Dorothy graduated from Waller High School in June, 1914. Since this occasion is nowhere mentioned in any of her writing, one assumes that it was an altogether routine affair insofar as she was concerned. There was no corsage, no prom, and no yearbook filled with protestations of friendship everlasting and predictions of future glory for her. When this tall girl with straight, bobbed hair walked across the stage to get her diploma, the applause that she got must have been slight.

She was, though, honored in a significant way. The Hearst Chicago *Examiner* had set up a competition in the form of an academic examination whereby twenty Cook County students could each win a three-hundred-dollar cash scholarship to attend college. Three students from each high school in the county were chosen to enter the competition, and Dorothy was one of the three chosen from

Robert Waller. When the examinations were graded, she was ranked fifteenth and declared one of the winners. This accomplishment she attributed to the hours of study she had put in during the mornings after taking care of her baby brother.

Was John Day among the parents at the graduation? Did he come to savor his daughter's honor? Perhaps not. The *Examiner* and the *Tribune* were locked in a mighty struggle to get subscribers, and, more and more, *The Inter-Ocean*, the Day family's means of existence, was being pushed to the brink. That Dorothy should receive assistance from a newspaper which used scandalous, strong-armed tactics to get subscribers was a consideration that may have turned him away. Within the year, *The Inter-Ocean* would fail, and once again John Day would be jobless.

But nothing dampened Dorothy's enthusiasm over the prospect of attending college in the fall. Of the summer of 1914 she later would remember nothing of significance happening— only the joyous anticipation of leaving home. Otherwise, the world went to war that August, and there began an acceleration in the process of history that ultimately would convulse and destroy the kind of life she had known in her youth. What she later remembered of the start of the war was only that there was talk about it up and down Webster Avenue, and the Germans who lived on the street were caught up in the subject.

✎ 2

Dorothy and Rayna

ONE MORNING in early September, 1914, sixteen-year-old Dorothy picked up her suitcase and took a streetcar downtown to Chicago's railway station. She was going to the University of Illinois at Urbana. In the concourse other students stood about, chatting animatedly about the prospects for the coming year, trying to give the impression that they were in control and knew what it was all about —what fraternity or sorority one should join, what courses to take, and what the prospects were for Coach Robert Zuppke's Illinois football team. Dorothy no doubt listened with interest but knew full well that such matters would be no concern of hers. From the first hundred-dollar payment of her scholarship grant she had had to pay a ten-dollar matriculation fee and twelve dollars for a semester's instruction. Then there were books and room and board. She would have to have more money, but she was not worried. She would work. The prospect of a new adventure, a break with her life at home, gave her considerable satisfaction. "I was sixteen and filled with a sense of great independence. I was on my own, and no longer to be cared for by the family. The idea of earning my own living, by my own work, was more thrilling than the idea of an education."

What did she want from "an education"? What was it for? She did not know. She had no vocational goal in mind, not even a degree. She vaguely wanted some clarification about her own life, and she thought college might give her that. Just to read more and to write more was her main expectation. Otherwise, she watched the students, all full of bright talk and ready laughter, all belonging to some group or other. She was alone. She had no group, and even on the train she began to resent them, their good clothes, their poses, and what struck her as their empty chatter.

As the Illinois Central train made its way southward through the rich black prairie land of Illinois that lay between Chicago and Urbana, she probably reread her university handbook of instructions to discover what she should do when she reached Urbana. She would find, at the Urbana depot, committees from "The Young Men's and Young Women's Christian Association." Committee members who met the trains could be recognized by the "distinctive badges" they wore. From the depot she should take a streetcar to the intersection of Wright and St. John streets, where the new YMCA building was located. For the time being, she would live at the "Y."

Whatever it was that Dorothy thought she would get out of college, that which had stimulated her imagination and had made her last summer on Webster Avenue interminable did not occur. The experience quickly became grim. With no thought other than to take those courses she thought she would enjoy most, she signed up for history, biology, Latin, and English. Almost from the first, it seems, she retreated behind a wall of critical contempt for her classes. The thing that "impressed her most in the course in American literature was the professor's futile attempts to implant in the minds of his students the love for the poetic phrase. She could still hear that class of sixty, yelling in every pitch: THE DESERT AND THE ILLIMITABLE AIR, after which the professor would ask ecstatically, 'Do you get the beauty and wing of that?' " Maybe some did, but not Miss Dorothy Day, sitting no doubt in the rear by a window, yawning, listening to the unceasing moan of the prairie wind outside and hoping that time would accelerate.

History? It was simply a memorization of facts in which she could see no meaning. Biology? She was "not interested" and "skipped courses recklessly." As for Latin, this subject for which she had had so much enthusiasm in high school held no interest for her in college. In the Latin class, too, her seat "was next to the window which looked out over the south campus to the forest where the pines were blue black." Later, when spring came and the window was open, she could hear the call of a meadow lark "which threw her into a trance out of which it was hard to awaken." In Rhetoric 3a, she adjudged the most valuable information she received there was that to avert a sneeze, one pressed the length of the forefinger firmly against the upper lip.

Yet, of the sixteen courses she took in the two years she spent at the University of Illinois, she failed only one—biology. In her other courses she got C's and B's. Her student file contains little that indicates she was a subject of special concern to the University officials. She did petition to be excused from gym the first year. "My reason," she wrote, "is that in the afternoon I desire to do manual labor in order to finish my courses here." The petition was granted, and the next year she again requested a deliverance from gym, this time because of a "sprained ankle." Again, she was excused. The reasons she gave were real, but it is difficult under any circumstances to think of her as a willing member of a gym class. Sports, whether she was to observe them or participate in them, interested her only occasionally. Perhaps her professors understood her better than she understood them. They recognized her intelligence and she, drawing from her reservoir of reading and high school study, avoided any academic trouble. But as she admitted later, "I really led a very shiftless life, doing for the first time exactly what I wanted to do, attending classes I wished to attend, coming and going every hour of the night as I pleased."

The reason for her "rebellion" is easy to locate. It might be making too much of the influence of her father on her to say that her realization that she was not bound absolutely to anything of his ordering had something to do with her unconventional behavior. Possibly that was part of it, but it was also her nature to defy convention when it suited her, and the mood of defiance was strong upon her. She was defiant because she was hurt. She had no friends. She seemed deliberately to have avoided socializing, feeling that she had nothing in common with the students she saw whose interests were football, fraternities, sororities, and the movies, and whose enthusiasms, as she heard them talking about these things, seemed affected and banal. She felt unattractive, conscious of being large and plain. She pursued her singular and solitary course.

While Urbana was only a two-hour train ride from Chicago, she apparently stayed at the university once she was there, and after the initial spell of excitement wore off, she became desperately homesick. "Hour after hour I lay awake, thinking of home. . . . Everything was cold and dead to me. I wanted the warmth of my home, I wanted my own, and I felt utterly abandoned. I was so completely homesick that I could neither eat nor sleep, and I paced the brick-paved walks of that small college town with tears streaming down my face, my heart so heavy that it hung like a weight in my breast."

She was "in the depths," but there was no thought of going home. In her unhappiness she began to enlarge upon the radical disposition toward life and society that had begun to appear in her thinking during her last year in high school. When she was filling out her student information card and had come to the space on religious preference, she wrote "Christian Science." It was just something to put there. Doctrinal preferences meant nothing to her, and to affirm this or that position when none of them had any effect on life was an exercise in pointlessness. "Religion, as it was practiced by those I encountered (and the majority were indifferent), had no vitality. It had nothing to do with everyday life: it was a matter of Sunday praying. Christ no longer walked the streets of this world, he was two thousand years dead and new prophets had risen up in his place."

One day in class (one that she decided to attend), she heard a professor make a comment on religion. Religion "was something which had brought great comfort to people throughout the ages, so that we ought not to criticize it. I do not remember his exact words, but from the way he spoke of religion the class could infer that the strong were the ones who did not need such props. In my youthful arrogance, in my feeling that I was one of the strong, I felt then for the first time that religion was something that I must ruthlessly cut out of my life."

So she "ceased to believe." She became critical of those who were pious. She "started to swear, quite consciously," so as to shock those she knew would be shocked. Of course, as she said, "I shocked myself as I did it, but I felt it was a strong gesture I was making to push religion from me."

It may have been at this time that she began a habit that for a good many years was almost a part of her personality. It was then, or soon after, that she took up smoking. Why not, after rejecting God, register her freedom by lighting, with carefree insouciance, a Fatima cigarette just outside the classroom door as the chattering scholars began to pass into the hallway and shock them, too? And just sixteen years old!

This rebellion against religion, however, was not just the result of her loneliness, nor did it come from her feeling that religion was a middle-class appurtenance that was used by "people who were so comfortably happy in the face of the injustices of the world." The "injustices of the world" seemed to her to be the legitimate object of human concern; the gospel of Christ was anachronistic and, by its nature, stood athwart the pathway of progress, the evolution of institutions toward that end where exact justice would exist. "The Marxist slogan, 'Workers of the world, unite! You have nothing to lose but your chains,' seemed to me a most stirring battle cry. It was a clarion call that made me feel one with the masses, apart from the bourgeoisie, the smug, and satisfied." She was in love with the masses; it was a love "that warmed my heart and filled it. It was those among the poor and the oppressed who were going to rise up, they were collectively the new Messiah, and they would release the captives. Already they had been persecuted, they had been scourged, they had been thrown into prison and put to death, not only all over the world but right around me in the United States."

Thus this sixteen-year-old college freshman gave herself over completely to a collectivist, time-involved view of salvation. "Pie in the sky" was for the weak and the fearful. In the battle for collectivist justice one had to be hard, unyielding, and tireless—and whatever stood in the way of this earthly beatitude had to be excised ruthlessly. She would begin her purification by excising religion. This is what she told herself.

There were, to be sure, several points she chose to ignore. What had happened to that "wise and dread spirit of nothingness," as Dostoevsky's Grand Inquisitor labeled the devil, a specter that had once pursued Dorothy in her dreams? And what did it mean if that point in the process of history when collectivist justice would reign were only a point? Could it be made retroactive for those millions and millions who had suffered, but who, beyond the grave, were nothing, and all their passion and hope were nothing? And at this point would community be real, final, and complete, or would it only be the form of community? But who, young and full of health, asks these questions? Not Miss Dorothy Day, who, after November 8, was seventeen and knew that she was invincible and immortal.

Something less than a dedicated student—the girl who sat by the window and who, no doubt, would sometimes let her consciousness fade into the warm caress of sleep as the instructor made his points as per the outline he had written on the board— what did she do with her time? She read. She read labor history and biographies of those heroes who had resisted capitalist exploitation. She got to know the Industrial Workers of the World— "Big" Bill Haywood, Arturo Giovanitti, "Mother" Jones, Elizabeth Gurley Flynn, and Carlo Tresca. She read about the Chicago Haymarket anarchists, some of whom had been executed by the State. "They were the martyrs." Yet she never became doctrinaire but remained a seeker, and her reading testifies to this. Labor history, Jack London, and Upton Sinclair, yes, but she read with even more abiding interest the writers of nineteenth-century Russia. She read the novels of Artsybashev, Turgenev, Gorki, Chekhov, Andreyev, and, above all, Tolstoi and Dostoevsky. She would in fact, throughout her life, be a passionate devotee of Russian literature, and in time the genius of Dostoevsky recommended itself to her so strongly that his effect on her was oracular and remained so all of her life.

As she was profligate in her reading she was also profligate in buying books out of the small sum that remained after she had paid her tuition and various fees at the university. "Before the two years were up, I had exhausted the money I had and many times I was out of work and money." From the first, she had reckoned on outside jobs to make her budget balance, but what with the books she could not resist buying and the low-wage jobs she had to take, it was inevitable that she should, from time to time, go hungry. There in fact were times when, with no prospect of food, she would awaken in her cold room, hear the ever-present wind rattling her window, and do no more than reach for a book from the stack on the floor and spend her class-time hours reading. Her jobs were in the late afternoon and evening, and being a late riser by nature, she put off her active day as long as possible.

Her first job was working in the dining hall at the "Y," setting tables and changing linens for a hundred and fifty students. For this she got her board, and possibly her room as well. From the congenial work of setting tables, peeling off dishes from a heavy stack as she hurried around the tables, then doing a second round in which she banged down the silver, she was demoted to the dish washer. She does not say why. It may have been that she preferred to work at a later time.

Anyway, she worked at the "Y" for several months and then moved out, realizing "how simple a thing" it had been "to wash dishes for a family of six." After that, she airily relates that "she moved her belongings into the home of a bootlegger to assist his wife in the care of the children and in return receive board and room." She had not known that the head of the house was a bootlegger, a circumstance that did not matter much to Dorothy, but his "howling troop of children" and his "evident amorous intention" caused her to leave after a week.

Apparently, her next job was with Professor John Driscoll Fitzgerald, who taught Romance Language and lived in the adjoining town of Champagne. Professor Fitzgerald's family consisted of his wife, mother, and three children, and Dorothy's job was to wash dishes for the two meals a day she had with the family. "They were Methodists and delightful people. I used to talk about books with the professor and faith with the old lady as she washed the lunch dishes and prepared vegetables for the evening meal."

One of the things that tended to compromise the position of the young atheist was that the Fitzgeralds always said a grace before meals:

> Be present at our table, Lord.
> Be here and everywhere, Adored.
> Bless Thou this food and grant that we
> May feast in Paradise with Thee.

But Dorothy said it, too, and seemed to feel no worse for it. Later she said that "remembering how much I liked the Fitzgeralds, I know I was happy in their religious atmosphere."

There was another job in the home of a "poverty-stricken instructor who had five children." She did not eat with them, since they had scarcely enough for themselves, but she got a room furnished with a table, chair, and a small stove on which to cook. Having no bookcase, she piled her books on the floor. At night, the room was so cold she went to bed, but the bed was cold, too, even with all her clothes thrown on top of the covers.

For these accommodations she did the family washing on Saturdays, house-cleaning, and even baby-sitting. Four of the children were under five years old, and "when one of them went to sleep, another would awaken it by crying. . . . It was smothering work." Occasionally she had to scrub the floors and beat rugs, and on Saturdays she washed baby clothes on a scrub board so long that all the skin was worn off her knuckles. She "swore over such work, but having accepted the job she could not turn it down when she found out what it was."

In *The Eleventh Virgin* she tells a story about working for another faculty family. This must have been toward the end of her first semester at the university, and the household head was a professor of psychology. The substance of this tale was the chit-chat between Dorothy and the professor's wife, who was three months' pregnant and expecting in June. As Dorothy tells the story, she would come into the professor's house at four o'clock after her last class and have to listen for a while to the woman's wailing over the prospects of having her second child at the age of thirty-eight. As time passed, the wife's conversational interests progressed to variations on the child-bearing theme. One was that if there was true justice in the universe, parents would take turns having children, the mother having one and then the father taking his turn. So it went until Dorothy had to go to the kitchen to get supper, and during the evening meal, the subject was rehashed again, with the professor presumably contributing erudite bits of information on the female-male roles in child-bearing. And who knows, maybe he even produced the "latest study" on the matter.

In subsequent afternoons, the professor's wife took up the subject of rape, and the speculative dimension to this discussion topic was "whether or not rape was possible" in marriage. The wife cited "cases in the newspapers, the opinions of her friends" and told "of things that had happened in her town when she was a girl; things that she had heard had happened in other towns." After all, said the wife, "the physical side of marriage was the most important one." In marriage, sex came first, and on this point one suspects the professor would have had to agree with his wife, since she did not seem equipped to contribute much else to the contract.

In short, all of this talk added up to Dorothy's "beginning to learn of sexual problems." Intrigued, she availed herself of books on sexual pathology in the professor's well-stocked library—books by Havelock Ellis, Forel, Krafft-Ebing, Brill, and Freud. "For the most part, she was repelled by what she read. She preferred her early glamorous idea of life and blotted out of her mind, as much as she could, the glimpse into the abnormal which her reading had given her."

Why was it that Dorothy, as intelligent as she was and as verbally facile as she was, had to become a household drudge in order to survive? Was there not more "genteel" work, like sitting at the front desk at the "Y," sorting mail, delivering messages, and giving information? Or could she not have, with a sorority pin perched on the crest of her breast, performed some of the other sociable offices attendant on university life—in the meanwhile eating well, sleeping comfortably, and meeting some of the more "interesting" people on campus?

Such jobs were not available to her for two reasons. First, as she demonstrated, she had her own vision and it allowed no ready mixing with the football and sorority crowd. But more to the point, one got jobs through the "Y," and the good people there were disturbed by Dorothy's iconoclastic tastes and blasphemous utterances. As a result, she did menial labor, and, so far as she was concerned, that was quite all right—for millions of others, perhaps more deserving than she, were doing it, too.

On December 15, 1914, the university student paper, *The Daily Illini*, noted that "a woman's section of the University Socialist Club, to be called the Socialist Study Club," was to be organized that evening. The purpose of the club "was not conversion to socialism, but the study of the relation of its theory to other social sciences." Each member was to make a study of "the various phases of the problem and then prepare a paper on the idea formed." What could be more thrilling than to hear a student read an hour-and-a-half-long technical disquisition on socialism and its relationship to some esoteric aspect of economics? It is, of course, the first principle of any form of socialist intrusion into the area of analytical scholarship that, before a paper or argument fulfills any other criterion of acceptability, it must first be dull. Dorothy soon learned the truth of this axiom at the meetings she attended. "I didn't attend very many," she said.

Rather than spend her time in political discussion which she regarded as boring, she continued to use her spare time to read and to do something that she had been doing for most of her life—writing. What did she write? It most certainly had to be re-creations of episodes out of her life because, through all of her years of writing, most of it was, in one way or another, autobiographical. The objective she had in mind for her writing during her first semester was to win admission into the "Scribblers," a club, said *The Daily Illini*, whose membership was "limited to students who show aptitude in literary composition." Admission could be granted at any time and was based on the submission of two manuscripts that club members judged worthy. Dorothy presumably submitted two manuscripts, but the one that caught the attention of club members was a narration of her experience of having to go three days without food during one of her "broke" periods.

One "Scribbler," an energetic, man-about-campus type whose writing appeared regularly in the major campus publications, suggested that Dorothy meet him and a friend in a coffee shop where they could have a leisurely chat about her work. This meeting, which must have occurred early in her second semester at the university, was the first time that Dorothy felt she had met people to

whom she could talk directly and receive an understanding response. Sitting over their coffee, they talked "for hours."

From that meeting Dorothy was invited to become a member of
the Scribblers, an honor which was signified by wearing a small
gold pen point. What mattered more in her life was that she now
had two friends who were understanding and responsive to the
probings of her mind and spirit, who liked her for her intelligence
and the passion they sensed in her, and to whom it was of no
account that her clothes were not the best, and obviously much
worn, and that there was no pretension in what she said or how she
said it. Yet she spoke well. She had a pleasant, well-modulated
voice with an unusual intonation that was hard to place. She always
spoke to the point and avoided affectations. As for looks, she was
no beauty and exuded no heavy feminine allure, subtle or otherwise. Yet she had a good figure and her face, because of its an-
gularity, was "interesting"—as those who knew not what else to call
it might say. As would be her custom all of her life, she braided her
auburn hair and wound it, crownlike, around her head.

So the three sat, dawdled over their coffee, and talked, and
when they parted to go home, Dorothy's heart felt lifted with the
first happiness she had known as a college student. Her two companions were Samson Raphaelson and Rayna Simons. Samson—or
"Raphe," as he was called—and Rayna were engaged. They were
Jews, but completely secular in their outlook. Secular or not, they
possessed something that was deeply Jewish: a deep sensitivity to
the richness and color of life, and a passion to do whatever it was
they did with feeling and intensity. Dorothy responded warmly to
this. Samson and Rayna were the first Jews that she had really
known, but over the course of her life she, in her strong and active
opposition to anti-Semitism, and in certain dimensions of her spirituality, could and did account herself as one with the Jewish
people.

In the years ahead, Raphaelson would become a well-known
writer of plays and movie scripts. His claim to fame in this latter
category now rests on his having written *The Jazz Singer,* Al Jolson's
"talking picture" of 1927. Raphaelson was born on Chrystie Street
on New York's East Side, a street that in time would be more familiar to Dorothy than it ever was to him. In his boyhood, he moved
to Chicago to live with relatives, going to McKinley High School
where he distinguished himself principally for his prowess as a
debater.

Rayna Simons also went to McKinley, and perhaps it was Samson's accomplishments as a debater and his "I can do anything" attitude that attracted her to him. Or perhaps it was a rebound situation, for Rayna had just been engaged to Milton Ager, who could play the piano and write tunes, one of which, composed in later years, was called "Happy Days Are Here Again." But the romance with Ager faded and Raphaelson was promoted to first place, a position he accepted because—well, it seemed to him to be the gentlemanly thing to do. When Raphaelson went to Illinois, Rayna decided that she would go, too—to be near him and to study, of all things, horticulture.

For a while, it was a three-way friendship, Dorothy and Rayna and Samson—Samson, of necessity, because of his closeness to Rayna, but Dorothy, too, was very fond of him, impressed with his energy and status as a big-man-on-campus, at least so far as his writing and involvement in the campus intellectual life was concerned. And Samson seems to have taken a mentor-like interest in Dorothy. Who but he, with Rayna's connivance (and with Dorothy looking over their shoulders), would have placed this newsnote in one of the issues of *The Daily Illini* that appeared sometime in the fall of 1915: "Dorothy Day, 18, has been appointed book critic and reviewer of the Chicago *Examiner*. Miss Day has always been a voracious reader. She is well informed upon all topics of the day and will be an able critic of the works of present day writers. This position is considered to be an important one on the large city paper, demanding well developed writing and a critical sense."

It may have been John I. Day who got this little work assignment for her, or possibly Dorothy just volunteered to do reviews, a proposition publishers could easily accept, since it committed them to little or nothing. As Dorothy does not mention doing any work for the *Examiner* among the various employment ventures she lists in *The Long Loneliness,* one might assume that the detailing of auspicious qualifications in *The Daily Illini* availed her little. Neither did she ever break into the circles of college publication, despite her admission into the Scribblers; a search of the major student publications over the two years that she was at the university indicates that she contributed nothing that was signed. A quarter of a century after leaving the University of Illinois, she wrote that the "only benefit those two years at college brought me was my friendship with Rayna and my own sense of complete independence."

Somewhere on the campus of the University of Illinois there

should be a plaque that tells the history of these two women, the passion for justice that consumed them and how they lived together in the bonds of closest friendship, one destined to be a Catholic and the other a communist. As Dorothy lyrically declares in *The Long Loneliness,* it was at the university that there came "in the midst of the bare hardship of my days, a new love . . . a new love of friendship that was . . . as clear as a bell, crystal clear, with no stain of self-seeking, a give-and-take friendship that meant companionship and sharing." A stainless friendship is a rare thing, itself almost worthy of commemoration.

Rayna was born in 1895. Her father, Joseph Simons, was a wealthy broker and once the vice-president of the Chicago Board of Trade. When Rayna was a senior in high school, the family lived in a plush apartment on Jackson Boulevard, and when they went down to the Chicago Loop, they rode in a big Winton automobile. In her high school days she had not been considered beautiful, or even very attractive, but by the time she went to college she knew how to dress and she stopped wearing glasses. Her picture in *The 1917 Ilio* reminds one a little of Janet Gaynor as the latter appeared in the movie, *Seventh Heaven.* Even so, the photograph may not do her justice because, finally, the thing that set her off from everyone else was her hair. Dorothy writes that she first saw Rayna "going down to the university. . . . She was the one person I remember on the train filled with students going back to school. She stood out like a flame with her red hair, brown eyes, and vivid face. She had a clear, happy look." Vincent Sheean, in his *Personal History,* also used the image of "flame" to describe Rayna: she was "the pure flame that gave such light and heat."

On the campus of the University of Illinois, Rayna was not the "flame" that Sheean saw. She was there to be near Raphaelson, to take her courses in horticulture, and when she got her degree, to get married. "She used to laugh at my absorption in Socialism," Dorothy once said. "She felt that I was unbalanced on the subject and was looking at life from only one angle."

Why was Rayna unmoved by the socialist cause on the campus? "Perhaps it was because on the only occasions she had attended the Socialist local in the town, two of her instructors had been there, and held positions as executives in the branch. This was sufficient evidence that socialists were not persecuted, as she had imagined, and that free speech was not merely a phrase in the constitution.

She could learn all she wanted on the subject from her economics professor, who was a well-read and non-partisan teacher. 'I am an instructor,' he once told them, 'not a politician.' "

Whatever this logic was worth, it seemed to satisfy Rayna for the moment, and although she could not follow Dorothy's socialist convictions, the two became inseparable companions—"soul-mates," an earlier time would have called them. What was the basis for their friendship? When the two women met, Dorothy had been leading "a hard life. . . . I had not had enough food or sleep for a long time and I had become morbid. Though I rejoiced in my sufferings, taking a grim pleasure in them, I took that pleasure defensively. I built up a consciously dramatic attitude to keep myself from becoming crushed. I was defiant so that I should not own myself beaten or frightened by life." So Rayna, generous, compassionate, and apparently appreciative of Dorothy's intelligence and, above all, her rare and determined spirit, made Dorothy her cause. And Dorothy, knowing that there was no self-serving in Rayna's action, loved her for it.

Thus Dorothy's life, which had been hard and somber, took on light and lyricism. She was brought into the circle of Rayna's friends, the people who put out *The Daily Illini*, young instructors with "advanced" ideas, the younger students who also had "advanced" ideas. The remainder of the school year was exhilarating for Dorothy, and when summer came, she took Rayna home to 417 Webster Avenue to meet her family, and, perhaps, to talk journalism with her father and two brothers. But they likely got little shoptalk from John. He did not think much of women in journalism and likened the profession to an old-fashioned barber shop— no fit place for a female who pretended to have some character. Dorothy did not stay home for long; most of that summer she lived with Rayna on a farm that Rayna's father owned.

When September came, they were back at Urbana, Rayna insisting that Dorothy live with her as a roommate, that she, Rayna, paid for the whole room, anyway, and nothing would be lost. Rayna did not have to insist very hard, and so Dorothy became a resident of a boarding house for Jewish girls. That Rayna lived there, Dorothy seems to suggest, was due to Rayna's not having been invited to join any sorority, despite her "outstanding personality, good looks and wealth." It was, said Dorothy, her first contact with anti-Semitism, a statement that seems a little improbable since she certainly must have heard her father give voice to anti-Semitic views along with his general distrust of "foreigners."

In addition to a room, Rayna shared with Dorothy whatever else she had. Dorothy wore Rayna's clothes at times, ate with her in the boarding-house dining room, and when Rayna's family insisted she drink a pint of cream a day to gain some needed weight, Rayna made Dorothy drink half of it. Indeed, Rayna even shared Raphaelson with Dorothy—or perhaps she had to share him, since Rayna seldom went to a meeting, a lecture, a concert, or even a picnic without Dorothy. It was a *ménage à trois,* but certainly one of utter innocence. As might be supposed, Raphaelson soon became annoyed. After Dorothy left the university, he wrote to tell her, not in anger but as one offering constructive advice, that she was altogether too ready to accept assistance from others.

In 1915 and 1916, Europe was at war, and the idea of progress, which in the last half of the nineteenth century had given a special illumination to Western life, began to fade. The tragedy of war seemed not to have oppressed Dorothy and Rayna. Apparently, they seldom discussed it, preferring conversations about serious matters, such as literature and their writing. And when those subjects became worn from overuse, there was still one theme that never grew old: the foibles of the fraternity-sorority crowd and their adoration of Coach Zuppke.

And, of course, there was the subject of sex, usually cast by collegiates, especially would-be intellectuals, in the lofty jargon of the psychology class, a resort which, among other things to recommend it, gave them the opportunity to feign a clinical objectivity in their treatment of it. Dorothy and Rayna enjoyed discussing sex as much as their fellows did, but the pose of academic disinterestedness affected by some seemed to have amused Dorothy. Six years after the event, she reconstructed, in *The Eleventh Virgin,* the conversation at an afternoon tea to which she and Rayna had been invited. Their hosts were English instructors, and campus rumor had it that two of them, "Miss Hubbard" and "Mr. Lord," were bedding down together—all of which gave a piquancy to the affair. In the following passage, the character "June" is Dorothy and "Regina" is Rayna. The scene begins just as Dorothy and Rayna enter the apartment:

"But how can one really *know* without a trial marriage?" Miss Hubbard was saying languidly, while her bright, sharp eyes sparkled around the group. And perhaps there was no answer because of the general rustle, attendant on the arrival of June and her roommate Regina. Then when Miss Hubbard assured June that there was plenty of room on the couch and Mr. Fenton had placed another chair for Regina, Mr. Lord brought back the conversation to where it had been when the girls entered.

"How can one really know?" repeated Miss Hubbard full of italics of earnestness.

"Know what?" Regina startled them all by asking.

But such a question could never be answered directly and Miss Hubbard went on.

"The only true mating is a complete harmony of the spiritual, mental and physical—preferably in that order my dear."

"But surely that's the usual order. We usually get acquainted with a man before we marry him," Regina put in. . . .

"Not at all," boomed Mr. Fenton. "Too many young things are attracted by mere physical passion." A slight stir went over the room. "They know little or nothing of their mate's intellectual or spiritual life and care even less. In fact," he went on in his best classroom manner, "it is by the sublimation of passion, or rather, the directing of it into higher channels that we arrive at the basis of an understanding."

The ladies nodded in agreement. Somehow it was more fitting for a man to speak of passion than women.

"But how long should a trial marriage last before one can really know?" spoke up Miss Smythe, English 2b, sitting on the edge of her chair and twitching with interest.

This question, couched in her own italics, was a little too direct for Miss Hubbard, who went on, "I don't know that I wouldn't advise a rather full experience for women before marriage. How else can we get into direct contact with the intricate nature of man?"

Another little stir, this time masculine. Mr. Lord "hawed" rather loudly, settling himself more firmly between June and Miss Hubbard, and the "haw" was understood to be the preface to a speech, every one kept silent.

"And when you speak of full experience, I presume you are speaking of a single standard for men and women."

"Yes, yes! That women should be allowed the freedom from condemnation that man enjoys, since in having freedom it is generally understood that they will exercise it with the moderation natural to their sensibilities."

"But isn't that presupposing"—June unconsciously fell into the didactic of the others. "But isn't that presupposing that the mental and spiritual can only be reached through the physical?" . . .

"You have to take into consideration the nature of the man and woman involved," Miss Hubbard said gently, as from a height.

"Then too," Miss Smythe reminded them, "one must remember the emotional wave line of women which stands in contradistinction to the steady even flow of that of man. After all, one cannot ignore recent tests made by Dr. Peraugh," . . . .

So there it was, a Sunday afternoon tea where the discussion was sex, but elevated to the level of literature, psychology, and of course, the "most recent study." That night as they were preparing for bed, Dorothy asked Rayna if it was the custom for the young instructors to "hang over their teacups and worry about sex every afternoon?" Rayna thought that if they were leading "full lives," as Miss Hubbard had called it, "then they wouldn't spend so much time gabbling about it." Nonetheless, the two girls continued to ruminate on the subject, speaking, as they probably felt, from the safe and proper haven of their own virginity.

At another time, Mrs. Rose Pastor Stokes, the feminist-socialist, came to the university to speak on socialism, and after her lecture Rayna and Samson interviewed her for *The Daily Illini*. That afternoon, after the interview, Rayna was "blazing with enthusiasm . . . and her eyes had red lights in them." Mrs. Stokes told Rayna that she too had once had red hair, that she had worked in a factory on the East Side, and that, finally, "this New York millionaire came along to marry her." Rayna explained to Mrs. Stokes that she was not a socialist but wanted to interview her about the birth control movement. She thought that she and Dorothy might write it up for publication in *The Daily Illini*. The article would be sensational, she thought—and so it would have been, except that the editor thought it ill-advised.

And so went the happy part of Dorothy's year. Dorothy remembered laughing from happiness as one afternoon she and Rayna played hockey on the field in back of the university auditorium. As she and Rayna giggled over their awkward play, they heard, welling from the auditorium, the organ notes of a mighty Bach fugue. Dorothy laughed from joy. There were truth, majesty, and beauty in the universe!

Together Dorothy and Rayna listened to lectures on socialism, heard John Masefield, Edgar Lee Masters, and Vachel Lindsay read their poetry, and went to concerts. When spring came, they picnicked in the woods south of the campus. One glorious day in May, with bright green alfalfa covering the fields and the song of the meadow lark piercing the air, Dorothy, Rayna, and "Raphe" took their lunch, books, and even a portable phonograph to a shaded area beside a field. Having eaten, they put an excerpt from a Beethoven symphony on the phonograph and began to read. "I can see Rayna lying on her side in a dull green dress," Dorothy later wrote, "her cheek cupped in her hand, her eyes on the book she was reading, her mouth half open in her intent interest."

In June, 1916, Dorothy took her final departure from the University of Illinois. "I had been there for two years and to this day I haven't the slightest idea what I learned in class. All my education had come from the outside." Whatever she missed in her education, she had had her friendship with Rayna, and Rayna, when she graduated, married Samson Raphaelson—as it had all been planned.

What else Rayna had planned—a life of domestic contentment, as helpmate to her gifted and energetic husband, with perhaps some children—did not occur. Perhaps it was "the flame" in Rayna that called her to something else, that made her other than what Raphaelson wanted for a wife, but the marriage lost its meaning, and they separated and were divorced. Afterwards, Dorothy loyally took Rayna's part. Of Raphaelson, she later wrote that "he writes Broadway plays now and has a yacht and a penthouse apartment. But that is not what she wanted. She was avid for knowledge and for beauty, and what she wanted him to be was a great novelist who would increase the world's store of beauty."

Rayna graduated from the university in 1917 and that summer she visited Dorothy in New York. Later, in 1921, when Dorothy was back in Chicago she saw Rayna briefly while Rayna was taking postgraduate courses at the University of Chicago. By then Rayna apparently knew the cause she wanted to serve, having been converted to Marxism, at least in some degree, by a journalist named Bill Prohme. She and Prohme were married, a marriage, presumably, plighted to find its meaning in their service to the cause of world revolution.

After their brief Chicago meeting, Dorothy heard no more of Rayna until, in the late thirties, she read Vincent Sheean's *Personal History*. His story of Rayna's odyssey to China and then to Moscow, where her death occurred, affected Dorothy greatly. She read and reread it, the last time just a year before her own death.

Sheean, a journalist of adventure at a time when the world still had remote and mysterious places, went to China in 1927 to interview two leaders of the Chinese communist revolutionary movement: Michael Borodin, a Russian who had lived in America and had been a communist since before the days of the Russian Revolution, and Eugene Chen, a British subject born in Trinidad who moved into the Chinese revolutionary movement and culturally became as Chinese as he could make himself.

Developing something of a sympathetic interest in the revolutionary movement, Sheean sought to broaden his sources of information. One day, Henry Missilwitz, a *New York Times* journalist, told him that one thing he ought to do "right away" was to "go and see Mrs. Prohme." Who was she? A red-headed girl, said Missilwitz, "mad as a hatter, complete Bolshevik. Works for Borodin. . . . There was some talk about her giving up her nationality. You can't pay any attention to what she says—she's the wildest Bolshevik in town—but she's a nice girl, anyway, and you'll enjoy talking to her." As for her husband, who was at the time in another part of China, he was as crazy as his wife, only he shouted at people.

So Sheean and Missilwitz walked over to the office of the *People's Tribune,* a propaganda newspaper of the Hankow government, and just as they got there, Rayna was coming out. Sheean described her as "slight, not very tall, with short red-gold hair and a frivolous turned-up nose. Her eyes were of the kind that anthropologists call 'mixed,' and could actually change colour with the changes of light, or even with changes of mood. Her voice, fresh, cool, and very American, sounded as if it had secret rivulets of laughter running underneath it all the time, ready to come to the surface without warning."

As they walked down the street, Sheean made some flippant remark about people's mistaking him for a Bolshevik, but Rayna solemnly assured him that no such mistake could be made. Rayna should be glad that he was not a Bolshevik, Sheean said. Otherwise, "I couldn't get anything printed in an American paper about your revolution, and, as it is, I do." Rayna said she understood, it was what was called "being fair to both sides. You sit on the fence and say, 'on the other hand.' "

This was the kind of talk they carried on, as if they could not move beyond it to something of substance. Sheean tried to figure out what had motivated her, and he decided that she was a romantic idealist that had to have a "cause"—any "cause." Later he concluded that Rayna was not a romantic, but was utterly convinced that revolution was the true means for mankind's salvation. Much of Sheean's chapter, while it does deal with the events of the communist revolution in Hankow in June of 1927, is the story of his developing love for Rayna. What was the character of this "love"?

"It was not a sexual relationship. . . . Neither in words nor in gestures did it take the forms of intimacy known to the readers of a thousand erotic novels." Rather it was "an all-pervading, all-controlling emotion that had no physical basis."

But, of course, there was a physical basis for his love. It was Rayna, flesh and bone, dust—but a dust that was translated by spirit. She was "unified, integrated, and burned with a pure white flame. . . . It was a marvelously pure flame, and even though I clearly could not hope to share its incandescence," Sheean acknowledged, it seemed to him that he must hover as close to it as possible. "Nothing else I had ever seen gave the same light and heat." What finally was the passion that fueled his light? Said Sheean: "She felt a genuine relationship to all forms of human life. That was the essence of it."

Yes, that was almost "the essence of it," but not quite. What Rayna had was not just a feeling for the relationships of all of human life, but for all of creation. The simplest Marxist would understand the involvement of the material world with human well-being and Rayna understood that. What Rayna had was a mystical sense of the oneness of all. She had a vision of community, and it was this that lighted her soul and gave her that special radiance that Christians ascribe to saints.

On July 5, Sheean left Rayna in Hankow in order to go on a journalistic adventure hunt. Shortly after that, the revolutionary government there collapsed and its leaders, Borodin and others, fled to Russia. Sheean did not know what had happened to Rayna, but on September 18, as he reached the top of the marble steps of the Hotel Metropol in Moscow, he saw Rayna, "coming swiftly across the hall, laughing, hands stretched out, her eyes alight beneath the conflagration of her hair." Rayna had escaped with the rest.

During October, Sheean was in England and Germany, but longing to see Rayna, he made his way to Moscow, arriving there on November 7, the day of the celebration of the tenth anniversary of the revolution. His train pulled into the Moscow station in the morning, and the first thing he saw on the platform was Rayna's fiery hair. She had found rooms near the center of Moscow and had reserved two for Sheean. He had scarcely deposited his luggage there when she had him on the move again. She had two tickets to get a front-line view of the parading in Red Square that had been going on since morning.

It was an impressive show, as Sheean described it: "The enormous square was filled with marching people. Crowded, disciplined, innumerable, they came into the square under the arch of the Iberian Virgin and rolled across it to the Cathedral of St. Basil, where they vanished. For half a day the delegations from all parts of European and Asiatic Russia had been riding or marching through the square, and there was [sic] still scores of thousands to come." In a high box, next to Lenin's tomb, stood Stalin, saluting repeatedly, glowing at the sight of this dense and disciplined mass of humanity—and surely thinking that nothing on earth could match this spectacle that the revolution had wrought.

Rayna and Sheean watched for hours, and perhaps Rayna believed that she was witnessing one of the signs that marked the advent of the community she longed for. Sheean, on the other hand, was disturbed. He wanted Rayna to give up her life and join his world—to divorce her husband, no doubt, even to go back to Chicago and become Mrs. Vincent Sheean, wife of the well-known journalist junketeer.

But Rayna was obdurate. Already she had decided to become a member of the communist party and join the Lenin Institute, where she would be trained in the techniques of spreading the revolution. On Friday, November 11, Sheean and Rayna argued all night long, but nothing was changed. Rayna was to enter the institute on November 14. Upset, Sheean, as if following a movie script, asked Rayna to go out with him once more, to give him a "bourgeois evening." They would eat at Moscow's Grand Hotel and dance—"dance away the night," maybe, as some of the songs in the twenties used to have it.

Rayna agreed. She would do it, although she would probably freeze to death in the gold dress that Sheean wanted her to wear. Nonetheless, she would try to borrow a coat and they would "run like hell when we got out in the street."

The next day, Rayna went to see Dorothy Thompson in her hotel room. Miss Thompson, a well-known journalist married to Sinclair Lewis, was in Moscow for the Red anniversary celebration. In the course of the conversation, Rayna fainted. But that night she was almost effervescent. She felt grand; she predicted that she would enjoy her "bourgeois evening." And though Sheean thought she looked grand, there was a quality in her appearance that touched him with foreboding and sadness. "She was only a thin girl with no particular stature or figure or conventional beauty," but

the "red-brown-gold of her short curls gave her the look of a lighted candle."

After a while Dorothy Thompson came to their table and sat
with them, and Sheean, a little drunk by now, told her what Rayna
was going to do. "It's the end of Rayna Prohme," he intoned. "No
more Rayna. Finished. Revolutionary instrument Number
257,849." Dorothy Thompson responded by looking slightly in-
credulous, and Rayna laughed.

They ended their bourgeois evening together in an unbour-
geois way. Rayna wanted to go to a mass ceremony of the Congress
of Friends of the Soviet Union. Sheean tells what happened:

> It was held in the old Hall of the Nobility of Moscow, a marble palace
> that had served the ladies and gentlemen of Tolstoy's aristocracy for their
> splendid entertainments. Now the immense staircase was thronged with
> Communists and Communist sympathizers from all over the world, and
> proletarian delegates. Great banners strung across the marble halls, and
> across the ballroom itself, shouted in letters of gold on red, in all lan-
> guages: "Workers of the World, Unite!" On the platform Vorishilov, the
> head of the Red army, was speaking from the midst of the throng of
> Russian and foreign delegates, and as we searched out places in one of the
> galleries he was just about to bestow the Order of the Red Flag on the
> aged German Communist, Clara Zetkin.
>
> Zetkin, the Frenchman Jacques Sadoul, and the Hungarian Bela Kum,
> were the heroes of the occasion. Zetkin's appearance was (even to me on
> that night) impressive. The old woman had spent her whole life in the
> revolutionary struggle, and her cracked voice trembled with emotion as
> she thanked Voroshilov for her bit of ribbon and the throng of delegates
> for their cheers.

Sheean was standing by Rayna in one of the galleries as the
ceremony went on, and "as the roars of the crowd came up to us,
crashing in successive, irregular waves like thunder, she looked at
me and I could see that her eyes were brilliant with tears."

At that moment Rayna surely felt what she thought was the
meaning and destiny of her life. The power of the dispossessed
had raised their voices; they had unity, and nothing, ever, could
stop this force that would bring humankind to its final community.

That night, at the Congress of Friends of the Soviet Union,
where Rayna was so deeply moved, Sheean left her and spent the
rest of the evening alone, drinking himself into a stupor. The next
morning, late, he walked to the Hotel Metropol to see Rayna, but
was met there by Anna Louise Strong, an American journalist who

had become a dedicated communist communitarian. She told Sheean that Rayna was again ill, that she had fainted and was lying unconscious at a small hotel where the Chinese communist delegation was staying. Sheean found her there and carried her to the Metropol and placed her in Anna Louise's bed. After a while Rayna regained consciousness, and for moments over the next two days, she seemed almost light-hearted. Sheean came to see her every afternoon and she would tell him about her morning visitors and, particularly, about the old days in Chicago. In fact, says Sheean, the week passed almost gaily.

But Rayna was dying, and on Sunday, November 20, she realized it. Would she go to Germany for treatment, Sheean asked her? She said that she would when she had recovered some of her strength, and that night, says Sheean, she sent a cablegram. To whom she sent it and what she said is not known, but there is a story that she asked Samson Raphaelson for a thousand dollars to make the trip to Germany and that Raphaelson immediately sent her money.

The next morning, Monday, November 21, 1927, Rayna died. On Tuesday, an autopsy was performed and the conclusion was that Rayna had died of encephalitis, inflammation of the brain. Her funeral was held on Thursday, and it was, from Sheean's description, an occasion to break the heart of anyone who loved Rayna:

On the afternoon of the funeral we all marched for hours across Moscow to the New Crematorium. There were delegations of Chinese, Russian and American Communists, many of them whom [sic] had never known Rayna. It was very cold, and as I walked along I became conscious of the shivering bent figure of Mme. Sun Yat-shen. . . . She had no winter clothing at all, and was walking through the dreary, frozen streets in a thin dark cloak. . . . The band played—out of tune—the revolutionary funeral march. . . . The maddening music, its lusty brasses a good half note off pitch, made the long procession hard to endure. . . . Eventually—it was dark by now, and the great bells of the nearby convent were ringing for the evening service—we came to the . . . crematorium outside the city. It was brightly lighted, square and spare. The bier, draped in the Red flag and covered with golden flowers . . . all the flowers of Rayna's own colours, a heap of gold and red and brown, were placed on the platform. . . . Then a signal was given, a switch was turned, and the golden mass of Rayna, her hair and her bright flowers and the Red flag, sank slowly before us into the furnace.

Five weeks after Rayna was to enter the Lenin Institute, Dorothy Day was baptized, and Dorothy, who believed that community could be found only in eternity, prayed over the years of her life that Rayna had reached that state.

❧ 3

The Journalist

WHEN THE *Inter Ocean* went out of business in 1915, John I. Day, at the age of forty-five, was confronted with having to begin again to put down roots in his career as a sports-page journalist who took care of the horse-racing news. Sometime in the spring of 1916 he got the word that the New York *Morning Telegraph* could use him, and so that summer the family moved back to New York City after a ten-year absence. It was this move that prompted Dorothy to leave college. "I could not bear to have them go so far without me. . . . I was not as free as I thought." That was part of it; the other part of it was that she had pursued an aimless course at the University of Illinois and she saw no point in continuing there. She knew she would miss Rayna, but in New York there would be a new life and a new excitement.

When the family moved in June, she went with it. It goes without saying that her return to the family was on terms quite different from those that had existed when she had left for college back in the fall of 1914. It was Della now who took care of baby John and the household tasks that Dorothy had once performed. And Della, now sixteen, seemed much younger to Dorothy; the close companionship that had once existed between the two sisters had, for the moment, changed its character. Now in her pose as the worldly wise, emancipated woman, Dorothy must have been a little difficult to take. Like her father, she was practically a chain smoker, and airily waving her cigarette, she would brightly and energetically chat with her mother on "modern" subjects, ranging from her own social views to the idea of sex before marriage. Grace, for her part, accepted with good-humored resignation Dorothy's pronouncement that the traditional mother-daughter relationship would not stand "between us in our friendship."

That was the way it was with her mother—but not with her father. John decided that his daughter had come out of the university a red-ripe communist on the way to losing all of her principles. He would hear none of her talk, even if she had been disposed to air her views in his presence.

In August, Dorothy began making the rounds of newspaper offices, trying to find work. Every afternoon she took clippings of her writing from *The Daily Illini* and the Urbana town newspaper and tried to show them to editors, having prepared a bright and artful commentary calculated to impress whoever would hear her out with her energy, resourcefulness, and overall journalistic acumen. In some places, she did not get past the office boy, but eventually she did get in to see two city editors. One told her that she "was very young and that newspapers weren't the place for young girls. So did the next one. He said he'd never allow a daughter of his to work on a paper." One of them suggested that a country newspaper would be a good place for her, and he gave her an address.

In *The Long Loneliness*, Dorothy blames her failure to get a job with one of the larger New York newspapers on her father. She accuses him of telling "his city editor friends to lecture me on the subject of newspaper work for women." She probably did not accuse him unjustly. From the corner saloon to the barbershop to the newspaper office, John Day was implacably opposed to any intrusions by women. Least of all would he have accepted his own daughter into this male universe.

But daughter Dorothy, as single-minded as her father and as tenacious in holding her position, got a job. One late afternoon, just before supper, she burst into the room where her mother was and told her about her success. She had been employed by "that little labor paper" she had brought home several days earlier. The paper was the socialist *Call*. Grace was dismayed. What would her father think? The question need not have been asked. She knew what he would think.

In view of her father's attitude, Dorothy told her mother she would have to leave home. The *Call*, she said, was "a morning paper and I start work at three in the afternoon and don't know exactly what time I'll be through. And it's quite possible I'd run into father around twelve or even get home later than he did. And it wouldn't be only one row but many of them. He'd quarrel about my working and about what I'm working at, and the hours I work.

You know very well, too, he wouldn't quarrel with me. It would be with you." The trouble with her father, she said, was that he did not "seem to realize that we're old enough to reason with. Why, only last Sunday at dinner he turned to you and asked you if I liked the breast or the dark meat, just as though I weren't old enough to speak for myself. And instead of coming to me he'd ask you why I wanted to work and why you couldn't persuade me that it was impossible for young girls to be out at night alone."

To this argument, Grace answered, "I know—I've always borne the brunt of the misbehavior of all of you."

So Dorothy concluded, "You can tell father I just decided to go away and be independent just as I did that last year at college. Then he can't blame you. He'll only commiserate with you at having a thankless child. And you know ... I always wanted to live away from home and be independent." Her mother asked why she wanted to be independent, saying that it was contrary to nature. "It's just a case of living one's own life," Dorothy answered.

All of this sounds as if, John Day notwithstanding, Dorothy was determined to move out. In *The Long Loneliness,* she says she left because "my father made it plain that no daughter of his was going to work and live at home." So was Dorothy, after all, "thrown out" by her father? Not exactly. Dorothy knew the terms on which she could live at home: she must live according to the tradition of womanly respectability that John Day had been taught to revere— that is, all of the tradition except the church-going part. But Dorothy was in a hard mood, too. When she thought about traditions or rules, "she realized she was capable of doing anything—capable of following her desires, wherever they led, and justifying herself for so doing." What it amounted to was her word against that of her father, and she was going to have it her way, no matter what. As for John Day, it was hard enough just to hold on with the help of the few certitudes he had—his wife, the beauty of horseflesh in motion, and his old-fashioned morality and sense of family order— without having to make concessions to a daughter who would go the opposite way.

Dorothy began her work for the *Call* about the first of September, 1916. Applying there for a job had been, for her, a last act of desperation. At least John Day's rescript to his professional associates concerning his daughter's vocational search did not reach down to the grimy lower East Side of New York City. He probably did not even know that the *Call* existed. But Dorothy had known, and the day she got her job, she presumably got off the subway at the foot of the Brooklyn Bridge, walked west on Park Row past pawnbroker shops, saloons, and, at that time, recruiting stations. At Pearl Street, she turned east toward the East River, walked past three saloons and two warehouses and found the *Call* offices in an upstairs warehouse room over the Meisel Printing Company.

It was smelly, dingy, and noisy, the air crowded with the sounds of banging, shouting, cursing—boat whistles on the river and elevated trains, a block away at Chatham Square, blotting out all other sounds with their clattering and squealing wheels that shook the ground on which she walked. It was enough to make an eighteen-year-old girl recoil in alarm. But not Miss Dorothy Day, who took it all in as part of the vast excitement of New York, and besides, she was on a mission and she had a hard-sell campaign plan. Climbing the stairs, she walked into a large room where, beyond a counter, men were working. A small man with blond hair walked by and Dorothy told him she wanted to see the editor. He said he was the editor. Then Dorothy told him what she wanted. He laughed. No money, he said. But Dorothy persisted. The paper obviously needed a woman reporter, someone who could talk to women—to waitresses, for example—someone who could write sob stories. It was going to be a hard winter and there would be a lot of bad, heart-breaking things to write about. Chester Wright, the editor, was interested, but he still pleaded poverty. Sometimes, he said, they even had to take up a collection from the office workers to get the paper through the next day's edition.

Then, according to Dorothy, she had an "inspiration." She told Wright about the "diet squads" around the country, particularly some "society women" in Chicago who were feeding themselves on a quarter a day. She would make herself a diet squad of one and live on five dollars a week. "Lots of factory girls are living on that and I had lived on nine in the country." Dorothy was referring to the previous summer when she had lived with Rayna on her father's farm. "I pointed out to him that working girls couldn't very well club together the way these 'squads' are doing and that I'd like to show how it would work out."

This vivacious and eager young woman could not be denied, at least by Wright, so he said that if Dorothy would take five dollars a week for a month and live on it he would hire her. At the end of the month, he would raise her pay to twelve dollars. So Dorothy dashed home, told her mother all about it, said good-bye to Della, and to whoever else was at home, and the next day lugged her heavily packed suitcase to the *Call* office. She got there shortly after noon, but Wright said she could come in at five since she still had to find a room.

Getting the room was another adventure. She walked east on Pearl to Madison and south on Madison to Cherry Street. On Cherry, she found "furnished room" signs, and wherever she saw one, she would stop and investigate the place. In her search, she "came across backyard houses, shut in between high walls of warehouses and factories and other tenements. I came across many a house with backyard toilets." The hallways were dark and evil smelling. There were tile floors, usually slimy with filth. The hallways were narrow with a door on either side opening into the front apartments. At the dusky end of these halls were two more doors entering the rear apartments. The stairs led up five flights with windows looking out into the areaways. Finally she found a room in the apartment of a Jewish family.

In *The Long Loneliness,* she says that her guardian angel must have been directing her because she took the first room she entered, and it turned out to be a good choice. Her room was in a fourth-floor, four-room tenement apartment; the other three rooms were inhabited by a Jewish family of six in which neither the mother nor father spoke English. Nonetheless, the mother conveyed to Dorothy the information that the family was Orthodox and that cleanliness was therefore required. That was fine; the only trouble was that the bed, with the thick mattress that looked so inviting, had bedbugs in it and, despite the landlady's repeated attempts to exterminate them, they always survived to marshall their forces and mount another attack.

It was a small and spare room, lit by a candle, and with a single gas burner on the table with which Dorothy could manage a breakfast and a late snack. On the table was a row of books and there were pictures on the wall of Amenemhat III, Stefansson the explorer, and Belmonte the bullfighter. One day she saw an advertisement in the *Call* that said for a dollar down and a dollar a week for fifteen weeks, one could buy a table phonograph. She bought it, and her mother contributed fifteen records of Fritz Kreisler's violin playing. When she got up in the morning, which was ordinarily late, she would put on a record, a Sousa march, fix a bowl of cereal, and eat it as she read a book propped against the milk bottle. With "Stars and Stripes Forever" ringing up and down the stairwell, it was not long before a bevy of children crowded around Dorothy's door. Her landlady would try to shoo them away, calling them "smootchy faces," the only English words she knew. But "Mrs. Gottlieb" herself, as Dorothy called her, was enthralled with the music—not with Sousa, but with Fritz Kreisler.

For the remainder of her life, Dorothy always said that her home in New York during this period of her life had been the East Side, and she would deny with asperity that she had ever been a Greenwich Village habitué. There was, for her at least, an atmosphere about the East Side, inhabited by Russian and Jewish immigrants, that was foreign and exciting, something in the tradition and spirit of the people there that appealed to her sense of the place of tradition in life. She found it in their belief in God as she saw, sometimes, shopkeepers and workmen reading psalms and saying their prayers during a moment of respite in their work; she found it in their attitude toward knowledge as something sacred for which one hungered. She noticed, for example, how Mrs. Gottlieb's twelve-year-old daughter spent all the time that she could in reading, how this girl had come to her own room to show Dorothy books that she had read and to borrow books. She found this tradition and spirit of the people in the joy and purposefulness of their sense of existence—singing together in the public showers where they washed themselves and their children, and she found it in their compassion and understanding, traits possessed by a people have who have long endured suffering.

While Dorothy in her autobiographical books makes much of her fourth-floor habitation with this Jewish family, she stayed there only three months. In *The Long Loneliness,* she tells of some of the unpleasant aspects of life in her room. In addition to bedbugs in the springs of her bed and in the walls, her room was cold and she had only the one-burner gas stove to heat it. Gusts of wind came down the airshaft and poured through the window, which looked into the dismal well. "The hall odor seeped in through the cracks and woke me with its stench," and "at night cats prowled in the halls and their howls wakened me so that I sat up in bed wet with perspiration and trembling all over. Sometimes they shrieked with almost human voices as though that stairway were haunted by lost souls."

There was also the walk home, usually between two and three o'clock in the morning. The streets along which she walked were Cherry, Madison, and Pearl. In the daytime, they were filled with the shouts of playing children and the admonitory voices of mothers standing on the fire escapes that fronted the tenements. But at night these streets were "strangely sinister." "It seemed at first that she, alone in all the world, was awake. Her footsteps so stirred the silence the first night she went home that she had rubber heels attached to her shoes the next day so that she could swing along without feeling so gruesomely alone."

After several nights of walking, Dorothy discovered she was not alone—"a whole silent world was alive, a world that slept at dawn as she did. There were huge sleek cats, furtive pariahs that prowled through the hallways and gutters. And their cries and calls answered the dreary rustle of the wind in the trash of the street. A dull murmur came from the coffee house, a subdued bustle from basement bakeries, the door of which opened sometimes to give out a warm, sweet smell of coffee, bread, and a glimpse of a perspiring and floury baker sniffing the night air."

She came across a phantom figure, an old woman who ran down the street, pausing occasionally to catch her breath and call out for someone. One cold night on her way home, she stopped, as was her habit, to chat with two policemen who kept a late-night station under Manhattan Bridge. They had warned Dorothy of the hazards on her homebound course and had even provided an escort service along Madison Street. This night they had a fire going in a trash can and a pot of coffee steaming on a grate that lay across the top of the can. As Dorothy drank the coffee they shared with her, the old woman she had seen calling in the night emerged from the darkness and approached the fire. The policemen encouraged her to come and warm herself.

"How about it, mother?" they said. "You haven't found him yet? Better come and get warm and have a cup of coffee. You've hunted long enough tonight. Better luck next time."

The woman was a prostitute, and to Dorothy's horror the policemen said that she was still at the business whenever she could induce some drunken sailor to pay for services performed in an alleyway. The policemen told Dorothy the woman's story as they had heard it from others. She had inhabited the area, a dock section, for most of her life. In recent years, she had become deranged, and her calling in the night was for a son she had had some forty years earlier and who, when he was eighteen, had been killed in a street fight. But it was not for the grown son that she called. It was for him as a child. Her name was Audrey, and the police, with heavy humor, called her "Dis-audrey conduct." As the old woman stood next to the fire and drank her coffee, she babbled of the injustices she had suffered from others who shared her life and from one in particular who had stolen her undershirt. To give evidence of her loss, she unbuttoned her blouse to show the padding of newspaper she had tied around her chest.

Leaving the safety and warmth of the fire, Dorothy faced the terminal part of her homeward course—climbing the three flights of stairs to her room. Garbage and children's playthings lay on the steps, and cats, looking for food, would sometimes dart between her legs.

The walk home and the bedbugs were reason enough to move, she may have decided, but the fact was that Dorothy never stayed anywhere very long. An available location that was novel, that permitted a flow of romantic fancy, would start her to speculating on its ideal qualities, and without giving the matter any considered reflection, she would jump, assuring herself and others around her that it was the perfect solution to her problem—just what she and everyone else needed. At least, it would be better than where she was. So one afternoon, as she was exploring an old Episcopal church down on the East Side near the river, she noticed that it had a parish hall with a sign in the window saying that rooms were for rent. Perhaps as she went through the church, a memory was stirred of the ardent religious feelings she had once had when she lived on Webster Avenue. Anyway, she took a room there and moved in the next day.

With her living situation improved, she could concentrate on her work. The *Call* was a socialist paper, but its "socialism" had no philosophically consistent or clear line. As Dorothy described its philosophy, the paper took roughly four positions, which corresponded to the interests of the editors. One position supported the American Federation of Labor, another spoke for the Amalgamated Clothing Workers, still another espoused the cause of the I.W.W. (or the "Wobblies," as such proponents were called), and there was one voice for the anarchist point of view, although what brand of anarchism, it was not clear.

Dorothy herself never was a card-carrying member of any of these groups, although she fully maintained her college days enthusiasm for whomever she regarded as a victim of a merciless capital. Naturally, as a young reporter, anxious to keep herself "professionally informed," she went to many lectures given by the radicals of the time. The most effective speaker she heard, she said, was Elizabeth Gurley Flynn. Flynn had come to New York to raise money for the relief of the miners' families and for labor defense. "Wherever she spoke, the audience wept and gave heartily to the cause. The night I heard her . . . I gave everything I had in my pocket, not even saving out carfare, so that I had to borrow the fare back to the office and go without lunches for some days afterwards."

Emma Goldman was another orator who had been stirring audiences for over twenty years in support of the anarchist philosophy, but Dorothy never met her or heard her speak, although they exchanged letters in later years.

Lectures, rallies, and picketing. It was all exciting—inflaming, even—for one never feels so selfless and noble as when bound to others in the action of a just cause. At least this was the way Dorothy felt then, just eighteen years old and glorying in it all.

Her job came first, of course. During her first two months at work, it amounted to helping get out the next day's paper. Her own by-lined stories began to appear in the *Call* on December 3, 1916. "New York *Call's* Diet Squad tries Life on $5 a Weak," ran the headline. Beginning the story, Dorothy explained what she was up to: "The average working girl receives five dollars a weak. We hear an awful lot of the barren statistics, but you never get the real thing. So I have taken a room on the East Side, down on Cherry Street, and I am going to follow the course of eating the Association for Improving the Condition of the Poor dietician gave me. I am going to live on five dollars a weak all by myself for one month, and each weak I'm going to tell how it feels. I am sure that it [the result of this experiment] will be quite different from the one that the diet squad in Chicago says it is." Dorothy's stories, four in all, which ran through December, turned out to be as flat as her intended humor in the first story where she used "weak" for "week." Her December 5 story was entitled "Reporter . . . Eats Farina and Cheese and Reads Wordsworth." On the 10th, she gave her report, telling her readers (by now, surely, declining in droves) that she had survived the week with forty-eight cents left over.

The series was supposed to run for a month but on December 27, with a week to go, the editor told Dorothy that that would be enough. As Dorothy said, "It is a frightful bore to have to state specifically what you ate, what you are eating, and what you are going to eat. Also how much you paid for it. And whether you have enough in your pocket or vanity case to pay for tomorrow's grub...." On January 28, 1917, she wrote a piece called "Plucky Girl on Picket Line Braves Knives of Scabs and Guerillas," and then on February 2, she did a major feature on Margaret Sanger's sister, Mrs. Ethel Byrne, who was on a hunger strike for birth control.

As Dorothy relates in *The Eleventh Virgin*, by February, birth control had become her first cause. "Of course birth control would solve all the troubles in the world. With birth control you wouldn't have any more children than you could afford to support and educate. Economic necessity would no longer be an excuse for the woman of the streets; and with education, a moral and social sense would be developed. No more poverty. And when women were not forced to have more than two children, they would have time to look into the laws. There would be a better educational system and a better industrial system."

Full of soaring enthusiasm for the "cause," the young reporter, age nineteen, attended meetings of the Birth Control League and made it her business to stand daily outside a clinic that had been started in Brooklyn. Her vigil was rewarded: the clinic was raided. Next came the trial of Mrs. Byrne, a nurse, who was taken to Blackwell's Island prison where she began her hunger strike. Rumors from the prison rolled out and over one another: she was being forcibly fed, brutally treated; she was dying. Mrs. Byrne herself became a cause, giving the governor little choice but to pardon her, which he did.

At this point, Dorothy's problem as a reporter was to guess where Mrs. Byrne would surface after leaving prison, since a good many people would be wanting a firsthand description of her physical condition. Dorothy supposed that she would go to her apartment on the West Side, and so, late in the evening of the day that had been assigned for Mrs. Byrne's 11 P.M. release, Dorothy knocked on the door of her apartment and was promptly admitted by a young "poet" who flitted about the room plumping pillows and arranging daffodils.

It was a quarter of twelve when Mrs. Byrne arrived in a taxi. Exiting, she gave Dorothy a three-sentence interview, the substance of which was that the horrors she had supposedly endured had been actually quite mild. The interview ended, she turned her attention to the versifier, and Dorothy went across the street to a telephone to get her story into the *Call*.

In *From Union Square to Rome,* Dorothy summed up her reaction to the Byrne affair. She had been assigned the story of Ethel Byrne, with the understanding that she was to present a picture of Mrs. Byrne and her sister as martyrs in a holy cause. She was "to paint harrowing pictures of the suffering of Ethel Byrne in jail and after her release. . . . Actually she did not suffer from her hunger strike and was perfectly well and strong when she was released from jail. . . . I realized that I was distorting the truth, and it sometimes irked me that my job was always to picture the darker side of life, ignoring all the light touches, the gay and joyful sides of stories as I came across them."

After Dorothy's move to the East Side, she did not return to her parents' home for visits, wishing, obviously, to avoid seeing her father. In one of her "diet squad" articles in the *Call,* she said that because of her loneliness she was "suffering the tortures of the condemned" and that she was "afraid" that she was getting homesick. Frequently, though, her mother and Della would meet her at the office for her supper break, and sometimes one of the three young men who worked in the *Call* office and whom she had gotten to know would go along with them.

One of these men, as Dorothy relates in *The Eleventh Virgin,* "was a young Jew, twenty-five years old, who had lived all his life in New York and who had worked for the last five on the *Clarion* [the *Call*]." This man, who would, in the thirties, achieve recognition as the hard-boiled editor of the communist *Daily Worker,* was Mike Gold, born Irving Granich. In *The Eleventh Virgin,* Dorothy calls him "Ivan" and says that he was the city editor of the *Call.* She describes him as an able and efficient journalist, who, after a period of intensive work, would fail to show up at the office. "It was generally understood on these occasions that Ivan was on one of his poker sprees which lasted until he returned to the office several weeks later, a nervous wreck and in debt to the extent of several hundred dollars." This failing of his aside, Dorothy liked him, and after several weeks at the *Call,* she fell into the custom of having pancakes and coffee at Childs Restaurant on lower Park Row with Gold and two other editors whom she labels "Chester" and "Emil." These meetings would occur in the early morning hours after the work on the next day's paper had been finished. Sometimes these gatherings went on until after 3 A.M. Having eaten, Dorothy would sit back in her chair, langorously inhaling the smoke from her cigarette, as she listened to Mike and the other two men talk about literature and "complexes." For how, in January, 1917, could a group of young people sit in Childs Restaurant in New York at three in the morning without invoking Dr. Freud's "complexes"? As they talked, Dorothy could hear the almost continuous ring of wheel flanges against rails as streetcars turned to cross the bridge over into Brooklyn, and every half-hour, the Third Avenue car clanged as it passed the bridge. When finally they went out onto the street, paper boys were already shouting news. It was about the war impending with Germany.

It was during this period that Dorothy and another *Call* reporter (it could well have been Gold) interviewed Trotsky, who was then in New York writing for the Russian socialist *Novy Mir.* Trotsky was so opposed to the parliamentarianism of the American socialists that the *Call* editor was unwilling to give much space to his remarks. So the interview was severely cut and its substance tossed into the trash basket. Otherwise, it might have gone as one of the high points of Dorothy's journalistic career. But Trotsky, relatively insignificant in the latter days of February, would, a few weeks later, become one of the world's prominent revolutionary leaders.

On March 21, Dorothy, with Mike and some of the others on the *Call* staff, went to Madison Square Garden where, she said, "I joined with those thousands in reliving the first days of the revolt in Russia. I felt the exultation, the joyous sense of the victory of the masses as they sang 'Ei Euchnjem,' the worker's hymn of Russia." It seemed to signify, said the *Call* the next day, "that the progress of human events was 'like the flowing of the river.' " And Dorothy almost believed that in the Russian Revolution a great new vista had been reached in the flow of the river, that all was beginning to converge, that time had not and could not betray the vision of final community now because it could be so plainly seen just ahead.

It was in March, too, that Dorothy suffered an affliction which temporarily replaced her revolutionary excitement with a prior concern with her own physical condition. She got a case of what in those days was referred to in elevated circles as *la grippe,* or the flu. Had she been living on Cherry Street, her landlady would certainly have nursed her as best as she knew how—perhaps even giving her chicken soup—but now that she had a room on the second floor of the gloomy and cold Episcopal rectory and did not know, or even see, any of the other roomers, she was on her own. And her landlady, the young wife of a rather elderly cleric, while apparently

realizing that Dorothy was ill, seemed to have tolerated her presence only when she could indulge in some self-righteous moralizing on the crude manners of her Irish servant girl.

For two days, Dorothy lay in bed, dragging herself twice to a
nearby bakery to get milk and bread. On the third day, she called
Mike Gold and asked him to bring her some whiskey, lemons, and
cough medicine. Mike, full of solicitude, said he would be there
that night after work, and Dorothy, to know when he was coming,
told him to whistle "Poor Butterfly" as he approached the rectory.
She would then go to the door and admit him; this way they could
avoid ringing the doorbell that would disturb the others.

So in the cold dawning hour of the morning, when all that
could be heard was a boat whistle on the East River and the fainter
sound of an occasional streetcar picking up momentum after it had
discharged a passenger, the sad melody of "Poor Butterfly" came
wafting up from the street below, and Dorothy, looking out of her
window, could see Mike's figure silhouetted against the flaring illumination of an arc light. Quietly, she descended the stairs and
admitted him.

Dumping the supplies on a table, he looked around the room
and was aghast at its dinginess, bareness, and moldy odor. Why did
she not move up to Eighth Street where the rest of them lived?
Dorothy explained that she liked the uniqueness of living in an
Episcopal rectory in a Jewish neighborhood, that the odor put her
in touch with antiquity, and that she liked living alone. They talked
about the politics of editing the *Call,* about whether or not the
editor was giving too much space to the American Federation of
Labor and too little to the Amalgamated Clothing Workers, about
"Chester" and "Emil," their companions at early morning breakfasts. Then Mike pulled out several poems he had written, read
them, and then read from a book he had found, *Gosta Berling,*
written by a Swede, Selma Lagerlöf, and first published in 1909.
What with the talking and reading, it was 6:30 before Mike got up
to go, but even then he returned, bringing Dorothy six pieces of
buttered toast and a large cup of hot milk.

Then she went to sleep and slept all day. That night she went to
work. The following day, up and dressing at noon, she heard a
knock on the door and shortly her mother came in. The occasion
of this first and completely unexpected visit had been a telephone
call from Dorothy's landlady to her mother. The landlady had
gone on at much length about Dorothy's questionable morals as

witnessed by her having a man in her room all night. Grace, though, was in no mood to listen submissively to a telephone diatribe against her daughter, and she said as much to the gabbling woman and hung up. Nonetheless she was concerned about Dorothy and forthwith she set out to see for herself what was going on. To find the place, she stopped at the *Call* office for directions and there she found Mike, who explained the circumstances of his presence in Dorothy's room. It was the landlady's fault, he said, because she had neglected Dorothy. At ease regarding Dorothy's behavior, Grace hurried on to Dorothy's room where she found her daughter recovering. While she fumed over the landlady's action in calling her, she did observe that in her day it was not considered proper for young ladies to receive men into their bedrooms, much less let them stay all night. Even so, there was no question at all but that Dorothy must move and she would help her pack then and there. It was done, and Dorothy moved to Eighth Street, as Mike had suggested.

It is possible that between moves Dorothy spent some time at home, but there is no record of it. Unquestionably, John Day, who was absolutely consistent in carrying out an edict once he had issued it, had had no change of heart about his daughter's living at home. If, as Dorothy says, he had ordered her out of the house once she had taken her job, there was no revocation of that order. What this cost him in personal distress is impossible to know, but surely it cost him something.

There is, of course, the question of what else might have occurred that night in Dorothy's room. Years later, one of those simple-minded unsophisticates who would occasionally account the Catholic Worker farm at Tivoli, New York, a home asked Dorothy out of the clear blue if it were true that she had had an "affair" with Gold. This person was, of course, treated to one of Dorothy's frigid silences—the hardness in her eyes and a growing paleness of her face that had the power of moving in waves of desolation from her, wilting the unfortunate blunderer. Another kind of Dorothy might have said, "No," and that would have been the end of it and the truth of it. But any prying of this sort represented an intrusion onto the most vulnerable parts of her person and none was ever permitted or even recognized.

It was, of course, true that, from the early months of 1917 through the following summer, she and Mike were close companions and later she would say that they had been "engaged." In one of her "On Pilgrimage" columns written in the later years of her life, when she frequently fell into a mood of reminiscing, she said that Cesar Chavez, the Mexican labor leader, had reminded her very much of Mike. "I was eighteen years old and used to spend a great deal of my time with Mike exploring the streets of the East Side, or sitting at the edge of piers over the East River and talking about life and the miseries of the working classes. Every now and then he would break into a song, whether in Hebrew or Yiddish I do not know." Occasionally, Dorothy said, Mike would "take me up to his home where his Orthodox mother wore the traditional wig of the Jewish women who cut off their hair at marriage. She used to look at me with great sorrow. All three of her sons, it seemed, were running around with Gentile girls." Dorothy said that if she ate at the Granich home, the mother would break all the dishes that had been used, since "it would not be kosher to use them again."

The thing that brought Mike and Dorothy together was their interest in literature and personal sensitivity to and concern with the establishment of new norms of "freedom," not only in terms of the social order but in terms of those values that society would have govern their lives. But if they ever were "engaged," it did not last long. It was sometimes laughingly said, among those who had been close to Dorothy over the years, that Dorothy did not have enough of the character of the *hausfrau* to suit Gold.

As for Dorothy, there is reason to think that her interest in Gold never moved into even the lower levels of romantic excitement. They were friends, not lovers, and perhaps scarcely hand-holders. Dorothy just was not "in love."

What leads one to this conclusion about the relationship between her and Gold? Because in *The Eleventh Virgin*, which was written no more than three years after this supposed romance, she speaks of him only as a "close friend." In *The Eleventh Virgin*, she describes herself as being "more sexless and unemotional" at the age of eighteen than she had been at the age of fifteen, a condition that she attributed to her "increasing mental activity." Mike Gold, then, obviously did not ignite the same conflagration of emotions as the lithe and muscular Armand Hand had when she had lived on Webster Street.

Still, the idea of sex "out of bounds" was not objectionable to her. In discussing the subject with her mother, she said that she had decided that in "all the books she read—English as well as

Russian and French translations—conventions were forgotten," and when they were, it seemed to her that "the race had benefited by the stimulating companionships of men and women even though they rested on the basis of sex." And what right did a man have to ask that his wife present herself to him as a virgin on their wedding night? Suppose, said Dorothy to her mother, the wife said to her husband, "Yes, this man was my lover and every moment I spent with him was beautiful. The experience made me more human because I loved so much. But it passed. We grew past it, and now we are not lovers, but friends."

Such a pronouncement might do for a novel, her mother told her, but it would not fit into the accepted order of things. She knew that, Dorothy said, but why was she having so much trouble thinking clearly on the subject? "God knows," her mother replied, "I don't. But I'll trust to your instinct, not your mind, to take care of you through life." If by this remark Grace Day meant that she would trust her daughter to conform instinctively to the conservative traditions of sex and morality, despite the latter's unorthodox views on the subject, she was trusting in something that Dorothy was already deciding to reject. This can be concluded from the attitude she took toward two opposite positions on the subject of sex, taken by two friends during this time. One friend she calls "Ellen Winter," and this Ellen, in a special way, one gathers, was the friend of one of Dorothy's journalistic associates, "Chester." Chester loved Ellen, wanted to marry her, but could not because of a disastrous earlier marriage that he could not, for the moment, legally dissolve. And Ellen, firm in her scruples, would not forfeit her chaste state until Chester was certified as her husband. It was after one of their early morning breakfasts at Childs that Chester urged Dorothy to go with him to Ellen's flat. She would be waiting up for him, would have hot coffee ready, and besides, the place was steam-heated. Willing to accept the favor, Dorothy went. She found Ellen a blond woman-of-the-world type and precise in her speech. At the moment she was writing a play, and that evening she and Chester fell into a long discussion of the contemporary state of the art. If they ever came to a conclusion, Dorothy did not know it, because the cozy warmth of the room and the softness of the cushion-strewn sofa on which she sat, and then reclined, dulled her senses and then blanketed them completely. She slept well into the day.

Perhaps sensing that Dorothy needed instruction and also feeling that she, by virtue of her ten-year seniority over this young and seemingly impressionable reporter, could be an influence for the good, Ellen Winter frequently telephoned Dorothy at the *Call* office and asked her to spend the night. And Dorothy, grateful for the physical comfort of Ellen's place, if for nothing more, would go and listen to Ellen's solemn warnings against the loss of her virginity. Whatever the world said or did, it was the sign of an affirmation of the special and unique place of woman in the design of creation. Virginity was the seal that could be broken only when the act of sex was solemnized by marriage. Whatever the impulses of the male and at whatever level he might account the value of the sexual act, it was for the woman to keep truth itself enthroned at this primary point—it was indeed her special and sacred prerogative, the magisterium of her supremacy over man.

But Dorothy was not impressed. As she confided to her mother, she disliked Ellen's continual "harping" on virginity. She was sick of it.

It was a month or so after Dorothy met Ellen that she met "Billy Burton," whom she described as "a pert little artist, whose one idea in life was to follow the whim." Billy Burton, in "real life," was Peggy Baird. Mike Gold had run into her some place in the Greenwich Village area and had introduced her to Dorothy. Soon Dorothy began to drop in on her. What attracted her to Peggy is still not entirely clear. They certainly shared no intellectual or literary interests, since Peggy scarcely read anything more elevated than the pulps. Her credential for Greenwich Village was that she was an "artist," and though some might question her qualifications in this area, she otherwise loved freely—a trait which also fit within the Village view of things. She was kind and an interesting conversationalist, and she smoked and drank to a degree that most persons found excessive. She was not beautiful, but she had a suppleness and a strong suggestion of readiness about her that men found hard to resist. She had a large number of friends, as do people who genuinely like other people, and doubtless she was admired by the company in which she moved for her seeming mastery of the problems of complexes and inhibitions. This quality, at least, initially drew Dorothy to her.

Dorothy found Peggy late one morning, as usual, in her small room, sitting in bed, smoking a cigarette in a long green holder, and sketching nude women on a pad propped against her knees. Peggy was a mess, her dark auburn-blond hair every which way over her pillow, and the kimono in which she was wrapped had seen uncounted days since its last washing. As Dorothy entered, she heard Peggy muttering a succession of "hells" as she worked with her drawing, but when she saw Dorothy her disposition soared. Dorothy had come in the nick of time: she needed a cup of coffee. Everything was behind a curtain that divided the room. So Dorothy lit the gas burner and fixed coffee. As she commented on the number of pages of incomplete drawings on the floor, Peggy suggested another favor. What? "Just strip off your clothes—the room's warm enough, and while you're drinking your coffee, I'll sketch you."

Almost nonchalantly, Dorothy stripped and curled up on a sofa, lighting a cigarette. Had men started making love to her yet? Peggy wanted to know, adding that Dorothy was "just the type." Yes, they had, Dorothy said. It was a kind of adolescent lovemaking, not done "violently enough to be convincing." There was "a sort of futility" about it. It was "purposeless—as though they did it because everyone else does it. I don't get half so many thrills as I thought I would when I became grown up and untrammeled." "Untrammeled," was not the word, Peggy rejoined. She was "unawakened."

Ellen Winter's preachments on the value of old-fashioned morality, delivered from behind her neatly set table with the electric percolater on it, had not touched Dorothy. Peggy, though, who made sexual pleasure a natural part of her existence, seemed to Dorothy to have taken the honest position. The difference between them was that Peggy was not disposed to give to sex the dressing of high drama that Dorothy would have for it. Dorothy, it almost seems, looked to some kind of Wagnerian passion. Whoever "Ellen Winter" was, she appeared no more in Dorothy's life. As for Peggy, her wandering path left Dorothy's, but then crossed and recrossed it, and finally remained with it for the last quarter-century of her life.

March came, and Dorothy, in her reportorial role—and also because she had found a cause that she fully affirmed—started attending the meetings of some Columbia University students who wanted to protest the nation's obvious course toward war. They had leaflets and posters printed, and at night, they—Dorothy included—would walk into the downtown department store area and paste their posters on store windows and the sides of buildings. It gave them much personal pleasure to placard the front of the Union League Club with peace posters.

It was apparently on Thursday, March 29, that Dorothy made

her mid-morning arrival at the *Call* office to find a note on her desk. Mike Gold wanted her to join the students on a peace trip to Washington. Rushing home, she picked up a few clothes and joined the group that was gathering at Union Square to board a hired bus. Out they rolled, across the ferry to Newark, and headed south to Philadelphia. As they entered towns, they would stop; the students would get off the bus and try to hand out leaflets and even make speeches. But the national mood was hardening in favor of war and the local police would hustle them on. That night they stayed at Philadelphia, where a "professor from Columbia" paid the bills for lodging and meals and otherwise chaperoned the group. The next night they were in Baltimore, and it was on a Saturday, apparently, that they tried to hold a peace meeting in an "auditorium." However, by then, "the war spirit had become so feverish that our meetings were broken up as fast as we started them."

And so it was at Baltimore, with a riot to boot. The gathering had started out, Dorothy says, as "a most dignified meeting," only to be invaded by a group of "Catholic college students," who began an assault on the peace advocates as "Jew radicals." A commotion followed that spread almost immediately to the crowd in the street outside the hall. Reverting to her professional role, Dorothy pushed toward one of the police wagons that had been pulled up, and she tried to see who among her friends was to be carted off. Struggling to get to the wagon, she was hit in the ribs with a club wielded by a policeman who was trying to keep a lane clear. She gives an account of this in *The Eleventh Virgin*.

The surprising thing, she discovered, was that you could enter into the spirit of the mob even when [the club] descended against her ribs with a hollow sound.... She felt it, but it did not hurt. She felt it, but it did not disturb in any way the curious, detached, mad feeling that flowed through her veins as the crowd seethed and shouted and fought.... [She] looked at the policeman who had used the club and perceived that he could see but dimly through a veil of blood that clouded his eyes. He had a cut across his forehead....

"Excuse me," he said politely, "I can't see."

On Monday morning, April 2, 1917, the streets of Washington filled. People, charged with an electric surge of expectation, moved outside the White House gates and up and down Pennsylvania Avenue. Many persons carried small American flags, but among the milling throng was a noticeable number who wore white arm bands—pacifists. Were Dorothy and her friends among them? They might have been, but she does not say.

Up at the Capitol, a leading proponent of war, Republican Senator Henry Cabot Lodge of Massachusetts, was sitting in his office when he was summoned to the door. A group of young people wished to register with Lodge their opposition to the war. An argument developed. One of the group reportedly called Lodge a "coward."

"You are a liar," Lodge was reported to have said, and he followed his declaration by hitting the offending spokesman in the face with his fist. The victim retired with a bloody nose. Lodge had given "the only appropriate reply," said the *Washington Post*. Moreover, said the *Post*, it was significant that Lodge's critic "was said to have a German name."

At noon, Congress assembled, while at the White House President Wilson restlessly awaited the news that the body was organized and ready to receive him. It was after 4:30 when the word came. The president could be received at 8:30. At 8:10, Mrs. Wilson left to sit in the gallery with the wives of cabinet members. And ten minutes later, Wilson left. With him were his personal physician, Cary T. Grayson; his secretary, Joseph P. Tumulty; and an army colonel.

Some three hours earlier, Secretary of War Newton D. Baker had received a message from State Secretary Robert Lansing. In the interest of the president's safety, could an army cavalry unit be provided to supplement the usual police escort to the Capitol? The procession was, for most of the people who lined the route, an unforgettable sight: their president with set features, sitting in the car, looking straight ahead, while stern-faced men of war sat ramrod stiff on their horses. A light rain fell, causing the streets to glisten with the reflected light of the buzzing and flaring arc lamps above them. Ahead of Wilson, the newly illuminated Capitol dome shone whitely against the dark background of the cloudy sky.

At 8:35, the Speaker of the House announced: "The president of the United States." Wilson walked in crisply, placed his manuscript on the rostrum, and with a hint of impatience, waited for the applause to cease. Then he began to read, deliberately and without oratorical flourish. What he read represented an epoch moment in Western history. The nation was asked to organize for killing so that an ideal might be established and then forever remain alive in the process of time. It was thrilling; it was apocalyptic—the vision of a luminously glowing new beatitude in time to be obtained by one final letting of blood. Was it worth the price to be paid? Yes, oh yes, said Congress in dutiful obedience to the obvious will of the American people. The high moment of community that war brought was worth all of it.

Was Dorothy touched by this patriotic fervor when the feeling for a national community rose to an ecstatic moment in which death did not exist and time ceased? Did her opposition to war, on the grounds that it was a capitalistic device, waver? Not at all. One of her enduring character traits was an almost complete immunity against the wash and flow of public enthusiasms. Besides, as she said, "we got to Washington too worn out and dirty to care whether war was declared. . . ." Wilson' s speech was "an anti-climax—at least in personal experience."

Back in New York, she told her mother and sister Della about her exciting trip and otherwise made plans to go to a dance at that mecca for large-scale Village socializing, Webster Hall on Twelfth Street. The affair, billed as the "Anarchist Ball," was to be held on Friday, April 13, and her "date" was apparently Mike Gold.

This dance turned out to be significant in Dorothy's life because it was the occasion of her leaving the *Call*. It happened this way: In the course of the evening, an acquaintance, a disheveled and slightly unbalanced person who called himself an anarchist and who at the moment, was awaiting a prison sentence for distributing anticonscription leaflets, saw Dorothy from across the dance floor. With a glad cry he rushed forward to embrace her. Taken aback by the ardor of his affection, she either slapped him or pushed him away. She could not remember which, but it is likely that she slapped him since the anarchist retaliated by slapping Dorothy. At this point, two gallants, reporters from the *Times* and the *World,* who were there to cover the ball, seized the man and hustled him out of the hall. It was Mike Gold's sharp criticism for having slapped a fellow radical that led her to resign her job—or, more likely, just walk off.

In *The Long Loneliness,* Dorothy writes of this slapping episode and then comments at length and with much contrition on her action. She had not been "a good radical," presumably because her response to the anarchist's embrace had resulted in violence and ignomy imposed upon him by two representatives of the capitalist press. Nor had she, as she reflected on the matter some thirty years later, acted like a Christian: "Had I been a Christian I would not have rebuffed the boy, and certainly would not have struck him had I been a true pacifist." Finally, once the incident had occurred, she would "not have wanted others to come to my rescue, making a mountain out of a molehill."

That Dorothy included this episode in her third autobiographical book and not in the first two suggests how her view of things changed as she grew older. That she could, when pressed, lash out, physically and verbally, was apparent on one occasion after another during her youthful years. In later life, of course, her assaults were only verbal and infrequent. And when they did occur, she was soon all contrition.

Having quit the *Call*, she worked for several weeks with the Anti-Conscription League. Most of its members were college students, and they needed someone to keep an office open and handle the mail. The league paid her fifteen dollars a week, which was three dollars more per week than she had been making at the *Call*. Also, working for the league meant no regular night work.

One day in late April, Dorothy May Day was long-striding along Fourteenth Street when she met Charles Wood, drama critic for the *Masses*, coming out of a saloon. She knew Wood from her reporting work with the *Call*, and sometime during that period, he and she had made an agreement that they would systematically investigate all of the saloons between the Battery and Canal Street, and the East and North rivers. For Dorothy, it was something "crazy" to do, something to talk and laugh about. On this occasion, Wood's intention may have been more businesslike, for he suggested to Dorothy that they re-enter the saloon so that he might have another drink to build up his appetite for lunch. She could have a glass of wine. After their refreshment, he would take her to meet Floyd Dell, the assistant managing editor of the *Masses*. Yes, Dorothy said, she would love to meet Dell, but she could do without the wine. So off they went to meet Dell who, at the time, was dining at a German restaurant on Third Avenue.

Floyd Dell was an aging (thirty-three-year-old) oracle of the "new" morality. Though he had never finished high school, he nonetheless developed an interest in writing and had some opinions about the state of contemporary literature. First a newspaper reporter in Davenport, Iowa, and then a book reviewer for a Chicago paper, he went to New York in 1911 to make his way in the editorial world. In 1914, he became the assistant editor of the *Masses*. In 1917, many who knew him thought he would be a famous man of letters someday, and his association with the *Masses* was taken as a certain sign of this.

They found Dell, as Wood had said, seated at a table at the restaurant, delicately and deliberately eating his food. Dorothy noticed that he was tall, slightly built, and that he had the appearance of a man who stayed up all night and slept through the day. She found that his eyes were "luminously sympathetic." At least Dorothy thought they were—so luminous and so sympathetic that she was emboldened to suggest to him that she write a review for the *Masses*. And Dell, liking her brightness and the assured way she talked and handled herself, said go ahead. A week later, he telephoned her, inviting her to have lunch with him at a little restaurant near the *Masses* office. So the next day, at the appointed time, she threaded her way through the tables to where Dell sat. He had a proposition: would Dorothy like to be his assistant editor? Max Eastman, then traveling, had agreed to allocate ten dollars a week for such a position to take the pressure off Dell of getting out the monthly edition of the *Masses*. He would teach Dorothy the technical procedures of getting out the magazine and otherwise leave to her the matter of choosing its material, for, as he said, he recognized that Dorothy had literary taste.

It was in these years, just before and during World War I, that an entirely new phenomenon arose. Because of an acceleration of the process of history, a cultural fault had begun to appear in the life of America's middle class. It was almost imperceptible at first, a rebellion of youth against their elders—a few young people who breathed a different air, who saw a new meaning for existence outside the traditional values with which they had been reared, who wanted to be "free," as they would say, for they were of the age of Freud, whose catch-phrases came glibly to their tongues as they celebrated their emancipation. And from what did they wish to be free? From the established view of sex and morality, from the Puritan ethic, which they could see only as a slavish devotion to capitalistic crudity and repressive and outmoded values. Time would redeem them; the old gods would not, nor would the everlasting God—if one existed. As a mark of faithfulness to their emancipation from the past, they assiduously practiced what they professed, and, like all who have seen a light, they sustained themselves, in the day and through the night, with one another's presence in the bare and cold flats of Greenwich Village.

It was largely persons of this disposition who supplied the material for the *Masses,* a magazine that began in 1911 as an insignificant socialist publication emphasizing cooperatives. As the publication strove to survive, its editorship was placed, in December, 1912, into the hands of Max Eastman, a twenty-nine-year-old Columbia University graduate student and assistant to the famous philosopher of process liberalism, John Dewey. Eastman had long since departed from the Puritanism of his forebears. He stood at the forefront of his generation's break with the past, the passionate apostle of a new freedom against outworn repression. He was tall, blond, charming at times, and he was literate. He was a Greenwich Villager, but one who liked his daily hot bath and his evening meals with candlelight and linen.

Eastman, unlike most Villagers, had managerial ability and an appreciation of the value of a dollar. Under his editorship, the *Masses* took a turn to the left, featuring writers such as John Reed, Randolph Bourne, and Upton Sinclair; poets Vachel Lindsay, Amy Lowell, and Louis Untermeyer; and cartoonists Boardman Robinson, Robert Minor, and Art Young. Some of the people who have written about the *Masses* refer, almost reverently, to its blatant irreverence, for it was the style of its youthful staff to jeer and laugh at the old order from which they, as they continually congratulated themselves, had escaped. Milton Cantor, in his biography of Max Eastman, refers to the journal as "the gaily irreverent *Masses.*" Cantor quotes the capacious and wide-ranging queen of Greenwich Village, Mabel Dodge, as remembering the *Masses* as "fearless and young and laughing at everything solemn and conservative." Her recollection was corroborated by Daniel Aaron in his *Writers on the Left.* The *Masses* people, he says, would gather at Mabel's "evenings," where they sat or lay in insouciant disarray around the floor, "happily subverting the social order by word and deed."

Dorothy began working for the *Masses* on a Monday in the latter part of April. The world might be seized in the convulsive agony of war, but never before had life seemed so pleasant to her. The East Side felt like home, and she had a circle of Village and East Side friends. Now she had an important job. She would be, in effect, the editor of the *Masses,* and though the publication would, as they all seemed to surmise, be submerged in the rolling wave of war, the position was for her completely new and challenging.

So excited was she that, on that Monday morning, she awakened before daybreak, two hours before she needed to get up. Watching the dawn break was also a new experience for her, since for seven months her usual procedure had been to pull the shades and sleep until eleven. But this morning her shades were up, and, turning in bed to watch the eastern sky, she saw it begin to lighten and turn violet. Sounds, separate and distinct, came so clearly into her room that she could hear them from some distance. It was first the birds, chirping and fluttering in the trees and under the eaves of houses. Then, from two blocks away, on the waterfront, she heard a man whistling the "Star-Spangled Banner." On the East River, a starting tugboat engine coughed and then settled into a steady chugging.

Her happiness at that moment—the coming of dawn on the Lower East Side on April 23, 1917—and the way in which the first sounds of day filled her senses combined to etch the experience so indelibly on her memory that she described it in *The Eleventh Virgin* some three years later in Italy.

By seven o'clock, she had darned her stockings and washed and dressed. Ready for her adventure, she went down the street into the fair air of morning. But first, breakfast—and what, she wondered, was better than breakfast "at seven in April. . . . Both the month and the hour are in [its] favor. Poached eggs on toast, the latter thick with fresh butter, coffee that is half milk, the paper . . . propped up against the water carafe before you. You can get such a breakfast in some of the East Side Jewish bakeries." Hooray for the East Side Jews! They could garnish a happy morning with rich fare.

After breakfast, she walked up Fifth Avenue to Fourteenth Street and over to the building at 33 West Fourteenth Street. On the fourth floor at that address, the *Masses* offices were located in three rooms. At nine in the morning, only the office girl was there, but Dorothy, with her competent air, asked the girl to take her to Dell's office, a room at the front of the building whose sole window overlooked Union Square and its park—a place for Village lovers to sit and stroll, as well as a haven for those concerned with less important matters, such as finding a bench on which to lay one's head or a spot on which to stand to call upon the world to follow the true road to salvation, either in eternity or in time—although mostly the latter, providing a revolutionary adjustment could be made.

Dorothy's business was not in the park but on Dell's desk, a pile of unopened mail six inches high. She was to go through it and reject or accept would-be contributions to the *Masses*. All letters had to be personally answered, even those from aspiring authors who did not stand a chance and probably never would. Going through the letters, she found one contribution called "Passerby."

> There were two of them,
> tight corseted,
> tight lipped,
> tight minded,
> jealous
> of my loose dress,
> loose breasts,
> loose morals
> the lover at my side.

Whether this poem was good or bad, Dorothy seemed not to be quite certain, but she liked it so well that she included it in *The Eleventh Virgin*. On the face of it, the poem fulfilled the standard Village criteria for a midnight, middle-of-the-floor reading in a cold flat: nothing rhymed, it was about sex, and it derided the "old" morality.

For several days, Dorothy answered letters. When she was not doing this, she sat by the window that looked out over Union Square and read books that had come in for review. Occasionally, one of the *Masses* artists would stop by to leave a drawing for an up-coming edition and would pause a while to chat. In this fashion she got to know the well-known Art Young, Hugo Gellert, Boardman Robinson, and Maurice Becker. Poets came in to read their works, and others came in to ask for advice. Within her limits, which she would have carefully set forth, she would give her opinion.

For three days, Dorothy was, in effect, editor of the *Masses*. Then Dell returned, looking pale and tired. He said he had been working on a novel at night and had been unable to sleep during the day. Besides, he said, he had spring fever—he was restless. Going into the main office, he shortly returned with David Karb, the advertising manager, and Merrill Rogers, the business manager. It was unusual, but Dell, Karb, and Rogers all happened to be there at the same time. They had decided, Dell said, to close the office and go on a picnic in New Jersey where, Dell said, he had "a little old shack." So off they went, stopping at a grocery store to buy food, charging it to the *Masses* "general expense" account.

The day was spent in talk. They talked about themselves, but mostly about themselves and sex. Karb, who had lived most of his youth in Texas, had graduated from Harvard and then driven an ambulance in France during the first six months of the war. Shell-shocked, he had returned home to recover, and, seeking light work, he had taken a job with the *Masses*. He sympathized not at all with the positions the magazine took, and he was, at the moment, trying to get back into the war in some branch of the American service. Where the subject of sex was concerned, Karb was, in Dorothy's view, another Ellen Winter, for he was an inflexible advocate of chastity in the unmarried state. Merrill Rogers was from Massachusetts. He was inarticulate, Dorothy thought, except that when the conversation took an interesting turn he would respond with an increased vigor of pipe-sucking that filled the air with wet sounds. This was annoying to Dorothy, but she soon got used to it and otherwise regarded Rogers as a most decent and good person.

It was Floyd Dell who led the conversation that day. Directing most of it to Dorothy, he revealed himself as an ardent feminist and an unqualified advocate of "sex for the single girl," a position he backed with a frequent invocation of "complexes." It was understood that to have a complex was to invite insanity and that the only way to avoid this fate was to yield freely to one's inclinations where sex was concerned. A woman, he told Dorothy, should not remain in the virginal state "after she had felt the first tingling of desire." To this Dorothy responded, as she had responded to Peggy Baird, that she had felt sexual excitement only once and that was when she lived in Chicago. By Dell's reasoning, she said, she should have had her first sexual encounter then. She supposed that the reason the subject had ceased to interest her was that the people with whom she now worked and associated were "so free in their discussions and I've heard so much about sex that it loses its importance the more I learn. It's no longer a temptation to indulge in desire. It isn't forbidden. You speak of it as a supremely right thing to do—to take a lover or as many lovers as you want. . . . We [in Greenwich Village] can't think about society and the condemnation of society, because we don't live in it." Look at the people on the *Call* and the *Masses*, she said. "Anything short of absolute promiscuity is disregarded as long as you can speak of sexual relationships as love affairs."

One suspects that Dorothy's speech represented a point of view not original with her, that she had heard the same thought voiced by her mother. Whether she actually believed what she said—that the reduction of sex to a response to a simple biological impulse had so cheapened it for her that she was without such an impulse—seemed questionable to Dell. He did not believe it, he said. He even went so far as to invoke one of the standard opening remarks used to inaugurate a campaign of seduction. He said, as Dorothy recorded it, "You make me furious with your pose of cool indifference; I know you're an exotic person. Don't you suppose my feelings tell me something? It isn't that I want you...."

He was lying, Dorothy told him. She recognized an "intellectual" approach to seduction when she saw one, and where she was concerned, she would just as soon be the object of a more primitive technique. But Dell, in her opinion, was too primitive. His love encounters "should take place on the stage of the Hippodrome before a packed house."

Dorothy's "no thank you" to Dell did not mean that she was subscribing to an Ellen Winter affirmation of virtue, no matter what. It meant that there was no stirring passion where she was concerned, and it certainly meant that she did not want to be chalked up as another episode in Dell's sexual adventures.

How much credence can be assigned to her recital of this picnic afternoon's talk about sex with its personal dimension? The essence of the incident is unquestionably entirely true, mainly because Dorothy was incapable of manufacturing the scene or of distorting what actually occurred. The words given in *The Eleventh Virgin* may not be the same words spoken that afternoon, but the sense was the same. Further, Floyd Dell himself affirmed this particular episode in her life. In his *Homecoming,* he says, "For a while my assistant on the *Masses* was Dorothy Day, an awkward and young enthusiast, with beautiful slanting eyes." She had written a novel, Dell said, one that contained "the quite true story of a very delightful though unusual summer."

It was at the end of the day that Dell suggested to Dorothy that she move into the apartment he shared with Karb and Rogers, a place on MacDougal Street right above the Provincetown Playhouse, one that had been loaned to the *Masses.* So Dorothy, always ready for a new experience, and feeling that the prospect sounded appropriately unconventional and exciting, moved in. Later, all would proclaim that the arrangement had "worked," and perhaps it had. Anyway, it remained intact only from the first of May through June. After that, Dell went to his "shack" in New Jersey to work on his novel, and Karb and Rogers, too, had places to go. So from July through September, when at last the *Masses* was suppressed by the government, the place was Dorothy's alone. Luxuriating in the room she had, she held open house for all who wished to come, talk, and even sleep, if they felt like it.

The summer of 1917 was a high point in Dorothy's life, a time when the enthusiasm and optimism of youth were full upon her, when days moved always onward, a fairyland of enchantment and excitement, when there was no sign of an abyss ahead. The world was hers; she would never die; she could do anything. At the Mac-Dougal Street apartment, she was up by seven, the first to take a cold, splashing bath in the tub, and while the others arose and bathed, she went to the bakery for morning bread. When she returned, the men had coffee ready, the table set, and were scrambling eggs and slicing tomatoes. Through with eating, they reached for cigarettes, more coffee, and then distributed sections of the morning paper around the bright orange table that could, when called upon, seat twelve. Almost invariably there was a guest for the evening meal, after which they sometimes played poker.

More often than poker, though, they fell to discussion, and increasingly the subject was the war and the upcoming draft on June 5. Particularly, Dorothy remembered the night of June 4, when a whole company of the male members of the Village's literary aristocracy assembled in the apartment to debate what course they would take the next day. Max Eastman was there, the blond, godlike Max, come back to the Village for the moment in the course of his summer lecture tour. There was Jack Reed, in whose restless soul was a call for community to which he knew not how to respond, except to plunge into the heart of those revolutionary causes that promised to free humankind from its misery and make the world into a paradise. Within months, he would be on his way to Russia to witness the Bolshevik revolution and, later, record what he saw in *Ten Days That Shook the World*. After that, he spirited himself out of the country and headed for the new Soviet Republic where, in October of the following year, he died from malnutrition and disease. How curious was the eccentricity of fate that the young Dorothy Day, no doubt sitting on the floor in one of the two crowded front rooms and listening to Reed speak, would a half-century later visit the Kremlin wall where his ashes were placed and pray that he had found his community at last.

Albert and Charles Boni were there as well. That year they would join with Horace Liveright to launch Boni and Liveright, a publishing house dedicated to bringing out material that reflected the age's new values. Six years later, the Boni brothers, by then publishing independently of Liveright, would bring out Dorothy's *The Eleventh Virgin*. Harold Stearns, who would shortly be editing *Civilization in the United States* for Liveright, was there, adding his voice to the discussion. And Mike Gold, again on the best of terms with Dorothy, was among the group. There must have been twenty persons present that night. It was an occasion, Dorothy said, that "she would never forget."

What radical decision did this radical group reach when their discussion ended at 3 A.M.? They concluded that they *would* register—not that they preferred it that way—in fact, some said, all things being equal, they would prefer prison. But in the end, the need for sleep and a higher logic broke their resistance. "It was better to prolong their usefulness in the radical world by sacrificing their principles." So early the next morning, they all registered. Some, though—and Mike Gold was one of them—escaped the draft by going to Mexico.

In *From Union Square to Rome*, Dorothy memorializes "the one true, consistent objector I knew at the time." He was the younger brother of *Masses* artist Hugo Gellert. When Gellert was put in a guardhouse camp on Long Island, Dorothy, Mike, and Hugo visited the young man and found him seemingly content with his lot, since his incarceration was not onerous and the guards seemed friendly. The day after one of their visits, though, they got the news that Gellert had committed suicide. It was shocking and unfathomable where Dorothy was concerned. Gellert, for his part, insisted that his brother had been murdered.

Yet there were lighter moments in those June days. Dorothy and her three housemates, tired of the cold and dreary winter, sallied forth in the warm evenings to embrace the world again. They went to burlesque shows. On other occasions, they took the ferry to Staten Island and then went by car to a deserted beach where they took off all their clothes and swam in the surf. Since there was no moon, Dorothy felt that her modesty had not been breached. One night they went to Coney Island, and Dell, who had never been there before, insisted on riding the roller coaster which, of course, provoked much squealing punctuated by Dell's kissing Dorothy in the darkness of tunnels.

When the men moved out at the end of June, Rayna came to visit. She had just graduated from the University of Illinois, and surely she and Dorothy looked forward to reestablishing the closeness of their friendship as well as the happiness of two summers past when Dorothy had stayed with Rayna on the Simons farm. It was a happy summer, judging from Dorothy's account of it in *The Long Loneliness.* "We walked the streets of New York with Mike Gold and Maurice Becker, sat on the ends of piers singing revolutionary songs, dallied on park benches, never wanting to go home to sleep but only to continue to savor our youth and its struggles and joys." There were parties at night, with Dorothy going out in the morning for rolls at a little French bakery on Sheridan Square. Many afternoons there were picnics along the Palisades, or a ferry ride to Staten Island and then a streetcar to the beaches where she and Mike dug for clams, lay on the sand, and talked.

As to what Rayna was thinking then about life and the world, Dorothy says nothing. Could it have been, though, that in that moment, when the world was convulsed with the failure of the Enlightenment vision to find a final solution to the hitherto errant character of social progress, Rayna had begun to glimpse a new vision? Did the singing of revolutionary songs on the piers of lower Manhattan in the star-jeweled beauty of the night bring some mystic sense of community rising out of chaos and lift her heart to new hope? It may have been.

Those late night hours of sitting on the pier could well have produced a different kind of mood in Dorothy. Singing revolutionary songs was fun, but when the singing ended and the talking lagged from weariness, she could lie on her back and look at the firmament, even to that all but invisible star. And as the waves washed quietly against the pilings below and the spaced and distant sounds of the harbor came to her through the warm, salt-scented air, she had the feeling that she and the star and the night were one and that all belonged to eternity.

But what of the *Masses,* with Dell writing his book, Eastman traveling, and the assistant editor frolicking, talking, and dreaming? The *Masses* was doomed; this became clear when, in June, Eastman got a letter from the postal authorities which said that the magazine's mailing permit was to be rescinded. So the last three issues were left for Dorothy to get out, and she, with everything in the doldrums, found that she could do all the work in several hours each morning.

Now that she was editor, she began to include some of her own work in the magazine. In the July issue, she introduced a poem, "Mulberry Street":

> A small Italian child
> Sits on the curbing
> Her little round, brown belly showing
> Through a gap in her torn pink dress.
> Her brother squatting beside her
> Engrossed in all-day sucker,
> Turns sympathetically
> Wipes her nose with the end of his
> ragged shirt
> And gives her a lick.

In the September issue she reviewed a novel, *Helen of Four Gates*, authored by "An Ex-Mill Girl." It seems obvious that Dorothy reviewed the book primarily because it gave her a platform from which she could express her opinion of the "modern" attitude toward love. It was, in substance, the same point of view that she had tried to register with Floyd Dell on their picnic afternoon, an attitude which was most un-*Masses*-like.

She knew, she said, that the idea of uncommitted love relationships "has taken pretty complete possession on the whole intellectual field. The conversations of intelligent people is [sic] conducted upon that premise." Increasingly, novels used this theme. And she could see in the personal lives of those who practiced this cult a set attitude toward love that amounted to "religious dogma." It was, she said, that "love—or rather love affairs—should be taken as passing phases, or as joyous adventures, or as new experiences— or, most discouraging of all, as incidents in an erotic education. The idea of permanence is dismissed as old-fashioned."

What those people who took this view of love would think of *Helen of Four Gates*, she did not know, because the book "tells of a love so profound as to be, I am afraid, quite unintelligible to them." But as for her, she liked it very much "because it tells the story of a man and a woman who can love each other, in spite of everything, to the end."

What Max Eastman and Floyd Dell thought of this, there is no telling, but they may have seen it as a matter of wry humor that the

Masses, with its long history of celebrating the new age of free love, would end on this note of affirming old-fashioned commitment.

In the November-December issue of the magazine—the last issue—Dorothy reviewed Upton Sinclair's *King Coal.* This book was about the hardships and dangers that attended the life of a coal miner. Dorothy was passionately at one with the miners, and in her review, she sounded off against her favorite malefactor—John D. Rockefeller: "It would be no comfort to go up to Rockefeller's Sunday school class and hear about the amelioration of working class conditions . . . because only a year ago in June, one hundred and sixty men burned alive in the Speculator mine of Butte, Montana, and only a few months ago, girls had their eyes and noses and fingers and ears blown off in the explosion at Eddystone. . . ."

In this last edition of the *Masses,* Dorothy included her description of South Street, and it was in this kind of writing that she caught so well the substance of small segments of life: "South Street, where the truckmen and dockmen sit around on loads of boxes and wait for a boat to come in, where men idle in the September sunlight and dream and yawn and smoke, where the horses clatter along the cobbles dragging huge heavy trucks with a noise resembling a mob of people aroused after long repression, and, where the kids sit on the edge of the dock and look with wishful eyes at the water below that swirls with refuse and driftwood." Occasionally, as she described it, there would be a lull in the noise and then one would feel "a wave of soft silence, golden in the September sunlight with the autumny smell." But characteristically, Dorothy could not leave her subject on a note of lightness. "The smells change too, . . . and the mellowness is replaced with a heavy foul odor from God knows what storehouse, and from the river that gulps and gulps at the docks all day long."

By the end of September, the work on the *Masses* was through. One night, Samson Raphaelson swept into the MacDougal Street apartment in the midst of a dinner party. His mission was to get Rayna to return to Chicago. Thus ended the happy days of the summer of 1917.

🌿 4

Adrift

MIKE GOLD did not go to the *Call* office on the evening of November 9, 1917. Instead he asked his friend and companion, Dorothy Day, to meet him at a Village basement restaurant and bar to get something to eat and to talk a while. There were subjects to be discussed: Mike's peril where the upcoming draft was concerned and Dorothy's unemployment. There was always the war to talk about, to denounce, and the revolution in Russia—a cause of joy. They were thus sitting, with a mounting number of cigarette butts in Dorothy's ashtray, when Mrs. Peggy Baird Johns, as she called herself then, came in and sat down with them. As usual, she looked a little disheveled, with her small white face and the startling red Cupid's bow painted on her mouth. Gold, who never thought about being tactful, told her she looked as if she were on drugs. Where had she been for the past month? In jail, she said. She had been evicted from her room because she could not pay the rent and, tired of the precarity in her life, she had impulsively joined a woman suffragist who was on her way to Washington to picket the White House. Peggy thought she would go along, too, and let somebody else take care of her for a while.

She told her story as she went through a succession of drinks. No, she was not committed to the cause; she would not vote if she could, but there was something exciting about the tension and atmosphere of conflict that came when the police herded the women into patrol wagons and took them off to jail. Some of the women had been quite defiant and she admired their spunk. In fact, she said, she was going back to Washington that night for what appeared to be a major confrontation the next afternoon. Would Dorothy go with her? Yes, Dorothy certainly would. With some of the young men she knew facing the prospect of prison for draft evasion, this would be her way of opposing "the system." Later that evening, Mike, who warmly approved the venture, took an exhilarated Peggy and a sober but determined Dorothy to Pennsylvania Station to catch the train for Washington.

Women's suffrage had been in the air a long time—certainly over a good part of the lifetime of Susan Brownell Anthony, the New England school teacher whose crusading zeal had been directed first against drink, then against slavery, and, after the Civil War, towards the emancipation of women, especially in the matter of voting rights. On her birthday, February 15, 1900, at the age of eighty, she retired, leaving one more cause for the new century, a century which in time would have more causes than it seemingly could digest.

After 1900 the suffrage movement grew at a new pace, energized by women who believed that suffrage for them could lead to the solution of many social problems—even to the end of war. It was further energized, as are all crusading movements, by persons who liked the sound of their own voices rising to declamatory heights and by those people, especially, who felt lifted out of the dull routine of life when they found what they considered to be a worthy cause to pursue.

In 1913, the campaign for a national suffrage amendment was launched and the issue moved to Washington. The amendment issue moved there in the persons of two young women, one of whom was Alice Paul, daughter of a Quaker family of Moorestown, New Jersey. After graduating from Swarthmore, Alice Paul took graduate degrees in politics and sociology at the University of Pennsylvania and then went to England for more study. In the course of all this academic work, she apparently had what today would be called "a consciousness-raising experience." She must have decided that to settle into a teaching position at some female institute or young women' s college would accomplish little in the face of the great changes the world needed. One change that was required was that women should be loosed of the shackles that bound them, and the first major step toward their freedom was to get the ballot.

In appearance Alice Paul was slight—even frail. Her dark brown hair was pulled low over her forehead and caught in a roll at the back of her neck. If there was anything about her looks that suggested the mystical and all-consuming way in which she embraced the suffrage cause, it was her eyes. They were clear and almost pale—eyes, which according to her sister suffragist, Doris Stevens, "strike you with a positive impact" and make "you feel the indescribable force and power behind them."

In *The Eleventh Virgin,* Dorothy, too, comments on Alice Paul's eyes. "There was something compelling" about them. "It was said around headquarters that she could make a fractious devotee do anything she wished by just looking at her." Dorothy thought at first that such comments "arose from admiration, but the more she saw of the suffragists the more she realized that it was something more than just admiration of her followers toward her. There was a quality of blind adoration."

Doris Stevens, who apparently adored along with the rest, characterized Miss Paul as a "flaming idealist," one who conducted the battle "with the sternest kind of realism, a mind attracted by facts, not fancies." She fought "fearlessly and with magnificent ruthlessness. Thinking, thinking day and night of her objective and never retarding her pace a moment until its accomplishment, I know no modern woman leader with whom to compare her. I think she must possess the same qualities that Lenin does . . . cool, practical, rational, sitting quietly at a desk and counting the consequences, planning the next move before the first one is finished."

The second woman who went to Washington in 1913 and brought the qualities of the zealot to the movement was Lucy Burns, a school teacher from Brooklyn. Alice Paul met Miss Burns in 1910 at London's Canon Row police station The two had been arrested, along with some hundred English women, for attempting to petition Parliament on the suffrage issue. All went to prison for thirty days, on which occasion the two American women joined their British sisters in a hunger strike. Doris Stevens thought well of Miss Burns, too. She was "the very symbol of woman in revolt. . . . Her body is strong and vital. She was the ideal leader for the stormy and courageous attack—reckless and yet never to the point of unwisdom." Dorothy described Miss Burns as "tall, deep-chested, red-haired and vigorous." She breathed "the atmosphere of combat," a type which Dorothy found more appealing than Alice Paul "with her quietly compelling and assured eyes."

A crusade usually requires a devil figure, and for suffragists, the villain was Woodrow Wilson. Over the years of his first administration, he was petitioned and visited by deputations of suffragists who pressed him to recommend to Congress an amendment to the Constitution that would enfranchise women.

No, said Wilson, he could not just "recommend" things; there had to be an "organic" welling up of policy issues from the people he represented and for whom he spoke. There was no clear call for a national suffrage amendment, and besides, suffrage was primarily a matter for the states to handle. When the Democrats convened in the summer of 1916 to make up their platform for the fall presidential election, they would go no further than to recommend that the states enfranchise women.

The re-election of Wilson in 1916 and the growing issue of war did not interrupt the suffrage crusade; to the contrary, suffrage leaders felt it was necessary to extend themselves even more. The campaign they had made in the West against the president had been successful, so the suffragists told themselves, and more than that, it had produced a martyr for the cause. Inez Milholland, of Vassar and a resident of Greenwich Village, had been a suffragist since 1909. Styled the "Amazon Beauty" of the suffrage movement because of her Wagnerian proportions and dark intensity, she found that declamation was one of her gifts and that plunging into the excitement of rallies and meetings suited her taste as much as the company of the literary and liberated companionship that she kept in the Village—people such as Floyd Dell, Max Eastman, and her husband, Eugene Boissevain. While speaking at a rally in California she fainted, but not before she had uttered her last challenge to Wilson: "Mr. President, how long must women wait for liberty?" After this she died—not immediately, but after some days and after she said other things, too.

That her death had resulted from pernicious anemia did not affect her canonization in the cause. She was, in the words of one sister suffragist, "the gallant and beloved crusader who gave her life that the day of women's freedom might be hastened."

Thus was introduced the tempestuous year of 1917, the year that shortly would bring America into the war in Europe and the year that the women's crusade would increasingly distract the nation's capital from an exclusive concentration on the war. On January 10, the first line of sentinels appeared before the gates of the White House, prepared to picket. For six months, this activity continued, with increasing annoyance to official Washington, whose primary concern was the war. On June 26, six women were found guilty of "obstructing traffic" and were sentenced to three days in jail.

That event was the beginning of a growing parade of picketers who received increasingly severe sentences. The demonstration on November 10 was planned for a special purpose. This demonstration was to be held on behalf of the rights of political prisoners. "We felt," wrote Doris Stevens, "that as a matter of principle, this was the dignified and self-respecting thing to do, since we had offended politically, not criminally." Mike Gold, who thought that this was an important issue, urged Dorothy to participate in the picketing. And Mike's approval meant something to Dorothy.

Doris Stevens's roster of picketers for the November 10 demonstration, which she includes in her book, *Jailed for Freedom,* lists forty-one persons. Dorothy says that she counted thirty-five. The women came from a wide background of situations, locations, and age groups. Some were wives of well-to-do husbands and thus had the means and leisure to promote a cause. Dorothy noted that a number were "middle-aged maiden ladies and straight-backed school teachers," who, perhaps because they were without husbands and children, had time for a cause. The youngest demonstrator was Miss Matilda Young, described by Dorothy as "a slim thing just out of school. . . . She was a quiet, gentle little creature and it was infinitely pathetic to think of her being locked in a cold solitary cell." The oldest demonstrator was Mrs. Mary Nolan, up from Jacksonville, Florida, who said that she was seventy-three, although Dorothy said she was eighty-six.

When Dorothy and Peggy got to Washington, they presumably went to the house that served as the Woman's Party headquarters, where they were put up. Here they soon learned that the picketing and prospects for prison that they faced the next day would require of them more than a few days in jail. Leader Alice Paul was already in jail on a hunger strike, but Lucy Burns was there on the scene, advising the women what they should do if, while in prison, they felt they were being abused. The women were also urged to hunger strike for their rights, as Alice Paul was doing, if they could.

On the afternoon of the 10th, the picketers, just prior to their departure for the White House gates, grouped themselves for pictures in front of a lattice trellis at the headquarters. All wore purple and gold sashes, draped over their right shoulders across their bosoms and joined under their left arms. Dorothy, it appears, carried her sash across her left shoulder. Most of the women look, in Doris Stevens' pictures, as though they were dressed in high fashion for an afternoon tea, the younger ones wearing skirts that were ten inches above the ground and revealed ankles delicately arched to present their best line to the camera. But not Dorothy, who stands solidly on her two feet, tall and angular and plainly dressed. Peggy is in the picture, too, looking a little dowdy in her flowery hat, a furpiece around her neck.

The parade began just as government workers were taking their Saturday afternoon off and heading home for the weekend. Starting from a park near the White House gate, where they had been marshalled, the women marched two-by-two in groups of six. Dorothy was in the second group, and as she walked, she thought of the stately processions that she had witnessed as a child in Our Savior's Episcopal Church in Chicago—the cross-bearing and surpliced acolytes moving down to the altar. She noticed that a "holy light shone on the faces of the suffragists." But, she concluded, it was the occasion and not the cause that had produced this "holy light." She felt "without doubt" that most of the women, like Peggy and herself, were there for reasons other than the cause of women's suffrage.

As they marched, they were beset by cries of disapproval from men, and some women, who thought that the parlous times demanded an exclusive devotion to the higher cause of defeating the Hun. As they approached the White House gates, the orderliness and solemnity of the procession began to fray. Dorothy had to wrestle with a red-faced sailor who sought to seize the banner she was carrying. In the commotion, which became general, a patrol wagon came clanging up the street, then another one, and the marchers were ushered into them. Since there was no room inside for the banners they carried, these were put on top of the wagons, and, thus bedecked, the wagons went clanging off again, this time to the Central Police Station. There, the women registered their names and addresses and were told to appear in court on Monday morning.

In court, it was Mrs. Harvey Wiley, looking "appealing and beautiful," who addressed the judge concerning the high purpose that had brought the women before him. Aside from her looks, Mrs. Wiley had stature as the wife of food chemist Harvey Wiley, who had done much to bring to the country's attention the extensive problem of food adulteration. "We took this action," she said, "with great consecration of spirit, with willingness to sacrifice personal liberty for all the women of the country."

The judge, according to Doris Stevens, responded in a less lofty vein. He admonished the defendants "with many high-sounding words about the seriousness of obstructing the traffic in the national capital." Then he went on to describe the situation in Russia and the danger of revolution, concluding with a pronouncement of "guilty as charged" for the picketers. As for sentencing them, he said he would have to think about it for a while. In the meantime, they were free to go.

And go they did—back to the White House gates where, again, they were arrested. At the police station, they refused to give their names or to make bail, so all were sent to a detention house in Washington where army cots were set up to take care of the numbers. The next morning, they were back again before the judge. This time he gave out sentences ranging from fifteen days to six months in the city jail. In some instances, as he pronounced sentence, the adjudged would make a speech employing a rhetoric which ascended to such flowery and oratorical heights that Dorothy and Peggy laughed. Dorothy felt sorry for the judge. He "looked like a miserable small boy who knows he is in the wrong but doesn't quite know what to do about it." He reminded Dorothy of her father, "with his patient Southern drawl. He seemed to feel that what he was doing was not what a Southern gentleman should do."

After the sentencing, the women waited in an assembly area in back of the courtroom and there resolved to begin their hunger strike. They waited in their detention room until four in the afternoon, when patrol wagons came to take them to jail. Dorothy noted that the wagons were windowless, having slits in their top to admit air. Their ride took them to the city prison on the outskirts of town. When the wagon's door was opened, they could see the prison "backed by a cemetery and surrounded by dreary, bare fields." But this was not their destination. In the wagon, Dorothy could hear, from a distance, some sort of argument going on at the prison entrance. Then the wagon's engines were started again and off they went. What did this mean? It meant, said one woman, that they were going to be taken to the "workhouse"— Occoquan prison. The wagons were going to the railroad station. This news started talk about the warden at Occoquan, a man named Whittaker. He was a rough customer, the women said. "We were afraid," Dorothy says in *The Long Loneliness*.

At the railroad station, the women were ushered into a waiting train, and Dorothy, with Peggy across the aisle from her, took a seat by a window. The train rolled out immediately and soon was lurching and rattling its way through the countryside. It was getting dark, but in the west the sky was still lit by the lingering light of a sun that seemed unwilling to give over to darkness. It was a cold fall evening, and as she watched the light gradually fade and lamps winking through the windows of farmhouses, Dorothy suddenly felt drained of the excitement that had buoyed her throughout the day. When they got to the Occoquan station, she told Peggy that "life and struggle seem very tawdry in the twilight. This bleak countryside makes me feel that I should struggle for my soul instead of my political rights. . . . I feel peculiarly small and lonely tonight."

In this train ride of scarcely forty minutes, Dorothy had experienced the sharp intrusion of a question that seemed to well up at times from some primal source of her being. There were others (perhaps most other people) who could find sufficient meaning for their lives just in the process itself of living—who could even give themselves to "causes" through which this process would presumably be harmonized and justice, abstractly conceived, would completely prevail. But what if "justice" were everywhere enforced and there were no causes? Then life would be reduced to a stagnation that only the mindless could endure. Dorothy sensed that there was something else, or ought to be, that was final and fulfilled, that was beyond time.

The mood soon passed, overridden by new tensions in the offing. Again the women found themselves in wagons, heading for the Occoquan administration building. It was seven-thirty when they got there. Mrs. Lawrence Lewis of Philadelphia spoke for the group. She informed a matron, who sat behind a desk, idly knitting, that the prisoners wanted to see the superintendent, the much discussed Whittaker. The matron kept on knitting, as if the request had been so absurd that no response was necessary. So again there was waiting, and the women, exhausted, began sitting on the floor, some even stretching out and sleeping.

It was ten o'clock before the feared Mr. Whittaker appeared. Described by Dorothy as "a large stout man with white hair and a red face," he burst into the room like a tornado. A porch adjoined the room, and through the door Dorothy could see many more men. Before Whittaker could say anything, Mrs. Lewis got up and announced that they were political prisoners and that they would go on a hunger strike until their demands were met. But Whittaker was not interested in pronouncements, and as Mrs. Lewis made her dignified statement, he turned to the door and summoned the men. In they dashed, two of them for each woman, seizing right arm and left arm, and escorting them to their cells. Mrs. Lewis was taken first and was pulled backward through the door, looking like "the stiff figure of a dressmaker's dummy."

As the melee commenced, Dorothy started to make her way across the room to where Peggy stood. Whittaker reached out to stop her, and at this point, Dorothy Day, who some three hours earlier had meditated on saving her soul, became a street-fighter. She bit Whittaker's hand and "had the satisfaction of seeing him start back and swear viciously before she found two men holding her fast by either arm." The two guards who laid hold of her held her arms above her head to escape her teeth, but even so she kicked their shins. Out she was taken, into the night, to a building with an American flag flying over it that caught the light coming from a nearby window.

Dorothy later observed that she had struggled every step of the way from the administration building to the cell block with the flag over it. No doubt she did, and no doubt, too, that while most of the women there probably exceeded Dorothy in the strength of their commitment to women's suffrage, none other erupted as she did to make the confrontation with Whittaker so personal and violent.

In the cell block, old Mrs. Nolan, who had gone along quietly, saw Dorothy being brought in. "She is a frail girl," Mrs. Nolan noted. "The two men handling her were twisting her arms above her head. Then suddenly they lifted her up and banged her down over the arm of an iron bench—twice. As they ran past me, she was lying there with her arms out, and we heard one of the men yell, 'The—-suffrager! My mother ain't no suffrager! I'll put you through—-.'"

As for Dorothy, though she had been slammed down on the bench, she still arose and started across the room toward Peggy. The latter stood laughing at the scene, turning the while to address light-hearted pleasantries to the two men who held her. Again, Dorothy was intercepted and again she struggled, this time against four men. Above the haze of passion and tumult within herself, she heard Peggy's laughter again, not from hysteria, but from a whole-hearted enjoyment of the spectacle. And Dorothy herself grinned, a vengeful grin such as she had seen on the face of her brother, Donald, when as a small boy he had given and received hard blows. It was "a grin of pure wrath."

Some fifty years later, Dorothy related to Professor Rosemary Bannon the circumstances of a legal consequence to her struggle with the guards. It was, apparently, sometime after the release of the suffragists that the Woman's Party instituted a suit against the government for a presumed injury done to Dorothy Day. As Dorothy related the story, the suit came about "because a guard tried to grab me when I was going from one side of the room to another and I resisted. He grabbed me by the arm and started to drag me. I fought back—I wasn't being non-violent—I fought back." As a result of this "little tussle," Dorothy got "maybe a bruise" on her back, but since she had "always had a slight curvature," she regarded her "injury" as nothing.

Be that as it may, the case was instituted on the grounds of a permanent injury having been done to Dorothy's back. The counsel for the Woman's Party was Dudley Field Malone, the almost-official male hero of the suffrage movement. Malone, once close to Woodrow Wilson, had resigned his position as customs collector for the port of New York and offered his services to the cause of woman's suffrage—all because of a conscience deeply troubled by the imprisonment of women who were only peaceably demonstrating for their freedom. According to Dorothy, though, the selflessness of his sacrifice was open to question since he was very much in love with one of the suffragists, whom he later married.

How the suit went, or whether she herself received any money from it, Dorothy did not say. Fifty years later, though, she had some strong opinions about the suit and lawyers in general. She had been "used," and since lawyers had become so much a part of this kind of chicanery, she had concluded that to use them was incompatible with honesty. They were not "anything like a St. Thomas More."

In a way, her epic battle with Whittaker and the guards had its compensation. She was cast into a cell with the famous Lucy Burns, who at the moment was straightening her hair and smoothing her dress. Wasn't it all just splendid? remarked Miss Burns. With all the influential women there, the newspapers would be sure to report how cruelly the women had been used.

Meanwhile, suffragists were being led past the door to be placed in cells along the corridor, and as they passed, Miss Burns called to each to ask how she had fared. Whittaker, standing at the corridor door, ordered her to be silent, threatening to gag and straitjacket her. He was studiously ignored, whereupon the superintendent ordered Miss Burns handcuffed to her cell door. This was done—much to Miss Burns's satisfaction. "Splendid!" she said to Dorothy, "her eyes shining. It gets worse and worse."

At least this is how Dorothy reported the episode. An hour later, Miss Burns was "cut down," so to speak, but the handcuffs were left on her. She would have to keep them on all night, the guard said, whereupon the old fighter turned to Dorothy and said, "Well, child, you'll just have to help me off with my shoes." Presumably Dorothy performed this service as well as getting, from the corner, two dirty blankets which she spread on the narrow benchlike bed. Since both were slim, both could lie on the slab. Tired as they were, they could not sleep immediately, so for a while they talked about Conrad's novels. Early the next morning, a guard came to take Lucy Burns to a special detention room used for sobering up alcoholics.

That morning Dorothy just lay on her bunk. There was a ventilator at the top of the rear wall of her cell, and for a while thin shafts of sunlight pierced the dim light of the room. It was noon, Dorothy thought, when a guard came and told her she could wash and use the toilet. On the way to the washroom she met Peggy, likewise being escorted to the washroom. There the two dawdled and talked until a guard started to pound on the door. Peggy responded by inviting him to enter.

Otherwise the day passed with painful slowness. When night came at last, the guards put a blanket over the bars of the cell door to shut out the light from the corridor. In the darkness Dorothy fell asleep and slept until late in the morning—then to be awakened by the sound of Peggy's singing in her cell. Her voice was not one to calm tempestuous passions; to the contrary, Dorothy hinted, it was more of the kind to produce riots, and the guards ordered her to shut up.

Always a hearty eater, and one who enjoyed the sociability of meals, Dorothy, then and throughout her life, found fasting most difficult. Nonetheless, she was determined not to eat. To some extent, at Occoquan she dulled her hunger by drinking water, but it was more than hunger that gripped her. Now there was no one she could strike, bite, or kick. There were just the dim light of her cell and an occasional voice from down the corridor, and through the ventilators there came the sound of pigs squealing as they pushed to the trough for their evening meal. The sounds tortured her. They became jumbled in with other thoughts that rushed through her mind, and, try as she might, she could not separate them out for what they were. For some strange reason, they made her feel as if something was about to happen, and she hoped with all her heart that something would. But nothing did.

This confusion of sound into the orderly process of her think-ing—this confusion of the relationship of things—was a sign of her weariness and perhaps, too, of how quickly she could be reduced when not buoyed by the excitement of conflict. When the tension was gone and nothing changed, there was no "cause" to sustain her. She began to wonder what good suffrage would do when it came. What would women do differently from how men were al-ready doing it, she asked herself. Her conclusion, as she ponders this question in *The Eleventh Virgin*, seems to be that women would do nothing differently. The war was an example. Most women were "blindly patriotic and accepted the idea of war without know-ing what war was." They had developed a war spirit "with more than masculine enthusiasm." Fighting would go on forever. Or take the birth control movement as another example. This was obviously a reform that the world needed, Dorothy thought. Yet many of the women who belonged to the suffrage party did not believe in birth control. So what difference did any of it make?

She was crushed by the thought that she might have to remain in the "sullen grayness" of her cell for thirty days. She would be "utterly crushed by misery before she was released." She thought of the stories she had heard—of bloodhounds roaming on the pris-on grounds, of a whipping post. They had been "documented." They were true—else why hadn't Whittaker taken the trouble to deny them, she thought. She says that, as the hours passed, she lost all feeling of her own identity. "A dull weight" had descended upon her, "the weight of the sorrow of all the world."

Her second night alone in the cell was a tortured one. When sleep came, vivid nightmares came with it. One dream had her in a theater that was filled with little children from some institution, perhaps a home for street waifs. The children were all chattering happily in expectation of the play. And then, as the play began, a dark and ominous pall descended over the children. The players wore hideous death masks and their bodies were distorted. One little child, leaning over the balcony railing, shrieked and died, his body falling down upon the children below.

One of the nightmares she had had as a child returned. Somewhere afar, a drumming, beating sound began. It came closer and grew louder and louder until it engulfed her, its demonic clamor taking possession of her very being. After a frightful struggle from the abyss of nightmares to consciousness, "she lay and sobbed . . . at the futility of trying either to sleep or to remain awake."

In one of her accounts of the prison episode, Dorothy states that, on the second day, she began asking for a Bible to read and that it was brought to her two days later. In another account, she says that one of the Christian Scientists among them had asked for a Bible and that Bibles were passed around to all of the prisoners. In any case, Dorothy read it "with a sense of coming back to something of my childhood that I had lost." Reading the Bible brought her some peace—and that fact troubled her. She and her radical journalist friends, Mike Gold especially, had been telling themselves that they were revolutionaries, and she must, therefore, resist this turning to God. Calling upon God was only an act of desperation. "I was like the child that wants to walk by itself. I kept brushing away the hand that held me up. I tried to persuade myself that I was reading [the Bible] for literary enjoyment. I prayed and did not know that I prayed."

Her anxious waiting for something to happen ended on the sixth day of her imprisonment. Three doctors and a retinue of guards and nurses came in to examine the women. It was decided that the six women in the tier of punishment cells, which included Dorothy, should go to the prison hospital. It was a clear, cold evening, the sun just setting, as the six walked out onto the Occoquan grounds, headed for the hospital building. For Dorothy, the last light of the sun touching the tops of the trees and the bite of the clear air in her nostrils brought a sense of new beginnings and happiness.

There were no nightmares for that night. The hospital was warm and lighted, and whenever she chose, she could stroll down the hall and take a shower. Moreover, Peggy's bed was on the other side of a partition, through which ran a radiator and a passageway for exchanging notes. Still, Dorothy persisted in her hunger strike, if for no other reason than she had taken the step and she would therefore follow the course. Her great fear was that she would be forcibly fed. Once she heard the doctors force-feeding an older woman in a room nearby, and the sounds of her gagging and thrashing around unnerved her.

It was Peggy who broke Dorothy's resolve to continue the fast. Feeling that no great issue was at stake, Peggy accepted food and urged Dorothy to eat, too. She would be a complete fool to persist, Peggy said. Whatever force this wheedling had with Dorothy was made pointless by Peggy's thrusting a piece of toast through the partition. Dorothy could not resist. Reaching out, she seized the morsel and savored each crumb as she slowly ate it.

The hunger strike ended two days later—in its tenth day. Word had been passed down from the White House that the women should be treated as political prisoners. Now everyone could eat; now everyone would shortly be going back to the Washington jail. The first food the strikers had was milk toast, followed shortly by a sumptuous meal of chicken. Other signs of the easing situation followed: their clothes were returned to them and their mail was given to them. This latter concession resulted in Dorothy's getting a "package" of letters from "admirers." Just who admired her, Dorothy does not say, but she probably got letters from Gold and her *Call* and *Masses* friends.

It is safe to say that no letter came from her father. If John Day knew that his daughter was in prison and was starving to death, he probably would not have succumbed to any warming influence of compassion and forgiveness. He probably would have commented sourly to Grace that their daughter was getting what she deserved and then asked where they had gone so wrong in rearing her, that she should even now, just beginning her twenty-first year, be possessed of a new devil. And then if the smoldering flame of concern should have begun to glow and to cause him pain, he would have doused it with two strong drinks—and then have doused it again, if need be, as many times as it took to put out the fire.

As for Dorothy, the ordeal was practically over. After the news of their victory reached them, the women were kept at Occoquan just long enough to get them ready for their removal to the Washington jail. This was a matter of two or three days, after which time they were all chauffered in limousines to the Washington jail. There they were received as guests, with the privilege of choosing their own cells. With Peggy, Dorothy made a leisurely tour of available accommodations, and the two of them chose a cell at the top and rear of the three-tiered cell block. Their considerations were light, ventilation, and distance from the matron's desk. But their cell location did not matter too much. From eight in the morning until eight at night they were free to wander up and down the corridors, visiting where they would and socializing as much as they chose.

In her narration of her prison experiences in *The Eleventh Virgin,* Dorothy provides a commentary on Negro women prisoners. It is interesting because it reveals her emphasis on the prevailing stereotypes where blacks were concerned. Black women were segregated in one section of the female block where, as Dorothy observed, they "kept up their chatter after eight o'clock at night and giggled and sang and quarreled, laughing at the matron who puffed up and down the steps to quiet them." There were card games on the third tier, "while one darkey kept a lookout for the matron; and shimmy dances up and down the corridor while a row of black faces gleamed along the line and hands beat time to the steps of the dancers." Saturday night was bath night for black women prisoners, an occasion of heightened tumult, since this ritual anticipated Sunday church. Even at church, minds and feelings were not wholly elevated to the domain of the spirit. "The men and women were separated by the width of the little hall, but during the two hours of worship they sat there casting hungry eyes at each other." Nor, for that matter, was Dorothy above it all. She "saw sex and felt it at its crudest and was stirred by it, yet somehow disgusted that the excitement should affect her."

If, as it seems, during this period of her life she accepted the stereotypes of behavior which popularly were thought to characterize blacks, still, her view was, after all, one shared by most of her "radical" associates. They were fervid supporters of a revolution in Russia with its causes, slogans, and drama that caught their imagination—certainly not what Dorothy later came to accept as the Christian personal revolution that would begin within herself and whose first consequence would be the obliteration of all stereotypes. As for sex, one is entitled to think that the only difference between the attitudes and habits of some of her associates and those that "somehow disgusted" her in prison was that her associates romanticized their Bohemian back-room-flat and street-corner encounters with some lines of turgid free verse, while the black prisoners were less encumbered with the necessity of embroidering the sexual urge with fictions.

How did Dorothy and Peggy spend their time in their cell-for-two when they were not wandering up and down the corridors? Peggy lay in her upper bunk, drawing pictures of black girls dancing in their prison garb and otherwise writing "free verse." Each opus was to commemorate a past love. At the time she was working on her twelfth, but when she was through, she said, she would have a book.

In the bunk below, Dorothy read and thought a lot about where she was heading. It would be simpler for her, she thought to herself, if she truly believed that socialism, or the Birth Control League, or woman's suffrage would benefit the world. But she was not sure that any of those things were solutions and, as for the woman's movement, she would "go crazy" among "these people with their single-track minds."

If Dorothy accurately recalls the chronology of events in her several accounts of her imprisonment, it must have been on November 28 that the women were released. The warden came into the cell area where the suffragists were, and in a voice effervescing with pleasure, he announced that all were pardoned by order of the president. His joy was not feigned; he had had enough of the women. But Lucy Burns demurred. The pardon could not be accepted because they had committed no crime for which a pardon was indicated. Just the same, said the warden, his hospitality had been overdrawn and he was turning them out.

That afternoon Peggy and Dorothy went to the best restaurant they could find and ordered roast duck. As they waited for their food, they leaned back into their seats and lit their beatific cigarettes. Deprived of the solace of smoking in jail, they now gulped into their lungs long draughts of smoke. That night they caught the train for New York.

The first thing Dorothy did on her return was to go and see her mother and her sister, Della, timing her visit, it can be assumed, to avoid her father. Grace rallied brightly from her worry over Dorothy's imprisonment and greeted her warmly. Young brother John, she said, had been telling it up and down the street that his sister was in jail. How the senior John took this, one can only speculate, but if he was driven increasingly to the racetrack, he could, at least, take some comfort in the fact that his two older sons were acting like well-balanced and decent human beings. Donald was going into the Navy Air Force, and Sam into the regular Navy.

As for Dorothy, she was, so she told her mother, going to an apartment on Waverly Place which she would share with her three roommates of the summer past: Floyd Dell, Merrill Rogers, and

David Karb. But this venture for some reason never came about. In *From Union Square to Rome,* she says that, after coming back from Washington, she lived in one furnished room after another, "moving from the lower East Side to the upper East Side and then again down to the lower West Side of town," and that she made a living by freelancing.

In her later years, when journalists and students sought Dorothy out for interviews, they frequently would ask her about her life in Greenwich Village. Suspecting that they were hoping for a revelation of some bit of hitherto unrevealed sensationalism about herself and the Village dwellers, she would vehemently deny that she had been a part of Village life or had even lived there. Her true formation, she would point out, was in the radicalism of the East Side. In the overall perspective, Dorothy was right. Her formation was the East Side— the *Call,* the *Masses,* Mike Gold, Hugo Gellert, and Maurice Becker. And it is true, too, that certain consequences of this formation remained with her throughout her entire life— in the way she viewed persons and issues. But it is also true that, during the cold winter of 1918, she was one of the central figures in the drama of Village life.

Why, then, did Dorothy, throughout her days, insist on completely exorcising the Village from her past? First, she was extremely sensitive about any discussion of her preconversion life that might give rise to irresponsible talk. More than once she would say that she did not want her example during these years publicized so as to beguile young people. "If Dorothy did it, why should not we do it?" But the fact is that Dorothy's deportment during this Village period was almost exemplary, and so something else must have caused her attitude. One can only guess at what it was—and then it sounds so trivial that one wonders how Dorothy, for the rest of her life, could have remained so sensitive to it. But Dorothy was remarkably thin-skinned, and even slight wounds would, in spite of everything she consciously tried to do to ignore them, fester a long time, especially when she felt that they were not deserved.

In 1934, literary critic Malcolm Cowley's *Exiles' Return* was published, and in it, Cowley, who had known Dorothy well in the early twenties, briefly mentions her in a chapter on Greenwich Village. His one-sentence comment was that the "gangsters admired Dorothy Day because she could drink them under the table; but they felt more at home with Eugene O'Neill who listened to their troubles and never criticized."

Why Cowley put in this sentence is not clear—perhaps partly in fun to draw a contrast between the young Dorothy and the Dorothy of later days who practically outdid Carrie Nation in her antipathy to alcohol. Anyway, the statement is not strictly true. The "gangsters" of whom Cowley spoke were the "Hudson Dusters," a band of bullying rowdies who hung out in Village saloons and, particularly, in a noxious rooming house-saloon at the corner of Sixth Avenue and Fourth Street, owned by Jimmy Wallace, a place that somebody in a fit of poetic extravagance had named "The Golden Swan." Since Dorothy was, for a brief period of time, one of its back-room regulars, she ran into the Dusters there, but she would not have gotten into any drinking bouts with them. Dorothy was always too possessed to pretend to any comraderie with an outfit like the Dusters, and she probably ignored them. As for O'-Neill, he affected a comradely relationship with them, a pose he probably cultivated as a protection against getting brass-knuckled in the jaw.

Cowley's remark, though, remained an irritant to Dorothy over all of her days, and at some period in her life, probably in the early sixties, she typed out her grievance on three pages and entitled it, "Told in Context." What she told was ostensibly about her Village association with Eugene O'Neill and some conclusions she had reached about O'Neill. But much of it was about Cowley's sentence. She said she had read "various books by literary figures, about life of the twenties, and found myself mentioned as the companion of Eugene O'Neill (therein was my glory, they thought) and as one who could drink longshoremen under the table." Cowley's comment, in particular, was "the first account of my flaming youth to reach the public," an account that had been made out of malice. The harm came from its being "taken up again and again by journalists and critics of The Catholic Worker Movement (for which I am responsible at the instigation of Peter Maurin, French peasant, teacher, and saint.)"

Further, the phrase had brought personal indignity upon her, on such occasions as when "Fr. Roger, S.J., a teacher at Fordham, asked me to speak to his students and spoke of a little get-together afterwards, [and] he said over the phone, 'And what is your drink —wine?'" If this wound had not been lacerating enough, there was the time when "Dr. Karl Stern, psychiatrist in Montreal and an old and dear friend, wanted to know whether I was an alcoholic and had been hiding this from him."

Well, she concluded, she "could only confess that when I was twenty, [though she was twenty-one at the time of her association with O'Neill] I did 'fling roses riotously with the throng,' as [Christopher] Dawson put it, but I could not really boast of the accomplishment with which Malcolm credited me."

In 1976, Malcolm Cowley, sitting on the porch of his home at Sherman, Connecticut, reminisced about Dorothy and referred to his sentence. Yes, "Dorothy was disturbed when I mentioned her reputation as a whiskey drinker," but, he emphasized, she was never anything approaching an alcoholic. It was only that "she was rather admired for her ability to put down several belts of whiskey and remain sober."

There remains, however, the temptation to wonder if Cowley's suggestion that Dorothy led a riotous life in the Village is worth all of the feeling she attached to the matter and if Cowley's comment was not a surface manifestation of something more fundamental that bothered Dorothy about the Village and her associations there. For a period of over a year, through 1917 and into 1918, and then on and off through 1924, most of her friends and associates, if they did not actually live in the Village, had some connection with its life. Primarily they were writers who thought they were ordained to prepare America, if not the world, for a new politics, a new life, and, as artists, a larger truth. Perhaps Dorothy, too, hoped that she as a writer would have some part in redeeming history from the stagnation into which, all were certain, it had fallen. Perhaps in some sense, Eugene O'Neill achieved this objective. But the others did not. Malcolm Cowley, to be sure, wrote high-class literary criticism; Floyd Dell, who in 1917 was assumed by many to be the most promising of the Village writers, trailed off into the obscurity provided him by a series of uninspired novels; and Max Eastman—who can remember anything of enduring significance contributed by him? Yet all of them, for a while, seemed to have thought that they had made a large forward step in bringing a truth about life into sharper focus. They were all opposed to any kind of moral order, and all of them, when they got a little older, wrote of the charming times back in the Village where it had all begun—times that had been so good, so prophetic, and so unique that they deserved to be memorialized in a personal account.

As for their companion, Dorothy, she had flunked out, regressed, turned to religion—a writer who, like themselves, would have moved to the forefront of American letters, had she not been lost by the wayside. This attitude was never made explicit, nor did

Dorothy ever say that she thought this was the case. Nonetheless, she sensed that this was a viewpoint held by some of her acquaintances during these years, and she reacted to it by focusing on the Cowley reference. Otherwise, she would consign her Village past to oblivion.

When Dorothy returned to New York from Washington, she would have, in the normal course of things, lived at home for a while. But there was her father, from whom she was now so completely estranged that it was impossible for her to go see him. So it was back to the old crowd, to Mike Gold and her *Masses* friends— back to sitting on the piers at night before it got too cold and dawdling over coffee in restaurants. This was in December, 1917, a time when she kept irregular hours, moved frequently, and seemingly achieved the Bohemian ideal of having no income for which she performed regular work.

It must have been around the first of December that Mike took Dorothy to the Provincetown Playhouse at 139 MacDougal Street and introduced Dorothy to Eugene O'Neill. Gold had business there, presumably to discuss the possibility of staging a play he had written about East Side tenements. Years later, Dorothy laughingly recalled how O'Neill talked about Gold's play. The story, said Dorothy, "was about clotheslines hung across alleys. Gene used to make fun of Mike: 'the short and simple *flannels* of the poor,' he would say of Mike's play."

After that, Dorothy began to spend a lot of her time at the playhouse where Gold's play was in rehearsal. It was an old brownstone whose downstairs rooms had been fashioned into a small theater, the creation of a small group of persons, relatively unknown at the time, who wanted to write and produce experimental plays. Before October, 1916, their "theater" had been Mary Vorse's old roofed-over pier at Provincetown, Massachusetts, a little community at the tip of Cape Cod. In early 1916, the enterprise at Provincetown attracted the interest of O'Neill, who for the moment was living in an abandoned hulk on a nearby beach. O'Neill submitted his *Bound East for Cardiff* to the group for a reading; the results were that he was immediately accepted into their midst and given, almost, the status of prophet-playwright of their vision. The MacDougal Street house was opened on October 31, 1916, with O'Neill's *In the Zone,* and the praise he got for it in the New York press raised him to an upper level of critical focus.

Why did Dorothy hang around the playhouse? In *From Union*

Square to Rome she says that "it was a bitterly cold winter and the rooms I lived in were never really heated. There was a coal shortage that winter and heatless Mondays were instituted. Usually it was pleasanter to stay out of my room, so there was a great deal of visiting friends, of hanging around the Provincetown Players." This is true, but then one wonders if Dorothy thought that she might act. She said once that she read some lines for a part and everyone agreed, including herself, that she could not act. Or, was she immediately attracted to O'Neill?

It seems likely that she was, partly because O'Neill had a quality common to all the men with whom Dorothy was ever seriously involved. He was, as a personality, a maladjusted egocentric, a type to which she was drawn as some people are to stray dogs. It was, one suspects, the quality of compassion in her that made them appealing, but where was the line between compassion and romantic fancy in a twenty-one-year-old who was both compassionate and romantic? And O'Neill outdid himself in commending himself to the compassion of certain types of women. He exhibited all the signs of the wounded and suffering soul: trembling hands, somber mien, dark and shadowed eyes, and he drank excessively.

In December, 1917, O'Neill was suffering deeply from a lost love. At least he gave it out that he was. The object of his passion was Louise Bryant. She was slender, dark-haired, and finely formed. Frequently, when she posed for a picture, her full lips were parted. With her large, dark eyes she could meet a man's gaze with steady directness, seeming to say that if the prospect was exciting, if it could be made to partake of her brand of poetry and passion, she would follow, no matter where. She was intense and extravagant, and although she seemed to have no talent for it, she thought of herself as a writer.

She met O'Neill in the Village, and in the course of affairs there, she became caught in the spell of the plays that he was writing, as well as his morose glowerings and shaking hands. She began to give O'Neill her steady, direct gaze—with lips parted—but he was possessed of scruples, not because she was still, so far as the law went, the wife of dentist Paul Trullinger, but because she was the mistress of his friend , writer-adventurer John Reed. Nonetheless, O'Neill could help Louise with her writing, and she, for her part, would lightly run her fingernail down his arm.

In the spring of 1916, Reed and Louise went to Provincetown, and O'Neill trailed after them. That summer, as they romped on the seashore, Louise told O'Neill that Reed was impotent because of a kidney disorder. O'Neill thereupon overcame his scruples. In the fall, when Reed went to Johns Hopkins to have a kidney removed, O'Neill took over the first position in Louise's life. He thought of himself as being deeply in love, even though Louise and Reed were now married. His bliss, however, was brief. Reed recovered and reclaimed his bride. In June, 1917, Louise went to Europe, and from there, several months later, she made her way to Russia to join her husband where he was shortly to witness the events that provided the material for his classic, *Ten Days that Shook the World*.

Dorothy knew all about O'Neill and Louise, and she may have even thought that she could, in a more constructive way, take the place of Louise. In any case, late at night when the Provincetown group finished their practicing, she would go around the corner to Jimmy Wallace's "The Golden Swan" and into its back room, which Village regulars called the "Hell Hole." There she would meet O'Neill.

Agnes Boulton, who arrived in the Village about the same time that Dorothy returned from Washington, tells in her *Part of a Long Story* of her visit to the Hell Hole one evening and of witnessing the arrival of Dorothy, whom she did not then know. Dorothy, she wrote, came in the Fourth Street door, followed by "two seedy, tough, middle-aged men who stood looking about, abashed and unsure. I saw at once that this girl was a personality, an unusual one." Agnes watched curiously as Dorothy took the two men to a table, overhearing her tell the men that she had promised the drink and she would buy them one. Then Dorothy paused as she saw the large and full-blown figure of Christine Ell, who ran a kind of house-restaurant for the Provincetown group upstairs over the theater, "Hello, Christine! Where's Gene O'Neill?" Dorothy asked. Christine laughed and replied with meaningful emphasis, "Well . . . you ought to know."

Apparently Dorothy did know, for looking through the swinging doors that separated the back room from the bar, she saw O'Neill standing at the bar. "Oh, there you are, Gene O'Neill," she called to him. Then she ordered three rye whiskeys. Returning to where Christine sat, Dorothy said casually that O'Neill would be there shortly. Sitting down, she began to sing, "Frankie and Johnny." Agnes Boulton describes the scene: "The two men were fascinated, but she paid no attention to them, stretching out her long legs and for the moment closing her eyes. She ordered another drink for them; then one of them, making for the toilet, stumbled over her legs." Then, suddenly it seemed to Agnes, the room began to fill up with people who had been drinking at the bar: some of the Hudson Dusters, a girl named "Grapes," and O'Neill.

Thirty years later, when Agnes recalled the scene, she could remember the face of Grapes and Dorothy's singing. O'Neill, she could recall only indistinctly, his "moving slowly around, his dark eyes alive and pleased, admiring Dorothy's strange almost staccato singing."

After she had gone back to her room that night, Agnes wondered about Dorothy. She had found out that Dorothy had run across the two men on the steps of a church, "where for some reason she had gone to pray." She wondered what Dorothy was doing in the Hell Hole. "It was odd because she looked and dressed like a well-bred young college girl." She was extremely attractive in a strange way and gave rather the impression of being a sort of "genius." Agnes thought further that "she had a sort of desperate quality beneath her extremely cool manner."

Later that night, the weary Christine went back to her apartment and Dorothy suggested that she, Agnes, and Gene go to a place she knew about where they could get something to eat. "We walked along the silent street together in the cold night and went down some steps to a place that was crowded with people eating at long tables. . . . Dorothy would say, once in a while, that she had to catch a train to go and see her mother." After a while Agnes, too, went home, her thoughts all of O'Neill. "Was I really in love with him that night when I left him in the restaurant with Dorothy?"

Yes, the reader of Agnes's prose knows full well that "in the hidden recesses of her heart," if not in the clear processes of her mind, Agnes was in love with O'Neill. She was beginning to quaver when confronted with his somber and stricken visage.

For the moment, however, it was Dorothy who whiled away the nights with him at the Hell Hole. There, sitting at the table with O'Neill, poet Max Bodenheim, and at times Mike Gold, she would listen to talk about literature and hear O'Neill indulge his enthusiasm for August Strindberg. One night as they sat there, Bodenheim began a poem and suggested that Dorothy and O'Neill in turn contribute a verse. Dorothy kept the poem for some years, but it was destroyed when, in the early forties, a fire burnt down her first beach cottage.

The occurrence of those nights that indelibly impressed itself on Dorothy was O'Neill's alcoholic recitation of Francis Thompson's "The Hound of Heaven." "Gene could recite all of it," Dorothy has written, "and he used to sit there, looking dour and black, his head sunk on his chest, sighing, 'And now my heart is as a broken fount wherein tear-drippings stagnate.'" It was, continued Dorothy, "one of these poems that awakens the soul, recalls it to the fact that God is its destiny." Agnes Boulton says that Dorothy listened "in a sort of trance" when O'Neill would recite the poem. "She even managed to get him to recite . . . [it] one night from beginning to end . . . while the Hudson Dusters listened admiringly."

One evening in February, 1974, Dorothy and a companion were riding along a north Florida highway after she had talked to students at Florida State University. With no reference to anything that had occurred that afternoon, she began to talk about her nocturnal episodes with O'Neill. Yes, she had been a part of O'Neill's life during that cold winter of 1917-1918, but the company they shared was not all confined to the Hell Hole. Sometime around three or four in the morning, Jimmy Wallace would close the place, and then she and O'Neill would venture out into the cold, making their way down to the East Side, stopping off frequently at taverns on the way that were still open. Dorothy had a room on the East Side, and when they got there, she would put the shaking and exhausted O'Neill to bed and then lie beside him under the covers and hold him close to her, trying to keep him warm. During such moments, Dorothy said, O'Neill would ask her, "Dorothy, do you want to surrender your virginity?" In O'Neill's usual sodden condition, this question may have been pointless. Even so, said Dorothy, she always turned the question aside. Early in the afternoon, when O'Neill awakened, he would call Dorothy, wherever she happened to be working then, and have her meet him at the Hell Hole to begin the cycle again.

Why Dorothy chose to reveal these details is unclear. She did have a habit of anecdotal narration, but she was never just garrulous; there was always a point to what she said, although the listener might sometimes wonder what it was. In this instance, her delicately phrased statement raises the question of why she chose to interject it abruptly into what otherwise had been a discusson of impersonal matters. It may have been that she was saying something for the record, namely, that the character of Josie Hogan in O'Neill's *Moon for the Misbegotten* was fashioned from several people that O'Neill knew and that she was one of them.

The play, O'Neill's last, was completed in 1943, and was about the last days of his brother, James. In it, the dissolute character of Tyrone [Jamie] is laid bare, but in the end Tyrone, after making a drunken confession to Josie, finds forgiveness and absolution from her, as it comes to him through the depths of her compassion for Tyrone's weakness.

In the biography of O'Neill by Arthur and Barbara Gelb (Harper and Row, 1973), the authors state that O'Neill modeled his Josie Hogan on Christine Ell, the woman of the large and admirable body but plain face who was the restaurateur for the Provincetown people and who, in 1917, had Jamie O'Neill as one of her favorites. This is probably true, partly because Josie, like Christine, is a large, Mother-Earth type. In the play, the description of Josie is that of a tall woman, just under six feet. "Her sloping shoulders are broad, her chest deep with large, firm breasts, her waist wide but slender by contrast with her hips and thighs. She has long smooth arms, immensely strong, although no muscles show. The same is true of her legs." Although Dorothy was a large woman and could, if she had weighed thirty more pounds, have matched the description, the picture is that of Christine. But Josie Hogan otherwise is not Christine. In the play, loose talk has it that Josie is almost profligate in her sexual activity, although actually she is virginal. Whereas Christine was something of a lost and bemused soul who tried to get consolation and help out of the wisdom of others, Josie has the strength to heal Tyrone. And if Dorothy, at the end of an alcoholic night, would take O'Neill through the frigid air to her own room and hold his shivering and trembling body close to her, Josie says to Tyrone in the closing lines of the play, " 'Come now. We'll sit down.' (She sits on the top step and pulls him down on the step below her). 'That's it—with my arm around you. Now lay your head on my breast—the way you said you wanted to do—' (He lets his head fall back on her breasts. She hugs him gently)."

There could, then, have been something of Dorothy in Josie, and it seems that Dorothy believed there was. It may have been, too, that in reciting her story she felt that, in creating the character of Josie Hogan, O'Neill was certifying, for as long as his art lived, that she had been part of the substance of its creation.

If there was that in Dorothy's spirit, or character, that touched the O'Neill genius, she did not have a brand of feminine appeal that would keep his attention focused. "Was I really in love with him?" Agnes Boulton had asked herself a week previous. And now came that special night when she and O'Neill "went down the slippery steps into a small, faintly lighted coffee shop." Dorothy was there, "of course, as we knew she would be, but the candlelight only brought out the long classic line of her jaw and the ends of her tousled short hair. Gene stopped listening to her and looking at her, as he always did under more normal light . . . for he was looking at me. . . . How do I know that it was the soft radiance of the little candles, . . . casting their light upward on my face, that did it?"

Agnes, it appears, was back to writing for the pulps when she wrote of her electric moment in the basement cafe. As for Dorothy, she probably observed something going on because it was about this time that she did something which by any accounting was unusual. One morning around ten o'clock, Agnes, who had a room on Waverly Place, got up from her typewriter, where she had been pecking out more lines about forbidden love, to answer the door. It was Dorothy. She had not been to bed all night, she said, and she needed sleep. "She looked gaunt but firm, and rather annoyed me by treating me in a superior way, telling me to get along with my typing. She would lie down and sleep. This she did, but not before telling me she had just left a church that she found open at an early hour that morning." Since Agnes had just moved into her room, she wanted to know how Dorothy had found her. "Gene" had told her, Dorothy said. So, Agnes concluded somewhat bitterly, Dorothy had been with O'Neill all night.

When Dorothy awoke from her sleep, she startled Agnes by proposing that she and Agnes share the room and that she would pay half the rent. No, said Agnes, her writing required that she be alone. But Dorothy was adamant, as Dorothy could be when a notion took hold of her. She told Agnes that she would help her with "ideas" for her writing. But, thought Agnes, "her only idea was a deep and increasing and, I am sure, a very real and important interest in Gene O'Neill. She could no more resist this than she could resist those sudden and unexplainable impulses to go into any nearby Catholic church and sit there." Agnes wondered about her going into churches, since Dorothy had no "religious background." The source of the habit was probably as obscure to Dorothy as it was to her friends, who considered it "amusing—Dorothy's way of dramatizing herself when she was not singing 'Frankie and Johnny.' "

Since Agnes Boulton was a kind and generous person, and since Dorothy was determined to have her way over the room matter, Agnes gave in and Dorothy moved in. As for Agnes's latter-day musings as to why Dorothy: (1) wanted to move in with her, and (2) went to church—one can only speculate. Years later, Dorothy told biographer Louis Shaeffer that she loved O'Neill's work and that Agnes loved O'Neill. Perhaps so. She held him, warmed him, but his gentlemanly propositions did not stir her. Nonetheless, she felt that she had some kind of proprietorial claim on him, and there was no explanation for her moving in with Agnes, except that she wanted to keep a check on him. But Dorothy's visits to St. Joseph's Catholic Church on Sixth Avenue were not publicity stunts. She went because she was tired and cold and the church was warm. She went because, by sitting there in the back pew, gazing at the altar, she got a sense of the holy, of something that seemed to let her rise above the hectic roilings of time which must have pressed upon her life so insistently at the moment. It was good to breathe the sweetness of incensed air and not that murky haze of cigarette smoke, alcoholic fumes, and sweat that one breathed in the Hell Hole and that clung to one's body and clothes long after one left. And who knows? Perhaps she looked at the figure of St. Joseph, dimly lit by votive candles beneath it, and drew a fatherly comfort from his presence.

This segment of Village life that moved into the winter of 1918 would shortly end. For several weeks, Dorothy, Agnes, and Gene kept company, but where the latter was concerned, it soon was all Agnes. Agnes was completely willing to live whatever kind of life O'Neill would have for her; she was submissive and clinging, and people said she looked like Louise Bryant. Dorothy, as O'Neill well knew, was not submissive or clinging.

Around the middle of January, the news started circulating around the Village that Louis Holladay was about to return. He was the brother of the almost legendary "Polly" Holladay who, like Christine Ell, also ran a restaurant on MacDougal Street. Both places were Village institutions, although Polly seems to have possessed an added attraction in the displays of temperament put on by her in-house lover, cook, and headwaiter, the anarchist Hypolite Havel. The mother of Louis and Polly, Adele, was likewise a Village figure who kept herself in comfortable circumstances out of contributions from her various male companions. Somewhere in the dim past, Adele had had a husband, the father of Louis and Polly, a college professor, it was said, who had been shot in a St. Louis bordello.

In January, 1918, Louis had been away for a year. He had been managing an apple orchard in Oregon, a job he had gotten through Louise Norton, the girl he planned to marry. His "year" had been one of rehabilitation and testing, to assure Louise that he could overcome the hold that drugs and drink had had on him. He had been successful, the talk went, and now, at his homecoming, he would announce the early date of his marriage to Louise.

This was the romantic framework in which the tragedy of Louis Holladay was set. In her various writings, Dorothy does not mention this episode at all—perhaps it was too painful for her to recall or, as likely, perhaps she did not want to open wounds that others still bore—but Agnes Boulton gives the story in detail. It was just after the Christmas holidays, she recalled, and everyone was excited over the news that Louis was returning. O'Neill was especially excited. "Gene was very pleased and gay when he heard it and went to the Hell Hole on the day Louis was expected back and started celebrating in the late afternoon." When Agnes got there at six o'clock, "there was a very convivial crowd."

That night everyone was supposed to meet at Christine's for dinner, for Christine, says Agnes, had a great affection for Louis and had early begun to celebrate "with many nips of gin," getting herself teary-eyed and flushed of face. So, after another hour at the Hell Hole, they went the short distance to Christine's. "Dorothy and some others came in, and everyone was waiting for Louis, who at last arrived—a beautiful strong young man, full of health and vitality, tanned and clear-eyed form his year in the open air, good food and hard physical work. . . . He had conquered [sic]."

He had "conquored," as Agnes had it, but she saw no bride-to-be beside him at Christine's. Louise had said she would meet everyone later, Holladay explained. So it was back to the Hell Hole, where near midnight Louise did come. By then Agnes was tired and decided to go to her room. O'Neill said that he would walk with her to Waverly Place and then return to visit with Holladay.

He left Agnes and she went to sleep. Sometime later she was awakened by O'Neill's voice at the door, and when she asked him what
was it he was saying, he could not respond. "Turn out the light!"
was his sole comment, and with that he rushed to Agnes's bed.
Without even taking off his overcoat, he hugged her close, trying
to stop the quaking of his body. Agnes decided that he was suffering some kind of alcoholic terror and went back to sleep. At three
o'clock she was awakened again. This time it was Dorothy who
stood over them.

Dorothy appeared to be in shock. She "gave the appearance of
being disheveled, as though she had forgotten about herself and
even who she was. Her coat was unbuttoned, her hair damp, her
face very pale. . . . For a moment she looked at Gene as if he were
a stranger; there was an emptiness in her face, as if some sudden
knowledge had shocked her into awareness. 'So you're *here!*' she
said, emphasizing the 'here.' " Holladay was dead, she said. She
had tried to find O'Neill at the Hell Hole to tell him. But now he
must go with her to Romany Marie's restaurant where the group
had gone and where Holladay had died. The police and the coroner were there, Dorothy continued, and had concluded that Holladay had died of a heart attack. "But I have this," she said, and took
a small bottle containing some white powder from her coat pocket,
which she had taken from Holladay's body. Holladay, presumably,
had died from a lethal dose of heroin. Sometime—either then or
later—Dorothy emptied the heroin into a toilet and flushed it. The
verdict of heart attack would stand.

The three went out into the street where the first light of dawn
had begun to make objects distinguishable. At a corner O'Neill
stopped. He would not go to Romany Marie's with the police, the
coroner, and the body still there. He would go to the Hell Hole, he
said in a firm way, so as to make it clear that he would take no
argument. And off he went, leaving Agnes and Dorothy to cross
the street and ascend the steps to the restaurant.

Inside, Agnes was struck by the silence of the place. There was
no animated talking or clatter and banging of dishes and eating
utensils. She and Dorothy stood for a moment at the door, just able
to make out the long tables. At the back of the large room were two
policemen who watched them enter. In a chair near them, with his
long legs stretched out in front of him and his head sunk on his
chest, was Holladay. As they approached, one of the policmen
greeted Dorothy and she withdrew with him for a moment, speak-

ing to him in a low voice. Agnes looked again at Holladay. A window had been opened to let in some air and the morning breeze stirred the curls of his head.

When Dorothy had finished talking with the policeman, she turned to Agnes to go. Outside it was now light. They walked the short distance toward the Hell Hole. On Sixth Avenue, a few cabs were parked, with the drivers asleep in their seats, waiting for the bar to open. Dorothy knew of a cafeteria nearby and she suggested they go there and have coffee before trying to rouse O'Neill at the Hell Hole. As they altered their course, Agnes says that "a certain shifty, elusive friend of Gene's appeared at our side and insisted on going on with us." He had been there the night before and wanted to talk about what had happened.

After Agnes had left the Hell Hole, the character said, Louise Norton had told Holladay that she was planning to marry another man. So Holladay made a general announcement to that effect and, for the next hour, bought drinks for the house. In the course of this, Holladay had contacted some of the sleazy hangers-on at the party and asked for heroin. Then, when the Hell Hole closed, they all went to Romany Marie's.

At this point in the recitation, Dorothy, who had ignored the character and continued to ignore him, interrupted to finish the story. Just after arriving at Romany Marie's, Holladay, seemingly quite self-possessed, looked around and let his glance linger on O'Neill and Dorothy, who were seated near him, if not beside him. It was then that he took the glass container and swallowed the powder. Soon, there were signs of impending death. Holladay fell into unconsciousness and began to foam at the mouth. The merrymakers, horror-filled, all fled—except Dorothy. "He died in my arms!" she said to Agnes. Then she began to cry.

After Dorothy had composed herself, she and Agnes went to the Hell Hole. The door was unlocked and there they found O'-Neill drinking Old Taylor. He appeared to resent their intrusion, and when Dorothy asked him to go with them for a grapefruit and more coffee, he laughed derisively. Dorothy and Agnes, unsure as to what they should do, sat there, hoping that O'Neill would get control of himself and go with them. As they sat, others came in, asking questions of one another, wanting to know what had happened. Polly Holladay came in, looking, as Agnes thought, "sinister and cold." She avoided looking at anyone, including O'Neill.

Seeing that they could do nothing, Agnes and Dorothy left.

They walked several blocks together and then, suddenly, Dorothy turned to walk down a side street. It was ten o'clock in the morning of January 23, 1918. Agnes noted that the sun was bright, making everything look hard. The people and the buildings "seemed to me like falsely colored pictures, pasted against empty space." That was the last time she saw Dorothy for a while. As Agnes watched Dorothy's retreating form, she wondered where she was headed.

Back to O'Neill, Agnes thought. But it was altogether likely that Dorothy was on her way home to see her mother and Della. For Dorothy had had enough of the Village. She had had enough of causes, of "characters," of bad free verse, drunkenness, and casual sex.

O'Neill, too, had had enough of the Village. Soon after Holladay's death, he suggested to Agnes that they get married and go to Provincetown. Agnes demurred. She preferred to wait until the both of them were in a more "marriageable mood," a state she thought they would achieve after they had settled in at Provincetown. Later they were married there.

Eugene O'Neill died on November 27, 1953. It was, apparently, in 1958 or 1959 that Dorothy wrote her "Told in Context," a statement about O'Neill. What, in her mind, was out of "context" and needed clarification is not clear. She did, of course, want to say to whoever she thought might read her statement that Malcolm Cowley had done her an injustice by suggesting that she had been a heavy drinker during her Village days. But what needed to be put into context where O'Neill was concerned? It was that she disagreed with Agnes Boulton and with O'Neill's last wife, Carlotta Monterey, that O'Neill had no interest in religion or the idea of God. To this proposition, Dorothy said, she could "only disagree." She thought of her discussions with O'Neill on Baudelaire and Strindberg, and what O'Neill had said about their art. O'Neill had not dismissed the God idea as so much trivia. "Gene's relations with his God was a warfare in itself. He fought with God to the end of his days. He rebelled against man's fate."

And she went on to say: "If ever a man had the tragic sense of life it was Eugene O'Neill. If ever a man was haunted by death it was Gene. Was it Gene himself or some friend of his who told me how he used to swim far out to sea when he lived at Provincetown and how he played with the idea of death in those deep waters in the ocean from which all life springs." Like Ivan Karamazov, "he wanted to turn back to God his ticket. His whole life seemed to be like that terrible dialogue of Ivan with Alyosha, and the problem of evil, and God's permissive will."

"I'll write my story one way, and others can write it in their way," Dorothy concluded, "and between us all we will have a picture of Eugene O'Neill to present to the world and no doubt it will be colored greatly by our temperaments, our needs, and desires." What Dorothy herself got from O'Neill was "an intensification of the religious sense that was in me." And, "since he brought me such a consciousness of God—since he recited to me 'The Hound of Heaven,' I owe him my prayers."

✳ 5

The Abyss

SHORTLY AFTER her return to New York from her Washington jail experience, Dorothy, thinking heavy thoughts about her future, applied for admission to nurse's training at King's County Hospital in Brooklyn. "I hate being Utopian and trying to escape from reality," she cites herself in *The Long Loneliness* as writing to a friend at the time. "Now that we are in the thick of war and there is so much work to be done, I might as well try to do some of it instead of sitting around playing at writing.... What good am I doing my fellow man?" She was still uncompromisingly against the war, but she did not think nursing would help the war effort. "It's the poor that are suffering. I've got to do something." When Dorothy submitted her application, so did sister Della, just turned eighteen.

The nursing class was not to be organized until April, and Dorothy, after the sad memories of her Village interlude had subsided, went back to those earlier established patterns of her life, before she began her association with O'Neill and the Provincetown group. In December, after her return from Washington, she began doing part-time work for the *Liberator,* the successor to the *Masses.* This new magazine was made possible financially through the fund-raising ability of Max Eastman and, even more, his sister, Crystal. The *Liberator* was not just the jibbing critic of middle-class values as the *Masses* had been. Reflecting Eastman's preoccupation with politics as possessing the answer to the question of human destiny, the *Liberator* was made into the American voice of the Russian Revolution. Early in 1918, it began publishing, on an installment basis, John Reed's firsthand accounts of the revolution, subsequently brought out by Liveright in 1919 as *Ten Days That Shook the World.*

Dorothy had found her work with the *Masses* exciting, mainly because she, almost alone, ran it in the closing months of its life. With the *Liberator,* the situation was different. Max and Crystal were on the scene, living in a house on Washington Square, Max with his mistress, actress Florence Deshon. Dorothy's responsibility at the *Liberator* were mainly those of an office girl, and one of her tasks was to take the morning mail to Max. Dorothy recalled that, as Max ran through the letters she handed to him, Florence hovered over his shoulder, wanting to see, Dorothy thought, if a rival might be bidding for Max's attention. Miss Deshon, from the standpoint of her interests, had good reason to inspect Eastman's mail. He was, in the phrase of that time, an "inconstant lover," and she felt his attraction for her waning. She was right, and two years later, alone and impoverished, she turned on the gas. A desperate attempt was made to save her life, and she was transfused with Eastman's blood in a hospital emergency room, but it was too late.

Eastman's imperious manner and Miss Deshon's jealous possessiveness made the mail delivery assignment an unpleasant daily routine for Dorothy.

Dorothy did get two pieces of her own writing into the magazine. In the March issue, she reviewed Sherwood Anderson's *Marching Men.* It was not a war story, she said, and she quoted Anderson as saying that "when a man marches with a thousand other men and is not doing it for some king, then it will mean something; . . . he is a part of something real and he will catch the rhythm of the mass and glory in the fact that he is a part of the mass. . . . He will begin to feel great and powerful." In other words, a man was really doing something when he marched for revolution.

Dorothy's other piece, a vignette called "A Coney Island Picture," was printed in the April issue. It was about the body of a girl found washed up on the beach, wedged between two pieces of floating ice. Dorothy was struck with the pathos of the news report: "She was poorly but neatly clad. . . . Eighteen cents was found in her pocket tied up in the corner of her handkerchief." The girl was labeled "Unidentified." In her story, Dorothy described the circumstances of the girl's life; the circumstances, though perhaps fictional, might, at the time, have been Dorothy's own. The newspaper account, she wrote, "said nothing of the blister on her frozen heel as tho she had walked—as we all have walked, to deaden the misery or to get warm. It said nothing of the many neat darns on her stockings—nothing of the thin cotton crepe underwear that was yellow because it had been washed and washed in the little bathroom of a rooming house, and hung over the heater to dry. Poor little chemise."

Dorothy, or so she claimed, performed one other service for Eastman and his former *Masses* associates that winter. On November 19, 1917, seven members of the *Masses* staff were indicted by a federal grand jury for violation of the Espionage Act—specifically, for obstructing the draft. Dorothy was not one of the seven who were indicted. During the course of the trial, which was held the following April, she was subpoenaed as a witness for the state. "I was a bad witness for the state and a good one for the defense," she said, but apparently her testimony was not very crucial to the interests of either side. It was not mentioned in the press accounts of the trial, and Eastman, in his autobiographical *Love and Revolution*, does not mention Dorothy in his chapter on the trial.

April came, and Dorothy began her work as a nurse probationer in a flush of enthusiasm, telling herself that this was what she was meant to do all along. Back in December, when she and Della had decided to begin the program, they had asked their mother for money to buy the prescribed patterns and material with which to make their probationer uniforms—six pink uniforms and a dozen white aprons each. And Grace was glad to help, greatly relieved, no doubt, that Dorothy was at last settling down and would be living an ordered life with predictable goings and comings.

Dorothy, too, thought that the new situation was good. "I liked the order . . . and the discipline." Up at six or earlier, the probationers were, by seven, on the ward, where they put in a twelve-hour day, interrupted by two hours of mid-afternoon class time. They had off Sunday afternoon and one week-day afternoon. After a day of work, Dorothy was usually so tired that she went directly to bed. When she got up in the morning, still tired, she took a cold bath, since sitting in warm tub water put her to sleep again. She had begun her training with twelve other probationers; after a few weeks, half had dropped out.

Her first assignment was learning to make a bed. "The sheets were folded in a certain way so that they could be unfolded and spread out on the bed in a certain way. There was no flapping open as you did at home with a sheet or table cloth to spread it smoothly. That might disturb germs that were in the air and set them in circulation." Assured that the germs were undisturbed, she went to the next step: tucking under the overlap. That had to be done in such a precise way that it took seven tries to satisfy the instructor. After she and Della had learned to make beds, they spent several days in an empty ward at this task. First, they had to whisk the mattress—always whisking away from themselves; otherwise germs would come cascading over their white aprons. Then the bed itself was washed. When six mattresses were whisked and the beds washed, then they were made up. And then on to six more.

After several days of this, Dorothy began giving baths to patients. Then she was assigned to the fracture ward to care for eleven elderly women with broken hips. It was in this ward that she encountered the case that "broke" her. One woman, a curiosity who had no breasts and grew a beard, was (for good reason, one would think) extremely anti-social. She vented her resentments by spitting on the nurses and throwing at them whatever was handy so as to dirty their uniforms. Dorothy, who had to grit her teeth while she washed the woman, was repaid by having a bedpan dumped over her shoes and stockings. Weeping hysterically, she went to the washroom and then to her own room where she continued to sob. Despite the fact that leaving the ward was regarded as a serious dereliction of duty, the assistant head nurse consoled her and transferred her to "ward fifty-four," a men's ward. She says that, at the time of her transfer, she had been in training for six months and, having passed the probationary period, she was now a formal trainee, wearing the blue-and-white-striped uniform with its heavily starched collar and small cap. She moved into the ward in October, a time when the lethal Spanish influenza was ravaging the world. Dorothy says that eight or ten persons would be brought into her ward daily and that they would fall unconscious as soon as their clothes were taken from them. In the evening, toward the end of her work day, she and her co-worker had to wrap sheets around the bodies of those who had died and send them off to the morgue. The press of work was such that she and the other student nurse began to skip their breakfast so as to be on the ward early enough to have the morning baths and bed-making finished by the prescribed 10:00 A.M. deadline. Then, after the head nurse had finished the crucial inspection, Dorothy and her friend would duck into the ward kitchen where Red Reynolds, a one-time Coney Island bartender, would fix them scrambled eggs and toast with, of course, the hot black coffee that Dorothy relished.

In the afternoon, Dorothy would take another break, likewise unauthorized. After her class, she would return to the ward by a circuitous route that took her behind the power house and laundries. There, sitting on a bench, she would smoke a forbidden cigarette, sucking quick deep draughts into her lungs.

As full as her days were, and as much as she kept telling herself that she liked the work, she felt her life coursing along on the surface, untouched by the passion her spirit craved. It was, as she knew and had said, a craving that could take her anywhere—into darkness or light. It was as she, in *The Eleventh Virgin*, says to her mother: when she "stopped to think about it, she realized she was capable of doing anything—capable of following her desires, wherever they led."

In her three published autobiographical works, Dorothy relates at some length her experiences as a nurse trainee. In the latter two, *From Union Square to Rome* and *The Long Loneliness*, which were written, as she says, to tell of what brought her to God, she mentions going to five-thirty Sunday morning Mass with a "Miss Adams, another nurse trainee." In *The Eleventh Virgin*, she says nothing of going to Mass. It is here that she narrates that part of her life, set against the background of her hospital training, in which she began her descent into darkness. It is this time, unquestionably, that she writes of in *From Union Square to Rome*, when she says that "though I felt the strong, irresistible attraction to good, yet there was also . . . a deliberate choosing of evil. How far I was led to choose it, it is hard to say. How far professors, companions, and reading influenced my way of life does not matter now. The fact remains that there was much of deliberate choice in it. Most of the time it was 'following the devices and desires of my own heart.' Sometimes it was perhaps the Baudelairean idea of choosing 'the downward path which leads to salvation.'" It was, she concluded, "the arrogance and suffering of youth. It was pathetic, little, and mean in its very excuse for itself." It was "grievous mortal sin and may the Lord forgive me."

She also might well have said, "may the Lord forgive them all" —the professors, the companions, and the writers—all of whose counselings were almost irresistibly persuasive, yet whose vision of what was good and true, as Dorothy later came to see it, ended in despair. But, as she said, it was her choice. The story of her life's movement into its period of intense suffering is told in *The Eleventh Virgin*. It is, as Dorothy herself has said, a true story. Since all of

the principals are dead, there is no other source—only the recollections of several people who knew Dorothy then, recollections that
provide some slight perspective on the matter but do not alter it.

In late April, 1918, with spring at full tide, Dorothy fell into a
distracted mood. Her attention to the afternoon class lectures was
not as sharply focused as it had been during the winter. One
Thursday afternoon, as the superintendent of nurses held forth on
anatomy, delicately turning a femur this way and that as she spoke,
blaring band music poured through the classroom window and the
superintendent gave up. The band was from a Catholic boys'
school and had come to serenade the residents of an old people's
home next door to the classroom building. Grateful for the respite,
Dorothy and sister Della went out to sit on a park bench and listen
to the concert for the remainder of the class time. "What did the
concert remind you of?" Dorothy asked Della. Della did not know.
Dorothy was thinking of Armand Hand conducting the concerts in
Chicago's Lincoln Park. It was the smell of cigarettes. "I can't think
of those park concerts . . . without remembering that odor of damp
grass and people's clothes and cigarettes." What she did not tell
Della, as she explains, was that "now and then a vague longing
came to trouble her—she felt a restless need of some one who
would clutch at her and not want to let her go."

Not long after this, the two were again in the park that surrounded the hospital and walking slowly back to the nurse's quarter after their day in the wards. Tired and wanting to enjoy for the
moment a seclusion that night gave to them, they again sought out
a bench. How many times had Della been in love, Dorothy asked
her sister. Three, Della said—once when she was thirteen, another
the year following, and just recently when she turned eighteen.
But Dorothy was not interested in Della's romances. The question
had been asked, Della told Dorothy, because "you probably just
want to get something off your chest." That was it, Dorothy said.
She had fallen in love and she herself was shocked at the explosive-
ness of it. She could understand knowing someone for a while and
then feeling a physical attraction for him. But "to see a man for the
first time and want to—. I'm ashamed of myself." She was so
ashamed that she could not tell even Della of the nakedness of her
passion.

This was no springtime budding of romance, a welling up of a
sweet crescendo of harmonic vibrations that began with conversations about life and books. She was a tinder box, it seems, ignited

by a vagrant spark. And what was it "that made me fall in love right away?" Dorothy asked Della. "It was this man's broken nose. It looked just exactly like Amenemhat's. You know his is broken, sort of hacked off so that it looks as though it were pushed to one side." This was the Amenemhat whose picture had hung on Dorothy's wall in the room she took in the fall of 1916 with the Jewish East Side family.

The man who had the off-center nose was Lionel Moise, and this physical irregularity in the midst of his rugged face gave him, no doubt, in the eyes of a young flaring romantic like Dorothy, a swashbuckling, man-of-the-world look. Such Moise was, and his bent nose was undoubtedly a badge of his propensity for barroom brawling. He was then an orderly in one of the kitchen wards of the hospital, and Dorothy ran into him there in one of her mid-morning quests for food. "You look just like Amenemhat III," she said as she burst into the kitchen. And Moise, turning in mild surprise to view the tall young nurse, asked "Who in hell is he?"

Moise was not, as Dorothy hastened to explain to Della, "an ordinary orderly. A good many of them were formerly professional men, doctors and lawyers, college graduates who had never fitted themselves for any work and who drank steadily until they found themselves in the city hospital either with some illness or delirium tremens." Whatever the background of the other orderlies, at least Moise tended to conform to the fallen but otherwise exalted status that Dorothy assigned to them. Moise, as Dorothy tells it, had been working with a moving picture company in Caracas and then got a job on a freighter for his passage back to New York. Once ashore, he headed for a saloon on Furman Street. "I always flattered myself that I was hard-boiled enough to take care of myself," Dorothy quotes him as saying, "but the trick those dirty Mexican sailors pulled on me was the simplest ever. . . . An overdose of knock-out drops, and they took all my money."

Maybe. Maybe not. In view of Moise's not infrequently demonstrated capacity to drink himself blind and end up in a melee, one is not inclined to blame, out of hand, "those dirty Mexican sailors." In any case, the insensible Moise was found under an archway at the foot of Montague Street and taken to King's County Hospital. It was there, a week later, that he regained consciousness. After convalescing , he probably decided to work a while at the hospital to pay off his bill and to plan his next move.

Moise (pronounced *Mō-ees*) was born in Emporia, Kansas,

November 30, 1888. He was a Jew of French background. He died in a sanitarium—a resort motel, it was called—at Desert Hot Springs, California, on August 8, 1952. He had been sixty-three, and the only surviving relation mentioned in his obituary was a sister. Twenty-five years later, a cousin-in-law, Mrs. Stanley C. Moise, remembered him only as a legend in the family. He had been a newspaperman and "apparently he was a perfectionist when it came to that." He was known as "a man's man, as well as being liked by the ladies. He also had a reputation as a heavy drinker."

Moise's legend, however, went beyond the family. He had been a colorful newspaperman, to be sure, who had worked for many of the country's major newspapers. He began this work in 1916 as a reporter for the Kansas City *Star*. Restlessly, he moved from job to job: the Boston *Record*, the Los Angeles *Examiner*, the New York *Daily News*, the Chicago *Tribune*, the San Francisco *Examiner*, and the Los Angeles *Express*, where he was the city editor. He had other jobs, too, which in that era were regarded as providing the stuff of raw, manly adventure: roustabout, lumberman, seaman, and, as Dorothy related, a member of a movie camera crew in Venezuela.

But there were other aspects to his character that made him greatly admired by some men and which, apparently, fascinated some women. He had a knowledge of the principal writers and thinkers of his time and he knew the literary classics. It was said that when he and some of his cronies would clean out a bar, he would quote Shakespeare to the bartender. While this story is probably apocryphal, it fits the substance of the legend.

There was also the cold, calloused "tough-guy" part of his makeup that seemed to have fascinated some people—including, apparently, young Ernest Hemingway, who for a while, worked with Moise on the Kansas City *Star*. Although Hemingway did not know Moise well, he was sufficiently impressed with him to write, in later life, a recollection of him:

Lionel Moise was a great rewrite man. He could carry four stories in his head and go to the telephone and take a fifth and then write all five at full speed to catch an edition. There would be something alive about each one. He was always the highest paid man on every paper he worked on. If any other man was getting more money he quit or had his pay raised. He never spoke to the other reporters unless he had been drinking. He was tall and thick and had long arms and big hands. He was the fastest man on a typewriter I ever knew. He drove a motor car and it was understood in the office that a woman had given it to him. One night she stabbed him in it out on the Lincoln Highway halfway to Jefferson City. He took the knife away from her and [broke her jaw: crossed out] threw it out of the car. Then he did something awful to her. She was lying in the back of the car when they found them. Moise drove the car all the way into Kansas City with her fixed that way.

Carlos Baker, Hemingway's biographer, says that Hemingway was impressed with Moise's "facility with words, his prodigious vitality, and his undisciplined talent. Whenever he drank, his active energy overflowed into violence. His writing style was forceful and flamboyant. Ernest admired him as a picturesque throwback to the older school of yellow journalism, though he could not help deploring his prodigal waste of his endowments."

This picture of Moise omits a contrapuntal element. He loved animals, especially horses. During the "National Be-Kind-to-Animals Week" in 1945, he wrote a story about the K-9 Corps dogs on Iwo Jima for the Chicago *Herald American.* It was an Albert Payson Terhune-like piece in which dogs assumed a stature above some humans. Dogs, one might have concluded, were worthy of love even if humans were not.

Why did Dorothy fall for him? Malcolm Cowley, when asked the question, ventured no particulars but said that many women "prostrated themselves before him." Cowley said that Moise "used to quote Nietzsche—something to the effect 'goest thou to woman and forget not thy whip.' That struck me as strange that Dorothy should be so infatuated and consent to live with a person of that sort." For those inclined to relish psychological dissection, it is obvious that there were some similarities between Moise and Dorothy's father. They commonly shared a Darwinian view of existence and they both loved horses. But to what conclusion these facts can be taken is not clear. What is clearer is that Dorothy had remained a virgin until the Moise affair, because she felt no attraction toward those wide-ranging Village samplers of all available sex. Their Freudian jargon and free verse that defied the moral order did not appeal to her. They seemed spent; there was no great passion within them, ready to spill over in drink and brawling. Moise was direct. Unquestionably, she was drawn to his profligacy and extravagance. He was a volcanic force that came crashing upon her.

From the first, she seemed to have cast aside as pointless the approaches, presumably traditional, by which the designing woman attracts the attention of the appointed male. She did not act the coquette; she did not plan encounters and effect surprise at his presence. She let him know immediately that she was his. "I've got to have you. I do love you. It's a fatal passion," the character June says in *The Eleventh Virgin*.

As for Moise, he was not unused to such declamations from women and he probably thought it was something at which he should be amused—certainly not take too seriously. It was the usual business of a young girl (Dorothy was twenty) falling for an older man (he was thirty). Whatever he told himself, it appears that he was interested. Recovered from his injuries, he could have left the hospital whenever he chose, but he stayed. Dorothy, unquestionably, was not the type to which he was accustomed—no spit curls, rouge, or giggly repartee. Dorothy was intelligent and the force of her personality could not ordinarily be turned aside. She was oddly attractive. If Moise was a force, so was she.

When Dorothy told Della of her infatuation, the latter probably thought that a passion so instantly conceived would as quickly fade. But as summer came and continued well into its course, there was no waning of Dorothy's ardor. Working on the men's ward, she saw Moise daily, and it became his custom to cook her mid-morning breakfast. They shared moments of drama involving patients, and after some arduous duty that involved washing, subduing, or capturing a patient who had fled the ward, Dorothy would seek out Moise, alone in a linen closet or the kitchen, and embrace him as if to get strength for the remainder of her day.

Then she began to sneak out of her room in the nurse's quarters and meet him—a park bench, some hidden part of the grounds, a deserted street. "I am becoming a common little slut," she has June saying to him. "I slink out at night without telling anyone where I am going and meet you . . . and we have so little time together that I catch myself scheming. Scheming to get you into back rooms of saloons—desolate, out of the way saloons, where the bartenders are always sleepy and there are never any customers so that I can look at you and you make love to me. I can't coordinate when you put your arm around me on the street— my knees wobble and I step on your feet."

Once, during one of these episodes, Moise responded to one of Dorothy's passionate declamations with sentimental badinage. Dorothy interrupted him. He was out of character being sentimental, she said. "You are hard. I fell in love with you because you are hard." Moise let it pass. He said he thought she had fallen in love with him because of his broken nose. "It was because I looked like the chipped and degenerate statue of Amenemhat." That was true, said Dorothy, but she thought that Amenemhat must have been hard. "He was probably skillful in his love-making and he victimized women. Women love to be victims."

What Dorothy should have said was that it was she who wanted to be a victim, a point that she explicitly made with Moise. "I should never be satisfied with a substitute," she told him. "I'll take what I can get out of you and if I can't get enough of you I suppose I shall just have to break my heart over it. I wouldn't compromise. . . ." With him, it was "as though a hunger were gnawing at me continually." And, said Dorothy, she knew what it was to be hungry. "One doesn' t forget days like those I spent down in jail in Washington. It's a continual pain."

Why should she be hungry? Moise asked. "After the wonderful breakfasts I've given you on the ward. . . ." He knew what she meant, but she made it explicit. "It's at night that I suffer so. . . . I dream of you all the time. I don't need to be a psychoanalyst either, to know what the dreams mean."

One dream was a nightmare, and like some nightmares she had had before in her life, it seemed to well up from a dismal area in her soul and emerged in the misty horizons of her consciousness as prophecy. Her dream was that she was again sitting on the docks, this time with Moise. "We were throwing daggers at each other and we were only a couple of yards apart so they always hit. We played leisurely as though it was a game. It was a hideous game. I kept trying not to start so as not to show that I was hit." Beneath his tough-guy, egocentric armor, something in Moise was touched by the desperate quality of this girl's passion for him. It was as if he were all that was left to save her from annihilation. She was ill. "You should wait for some nice young man who will marry you . . . and give you babies . . . you know you love babies. And if you had one I'd leave you."

"I don't want anyone but you," June replied, and then voiced opinions that she regarded as representing the higher insights of the Birth Control League. "When women are really in love they don't want babies. They only want them when they aren't satisfied with the man they have and feel the need of something else."

Thus Dorothy depicts herself as waging a relentless campaign that had as its ultimate object the seduction of Moise. But he, the worldly wise and ever ready lover, kept his distance. "I have never had a virgin," he once said to her, but she did not react to his callousness. "Nothing you can say will hurt me. Nothing will persuade me to give you up. You're mine, I know it."

So went the state of things into November. One morning when she came on duty, she found Moise prancing around the ward holding aloft a sheet that trailed behind him. "Good-bye, boys, I'm through," he sung out. He had said before, more than once, that he would leave, but she thought she could hold him. Now, it seemed, he really was leaving. When he saw her white face, he came over to her and said, "Poor child, I'm going to leave you." Her reply was to the point and completely in character: "No, you aren't. . . . Come on out in the kitchen."

There, alone, Moise—the character "Dick" in *The Eleventh Virgin*—took her in his arms. How could he leave her? She had become "a part of my heart" now after these months, and it would be difficult to leave. Nonetheless, he was going.

"You won't."

Yes, he would. "What in hell would I do with a woman around?"

It made no difference. Wherever he went, she would go. "I can't live without you and I don't intend to stay here and suffer. You can run away all you want to, but I'll just run after you. . . ."

It turned out that Dorothy would not have to run very far. Moise had an apartment on Thirty-Fifth Street, and he was going there for a while. That afternoon, while Dorothy was in the linen room, he came in, took her face between his hands, and kissed her. He had decided to let matters take their course. So saying, "he slipped a little card down the bosom of her dress." It was his address. Dorothy could meet him there, if she chose. He would wait for her.

At this point, Dorothy decided that the matter required a "consultation" with the family, meaning Della and her mother. She told Della that night. Della commented that she knew that Dorothy had always said that she would live with a man rather than marry him, but, still, it was a shock. And, said Dorothy, she was not going to give either Della or her mother her address, lest they become victims of "a conscience-stricken impulse . . . to come and urge Dick to make an honest woman of me and all that sort of thing." And this would be ridiculous since "he's not seducing me, I'm seducing him."

Was this the "downward path to salvation," the phrase that Dorothy uses to characterize her life at this time? Perhaps it was. Perhaps, out of those shifting elements of shadow and light that had made her life, there appeared for the moment the focused object of Moise as the final and constant end of her passionate seeking. Later she would think that she had been transfixed, drawn into a well of darkness.

That night she and Della got a telephone call at the nurse's home from a doctor. Grace Day was ill with a "diptheritic sore throat" and someone would have to nurse her. It was an emergency, and Dorothy was given leave to go home.

As it turned out, Grace did not have diphtheria, but she was sick enough to require Dorothy's care, or so she said. But it was not just Dorothy's nursing she needed. She probably wanted to have her home once more, and for this reason she had asked for Dorothy rather than Della. Surely she worried about her oldest daughter with her unconventional ideas, who with every move she made seemed to estrange herself further from her father, and who, though seemingly so self-assured, was never able to settle on anything.

Grace's moment of relaxation did not last. One afternoon as she sat sewing, robed in her new black silk kimono (still with the storks on it), Dorothy broke the news. When addressing delicate situations, Dorothy could be painfully direct, and she was direct now. She had fallen in love, "terribly in love." The man was not nearly so fond of her but, even so, she was going to live with him. "You know I've always told you that I didn' t think marriage was so important."

When did she plan to move in with the man, her mother asked. She wanted to go immediately, Dorothy said. The man was expecting her, she had already been away much too long without his knowing why she was away. She asked her mother if she could go.

Grace took the announcement with the long-suffering resignation to which she had become accustomed. She knew, she said, the utter futility of trying to change Dorothy's mind. "Oh, why ask me what to do? You know you'll only do just what you think best for yourself and pay no attention to me anyway. It's after five. Leave me alone to think."

Dismissed, Dorothy immediately packed and flew to the streetcar stop to begin her pilgrimage to Moise's doorstep, frantic to surrender her virginity. Had he waited for her? If he was there, would he take her in? Atremble, she knocked at the door of his small apartment. He was there. He opened the door, holding a half-finished cigarette and a book in one hand. With the other hand he closed the door as she entered. Barely acknowledging her presence, he went back to his chair, and with his face a mask of cold indifference he resumed his reading.

"June took off her hat and gloves and put them on a table at one end of the room. Then she slipped down on the floor by his knees so that he could not get up and he picked up his book again. . . . She was with him again." So she was, and Moise, tackled, as it were, by the tight hold she had on him, recognized the necessity of addressing the situation. Where had she been, he asked. "I thought you said you'd be here a week ago!" In the meantime, he had burned. He did not say this, but his wounded indifference to her presence was the classic symptom of the male rejected.

Dorothy explained her absence. Why hadn't Della taken care of her mother, he wanted to know. Dorothy explained this, too. "I had to stay with her," Dorothy said. "I knew I was going to hurt her enough when I told her I was going to live with someone." Moise's mood softened and, "finally he drew her up in his arms and held her closely." In his arms, the conflagration began, "the bright flame searing her, leaping up in her again and again until it was almost anguish."

So much for the welling tide of impending ecstasy. Dorothy, it should be remembered, wrote the phrase when she was twenty-three. At any rate, Moise knew that he need burn no longer. "Do you want me?" Dorothy asked. "Yes," said Moise, knowing he could not fight against it. Besides—"what does it matter? A month or two months, and it will pass and then I'll be free again."

Dorothy remembered the strange mood that came over him. For some time he was silent and vagrant sounds crept into her consciousness. From down the street came the mechanical rhythm of a player piano, and closer, a phonograph played. Outside, an occasional soft wind stirred the stunted trees in the small yard and drifted through the open window into the room. It was September. Then Moise talked, and his words, as Dorothy remembered them and as she remembered words that he spoke later, described his feelings for Dorothy. "Women—all I ever thought before was that you take something that you need from them. It's physically impossible for a woman to take a man. She always gives, gives herself up.

And now I hate you—I don't want you because I feel everything going out of me." Had he, finally, encountered someone more ruthless than he, who could take more than he?

Dorothy was in no mood for situation analysis or personal dissections. "She bit his neck contemplatively." Suddenly Moise shook her. Then he gave up; he turned down the lamp.

Their first days together passed in a velvet flow. Moise left at noon to work at an acting job he had found, and Dorothy took on the role of housekeeper. When he was there, and passion's demands had been met, for the moment, they discussed literature. On this subject, Moise took a proprietorial air. "You are nothing but a damn little fool so don't you dare tell me Conrad knows how to write a story," he told Dorothy. "I'll never read Conrad again," said Dorothy, in glad obedience, although in saying this she recognized that he would take her statement as a lie, and by so taking, the truth would be reached. What would he have her read? *The Count of Monte Cristo, The Three Musketeers,* Heine's prose, and "any Scandinavian literature."

She was the contented and purring housewife—"my woman," as Moise said. As for her, "it was sweet to be his woman," to lovingly hang up his clothes, caressing them as she did so, to inhale deeply the lingering scents of his morning shave, to exchange knowing glances with Amenemhat who saw everything from his place on the wall over the bed. In the afternoon, she made clothes for herself from material she had gotten from the cotton remnant table at the department store. She also acquired some silk remnants, "very thin," from which she could make a nightgown. Later, as she sat sewing on this item, she smiled to herself as she remembered a story Peggy had told her. A "lover" had gotten Peggy to bed, but as matters had progressed toward their final action when passion would be resolved, he had been overcome by a fit of artistic fancy. Taking Peggy's lavender chemise, he draped it around the light bulb above the lover's couch. Then, in the shadowed shade of lavender, as the rolling waves pounded with incessant hammering upon the surf, as Wagnerian chords rolled to peak crescendo, the chemise burst into flames. Perhaps Peggy had assured her that it was only the light bulb that had done it.

After two honeymoon weeks, Dorothy called her mother. Could she come home that evening and have supper? Of course she could, said Grace. She was doing some cleaning and Dorothy could help. When Dorothy got there, her mother greeted her with a kiss and told her that she had a wedding present for her. It was flatware, service for six.

During the visit, Dorothy chattered brightly about Lionel—how careful he was about his appearance, how he himself would occasionally cook. Obviously, Dorothy was trying to reassure her mother that it was all working out well. And Grace, whatever she may have thought, played her part. She soon began referring to Moise as "the new member of the family." Before she left, Dorothy added another bit of information that she felt was positive. She had introduced Lionel to Peggy, Mike Gold, and Floyd Dell. He had seemed to like them all well enough and had even agreed to go to parties with them. But, said Dorothy, "he objects to my seeing any of them when he isn't with me. I think he's jealous." "Jealous" was not the right word. One suspects that Moise, believing that he had compromised his freedom by admitting Dorothy to his bed and board, felt that he could exercise an absolute proprietary right over her. When he spoke of her as "his woman," he was not just making idle boudoir chitchat. And one can believe that only a completely docile and adoring Dorothy, forever confined to quarters, could have kept him with her for any length of time—if even then such a thing were possible.

It was impossible with Dorothy. She was sociable like her mother; she liked conversation about ideas and books; she liked to laugh, too. Sometime in early December a blow-up occurred. She, Moise, Peggy, and some of Peggy's friends had congregated at a Village restaurant for a late evening supper. Dorothy, happy to be out and mellowed by a drink she had just had, leaned to one side to talk to Peggy and, in so doing, rested her hand on the shoulder of the man who sat next to her. Observing this rather innocent familiarity, Moise suddenly pushed back his chair, stood up, and looked down contemptuously at Dorothy. He was leaving, he said, and Dorothy could remain "to embrace the gentleman on your right."

Dorothy, paralyzed, did nothing. Instantaneously the scene, which moments before had been warm and happy, became discordant and ugly. She gulped down another glass of whiskey, and when the "gentleman on her right" turned to her to ask her what had happened she rudely repulsed him. Peggy came and sat in the vacant chair beside Dorothy and held her hand. Men were brutes, she whispered to Dorothy, but this opinion did not prevent her from energetically pressing her conversation with an artist sitting across the table. Peggy considered herself in love with him, but his love was confined to his painting and alcohol. Another man at the table looked at Dorothy and grinned sardonically. He laughed, he told her, so as not to weep. It was one of the richer Village aphorisms, appropriate to a tragic moment—like the one that had just engulfed Dorothy. He told her that it was rotten to be in love.

For a while Dorothy sat swiveling her head in the direction of whichever of the three doors of the restaurant that she heard opening, hoping to see Moise reappear. Then she began to cry. "Before I had everything in the world, and now—now I don't see any use in living."

When closing time came for the restaurant, Dorothy had no place to go. She had no key to Moise's apartment, and since it was in the back of the building she was sure she could arouse no one— or so she told the grinning man who laughed because he could not cry. She decided to go home with Peggy, and Peggy, full of solicitude, said she would give Dorothy so much wine that Dorothy would forget everything. But the wine was not needed. As soon as Dorothy lay down on Peggy's bed, she fell fast asleep. She awoke at last to see flecks of dust dancing through a bright shaft of sunlight pouring through the window. Across the room, Peggy sat up from the couch on which she had been sleeping. It was almost eleven o'clock. After a bath and coffee, Dorothy's impulse was to go back to the apartment, knowing that Moise would be there until noon, at which time he would go to his acting job. But Peggy convinced her that she should stay. Moise should come for Dorothy; it was he who had gone off in a huff. Dorothy stayed and then wished that she had not, but by then it was too late. Moise, she knew, had already gone. Then burying her face in the cushions of the sofa, she cried repeatedly, "God, how I want him." It was very dramatic, but then Dorothy had just turned twenty-one and even may have seen Norma Talmadge do something like that in the movies.

So there was another night with Peggy. The next morning, though, she was up and off early. She found Moise, as she had found him the first time, sitting by the window. He looked up from his task of filing his fingernails and eyed her coldly. Had she come for her things? No, not for her things. She sat on his lap and put her arms around his neck, a move which interfered with his nail-filing. Soon his stern indifference became irresolute. "She could feel him trembling as he picked her up and carried her into the next room."

Yet it was always a part of what was unusual in the make-up of Dorothy Day that she could never, figuratively speaking, use ellipses to avoid a confrontation with the truth of a situation, however unpalatable. So the trembling Moise carried her into the bedroom—then bliss. Oh yes, but afterward Moise, with his trembling cured, tells her to leave; he could get along without her. Hating him "desperately," Dorothy begins to pack but suddenly stops. She will not leave, she tells him. She must go, he tells her firmly, and she realizes that he means it.

Where Dorothy went, she does not say, but at this point in her life the recollections of two people who knew her then provide elements of the story. One is Mrs. Sue Brown, who then was the wife of Provincetown Playhouse director, James Light. The other is Malcolm Cowley. In her home in Sherman, Connecticut, in the early afternoon of August 6, 1976, Mrs. Brown, with Cowley adding comment, told of episodes in Dorothy's life.

She and her husband were living at the time at 86 Greenwich Avenue, Mrs. Brown said. They had the top floor of the building that they called "Maison Clemenceau." The Irish family that owned the place lived on the first floor, one room of which they rented to Dorothy. "Dorothy thinks I saved her life at Maison Clemenceau," Mrs. Brown said and went on to relate circumstances. She had just come home from shopping one day and was unpacking her groceries when one of the family sons, unkindly called "Weary Willy" because he was spastic and walked with a slow, uncertain gait, pulled himself upstairs to tell Mrs. Light that he smelled gas coming out of Dorothy's room. The two went there immediately and, with Weary Willy helping "and my own muscles," they dragged Dorothy upstairs. After five or ten minutes, Dorothy regained consciousness and drank some tea that Sue had made for her. Mrs. Brown said that she had wanted Dorothy to go to a doctor, but Dorothy refused, saying she was all right and would just stay where she was for a while. Then Mrs. Brown went out again to get something, and when she came back, Dorothy had gone.

Dorothy did not explain what had happened, and all that Mrs. Brown could recall was that the gas hose was disconnected from the heater when she had gone into Dorothy's room. Cowley, sitting there and listening to Mrs. Brown relate the episode, speculated that Dorothy had tried to commit suicide. Then he àdverted to a time, shortly after this, that she had taken an overdose of sleeping pills at "Spanish Willy's." Of this latter incident, he could supply no facts, only that it had been part of the talk of the time.

Had Dorothy actually tried to kill herself? Sue Brown said she had never noticed anything in Dorothy's personality to suggest that she might be suicidal. She never seemed depressed; on the contrary, she was usually "happy and jolly." As for the disconnected hose, she might have been so tired that she tripped over it, not realizing what she had done. Still, in Greenwich Village suicide was not unusual—it was the final and ultimate statement that without love, life could not go on. Even so, and as infatuated as she had been with Moise, it is difficult to think of Dorothy, with a set and final determination, taking her own life. One cannot, however, reject the thought that she may have played with the idea and even "acted out" a requirement of the code as it existed for persons of her age and place. She was, after all, just twenty-one.

In January, 1919, the Lights temporarily provided hospitality for two of their friends at Maison Clemenceau. Sue Light had known Malcolm Cowley in high school, and he, back from the war, had gone to New York to begin his writing career. Cowley brought with him to Maison Clemenceau another hospitable soul, the belle of Village bohemia, Peggy Baird. He and Peggy had just gotten themselves settled when it was Peggy's thought that they should invite Dorothy up to visit. Cowley said that Peggy "kept exclaiming about the line of Dorothy's jaw, which was extraordinary, this long straight line of the jaw." Cowley did not say what they talked about when Dorothy came, but he did remember "being impressed by her as a handsome young woman."

Dorothy's expulsion from Moise's apartment was not the last of the affair. When she left, she told him that he could find her in the Village restaurant where she and her friends had been hanging out. Soon she began to station herself there, remaining until closing time. Eventually, he came in. How was she, he wanted to know. His manner bespoke affectionate interest. He saw the book that she was holding—Max Beerbohm's *Zuleika Dobson*. He picked it up, looked inside the cover, and read the inscription made out to Dorothy by a male friend. Instantly jealousy took hold.

"You're a fool," Peggy had told her the night before. Now with Moise sitting beside her, she thought of what Peggy had said and laughed. Flashing through her mind was a phrase of St. Paul's:

"We are all fools for Christ's sake." Moise took her hand. He burned. "Let's go home," he said. Well, she *was* a fool, she thought, but she got up and went with him.

So the affair was resumed. Yes, Moise told Dorothy, he loved her. She was not beautiful, but she appealed to his imagination. "When I hold you in my arms at night . . . I'm kissing a little street girl from Montmartre whom I'm keeping for the night; or you're an eastern woman capable of any viciousness and with a knowledge of all the secret sins."

This, at least, is what Dorothy reported him as saying and no doubt he did. They were fine words, right in the Village tradition. But the Village tradition made for parting, too, and that was what festered in Dorothy's mind and lay over her days like a pall. When Moise was in the apartment, she lived in a fever of excitement, clinging to him physically so as to enforce his presence. When he was away, she fell into a desperate mood of apprehension, full of fear that he might never come back.

It was May, 1919, and life for her became jarringly discordant. It seemed to her that everywhere she heard "The Missouri Waltz." Vendors played it on their hand organs; she heard it over and over, pumped out with mechanical precision on the player piano down the street; she heard it on phonographs in the apartments around her; and she even heard it sung by two little girls from upstairs who played in the small yard outside her window. What difference did it make that the country was filled with rumors that the Reds were preparing to take over; that one of the navy's giant Curtiss flying boats had, stage by stage, flown its way across the Atlantic; and that Mike Gold had gone to Mexico to avoid prosecution for draft evasion? *"What is the matter with you?"* Peggy had written to her, underscoring the question herself. "Are you dead or something?"

The problem was that Dorothy had discovered she was pregnant. It was a possibility that her mother had repeatedly warned her of. "Don't get caught. . . . Whatever you do don't get caught," her mother had said to her. Well, she was caught, she thought to herself, when the full realization of her state came upon her. She described the moment as a painful one: hysterical sobbing and clenched-fist pounding of the bed.

From the first, she ruled out two courses she might have taken, had she decided to have the baby. One was to return home. It was a choice she ruled out immediately. Her mother had warned her, and she had told her mother that, no matter what happened, she could take care of herself. Now she would have to keep her word. And, although Dorothy did not mention it, there was her father to be considered. Confronting him with her problem was something she could not face. Her other choice was to go to a home for unwed mothers. She knew of such a place but, again, she could not submit to the humiliation of asking for succor there. It was all a matter of pride, she said.

And what about Moise? If only she could tell him and hope that some overwhelming compassionate response would come welling up to cause him to put aside the pronouncements he had already made as to what he would do should she become pregnant. He would "never consent" to having a child, he had said. "He had impressed that on her mind many times. If she insisted on having it, he would leave her—leave her as soon as it began to show." Moise had said that, but Dorothy, as usual, excused him. "He hadn't wanted to love her or live with her. She had started the whole thing . . . God knows he hadn't wanted to live with her."

The only person with whom she could discuss her problem was Peggy. Peggy's opinion was that Dorothy should have the baby. That was what she, Peggy, would do. In fact, Peggy said, she would "give anything in the world" to have a baby of her own, but she was incapable of having one.

This advice was not what Dorothy wanted to hear. Her mind was made up, she told Peggy. She was there to get the name of an abortionist and to see if Peggy could lend her the money she would need. Yes, she wanted the baby, but she could not have the baby and have Moise—and it was Moise that she wanted. She would lose him "unless she went to a doctor immediately and said nothing at all to him [Moise] about it."

She was out of her mind, Peggy told her, but Dorothy went talking along, indulging herself in that great sophistry, so frequently used, that it would be "the height of selfishness to bring children into the world . . . unless they're going to have a fair chance at happiness." It was, of course, *her* happiness that was at stake. Or so she thought. She may also have thought, in a penetrating moment of lucidity, that the person of Moise had catalyzed forces within her that she could not resist and would take her to hell.

Immediate action was necessary, she had told Peggy, but, curiously, she did nothing. One supposes that she kept delaying the abortion in the hope that Moise, finding that life with Dorothy could be good, would become domesticated, even to the point of marrying her. So a month passed, and then two. With "The Missouri Waltz" gouging itself into her consciousness and a lowering mood gripping at her soul, she took to walking the streets and riding buses. She watched "the women shopping on Fifth Avenue," and looked at "the homes of all those people who accepted permanency as the undercurrent of their lives. Those women were buying things to take home to their husbands—to their babies. . . . Why couldn't she too have a home, a husband, and babies? A dull resentment smouldered in her breast."

Malcolm Cowley tells of a visit that he and Peggy had from Dorothy about this time. "She came down to see Peggy and me at 107 Bradford Street. Dorothy and I went out shopping to get things for supper. We passed I think it's St. Peter's Episcopal Chapel on Hudson Street, and Dorothy said, come in with me. So we went in. The service was an Episcopal Evensong and after a while Dorothy got down on her knees and prayed. I saw tears streaming down her face and then she said, don't tell anybody about this. We went back and cooked dinner with Peggy."

It must have been sometime around the first of September that Moise told her that he was leaving. Faced, finally, with the necessity of resolving her problem, Dorothy made her last stand. She told Moise she was pregnant. Whether or not this was news to him is another question, but at this point, presumably, he insisted that Dorothy have an abortion. It was several days later, early in the morning, that Dorothy appeared at the upper East Side flat of "Dr. Jane Pringle." She was shown immediately into a small room and, as Dr. Pringle laid out her tools, Dorothy undressed and put on what must have been to her the familiar hospital gown. The abortion was induced by passing an instrument into the uterus, manipulated so as to tear the fetus from the uterine wall. It was a process that also mangled and killed the fetus.

When this ordeal was over, Dorothy was put on a cot in another room. It would be only a few hours, the doctor told her. Her lot now was "just to lie there and endure. Three hours seemed an eternity . . . one pain every three minutes. . . . The pain came in a huge wave and she lay there writhing and tortured under it. Just when she thought she could endure it no longer, the wave passed and she could gather up her strength to endure the next one."

Just before nine o'clock, she heard the doctor's little boy tramping down the hall on his way to school. Then the doctor went out. She had to make some calls, she said, but she would be back at noon to see how things were and to make lunch for her son. In the next room, Dorothy could hear the "sing-song" ticking of the clock, and welling up through the airshaft near her came the sound of a woman's voice, singing an aria from an Italian opera.

She thought of the immediate future. She, Della, and her mother had concocted a story that covered Dorothy's long absence from the hospital. Her mother had gotten in touch with the hospital people and had told them Dorothy had gone out West to take care of a failing aunt. When the crisis was over Dorothy would like to return. Could she? Yes, she could, Grace reported the hospital as saying. Dorothy thought of Della, now finishing her last year of training. She might even be one of the senior nurses on the ward to which Dorothy would be assigned, giving her orders.

She thought of Moise and her thoughts followed the same old paths—the same desperate things she might do to keep him. It was over, she knew. Having done this final thing she no longer cared—she was too tired to care—"tired of being precariously poised on the edge of an abyss of unhappiness. She had fallen into that abyss now. No one had reached out a hand to keep her from falling."

Finally it was over. A life that had begun an unwilled journey into time, a life that was guilty of nothing, had been assaulted and made to die because it stood in the self-willed course of others. Its destiny, for whatever meaning, had no further business with history. Now only a bloody and battered blob of tissue, it lay on the receiving towel to be wrapped, no doubt, in toilet paper, and flushed down the drain. It was the realization of this that became a part of Dorothy's person and, finally, changed her life.

For the moment she slept, deeply and dreamlessly. "She no longer thought of the child. That was over and done with." That evening, Dr. Pringle made her final inspection and told Dorothy that everything was "just fine." Perhaps wishing to end the day with some relief from its grim character, Dr. Pringle went to a picture show, taking her son with her. By eight o'clock, Dorothy was dressed and ready to leave. Before leaving the apartment that morning, she and Moise had talked of the day's prospect, and he had said that he would come for her when it was over. Tired from dressing herself, she lay on a lounge in the front room to await his coming. Minutes dragged by. Cars passed on the street below, and when she heard one slow down, she held her breath in a rising fever of expectation, hoping that it was a cab and that he would be let out at the door. But then there was only silence—no reassuring sound of steps in the stairwell outside her door. She strained to hear the telephone, willing it to ring, wanting to hear him say that he would be there shortly. The phone always gave a buzzing sound before it could muster the energy to erupt into a full ring, and when she heard this sound, she was on her feet to answer it. Twice it rang, but the calls were only patients. By ten o'clock, she knew that he would not come.

Dr. Pringle would soon be home, and not wanting her to know that Moise had not come, Dorothy hastily put on her hat and coat and went out to the street to catch a cab.

What did she think, as she rode down through town to the Thirty-fifth Street apartment? She does not say, but her spirit, anguished as it was, was to receive another blow. Arriving at the apartment, she found no Moise, only a note. Dorothy cites the note, although one wonders if it was as he had written it. Yet it does sound like him. He had left, he said, because his new job demanded his immediate departure. Nonetheless, he had suffered with her in the ordeal she was undergoing, but after all, she was "only one of God knows how many millions of women who go through the same thing" and he would have to keep the matter in the right perspective. When he returned, he would probably find her married to a rich man. "And be sure it is a rich one, for it is quite likely that I shall want to borrow money from you." Speaking of money, he had "committed a last little crime. I cashed a check on a bank where I had no account . . . the money you will find in the enclosed envelope." It would take care of her for a couple of weeks, or "until you return to the hospital."

He concluded with sober advice: "Don't build up any hopes" of reconciliation. "It is best, in fact, that you forget me."

Here ends the account of the episode in *The Eleventh Virgin*.

⚜ 6

Chicago

WHAT DOROTHY did immediately after the ending of her affair with Moise is not known—at least not known by anyone willing to tell about it. In *The Eleventh Virgin,* she mentions the plan to go back to the hospital, and then in a brief conclusion of one page, which she calls "Monologue," she portrays herself sitting on the bench in the hospital grounds and talking with Della. She tells Della that she will have a husband, that she will have a child, and that she will live in the manner and with the security to which middle-class wives were accustomed.

As it turned out, she did not go back to the hospital but she did get married. The man's name was Barkeley Tobey, and she married him, it seems, in the early spring of 1920, just months after the tragic denouement of the Moise affair. The marriage is a matter that Dorothy was loath to discuss. "About my marriage," she wrote to a friend, "I'll tell you more about it sometime. It lasted less than a year. I married a man on the rebound, after an unhappy love affair. He took me to Europe and when we got back I left him. I felt I had used him and was ashamed."

It is again Malcolm Cowley who supplies the information that is available on Tobey. "Another strange character," Cowley mused. "He was a promoter—that is, he promoted ideas for publishers, including, I think, the first idea for the Literary Guild. But always he would get these well-paying jobs for *The New Republic,* later the Literary Guild, and always it would be discovered that he wasn't doing anything at all after getting the brilliant idea."

Then Cowley told a story to give substance to his point that Tobey was "strange." It was also a story that Cowley obviously enjoyed telling and had, no doubt, told before. "At that time there was a quirk in the Connecticut state marriage laws that Barkeley took advantage of. He used to court a young woman, offer to marry her, and take her up to Greenwich to be married at high noon and then promptly take her back to New York and never again set foot in Connecticut with her for the rest of the marriage." The legal "quirk" was, he said, "that no marriage performed in Connecticut was legal unless it was consummated in the state of Connecticut. Barkeley was very careful not to consummate a marriage in the state of Connecticut, and thereupon when the marriage broke up, as they all did, there would be no question of a divorce. Simply the slate wiped clean."

Cowley had another story: "Barkeley and Dorothy had invited us—Peggy and me—to dinner and this would be in the spring of 1920 on the southside of Washington Square in a big apartment. Barkeley always had money." At dinner, "we ate off the Tobey family silver—quite grand family silver. Two days later Dorothy appeared at our tenement and said the most awful thing happened. 'All our silver has been stolen. And it must have been one of the people who were at dinner with us on Tuesday night.'" Then Dorothy mentioned all the others who had been there. "And I said to Peggy," continued Cowley, " 'I won't pay a damn bit of attention to this; it's all a bloody detective story from a cheap English novel. I don't believe it.' Later we discovered that every time our good Tobey married a young woman, the family silver was given to her and then stolen a couple of months later."

So much for Cowley's stories. When Tobey died in 1964, he had been through eight marriages. If it is true that any of these matrimonial ventures came from his having hoaxed young maids into his bridal chamber, Dorothy was not one of the ill-used ones. Rather than Tobey's having deluded her, it may have been she who was the designing party in the matter. Speculation aside, the fact remains that this marriage occurred so soon after the shattering collapse of the Moise affair that it was obviously contrived—a "rebound" matter, as Dorothy said. One can imagine how she hastened to tell her mother and Della how well she had straightened everything out—she would marry a man with means, she would have children, she would write. In fact, she and Tobey were going to Europe where most of the people she knew who could write were going, or had already gone. And Tobey, then forty-two years old, considered the bright exterior of this intelligent and vivacious girl and braced himself for a new venture.

So they went to Europe, apparently in the summer of 1920.

How long did they remain? "Less than a year," Dorothy said in one instance. "A year," she says in another. Dorothy was never more at peace with herself than when traveling, and especially on a ship. The voyage was good medicine. Their first stop was London, where, says Dorothy, she "walked and took bus rides and explored and thought of DeQuincey and Dickens." DeQuincey she had read and liked from her days at Waller High School in Chicago, and Dickens, like Jane Austen, was an author she would read and re-read for the rest of her life.

After exploring London, the Tobeys went to Paris, and for Dorothy, there were again more long walks and bus rides. There was also a lot of drinking, if one is to judge by an offhand remark she once made. She told a friend once that her first awareness of Paris was that of waking up in a hotel room there. Comments she made in later life about the French lead to the judgment that she was not warmly drawn to the country. The people there, she said, did not bother to answer questions. Perhaps. But one is inclined to wonder if her judgmental attitude toward the French was not affected by a growing sense of the impossibility of her marriage to Tobey. In any case, she, alone or with Tobey, left Paris for Italy.

In Italy, her mood brightened. "Italy I loved; the six months I spent in Capri meant that forever after, the smell of Italian cooking, the sound of buzzing flies, the loud strong voices of my Italian neighbors, the taste of spaghetti and polenta and the sour red wine brought me back to the months I spent beside the Mediterranean, or wandering around the streets of Naples, or driving on sightseeing trips behind the shabby horses with their voluble drivers." She was affected by the drivers' kindness to their horses, "even to the point of fanning them and wiping their faces." Yet the same drivers were "inconsiderate of their wives, who carried heavy burdens and worked long hours and were always gracious, with dignity and beauty far surpassing that of any other women I have ever seen."

Dorothy says that she spent a year in Italy, during which time she wrote. It was a time when Mussolini's black-shirted legions were beginning to fill the streets, but that was something to which she paid little attention. "I was living through a time of my own personal joy and heartbreak and what happened in the world had little effect on me." What was the source of the "personal joy" she had? It was likely the experience of living in Italy, of living simply, of finding in the existence of even the poorest some mark of an ancient order that put grace into their lives and made them human beyond anything she had known.

And her "heartbreak?" Her marriage had become oppressive to her—a cacophonous experience when compared with her memory of the thrilling urgency and single-focused passion that she had felt for Moise. And always there was the other memory of the child that might have been, the child that was destroyed when it could have been the seal of life upon their union. It was her fault; it was she, the woman, the keeper of that seal, who had failed, who had allowed that seal to be broken.

What reason is there to suppose that these could have been Dorothy's thoughts? One finds them in the latter part of *The Eleventh Virgin*. It was in her room in Capri that she wrote of that May morning in 1917, when awakening early to go to the *Masses* office for her first day of work, she recalled those separate and distinct sounds that came from the East River. There was the man whistling the "Star-Spangled Banner" off-key. She heard the backfire of a starting tug engine and then the creaking and groaning of pilings as the boat pulled away from them and began to move into the mainstream of the river. "Then the boat swished past leaving only the tentative caress of the waves against the little beach; like a baby's lips pressing against its mother's breast when it is not quite hungry. . . . A tender, happy sound."

In this passage, one suspects that her memory of the tugboat's foaming through the river was real, but that the gentle washing of waves on the beach was an image she created so that she could express the thought of a contented baby at her breast.

Then there is that good-bye letter from Moise with which Dorothy closes the main narration of her manuscript. The substance of this letter, it may be recalled, was an explanation for Moise's not showing up at the doctor's office after the abortion and his counseling Dorothy to forget him. There is, however, her final paragraph in *The Eleventh Virgin*, and a reference to it seems more appropriate to Dorothy's state of mind when she wrote it in Capri than to the time that she was recalling. It is Moise who speaks: "Child, don't be unhappy. Who knows. Perhaps my heart, scarred with the shackles of a hopeless passion, will creep back some day like a frightened convict to the scene of its serfdom. Bleeding, torn from contact with an unsympathetic world, it may ask, who knows, that it be permitted once more to take its place in that least anchoritic of cells which you have provided it."

These words do not sound like words that Moise would use, and, likely, it is actually Dorothy who is speaking as she concludes her story. If it is, and if one substitutes the phrase "perhaps my unborn child" for "perhaps my heart," then one gets a sense of a hope that was beginning to form in her mind. She would yet have a baby and, more than that, Moise would be its father.

In the "monologue," Dorothy explains it all to Della. Once, "I thought I was a free and emancipated woman and I found out that I wasn't at all, really. I got excited over socialists and the I.W.W.'s, and anarchists and birth controlists and suffragists and if I had not been working on a newspaper and bumped into them all at once, I would have gone on from one to another of them and joined them all and kept on being fervent for years."

As it turned out, though, "I fell in love, happily at an early age, and I'm still in love. And it looks to me that this freedom is just a modernity gown, a new trapping that we women affect to capture the man we want." She knew exactly what she wanted. She wanted Moise "and marriage and babies! And I'll have them yet. Wait and see."

This was, of course, desperate thinking—desperate planning— but caught as she was, any glimmer of hope no matter how dim and how distant, or how illusory, seemed in her fevered mind to represent the grand avenue to happiness. Her "wait and see" was not spoken idly. Dorothy knew her strength and her determination.

It was, presumably, the summer of 1921 when Barkeley and Dorothy returned to New York. And there, as she said, she left him. Her marriage, she doubtless assured herself, had been a great mistake, unfair to Barkeley and intolerable to her. Her vision was back in focus: it was Moise she wanted and he was in Chicago working on a newspaper. She would go to Chicago.

Before settling there permanently, she made a preliminary visit to the city. Would Moise accept her back into his company? Could she support herself? She contacted Rayna and the two met on several occasions, but Rayna, full of a zeal that came from her newly acquired Marxist faith, seemed preoccupied. Their days of close comradeship, when Dorothy was the radical, were over.

As for Moise's position in the matter, one can speculate only in terms of what occurred later. Dorothy did shortly return to Chicago; she did take up with Moise again, and probably there was some kind of "relationship." No doubt Dorothy pursued him and tried to pinion him with the force of her personality and will. Moise, though, was elusive, and their association never attained the ardor or the exclusive mutuality that presumably existed the first time. Finally, after a year of it, Dorothy realized that the happy ending she had so confidently looked for, as she concluded her book at Capri, had become a bottomless pit. Moise was unobtainable; she had failed in her effort, and in the process she had fallen again into depths that seemed to have reduced her spirit to a state of hopelessness.

In her own published narrations of this part of her life there is, of course, no mention of Moise. That he was the prime object of her Chicago interlude was known only to her family and possibly to a few of her confidants who were absolutely mute on the subject, as they were about the entire Moise episode. That Moise was her object is indicated in the concluding page of *The Eleventh Virgin*. That he was a part of her Chicago life is clear from the several references she makes, in her own story of this period, to a "man with whom I had been deeply in love for several years." Further, there are two other connections that tie her to Moise. One is a letter to Dorothy, dated December 22, 1965, written by a Charles Shipman. "Many years ago, in a previous incarnation, when my name was different, I knew you," Shipman wrote. He had been to Floyd Dell's apartment in the Village and had remembered her there. Then again, "when Eleanor Owen and I were in the Collegiate Anti-Militarism League together and you worked for a time in our office near Columbia University (helping to get out the magazine *War*), and finally in Chicago during and after your Lionel Mauice [sic] episode."

Another connection is suggested from evidence that comes from a jailing episode that Dorothy experienced in Chicago. The story, despite its somewhat sordid features, is straightforwardly told by Dorothy in *The Long Loneliness*. "During the past year," she says, "I had come to know intimately a rough young woman who had been a shoplifter and a drug addict but had cured herself after many years of addiction. She had fallen in love with a newspaperman who had introduced her to our group and she had been our constant companion on evening parties for some months." Then Dorothy goes on to say that this woman, about thirty years old, Dorothy judged, had, in "a fit of depression," swallowed some bichloride of mercury tablets and had been taken to the county hospital. "The tie between us," Dorothy writes, "was that we were in love with the same man."

The *Chicago Tribune* provides details in its July 18, 1922, edition. It said that a Mae Cramer, "butterfly of Chicago's bohemian quarter," had made her second attempt to commit suicide. She was further described as "an artist's model and a figure in Chicago's Greenwich Village on the lower North Side." She had swallowed poison during a " 'Bohemian' frolic at the Grey Cottage, a tearoom at 10 E. Chestnut Street," all because of an "unhappy love affair with Lionel C. Moise, a writer."

In this news account, the *Tribune* recalled Miss Cramer's first suicide attempt, again because of "unrequited love" for Moise, made the previous March 22. But this was not all to the story. At the same time Miss Cramer was being admitted to the hospital on March 22, another would-be suicide was recovering at Columbia Hospital from an attempt she had made on March 8, also because she had been spurned by Moise.

From the March 9 *Tribune* account of this pathetic story, one can gather something of the style and life of Moise. The principal in this instance was a Mary Lieberman, seventeen years old, "artist's model and vers libre poetess." Miss Lieberman, in accordance with what seems to have been the approved ritual for such matters, walked into a rendezvous for Chicago's bohemia, the back room of David Luchesi's saloon at 2 East Chestnut Street, asked for a drink of water, wrote a note to a "Lionel Moise," and then swallowed twenty-five bichloride of mercury tablets.

The note is that of a despairing seventeen-year-old whose reading fare, apparently, was "true confession" magazines. "Dearest," she began, "I wish I could say everything to you now in this note that I always wanted to say. However, nothing seems to matter now except that I love you. Everything else is so futile, meaningless, fruitless, and blank. Everything seems to come to a nothingness, and as I go beyond that I go mad. Please don't say, 'Damn fool,' in that emphatic way of yours. Really, dearest, nothing seems to matter. People and things are horrible and rotten, and while I may sit back and laugh at them I have loads of fun. But I'd rather not. My laughter would be too self-conscious."

Then she wrote a paragraph that contained sentiments similar to those Dorothy could have expressed three years earlier. "I realize your need for . . . perfect happiness. Dear love, I know I didn't have so much to give you, but I did want to give you everything. But when I came to you I found myself floundering miserably, because I would realize you didn't want anything of me, no matter how much or how little I gave. I might ask you to remember me every time you take the fifth drink, but that would be asking too much, I fear, and then, that is such a cheap attempt to add a wonderful touch of burlesque to the tragic story of a young girl who loved not wisely, but too well."

Seventeen-year-old Mary Lieberman looked up from the note she was writing; her glance swept around the room, searching for some miraculous intervention that might break the grasp that a malignant fate seemed to have on her. She looked for Moise, coming from the bar in the next room, a Moise who would approach her, take her by the hand, and, as the angelic chorus swelled, lead her into the light. But Moise did not appear and Mary wrote: "Dearest lover, I have no illusions about you, but am almost the disillusioned person you represent yourself to be, and you said you didn't care at all. Remember me, I love you." She signed her name, opened the bottle, and with an intermittent swallowing of pills and gulping of water, attempted to frustrate the deadend affair that life seemed to be. Mary Lieberman recovered, and the next July— about the 25th, one guesses—Mae Cramer began to recover. Insisting that she be released from the hospital, she signed herself out and went to the Chicago headquarters of the I.W.W., where she felt she would be taken in.

One of the common areas of association for Mae Cramer and Dorothy at this time was in the activities of the I.W.W. Miss Cramer, apparently having nowhere else to go, went to an old rooming house managed by the Wobblies, where, despite the fact that it was ordinarily used for men, she felt she could get hospitality. When she got there, she telephoned Dorothy and asked her to bring her something to eat and to wear. Dorothy went immediately, and finding Mae still shaken and ill from her experience, she decided to spend the night with her. Most likely, Dorothy felt that the woman might again try something desperate. "We were undressed and getting into bed," wrote Dorothy, "when a knock came at the door and four men burst in telling us that we were under arrest for being inmates of a disorderly house."

Dorothy explained this invasion as an indirect result of the Red Scare: the Wobbly house was under surveillance, and when two women were seen entering the place, the police decided to raid it. And so Dorothy, whose immediate impulse was to help this desolate woman, found herself, along with a loudly cursing Mae, being rudely led into the street, and there under a buzzing and popping arc light, she and Mae stood with their captors, awaiting the arrival of a patrol wagon. When she later wrote of the scene in *The Long Loneliness*, Dorothy recalled a theater advertisement she had seen that depicted "a girl of the streets," standing beneath a street light, and she was reminded of her own plight some thirty years previous.

Was Dorothy, in this latter day, able to laugh about it? The horror and shame of the experience was still with her. She was not, ordinarily, a quick healer where such wounds were concerned. The abiding character of this bitter memory remained in her mind, "because of my own consciousness that I deserved it." She had been a "victim of my own imprudence, of my own carelessness of convention." Her and Mae's presence at the I.W.W. lodging house "meant only one thing to the men who arrested us, and when we were booked in the morals court, they had the law on their side."

Standing under the street light, with gall rising in her throat, was just the beginning of her ordeal. In the late hours of the night, the patrol wagon took them through the vacant streets to the West Chicago Avenue police station. There they were questioned, searched, relieved of their possessions, and booked to appear in court two days later. Dorothy gave the clerk a fictitious name—what name she used, she does not say.

Her first jail experience, five years earlier, had been something of a sacrificial offering of herself, made in the company of other self-sacrificers who carefully enunciated their words and used them at dramatic moments in the construction of lofty periods having to do with justice, freedom, and sacred rights. Her sister inmates in this Chicago matter, as it turned out the next day, had been caught in the net of vice raids in the area of Twenty-second Street. Fifteen or so were put into the cell with Dorothy and Mae. As Dorothy related it, the first activity of these whores, after the cell door had slammed, was to take off their dresses, carefully fold them and lay them aside, and then caper around in their shifts. When a guard brought in another of their profession, to add to their growing number, he was greeted with obscene raillery and provocative posing. The "girls" took their incarceration as something that was little more than a coffee break in the rigors of their work-a-day lives.

Throughout the first day of their cavorting and chatter, Dorothy remained glumly silent. The other girls took this as a sign that Dorothy was new in the business and this was the first time she had been caught. They tried to console her, and as the day wore on,

Dorothy witnessed them performing little kindnesses, for her and for one another. She came to have a feeling of community with them that probably exceeded anything she had felt for her suffragette associates in 1917.

The next day Dorothy found herself back in the patrol wagon, she and her new friends hustled off to the morals court. Fortunately, said Dorothy, she met a newspaperman in the courtroom whom she knew. Could this have been Moise? Perhaps, but more likely it was one of his associates. This man apparently assured Dorothy that he could get her out, although Dorothy had refused the use of both lawyers and bail offered by her companions. It was not because she felt ungrateful, or that her case was "different" from theirs, but because she had some feeling of community with those "others," whoever they were, who had no recourse other than to go to prison for their misdeeds. "I would have preferred to spend the ten days at Lawndale Hospital and take any sentence they chose to inflict. What right did I have to avail myself of the friendship of those in power?"

Apparently, because the judge who was supposed to make the disposition of Dorothy's case was out playing golf and could not take up business again until the weekend was over, Dorothy was sent to the county jail. As she was going out of the building, she recognized a friend, "Manny Gomez." She had known him first as a Columbia University student with whom she had worked in the Anti-Conscription League in the early days of the war. "Gomez" was, of course, an assumed name for this black-bearded man, and well might he have taken one. Having fled to Mexico to avoid being conscripted, he had then gone to Russia for the communist meeting of the Third International. Afterwards he returned to the United States, via Mexico, to take up the work in Chicago. Now, standing on the sidewalk, Mr. Gomez looked wonderingly at Dorothy, whose acquaintance he had recently re-made in Chicago, and asked how she was. Her brief explanation brought from him the comment that he seemed to run into her in the most unusual places, but that he knew lawyers and would soon have one for her.

At the city jail, Dorothy and her friend Mae were made to disrobe and then searched for drugs in a manner that Dorothy found somewhat more exacting than necessary. Then they were given prison clothes and put into a cell.

The most difficult part of the experience, as Dorothy narrated the story, was witnessing the agony of a drug addict in the cell next to her. This unfortunate person "beat her head against the bars or against the metal walls of her cell and howled like a wild animal. I have never heard such anguish, such unspeakable suffering. No woman in childbirth, no cancer patient, no one in the year I had spent in King's County Hospital had revealed suffering like this." What struck Dorothy about the woman's plight was the "madness, the perverseness of this seeking for pleasure that was bound to be accompanied by such mortal agony.... To see human beings racked, by their own will, made one feel the depth of the disorder of the world." She thought of the "sadness of sin, the unspeakable dreariness of sin, from the first petty little self-indulgence to this colossal desire."

Dorothy spent two days in the county jail and then was released by the judge that Gomez knew. At least, this is one account of what happened. Gomez's lawyer friend never appeared, but then one may excuse him on the ground that Dorothy's case was not in his usual line of practice.

Her prison experience was, in a way, the consequence of her relationship with Moise. It is most likely that, after it, she went over and over in her mind the course she had set for herself and bitterly wondered if she had not been the world's greatest fool. She had been in Chicago nearly a year, and the high hopes she once had, that this homecoming would bring about some kind of stable relationship with Moise, she certainly knew by this time were completely unreal. And there was that other hope, which she surely still possessed, so poignant in its character—the one that had impelled her into this wild Chicago venture. This was the hope that she would yet have a child by Moise, a reincarnation of the one she might have had.

Whatever Dorothy's dreams, they did not reach down to the reality that she encountered. Moise was a person who seemed almost completely unstable, who could make no final commitment to any value that lay athwart the mood or impulse that promised the next excitement. And Dorothy, who probably thought that she could raise his vision and order his life, found that it was she who was changed. Her association with him had, to some extent at least, been established by her joining "his crowd." There were parties night after night in Chicago's Greenwich Village, an area that began at Ohio Street and ranged north to Division. It was a place where many old mansions and more ordinary structures had been converted into flats and studios for artists. In New York, the favorite nighttime gathering place for Village bohemia had been the Golden Swan. In Chicago, it was the Wind Blew Inn, and as Dorothy had known the former, she probably knew the latter. But in the Wind Blew Inn there was no Eugene O'Neill, no Max Bodenheim, none of those visionary and demented characters that excited her imagination and raised her vision. There were only Moise and his companions, and the atmosphere they created was raucous and vulgar, untouched by graciousness.

Their better moments together came from their discussion of books and Moise's instruction to Dorothy on how to discipline her writing. Dorothy said that Moise was a great admirer of Pascal, and so she read Pascal but did not understand him. Dorothy was reading James Joyce's *Portrait of an Artist as a Young Man* at the time and found something interesting about it. But once, when they were riding Chicago's North Avenue elevated and she was reading the book, Moise became so incensed at what he considered her depraved taste that he tore the book from her hand and threw it out of the train window.

They did, though, share a common love for Dostoevsky. Dorothy had read him in high school, but in Chicago, she read him with a new sensitivity to something she had missed the first time. "I could not hear of Sonya's reading of the gospel to Raskolnikov in *Crime and Punishment* without turning to it [The New Testament] with love. I could not read Ippolyte's rejection of his ebbing life and defiance of God in *The Idiot* without being filled with an immense sense of gratitude to God for life and a desire to make some return." At another time she wrote, "the characters, Alyosha and the Idiot, testified to Christ in us. I was moved to the depths of my being by the reading of these books during my early twenties when I, too, was tasting the bitterness and the dregs of life and shuddered at its harshness and cruelty."

The shiftlessness of Dorothy's life during this time is suggested by the frequency with which she changed jobs. "I worked at Montgomery Ward's . . . another time I took work as a copyholder to a proofreader; there was a job in the public library as a helper at fifteen dollars a week and another as a cashier in a restaurant." She did courtroom reporting, and said she got to know Ben Hecht and Charles MacArthur through her newspaper work. She even earned extra money by posing for art classes.

If she ever lived with Moise in Chicago, there is no mention of it anywhere, no hint, even, that this may have been the case. She says that when she first got to Chicago she lived in a slum on On-tario Street, that she had a "huge" room for which she paid twenty-five dollars a month and which she shared with a student. She mentions artist friends living downstairs; possibly it was through them that she got her modeling jobs. Then she mentions a "little apartment on the North Side" where she found a furnished room she shared with "a French Canadian milliner" who did most of her work in their room.

It was while she was living in this place that she spent her des-perately unhappy winter of 1922/23. Not only did the discordan-cies of her life weigh upon her with almost unbearable pressure, but she was ill. Twice, she said, her indisposition, whatever it was, was so severe that she had to miss work, staying in bed for several days at a time and brooding the while over her state.

Misery, it is said, loves company, and Dorothy to some extent that winter was the confidant of two young women who were suf-fering from despairing romantic problems. One was her room-mate, "Blanche," a Catholic, "who suffered because she was in love with a Mason and was forbidden by the Church law to marry him." Nonetheless, poor Blanche kept a hope chest and "prayed long and fervently on her knees, every night and morning," presumably to the end that her fiance would forswear his Masonry. The other was "Bee," daughter of the couple who owned the house in which Dorothy lived. Bee was in love, engaged, and she spent the wages she earned from the streetcar company on her hope chest. Bee, said Dorothy, passed long hours on Wednesdays and Saturdays in the cold front room of the house with her young man. Her prob-lem, as she confided to Dorothy and Blanche, was the extent to which she was sexually aroused, even in the cold front room, and what such feelings portended in the way of the danger of premari-tal intimacy. Bee, too, was Catholic, and her scruples about sex had their origin in her religious training.

Dorothy's response to the problems of Bee and Blanche was not, as it well might have been, one of ridiculing their qualms and laughing at their innocence. She felt, to the contrary, that they had in their lives norms of order whose preservation was crucial to them, and whatever their frailties in upholding these norms, they could get strength from their saints and their God. In her own case, she thought, "resentfully," she says, "I had nothing." She wondered why they never tried to interest her in the Church, in things like making "a mission," or praying "for someone's intention"—words she heard them use which meant nothing to her. Perhaps it was because they were "most ordinary" Catholics, fearful of exposing to ridicule the ordinary routine of their faith. After all, they knew "that my standards were not theirs, that I belonged to radical groups who had a different code of morals, who did not believe in God."

"Different" though Dorothy may have been, she felt drawn to these two women and was grateful that they accepted her as she was. "Perhaps they did gossip about me behind my back, but their behavior to me was ever kind and good to my face. I have long since come to believe that people never mean half of what they say and that it is best to disregard their talk and judge only their actions."

On February 3, 1923, Lionel Moise was back in the news. The Chicago *Herald Examiner* reported a fight among the publishers and editors of a newspaper called *Tolerance* and named Moise as one of the principal combatants in the matter. *Tolerance,* whose aim was to fight the Ku Klux Klan, apparently had only two working journalists, one of whom was Moise, and both had been fired a month prior to the incident. Moise, apparently on a sleuthing mission, had returned to the *Tolerance* office and, it was charged, had been found rifling the desk of one of the *Tolerance* officials. Thereupon a fight erupted. The paper's management went to court asking that Moise be enjoined from entering its offices. Moise, as usual, was all innocence, claiming that he had been blackjacked while on an innocuous mission.

This affair probably set Moise on the move again. He may have left Chicago to take newspaper work in Wisconsin, perhaps in Milwaukee. At any rate, his next major public appearance was in April, 1933, when he appeared on a Columbia Broadcasting Company network from Milwaukee to tell the world that "Milwaukee beer is good beer." As a reporter for the Milwaukee *Sentinel-News,* he had somehow gotten a job as an assistant brewmaster with Milwaukee's Cream City Brewery, which was just beginning its production of 3.2 beer for the market soon to be legal. On the newscast, Moise, called the "Paul Revere of Beer," told how he, in his job with Cream City, had followed a rigorous regimen of taste-testing the Cream City product and how he had found it good. In fact, he said, the beer was comparable both in taste and stimulating effect to pre-prohibition beer. After drinking two quarts of it, he felt "light and giddy."

If Moise did leave Chicago in early 1923, his departure coincides with the approximate time that Dorothy reached a final conclusion that her dream-world construction of him, the constant lover, the father of her child, had been a hellish caricature. Back when she was in Capri, writing her conclusion to *The Eleventh Virgin,* she had disavowed all of her radical crusades in favor of married love and children. So for a second time, she had pursued Moise with the whole force of her person, driven by a tenacious and unremitting will, and for a second time, she found herself in the wasteland that Moise was for her. Having given up a part of herself in the first experience, she hoped in the second to redeem all that had been lost. And now this too had failed. It was not his fault; he had said all along that there was no hope at all that her dream could be realized. She could not blame him at all. Nor did she. Nor would she ever.

With Moise out of her life, Dorothy took up again her radical crusade. "I was happy to be with friends again who were active in the work of changing the world." A particular friend, in this instance, was the "Manny Gomez" who had tried to help her at the time of her Chicago imprisonment. "We spent Sundays together at workers' picnics on the outskirts of Chicago and at meetings." It was good, she wrote, "to get out of the city . . . to listen to the playing and singing of the foreign-language groups and to see their national costumes and watch their dancing."

It was during this period that Crystal Eastman's *Liberator,* the successor to the *Masses,* was reissued in Chicago as a communist monthly. Cartoonist Robert Minor was its editor, and Joseph Freeman, its managing editor. For a while that summer, Dorothy worked as Minor's secretary. Beyond typing Minor's letters, she did one book review for the magazine that appeared in the September, 1923, issue. The book she reviewed was Floyd Dell's *Janet March,* and no doubt she assigned herself to the job of doing it.

She begins her review with a prefatory comment. Five or six years ago, she said, she had written reviews for the *Masses,* and Dell, who was its managing editor then, had made her rewrite them. "I'd like to be able to pass this across the desk to him now," she said, "and get it back with sentences and even paragraphs neatly rewritten in bright green ink."

So much for old times. What Dorothy really wanted to do in her review, Dell's *Janet March* notwithstanding, was to write about Dorothy's Janet March. That is, Dorothy saw the character, "Janet

March," as very much the person Dorothy wished to think of her-self as being. In fact, Dorothy *was* "Janet March," and as she char-acterizes Janet March in her review, it is almost as if Dorothy were working out a comforting rationalization for her own life's course. She addresses her initial comment to Dell personally and continues in this mode as she discusses Dell's subject:

I'm inclined to believe that before you were done with . . . [her] you made Janet a hard-headed, strong-bodied woman who walks with her eyes wide open into any experience life has to offer her. She finds out that she doesn't want to finish . . . [college] and teach school, and she doesn't want to enter the business world. She tries it out one summer as a file clerk in an office. But she doesn't cling to any dream of finding independence. She doesn't want to be free. . . . She just is. When she wants to go to Chicago she goes. When she decides to have an affair . . . she goes to the man she has chosen. . . . When she finds that he does not need her, that her love might hurt him as well as herself, she doesn't romanticize about it, but kisses him a cool good-bye and goes away, leaving him, I am sure, with a very sweet taste in his mouth. . . .

I like your Janet March and I'm sure you too must have been tremen-dously fond and proud of her as she walked steadily through your pages.

Then Dorothy expounds, with some detail, what ostensibly is Ja-net's view of sex but which more likely is her own:

She had no idea of sin when she took him for a lover. As she thought, "sin and laughter didn't go together." As for sex—"what was it?" Beauty. Strange that it should be so many different things, such a melange. Play, a frolic, as of romping kittens, silly laughing childishness, a release from all the sober constraints of everyday life, a discovery of an Arcadian realm in which the only reality was play. Strange too, that the Arcadian realm was but a single step from the world of common place—and another step might bring one into a world of bewildering wondering in the dark! But it hadn't been merely play, there had been something antique and noble in its very naturalness, it was a rite that took one back out of civilization into some earlier world, it was a solemn and sacred ceremonial of the worship of nature. And it was the satisfying of some deep impersonal need, like hunger, like thirst, like the wish for sleep; it was rest, healing, quietness after tumult—it was finding hints, through one's own body, of something that might be one's soul; it was taking of wings and soaring into perilous heights of ecstasy alone.

This discourse on sex reveals a different Dorothy from the one who, back in her Village days, had listened with critical reserve to the ecstatic soarings of Dell and others on the subject of uninhibited, wide-ranging sex. The question is at this point—and it remains a question—had sex, in her hurt and bewilderment, become a bromide with her, justified, for the most part, by the standard Village rhetoric that she had heard from Dell and others: "Play, a frolic, as of romping kittens, silly laughing childishness, a release from all the sober constraints of everyday life"? Perhaps it had, but there is also the feeling that Dorothy was too intelligent, too critical, to be taken by a view of sex as "romping kittens" and the like. Yet she had written down all of this, and for the moment, she may have told herself that she did believe it and that everything would be all right.

It was soon after the departure of Moise from Dorothy's life that Della came to live with her. If Dorothy, as it seems, is referring to Della when she speaks in *The Long Loneliness* of a "friend of my disorderly life, who afterward became a communist and was active in the work for Loyalist Spain," then Della, too, had acquired a taste for the radical cause.

Della's radicalism may have come, in part at least, from the company she kept. Through Dorothy, one suspects, she had been brought into the radical, literary group of Greenwich Village, and youthful, unaffected, and intelligent as she was, what she heard from her radical companions made sense to her. But she was no gimlet-eyed doctrinaire. She was, to the contrary, a big, well-developed blond who laughed readily, who was personable and innately kind to people. She lacked Dorothy's quality of passionate and ruthless seeking, and the role to which she was destined, wife and mother, came naturally to her. She was, of course, most attractive to men, and a comment Dorothy made years later suggests that Grace Day, on one occasion, sent Della out of the country to put her beyond the range of what Grace thought were the ill-advised attentions of one young Village scholar who had already made his matrimonial commitment. Perhaps Della's presence in Chicago was connived by Grace, who thought to kill two birds with one stone. Despite glowing accounts Dorothy may have written to her mother about her life in Chicago, Grace knew her daughter too well to be misled. Della, she knew, would provide companionship and solace for Dorothy. At the same time, new interests would be good for Della. Dorothy says that she was "glad" to have "Mary" [Della] with her, that she liked her "irresistible sense of humor and a huge appetite for such a 'good time.'"

It was sometime during the fall of 1923 that Dorothy and Della decided to leave Chicago. Della, it seems, wanted to try life in New Orleans, and Dorothy, "tired" of Chicago, was happy to go. "I had a book finished [The Eleventh Virgin] and accepted by a publisher and I was at loose ends, waiting to see what would happen to it, whether I would get enough to live on it [royalties] so as not to have to think of a job for a while."

One thing is certain. New Orleans did not attract Dorothy because of its musical reputation. Never, then nor throughout her life, did she ever show the slightest interest in jazz or in its evolved form, the sophisticated swing style of the big bands of the forties. She and Della went there probably because of its reputation for color and excitement and because it promised relief from Chicago's dreary winter dinginess.

The room they found was in the heart of things—on St. Peter Street in the French Quarter and near the cathedral that faced Jackson Square. "There was a kitchenette and a gas meter into which we put quarters. The gas was apt to run out just when we had spent our last cent on a rabbit stew which took hours to boil. Rabbit stew, rice and shrimp seemed to be our staple dishes that winter."

Dorothy writes briefly of her social life in New Orleans. She and Della got to know some girls in the area who "like ourselves . . . were out of work and were only too anxious to go taxi dancing with us." There were "occasional young men," one "a wounded cameraman from Hollywood who had gone through the war and come back with many scars and minus a leg, and another silent, mysterious young man on his way to South America who told me he carried a revolver in a holster under his arm and slept with it under his pillow."

Ever resourceful, Dorothy got herself a job as a reporter on the New Orleans *Item*. Her special qualification, as she probably represented herself to the *Item's* editor, was her knowledge of the taxi dance halls. She would be a taxi dancer and write a series of articles on those festering sinks of iniquity. And the editor, hat low over his eyes, reached down into his drawer, took a pull from his bottle, looked through narrowed lids, and sized up his woman. She was hired.

Dorothy's first story was a straight reporting job. She was sent to the Roosevelt Hotel to interview Eleanora Duse, "Italian trage-dienne," who was vacationing in New Orleans. The headlines told of Dorothy's failure: "Mme. Duse Here as a Recluse; Even Sleuth Tactics Fail to Break Actress' Privacy." On Sunday, February 3, the *Item's* front page headline told of Woodrow Wilson' s approaching death. On the same page was the first installment of Dorothy's dance hall articles: "Dance Hall Life of City is Revealed." The next day's headlines carried the news of Wilson's death. Dorothy was still on the front page, too: "Dance Halls Flooded by Drink, Dope." Tuesday's headline suggested that things were pretty bad: "Hangers on Scramble to Gain Dance Hall Girls, then Offer Them Whiskey, Dope, Smokes."

The February 5 issue of the *Item* had a front page headline that suggests Dorothy had aroused the conscience of the good women of New Orleans. "Women's Club Favors War on Dance Halls," it read. The Business and Professional Women's Club, at its weekly luncheon at the Young Women's Christian Association, "went on record as approving and thanking the *Item* for publishing reports of 'true conditions in the dance halls.'" A committee was appointed to visit the *Item* and urge that the spotlight of publicity be kept on the dance halls, as an effective means of freeing the city of a menace.

Another "revelation" came on February 7. Dorothy wrote of getting in line with the girls available for dancing and then being "confronted by a genial young drunkard who fumblingly poked a ticket at us and clutching us around the waist tried to dance." He "believed himself to be possessed of rare gifts in the way of dancing and painstakingly held us off at arm's length while he gazed at his feet and executed strange and complicated steps. Realizing finally that we were not gifted as he was, he contented himself with strolling rhythmically around the floor simpering inanely." Then, after a while, he began to repeat over and over a line that had gotten hung in his mind: "Four hundred concupines uttered a very vulgar expression."

"Surely you mean porcupines," said Dorothy—or maybe it was "concubines." But no, the young man assured her he knew whereof he spoke.

After this, Dorothy's dance hall articles flagged. What happened was what had happened when she was writing her "diet squad" articles for the *Call* back in 1917. She had said everything that could be said on the subject. Her last signed articles for the *Item* appeared in mid-March of 1924.

On evenings when she had no special reporting assignment, she would go across Jackson Square to the cathedral to make a visit and, when it was scheduled, attend the service of Benediction. Wanting to know what hymns and prayers were used at this service, she bought a prayer book and studied it. Observing this interest in religion, another girl who lived with Dorothy and Della gave Dorothy a rosary for a Christmas present. "She was a Russian Jew and did not understand my interest in Catholicism. She just wanted to give me something she thought I'd like." After this, Dorothy began saying the rosary at the evening cathedral services.

In February, Della went back to Chicago, but Dorothy, getting some serious reporting assignments, stayed with her newspaper work. In April, *The Eleventh Virgin* came out, published by Albert and Charles Boni. She "affectionately" dedicated her book to "H. N., to J. K., to a girl whose initials I cannot remember, and although it is not customary to include oneself in dedications, to myself; according to agreement." Except for Dorothy, just who the recipients were of this rather bubbly dedication is not known. But then Dorothy, apparently, was not altogether sure, either.

The book was given minor recognition by an unnamed reviewer in the *New York Times*. The reviewer headed his comments, "Truth Incoherent." Everybody but novelists, he said, was writing books. "Apparently there is a strong movement on foot to tell the truth at any cost—as if the truth was something particularly new and novel discovered in this age of confusion. Pseudo-confessions and autobiographical novels burst with the truth of life. Truth is so prominent that there is practically nothing else." The book had none of the elements that ordinarily were used as a basis on which to make a judgment of its quality. It had no form, and no coherence, and nowhere, by any standard, did it contain "truth and beauty." Yes, said the reviewer, he understood that "the defenders of all that is ultra-modern" would say that such a novel was defining "a new sense of values," something "solid on which to erect the future." But was this "new" an advance over the past? The only difference that he could see was that the "fallen" heroine of the past could blame her state on a harsh fate. But not "June" of *The Eleventh Virgin*. "Not blindly is she ensnared in the web of life—but fully conscious—even forewarned—she will hazard her chances with the loaded dice of fate. . . . It would almost seem as if she were a bit of a fool."

What was there left of the book to recommend? Nothing. "If

'The Eleventh Virgin' was an experiment in a new technique that had failed to come off, there would be some excuse for its jumbled mixture of reporting, observation and fiction. As it stands there is nothing new about it—just one more adolescent novel."

Why did she write this book, laying out matters so painful and personal that ordinarily one would consign them to the most hidden recesses of one's person and erect a barricade around them? From her earliest days, Dorothy had been possessed of the idea that she wanted to write. This idea came to her naturally because she was highly literate, and within a kind of reportorial dimension, she could be creative. It is likely that this idea, to the point of becoming a passion, was reinforced in her as a reaction to her father. Inwardly, she was as super-sensitive and vulnerable as he was, but she also had, as he had, a determined, implacable streak in her. The breach between them had set her on a course of proving herself, and her vehicle, of course, like his, was writing.

Beyond this father factor, there was her history as one of the would-be members of the coterie of Village writers who espoused the new radical vision. In 1919, when Floyd Dell, Max Eastman, and Jack Reed, especially, had achieved a large recognition, she was scarcely known. Then there was Eugene O'Neill, beginning to be recognized as a great playwright. And she was only a hanger-on, reduced to nothing and cast into that ash pile of oblivion, along with all the other self-deluded visionaries with their pedestrian talents. Well, she would write a novel of realism, more real than anything written before. In one action she would recoup all that had been lost and establish herself as the O'Neill of the novel form. She knew she would be laying out for public scrutiny her own private life as well as that of her family, but that was what art required.

So much for conjecture. Years later, Dorothy would agree with the *New York Times* reviewer. "I wrote a . . . very bad book," she says in *From Union Square to Rome.* To be sure, but at the time it brought her something she needed more than fame: money. One spring day she got a long-distance call from the Boni publishing house— the sort of flamboyant gesture that the editorial office of a Village publishing house might make. Big news: moving picture rights to her book had been sold for $5,000. Dorothy's share was $2,500. And that was all there was, or would be. Malcolm Cowley said that the movies had bought the book simply for the title. "They threw the book away and wrote another movie to go with the title, and then decided they couldn't use the title."

For the moment, though, Dorothy was giving no thought to anything except to luxuriate in the pleasure of knowing that by her accounting, she was wealthy. She would return to New York, forthwith, to live in the glow of this minor triumph.

🌿 7

The Beach

It was early April, 1924, when Dorothy got back to New York, glad, surely, to have behind her the two dismal and despairing years she spent in Chicago. It was something of a homecoming for her because she went back to the area where she had worked and lived during her first four years in New York. Many of her friends were no longer there but, as she commented years later, she spent her first two weeks profligately wining and dining those who remained. She felt she could afford it.

One interrupted friendship that was immediately renewed was with the Cowleys. Peggy and Malcolm had been in France for three years, returning in early 1924 to live in an apartment at 25 Bank Street. It is possible that Dorothy was "put up" by the Cowleys during those first days of her return, since Cowley cites, from first-hand knowledge, an occasion when Dorothy "seduced" a friend of his in the apartment. This was at a time, Cowley says, when Dorothy was "almost contemptuous of the flesh."

How is this to be taken—that Dorothy, in the buffeting she had received in the prior five years, had reached a completely amoral position regarding the matter of sex? Was it just "play," like "romping kittens," as she put it—the sheer enjoyment of it—the culminating ecstasy where she found that brief moment of becoming one with someone else, of being held and loved and taken to some oasis beyond care and time?

Perhaps this was it, and if so, it is understandable. However, there is another likely explanation for this behavior. In her conclusion to *The Eleventh Virgin,* Dorothy had said that she would have a baby. She even suggested that, in some sense, the one she would have would be a reincarnation of the one that had been lost. Whatever the nature of her association with Moise in Chicago, there had been no baby. Now, twenty-six years old, she began to wonder if she could still have one—if she had not been made sterile by the abortion. She wanted a child desperately, and the matter seems to have become obsessive with her.

Within weeks, Dorothy had established herself with friends of the Cowleys and had made them her own friends. These were first, the Lights, Jimmy and Sue, whom Dorothy had known when she had previously lived in New York. Cowley had known Sue in Pittsburgh, where she had been editor of the school paper. He had submitted his fledgling writing attempts to her. Cowley had also known Jimmy Light in high school, and when Cowley settled in the Village after his return from the war, he renewed his friendship with the two. Years later, the Lights were divorced and Sue Light became Sue Brown.

The Ohio connection did not end there. Mrs. Brown said that when she went to Ohio State as a student, she met three sisters, Rose, Lily, and Margaret Batterham. Later, after Sue and her husband had settled in Greenwich Village, the Batterham family moved to New York and the girls looked up Sue. Cowley, too, had a friend who came to the Village from Pennsylvania, Kenneth Burke. He and Burke had known one another in grade school and high school in Pittsburgh, and then, when Cowley moved to the Village, Burke would sometimes visit him there. It was probably in the socializing between the Lights and the Cowleys that Burke met Lily Batterham and soon married her.

As a result, when Dorothy arrived in New York, she was brought into this circle, and it was not long before she and Lily Burke became close friends. It was at the Cowleys one day that Dorothy met Lily's brother, Forster, pronounced "Foster." A year later she "entered into a common-law marriage with him." "The man I loved . . . was an anarchist, an Englishman by descent and a biologist. . . . His friends were mostly liberals and his sympathies were decentralist and anti-industrialist, though he loved the machine and the illusion of progress. . . . He was never active in any of the groups in which we mingled. His position probably approximated that of those who came later to be called the Southern agrarians."

Dorothy's characterization may be overly romantic. Batterham's anarchism, apparently, was not a thought-through position so much as it was the result of his unwillingness to be bound by anything. Sue Brown said that he had developed "iconoclastic ideas about life," that he was critical of any convention or moral code that he thought limited his freedom. He was "kind of an acerbic person—indignant with the tragedy of existence—having nothing to do with anything that would limit his whims." Cowley thought that Batterham "was marked for life by having too many sisters. Apparently he had no ambition except to catch many fish." Physically he was "tall and slim with straight sandy hair, pink-brown complexion, and a high forehead." He made "abrupt gestures—did not talk much about his ideas—talked about fishing . . . everybody knew he was a philosophical anarchist who didn't believe in marriage." Thinking back, Cowley said he could "still hear" Batterham's "flat Carolina, hill-country voice."

In her book, *Thomas Wolfe and His Family,* published by Doubleday in 1961, Mabel Wolfe Wheaton, the sister of novelist Thomas Wolfe, gives a brief sketch of the Batterham family as she knew them in Asheville, North Carolina. "They were typically English folk and the father and mother had been born in England." Altogether, they were "fine people" who "loved the outdoors." This penchant for outdoor life led Mrs. Wheaton into a story that concerned her brother, Fred Wolfe. Every time they got a chance, Mrs. Wheaton said, the Batterhams would "ride out into the mountains and sometimes they would take their tent along and spend a night or two." There was one particular trip, shared by Fred Wolfe, where "they had taken a wagon along on which to carry the tent and food, and I believe some children rode in it." Finally they got to the top of Craggy Mountain, "one of the most beautiful spots in our entire region," and there they put up the tent and started to prepare supper.

But wait a moment, Mrs. Wheaton says. Before continuing her story she must introduce "Bess," the Batterham horse. "She was a mare, a roan, and she was a frisky, spirited animal." Also frisky and spirited, it seems, was Fred Wolfe, along on the trip. Playful Fred, waiting for his supper, approached the contentedly browsing Bess from behind and slapped her smartly on the rear. Rearing, Bess lashed out with her hind legs and hit young Forster "squarely between the shoulder blades," sending him about twenty feet down a slope and knocking him out. As his inert form was carried back up the hill, Mrs. Batterham sent up a series of wails, all to the effect that her son was dead. No, responded the stammering Fred, "'F-F-F-Foster ain't killed! He just had the h-h-hell knocked out of him. But I know what'll bring him around right quick!'" Whereupon

Fred raced up the mountain, "where some mountain men had gathered," to get a jug of hard cider. He never made it back. Like his brother Tom, he apparently found that going down a mountain set up a craving for spirits. Weary, he sat down a moment to rest and to slake his thirst. "When the Batterhams found him an hour later he was singing with the jug in his lap."

Forster recovered handily and later was Fred's roommate at Georgia Tech. From what Forster would tell Dorothy years later, he and Fred were not compatible types. His experience with Fred as a roommate and with the Wolfe family in general led him to characterize them as "wild" people.

As the only boy in a family of seven girls, Forster probably matured in something of a hot-house atmosphere. When the war came, he either enlisted or was drafted, but the flu kept him from service, hospitalizing him for a year. As Sue Brown tells it, "he finally got better—and moving around—and then went back to live with his family." When the Batterham girls gravitated toward the Village, Forster was "taken in" by them. Mrs. Brown remembered him as "blond and anemic looking."

What, then, was the attraction between Dorothy—vivacious, sociable, verbally expressive, literate, impulsive, and passionate seeker—and Forster, who in most ways was the antithesis of all of these things? Mrs. Brown thought that Dorothy felt attracted to him because she "felt a sense of, perhaps, motherliness towards him." Dorothy regarded him as a "misunderstood cast-off."

Dorothy, it is true, was warmly drawn to "misunderstood" and "cast-off" types. Also, she badly wanted some stability in her life. Forster would be her man, and unlike Moise, he represented no potential for a draining and destructive passion. She would not try to order his life, and for her part, she would go on with her writing.

The summer of 1924 was, it seems, a round of parties and perhaps some attempts at writing on Dorothy's part, although none of it has survived. Dorothy kept in close touch with her publishers, the Boni Brothers, hoping that despite the bad review, her book would blazon forth. But royalties, if she got any, were meager.

The winter of 1925 must have been interesting. Caroline Gordon and her husband, Allen Tate, lived across the street from Della's apartment, and Dorothy and the Tates—or Caroline, at least—became quite chummy. Caroline was writing her first novel then,

Dorothy recalls. "Hart Crane used to drop into all our homes for coffee and conversation." He was just then receiving the favorable attention of critics for his poem, *The Bridge.* "I knew nothing about poetry," says Dorothy, "and had little knowledge of the techniques of writing." Kenneth Burke was then editing *The Dial* and, says Dorothy, "writing the first of his strange books." Cowley, who had not found his niche, was editing an architectural catalog and making only a precarious living. Sometimes the lofty heights to which Dorothy's friends went in their talk about literature and writing left her stranded on the shoals. "I can remember one conversation among Malcolm, Kenneth and John Dos Passos which stood out especially in my memory because I could not understand a word of it."

There was one personal cross-current at work during that winter of work, philosophizing, and extensive partying. Sue Brown says that Cowley fell in love with Della. She remembered that during the parties "Peggy would get so drunk that she didn't know what was going on and Malcolm would say to someone, 'You take Peggy home' and then he would go to Della's." Cowley himself talked of his feeling for Della. The parties, he said, were "rather boisterous," and Peggy would frequently drink too much. "At that time I fell in love with Dorothy's younger sister, Della, and that went on with intermissions for three years—finally broken up when Della married Franklin Spier—to my great sorrow."

It was Peggy, though, who urged Dorothy to take the step that turned out to be a significant factor in reversing the course of her life. Dorothy was foolish, Peggy told her, to spend what was left of her money in partying and indulging her friends. Why not buy a place in the country, like some others in the old radical group were doing, to get away by herself and lead her own life? It would be a place where Dorothy could concentrate on her writing. That was true, Dorothy thought, for in the city, "there was always a great deal of partying and drinking."

Several years later, Dorothy recalled the day in early spring when she and Peggy "found the little house which was the scene of my conversion to the Church" on the west end of Staten Island. "On the train we pored over real estate advertisements." Even before talking to the real estate agent, "we sat on the bare porch in the spring sunlight and Peggy immediately drew paper and pencil from her pocket and started planning an elaborate garden for me. 'I will help you, Dorothy,' she said enthusiastically. 'You must have climbing roses over the side of the house, and we will transplant violets from the woods—those long-stemmed kind, yellow and purple. And sweet williams and ... daisies of course. They come up year after year and are no trouble at all.' "

It was not much of a place, a fisherman's shack on a piece of ground that measured only twenty-five by fifty feet. But what is better to live in than a shack where a tin roof holds back the rain that comes to pound thunderously on it and gives one, amidst all the din, a sense of inviolable security—where the inside air is touched with the pleasant smell of old dust lodged between boards —where the crackle and flare of driftwood fire holds at bay the raw dampness of a stormy night—where from the porch one can watch ships moving slowly toward the Jersey shore, so easily seen— where waves roll in to churn the sand, leaving the marine life buried there gasping and bubbling—where gulls wheel and cry and then dive to skim along the top of the water—where the cool salt air fills lungs with life—where, behind the house not too far away, the new green of trees shades a boggy earth, alive with flowers— and where, at the moment, as Dorothy stood in the bright sun, the beauty of it all fell upon her with such warmth and love, almost, that she had an unaccustomed feeling of peace.

Dorothy was no cautious buyer who filled a pad with questions and notes concerning what was wrong with the house. She would take it at once. A payment was made, and as she and Peggy rode back to New York, on the train first and then the ferry, they talked of how they might furnish it. In the city, Dorothy told Forster about the day and they laid their plans. She would move into the cottage and write; Forster would stay during the week in New York, where he had an off-and-on factory job, and go to the cottage on weekends.

Forster probably fell in with the idea wholeheartedly. Like his parents, he loved nature and especially the water. Alone in a boat, either fishing or just rowing, his soul was at peace.

Dorothy lived in her cottage for nearly four years, and since it was such an important time in her life, she writes at length about it in *From Union Square to Rome* and in *The Long Loneliness*. Further, she began keeping a journal, and much of the material she uses in these two books is taken from the journal. All of this represents an extensive body of source material in her life during this period, but the difficulty in using it is maintaining a perspective as well as valid chronology. Dorothy wrote of what touched her, but she was often vague, confusing, and even incorrect about dates.

She lived at the beach cottage from the spring of 1925 until the winter of 1929. One principal theme that appears in her writing during this period is nature. Then, and throughout her life, it was nature that produced in her the most direct sense of goodness and peace. Nature was for her truly the handiwork of God. The seemingly most insignificant things of nature were beautiful to her, and she attributed to Forster the awakening of her consciousness to little things as well as to nature's grandeur. Sometimes, as a writer, Dorothy would speak of herself as primarily a journalist. True, but her best reporting was that in which she was describing the beauty of creation.

The first entries in her journal for 1925 are descriptions of the beach: "The shore line down by our house is irregular with many little bays and creeks wandering inland every few miles." There were "small piers and breakwaters" that either eroded the sand or piled it up. "Some years before, a pier a quarter of a mile down the beach towards the ocean fell to ruin in a storm with the result that the sand is washed away from our beach to be piled up on the next one." This left "a big expanse of rocky wasteland, varied in color and mottled with green and red seaweed. It is a paradise for children, though hard on their bare feet. They grow accustomed to it, however, and can soon walk lightly among the stones, finding all kinds of crabs and little fish and eels caught in the pools at low tide."

Old men, "gaunt and weatherbeaten," came from miles around to dig bait, "most of them bending for hours over their digging forks, getting foot-long sandworms and bloodworms and which they sell for fifty cents a dozen. . . . I go down to the bait diggers and pick up clams as they turn them up in search for worms." Overhead, "the seagulls scream over the rocks, blue and gray and dazzling white, winging their way from the wreck of an old excursion boat, now used as a pier, to the larger rocks in the water, diving with a splash into the shallow gray water for a fish. The waves, the gulls, and the cawing of the crows in the woods in back of the house are the only sounds on these . . . days." Away from the bay, up and down the beach, "the swells roll in from the ocean, smashing dull and ominous on the sands, but here the waves are gentle and playful."

In both her books and her journal, Dorothy gives much attention to her neighbors because, as she recognized, they were an unusual assortment. Down on the beach, near her house, was a small shack, inhabited by an old beachcomber named "Lefty." To get a little money for staples and whiskey, Lefty dug sandworms and sold them as bait. His main occupation, when he was not digging bait or sleeping off a binge, was gourmet cooking. At least that is what Dorothy suggests. "He prepared his small fire on the sand, banked up with bricks; carefully scrubbed the clams in the pools among the rocks; steamed them with just a little water"; and then, after draining off the clam juice, he put the clams back on the fire "to warm with a dash of butter, salt and pepper." He sipped the clam juice and ate a slice of buttered toast. Clam juice, he said, was the best thing in the world for a hangover. Lefty frequently had lobster and crab, also served with butter.

Dorothy sometimes shared in his feasts. "I often sat down on the sand in front of his cabin in a steamer chair which he kept especially for me, and watched him cook." Coffee? Lefty would ask. Yes, of course, coffee was always good. "I accepted the big cup from his hand and bit into a thick slice of buttered toast with fried mushrooms on top." Placing her toast on her lap, she would lean back in her chair, holding her hot cup in her hands, and watch the western sky become aglow with the setting sun. "The waves lapped the shore, tinkling among the shells and pebbles, and there was an acrid odor of smoke in the air." Down the beach she could see some people loading rocks into a cart that was hitched to a white horse. They were Belgians. When the nearby St. Joseph's Church began chiming the Angelus, they stopped their work and stood as if in prayer, their figures outlined against the brilliant western sky. Dorothy was very affected by the beauty of the scene and did something which she suggests she had not done in a long time. "I found myself praying, praying with thanksgiving."

Her neighbors constituted an international set and most of them, it appears, were bootleggers. The prayerful Belgians, "Pierre and his wife," had as their "sole aim in life . . . to wrest from the beach and the waters of the bay a fortune to enjoy in their old age." They also sold wine and booze—the Catholic "olive oil"—when it was ordered over the telephone, which, apparently, Dorothy or her neighbors sometimes did, since Dorothy was the only person in the immediate neighborhood who had a phone. The village hotel keeper sold whiskey and drank from his stock, only to fall down the stairs and break his neck. The policeman, who made his rounds in a Model T Ford, sold spirits from a deserted shack on the beach, and according to Dorothy, he antagonized his rivals by underselling them. Mrs. Mario, the Italian woman from Bleeker Street who ran a kind of hotel next to Dorothy's house, would occasionally sell "very good wine," a product on which Dorothy felt qualified to render a judgment.

Some weeks after Dorothy moved to the island, the Cowleys, too, bought a house nearby. "I had an idea," Cowley said, "that I wanted to get away from working for Sweet's Architectural Catalog and support myself by freelancing and living in the country. So I . . . saved up enough money to buy a Ford for $125—on which I was cheated—and finally some garden tools as well, and had a garden and a house way in the back country near Huguenot, but . . . only a mile and a half or two miles from Dorothy's place." Cowley said he lived there nearly two years and that during that period he and Peggy saw Dorothy and Forster quite often. "We swam off their beach. I sometimes went fishing with Forster—a great fisherman—and sometimes we had a party there on Saturday night, the parties becoming rather boisterous, although Dorothy, I must add, was never a great drinker." And thus Cowley straightened out the record for history's sake where the subject of Dorothy's drinking was concerned.

In characterizing her neighbors in *The Long Loneliness,* Dorothy described the Cowleys as being the somewhat "smart and sophisticated" element in her beach community. This was not something they affected; it was only that Malcolm, educated and intelligent, had a bookish and scholarly aura about him and that he and Peggy, with their three years of France behind them, reflected a kind of international intellectual cosmopolitanism. The picture Dorothy gives of Peggy at that time is, in fact, that of a person who is anything but poised and sophisticated—rather a character. Peggy, she says, would likely as not spend her day doing crossword puzzles or playing endless games of solitaire. In the meantime, the house would grow into a confusion of disorder—dishes in the sink, beds unmade, and ashtrays full. Then, sometime after supper, she would commence a riot of mopping, sweeping, and dusting. One cold night Dorothy went to the Cowley's house to take a bath, since their house had a tub and a hot water heater. As she settled in the hot water, cigarette aglow and a copy of Balzac's *Cousin Pons* in her hand, Peggy went out the back door, letting in a cold draft that chilled Dorothy. What was going on, Dorothy wanted to know. Peggy said she was going out to pick what flowers were left in her garden because the frost would certainly get everything that night. Dorothy could envision the picture, and warmly immersed in the water, she smiled to herself at the spectacle that she knew Peggy made—her pallid face with its patrician nose and chin just emerging from her fur coat, her slender hands in "a pair of gaily colored Bavarian mittens with *Aus Muenchen* woven into them," and a basket hooked over her arm in which to put her flowers.

Peggy had two passions: flowers and cats. Her summer gardens were filled with flowers, and when during the cold winter months she and Malcolm moved into their little apartment in the city, she had them in window boxes. Her devotion to her cats was such that on her journeys between the island and the city she entrusted them to no one, carrying them with her in a brightly colored basket. That color, in fact, was an aspect of her person was evident in the clothing she wore. In the mid-twenties, when hemlines were rapidly moving upward to the knees, she wore flaming stockings and gaudy dresses.

The first year of Dorothy's life at the beach was not always a time of quiet and solitude for her in contrast to the hectic character of her days in the city. There were walks on the beach and contemplative moments when she was touched by the beauty of nature, but during the winter weekend trips to the city, there were parties in some Village flat where they drank, laughed, posed as enlightened sophisticates, and exclaimed over the insensitivity and stupidity of those Americans who lived by the editorials in the *Saturday Evening Post*. Then later, when alcohol sent spirits soaring, there was dancing. After a while, there would develop the inevitable clamor for one of the women among them to do the Charleston, and she, with legs flashing and beads swinging, would kick and shimmy her way through the 1925 hit, "Yes Sir, That's My Baby."

During the summer, Dorothy's place was the favorite gathering point for weekend parties. She had the indispensable phonograph, but, more than that, she had the beach, which, considering the distance from the city, made for weekend-long hilarity. After a while, these gatherings, which occurred during the first part of the summer of 1925, began to wear on her. Now twenty-seven years old, she plunged into one of those introspective moods to which she was sometimes given. Where was she going? What did all this partying add up to? Besides, her guests were perpetually tracking in sand from the beach and leaving their wet bathing suits all over the house. She decided to end the parties and, having decided this, she found that her "virtuous resolutions to indulge in such pleasure no more are succeeded by a hideous depression. . . . I think of death and am overwhelmed by the terror of blackness of both life and death."

Parties or otherwise, she had one guest during these days who was always welcome. Sister Della liked parties, too, but Dorothy remembered especially one springtime when Della was visiting her. They went walking every afternoon and once they came onto a farmyard where there were some goats. "They were so sweet," says Dorothy, "that Della insisted on going back there every visit to hang about their necks garlands of flowers, which they promptly ate."

Dorothy's writing took much of her time. She worked on a serial for a syndicate, one of those day-by-day episodes of adventure and romance that appeared in newspapers during the era. She wrote pieces about gardening for a Long Island newspaper, and she wrote in her journal, which she tended to keep in tranquil moments.

And there was Forster and her life with him. In *From Union Square to Rome,* his name is "Fred," but he is mentioned infrequently. Since this part of the book is almost entirely a duplication of the journal that she kept during these beach years, it would seem that "Fred" was not uppermost in her mind, at least when she was doing her journalistic musing. In *The Long Loneliness,* she gives Forster a page in the way of a critical examination, and some of her findings were negative. "He worked as little as possible, he shared in all the expenses of the house, but he never spent any money if he could help it. He hated social life and fled from it, and seemed afraid of any actual contact with the world." It would seem, then, that when Dorothy was partying, Forster was probably out on the pier fishing. In the mornings at breakfast, he "read the *Times* faithfully, and all I knew of the political and foreign situation I knew from his reading aloud." She realized that she could tune him in or tune him out, as she chose, but he read so indignantly and passionately of the woes people were suffering that she listened. The situation was not anything that he had experienced, and certainly it was nothing about which he would do anything, except rage at the very fact of its existence. His response was to go off by himself— fishing, rowing, or tending his garden. "It was hard for me to see at such times why we were together," Dorothy writes, "since he lived with me as though he were living alone and he never allowed me to forget that this was a comradeship rather than a marriage."

From Dorothy's journal one gathers that Forster did not mind her indifferent housekeeping since he contributed more than his part to the disorder. Her journal at one point tells of how she had just scrubbed the living-room floor. Then she describes the interior of the room. Hanging on the wall and thrown around on chairs and boxes were "horseshoe crabs, male and female, spider crabs, and a dried sturgeon, the jawbone of an ass, an assortment of skulls of every kind of small animal, the wings and tails of brightly colored birds, the shell of a huge sea turtle, two birds' nests, a wasp's nest, whelks' cocoons, hanging like false curls, several mounted fish heads ... sea horses, pipe fish and file fish." That particular morning the place was "especially messy. There were fish hooks on the window sills and fish lines reeled out to dry all over the floor. A few clams had fallen from the pocket of Forster's sweater, which was hanging damp with salt water, over the foot of the bed." There was, too, Dorothy's mess: books randomly stacked in the corner, on orange crates and on the lounge. Surrounding her typewriter on her desk were the scattered sheets of the serial she was writing.

Mess or not, Dorothy deeply inhaled the peace around her, and as she continued writing her journal, she turned her look outward. "It is a sunshiny hazy day and the boats on the bay look ghostlike and unreal. The morning sun makes each blade of grass, each dry twig, stand out and the grasses in the field next to the house do not stir. There are only the starlings to break the silence and occasionally the far-off whistle of the train. Even the waves make no sound upon the beach for there is an offshore wind."

The bay was a picture and the train whistle from the Jersey shore seemed to blot out time. Then sounds immediately at hand brought time again into focus. "The cats have just been fed a dogfish apiece and are growling at each other under the porch. Forster caught the dogfish last night on the pier and he has been cutting one up to study its insides. No one around here eats them, thinking them not fit for food, except Mrs. Mario who assures us that all Italians think them delicious. So we shall try them for lunch today." After this entry had been made, another sound intruded itself into her consciousness: "There is a bucket of soft-shelled clams out in the pantry and they squirt now and then and sound as though they were gasping and sighing."

She wrote on, discussing the odors of which she was then con-

Grace Satterlee Day, ca. 1910.
Courtesy John Spier.

John I. Day, 1932. Courtesy *The Catholic Worker.*

Dorothy and her older brothers.
Courtesy John Spier.

Dorothy and Della. Courtesy John
Spier.

Scribblers' Club: back row,
Dorothy, center; Samson
Raphaelson, right. University
of Illinois Yearbook, 1915.

(Right) Rayna Simons,
University of Illinois
Yearbook, 1916.

(Below) Dorothy Day,
February 9, 1917. Courtesy
UPI.

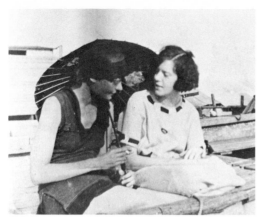

Dorothy and Della.
Courtesy John Spier.

Forster Batterham,
Dorothy, and brother
John. Courtesy John Spier.

Dorothy in Staten Island cottage.
Courtesy John Spier.

Dorothy and Tamar, ca. 1932.
Courtesy Dorothy Day-Catholic
Worker Collection, Marquette
University.

New York, 1930s
(Peter Maurin,
center). Courtesy
*The Catholic
Worker.*

Catholic Worker
House,
Milwaukee, late
1930s (Dorothy,
Nina Polcyn,
second and third
from right).
Courtesy
Dorothy Day–
Catholic Worker
Collection,
Marquette
University.

Easton Farm,
ca. 1940 (standing:
Dorothy,
Fr. Pacifique Roy,
PeterMaurin,
third, fourth, and
sixth from left).
Courtesy
Dorothy Day–
Catholic Worker
Collection,
Marquette
University.

scious. "There is a smell in the house of apples and fermenting elderberry wine. These smells drift in from the kitchen and compete with the smell of sweet clover, bayberries and driftwood. Which reminds me that I must throw out the armload of sweet clover which hangs over the mirror and hunt around to see if I can find some fresh. . . . And I must go down on the beach and pile up drift wood before the tide comes in and carries it out again. A pleasant task."

These frequent sighings in Dorothy's journal, over the peace and beauty of it all, indicate that her life had moved, for the first time, away from a coursing flow of strident discordancies into calm depths. There is warfare and destruction in nature, but there is healing, too. Nature is always busy with the creation of beauty, and whoever takes time to be sensitive to its work cannot help responding with hope and love to its goodness. In a particular way, this was true for Dorothy, whose spirit, even through the turbulent years just past, had been dominated by one passion. She wanted to love, and now she began to experience the joy of her harmonious response to creation. The beauty of nature "spoke to my soul," as she would say years later.

Forster, she says, was the agent of bringing her this peace. "He had all the love of the English for the outdoors in all weather. He used to insist on walks no matter how cold or rainy the day, and this dragging me away from my books, from my lethargy, into the open, into the country, made me begin to breathe. If breath is life, then I was beginning to be full of it because of him." She sat with him on the pier as he fished, and rowed with him over the bay. In her journal, she mentions one rowing episode that was especially pleasant. "The oyster boats were all out and far on the horizon, off Sandy Hook, there was a four-masted vessel. I had the curious delusion that several huge holes had been stove in her side, through which you could see the blue sky. The other vessels seemed sailing in the air, quite indifferent to the horizon on which they should properly have been resting." Forster tried to explain the phenomenon to her in terms of mirages and atmospherics.

He gave her elementary instruction in marine life. "Yesterday was a busy day. We studied biology for an hour or so in the morning in the shape of the larvae of a mussel." After that "we went for a long row along the shore . . . every now and then stopping to investigate the flotsam and jetsam on the water." Yes, she knew the difference between "flotsam" and "jetsam." They were not terms that necessarily were used together. "I read a definition of them the other day, according to a Merchant Shipping Act. Flotsam is floating wreck and jetsam is property thrown overboard to avoid wreck, and in early days was distinguished from wreckage cast on the shore by the waves."

There was gardening, "thanks to F., who . . . has a green thumb." She had roses growing alongside of the house "and violets from the woods are there—huge clumps of them, and yellow and purple iris." Next year she wanted to have "heliotrope and mignonette."

Writing about her garden made her think of Peggy, whose little yard "was a riot of flowers," so thick "you could not walk through it. Peggy utilizes every inch of soil, and it was only so that Malcolm could have his afternoon tea on the lawn that she left a space for a tiny square of grass, just big enough to hold a tea table and some benches."

Dorothy owed Forster much, she knew, and in *The Long Loneliness,* she writes a hymn of her love for him. "Sometimes he went out to dig bait if there was a low tide and the moon was up. He stayed out late on the pier fishing, and came in smelling of salt air; getting into bed, cold with the chill . . . he held me close to him in silence. I loved him in every way, as a wife, as a mother even. I loved him for all he knew and pitied him for all he didn't know. I loved him for the odds and ends I had to fish out of his sweater pockets and for the sand and shells he brought in with his fishing. I loved his lean and cold body as he got into bed smelling of the sea, and I loved his integrity and stubborn pride."

She might have added that she loved him the more because he was the co-creator with her in fulfilling the most fundamental longing of her heart. It was in the first days of June, 1925, that she thought she might be pregnant. Novelist Caroline Gordon tells of going to Staten Island to see the Cowleys about this time and, while there, of visiting Dorothy with Malcolm and Peggy one evening. "I remember when Dorothy saw I was pregnant, she said, 'oh, I hope *I* am pregnant.' We had a good time in the cottage, staying until 1 A.M. Her last words were still, 'I hope I am pregnant!'" She was finally sure on a "beautiful June day." She, Forster, Peggy, and Malcolm were going to Tottenville to see a circus. "We brought dandelion wine and pickled eels and good home-made bread and butter." It was wonderful fare, "but I remember enjoying the root beer and popcorn later and feeling so much in love, so settled, so secure that I now had found what I was looking for." She does not say how she knew that day that she was pregnant, but it may be assumed that the combination of dandelion wine, pickled eels, root beer, and popcorn produced the classic symptoms: nausea, faintings, and palpitations—all so unmistakable in their meaning, that all doubt about her condition was removed from her mind.

She would never forget that "blissful joy" that overcame her when she was certain. Six years before, she had wept and railed at fate as the awareness of the same state then had dawned upon her. Now she was ecstatically happy. "For a long time I had thought I could not bear a child, and the longing in my heart for a baby had been growing.... I felt myself unfruitful, barren." She felt now that some disease of her soul had been cured, that God had forgiven her, that a pall that had hung over her had been removed.

The rich time of autumn came. "There are little waves on the shingle, a little breeze rustling the dead leaves on the paths in the garden, the sound of the rags ... [and] iron man with his bell-strung cart on the road." She thought of her past life, the time of "fret and strife," even of sadness and despair. How curious it was that then she felt she was "free," but now she felt that "I had not known real freedom nor even had a knowledge of what freedom meant."

As she relates in *The Long Loneliness,* she began to pray. To pray was not a conscious decision. She did not, at the end of the day, get down on her knees and pray. This would have been too calculated. She prayed when she walked to Huguenot in the morning to get the mail, "holding the rosary that Mary Gordon gave me in New Orleans some years before. Maybe I did not say it correctly, but I kept on saying it because it made me happy." She prayed because she "wanted to thank Him.... No matter how dull the day, nor long the walk seemed, if I felt sluggish at the beginning of the walk, the words I had been saying insinuated themselves into my heart before I had finished, so that on the trip back I neither prayed nor thought but was fulled with exultation." She began to make visits to the Catholic chapel on Hylan Boulevard, near where she lived.

The prospect of fatherhood was one that Forster found unattractive. As Dorothy had said, there was something of a child-mother relationship between them, in that Forster seemed constitutionally incapable of taking any ordering role in working out the circumstances of their lives. He would take no responsibility for anything, only wanting his "freedom" to go where he would when he chose—which usually meant out on the bay in a boat. A child would complicate their lives and involve him in responsibility. He wanted no child and possibly he even felt that he had been ill-used in the matter of Dorothy's pregnancy, since she undoubtedly had told him that such an eventuality was most unlikely.

Dorothy's interest in religion made him more resentful—apparently for the same reason that he resented her pregnancy. Their love together was enough. To have the idea of God in the picture would only weaken their love. Dorothy rejoined that without faith, without commitment, their love would evaporate, but Forster was completely incapable of seeing her position. As Dorothy tartly comments, the introduction of the subject of religion into a conversation between them would cause Forster, "the inarticulate," to become "garrulous . . . in wrath." The turn of events, it appears, so upset him that he took to staying away from the house, spending days in the city.

His absences did not seem to weigh heavily on Dorothy. Her journal during this period begins to be filled with pages of comment on a neighboring family, the Maruchesses, Sasha and Freda, and their son, Dicky. They were Russian Jewish emigres. Sasha as a youth had turned to political radicalism and had narrowly escaped death on several occasions from the bullets of the Czarist police. Making his way to America, he, with his family, lived in one of the cottages in a group of six that made up Dorothy's immediate neighborhood.

Dorothy wrote at length about the Maruchess family because, one suspects, she wanted to use them in a story. And they were colorful. Sasha, a sometime actor and musician, went around the neighborhood wearing blouses of bright hues and sometimes a sash to go with them. He had coal-black hair and kept a cigarette tucked behind his ear. His eyes were dark, and, as Dorothy describes them, "there was a warm, kind look in them usually; even when he was harsh and impatient, or cruelly satirical, his eyes never became cold but seemed sadly morose, as though he were indulging himself merely to escape an unutterable melancholy." In his leisure moments he would play the guitar, drink black tea, and eat jam, or, when he was in a festive mood, he would drink vodka. At times, he would treat Dorothy to long episodes of what she called his "riotous enthusiasms . . . for people." On other occasions, he would expatiate on the agony of existence and his fear of death, a fear that at the time he thought he could overcome only by killing himself.

Freda is described by Dorothy as a large, noble-looking woman who was indifferent to the commonly accepted conventions of housekeeping or attire. Her house was usually untidy, her only concern being to sweep up the sand tracked in from the beach by her husband and son. Entering middle age and beginning to put on weight, she nonetheless went about in old evening gowns, daringly cut to reveal a lovely expanse of her large bosom and strong broad back. She loved Sasha deeply, but she sometimes felt hemmed in by her domestic role, and she spent much time dreaming and reading. Reading drew her and Dorothy together, and there were many afternoons of drinking tea and discussing books.

Sometimes, after Sasha had been paid for an acting job, the Maruchesses would have a party. Then above the sound of wind and washing waves rose the wild strumming of Sasha's guitar and shouts of encouragement to whirling dancers. Dorothy loved these people because they were of an ancient race, wise and rich in their suffering. They, for their part, seemed interested and pleased with Dorothy's growing interest in religion, but as Sasha said, "Religious faith is a talent, a gift which I do not possess. I cannot believe."

In December, Dorothy took an apartment in the city to await the arrival of the baby. She says that Della came to stay with her to help her "through the last hard months." She was glad, she writes, to be back in town, close to her friends and close to a church where she could go and pray. She read *The Imitation of Christ* and resolved to have her child baptized, "cost what it may." If she had any long-range expectations about life with Forster, it would cost plenty. As for herself, "I prayed for the gift of faith." She was sure, "yet not sure."

Otherwise, she did everything she thought necessary to enable the baby to go full term. She was, after all, twenty-nine years old, and with a history of gynecological problems since the abortion, she was apprehensive about a miscarriage. She gave up going to radical meetings and socializing with friends. Since she was never one to visit a doctor except under urgent circumstances, assuming that nature was the better physician, her registration at a public clinic at Bellevue hospital for pregnancy care and then delivery indicates the degree of her concern that the baby be well delivered.

In February, 1927, a clinic nurse gave her a "red" ticket, which admitted her to the clinic for weekly examinations. On the morning of March 2, she went to the clinic for what she felt would be her last visit before birth. It is at this point that she began the narration of events that ended in the birth of her child. This narration later appeared in the communist *New Masses* in the June, 1928 issue.

As usual, the clinic that morning was filled with women in various stages of pregnancy. Sitting on a bench, Dorothy was "astonished and discouraged" to see a girl there that she had seen the week before. The girl had been overdue then, and here she was still. She was "a pretty brown-eyed girl with sweet full lips and a patient expression. . . . She said 'Ma'am,' no matter what I said to her." Because the place was so crowded, a young Greek girl had to stand. "She wore a turban and a huge pink pearl necklace with ear rings, a bright dress and flesh colored stockings on . . . slim legs. She made no attempt to huddle her coat around as so many women do . . . and she poised herself easily by the door, her head held high, her coat flung open, her full figure most graciously exposed. She rather flaunted herself, confident of her attractions." Dorothy could always recognize a woman who took satisfaction in her physical attractiveness—even one who was pregnant.

As for Dorothy, after her examination the nurse in charge exchanged her red ticket for one that was white—meaning that labor was imminent and that she had an open admission to the clinic. "You'll probably be late," the nurse sighed. "They are all being late just now."

That afternoon, feeling in a state of suspension, Dorothy packed her bag and settled herself into a tub of warm water for a bath, taking an Agatha Christie novel with her. She had fifteen pages to go when the first pain struck her. Well, she would finish the book and see what happened. Just as she finished, the second pain hit her. She called Della. "The child will be born, before tomorrow morning." Nothing but false pains, scoffed Della. Even so, Della's knees were trembling and, thinking that further discussion would be superfluous, she ran into the street to hail a cab. "A few minutes later we were crossing town in a Yellow, puffing on cigarettes and clutching each other as the taxi driver went over every bump in his anxiety for my welfare."

Did Dorothy remember the long taxi ride to Chicago South Side they had taken in 1923, going to the Mad Hatters' Ball, Della asked, and she then went on to say that she supposed that even then, as people looked into the cab, they would assume that they

were just two girls out to have a good time. This chatter was somewhat insane, to be sure, but it filled time. At Bellevue, the two sat
for half an hour. When the doctor came, the two women stood,
and he, being the witty kind, asked which one was the maternity
case. They giggled.

An examination confirmed that the infant had already begun
its venture into the world, and Dorothy was wheeled into the
preparation room. While she was there, she was joined by "a colored woman with a tiny pickaninny, born that morning, clutched
to her bosom, yelling that she had an earache. . . ." This comment
suggests that in 1927 even the most enlightened could use offensive colloquialisms.

For the next hour, Dorothy was "prepped," as the medical
people say. "The nurse who ministered to me was a large beautiful
creature with marcelled hair and broad hips which she flaunted
about the small room with much grace." She was a flippant creature and talked of Douglas Fairbanks and the film she had seen
that afternoon, while she wielded a long razor with abandon."

At this point, Dorothy introduces an aside into her narration.
"Abandon, abandon. What did that remind me of? Oh yes, the
suitor who said that I was lacking in abandon because I didn't respond to his advances." Why did she put this in? Probably she had
been writing too many true-confession-type serials in which such
asides were a stock in trade.

As her pains mounted, she says that she thought again of where
she might place the baby when she took it back to the apartment.
All she could think of was the bureau drawer. For several years,
she had wanted a cradle. "A long time ago I saw an adorable one
on the east side in an old second hand shop. They wanted thirty
dollars for it and I didn't have the thirty dollars and besides, how
did I know then I was ever going to have a baby?" Anyway, "if
Sarah Bernhardt could carry a coffin around the country with her
there is no reason why I couldn't carry a cradle around with me."

Another wave of pain rolled over her, making her "sick to my
stomach." Then she wondered, should one say "sick *at* your stomach or sick *to* your stomach?" She had said *to*, but debated the
point. "William [Forster] declares it is 'sick at your stomach.' Both
sound very funny to me. But I'd say whatever William wanted me
to. I am tired of it. Doing without milk in my coffee, for instance,
because he insists that milk spoils the taste of coffee. And using the
same kind of tooth paste. Funny thing, being so intimate with a

man that you feel you must use the same kind of tooth paste he does. To wake up and see his head on your pillow every morning. An awful thing to get used to anything. I mustn't get used to the baby."

The broad-hipped nurse came in again, bringing with her "a flip young doctor and three other nurses to joke and laugh about hospital affairs." The doctor and the other two nurses sat on two vacant beds, "but my nurse sat on the foot of mine, pulling the bed askew with her weight. This spoiled my sleeping during the five minute intervals and mindful of my grievance against her and the razor I took advantage of the beginning of the next pain to kick her soundly in the behind."

The night wore on. "Every five minutes the pains came and in between I slept. At each pain I groaned and cursed. . . . And then when it had swept over with the beautiful rhythm of the sea I felt with satisfaction 'it could be worse,' and clutched at sleep frantically."

The baby, a girl, came in the early hours. No one would ever know "the terrible joy I felt when I first looked at my baby," Dorothy wrote years later. In her article, "Having a Baby," she refers to her daughter as "Tamara Teresa," a name that was sparkling and dewy, just right for a girl baby who would undoubtedly become a great dancer, writer, or actress. "Tamara" actually had started out as "Tamar," and that was what it shortly returned to, although for a while, until her daughter was eight or so, Dorothy called her Teresa. The name *Tamar* was Hebrew, meaning "little palm tree," and Dorothy got it from Sasha's sister, who had chosen it for her own daughter. The "Teresa" was added because Dorothy had read a biography of St. Teresa of Avila and was taken with the saint's vibrant personality.

With her baby in her arms, Dorothy felt as if that which for so long had left the taste of hell in her mouth had been cleansed from her soul. Lying in her hospital bed during the first morning of Tamar's life, she wrote of her ecstasy. "Tamara Teresa's nose is twisted slightly to one side. She sleeps with the placidity of a Mona Lisa so that you cannot see the amazing blue of her eyes which are strangely blank and occasionally ludicrously crossed." Her wisp of hair was auburn, her eyebrows "golden," and her complexion was tan. "Her ten fingers and toes are of a satisfactory length and slenderness and I reflect that she will be a dancer when she grows up," but "just now I must say she is a lazy little hog mouthing around my nice full breast and too lazy to tug for food. 'What do you want, little bird? That it should run into your mouth I suppose.' "

Propped in bed, Dorothy surveyed her "beautiful flat stomach" and then turned her gaze outward. Again, she saw the sights and heard the sounds that had become a part of her being and always would be. Streaming toward her was "the wide path of the early morning sun on the East River." Tugboats and barges, tooting their whistles, plowed through the water, and down below her room she could hear some men singing on the dock. "The restless water is colored lavender and gold and the enchanting sky is a sentimental blue and pink. And gulls wheeling warm grey and white against the magic of the water and the sky. Sparrows chirp on the windowsill, the baby sputters as she gets too big a mouthful, and then pauses a moment to look around her with satisfaction." It was a rare and golden moment in her life, like that May morning in 1917 when she had awakened to the same sights and sounds to begin her first day with the *Masses*. That morning had been one of happiness, but this was one of joy.

In the bed next to hers was a "Catholic girl," a "young Italian" who "had just had her third child. She had some kind of heart condition that led the clinic physicians to tell her that she should have no more children. Several times they stood there giving her information on birth control and she listened with her eyes cast down, not answering them. They assumed she was stupid and repeated in the simplest phrases their directions, speaking in phrases as they spoke to foreigners who cannot understand English. Then when they looked on her chart and saw she was a Catholic, they expressed their impatience and went away." She paid no attention to the doctors, the girl told Dorothy. God would take care of her. She knew she had to be careful.

Once the girl asked Dorothy what she was going to call her daughter, and Dorothy responded, "Teresa," and the girl offered her a medal of St. Therese of Lisieux. Dorothy could be abrupt, and she was in this instance. "I don't believe in these things," she said. But the girl was not offended. "If you love someone, you like to have something around which reminds you of them," was her rejoinder. It was, said Dorothy, so obvious a truth that she was ashamed.

And through all the drama of new life, where was Forster? It was obviously Dorothy's show; he had stood mutely by, staying at the apartment with Dorothy and Della, doing the manly thing as he may have viewed it, adding a touch of propriety to the affair.

In mid-April, bearing the new life that was so profoundly of them and which in some mystic sense indissolubly bound them, they returned to the beach. Living, as they had been doing over the past two years, in a state of financial precariousness, they were now the more pressed because of a reduction in Dorothy's earning power, which had always been meager at best. It was sometime in this period that an arrangement was worked out with Dorothy's father by which he would pay Dorothy to keep her brother, young John. Day Senior, it appears, was in the process of establishing a base in Miami, where he was involved in the development of the Hialeah racetrack. So John Junior moved into the attic room and soon established himself there with "bits of broken glass, empty test tubes, a chemistry set and *The Microbe Hunters;* pieces of wire from a radio; rubber cigars and matches which exploded as you lit them; and for serious reading, a copy of Nick Carter's *The Vial of Death.*"

Dorothy, settled into a mood of solid contentment, began writing her journal again. "John, of course, is last out of bed. Though I sympathize with him and would delight myself sleeping late I've never been able to since the baby was born, and I find my recompense in the early rising." Every morning she could see Mr. Harding, standing on the bank in front of his house above the beach, going through his exercise routine. She could not do that, "but I must indulge in physical exultation of some sort, and take it out in going down on the beach. There, picking up driftwood for the fires, I recite psalms, or even sing at the top of my lungs, if the waves are loud enough to drown the sound of my voice." What she really wanted to do was to "dance and leap," but "being a staid mother ... I have to restrain myself."

Coming up from the beach, she prepared a big breakfast because "F. insists on huge breakfasts." "This morning we had tomcods, the roe and milk to spread on toast, coffee and french-fried potatoes. The coffee and toast would have been enough for me," but with Forster, such a breakfast meant that he could read everything in the *New York Times.*

When the dishes were done, Dorothy built up the fire in the stove and gave the baby her morning bath. "There is a driftwood burner in one corner and I cram it full of paper and chips and odd chunks of wood and in a moment there is a satisfactory roar. It snaps and crackles cheerily and the heat spreads round and what does it matter if it occasionally reeks of chemicals and tar and coal oil and seaweed and other strange smells?"

Tamar was fed and then put in her bed on the front porch. "The sun is hot and I am without hat or coat and there is no wind to chill. The only sound is that of starlings, occasionally the trill of song sparrow and the little spring waves on the beach." Looking out on the bay, she sees an "enormous freighter pulled by a tug . . . and off on the horizon there are two or three little sailing vessels." There had been "much traffic in the bay this morning—several four-masted sailing vessels, a lake boat, long low and squat . . . two freighters and three tankers."

Later in the day, with Freda, perhaps, to watch out for the baby when she took her afternoon nap, Dorothy and John walked through the woods, looking for pussywillows. "We lunged for a long time through swampy ground and finally found some and now we have a fine collection of twigs and branches filling the room. . . . Other acquisitions today were two live cocoons and some dead ones which we cut open to examine the pupa shell and we could not tell whether they had hatched out or died an unnatural death." Since dissecting cocoons was not Dorothy's style, she was either assisting John in a biological exercise or arming herself to stimulate Forster into conversation.

Later, as supper cooked, she wrote again. "It is five-thirty now and not yet dusk, and I am sitting on the porch. The tide is coming in fast and the sound of waves is pleasant. . . . Although nothing is green yet, everything suggests green to me. There are lovely hazy shadows, violet and heavy blue on the horizon."

Increasingly, she reflected on her spiritual condition. "In spite of my activity it has been one of these melancholy days which usually follows a week of exhiliration. It is strange how some days I am so overflowing with animal spirits that I can wander around the house and beach with a continual song on my lips. Other days I am so dull I must keep continually occupied. And I can usually trace these moods of mine to my spiritual state—to faults and negligences—slothfulness of mind and body."

Not having forgotten her resolution to have her baby baptized, Dorothy persisted in that intention. In some "notes," written some years later, she says that "when one has a child, life is different. Certainly I did not want my child to flounder as I had often floundered, 'without a rule of life an instruction.' Faith! I wanted to believe, and I wanted my child to believe and if belonging to a church would give her so inestimable a grace, as a faith in God, and the companionable love of the Saints, then the thing to do was to have her baptized a Catholic. She would be incorporated into the Church; it was to be hoped she would grow in wisdom and grace and in following the footsteps of Jesus and have all the safe-guards and helps that a universal Church would give."

As she says, it never entered her mind to have Tamar baptized anything but a Catholic. That it might be well to weight the claims of other churches before taking this step did not occur to Dorothy. She only knew that in those years just past, when she had felt so God-forsaken, it was in a Catholic church that she had felt God's presence. She says, in *The Long Loneliness,* that even without exam-ining in any depth the history and character of the Catholic Church, she was ready to declare that "for me she was the one true Church. She had come down through the centuries since the time of Peter, and far from being dead, she claimed and held the alle-giance of the masses of people in all the cities where I had lived." Dorothy saw the Catholic Church as the church of the immigrants, of the laboring class. And if the Church took hard positions on some matters—even on that of going to Mass on Sunday—what of it? The hard way appealed to Dorothy. If the Church offered the hope of eternal life with God, then however hard the way, it would be glorious at every step.

Still, there were problems. There was Forster, the father, who deserved to have something to say. Ordinarily, Forster was voice-less where most things were concerned, but in this matter, as well as in Dorothy's growing preoccupation with religion, he took a po-sition. With vehemence, apparently, he told Dorothy that her "yearnings toward the life of the spirit" were "morbid escapism." He was a complete materialist, yet with a passionate feeling for the dignity of man. "He thought of . . . baptism only as a mumbo jum-bo, the fuss and fury peculiar to woman." Why could Dorothy not just love him? That was all that was necessary. This intrusion of God into their companionship was bound to ruin it. He sensed, no doubt, Dorothy's ruthlessness. If God was to become the object of her great capacity for passion, their relationship, as if it had been nothing, would be swept aside by the great force of that passion. He became jealous of her God preoccupation; and when he came for his weekend at the beach, he spent most of his time on the bay.

Dorothy well knew how things were, but as she saw it, there was much more at stake than a continuing affability between Forster and her. Tamar was, in a special way, she felt, her child. If Forster's role in her conception had been unwitting on his part, an unwanted consequence, she knew only this time she would gladly die to preserve that life and to give it what she could see as its fullest human due. She regretted, even trembled, over what she knew would be the consequence of her course, but it was a matter of the highest conscience with her that she fulfill at every crucial point her commitment to that life. Baptism could not be avoided, or even delayed.

In both *From Union Square to Rome* and *The Long Loneliness,* Dorothy has written in some detail how it came about that Tamar was baptized.

As she says, she knew no Catholic to whom she might speak about her concern. "The grocer, the hardware storekeeper, my neighbors down the road were Catholics, yet I could not bring myself to speak to them about religion." Her reserve is understandable. Dorothy and her neighbors in her little community were understood to be Bohemians and radicals—communists, even, a word that had Satanic overtones for many people in the mid-twenties. So, thought Dorothy, she would bring up the subject to a nun, since St. Joseph's Home, run by the Sisters of Charity, was on Hylan Boulevard, just two short blocks from where she lived.

There was, however, a problem. St. Joseph's Home had been given to the Sisters of Charity by Charles Schwab, former head of Bethlehem Steel, and it had been Schwab, so Dorothy averred, who had moved so ruthlessly against the workers in the Homestead Strike of 1892. "I could not but feel that his was tainted money which the sisters had accepted. It was, I felt, money which belonged to the workers. He had defrauded the workers of a just wage. His sins cried to heaven for vengeance. He had ground the faces of the poor."

It was almost a sacred precept in radical politics that the dehumanizing consequences of corporate power should be personalized into the particular villainy of the corporate head, be it Schwab, Morgan, Vanderbilt, or Rockefeller. This dramatic outburst against Schwab was, and to some extent always would be, a characteristic reaction by Dorothy to those builders of great corporate structures, especially if they were associated with repressive action against labor. As she says, she experienced again "that bitterness felt by so many in the radical labor movement towards what they call 'organized religion.' " But she says, "I would not blame the Church for what I felt were the mistakes of churchmen. I could always console myself with Christ's words that the greatest enemies would be those of the 'household.' "

Thus consoled, she set out one spring afternoon, wheeling baby Tamar in her carriage up Hylan Boulevard toward St. Joseph's Home. In the vicinity of the Home, she encountered a nun, on her way, as it turned out, to visit one of Dorothy's neighbors. In the first draft of *The Long Loneliness*, Dorothy described the nun as "a simple old sister who had taught grade school all her life in religion and was now put to taking care of babies." It was the "babies," with their unmarried mothers, who stayed at the Home. "I went up to her breathlessly and asked how I could have my child baptized."

That Dorothy, who always radiated such presence and controlled assuredness in any situation, could be "breathless" in approaching this nun seems implausible. In any case, Sister Aloysia accepted the question very matter-of-factly and said that she would begin the process. It was, as such matters go, a long process, due apparently to what Dorothy called "irregularities" in her marital state. Mainly, though, the priest who was consulted wanted to be certain that Dorothy was not acting on a whim and that the baby would be reared as a Catholic. Sister Aloysia should begin by instructing Dorothy in her obligations on this point. "She took me under her protection immediately. She did not make little of my difficulties, nor did she think for a minute that they were insurmountable. There was a hard row to hoe in front of us, was her attitude, but we could get through it. She would hang on to that long, formidable-looking rosary of hers, hang on to it like an anchor, and together we would ride out the gale of opposition and controversy. All we had to do was depend on prayer."

There were, of course, assignments for Dorothy. "She gave me a catechism and brought me old copies of the Messenger of the Sacred Heart which was filled with the Kathleen Norris type of success story and had besides some good solid articles about the teachings of the Church." Dorothy read it all, went to Mass at the sisters' chapel, and regularly said the rosary. What an excitement and subject for discussion it must have been for her radical friends who, dropping in for a visit, found reading material and religious objects that gave evidence of Dorothy's blossoming piety. Perhaps they wondered at her sanity.

Meanwhile, three times a week, Sister Aloysia trudged up the little road at the back of the cottage to give her catechism lessons. These lessons were not intellectual, in-depth examinations of the principles of Catholic belief, carried in the atmosphere of warmth, sincerity, and mutual respect characteristic of a psychiatric counseling session. Sister would settle herself on a chair, have Dorothy state from memory the question as it was given in the catechism, and then enjoin her to repeat verbatim the answer. When Dorothy stumbled, she was treated to a verbal chastizing. "And you think you are intelligent!" the nun would say scornfully. And Dorothy, contritely, would answer that she was sorry and would certainly have her lesson well prepared the next time.

When the lesson was over, the sister would likely as not criticize Dorothy's housekeeping. "Here you sit at your typewriter at ten o'clock and none of your dishes done yet," Dorothy would quote her as saying. "Supper and breakfast dishes besides. . . . And why don't you calcimine your ceiling? It's all dirty from woodsmoke."

The sister was very concerned about the baby's health, afraid that she might die before being baptized. One morning, Dorothy writes, the nun came rushing onto the front porch of the cottage and asked if the baby was dead. Assured that the baby was hale and hearty, she praised God that Tamar was alive, adding that she was sure that "the powers of darkness were struggling hard for my little one." Then bending over Tamar's crib, she would address little Tamar in baby talk, all of which Tamar presumably understood, since she would respond with a "toothless smile, embellished by a delightful dimple which she has since lost."

Usually on her visits, the sister made a cautious approach to the house, fearful of Forster's presence. "Is he here?" she would ask Dorothy in a loud whisper as she peered through the back window. If he was there he would usually go out the other door, slamming it as he went.

Tamar was baptized in July. Afterwards, there was a feast at the cottage of garden vegetables and lobster, provided by Forster. But, says Dorothy, he then became angry, "with some sense of the end to which all this portended. Jealousy set in and he left me."

In fact, "he left me quite a number of times that coming winter and following summer, as he felt my increasing absorption in religion," Dorothy says. This means that for more than a year there were times of tension, even scenes. Frustrated and angry, he would leave. Of course, he returned. He had become fond of his child; she was, in fact, "his delight." And, no doubt, he longed for Dorothy's presence and warmth, hoping that when he returned, he would find her as she had once been—that her turn to religion had been a temporary aberration.

Whatever his hopes, he would find Dorothy more resolute in her course than ever before. Tamar's baptism came after "I had become convinced that I would become a Catholic," although she knew full well that "obstacles . . . were there, shadows in the background of my life." The obstacle was that, as the Church viewed it, she was already married and that to continue to live with Forster would make her an adulterer. "I wanted to die in order to live, to put off the old man to put on Christ. . . . Why should not Forster be jealous?" And, she noted, "In the eyes of God, any turning towards creatures in the exclusion of Him, is adultery and so it is termed over and over again in the Scripture."

The only way the matter could be worked out was by Forster's agreeing to marry Dorothy. Then she might live in the hope that somehow her first marriage could be voided by the Church, thus removing the "shadow" over her. This was the solution for which, surely, she hoped. "I had known enough of love to know that a good healthy family life was as near to heaven as one could get in this life." She was fully conscious of the difficulty of rearing Tamar without a father. It was a solution, though, that Forster would have none of. He was obdurately "averse to any ceremony before officials of either Church or state. He was an anarchist and an atheist, and he did not intend to be a liar or a hypocrite." And that was that. So Forster, when he was at the cottage, spent many nights fishing on the bay.

Thus Forster was expendable, but expendability was, after all, implicit in the nature of the arrangement that he had decreed. Yet, apparently on the advice of the priest at Tottenville, it was over a year before Dorothy took a stand on the matter. As the priest probably saw it, Tamar's right to the presence of her father took precedence over Dorothy's wish to be baptized. And this, it seems, was Dorothy's feeling, too. In her journal, which could have been written in the early summer of 1927, she ruminates over the impending separation. "It is Saturday so John does not have to go to school. While he glowers over his microscope I sit by the window and knit, because knitting allows me to muse over my day. . . . I find the mornings too happy to spend over writing and leave it until the evening too, because the new serial I am doing is hard work, and hard work keeps me from thinking or being lonely. . . . I wonder how I am ever going to be able to live alone."

So, after supper, she set herself up in the living room to write, but Tamar, now almost a year old, was beginning to get into everything. "If she is with me she wants to crawl all over me or do what I am doing. She gets her little hands entangled in my knitting or mixed up in my typewriter keys and life becomes a burden for both of us." Or, if Dorothy tried to read, Tamar seemed to object to that. "She used to be content to imitate me, taking a book or magazine, lolling back on the couch with it . . . and looking up to giggle now and then. But now she has come to resent novels just as F. resents them. She feels that I am escaping from my duty when I become absorbed in them, and she feels she must recall me to it."

According to one note Dorothy made, Tamar's presumed resentment was justified. "I have spent the last weeks in reading," Dorothy narrates. Altogether, she had read fourteen books, among them *War and Peace, The House of Seven Gables, The Scarlet Letter, Passage to India,* and others of almost equal weight.

One of the books she read in this period was the first volume of Sigrid Undset's *Kristin Lavransdatter.* Dorothy's neighbor Freda read it first and began to exclaim over it to Dorothy. "Reluctant to start a new author whom I had never heard of before, I paid little attention to Freda's ravings until Sasha began to complain. 'We are around the house starving,' Sasha groaned. 'First thing in the morning she picks up those books. She's at it all day—she talks about it. She tells the plot, she brings in William James and his *Varieties of Religious Experience,* including yours, Dorothy. Unless I cooked myself I swear we would have starved.' "

Dorothy was interested. "I took up volume one as she finished it and . . . am engrossed. . . . I have been living with Kristin these days, I have sinned and suffered with her. I have worked with her and worshipped with her. . . . These books with their whole picture of Catholic life colored my days and do much to help me in the struggle I am going through."

Dorothy was "engrossed" because Kristin's experience in her love for the weak but fascinating Erlend, had been, in many ways, similar to Dorothy's love for Lionel Moise. The difference, which Dorothy surely saw, was that Erlend loved Kristin.

There was outdoor work, which Dorothy preferred to washing dishes or picking up after Forster and John. One work episode which involved a reluctant John was that of eviscerating and salting down fish—two bushel baskets full that were on the front porch. "We take sharp knives, spread out newspapers and set to work. Right at hand are pans of warm water for us to thaw our hands in during the course of the work. At first it is an agony. 'This is the hardest work I ever did,' I groan, blowing on my hands. . . . 'I'd rather live on rice and tea and do without salt fish.' "

John demurred, telling Dorothy that she was "always talking about living on rice and tea." Then Dorothy told her brother how it was—down in New Orleans, "years ago. My salary was scarcely enough to live on, and toward the end of the week I always found myself living on rice and tea. But if I just had eight cents for a half a pound of shrimp I could make a delicious meal of rice and shrimp." The memory of New Orleans brought her to a different thought—cities. "I do love cities."

That she did, and always would, but the subject of cities provided her with an opportunity to raise the level of her task with John to final things, "yet here we have no 'continuing city,' Thomas à Kempis says." Well, she knew that she had, in fact, always been conscious of that. "But here I am sodden with contentment, nestled into this scrap of land and filled with a hideous sense of possession."

John was not taken with the thought. "There you go again, worrying about your soul," said John, who hated to hear his sister "talk in this pious manner."

Both baskets of fish were finished before lunch. "We were so relieved that we ran out of the house and chased each other all over the beach. . . . After he had brought up enough wood to last over Sunday, and had his lunch, I extravagantly allowed him to go to the movies in the village and the baby and I settled ourselves for naps." Later that afternoon, she wrote of the day's doings, and settled into a tranquil mood. "I love the somnolent atmosphere of the house on a winter afternoon. The fire crackles, the tea kettle sings, the clock ticks on and on and outside the wind rises and the waves crash on the beach." A cloud of discord moved into her consciousness but she walled it out of her mind. "I am refusing to think about F. and this whole issue of religion." So resolved, she nestled into her "huge knitted afghan," which she used "just for napping" and was soon sound asleep.

The felicitous moment passed, and no doubt there were others like it that winter, but on those occasions when Forster returned to the cottage, as he always did, household tranquility went out of the window. Had the matter come down to what Dorothy said for her was a choice between God and man? Very likely it had, but in the process elements of their basic incompatibility had become swollen and inflamed, imposing a monumental strain on any aspect of an association between them.

In August, 1927, the impending execution of two anarchists, Nicola Sacco and Bartolemeo Vanzetti, for what the courts said was their murder of a shoe factory paymaster at Braintree, Massachusetts, reduced both Dorothy and Forster to a state of numbness. Ordinarily, Dorothy would have joined her friends, including her sister, Della, who had gotten married the preceeding spring, in the protest demonstrations in Boston. But Dorothy could not leave Tamar, and Forster, who was constitutionally incapable of becoming a part of any organization for any objective, could do no more than keep his grief to himself. He was, says Dorothy, "stricken over the tragedy. He did not eat for days. He sat around the house in a stupor of misery, sickened by the cruelty of life and of men. He had always taken refuge in nature as being more kindly, more beautiful and peaceful than the world of men. Now he could not even escape through nature." In the days that followed the execution, "he stupefied himself in his passion for the water, sitting out on the bay in his boat." When he began to recover, he collected marine specimens and peered into his microscope at their dissected parts for long hours. "Only the baby interested him."

Neither did Dorothy hold up too well. She says that, what with the continuing and mounting tension between Forster and herself, she began to have "spells." One night she woke up choking. Concerned, she went to the Cornell University medical school clinic and had a complete physical examination. Her problem, said the doctors, was "nerves." And, no doubt, it was.

It was in December, apparently, that "an explosion" occurred between them. Again Forster left, but this time Dorothy resolved to end the matter. When Forster returned, as she knew he would, she would not let him come into the house. Their life together was over, finally and forever, she told him.

One of the very characteristic things about Dorothy over her entire life was the impulsive way in which she sometimes made far-reaching decisions. It must have been moments after her confrontation with Forster that she called the priest at Tottenville to ask for baptism the next day, a Wednesday, December 28. That afternoon, apparently, she took Tamar to the city, and the two of them spent the night in an apartment with Della and her husband of some seven months, Franklin Spier.

The next morning, with Della minding Tamar, Dorothy set out

for Tottenville. The entire trip was without the relief of one glistening moment of certitude that what she was doing was right. As she rode on the ferry to the island, the sun beat no sparkling path across the water to her feet. It was a gray, foggy day, and as the ferry plowed through the oily water, all that she could think was that she was being too precipitate. "I had no sense of peace, no joy, no conviction that what I was doing was right. It was just something that I had to do, a task to be gotten through." Getting up from her seat on the passenger deck, she "walked around and around the deck, . . . almost groaning in anguish of spirit." Maybe "the devil was on the boat."

Maybe he was, lurking out in the fog, darting in when he saw an opening to place a doubt in Dorothy's mind. If Satan was there, he knew not with what he reckoned. Short of the ferry's sinking and the trolley's running off its rails, Dorothy was going to Tottenville. The implacable in her nature had taken over. There was no turning around.

When she arrived at the little town at the tip of the island, she got off the streetcar and walked to the church. Sister Aloysia met her there to be her godmother. She does not remember the name of her godfather. He may have been just someone at hand who could stand for her and sign her baptismal certificate.

After baptism, she immediately made her confession, which, she says, Father Hyland heard "gently, with reserve, with matter-of-factness." The next day she went to her first Mass as a Catholic. Again, the devil must have been hovering about. "I proceeded about my own active participation in the mass . . . grimly, coldly, making acts of faith, and certainly with no consolation whatever. One part of my mind stood at one side and kept saying, 'What are you doing? Are you sure of yourself? What kind of an affectation is this? What act is this you are going through? Are you trying to induce emotion, induce faith, partake of an opiate, the opiate of the people?'" When she knelt, she felt "like a hypocrite" and "shuddered at the thought of anyone seeing me." She committed the gaffe of going to the communion rail at the Sanctus bell, and then, not knowing what to do, she knelt there through the consecration, the Our Father, and the Agnus Dei. Well, she thought, the humiliation was good for her.

Yet even with the purgation of humiliation, she left the church unmoved and with her spirits anything but lifted. Perhaps, as she walked back to the cottage, she may have wondered how she, a political radical, a Bohemian, had come to this position. As is the wont of converts, she gives "reasons" in the form of a statement to her brother in the last chapter of *From Union Square to Rome*. This statement aside, one may think that Dorothy's conversion was not the consequence of some mystical change in her character. Through all the misdirection and pain of her life, even when she had approached suicide and tottered on that brink, she wanted to love and be loved. Even then, as she would say later, it was God who had been the object of her passionate seeking. Years later, in some undated notes, she wrote of those dark days of the summer of 1919 and of her awareness, even then, that God was close to her. Yet there was "something within me which rebelled at turning to God in sorrow, in the woe which came so often from sin, or the result of sin. Perhaps I felt a grim determination to accept suffering as expiation, not asking comfort, knowing perhaps all the while that comfort was there, that it would come, that I could not indeed escape it." Yes, she added, "I know what remorse is, what shame is. I know the bitter aftermath of sin. I knew what a disordered life was." It was a condition that Job had described: "where no order is but everlasting horror."

So it was not suffering that had brought her to this position. It was "gratitude and joy," and "the object of this love and gratitude was God. No human creature could receive or contain so vast a flood of love and joy as I felt after the birth of my child." It was as she found it said in the Scripture: "Thou shalt love the Lord thy God, with thy whole heart, and with thy whole soul, and with thy whole mind and with thy whole strength." And it was this wanting to love entirely, she says, that led her to the Church. "We are only too conscious of the hardness of our hearts, and in spite of all the religious writers tell us about *feeling* not being necessary we do want to feel and so know that we love God." The Church, so it claimed, was the tangible union between heaven and earth, between eternity and time. This was a proposition she could affirm. It also provided her with a substance to which she could attach herself. "Sooner or later," she writes, "one is given a chance to prove his love. . . . It was all very well to love God in his works, in the beauty of his creation" and she had "heard people say that they did not need a church in order to worship. But I did not agree to this. My very experience as a radical, my whole makeup, led me to want to associate myself with others, with the masses, in loving and praising God."

There were, to be sure, her own questions about the Church. "Of course I criticized the luxury of the Church. Rectories to house a half a dozen priests were as large as the homes of the rich, the Schwabs, Morgans, Rockefellers. In a big city like New York, or Philadelphia, or Boston, priests live like Cardinals, like Princes of the Church. I am not judging them as to whether they were poor in spirit, to make up for their 'appearance' of wealth. . . . It is the scandal of our day in America." Yet, finally, as she says in *The Long Loneliness:* "I loved the Church for Christ made visible. Not for itself, because it was so often a scandal to me. Romano Guardini said the Church is the Cross on which Christ was crucified; one could not separate Christ from his Cross and one must live in a state of perpetual dissatisfaction with the Church."

Yet she did not give herself over to the always-inviting role of the carping critic of the Church. As she came to understand the history of the Chruch, its traditions and teachings, she found herself drawn more and more to it. Years later she would say that "I never regretted for one minute the step which I had taken in becoming a Catholic."

Her baptism must have caused intense discussion among her friends. She had flung into their faces, almost, an institution which, as they saw it, was diametrically opposed to all that she had seemingly professed—an anachronistic but still dangerous remnant of medievalism. Much of what went on Dorothy probably let pass, but there was one story making the rounds to which she took unusual exception. It was that she had become Catholic because sex no longer interested her. No, she said, sex was a "sample of Heaven, of the enjoyment of God. The very sexual act itself was used again and again in scripture as a figure of the beatific vision. It was not because I was tired of sex, satiated, disillusioned, that I turned to God. It was because thru a whole love, both physical and spiritual, I came to know God."

Then there was author Charles Harrison, "who said I probably became a Catholic because of the beauty of the ritual of the Church." This, she said, might be plausible except that "one sees little ritual . . . in our parish churches. The Low Mass is a plain, unadorned offering of the Sacrifice, two candles lit, no music, no participation of the laity."

Over the years, though, her radical friends—or many of them at least—seemed to be more comfortable with her conversion than did many of her co-religionists who were staunch defenders of the values of bourgeoisity. As her radical friends seemed to appreciate, conversion had not lessened her passion for a better world; it had started her along the path toward a vision that they shared, no matter what they called it or how they defined it. Both Dorothy and her radical friends were seeking community, the final and complete harmonization of all. The difference was that her friends talked of this goal as something that would crown their revolutionary struggle—that would be found in time. But for Dorothy, as she came to see, the way was love and the end was eternity. "All my life I have been haunted by God," she says, quoting the character Kirilov in Dostoevsky's *The Possessed*. And she believed that this was true of her friends, for as she says, "I do believe every soul has a tendency toward God."

🌿 8

The Search for a
Vocation

AFTER HER baptism, Dorothy closed the beach house and again moved into the city for the winter months. In biographical notes, typical of a kind that she made throughout her life when her memory happened to settle on some past time, she says that "I lived on the West Side then, in a ten-dollar-a-month flat with open fireplaces. There were a half a dozen friends living in other apartments there, and one of them made a living by salvaging the lumber from the subway which was being built thereabouts and splitting it and selling it for firewood in the neighborhood." Dorothy's job then was synopsizing novels for Metro-Goldwyn-Mayer at six dollars a novel. Each synopsis had to be six pages, typed single-spaced, and with six copies. "If you worked hard you could do a book a day."

She says that "another job that I had at the time was with the Communist affiliate, the Anti-Imperialist League, handling the publicity about our agression in Nicaragua, getting aid for Sandino, who was resisting our marines." It was a job that she could hold "in good conscience as a pacifist though I knew of course that my associates were not pacifist." There were many evenings, too, that "I went out . . . to meetings and demonstrations, of which every radical's life is full."

She does not explain how her "pacifist conscience" was appeased in getting aid for Sandino, but working out a logically consistent position where folk heroes were concerned was a problem she could bypass, then and in the future. Nor did her evenings out create a domestic dilemma insofar as Tamar's care was concerned.

"There was the Horatio Street nursery where you paid ten cents a day and where there was wonderful equipment and a playroom and garden, but where the children were bundled into their coats and hats an hour or so before you came to call for them." Otherwise, "there were enough of us living there so that there was always a friend to take care of the baby."

Amid all of this activity, with its causes and meetings—as well as her synopsizing work—what of her life in the Church? She knew next to nothing about what this life could mean to her; with all her radical activities, it almost could be expected that she would put it aside and, in time, forget it. But there was the other part of her, impelling her to an answer to the problem of existence, an answer that only a faith could provide. Causes, activism—yes. They took her energy, her need to be doing. But beyond time's turbulent flow, there was eternity, finality, completion. There was God, and God, she knew, was the end of life. Seeking God, she said of this time in her life, was "a struggle," in which she had "little joy."

She went to Mass and confession at a little church on West Fourteenth Street, Our Lady of Guadalupe. The church was staffed by Augustinian Fathers of the Assumption, and in the morning, before Mass, a priest would come over from the rectory to hear confessions. Dorothy, with her struggle and spiritual dryness, was there frequently, determined to tap that source where the Church had told her to find sustenance for her life—the sacraments. Her confessor was a Spanish priest, "a gentle old man who was good and patient with me." After hearing her out and giving her absolution, he would question her on some of the particulars of her life. It must have been a matter of some bemusement to him to find that his penitent, who voiced her problems so explicitly and clearly, was a thirty-year-old convert, engrossed in radical causes—whose friends were all radicals, most of whom, presumably, felt that the Church was the enemy.

Well, a soul was a soul, the old man probably told himself, radical or not. And a job was a job, so he advised her to keep the one she had with the communists until she could find another. He gave her a book of meditations and a St. Andrew missal so that with the latter she could follow the seasons of the Church and the saints of the day. Later, she would write of this missal that, every now and then, she could find "evidences of anti-Semitic feeling" in it, "just as one found it in the conversation of friends." She only mentioned it then, she said, because of her "great love and gratitude for the book which was a veritable encyclopedia to me" and because of her hope that it would have "a scholarly revision some day."

Since Dorothy speaks of this period as one of spiritual dryness, if not of incertitude, her frequent use of the confessional, as well as conferences with this priest, suggest a grim determination to progress in faith. This determination seemingly bore fruit, for she was confirmed on Pentecost Sunday and after that, she says, she felt certain on her course.

In mid-March, Dorothy and Tamar returned to the beach house, where they were again joined by her brother, John. Forster, it appears, had returned to the city. While her journal for these years is undated, it seems that parts of it are applicable to this period. "All during the days which are becoming longer and brighter, we occupy ourselves with spring housecleaning, housepainting and gardening. I have been busy with painting the smoky living room and kitchen and John and Dick [Maruchess] have spent whole days on the beach, caulking and painting their row-boats. We have the smell of paint on our hands and the smell of smoke in our clothes and hair, for we have burnt the stubble in the gardens around the house."

Scarcely had they gotten into the work of refurbishing the cottage than spring rains began to come, continuing "without interruption for weeks." A particular difficulty caused by the weather was that of getting driftwood from the beaches for her stove. "It is in the fall that most of the wood comes up on the beach, it seems, but these days it is swept clean." It was especially hard on the Maruchess family because they had only a woodburner in their living room and otherwise had to use an oil stove. "The only thing Freda and Sasha can do is to light the ... stoves and burn four gallons of kerosene a day in an attempt to keep warm and dry."

One afternoon, though, the rain stopped for a while, and a heavy swell on the water brought piles of wood up on the shore. It was "hailed with delight. The tar soaked pieces we collected right away, and soon in both our houses the wood burning stoves were roaring, the temperature went up to eighty-five and everybody basked in the heat and was content." That evening Dorothy went over to Freda and Sasha's, where they drank tea and ate elderberry jam on bread.

In fact, Dorothy frequently basked in the contentment of Freda and Sasha's living room. One day, as she sat there, they heard a woman's voice outside the window. "Mabel," who did Freda's washing, was telling Dickie and his cousin, Shura, how lynchings were conducted. "They string up their victims, then they let them down again and then string them up again, and do it over and over so that they won't die too quick. And then sometimes they take all their clothes off and pour boiling hot tar all over them, and stick feathers into them. . . . That'll teach 'em a lesson how to behave with white people. . . ."

"Even before we could call them," Dorothy says, the boys came in, completely aghast. Dickie was inclined to believe it was all a gigantic fiction, that Mabel, who was given to talking about dreams, reading tea leaves, and doing other things of that sort, was betraying a lapse of reason. Shura, older, took a different view. "They *do* do those things," he assured Dickie, "but it's only stupid people like Mabel who think it's right. It's people like Mabel who belong to the Ku Klux Klan." Whereupon Shura went into an animated description of sheeted and hooded figures convening in the deep dark of night beneath moss-hung trees where they burned a cross and then perpetrated their fiendish brutalities on hapless blacks and Jews.

The episode left Freda shaken. "That settles it," she said. "I could put up with her drinking now and then and being helpless for days at a stretch so that I had to wait on her. I could even put up with the boredom of having anybody like her around. But when it comes to her indulging in such horrible gloating over the torture of another human being and talking to Dickie about it—I can't stand it—I really can't stand it—I can't have her under the roof another night."

But Sasha took a less harsh view. The woman was a victim of ignorance. Let her stay until she could get another job. They would say to her that she should take it—they did not have the money to continue to pay her.

That summer Dorothy and Freda collaborated in taking care of a "dozen" children, students at the "Hoffman School of Individual Development," located at Spuyten Duyvil, several miles up the beach from Dorothy's place. Maybe the head of the school thought that "individual development" would be put to its highest testing with Freda and Dorothy, or maybe she wanted a little peace for a while. In any case, it seemed to have worked out quite well, as Dorothy thought of it. Dorothy took the smallest of them, bedding them on her front porch, while Freda put the rest, "dormitory style," in one of her bedrooms. Ordinarily, Freda did the cooking and Dorothy the dishwashing. Many times, though, there were picnics on the beach, where eating was of the sort to which beach-combers were probably accustomed—lots of sand in the food.

Dorothy's mood of spiritual tranquility continued. Most summer mornings she would get up early and go to Mass at the chapel at Huguenot. Walking home, she would say the rosary—the Joyful Mysteries every day of the week except Tuesdays and Fridays, at which times she said, as was the custom, the Sorrowful Mysteries. At first, when she began to say the rosary, she had trouble with the Sorrowful Mysteries with their meditations on certain events that prefaced Christ's crucifixion. "In reciting the sorrowful mysteries in the past, little devils have suggested to me that other men have suffered besides Christ, and that their sufferings and tortures have actually been greater than His." This bothered her, she says in her journal, because "my heart was not saddened, yet finding it almost impossible to grieve except intellectually over a tragedy which took place more than nineteen hundred years ago."

It was one of the problems that converts sometimes confront and with which they have to struggle. In the course of the summer, the matter was resolved. "Various things I read, St. Teresa, perhaps, and a book on the Sacred Heart and the life of Margaret Mary by Bougaud, gradually forced upon me the comprehension of Christ as a man. I felt and realized His humanity, and realized suddenly that He was suffering not only His own tortures, but the tortures of the entire world which He took upon Himself. His agony in the garden was not only the agony of one night, but the agony of all the countless nights spent by miserable and agonized souls. He shed all the tears which have ever been or ever will be shed and His despair was the despair felt by the entire world."

And Christ, "true man," had asked "that His cup of sorrow be taken from Him, if it were possible, even though He knew His end and had always known it and suffered it.... His scourging was not only His own but the scourging of ... the ... colored victim of the Ku Klux Klan. His crown of thorns was the weight of humility and indignity which the world always has [pressed] and always will press down upon the foreheads of its martyrs. And in His end He suffered every death. No man has ever died, nor ever will die whose end has not already been endured by Him."

And so she clarified a question that had bothered her. The remarkable thing about Dorothy, then and later, was the direct way in which she seized upon every aspect of Catholic affirmation to enlarge her faith. If at first she found certain practices or beliefs to be meaningless, she practiced them and affirmed them and invariably, it appears, found them a real nourishment for her spirit.

In a draft of *The Long Loneliness,* she says that the summer went well, "in spite of my missing Forster"—a phrase that she lined through. In her journal, she frets at living an isolated life; having her daughter was not enough. Still Tamar, or "Babbie," as Dorothy called her for a brief period, was beginning to take an active part in her mother's life. "If I tell her to set the table for herself, she gets plate and spoon, puts a table cloth on her little table by the window and sets it. She is already running little errands for me, going to the kitchen to get a match [for Dorothy's perpetual cigarette], fetching her hat and coat, the book I was last reading, or my sewing."

Even so, she thought Tamar tended to be "inarticulate and unresponsive" and she began to feel guilty that she did not talk more to her daughter, as did St. Francis who talked "to God's inarticulate creatures." So Dorothy, according to her journal, began to talk to Tamar, calling her "Teresa"—presumably in the manner of St. Francis:

"Do you hear all the little birds, Teresa?" she asked her. "They are all singing songs to God because it is a sunny day."

"Noisy birdies," responded Tamar, articulate enough.

Dorothy persisted: "They are all singing thanksgivings because they are happy. They have their nests and little birds and plenty of worms to feed them with, and the sun is shining."

At this point, Dickie Maruchess added his part to the Franciscan theme: "And the wind laughs 'Praise the Lord' and the angels are riding the clouds singing. I can hear them," he screamed. "Listen Teresa, and you can hear the angels. They are having a pillow fight with the clouds, aren't they?"

All of which was extraordinary for a little Jewish boy whose parents were radicals. At least, Dorothy thought it was, "so I gave up the idea of sermons . . . and have taken to reading the children psalms instead."

Late in the fall, there was a final supper on the beach—a memorable occasion, apparently, because Dorothy wrote about it and may even have planned to use this journal material for a story.

It was a cold day, and she began her tale by observing that she and John, with "Babbie" tagging along, had been scouring the beach all morning, looking for driftwood for their stove. Since John lacked both the strength and experience for chopping the big pieces of oak that had drifted in, they looked for pine. But "pine burns up very fast and we are continually under the necessity of replenishing the woodboxes." Although the beach had been well scoured for driftwood, they finally found "piles of it on the other side of Mr. Schmidt's breakwater. There were plenty of small pieces cast up by the last high tide to dry out in the . . . sun."

Meanwhile, three girls who lived down the beach—one of whom, older than the other two, may have been interested in John —began to help them scavenge the wood, and eventually it was all gathered. "Then we built a roaring fire, dragged down the steamer chairs from the garden, lined them comfortably with blankets and sat there blissfully." John put potatoes in the accumulating ashes, hung a kettle of grease over the fire, and then "went up to per-suade [the name is blotted out] to mix us a batter for clam fritters."

Comfortably settled, one of the children asked Dorothy "to start that story you were talking about." All right, said Dorothy, she would tell a story about a "little Mexican girl who lives in New Orleans, an orphan taken care of by her aunt and uncle." She would call the little girl "Bibiana," after a saint, "a Roman virgin who was scourged to death in 363 A.D. in the persecution of Julian the Apostate."

Dorothy was beginning to have a new feeling for the meaning of community. It was not just the present moment projected, as radical thought would have it, toward a completion in time. It tran-scended time. Bibiana, was at that moment there on the beach. "She must be very strong and noble," said Pilar. "I like to read stories of strong and noble people. All the books you read nowa-days are about people who are beyond good and evil."

"Pilar," whoever she was—perhaps one of the girls from the Spanish community—was expressing a sentiment that was Doro-thy's.

But back to the story. Bibiana, the little Mexican girl, lives with her "very devout aunt and uncle," who had left Mexico because of the persecution under Calles; daily she went to the French market to buy a few pennies' worth of "ground artichokes, or something like that. Once a week they have a rabbit, which costs twenty-five cents, excepting during Lent when they have nothing but vegeta-bles and fruit."

In her goings and comings, the little girl would always stop in at the cathedral to pray to the saints, mainly "St. Rita, Saint Ann and Our Lady of Lourdes."

Living next door to Bibiana is "an old colored woman" who works for a French mistress of a rooming house. "The old colored woman [is] just like the one who worked in the house I lived in in New Orleans. She always went around barefooted even in very cold weather, and she carried up piles of wood on her head from the river, or wherever she got it. She wore earrings which were made from safety pins and old teeth and bones and her necklaces were a conglomeration of knicknacks held together with pins and bits of wire." When this "old colored woman" got sick, Bibiana took care of her and spent "her last penny for a candle to burn in front of St. Rita." One day "old Columbine," the "old colored woman, gave Bibiana a little silver pendant, the figure of a kneeling saint with a halo around its head." After that, Bibiana began to pray to her "silver saint."

Time passed. Bibiana was now sixteen, "working as a seamstress, making christening clothes for little babies." As she sat sewing, she always sang to herself. Of course, "she sang hymns, the Agnus Dei, Tantum Ergo and O Salutaris Hostia." Once as she sang, Bibiana addressed a petition to her Silver Saint. "Silver Saint, pray to Our Lady to pray to the Lord to send me a marvelous voice so that I may sing His praise the better." Then, one "bright sunny afternoon," when the air was heavy with the smell of magnolias, a handsome young man who was always good "sat [beneath the magnolias, one assumes] courting Bibiana. Bibiana, overcome by the beauty of the day and the goodness of her young man, suddenly burst into song. And what was the surprise to everyone to find that she had the most marvelous voice—a voice which would have put to shame Jeritza and Farrar.... Bibiana kept singing and singing, obligingly, until she finally realized herself that a miracle had occurred and she [had] been given what she so unthinkingly had asked for."

Here ended the story, just as John came hurrying down the embankment with the batter and the frying pan. He was probably just as pleased that he had missed the recitation—which he could have guessed would have been laden with saints, medals, and even a miracle.

But Dorothy was awash in it all. She could believe it all because, as she saw it, what had happened to her was unbelievable. She had come through her dark night into light, and never, perhaps, did she feel the miraculous character of her own transformation more than that evening with the winter just upon them. "The tide had come in while we were talking and the cold breath of the water fanned our faces. There was no wind, but there was a huge swell and the waves crashed in and roared in our ears. I had to hold on to Babbie, who suddenly decided that she wanted to run into them, but as soon as the pancakes began to come off the fire she stayed willingly enough by my side." They stayed on the beach until darkness began to fall and the tide had come up so high that it almost reached the fire. "When we left our noses were stiff with cold, and the house felt deliciously hot in contrast to the beach."

It was winter and time to move again into the city. New York was merry that winter, but Times Square never attracted Dorothy. Her part of town was Union Square, and that winter she got "housekeeping rooms" on West Fourteenth Street, to be near Our Lady of Guadalupe Church. The previous fall Freda and Sasha had moved into town, bent on opening a restaurant. They rented a large ten-room apartment on Fourteenth Street and made three of its rooms into a dining hall. Across the street was a theater, and they counted on theater-goers becoming their patrons. They had at least one regular customer—Dorothy, who says that she spent "a great deal of time with them." In *The Long Loneliness*, Dorothy falls to musing as to how she "could never understand" how it was that Freda and Sasha left the business poorer than when they started, even though Sasha served liquor as well as food. Perhaps, she says, it was because they were "typically Russian, large-hearted, generous, so doubtless they fed many who could not afford to pay."

For employment, Dorothy worked with the Fellowship of Reconciliation. Again, she was working for a radical cause. It was easy work and her hours were from ten until three. Again, too, Tamar was put in a day nursery on Fifteenth Street, and this gave Dorothy several hours a day for her writing—in this instance, she worked on a play.

Still, it was a hard winter. A flu was making its rounds in the winter of 1929, and Dorothy got a severe case. She was so ill that she could only lie in bed and wonder, between her fevered dreams, what if she should die and no one would know about it until the landlady came to collect the rent. Meanwhile Tamar, always accepting life's buffetings, "played in the long gloomy dark room which faced north to a high apartment house on the next street." When she could summon the strength, Dorothy would drag herself out of bed and feed and bathe Tamar, now almost three years old.

Where were her friends? They were "busy and did not know

how ill I was." Della, the good, who never failed her sister in her trying moments, was herself going through a trying moment. She too was sick—"expecting." So Dorothy, alone in her gloomy room, fought it out and survived. Her solitary experience caused a welling up of something like bitterness, and it touched her later memory of that time. "I shall never forget that siege of illness in a rooming house where each one was isolated from the other, each afraid another would ask something from him." Had she been living on the Jewish East Side it would not have been that way, "where neighbors ran in to see how you were getting on, with offers of a bowl of soup or a dish of fresh rolls." Thereafter she resolved, she would live on the East Side. It was an unkept resolution.

When spring came, it brought little in the way of an echoing response of rising feelings to her. The aftermath of her illness had left her depressed; possibly because she felt that some helpful gesture to another would lift her out of her loneliness and weariness, she asked a friend, more desperate than she, to come and live with her. Dorothy refers to this friend only as "Lallah." Lallah was an older woman, and the friendship between her and Dorothy seems to have been of brief duration. Lallah's husband had died sometime previous, and she had just suffered the shattering blow of the suicide of her eighteen-year-old son. The woman's grief did not draw Dorothy out of her dark mood; to the contrary, it intensified it. The suicide of Lallah's son bothered Dorothy—to the point, it seems, that she discussed it with a priest. He told her that she should pray for the young man and put her life to the end of that goodness which to the dead boy had seemed lost. Her own efforts and prayers would be meritorious for his soul. But he was dead; he had killed himself, said Dorothy. How could she help him now? She was thinking of a time relationship, said the priest, and with God there was no time. This observation consoled Dorothy and clarified some questions she had had about praying for the dead.

Worry about money also depressed Dorothy's spirits. With her meager income, she had an accumulation of taxes on the beach house. Returning there for the summer seemed out of the question, so she decided that she would try to get a job as a cook in a summer camp where she and Tamar would be lodged and fed. She could then rent the cottage.

One May weekend, Dorothy, having fled to the beach, went, like a conscientious Catholic, to Saturday-evening confession at

Our Lady, Star of the Sea, the church in Huguenot. This Saturday, some Marist fathers were there to hear the confessions. Afterwards, she sought out one of the priests and asked him about the possibility of her working in one of the summer camps run by the Marist Fathers. Why, he asked, did she not come and cook for the few priests and brothers who would stay that summer at the Marist novitiate on Prince's Bay? It was just a mile or so down the beach from Dorothy's cottage. That would be fine, Dorothy said.

The summer was pleasant. The priest to whom Dorothy had spoken that Saturday evening was Father McKenna. "We became good friends at once," Dorothy said. Father McKenna, like Dorothy's confessor in the city, was unperturbed by the fact that Dorothy had a number of visitors who, finding no one at her cottage, sought her out at the novitiate. "When my guests came, he brought candy and cigarettes for them, and drove them to the station as they came to and from the city. He had never seen any Communists and anarchists before, and they had never been so close to a priest. They were a little wary of each other and there was not much conversation between them."

As for Dorothy, the presence of her radical friends that summer did not deter her at all from learning more about the Church. She read books supplied by Father McKenna, one of which was Karl Adam's *The Spirit of Catholicism*. The priest also taught her how to say the Little Office of the Blessed Virgin.

Dorothy, too, tells of Father McKenna's interest in Tamar. He took her with him to the barns where the Brothers milked cows and then to the chickenyard, where Tamar imitated him by throwing out corn to the clucking, crowding fowl, poised to run in whichever direction the grains fell. Once, when hay was being cut, she found a nest of field mice and brought them home, Dorothy says, to make a new home for them in a muffin tin.

On August 15, Dorothy relates, she got a telephone call from the Pathé Motion Picture Company offering her a three-month contract to write movie dialogue. Some of the Pathé people had read the play that Dorothy had written the previous winter, and they thought it was little short of pure genius. Dorothy, who usually was not taken in by extravagant praise, was nonetheless ecstatic. Yes, she would sign the contract. It was for one hundred and twenty-five dollars a week, and, "like all Hollywood-bound authors, I thought of the money that I would make that would free me for a simple life in the future and for work on the novel I was writing."

She was to leave for Hollywood in the last days of August, and that was just right because the Marist novitiate was to open on September 1. Despite her heady expectations where Hollywood was concerned, she left the Marist novitiate with genuine sorrow. Father McKenna, she was sure, had driven away the demons that had caused her depression. It was during one of her first days there that he had come into the kitchen and had found her weeping as she sat at the kitchen table. Unable to learn what troubled her, he said he would offer a Mass for her. After that, her sadness left, "thanks, I firmly believe, to that good man's prayers, and the power of the Sacrament."

When Dorothy and Tamar arrived in Los Angeles, the city was in a state of high excitement. The Graf Zeppelin had just arrived from Tokyo on its round-the-world tour. But Dorothy, who had gotten through the year 1927 without mentioning the Lindbergh flight in her journal, was likewise unconcerned about the presence of Germany's mammoth vessel of the sky. She had her own business to attend to—finding a place to live in Culver City, where Pathé was located, and getting Tamar into a nursery school.

Her experience in Los Angeles was worse than anything she had anticipated. She was given a small office, tastefully furnished with lounge and desk, but she had nothing to do. She says that once in a while "a group of us, not knowing each other, were summoned in to a most comfortable lounging room, where we sat in chairs with ash trays by our sides and viewed some stupid production . . . and were invited to give our views on it." Since Dorothy was incapable of dissimulation, her comments probably set the Pathé officials wondering about her. Dorothy at Pathé was, in one respect, like Dorothy at the University of Illinois—an outsider, completely incapable of affecting even the innocent artifices necessary to ingratiate herself with people whom she regarded as insincere and lacking in intelligence. Later she recognized that she could be wrong in her judgments of people.

So she sat in her office, read, smoked innumerable cigarettes, and waited for mail. Once in a while, she ventured out into the production areas, but, so far as she was concerned, it was all noise and confusion. "I was lonely, deadly lonely," she says, and then adds a statement that may be taken as one of her few expressions of feminist feeling. "And I was to find out then, as I found out so many times, over and over again, that women especially are social beings, who are not content with just husband and family, but must have a community, a group, an exchange with others. A child is not enough. A husband and children, no matter how busy one may be kept by them, are not enough. Young and old, even in the busiest years of our lives, we women especially are victims of the long loneliness."

This statement, though, describes Dorothy Day far more than it does women in general. Women, to be sure, "must have community," but so must all, and Dorothy's loneliness at Pathé, as throughout her life, came from her extraordinary craving for community. It was this craving that produced her restlessness, her continual moving about—perhaps, even, all of those words that throughout her life she wrote of herself—words that were meant to take a part of herself to all who would hear them and thereby empty out her loneliness.

Neither did she find a reprieve from worry about money. Five hundred a month seemed like a princely income to her, and from it she probably paid up her taxes on the beach house and indulged herself by buying some clothes. Wanting to do her best for Tamar, she put her in the daytime care of an English family, which probably charged premium fees on the grounds that their accent was worth a lot. With every move, it seemed, people stood before her with open palms. Once when Tamar was invited to stay at "a comrade's little ranch" for a week, Dorothy accepted, thinking this to be a laudable, comradely gesture. But when Tamar got home, she brought with her "a large bill for the hospitality."

Then, because she was lonely, Dorothy invited Lallah to visit her and sent Lallah money for a train ticket. When Lallah got there, she became ill and had to be hospitalized. Dorothy paid the bills.

The one aspect of relief from this otherwise trying time came when she purchased a second-hand car—a Ford Model "T," presumably—and learned how to drive.

As she fully expected, her contract was not renewed. She says that she would have gone back to New York, except that New York was then "an occasion of sin" for her. She "hungered too much for Forster." In an article written for the *Oratory* for April, 1956, she says that she wanted to go to Mexico "to get away from uncomfortable situations attendant on my conversion," meaning Forster and likely, too, a style of life in New York that she found increasingly at variance with the course on which she had set herself. Also, "I wanted to go to Mexico and spend some months there to see what it was like to live under a persecution, such as was going on during 1928."

This "persecution" to which she refers found its substance in the Mexican Constitution of 1917 and thereafter in a series of anti-clerical state laws. Essentially, the Catholic Church in Mexico, as were other churches, was placed under the direct and repressive control of the state. Priests were disfranchised—"confined to quarters" when in clerical garb—and monasteries and convents were prohibited. And, coming out of Mexico during this period were innumerable stories of the harassment and persecution of churchmen.

Although it might be concluded from what she says in *The Long Loneliness* that Dorothy went directly from California to Mexico, it is probable that she went first to New York. But with the Forster matter still in the background, it may have been that she decided to go to Mexico—but not before going to see George Shuster, the editor of the liberal Catholic weekly, *Commonweal*, and lining up some writing commissions.

Arriving in Mexico City in January, 1930, she rented a room from "an old one-armed woman, her daughter, and their orphaned nephew and niece." She says that she lived there as she lived in New York—"with the poor." The description she gives of her room, though, suggests a pleasant abode. "On the terrace outside the door were potted plants and hanging bird cages. The kitchen itself was open to the sky, and the stove was a strange out-door affair, constructed of stone, and made to burn charcoal. One stood in front of various apertures and waved a fan, and the bed of charcoal sparkled like fourth-of-July sparklers, and the delightful smell of charcoal fire mingled with meat and vegetable oil." The main family meal, in which Dorothy shared, was at midday. It was always "delicious," Dorothy says. Otherwise, she did her own cooking on a small oil stove in her room.

All of the writing that she did in Mexico was published in *Commonweal* in the winter and spring of 1930. She had initially thought that she would write about politics in Mexico, but she quickly recognized that politics was a subject about which she knew practically nothing. So she reverted to the themes she had always used and always would use—herself and the life around her.

Much of her writing for *Commonweal* had to do with her church-going and Tamar, who, as Dorothy saw it, was beginning to develop distinct attributes of piety. "Every morning I first go to the old Church of San Jose, and thence to the market, just as all the women do here. The Niño Perdido streetcars pass the Church, so named not for any lost child of the neighborhood as I thought rather tragically at first, but for the lost Child Jesus, when He was separated from His holy mother and foster-father for three days."

One *Commonweal* account was of her visit to the shrine of Our Lady of Guadalupe, a twenty-minute bus ride from the center of Mexico City. The trip was taken mainly for Tamar, who, just four years old, was "at a very precious age, the age when the apocryphal stories tell us that Saint Ann introduced the Blessed Virgin to the temple." And Tamar, for her part, seemed to possess a pious strain that warmed her mother's heart. In the church, she "blessed herself with holy water, and made her rather lopsided genuflection." But that was enough. She "skipped out of the Church again that she might lean over the low walls and peer into doorways at the chickens, pigs, lambs and pigeons, not to speak of cats and dogs which shared the house and gardens." After her inspection, which was probably the highlight of her day, she heaved a sigh. " 'And now, no more churches today . . . but a lollipop and peanuts instead.' "

In another *Commonweal* article, she wrote of a Palm Sunday service she had attended. She had gone with Soledad, the landlady's niece, to the parish church, "as large as the church of St. Francis Xavier in New York." "Crowded to suffocation," as the church was, the service was still "a tremendously uplifting and glorious spectacle, and my eyes were filled with tears often." All of the people held palms, not "palms such as we have in New York, but palms braided and plaited and woven into crosses, little altars, long plumes and the semblance of stalks of flowers and interwoven with flowers of every color and delicious odor." Many of the palms were as tall as a man, making the church like "a field of wheat, blossoming with flowers, waving and stirring triumphantly."

When the priests began their procession to the altar, "the people raised their palms on high so that one could see only palms and the dark, gleaming faces of the Mexicans, uplifted like palms and radiant. It seemed impossible, but the procession was able to pass through the church to the rear, and out the side doors." Then, after a number of minutes, while the organ played, "the huge doors, fifteen feet high, opened, letting in a flood of sunlight. At the doors three life-sized figures of Christ, one crowned with thorns, one after His scourging, and one carrying His cross, a grim reminder of what was to come, met the incoming procession." The spectacle was so powerful that Dorothy was nearly overcome, wondering when she left "how these people could celebrate the Resurrection of Christ more gloriously than they did this day of His triumphal entry into Jerusalem."

Easter Monday was another great celebration in the Mexican Easter cycle. "And now it was Monday and the cobbled roads and paths across fields to the church were filled with gayly dressed Indians, children in pink and blue satin, the men in white cotton and linen colored blouses." Inside the church, it was so crowded that Dorothy, like many others, had to sit on the floor. Then the Mass began, the three priests in their white and gold robes moving down the center aisle to the altar. As they walked with measured tread to joyful music, "showers of blossoms of all kinds began to float down through the church in steadily increasing density. The Mass was being said at the altar of the black Christ, blacker by far than any of the Indians in the congregation. During the Gloria in Excelsis little Indian boys appeared at windows high up above the altars, looking like cherubs painted there, and came to life to hurl down handfuls of roses and poppies which fell softly before the altar. The steady storm of blossoms was coming from five other apertures in the dome of the church." It went on throughout the Mass, "petals of carnations, violets, roses and poppies and shreds of calla lilies came floating through the air, falling on everyone, until the flowers were so heaped up around us that there was actually a wet sound of falling petals."

Thinking about it all, she may well have wondered how persecutions could ever touch something like this: an action of worship that meant so much to the worshippers that it literally produced a torrent of beauty.

Of persecution, Dorothy says little. In her *Commonweal* article, "A Letter from Mexico City," she tells of going to see a Father Thwaites, an Englishman who had been in Mexico City for thirty years and who was the only priest who could hear confessions in English. "When I reached his house I had a hard time gaining admittance. The porter professed to misunderstand me, and it was only after questioning several people that one woman whispered fearfully, 'El Padre?' and showed me where to go. The people still tremble for the liberty and lives of their pastors."

Living quietly and very contentedly, it seems, Dorothy wrote of her life and her impressions of Mexico, avoiding large judgments of politics and of life. Living, as she said, with the poor, she found their lives ordered by a tradition that was rich and beautiful. One aspect of Mexican life that she saw bothered her. The men spent hours in recreation, but women "have no time to play. They go to market and to Mass. They are always washing clothes. When they have nothing else to do, they are fanning the charcoal fires in order that the men and children may eat."

Compared to the people around her, Dorothy was exempt from poverty's necessities. She could write, and she could come and go as she chose. She even had a country retreat, "a little stone house in Xochimilco" that had "a thatched roof, and geraniums, roses and cactus." The place was on a ten-acre site that had a lagoon "where my funny flat-bottomed boat is tied to the bank."

The house was not much—just one room. It had no glass panes; there were no pumping facilities, which meant that water had to be brought in jars to the house from a nearby village well. When she wrote, she took her typewriter outside and put it on a low stone wall where she had melons and squashes ripening.

How did she come by this place? She does not say, but perhaps, for the moment in disuse, it belonged to some of her Village friends of a decade earlier. Some of these people, including her friend Peggy Baird, had taken to going to Mexico City in the late twenties and early thirties. That Dorothy had the use of a "country home" probably impressed some of her friends back in New York, since the rural retreat was considered one of the requisite appurtenances of the successful writer.

While she was in Mexico, she met the artist Diego Rivera. She remembered him as a "huge man, hearty and genial—against the Church and not at all religious." This did not offend Dorothy. "I had come up against enough anti-Church and anti-religious sentiment amongst some of the artists and writers in the old *Masses* that I was not shocked at it. I had been a Catholic only a few years and knew no Catholics as yet, and had read little of modern Catholic writers. I probably agreed with much of the criticism of the church, especially as to her wealth and disregard of the poor. My faith was an act of faith. 'That he may slay me yet will I trust in Him.'"

In *The Long Loneliness*, Dorothy says that she stayed in Mexico for six months, departing reluctantly only because Tamar was ill with a malarial fever. Her departure would have been in July or August, 1930. Where to then? Back to New York? The narration in *The Long Loneliness* suggests this when she says that Tamar "recovered as soon as we returned to New York, where we arrived just after the May Day riots in Union Square." Then she goes on to discuss the "beautiful clear" summer of 1932, with its sparkling weather." What happened to the year 1931?

The answer, it appears, was that she had been in Florida during the fall of 1930 and the winter of 1931. These were flush years for her father, what with his Hialeah racetrack connection, and however tough and unbending he could be toward Dorothy, he was neither ungenerous nor neglectful of family duty. One suspects that there were a good many times in Dorothy's life when her mother helped her financially and that this help came out of John Day's purse. Leaving Mexico with little or no money, and with a sick child, Dorothy may have asked for hospitality from her mother and father.

How things worked out is a question. Dorothy, in all of her journal-keeping and reminiscing, never mentioned the winter of 1931. Perhaps it was a time of such unhappiness for her that she excised it from her life, or perhaps she does not mention it because she well knew the extent of her father's holy horror at the thought of being introduced into any autobiographical narrations.

The next opportunity one may have to learn anything of her life from her published writing comes in the August 19, 1931 issue of *Commonweal*. Certainly, editor Shuster was doing his best by her in these days. In an article, "Now We Are Home Again," Dorothy tells of her spring arrival at her beach cottage—"to find the garden overgrown with weeds, my perennials strangely distributed around the neighborhood and no longer in my flowerbeds, fish-lines and ten-foot poles strung around the room, a box of dead and dried worms and clams left under a couch on the back porch, and fish-hooks stored on the little shelf over the door where a cross used to be and where now a giant spider crab hangs on the wall." It sounded as if Forster had been living there, but no, says Dorothy, "we had rented it to friends." The "friends" had put the cross in the attic, so the first thing she did was to dust off the shelf, drape it with a shawl she had brought from Mexico, and restore the cross to its position of prominence in the living room. Then she and Tamar went into their small backyard and found a few hyacinths, which they placed in front of the cross.

"We both slept very well that night, in spite of the howling of the wind which sounded like devils battering against the little house. I can laugh at myself for my Irish forebodings, but I believe in devils as I do in angels. I have heard them before in the gloomy melancholy of the wind and have felt that I have had a glimpse of hell in a sudden knowledge of the horror of the absence of God. I have felt a devil in the shape of a little fly which buzzed about my ear as I walked two miles home on a hot summer afternoon, after I had been gossiping with a friend about a neighbor."

She earned what must have been a precarious livelihood that summer by interviewing members of horticultural clubs. What objective her "garden interviews" was supposed to achieve is not known. To do this work, she needed a car, and so she bought a Model T Ford. It cost thirty-five dollars, but since she had to buy four new tires, a coil, and several other things, the total came to seventy-five dollars. "Now it is running smoothly and ... I whirl around the country roads ... and stop off at old farmhouses and beautiful estates and dingy, little new houses and bright and shining new houses, and talk to their occupants about flowers."

She was thirty-three that summer, and Tamar was five. Together they bounced over the roads of Staten Island, turned into driveways, and parked alongside cottage fences, all to the end of discussing with the lady or lord of the house the flowers they grew. And Dorothy, looking about, would exclaim over their flowers, complimenting the people on their eye for color and their planting arrangements.

In the course of her comments and queries, she made her notes, and when she was finished, she did not linger. It was back to the Ford, retarding the spark lever all the way, advancing the gas lever just a little, turning the switch on to "battery," and then pulling up on the crank with a smart surge of strength. When the engine caught, the levers readjusted, and the switch turned to "magneto," she and the Ford were ready to go. She did it all mechanically, having little feeling for the inner sensitivity of mechanical things. But she enjoyed driving and always excepted the automobile from sharing in technology's oppression of humankind.

If she left journals describing her life on the beach that summer, they were burned in the fire that consumed her little house a few years later. The Maruchess family probably still lived next door, and the Granichs had bought a cottage down the road behind her house. As she had in the past, she probably enjoyed companionable moments with Mike Gold [Granich] and his two brothers. Years later, she would remember old Mother Granich coming out to the island on weekends, bringing with her all that was necessary to maintain dietary orthodoxy in the pagan atmosphere of beachcombers and freethinkers.

Still, there is no mention of the inner tensions and problems that weighed on her mind and soul during this period. In fact, there is no indication of what she did in the fall of 1931. Presumably, she stayed at the beach cottage until the weather turned cold and then went again to Florida to stay with her mother. In another *Commonweal* article, "Notes From Florida," published in the June 22, 1932 issue, she writes, "We are visiting my mother in Florida," and that is all she reveals as to the source of her shelter and sustenance. Where was her father? He could have been staying, as he sometimes did, in New York, attending to business there.

And Dorothy? She rode her bicycle along palm-lined streets to the Church of the Little Flower in Coral Gables, three miles from her parents' home. A block away from the church was a Catholic school run by the Sisters of St. Joseph; there Tamar went to kindergarten. But, she writes, "it is not a Catholic country—as Mexico or even New York is Catholic. There are only four Catholic churches in Miami and the vicinity."

Otherwise, Dorothy visited with her mother and wrote, noting in her *Commonweal* article that "as I write, big black storm clouds are rising in the south. To the east, through the open French doors, the sky is delft blue with little feathery clouds. The Florida pines rear their plumed masts to the sky, and under them, dotting the open fields, are seedling pines, bright and green. There is a heavily wooded hummock at the end of the road, and only one house [is] in sight surrounded by scarlet crotons and a field of tomato plants."

In her article, she writes of another scene, a quarter of a mile away in Cocoanut Grove. It was a "colored town, where the little frame houses are ... thickly surrounded by royal poinciana, ... fig, mango, orange, grapefruit and other low-growing" trees, over which towered the palms. This "colored town" held a story for her and she told it. It was about "Toto," the black woman who worked for Grace Day. Toto's eighteen-year-old daughter, Evelina, had just died, and Dorothy told of Evelina's death as she heard it from Toto. The night that Evelina died, the family and some neighbors sat around her bed and sang. Among those there were "Frankie, her most loved brother; her father; the minister from the church;

and her two little brothers.... Every now and then ... [the two little brothers] went out to nibble at the fudge which I had sent over to Evelina the week before. The tuberculosis had gone to her throat and she had said that it helped to suck on the sweet candy."

As Evelina began to die, Toto went out to sit on the porch for a moment. "Overhead the moon flickered through the leaves of the poinciana trees, and the rustling of the dried pods of the tree, which hung in yellow festoons during the day, sounded like the clapping of many hands." When Toto went back into the room, Evelina asked her, "Have you given me up yet, Mother?" And Toto said, "No, I can't give you up."

Then Evelina said, "Go and talk to the Lord, Mother, and see if you can't give me up. You are keeping me here and I want to go." So Toto went out on the porch again and talked to God. When she went back into Evelina's room again, Evelina asked her a second time, "Mother, have you given me up?" And Toto said, "Yes, child, I have given you up to the Lord." With that, Evelina went to sleep, and in her sleep, she died.

Dorothy concluded her story: "As I listened to Toto talking of Evelina, and of the children who are left to her, I thought of the dense gloom of that little porch, which is in reality but a platform since the porch blew away during the hurricane of 1926. I thought of the overhanging trees ... which Toto's children had planted around the house. I thought of the happiness that house has seen and the misery it now contains. I thought of those night hours on the porch, and I heard again that awful wailing in the church." She thought of Toto, as she sat there at her mother's kitchen table, telling her the story of Evelina and of Toto's final remark: "But it is God's will." Then Toto, "her eyes strong and shining," got up from the table and went back to her ironing board, set up outside in the afternoon sun.

Dorothy and Tamar returned to New York in late April, finding "a cold tang in the air," which was "very refreshing after the torpid heat of Florida." Again it is *Commonweal*, in its November 30, 1932 issue, that provides some of the circumstances of her homecoming. She called her recital "East Twelfth Street," the place where, once again, she and Tamar had found a tenement that they could call home. She had gotten it hurriedly: "Hotel bills were exorbitant, we were in a rush." She paid twenty-eight dollars a month for it, a price which included the expense of hot water and steam heat. And, if among all of those rooms, flats, and apartments in the

City of New York where she had lived none could be described as other than squalid, still she always found in each new abode something that redeemed it and made it desirable. Here her rooms got "plenty of sunlight" and the neighborhood was "warmly crowded." She says that there was an Italian church across the street. Often there were funerals, and in Italian funerals, a band led the hearse as it approached the church. To Tamar, "this glimpse of death with its massed flowers, the dignity and solemnity, has lent a new aspect to heaven."

Tamar's enlarging consciousness included more than a confrontation with the idea of death. There was also life, and she and her little Jewish friend, Anita, would "play like" they had a herd of babies. Always quick to detect signs of a budding piety in Tamar, Dorothy portrays her and Anita as wheeling their doll carriages, loaded with babies, before the statue of Mary that was on the mantelpiece. There, "the figure of Our Lady of Grace, which had been blessed by a Pope and has traveled from Rome to Spain, to South America, to New York, presided with a benign smile over two little girls of East Twelfth Street. And Lady Mary, no doubt, was happy to have Anita, one of her own nation, there with her."

The felicities of East Twelfth Street notwithstanding, Dorothy did not long remain there. She found a flat on Fifteenth Street that went for twenty dollars a month. It, too, had advantages. The German family upstairs, managers of the property, kept it very clean. But the feature that attracted Dorothy was the backyard, one of a succession of "beautiful back yards, separated by wooden fences. Each house had its flower garden, divided by a home-built wire fence from a cement-paved yard where the children could play without trampling flowers." A tall privet hedge along the back gave privacy to the area. The flower garden contained perennials, specie separated from specie by brick walks. In the center of each little garden was a fig tree. It was, in Dorothy's eyes, a charming place in which Tamar could play and where, too, on hot afternoons, she could set up her typewriter and work.

That summer one of the popular songs was "Brother, Can You Spare a Dime?" It was a time when the more enterprising—or desperate—of the unemployed took to the streets to sell apples. But, says Dorothy, it was for her, "for some reason or other," a time in which she was "extraordinarily happy." Perhaps her contentment came from having "sufficient leisure for my own reading and writing." This summer, she says, was "beautiful and clear . . . with sparkling weather, not too hot, so that after some of the research work I was doing at the library I was able to walk home and savor the beauty of the city." Yes, she adds, "there is a beauty of the city, of the wide avenues, of the clean houses on orderly streets, of trees and little porches, and there were streets I loved and walks I loved that were not in the slums where I was living."

The writing of which she speaks was another attempt at a novel. "I have always been a journalist and a diarist pure and simple, but as long as I could remember I dreamed in terms of novels." This novel was "to be about the depression, a social novel with the pursuit of a job as the motive and social revolution as its crisis. There was to be the struggle between religion and otherworldliness, and communism and thisworldliness, replete with a heroine and hero and scores of fascinating characters." Still, the book was, as usual, autobiographical. "I put my own struggle and dreams of love into the book and was very happy writing it."

With its "otherworldliness," her novel was not "realistic" enough to meet the specifications of a communist John Reed Club publication, nor, presumably, was the subject of job-hunting likely to intrigue the public. As novels went in the thirties, she would have done better to have written of enchanted kingdoms and princes and princesses. But, as she says, the writing made her happy, although she seems to have thrown out her summer's literary venture.

Her contentment that summer was also due to a sense of the rightness of the course on which she had set her life. She began to go to an early Mass every morning at a church on East Twelfth Street, Our Lady, Help of Christians. "This was at the urging of a priest whom I never happened to see, to whom I spoke in the confessional, to whom I confided my struggles from week to week." The priest was "Father Zamien, a Salesian who advised daily Mass" and "made you know your importance as a child of God." Sometime that summer he was sent to Yugoslavia.

What were these struggles that brought her so frequently to confession? Was it the temptation to go back to her old ways? Her resentment at having to raise Tamar alone? Her loneliness at her estrangement from much of her family? If so, her feelings were not based upon self-pitying imaginings. Her circumstances were real, but through daily Mass and prayers, she seemed to be able to transcend her feelings, to see the meaning of her life in a more final perspective. From this summer on, daily Mass, when possible, became the habit of her life, and when, for some, it became fashionable to rail against priests for their worldliness, Dorothy would remember Father Zamien and the old Spanish priest at Our Lady of Guadalupe. They were simple men, but they had helped her keep faith within her grasp, and nothing else seemed as important to her as that.

That fall Dorothy's brother John and his wife, Tessa, moved in with Dorothy. Tessa was Spanish, born in Argentina. John, it seems, had met her when he had lived with Dorothy on Staten Island. Tessa's family were radicals and, at some earlier period, had moved to Dorothy's part of the beach to be with others of like-minded views. According to Dorothy, Tessa was "one of these harsh Spanish beauties. That is, she was really homely, but with her blonde, straight hair, full lips, bony face and wide, steady eyes, she was most attractive."

Homely or attractive, Tessa appealed to John who, radical himself, probably found her social views compatible. After their marriage, they lived for a while with Tessa's parents, and then accepted Dorothy's invitation to live with her. John was the brother with whom Dorothy had been closest, and now, wanting to do something helpful for him and Tessa, she offered to share her flat. That Tessa was pregnant made Dorothy's offer of hospitality the warmer.

Dorothy mentions a change in her style of living that began to be apparent that summer. "After I had become a Catholic I began little by little to lose track of my friends. Being a Catholic, I discovered, put a barrier between me and others; however slight, it was always felt."

How could it have been otherwise? In some final reckoning, Dorothy could not but be the outsider. She sought another kingdom, one which, as her friends saw it, was at war with the one they would have. That her kingdom, as she saw it, might also fulfill their own vision was beyond their belief. They could only think that her vision had failed. She was an anachronism. Now it was their time.

Still, Dorothy says, she continued to see her Staten Island friends, Freda and Sasha. They knew Dorothy well enough to know that whatever the intensity of her religious feeling, there would never be anything exclusive or judgmental about it.

She also continued her association with the Granich family. "Mike Gold and his brothers George and Manuel and their wives

... bought a house in Staten Island down the road from me. We were still very close. In the fall when Tessa and John came to live with me Mike used to drop in often. It was before his marriage, and he longed for children. 'All the world loves a pregnant woman,' he would say wistfully, and he would lay his hand on Tessa's body." This action, as Dorothy appeared to take it, was a kind of blessing.

That fall, George Granich worked for the communist Unemployed Councils, organized to combat the spreading effects of the depression through direct action—parades, rallies, banners, and oratory. In November, Granich told Dorothy of plans to rent trucks and take groups to Washington, there to meet with similar groups from around the country. In Washington, council members would stage a "Hunger March" to dramatize the plight of the poor. It was Granich's task to assemble the trucks, hired by funds collected from neighborhood councils.

Dorothy, alert as usual to the possibilities for a journalistic enterprise, proposed to her faithful benefactor, *Commonweal*, that it stake her to the trip to Washington in return for her story of the march. *America*, the Jesuit monthly, offered to buy her story on a protest assemblage of small farmers and tenants that would also be in Washington then.

On November 30, seventeen moving vans and three old cars left Union Square, carrying about six hundred marchers. "Column 8," they called themselves. Before they left, there was a brief ceremony. A band, also making the trip, played the "Internationale," as marchers went around the square, some bystanders cheering and others jeering. Several days later, Dorothy boarded a bus for Washington.

It had been seventeen years since her last trip to that city, and surely she must have thought of her imprisonment there and the course her life had taken since that time. Her companion on the bus was Mary Heaton Vorse, a journalist and story writer for popular magazines. Dorothy had known her from the *Masses* days, and for a time, their interests were much alike: workers' causes, social change, and even revolutionary expectation. After Mrs. Vorse's first two marriages had ended with her husbands' deaths, she had married Robert Minor, the man who had been Dorothy's employer in Chicago back in 1923, when Minor was editing the new communist *Liberator*. Dorothy quotes Mrs. Vorse as saying that "Bob had struggled through from a faith in the I.W.W., the anarcho-syndicalist [movement], to the communist, with much soul-searching and study." He was a "sincere" revolutionist. In the forties, when Earl Browder was jailed, Minor became the party's secretary. Later, he and Mrs. Vorse separated, "he to marry a younger woman . . . and Mary to continue her work as a world reporter."

So Dorothy and Mary talked as the bus made its way to Washington. When they got there, they took a dollar-a-night room in a tourist home on Massachusetts Avenue, and, as Dorothy says, they ate in lunch wagons—not necessarily a great trial, since in 1932 some of the best hamburgers made could be gotten from such establishments.

Meanwhile, the vans and cars transporting the would-be marchers had, after much harassment from mayors and police chiefs along the way, arrived in Washington. Out of a fear that this rag-tag horde might try to overthrow the government, the caravan was stopped on U.S. 1 as it entered the city; there the Washington police cordoned it off as other traffic was rerouted. For some hours the demonstrators, hungry and tired, were confined to their vehicles. But the call of nature had its inevitable way, and the marchers got out and used the railroad bed that ran alongside the highway. Finally, too, the police permitted one truck to leave the cordon to go into the city for food. This state of affairs continued for three days, produced, the police explained, by the marchers' not having pre-arranged lodging in the city.

Dorothy ascribes the inhospitable reception of the marchers to a "red scare" mentality in Washington and around the country, and she writes that while the demonstrators were sleeping in the open in "bitter" weather, "the respectable citizen slept in his warm bed and read comfortably of the 'reds' who had come to take over Washington."

This pronouncement makes Dorothy sound as if she had over-shot the truth as much as had the newspapers with their buildup, as she says, of the threat of "communism at home and Communist atrocities in the rest of the world." With the country in the bottom sag of the depression, it can be assumed that every true believer in the communist ranks hoped for an electric moment when affairs could be turned to their end. The newspapers, as Dorothy says, may have been guilty of overplaying the threat of a communist takeover, but the police were doing what to them seemed prudent.

The marchers were finally able to stage their parade on the morning of December 8. Dorothy says that she "stood on the curb and watched them, joy and pride in the courage of this band of men and women mounting in my heart, and with it a bitterness too that since I was now a Catholic, with fundamental philosophical differences, I could not be out there with them. I could write, I could protest, to arouse the conscience, but where was the Catholic leadership in the gathering of bands of men and women together, for the actual works of mercy that the comrades had always made part of their technique in reaching the workers?" Even her "summer of quiet reading and prayer . . . seemed sinful as I watched my brothers in their struggle, not for themselves but for others."

Marching men and banners—the call to action! What was there of this that made her feel that her summer of reading and prayer had been selfishly spent? She sounds like the old radical again, one who had trifled with religion but who had seen the light. She was ready to walk with the comrades and battle the forces that repressed them.

Why did it have to be this way with religion—with her life as a Catholic—that she could not join these marching men and women? Christ most certainly was with the marchers. They were "His comrades."

She was emotionally overwrought, obviously, but her feelings, nonetheless, were expressive of a profound illness that had become acute in the body of Christendom. Those who professed Jesus had not made him Lord of history but history's lackey. And Dorothy, whose heart had always been drawn to the dispossessed, who had always stood aside from the main course that was crowded with persons struggling toward their bourgeois heaven, knew that the Christ they said was helping them in their struggle for bourgeosity was really the anti-Christ.

"Is there no choice but that between Communism and industrial capitalism?" she asked. "Is Christianity so old that it has become stale, and is Communism the brave new torch that is setting the world afire?" How strange it was that "when Catholics begin to realize their brotherhood and betake themselves to the poor and to all races, then it is that *they* are accused of being Communists."

"When the demonstration was over and I had finished writing my story," she said, "I went to the national shrine at the Catholic University on the feast of the Immaculate Conception. There I offered up a special prayer, a prayer which came with tears and with anguish, that some way would open up for me to use what talents I possessed for my fellow workers, for the poor."

🌿 9

The Gentle Personalist

DOROTHY probably stayed in Washington the night of December 8, going from the shrine, where she had prayed with such fervor, to her room at the tourist home. Later she may have met Mary Vorse for supper. If this was the case, she surely lingered after the meal, with cigarette and coffee, discussing the day's events, omitting, of course, her visit to the shrine. That was her own business, and a kind in which she could expect Mrs. Vorse to take little, if any, interest.

The next day she took the bus back to New York, reaching her apartment that evening. Worn out, she wanted nothing more than to enjoy her reunion with Tamar, to catch up on the news with John and Tessa, and to dawdle over something to eat. The anticipated intimacy and community of the kitchen escaped her. Entering first her room on the street front, then going through Tamar's bedroom, which was little more than a big closet, she went to the kitchen. Standing there with the rest was a man who identified himself as Peter Maurin. Although he spoke with a decidedly French accent, he pronounced his name "Maw-rin," the American way, probably because he did not want people to have to struggle with the French version. Peter had been there several nights before, looking for Dorothy. Tessa, who possessed "beautiful courtesy and hospitality," had asked Peter to stay for supper and told him when Dorothy was expected.

In an article she wrote for *Jubilee,* that bright magazine of the fifties that concerned itself with Catholic themes, Dorothy recounts her impression of Maurin at their first meeting. He was "a short, broad-shouldered workingman with a high, broad head covered with greying hair. His face was weather-beaten, he had warm grey eyes and a wide, pleasant mouth. The collar of his shirt was dirty, but he had tried to dress up by wearing a tie and a suit which looked as though he had slept in it. (As I found out afterward, indeed he had.)" In another instance, she referred to him as "a real St. Benedict Joseph Labre in our day when we put such emphasis on showers and daily baths and the toilet in general. Peter was hard to take, for us all, I think, in some ways."

Peter stayed for supper that night, but otherwise his visit must have been brief, not out of a recognition of Dorothy's exhausted state, but because Dorothy may well have told him to go.

Whatever the case, Peter was able to explain to her why he had sought her out. He had heard of her from George Shuster. She had not had a Catholic education and it sounded to Peter as if she needed one. He would be her teacher. And Maurin, pleased with the bright appearance of his prospective scholar, took his hat and walked out into the darkening night, heading for who-knows-where—Columbus Circle or Union Square—to talk to whoever sat there on benches and would suffer him to make his "points."

Twenty years later, Dorothy wrote some three hundred pages of manuscript material on this man, hoping to make it into a book. It would be a book, she said in her preface, that would "be filled with digressions just as Peter's conversations seem to be filled with digressions, so that it is hard to pin him down. But it will be seen when I have finished that with all these digressions, all these perambulations, there is a picture presented, a point made, history being written, even history being made." Her story was about "a genius, a saint, an agitator, a writer, a lecturer, a poor man, and a shabby tramp, all in one."

And so it was, and the publisher to whom she submitted her manuscript rejected it because of all her "perambulations." Still, as she said, "a picture is presented," and, though roughly drawn, it did reflect truly those elements of brilliance and saintliness that Dorothy, like few others, saw in Maurin.

Since Maurin never talked voluntarily about himself, the circumstances of his life before he met Dorothy are hazy. He was born in 1877 in the province of Languedoc, southern France. He came from a family of peasants who had lived on Maurin land for centuries. "I have roots," he would exclaim proudly. It was, as they used to say, a God-fearing family. "My grandfather ... died at the age of ninety-four," Maurin told Dorothy. "He worked in the fields until he was eighty-five, and after that he could not because of his eyes. So he stayed home and made baskets and recited his rosary."

There was a large family of brothers and sisters, but Maurin was not sure what had happened to them. "My youngest half-sister was a weakling but got stronger as she grew older. She studied in England and she is a nun, I don't know what order, and is head of a school in Bolivia." A brother was the head of a school in Paris, "St. Clotilde's, a parish school." He had been a Christian Brother, but when the order was secularized, "they no longer wore the garb but went on teaching, just the same. One of my half-brothers taught for the Christian Brothers' School and he was married to a school teacher, who taught in the public school. In the first world war he had a bullet in his body seventy-one days when he was taken prisoner by the Germans."

"We did not eat the calves, we sold them. . . . We ate salt pork every day. We raised no hops, and there was no beer. We raised no grapes, so no wine. We had very little meat. We had plenty of bread—there was a communal oven. We had plenty of butter to season things with; we had eggs. We had codfish from the Brittany fishermen. They went all the way to Newfoundland and Iceland to fish. We had vegetable soups, salads and cheese.

"It was in 1882 when the public school system started: I was five years old. It was obligatory in every village. My mother and father could not speak French, only a dialect like Catalan. . . . Our home language was more Latin than French. The name of our town was a Latin one, Oultet.

"The seat of our diocese was twelve miles away, and our parish church two miles away. Oultet had fifteen families and in the parish there were ten villages. There were two priests, and they worked very hard. To help make their living they worked in the garden. The villages provided them with wood, and they got some little pay from the State, a compensation which was regulated by the concordat made by Napoleon. . . .

"My family owned eighty sheep and there was a herder for all the village. He had an assistant in summer. There were probably three thousand sheep in the flock and they grazed on what was still communal land. It was very cold in winter. The fuel we used was branches from the trees. We used to cut the branches every three years. The leaves were for the sheep and the branches for firewood. We cooked at the open fireplace.

"My father is dead, and my stepmother must be seventy-five by now. . . . She was nineteen when she married my father.

"I lived there in the southern part of France, a peasant, on the soil, until I was fourteen. For a time I was a cocoa salesman traveling around France. Then I went to the Christian Brothers' school near Paris, and five years later I was teaching there. I was a member of a study club in Paris. It was the same time that Charles Péguy was there, but I did not know him, nor was I influenced by him, though people say I write like him. Instead I was interested in a group which published a paper which came out twice a week, called *Le Sillon [The Furrow]*. It had nothing to do with the decentralist movement . . . but it was interested in ethics. It understood the chaos of the times. Marc Sangier was editor and backer of the paper. Later my friends got out a weekly paper called *The Spirit of Democracy*. They were looking for an ideology. They were preoccupied about the idea of an elite in a democracy.

"I did not like the idea of revolution. I did not like the French revolution, nor the English revolution. I did not wish to perpetuate the proletariat so I never became a member of a union even though here in America I did all kinds of hard labor. I was always interested in the land and man's life on the land.

"That is why I went homesteading to Canada, but after two years, when my partner was killed, I went around the country with work gangs and entered this country in 1911, where I have been ever since."

This was Peter's story, as Dorothy got it from him and as she wrote it down. The remainder of this biographical sketch she filled in herself. "It was the sight of the poverty of Paris slums and the thought of his peasant background, and the reading of Prince Kropotkin, that first led Peter to think of moving to Canada to settle on the land."

One story Peter told Dorothy recounted how he had been jailed once in Illinois. "He had been working for a railroad, and when the job was finished he set out for Chicago where he was to be paid. The 'gandy dancers,' as these workers were called, had to ride a freight, which was illegal, in order to get back to the city. They were taken off, arrested and confined to jails as vagrants and set loose again. . . . Yes, Peter was well acquainted with poverty and injustice, rudeness and abuse."

As Maurin had said, he did all kinds of work. He worked on farms, "in brickyards, in steel mills, at every kind of unskilled labor from Chicago to New York." "At one time," Dorothy continued, "he settled in Chicago for a time and gave French lessons, using the methods, as far as I can make out, of the Berlitz School, and he was successful at it. In the hours that he was not doing manual labor he read."

In the seven years before she met him, Dorothy said, he had worked at a boys' camp. "In the course of his wanderings around the United States, he arrived one day at a . . . camp in the Catskills, which was run by the pastor of one of the large and prosperous parishes of New York. He probably stopped there for food and offered to work. He also probably entered into conversation. The priest appreciated his conversation and invited him to stay, and so for seven years, he lived winter and summer in the camp, coming to New York when the mood seized him and living on an allowance of a dollar a day."

How did he live? At the camp, Dorothy says, "his most constant companion was an old horse and from the way Peter talks, I believe he shared the barn with him." As for his days in New York, he stayed "at Uncle Sam's hotel where one can get a cubicle for thirty cents a night. There is just such a hotel on the corner of Hester Street and the Bowery." Otherwise, he spent his time reading in the New York Public Library or visiting people he thought might be interested in his ideas. Since, as Dorothy said, "he was no respecter of persons," he visited bankers, professors, and journalists, as well as his acquaintances at Union Square.

"It was hard to get facts from Peter about his life," Dorothy wrote, and "of course," there were "some things" about which "one does not question too deeply." Nonetheless, Dorothy asked if he had ever married: "And he said no."

"Peter, were you ever out of the Church?" Yes, he had been once, for about ten years.

"Why?" Dorothy asked.

"Because I was not living as a Catholic should."

"There was a finality about his answer that kept me from questioning further," Dorothy said. "So I have understood from that that his difficulties had not been intellectual but moral. . . . I could only suppose that he was living as most men do in their youth, . . . following their own desires." She could not forebear adding a moralizing editorial: "Indeed if a draftee or volunteer at the present day admits virginity to the army psychiatrist, it is assumed either that he is impotent or perverse. Purity is not acknowledged as a virtue." But this was Dorothy in 1952, not 1920.

Maurin's appearance in Dorothy's kitchen on the evening of December 9 can be accounted for in no way except, as she declared, by a special and direct Providential intervention—unless one accepts the proposition that in the infinity of random connections that occur in time, none are truly random, that all are, and always were, of the mind of Providence. Otherwise, their meeting seemed as improbable as one of those random collisions of molecules in some remote corner of the universe that happens to ignite a sequential chain of interactions to produce a spectacular cosmic phenomenon. Maurin, whose mind burst with the explosion of an idea, had apparently spent the previous seven years of his life going from person to person, searching, as the true teacher always searches, for the student who comprehends the idea and will act on it.

It was, again, the *Commonweal* editor, George Shuster, who figured in Dorothy's life. Poet John Brunini, then working for *Commonweal*, later told Dorothy that Maurin had come to their office frequently, wanting to discuss his ideas with Shuster. And, as Brunini related to Dorothy, "thinking to save George Shuster's time, I was politely urging him to come another day ... and George rebuked me for it afterward. 'You might have been entertaining an angel unawares,' he said."

As angels, who exist outside of time, invariably accomplish their missions, so did Peter. He soon talked to Shuster, and Shuster, Dorothy relates, knowing of "my background of Socialism and Communism and my conversion to Catholicism, referred him to me." So Peter "obediently began to find me." And he, "not thinking in terms of either time or space, had forgotten to get my address. . . . Anyway, he started out looking for me without an address. That was like Peter." His method for finding her was to ask people he met if they knew her. He asked priests, especially. Finally, he "ran into a clue over in Union Square. He met a redheaded Irish Communist who referred him to me." The "redheaded Irish Communist" told Peter that he talked like Dorothy Day. "You should look her up." This time Maurin found out where Dorothy lived.

In the years ahead, Dorothy would assign to Peter a crucial and indispensable role in beginning the Catholic Worker movement. In the *Catholic Worker* of May, 1939, she wrote that "if it had not been for Peter Maurin, there would have been no houses of hospitality throughout the country. When he came to me in 1932, urging me to start a Catholic Labor paper, he had in neat and orderly outline, his program of action." In a letter to a student who was working on a thesis dealing with Maurin, she said that "Peter Maurin is most truly the founder of The Catholic Worker movement. I would never have had any idea in my head about such work if it had not been for him. I was a journalist, loved to write, but was far better at making a criticism of the social order than of offering any constructive ideas in relation to it."

This was a theme she repeated many times and from which she never deviated. Was Peter fundamentally vital in providing for her a coherent vision of the heights to which a person might aspire—or was he a saintly eccentric whose disorganized life appealed to Dorothy's contempt for the middle-class ideals of efficiency and order?

"Liking Peter was not the issue," Dorothy insisted. "It was not the attractiveness of person, or personality that won people to him, but simply what he was." She went on to recall something that a French priest, "whose name escapes me," had once said. This priest, who died in a concentration camp during the war, had "pointed out how we should be careful not to exert personal influence to win people to ideas—that their freedom is so sacred a gift that they must not be constrained, or forced in any way. It is the truth which should attract. Or rather Jesus, who is the way, the truth and the life, who attracts. More often than not, we ourselves get in the way."

It was not Peter's personality, accommodating and ingratiating, that made a lasting impression upon Dorothy. In a sense, he had no personality. "He was oblivious to little things. He was a French peasant, and if he found himself in a drawing room it was because he had something to say. Manners were not important, and he would precede others through the door, forget to take off his hat, nor give up his seat to an old woman unless he was told, nor say thank you when given anything. He was unconscious of the need for such courtesies. Or perhaps he did not have the habit of them." Neither was he self-conscious about his lack of manners. "To him 'a gentleman was one who did not live off the sweat of someone else's brow.'" He liked to talk of "the gentle personalism" that should be at the heart of one's attitude toward others.

Peter, as he said more than once, disliked organization. Attending to the matter of making things fit together interfered with thinking. "Peter had no income so did not need to worry about taxes. He used those things he needed, in the way of clothing and food, 'as though he used them not.' He had no worries about style, fit, fashion. He ate what was put before him, and if he preferred anything he preferred vegetable stews to meat, a hot drink to cold, olive oil to butter. He did not smoke, he did not drink wine, 'because it causes his brother to stumble.' Otherwise, he believed in feasts as well as fasts, and there are, after all, feast days and days of rejoicing."

Whether or not Maurin was a genius, Dorothy thought he was. And she, who later would sometimes be dismissed by her critics as a "romantic," had a mind that was logically critical far beyond the reach of most. To her, Peter was a thinker without flaw. He was almost totally cerebral. He raised reason to a crucial position in dealing with the very problem of existence. His concern with ideas —his overall synthesis of history and of ideas—was such a passion with him that he could think of nothing else. As he saw his structure, all its parts fitted together so completely that he could not restrain his excitement. He was filled with the need to tell about it.

The elements of his "grand idea" came from years of reading. He read, not to engorge facts, but for ideas—to see how things went together and where they tended. In writing of this trait of Maurin's, Dorothy quoted some lines from "Bishop Prohaszka's *Meditations on the Gospels,*" which, she said, "made me think of Peter": " 'He wished to know much, so as to be able to love much. Let us therefore read and learn, not for the purpose of killing time or loading our memory but for refreshing our spirits and kindling our hearts to divine love.' " Always, continued Dorothy, "he was bringing me sheaves of paper on which were neat digests of what he had been reading and studying. The first of these digests I can remember was Kropotkin's *Fields, Factories and Workshops.* I still have that little sheaf of quotations, arranged with headings and subheadings, neatly written in slanting, printed script."

An important consideration, of course, is what he read, who "influenced" him. It is impossible to know all that he may have read over the obscure years of his life, but Dorothy mentions some of the books he had her read. "Besides Fr. Vincent McNabb and Eric Gill, there were Jacques Maritain, Leon Bloy, Charles Péguy of France, Don Sturzo of Italy, [Romano] Guardini and Karl Adam of Germany, and [Nicholas] Berdyaev of Russia." Then she says that "the books Peter brought us enriched us immeasurably."

According to Dorothy, he read much history, especially histories of the Church. He read history not to use it as the predictive instrument of the "social scientist," or to whet some pet theory as to why one thing and not another had happened. Rather, he read history because through it he could discern the workings of those large ideas that had, at one time or another, won the minds and spirits of humankind. In history, he could see the relationship between an idea-climate and a culture. History, too, as he saw it, was the catalyst of tradition, the tool by which tradition can be humanized. It was also the agency of community. For, as a traditionalist, he affirmed that if the human vision was to be kept clear, the past must not be disassociated from the present. All that had been possessed an organic unity with the present. The past was not a carcass to be picked over and then cast onto the refuse pile.

He studied the lives of the saints and recommended their biographies to Dorothy as examples of particular qualities of spirit on which a true humanism could be built. "Peter was always getting back to Saint Francis of Assisi, who was most truly the 'gentle personalist.' In his poverty, rich; in renouncing all, possessing all; generous, giving out of the fullness of his heart, sowing generously and reaping generously, humble and asking when in need, possessing freedom and all joy."

As for philosophy, Peter read Jacques Maritain. "These Catholic philosophers have encyclopedic minds. Agnostics have specialist minds." However, Maurin also read one philosopher who was not Catholic—Nicolas Berdyaev.

To possess a vision is also to profess that vision, and Maurin, as Dorothy saw him, was the angelic professor. "Peter was a teacher and undoubtedly it is proof of his genius that he left much for people to find out for themselves and by their own reasoning. He held a high ideal and was not disillusioned when his fellow workers reached only half way. At any rate, they had made a start. He leaped, as it were, from crag to crag of thought, expecting his listeners to fill in the gaps."

To be sure, there were very few of his listeners who could do this. Most, unfortunately, became "disjointed in their own reasoning." By this, Dorothy meant that they could not see the overall coherence of what Peter was saying, but would emphasize some particular aspect that happened to catch their fancy. Dorothy was perhaps the only person who could not only see Maurin's "crags," but also the substance of what filled the spaces between. She also singularly possessed the passion and the will to begin building his vision.

"He never tired of teaching," Dorothy said. In the summer of 1933, as young people began to gather at Dorothy's apartment to hear Peter's ideas, the meetings went on "night after night." Dorothy remembered one evening she spent "leaning wearily over the kitchen table" and listening to Peter's voice out in the backyard. A seventeen-year-old Lithuanian boy, Stanley Vishnewski, sat at the table drinking coffee with Dorothy while another woman, Mary Sheean, busied herself with kitchen work. " 'Gee,' said Stanley, in an awe-struck voice, 'if he were teaching at Fordham now, how much money he would get for these hours of lecturing he puts in!'

" 'And why aren't we out there listening to him, if he's so great,' Mary said in her usual tart way. But we went on drinking our coffee and I was longing for the meeting to be over so I could get to bed.' " Dorothy was reminded of Saint Paul, "who talked so long that the young man fell off the window seat, out of the open window, and was picked up for dead; St. Paul had to revive him." Dorothy was further reminded of Saint Catherine of Siena "and how she used to talk. There is a story told of her that she could talk for twelve hours at a stretch, and when the listener, whether he was a priest or bishop, fell asleep under the barrage, she used to wake him up and insist upon his continuing to listen."

Mary Durnin, a lifelong friend of Dorothy's, remembered Peter's teaching sessions. What impressed her most about Maurin was the way in which the ideas he expressed were everything and his personality a shadow to them. Of course, Mrs. Durnin explained, the young people had their own ideas and wanted to state them. Peter would listen quietly for as long as they had something to say. But if they said something that illustrated the idea he had been trying to develop, he would exclaim almost triumphantly, "See the point! See the point!" She could still picture him standing there, his leveled forefinger snapping up and down in brief arcs to give emphasis to his words.

Dorothy provides another aspect of Maurin's selflessness. "I've seen him again and again at meetings cut short by the chairman and with no sign of resentment, even when he had been stopped in the middle of a word, he will just say, 'oh' in a little apologetic tone, and take his seat. He neither takes offense, nor bears resentment. He continues to bring his message to those who will listen. He is entirely unsuspicious, and never thinks ill of anyone. On the contrary, he sees their good points to so extravagant extent that his friends say indulgently, "He has no judgment in regard to people.' " Without exception, he "loved" those people who listened to him and discussed ideas with him "as sons and brothers." He "has told of their accomplishments and attributes with enthusiastic joy to all his other friends and listeners." Dorothy found something "quite childlike in this hopefulness, in this enthusiasm, and how beautiful an attribute to see the good!"

Teaching whoever would listen seemed such a haphazard business that Peter was sometimes asked why he did not have a plan. "Our Lord had no plan," Dorothy quotes him as saying. "He did this on the principle that you never knew where you were going to find a disciple and that there was a spark in every man that could be kindled if you could but find the proper word. Of course you planted the seed and God gave the increase. Everything depended on God's good pleasure, whether or not He chose to call this one or that. But he, Peter, would go around planting his ideas hopefully, watering them with his kindness and persistence and faith and hope, and leave it in God's hands as to whether they would grow and bear fruit."

That anyone could fail to be interested in his ideas was inconceivable to him. "He had a gentle insistence, an enthusiastic generosity, an assumption that one was intellectually capable of grasping the most profound truths and was honestly ready to change one's life. . . . I have seen him buttonhole an acquaintance on a street corner, engage a casual friend in conversation, start propounding to casual acquaintances in coffee shops; and . . . he was quite as happy talking to workers on the Bowery as to Bishops."

His one "teaching aid," aside from the pointed forefinger, was the written word, either that which was printed or which he wrote out in his own script. "His pockets are full of pamphlets, pages torn from books. . . . He tears pages from them ruthlessly—those pages which illustrate his ideas—and brings them out to enforce his points."

Dorothy did not think it necessary to add that the books he so unconcernedly ripped up were his own. She mentioned this practice because to her it illustrated his freedom from an attachment to objects. "He has no respect for magazines and books as such."

Some books he left intact because he thought people ought to be using them. When they would not read these books, he would digest them into a series of short phrases. His writing was soon given the title of "Easy Essays" by Dorothy's brother, John. The title was apt, and "Easy Essays" remains today the heading under which Maurin's writing appears.

It is interesting to reflect that in the thirties, when the world was ringing with the oratory of figures calling millions to the vision of a new community of Caesar, there were a number of persons in Paris, remarkable for their brilliance, who like Maurin were affirming a diametrically opposite kind of community—the community of spirit. These Christian personalists, as they were called, included, preeminently, philosopher Jacques Maritain, Emmanuel Mounier and his circle of intellectuals, and the Russian exile, Nicolas Berdyaev. It is Berdyaev who best provides a philosophical statement of Maurin's "synthesis." Berdyaev did not "influence" Maurin in an exclusively primary way, but Maurin read him, wrote digests of his ideas, and in his own teaching emphasized many of Berdyaev's principal points.

In particular, there are two substantive positions taken by Berdyaev that are integral to Maurin's thinking. One is Berdyaev's denial of the idea of "progress." He saw nothing at all in the character of contemporary history to justify any optimism for the future. He was, in fact, quite pessimistic about it. "A terrible judgment hangs over history and civilization," he wrote. "History shows constant signs of a fatal lapse from the human or divine-human to the subhuman or demonic. Out of his idolatrous and demonelatrous instincts man conjures up real demonic powers which in turn seize control of him. 'The beast rising out of the sea' [an image in the Book of Revelations] is a highly suggestive apocalyptic image of the last demonic attempt of the kingdom of Caesar to dominate and to enslave man and the world."

The other significant position that Maurin shared with Berdyaev is the denial of the Enlightenment dogma that the truth which serves a true human progress can be found in an analysis of the "objective." This passion for the "objective" transfers the criterion of reality from a subject reference, the person, to an object reference, the datum. The "objective," which has become the great driving force behind modern scholarship, expresses its social usefulness in the production of patterns in "hard data" that provide norms to which society, and the person, can be adjusted so that passing time can flow more serenely on its way. Thus the person, who once found a meaning for existence from a value climate that was ordered to the eternal, now finds his freedom and creativity thwarted by the necessity of conforming to the new behavior norms based always, of course, on the latest "new study."

Suddenly, it seems, the individual of the hour is the time-server, who, armed with computers, memo pads, jargon, directives, questionnaires, and the hard enamel of "professionalism," plots the course of "progress." And, miraculously, the font of data never runs dry. To the contrary, each datum has the potential of proliferating endlessly, like the cells of a cancer.

According to Dorothy, Jesuit Daniel Lord told this story about Maurin: "As a young priest, I was talking with Peter Maurin, father of the Catholic Worker and philosopher by right of innate genius and zeal for souls. He was telling me of his recent invasion of a great Catholic University campus. He told me how he had grasped by the arm a priest who was a great scholar and a man of power in the world of learning. 'I shook my finger under his nose,' said Peter, and demanded 'What are you doing for the Catholic social revolution?' Do you know what he answered me? He said, 'That is not my field.'"

The fragmented minds of many college professors bothered Peter, and he wrote about this in some of his phrased essays. "College professors enable people to master subjects, but mastering subjects has never enabled anyone to master situations." Peter himself "did not want to be fragmented," Dorothy said, giving the phrase her own emphasis. "He did not want to be called a pacifist or an anarchist, or anything, for that matter, except Catholic."

The picture emerges: The "beast rising out of the sea," as Berdyaev phrases it, is the inundating flood of mechanical interactions that are necessary to keep time's flow moving without civilization's experiencing catastrophic turbulences and backwashes. But in Berdyaev's view, neither the human mind, nor the human psyche, nor society could keep up with the accelerating factor of fragmentation that came from the singular pursuit of the "objective."

Against this cascading inundation of the "object" that would claim all of humankind stood Peter Maurin, the peasant, the traditionalist, and, above all, the radical. He did not believe, as did those who represented the mind of the Enlightenment, that the reality on which all rational structure was built was the unchanging mechanical order of creation and that all humankind had to do to reach utopia was to build institutions on the model of universal order. He did not believe, as did England's Herbert Spencer and Yale University's William Graham Sumner, that the person could dispense with reason in clarifying a vision of a true humanism— that all that needed to be done was to let history's process sweep society toward that final triumph of evolution, the heavenly city of history. Nor did he believe, as this age seems to hope, that "the best and the brightest" can save society, even with the assistance of the computer.

And so Maurin was a radical because he denied the Enlightenment proposition that reality lay in a discernment of order in the object and because he denied the nineteenth century idea that history was evolving toward its own heaven. Therefore, he rejected the two main contemporary positions that presume to bring things aright. The first position is that of liberalism, which holds no promise of a final beatitude for history but uses the pragmatic method of keeping the process going, of avoiding those cul-de-sacs where cataclysm lurks. The second is Marxism, which uses the nineteenth-century idea of evolutionary struggle and the inevitable completion of "progress" in the attainment of an earthly paradise.

Seemingly at war with one another, these two positions are in many respects similar. Both are based on principal elements in nineteenth-century evolutionary thought. Both affirm that only through the linear route of time can things be made better, and both are materialistic and atheistic—Marxism specifically and aggressively so, and bourgeois liberalism implicitly but perhaps more effectively so.

Maurin stated his objection to liberalism in several of his short essays. Liberalism was "the logical consequence of the so-called age of enlightenment.... By spreading nationalism and capitalism modern liberals have given up the search for truth and have become paid propagandists." What did he mean by "propagandists"—propagandists for what? He meant propagandists for capitalist materialism and the bourgeois mentality, each feeding on the other. "The fruit of Liberalism is secularism and secularism is the separation of the spiritual from the material." That separation, when maintained philosophically and then expressed in education, politics, and even business, acted, in Maurin's view, to sever the roots from an authentic humanism. "When religion has nothing to do with education, education is only information. When religion has nothing to do with politics, politics is only factionalism. When religion has nothing to do with business, business is only commercialism."

This "separation of the spiritual from the material," said Maurin, had opened the way for the rise of the bourgeois mentality, something that he saw as a virulent disease of the spirit. Paraphrasing some of Berdyaev's thoughts, Maurin wrote that the bourgeois mind had "enslaved human society and culture at the summit of their civilization." Because the Enlightenment had excised the spiritual from life, "bourgeoisity" was "no longer restricted by man's supernatural beliefs as it was in past epochs. It is no longer kept in bounds by the sacred symbolism." The rise of bourgeosity spelled "the triumph of mediocrity" for culture, something that had been denounced "with uncompromising power" by "a few deep thinkers . . . Carlyle, Nietzche, Ibsen, Leon Bloy, Dostoievski, Leontiev." All, continued Maurin, "foresaw the victory of the bourgeois spirit over a truly great culture, on the ruins of which would be established its own hideous kingdom."

"History has failed," Maurin continued. "There is no such thing as historical progress. The present is in no wise an improvement on the past. A period of high cultural development is succeeded by another wherein culture deteriorates qualitatively. The will to power, to well being, to wealth triumphs over the will to holiness, to genius. The highest spiritual achievements belong to the poor. Spirituality is on the wane and a time of spiritual decline is a time of bourgeois ascendency."

The mark of bourgeosity was the elevation of acquisitiveness to a transcendental truth; the eminently worthy are those who possess great empires of "things." The bourgeois recognizes the material basis of life only for himself, not for humankind. And then, having exalted himself above those who possess less, he claims as his just reward the first seat in heaven.

Maurin agreed that the communist criticism of bourgeois capitalism was just. However, he disagreed with communism because "a proletarian dictatorship and class struggle are not sound means. They are not pure means; they are impure means." Since "a pure end requires pure means, Christian charity and voluntary poverty are the pure means for the realization of a Communist society." So Christianity "has nothing to do with either modern capitalism or modern communism," for Christianity has a capitalism of its own and a communism of its own.

What Maurin wanted was a new world, a world in which the truths of Abraham, Isaac, and Jacob, and the truths of Jesus, would inform and reform the myth that provided the transcendental model of how people should think and act. The myth form that lay over humankind in the twentieth century had become a pall, a sullen, inchoate transmitter of evil, ordering life to slavery and death. Reordering institutions in the flow of time, either by "peaceful" or revolutionary means, could change little in the long run.

The rebirth of the world would occur when the myth of slavery and death give way to the light of the divine, where life and freedom found their true focus in eternity.

Berdyaev had seen the world ending because of what he took to be the triumph of time—that point at which the "system" became all and the person became nothing. But in the end there would be the "victory of the Lamb over the Beast," the victory of "freedom and love over force and hatred. The beast will then be cast once more into the abyss of hell and shackled, not to eternity, but to time: for hell is that which remains in time; that which, obsessed by its evil nightmares, does not pass into eternity."

In an age when some have come to think that the demonic flows unchecked, Berdyaev's "victory of the Lamb" is not that of the traditionalist's expectation of the "saved" being swept out of it all, leaving the rest of humankind bubbling in the molten fires of eternal damnation. "It may be possible," he says, "to await passively the judgment of a revengeful deity, but no such attitude is compatible with the Second Coming." This event, he says, will be a "transition from a historical Christianity, i.e., from Christianity this side of the end, to eschatological Christianity, which foreshadows the end of this spellbound world of ours." This "Second Coming" era would be a time not "of fear, inertia and frustration, but one of daring and creative endeavor." Historical Christianity has grown "cold and intolerably prosaic; its activity consists mainly in adapting itself to the commonplace, to the bourgeois patterns and habits of life. But Christ came to send heavenly fire on earth. . . . That fire will not be kindled until the fire of man is set ablaze."

Then Berdyaev gave the signs of the "heavenly fire." "Every moral act of love, of mercy and of sacrifice brings to pass the end of the world where hatred, cruelty and selfishness reign supreme. Every creative act entails the end of the kingdom of necessity, servitude and inertia and the promise of a new and 'other' world, where God's power is revealed in freedom and love."

It was in this light that Dorothy saw Peter, a person ablaze with "heavenly fire"; one who lived outside of time, beyond the spirit of bourgeosity, the new but old Christian who would "bring to pass the end of the world where hatred, cruelty and selfishness reign supreme"; where the determinism of a mechanical, objectivized mold to which all life must conform would be broken and humankind restored again to the freedom that permitted true creativity.

This was the "revolution" that Peter taught, and however exalted, it was not beyond the reach of Dorothy's spirit. For her, it was the highest realism. Objectively, it was true because, in the logic of those elements that fit into the equation summing the problem of existence, it took into consideration the whole of the equation— time and eternity, spirit and matter. Subjectively, it was true because of Peter's sanctity. This, as Dorothy saw it, made him the believable teacher, a point she made time and time again in the latter years of her life.

"I'm not saying that Peter is *the* only saint of his day," Dorothy wrote. "There are many saints, I am convinced, here, there and everywhere and not only the canonized ones that Rome calls to our attention." She thought of how Saint Paul "used to address his readers, common ordinary folk like us all, as 'called to be saints.' " So there were many saints, unremarked but following the counsels of perfection just as these counsels had been enjoined upon them by Jesus: " 'Be ye therefore perfect,' our Lord said, 'as our heavenly Father is perfect.' "

Peter, though, was "different." He was the saint-teacher. "He was an apostle to the world. It is this which set him apart from other men, from other saints of the Church of God who went around preaching penance, reminding men of their relationship with God and eternity. Peter thought not only in terms of eternity, but of this present life, even though it be but a second in eternity where one day is as a thousand years. He made one feel the magnificent significance of our work, our daily lives, the material of God's universe and what we did with it, how we used it."

He emphasized "the dignity of the worker, the dignity of work, the goodness of God's goods. Man as a co-creator. These were the things he believed in. He had faith in himself, in his own importance as a lay apostle, and that faith was sufficient for him to rise above any and all rebuffs from whatever source they came. He knew, he was confident, that he had a message. He always talked of the necessity of the long view, of the vision, in order to give ourselves the perspective we needed to see things in the light of eternity." That "very long view made the work of the day, what we did here and now so important that each thought, each decision, each step we took determined the future, not only for ourselves but for the world."

Peter, the teacher, saw the world so full of potentiality for heaven that "he did not even converse on spiritual things. . . . He never preached. He never talked about the spiritual life of the world around him. He was an apostle to the world." Dorothy observed that people found it curious he should be so preoccupied "with business, with economics, with agriculture, with labor, with capital, with unions, maternity guilds, with cooperatives, his unceasing emphasis on the fact that these are vital concerns of religion." His dwelling on these subjects led people "to think of him as a MATERIALIST! 'Laying too much emphasis on the material,' they say, piously, and return to their prayers. 'After all, we must use our spiritual weapons; we must devote ourselves to religious service and all these things will be added unto us.' So they withdrew themselves, 'keeping themselves unspotted from the world,' they again are guilty of secularism, of using religion as an opiate."

If, as Peter had said, he disliked political revolutions, nonetheless he did affirm a revolution: the revolution of the person. The true revolution began with the subject and not the object. As a teacher, Peter stressed that the revolutionary spirit in the person was kindled by understanding the overall logic of the human condition. The course of history had always been moved by the great rational designs postulated by thinkers who, expressing the mind of the age, urged their designs upon humankind as the true means by which human destiny could be fulfilled. As Maurin saw it, the complete design had to take in all of the polarities of the equation —time and eternity, matter and spirit. The design also had to provide the person with the highest vision of what it meant to be human, the heights to which the person might aspire.

This was the personalist revolution, the revolution of the Second Coming, the revolution that began with the subject and not the object. This "subjective" revolution, which began with the person and worked its way toward the reordering of all creation, was characterized, as Dorothy noted, by certain personal dispositions that Maurin repeatedly emphasized: " 'Be what you want the other fellow to be,' he kept saying. 'Don't criticize what is not being done. See what there is to do, fit yourself to do it, then do it. Find the work you can perform, fit yourself to perform it, and then do it.' " Another saying he used many times was, "We should be announcers, not denouncers." And others: "Everyone taking less, so that others can have more. . . . The worker a scholar, and the scholar a worker. . . . Each being the servant of all; each taking the least place."

Personalism, as "Peter was always stressing," meant "that to turn to the state was to repeat with Cain, 'Am I my brother's keeper?' and that personal responsibility was to be put before state responsibility." Dorothy then added her own sense of how this was: "Only when all other means had failed, when one's own resources, the parish resources, the Church resources had failed, was one to turn to the state. The parish, the union, the group were to combine for mutual aid and the functioning of these smaller bodies would be more efficient than the cumbersome machinery of city or state."

To give personalist substance to what he said, Peter lived the life of voluntary poverty. "When Peter talked about asceticism, it was matter-of-factly, as the word implies, 'an exercise' of one's religion. To him, religion and asceticism go together. It is inconceivable, for instance, that one can be truly 'religious' and not embrace poverty."

After World War II, Maurin's ability to think left him, and he wrote no more of his phrased digests of reading he had done which he felt was significant. One of his last digests was of thoughts on poverty he had gotten from the English craftsman-artist, Eric Gill. It was on poverty.

And whatever may be said about Christianity in other respects, this at least is clear, crystal clear, clear as the stars: Christianity is the religion which blesses poverty and blesses the poor.

And whatever may be said about Christians today in other respects, it is clear that they do not keep the blessedness of poverty uppermost in their teaching or in their lives.

For poverty is not only blessed, it is uppermost. For poverty is no privation. It is indeed strictly and precisely the opposite.

The poor man, in the sense of the Gospel, in the meaning of Jesus, is not he who has been robbed but he who has not robbed others.

And it is a positive thing. For the poor man in this sense is not he who has not been loved, but he who has loved others rather than himself.

"Blessed are the poor in spirit," says Matthew. "Blessed are ye poor," says Luke even more simply.

And that thought, that recommendation, pervades the whole of the teaching of Jesus. Jesus of Nazareth, son of a village carpenter, a poor man, followed by poor men.

Dorothy saw the point: Maurin's poverty "was not an end in itself. It was a means to an end, a way of sharing with others, showing his love for others by deed rather than by word. Then when he had nothing further materially to give, he gave the richness and wealth of his mind and heart, without question, to whoever would listen. He himself always followed the program of the works of mercy. He did this so consistently over so many years that we used to think he spent himself too profligately, that he cast his pearls before swine, to use the brutal words of the Bible."

"What a mysterious thing poverty is!" Dorothy exclaimed. "To the religious-minded, it has had an enormous attraction down through the ages. To simplify one's life, to cut out the superfluous, to go against the sensual inclinations of one's own nature—Christians and non-Christians have emphasized these teachings." But there was, in the Christian sense, a paradox to poverty. One did not, objectively, try to banish poverty. "Christ did not try to rescue people from their poverty," Dorothy wrote, so as to clarify Maurin's position. "He came to preach the Gospel. When He fed the multitudes, first the Jews and then the Gentiles, the people must have wanted Him to go on feeding them. But He fed them once, taking compassion on them so that they did not go away hungry. It must have been a suffering all through His life, i.e., NOT to feed people in their poverty. It would have been so easy for Him to feed men, to relieve their hunger."

Here, of course, Dorothy was echoing the point that the Grand Inquisitor, in Dostoevsky's *The Brothers Karamazov*, made to Christ, as the latter sat mute before the Inquisitor. Christ indeed had not come to fill men's stomachs. "Seest Thou these stones in this parched and barren wilderness?" the Inquisitor asks Christ. "Turn them into bread, and mankind will run after Thee like a flock of sheep, grateful and obedient, though forever trembling, lest Thou withdraw Thy hand and deny them Thy bread. But Thou wouldst not deprive man of freedom and didst reject the offer, thinking, what is that freedom worth, if obedience is bought with bread?"

So freedom stood above bread, and, wrote Dorothy, "Remembering this, and living in poverty ourselves is the only way we can endure life which is so filled with suffering these days." Poverty, the great mark of human woe, stood as a sign, dark and forbidding, but which through love, the personalist way, could be changed into radiance. "And Peter has amongst us all, most exemplified the man who was poor."

Community, as Maurin described it, is integral to another of his themes. Dostoevsky's Inquisitor, in confronting Christ, dealt with the subject as central to existence and thus central to history. Community, as the Inquisitor declares, is the ultimate quest of every person, more powerful than the need for bread, although the two are curiously and inextricably interwoven. Of community, there are two visions. There is the vision of a community of eternity that has been sustained by hope over much of the history of humankind by the belief in immortality. The other vision, which has arisen in this recent moment of history, is one of a community that can be achieved in time as the only community that can be had because there is no eternity. Since the Inquisitor is "wise," he knows that there can be no community in time because time destroys all that it touches. Thus, says the Inquisitor, all that can be done for people to satisfy this—the main "craving" of every soul—is to give them illusions of community: rallies, parades, stirring exhortations, games, and "innocent dances."

This illusion of community, as Dorothy expresses Maurin's thought, was the main "heresy" of communism. It was Maurin's mission "to bring back the communal aspects of Christianity." It would not be the "I," but the personalist "We" that would mark the Second Coming.

What Peter Maurin did for Dorothy was to reorient her vision from the object to the subject, from collectivism to Christian personalism. He also provided her with something she had not had—an understanding of the meaning of the Church and her position in it. Peter saw the Church as the logical and necessary instrument of re-creation. It was logical and necessary because the whole of human history had been cluttered with the wreckage of lives and of cultures that had been victimized by the ambitions and vision of those who would have their own beatitude in time. No such heavenly city of history had ever been achieved, but were it approximated, it would impose an absolute tyranny upon every person that lived within its bounds. True freedom, true creativity, true humanism could be achieved only when a people were set upon the path to God. The Church provided that path; it was the voice of God made audible in time, giving humankind "an instruction and a way of life."

Yes, Peter would agree, the Church itself—that part of it that showed itself in history's process—had been caught in time. But now all of history was at its critical moment and a "clarification" was required. An intellectual revolution was necessary. The truths of eternity had to be made understandable to the minds of ordinary people. Further, whatever part of the Church had been beguiled by time, the mark of its long embrace with the spirit of bourgeosity, had to be excised. That which should remain as the heart and spirit of the life of the Church was the Gospel message of love. This love was not a sugar coating on the process of time, a sentimental bandage on the wounds of life so as to hide their character. It was the love that moved one to take goodness to the heart of affliction, to begin there the work of re-creation.

"Peter," Dorothy concluded, "has a message for all, though all are certainly not called to go out as he did among the poor, as a teacher and worker. The doctor, the laboratory worker, the teacher in his classroom, the worker at his machine, the farmer at his plough, the student at his books—all have their vocations. . . . Poverty is a thing of the spirit as well as of the flesh. But we do not see enough of Peter's kind of poverty. His message of poverty is for all, and his message of personal responsibility is for all." He had "pointed a *little* way. . . . He built up a new apostolate. He reached the poorest and the most destitute by living always among them, sharing their poverty and sharing what he had with them. And this expression of love is rarer than one thinks."

And now, wrote Dorothy, "We must build up leaders. And the leaders must first change themselves. And the job is so hard, so gigantic in this, our day of chaos, that there is only one motive that can make it possible for us to live in hope—that motive of the love of God. There is a natural love for our brother, our mate, yes, but even that does not endure unless it is animated by the love of God."

What had Maurin meant to Dorothy? "Peter with his 'correlation of the material and spiritual' was a revelation to me." And she said, "I do know this—that when people come into contact with Peter . . . they change, they awaken, they begin to see, things become as new, they look at life in the light of the Gospels. They admit the truth he possesses and lives by, and though they themselves fail to go the whole way, their faces are turned at least toward the light."

❧ 10

The *Catholic Worker*

"It was depression time," Dorothy wrote; "canned beef was being doled out and more people were going on home relief and work relief and were submitted to questionnaires and bureaucracy and the bitter worm of despair was gnawing at the human heart. To be questioned as to every bite you ate, every mouth there was to fill, every moment of the time one spent. 'What right have you to have another baby for the state to support?' That was the kind of inquisition that went on. And rent money was not an emergency until one was put on the street, sitting in the midst of one's furniture."

Dorothy's main problem in the closing days of 1932 was Maurin. Having treated him with scant hospitality during his first visit to her apartment, she was not overly disposed, even after she had had her night's sleep, to have him underfoot. Daily she went to the New York Public Library to do research for the Paulist fathers. When she got back to the apartment, around three o'clock in the afternoon, Peter was waiting for her to continue what he called his "indoctrinating." "No matter what it was that I had to do, housework, shopping, ironing, mending, cooking, Peter followed me around, not only interpreting daily events in the light of history, but also urging a program of action." And Dorothy, grim-faced and occasionally begging for respite, listened in spite of herself.

She recalled one of his discussions in those first days of his teaching: the necessity for the worker to own the means of production, "an ownership that brought responsibility and not a share in the stock which was a bribe, 'a stock which got the worker stuck!'" Peter would say triumphantly, "his face beaming, thinking he had made a specially clever play on words." Maurin's penchant for the use of catchy phrases, said Dorothy, "used to make me blush, but they were as much a part of Peter as his clothes, so that I soon realized that intellectual disdain of the one was almost as bad as snobbish disdain of the other."

Still, "of course," it was "exhausting." "One could not live at Peter's intellectual level all the time." There was one evening— when John was out, working at night on a newspaper—that Dorothy and Tessa wanted to listen to some symphonic music on New York's classical music station, WQXR. Tamar was in bed with the measles and "Tessa and I were most anxious to hear the symphony, I think it was Tschaikowsky's 'Pathetique.' But Peter was there. . . . We begged him. 'Peter, a symphony! Just an hour. Do sit quietly.' "

He did his best, but sooner or later, "his face started working, his eyes lit up, his nose twitched, his finger began to mark out points in the air before him. Usually he'd take out a notebook and start jotting down points. Finally, when he could bear it no longer, he looked at me wistfully, and then, seeing my adamant expression, turned to Tessa. I remember that night especially because he went over and knelt down by her chair and began whispering to her, unable to restrain himself longer."

Sometimes when Peter came he brought a friend, someone with whom he had become acquainted at Columbus Circle or Union Square. There was a young Jew, "Klein," who, though a socialist, was also religious. "Peter did not talk about religion with him but Klein was always conscious that we stood for the primacy of the spiritual. 'You use the name of God so freely,' he used to say. 'Jews would be terrified to speak so freely, so often of Him.' "

There was Dan Irwin, an unemployed bookkeeper, and Frank O'Donnell, an Irishman "with a troubled conscience" because he was trying to make a living by pressure-tactic salesmanship—"selling the idea to poor housewives of having family snapshots enlarged and hand-colored." Charles Rich, also Jewish, sold gardenias on the streets. "The smell always reminded him of police, he confessed to me, they so often told him to move along, threatening him with arrest for street-selling without a license." But Rich was not a convincing salesman. He "spent most of his time in the library, studying. . . . He starved himself most of the time." Another guest, a young college student, had been sleeping in Central Park, although he was arrested regularly for doing so. He would spend the day in jail, and then be released in the evening for a few hours of relaxation before he retired again to his bench in the park. "Occasionally he got a job dishwashing, but those were hungry days for all."

The most interesting of Peter's friends was Homer, the "mad sculptor." It was a curious story, that "I must speak of," Dorothy wrote, "because telling of him illustrates that aspect of Peter which was not only amusing but often irritating and the cause of complications in the work." Homer was not only a sculptor. He also played the flute, and once in a while, he would "drop in of an evening and while Peter talked, he would take out his flute and play. When Peter spoke to him especially, when Tessa and I were not attentive, the flutist would answer with some unintelligible remark, which somehow satisfied Peter so that he went on. Once when a woman friend paid a call and was introduced to Homer, he acknowledged the introduction and said courteously, 'Yes, I think I met you last year. You were sitting nude on a mantlepiece.' " The "poor woman," related Dorothy, "the respectable mother of three children, was overcome with confusion."

But Peter, so caught up in his own thoughts, paid no attention at all to such incidents. He went on talking, incapable of thinking that anyone could be indifferent to what he was saying.

But, as Dorothy said, Peter was "no respecter of persons" and he had friends who were of a "higher degree," as the world is accustomed to making such judgments. Thomas Woodlock, editorial writer for the *Wall Street Journal,* was one of them. Dorothy was certain that Woodlock had "contributed to Peter's thought, as I know Peter contributed to his." What interested Woodlock, as it did Maurin, was the Thomistic idea of the common good, and this was usually the subject of their conversations. "Mr. Thomas Aquinas Woodlock" they used to call him at the *Wall Street Journal.* Another friend of Peter's was John Moody of Moody's Investment Service.

Maurin, to be sure, did not bypass the academic community. No doubt he was rebuffed many times by professors busy with their "research," but one with whom he became acquainted was Carlton Hayes, professor of European history at Columbia University. A story is told of how Maurin once went to the Hayes home to talk with Professor Hayes—and how Mrs. Hayes, thinking that this shabbily dressed man had come to fix the plumbing, asked him to go to the basement where, presumably, the job was located. When Hayes got home, he found Maurin patiently sitting there.

There were many such stories about Maurin. Too many, Dorothy thought. People would laugh at the stories about him, almost as if they used his seemingly eccentric behavior as an excuse to avoid a confrontation with his thinking. In the case of Hayes, the situation was not one of Maurin's being a saintly "character" whom the professor condescendingly agreed to see. Maurin was sure that Hayes, a Catholic convert, would be interested in his "outline of history." Hayes was interested, for as Maurin told Dorothy, he had gone to the Hayes house to read the "outline." And after he had read it to Professor Hayes, he read it to Mrs. Hayes, who no doubt thought that listening to Peter was her due for having sent him to the basement.

It is perhaps the character of the authentic nuisance that the longer one is around him, the more irksome he becomes. Where Dorothy's reaction to Peter was concerned, it was the opposite. However short she may have been in her speech to him, he persisted. In time, she began to see something of the mind and spirit that moved him. His "outline of history" began to make sense to her. He began with the prophets of Israel and moved into the history of the Church, pointing out where civilization had taken the wrong turns that had led to its present state of chaos— the Enlightenment, the secularization of society, the rise of nationalism and of finance capitalism. There were, on the other hand, clear maps as to how society could regain its balance, its sanity, and a true human character. These were the papal encyclicals. He wanted to make "the encyclicals click," he said.

Continually he urged a program of action. "He proposed the publication of a paper, round table discussions, houses of hospitality and farming communes; the paper to carry his ideas of unemployment and what to do about it; to popularize the Personalist and Communitarian Revolution, and round table discussions for the clarification of thought." The houses of hospitality were to be "centers of parish life, hospices where the Works of Mercy could be practiced and craft schools started. Farming communes, or agronomic universities, were to restore the communal aspect of Christianity, and were to be in imitation of the Irish universities back in the tenth century to which men came from all over Europe to live and study."

The idea of having her own newspaper appealed to Dorothy and, more than that, she felt quite capable of putting one out. The question was, how to finance it? Peter had a ready answer: "The thing to do is just to start," adding that "in the Catholic Church money is never necessary." All right, thought Dorothy, she would start. She had been reading the life of Nathaniel Hawthorne's Catholic-convert daughter, Rose, who had started a Cancer Hospital down on the East Side. If Miss Hawthorne could begin with little or nothing, why couldn't she? Dorothy was also reading St. Teresa's *Foundations,* wherein the Saint had said, "Teresa and three ducats can do everything." Considering her bills, Dorothy did not have "three ducats," but she had the help of her brother John, so she began the work of putting together a paper on her kitchen table.

Even so, Dorothy immediately was confronted with the need for money, since she wanted to have the first edition ready for May Day. "If we had had a mimeograph machine, it would have been a mimeographed paper. But we had nothing but my typewriter." In the meantime, Peter had confidently spoken of prospects of getting money from the priest for whom he had worked at the camp at New Rochelle. In any case, Peter said, the priest, a pastor of a large uptown church, would probably let them have a room in the basement of one of the church buildings, and there, with a mimeograph machine, they could get out the paper. So one morning Dorothy took the train uptown to the parish, hoping to meet the priest. Finding him away, she went into a nearby church to make a visit. One person was there. It was Maurin, kneeling in one of the front pews and looking at the altar. Praying, no doubt, Dorothy thought. But as she watched, she saw him raise his forefinger and slowly count off whatever points he was making. "The conviction came over me that Peter ... was a man of vision."

Fearing that she pursued only a will-of-the-wisp in expecting help from the priest, she went to the Paulist Press to see what it could do for her. For fifty-seven dollars, she was told, she could get 2,500 copies of an eight-page, tabloid-size paper. All right, she would take it, although it probably meant that her electricity and gas would be cut off and that she would be turned out on the street because her own bills would go unpaid. "I had a small pay-check coming in for the research job which was just finishing; two checks were due for articles I had written," and there was some money she had been given by Father Joseph McSorley, the Paulist, for some bibliographical work she had done for him. Altogether, it would pay for the paper.

First, though, she had to go and get the fifteen dollars that she was due from *Sign* magazine for an article she had written. There she found Father Harold Purcell, "a first-rate editor," dreaming of something more than editing a magazine. "On the office wall was hung a blueprint and painting of his dream—the City of Saint Jude, which he envisioned as a complex of school, hospital, clinic, and settlement for blacks in Montgomery, Alabama." Within the year, Purcell would begin this work, and as Dorothy lamented, when he departed, he "walked off with two of our first Workers."

Though she was to lose those two young helpers later, she gained a lifelong friend there in the office that day. She met a nun, Sister Peter Claver. Sister, one of fourteen children, had been born in Rome, Georgia, at the turn of the century. Her father was Irish and her mother, Jewish. Gracious and intelligent, she had, as a young woman, left her small town in the north Georgia hills and gone to New York to become a dancer. But the life of a ballerina, she came to realize, was not what she wanted. The question of a religious vocation had been in her mind for some time, and now it seemed to demand an answer. In 1926, she entered the Missionary Servants of the Blessed Trinity. A prayerful woman, she too wanted to change the world through the use of "weapons of the spirit." Perhaps she was in Father Purcell's office that day to learn more about his Montgomery project. In any case, she and Dorothy talked, and when she heard what Dorothy was trying to do, she gave her what she had—a dollar.

In addition to this donation, Dorothy got ten dollars from a Father Ahearn, pastor of a Newark parish of blacks. "These were our finances," wrote Dorothy. With her several checks and eleven dollars in cash, she had enough to pay for the paper. The only problem that remained was what to call the paper. Peter, who had taken no part in making it up, wanted to call it *The Catholic Radical,* but Dorothy chose the *Catholic Worker.* Peter deferred. "Man proposes and woman disposes," he said. There was never any bitterness in Peter, Dorothy added. When things did not suit him, he was silent.

In the long view, Peter's proposed title may have been the better one. But 1933 was a time when the worker, the factory worker, with or without a job, appeared as a class upon which the evils of the time effected their greatest oppression. Anyway, the *Catholic Worker* sounded just right—the true *Worker,* the Catholic response to the communist *Daily Worker.*

By May Day, 1933, all was ready. Twenty-five hundred copies of the first edition of the *Catholic Worker* lay bundled on the kitchen floor in Dorothy's apartment. Dorothy had already decided that the paper would sell for a penny a copy. As she later told Professor Rosemary Bannon of DePaul University, it might have been better to have given it away, "but you can't get a second class mailing permit if you give away a copy; so you put the least possible price on it to indicate what you feel about money."

There to help Dorothy sell the paper was Joe Bennett, the college student who slept nights in Central Park and spent his days in jail. This day, gainfully employed, he was out. Two others came to help—"commission" salesmen, probably sent by a priest from a nearby parish.

May 1, 1933, was a day full of signs of the time. The Soviets celebrated the largest May Day in their history. A million soldiers and workers paraded through Red Square and saluted Stalin as he stood with other government leaders on the terrace of the gleaming red granite tomb in which lay the chemically reconstructed body of Lenin, representing materialist immortality, as it were. In Germany, a public ecstasy erupted. Throughout the day in Berlin, there was a continuous succession of bands and marching groups singing the "Horst Wessel" song. "In all the world," wrote the correspondent of the *New York Times,* "never previously had there been anything to compare with this first labor day of the new Third Reich."

In the United States, Franklin Roosevelt was well into his "hundred days," and whatever he was then doing about the banking situation, the people of the nation could at least look forward to having their beer again. In Union Square, fifty thousand radicals assembled to hear speeches that denounced Hitler and called for a revolutionary change in the social order. At 4:50 P.M. the crowd reached its peak when two communist parades came marching down Broadway and spilled into the square, transforming it into "a hot undulant sea of hats and sun-baked heads, over which floated a disordered array of banners, placards and pennants." And into this "undulant sea" waded the four from 436 East Fifteenth Street, crying out the revolution they had in mind.

There were no mass conversions. There was not even one conversion that Dorothy could remember. Early, the two commission salesmen slunk away, disheartened by jibes and poor sales. But perhaps some of the people who had a *Worker* thrust into their hands and who then bothered to read it were surprised at what they read. The invasion of Union Square had been symbolic: a slender, plainly dressed woman of thirty-five and a boy, short of breath from a rheumatic heart, moving among jam-packed thousands—David and Goliath—the first pinprick of an innoculation of truth against error, as Dorothy saw it. Anyway, when she and the weary Joe Bennett reached her apartment, she felt the venture had gone well.

What she did during the next several weeks she does not say, but what occupied much of her time is apparent. She waged the battle on the economic front by sending out copies of the *Worker* to anyone she thought would read it—and then she let them know that a donation would help. One of her first contributions, surprisingly, came from that Catholic journalistic bulwark of conservatism and traditional piety, the *Brooklyn Tablet*. Editor Patrick Scanlan thanked Dorothy for her letter of May 6 and hoped that her "adventure meets with success. Enclosed is a contribution for the work."

More donations came in. They were small, but Dorothy was able to keep the gas and electricity on, and eventually she paid the rent. One shadow having passed, another dimmed the prospect. Peter had gone. He had wanted a paper that would print his essays, make the points that he made, and then relate them to the condition of the world in 1933. But the paper, declaring its solidarity with labor and its intention of fighting social injustice, was not, by Maurin's standards, a personalist newspaper. He might have said that the first edition of the *Catholic Worker*, by its appeal to a class, had something of the tone of its communist counterpart, the *Daily Worker*. So he had gone back to the boys' camp at Mt. Tremper.

Returning in mid-May, he walked into Dorothy's kitchen as if he had never been away. There he took some papers from his pocket and began to discourse on a "point" of economics. Overjoyed with his return, Dorothy made Maurin's essays the feature of the June issue and suggested that he become one of the editors of the paper.

When the *Worker* came out, it carried a brief statement by Maurin. He said that he did not want to be an editor, only a contributor. "I would rather definitely sign my own work," he said, because he felt that there could be things in the paper with which he would disagree. Then he outlined his "program for action," about which he otherwise talked and wrote under the heading of "Cult, Culture and Cultivation." "Cult" involved religion—the recognition of the

Catholic Church and what it taught, especially in the social encyclicals, as the ordering center of his idea. As one's faithful participation in the liturgy of the Church, "cult" should be the central, cohering action of daily life.

"Culture" was the medium in which this liturgically oriented life of the person would operate. The desired revolution of culture would occur when the spirit of "gentle personalism" took precedence over bourgeosity and class-struggle ideology. "We are interested in standards of loving and not in standards of living," he would sometimes say to Dorothy.

"Cultivation" was the instrumentality for bringing the new life into effect. People in crowded cities would re-establish themselves in "agronomic universities," or farm communes. Maurin believed that a fulfillment of the need for creative work was necessary to a complete humanism and that by going back to the land in agrarian cooperatives, by initiating the "green revolution," the inhuman effects of complex industrialization could be relieved. In a phrase he used many times, his agrarian commune would be a place where "the worker would become a scholar and the scholar would become a worker." It would be a place, as Dorothy explained, "where a man can develop his personality." In his *Worker* article, Maurin said that he knew his idea was "Utopian Christian communism," but that he was not afraid of the word *communism:* "I am not opposed to private property with responsibility. But those who own private property should never forget that it is a trust."

While Peter emphasized farm communes—a back-to-the-land movement—in his article, he also discussed briefly his idea of having "houses of hospitality" for the urban dispossessed and "round table discussions for the clarification of thought." On this latter point, he had an announcement. He had put a rental deposit on the Manhattan Lyceum at 66 East Fourth Street for a meeting on the last Sunday of June. "I have no more money now but I will beg the rest. I hope everyone will come to this meeting. I want Communists, radicals, priests and laity. I want everyone to set forth his views. I want clarification of thought."

Peter had his Sunday afternoon meeting and Dorothy managed to prod six people into going. Although he talked for three hours, it is questionable if anyone's thought was "clarified." Each of the six had his own clarification to advance. But Peter, knowing that clear heads and a vision were needed, had tried, and he would try for the rest of his days, for as long as his mind would work.

Meanwhile, the character of Dorothy's household had changed. Before the second issue came out, John and Tessa moved to Dobbs Ferry, where John had a job as editor of the town paper. Tamar had gone to spend the summer with Della. Peter, on the other hand, brought in more "friends." One was a "Mr. Minas," an Armenian poet whose whole family in Armenia had been slaughtered by the Turks, "and now he lived unknown in New York, tiny, huddled in a great coat most of the year." At the time, he was working on an "epic" poem. Once he lost it in the subway and, recounted Dorothy, "Margaret, the Lithuanian girl who came to cook for us, prayed it back for him, she said."

Another who came to remain was Steve Hergenham, "a vigorous forty-seven when Peter met him in Union Square. He was a carpenter, a skilled craftsman who wished also to be considered a scholar. He scorned the Worker emphasis on the 'works of mercy,' saying 'If man will not work neither let him eat.' No matter what help others might try to give him in repairing furniture, putting up shelves, or making benches, he repulsed their efforts, citing their lack of skill, and pointed proudly to the fact that he had done the work alone."

The third issue of the *Worker* came out for the months of June and July. With people there to help with the production and mailing of the paper, and with others like "Big Dan" Orr, a large Irishman who had come in off the streets, and a seminarian helping out for the summer to sell it, Dorothy had ten thousand copies printed. It was in this issue that Dorothy began the column she would write for almost fifty years. She first called it "Day After Day," then "Day by Day," and finally, in 1946, after a decade of groping for the right title, she settled on one that would stick: "On Pilgrimage."

"By this time," Dorothy said, "as people accumulated around us, we rented the store downstairs for an office, the store next door also, then a few more apartments down the street, and part of a dilapidated building on Jackson Square a few blocks away. These were the beginnings of our hospices."

Starting the paper had been Dorothy's business. Peter's business was to "indoctrinate" the people who were beginning to congregate at the Fifteenth Street apartment, its basement store adjunct, and the abandoned building over which Dorothy exercised domain. Since Peter, Mr. Minas, and Steve Hergenham had moved into the room that John and Tessa had occupied, it was eminently convenient for Peter to hold his "round table discussions" at any time he could find a group together, whether it was in the kitchen or in the backyard. "Clarification of thought went on apace. Our life was made up of discussions." Perhaps, said Dorothy, "there is too much small talk, too much hanging around, too many . . . people bantering, too much staying up late, but that is unavoidable. . . . As for the kind of talk one gets from Peter . . . there could never be too much of it."

There, in the backyard of the Fifteenth Street apartment, Peter would pull notes from his pocket and begin to "indoctrinate": "We read in the Catholic Encyclopedia that during the early ages of Christianity the hospice (or house of hospitality) was a shelter for the sick, the poor, the orphans, the old, the traveller and the needy of every kind. . . .

"The fourteenth statute of the so-called council of Carthage, held about 436, enjoins upon the Bishops to have hospices or houses of hospitality in connection with their churches.

"Today we need houses of hospitality as much as they needed them then. If not more so. We have parish houses for the priest, parish houses for educational purposes, parish houses for recreational purposes, but no parish houses of hospitality.

"Boussuet says that the poor are the first children of the Church, so the poor should come first. People with homes should have a room of hospitality so as to give shelter to the needy members of the parish. The remaining needy members of the parish should be given shelter in a parish home."

Later, in writing about Peter, Dorothy put his idea in her own words: "Every house should have a Christ's room. . . . It is no use turning people away to an agency, to the city or the state or the Catholic Charities. It is you yourself who must perform the works of mercy. Often you can only give the price of a meal, or a bed on the Bowery. Often you can only hope that it will be spent for that. Often you can literally take off a garment if it only be a scarf and warm some shivering brother. But *personally,* at a *personal sacrifice,* these were the ways, Peter used to insist, to combat the growing tendency on the part of the State to take the job which our Lord Himself gave us to do."

"We printed these essays," Dorothy said of Peter's writings on houses of hospitality, "and by mid-summer the *Catholic Worker* ceased to be just a newspaper but the voice of a movement." The Fifteenth Street apartment had become a house of hospitality for men. But this male predominance did not last for long. An unemployed young woman, having read Peter's essays, visited Dorothy and "demanded that we start such a house" for her—and "at once." So "that very afternoon," with money Dorothy begged from a friend, Mrs. Porter Chandler, "we rented our first apartment, moved in some beds and sheltered this one unemployed woman. Within a week we had a score of applicants at our doors. . . . Since then . . . we have had rooms for women. . . . We have never tried to think in terms of bigger houses, but have kept stressing the need for more and more shelters in Christian families as well as in parishes."

For the unemployed, it was a hard summer. "Every day there were evictions. People were dispossessed for non-payment of rent. In the morning the sheriff came, and with his helpers put all the furniture that had not already been sold out on the sidewalk. Sometimes people . . . sat on the broken-down chairs and begged, trying to get enough money to pay rent someplace else. Most of the time they slunk away, leaving their things there to be picked up by trash trucks and carted off and dumped."

Occasionally, said Dorothy, families who were being evicted came to her to get help in moving. "We borrowed a horse and wagon [driven by Dan Orr] and push cart and with the help of the neighborhood helped people move. We saw at first hand the actual destitution there was behind the closed doors all around us."

But Dorothy could tell of things less grim than evictions. Writing in the *Catholic Worker* of July/August, she said that all up and down the street "benches have been set out in front of houses and boys sit around tables on the sidewalks playing cards. Wagon loads of fragrant pineapples are passing by. The Italians in the neighborhood are making cherry brandy. All the babies are tanned brown and the benches in the square are crowded. Street cleaners flush streets and the children run screaming." She observed, too, that with people sitting on the sidewalk, radios were turned up. One of the hit songs that summer was "Annie Doesn't Live Here Anymore"—evicted, no doubt, the East Siders may well have thought.

When fall came, Dorothy believed that she had found her vocation. Twenty-thousand copies of the *Worker* were printed for the September issue. Granted that bundles were sent out pell-mell, the paper's growth was nonetheless phenomenal.

Why was this? Dorothy's energy and personality had something to do with it. She was thirty-six years old in November, 1933, and her health was probably better than it had been for some time. Weighing between 125 and 130 pounds—almost thin for her height—she had a rapid-striding energy and a prodigous capacity for work. Much of her work was writing, and in the summer of 1933, many people got a letter from her telling them about the *Catholic Worker* and what she and Maurin were trying to do. Would they please help? Yes, many of them would help.

But there was more to it than that. Dorothy had, as her mother had said, a "presence" about her, a controlled strength, unobtrusive but still a force. Without ever betraying the ordinary and usually unpleasant marks of assertiveness, she had a "take charge" approach to things, and such was her poise, intelligence, and acumen that people were convinced immediately of the honesty and integrity of this plain but well-spoken woman. She visited many parish priests to tell them about the venture she and her friends were undertaking. It would have been a pretty ho-hum-off-to-the-golf-course kind of cleric who refused to give her a hearing. That many priests and nuns listened and were impressed is indicated by the letters and offerings that came in to the Fifteenth Street apartment that year. The great majority of contributions came from those who were in religious life—a dollar bill or two, but sometimes just a quarter folded up in a piece of paper.

But Dorothy, the convincing and industrious saleswoman, was not by herself responsible for the mushrooming circulation of the *Worker*. Communism was a big issue in 1933, and its upsurge alarmed many. On September 12, 1932, fifty-three writers, artists, and composers had signed a statement affirming communism, a statement carried in some of the larger city newspapers. "We believe," it said, "that the only effective way to protest against the chaos, the appalling wastefulness, and the indescribable misery inherent in the present economic system is to vote for the Communist candidates." Then, in October, in the personal testimony tradition of the sawdust revival, a number of those who had signed this statement held a meeting at Cooper Union so that all might hear how the new converts had come into the light. Dorothy was there, not to testify, but to report the meeting for *America*. What interested her was the presence of some of her old friends, especially Malcolm Cowley.

The article came out on April 29, 1933, and she called it "The Diabolic Plot." It was "because of the Communist party's ideals, not because of its essential anti-religious aspect; because of its love of the ordinary man, and not because of its hatred towards God, that so many young people are being attracted towards Communism. And being attracted by what is good in their natures, and fervently embracing it as a cause, they come eventually to accept whole-heartedly all that the party teaches." So young idealists, drawn to the good that communism seemed to represent, were drawn also into atheism, and that was the diabolic plot.

This article could have done little to enhance Dorothy's status as an authority on communism, but it did add to her recognition as a former contributor to publications that were considered radical— a past history she stated in her article. Now that she was the editor of a socially crusading newspaper that proclaimed itself Catholic to the core, her paper acquired readers who thought of it, with its social concern, as the intelligent Catholic's answer to communism. As a Fordham Jesuit wrote to the *Worker,* "It is the best literary antidote I know against its mendacious namesake, the *Daily Worker.*" This viewpoint was reinforced by many letters to the paper in the first year of its publication.

Dorothy's attitude toward communism was anything but inflamed. Communism was a heresy, but, as she said in her *America* article, she regarded the communists she had known as good people. In their generosity and self-sacrifice in the cause of human values, they were unlike any other people she knew. In those early days of the *Worker,* she may have even thought that communists would be especially susceptible to the appeal of the paper. "We do a great deal of distributing at Communist meetings," she said in one of the early issues.

What of her communist friends? When she had first moved into the Fifteenth Street apartment, Mike Gold and his brother, George Granich, frequently visited her. But "after we began publishing the *Catholic Worker,* our communist friends left us. When religion was a private matter with me it was all right to come and pay a call. But when Peter and I became editors of a paper, we were enemies. After that first year, many friends fell away."

Interest in the issue of communism did not account for all of the paper's rapidly increasing circulation. The thirties was a decade —perhaps the last one for a while—that saw a good share of the world's population seeking and making commitments, wanting, as Dostoevsky's Inquisitor said, "to be together" in something. Idealism, no matter from what sources, human or subhuman, filled the spirits of youth and beckoned them to great adventure and trial. Catholic idealism had long since been muted with stodginess, and the Catholic press constituted a good part of that condition. It was a press that upheld the standard and frequently reactionary wisdom of the political rostrum and the marketplace, while faith was a matter of taking flight into an escapist imagery. Many Catholics in 1933 found little meaning in the saccharine effusions of much of the Catholic press. As Maurin frequently said, "The truth has to be restated every twenty years." The Catholic press was several centuries behind the times. During a period when positions were being affirmed and lines drawn, Dorothy and Peter placed the Church at the center of affairs and said that it was the only idea, the only institution, worthy of the most exalted reaches of idealism. Its potential for changing society was beyond anything of which the human mind could conceive.

It was the idea of a cause that, in the years ahead, drew young people to the Worker movement—young people who wanted to make their lives count in the service of the Church. Stanley Vishnewski was the first of these young idealists to come, and he remained the longest, dying at Maryhouse, the New York Catholic Worker house for women, at the age of sixty-three. Stanley's forebears were Lithuanian, peasants in the old country and factory workers in America. His name on his baptismal record was Visniauskas (a spelling that Dorothy sometimes used), but in a Brooklyn parish school, a nun had changed it to Vishnewski, a Polish version. Maybe the nun was Polish, but the name suited Stanley. In "Days of Action," his unpublished account of his life with the *Worker,* he said he liked the Poles, too.

As a high school student, Stanley seemed to have more than the ordinary amount of concern about what he was going to do with his life. He sometimes stopped in at a church to pray about it. And, inevitably, he sent off for material on religious vocations that he had seen advertised in the *Sacred Heart Messenger.* The material, he said, was so "lurid" that he decided he had no vocation. One piece, addressed to young women, urged as the advantage of a religious life the fact that they would never have to submit to a drunken husband. "I love the story," Stanley wrote, "of the young man who entered a strict religious order where the emphasis was placed upon mortification and complete custody of the eyes—where the new postulants, upon pain of expulsion, were forbidden to look up from the ground; their eyes were to be closed at all times. Imagine his consternation when the time came to take his vows and he discovered that all along he had been in a convent of women."

A far-fetched story, to be sure, but Stanley's humor was at times far-fetched. Over his years in the Worker movement, it would come sparkling through in the grimmest and most desperate situations, and it was his ability to recast what was dark into light absurdity that enabled him to endure—and, no doubt, helped others, too. When he began writing his memoirs, he said that "I could honestly call this book 'Life Among the Insane, The Troubled and The Perplexed.'" So might he have, this man who was the intelligent, completely normal embodiment of Maurin's "gentle personalism."

Stanley first learned of Dorothy Day and what she was doing while reading the *Brooklyn Tablet*. A news note said that Dorothy Day and Peter Maurin had started a paper to combat communism, so Stanley wrote a letter to Peter and Dorothy, asking if he could be a part of the new group. Dorothy answered yes, come when he could; they needed help putting out the paper. Shortly afterwards, Stanley, seventeen years old and weighing 110 pounds, walked across Brooklyn Bridge to the Fifteenth Street address. When he got there, he went down the stairs of the basement store, but could rouse nobody. "To pass away the time, while waiting for someone to come, I studied the window display. It consisted of a large tryptich cardboard on which two copies of the paper were pasted. It also gave a list of books to read: 'The Great Commandment' by the Apostolic Delegate; 'The Valerian Persecution' by Father Patrick Healy. I began jotting titles in my notebook: 'The Making of Europe' by Christopher Dawson; 'Nazareth and Social Chaos' by Father Vincent McNabb, O.P."

After an hour, one of the household, Margaret Polk, let Stanley in. That was the beginning. Years later, he would say that "I believe that it is impossible to be able to present in print the inner feeling of vitality and the spiritual forces that give depth and meaning to a Movement such as the Catholic Worker." He never got over what he felt was the glory of those first years; he never outlived the idealism of his youth.

It was fall, 1933. "A haze hangs over the city," Dorothy wrote in the November *Worker*. "Fogs rise from the river and the melancholy note of the river boat is heard at night." Surely, when she heard the sounds of the East River, after the noises of the day had faded, time was erased and her consciousness was touched with the sensation of reliving past moments. She was working in the *Call* office—she could smell again the dark-varnish mustiness of the room she had in the Episcopal rectory in the winter of 1916—she was lying in a bed in May, 1917, swept with the excitement of going to her first day's work at the *Masses*.

But surely, too, with the first cool day of fall, when the wind came from the north and cleared the city of the heat and smells of summer, she felt something of the hope and gladness that youth feels when summer ends. "It was just one year ago," she wrote in the December *Worker*, "that I spent the morning at the National Shrine of the Immaculate Conception in Washington.... We do not know how to get along. But we know that we are making progress."

Yes, "we" were making progress. She had made progress—a giant leap forward in comprehending Maurin's synthesis. It had put her on the high road; she had a direction, and the "progress" of which she spoke was that of having set out on the course. Things were in motion, and the "movement," as she chose to call it, was gathering momentum. "A spiritual revolution is upon us," she wrote in the December, 1933, issue of the *Worker*.

The next two years were filled with almost explosive activity. In the late fall of 1933, the Workers' School was inaugurated. Classes were held nightly on weekdays from eight o'clock until eleven. One of the early speakers was Paulist Father James Gillis, a well-known columnist for the Catholic press. Father Gillis received approving comment in the *Worker* for his comments on capitalism. The Church, he said, "does not stand or fall with Capitalism. She was here a long time before Capitalism and she intends to be—and will be—here when Capitalism is gone.... If Capitalism cannot or will not reform altogether, we shall have to take upon our lips words ... from Sacred Scripture, 'Why cumbereth it the ground? Cut it down and cast it into the fire!' "

When Gillis finished, his audience, sitting around in chairs and on the floor of the basement room, applauded vigorously. The *Worker* mentioned, almost breathlessly, that a young "communist" was one of an audience of fifteen or so and that, surprisingly, he was "a well-dressed, good-looking young fellow who might have passed for a Catholic college student."

Throughout 1934, people with prestigious names came to speak. Professors Carlton Hayes, Parker Moon, and Harry Carmen of Columbia ventured down to Fifteenth Street and gave their wisdom to the street people and students who had found a home at the Worker houses. Distinguished Jesuits came: John La Farge, Gerard Donnelly, and Wilfred Parsons, the latter two of the *Amer-*

ica staff. Paulist Father Joseph McSorley came to give a talk, but on occasion he came just to visit. There were, said Dorothy, "many other priests and laymen of renown" who "gave generously of their time and work."

The *Worker* made distinguished friends that year. Hilaire Belloc, the English poet, biographer, and essayist, visited Fifteenth Street. Jacques Maritain, regarded by Catholics, in 1934, as the peerless philosopher, came also. In November, Dorothy had received a letter from H. L. Binnse, Executive Secretary of the Liturgical Arts Society. Binnse was writing for the philosopher who "particularly asked us to arrange a visit at the 'Catholic Worker' headquarters this Friday, when he will be back in New York. We shall appear on the scene about 10:30 in the morning, and I think he could stay for about an hour." Maritain did appear, and no doubt Peter glowed with joy over the presence of his distinguished fellow countryman whose social ideas were so like his own. When Maritain and Mrs. Maritain left for France, Margaret Stasarvage, the Lithuanian girl who helped cook, and who otherwise, as she claimed, once prayed lost items into reappearance, gave him a box of homemade fudge to take on the boat to his wife "as a little going away present."

Several weeks later, Maritain wrote to Peter: "Tell Dorothy Day . . . how very happy I was to visit her, and how touched at the reception given me by your friends. I wish I could have said all that was in my heart—never was I more vexed by my inability to speak fluent English. It seemed as if I had found again in The Catholic Worker a little of the atmosphere of Péguy's office in the Rue de la Sorbonne. And so much good will, such courage, such generosity. . . ."

The paper that year continued its explosive increase in circulation, reaching sixty thousand by December, 1934. At a time when the Catholic press scarcely mentioned the subject, the *Worker* carried editorials on the injustice of racism. The 1933 Scottsboro trial, in which nine Alabama blacks were charged with rape and stood in jeopardy of execution, if not lynching, elicited concern from the *Worker*. Both "the poor whites and the poor blacks" were "victims of the industrialists who grind the faces of the poor." This sentiment, of course, did not square with Maurin's position that Workers should be "announcers" and not "denouncers," but then it would be quite a while before Dorothy managed to curb her tendency to lapse into denunciations of "capitalists," "the rich," and "oppressors" of the poor. "The bottle always smells of the liquor it once held," she would say in her defense.

On May 15, Dorothy wrote a letter to editor Scanlan of the *Brooklyn Tablet*. Would he please publish "this plea for a large attendance" at a "Cathloic Interracial Mass Meeting" to be held under the auspices of the "Laymen's Union," the "first to be held in the East"? Father James Gillis was to be the main speaker, and, said Dorothy, "We know that negroes in large numbers will be there.... Let us hope that white Catholics will attend the meeting in large numbers.... Let nothing stand in the way!"

Lest the urgency of the matter be minimized, Dorothy said that it just so happened that she was at that very moment "glancing at one of the pamphlets" of the communists and that "two statements catch my eye." First, the "negro question is for our party," said the communist statement, "a question of fundamental principle [sic] importance," and, second, that "the party cannot become ... a Bolshevik party, unless it wins masses of negroes."

"Our paper, the *Catholic Worker*," said Dorothy, "is for both negro and white." Scanlan printed Dorothy's letter in his May 19 issue of the *Tablet*. It is unlikely that many of the readers trekked to the meeting across the Brooklyn Bridge. Still, the meeting must have produced something positive, for it was at this time that the Workers opened a house in Harlem. Peter and some of his friends would staff it.

Several days after this Harlem storefront was opened, Father La Farge, then one of the most vocal members of the Catholic clergy in the cause of justice for blacks, went up to Harlem one evening to visit Peter. Since there was no money for electricity, or even candles, Peter sat there in the dark. Father La Farge said that "all he could see in the ... gloom was Peter's forefinger motioning in the air as he was making points." Where blacks and their hope for a better day were concerned, Peter felt that their own spiritual tradition held the answer. Pursuing the bourgeois goals, so prominent in white culture, would only compound their slavery.

The *Catholic Worker* had another running theme that summer. Occasionally it would carry statements critical of the proscription of religious freedom in Mexico. Dorothy probably felt a little ill at ease at giving this subject prominence in the paper. But it was a popular one in the Catholic press, and some of the young Workers wanted it aired in their paper.

At the urging of one young Worker, Tom Coddington, Dorothy planned a demonstration to picket the Mexican consulate in December. Invited to participate were the female students of Cathedral High School. A number at the school volunteered, and so Sister Bernadette, a Sister of Charity, met with the group and asked that someone report to the senior class what had happened in this significant demonstration of "Catholic Action." Everyone seemed reluctant to take on the chore, but finally a dark-haired senior raised her hand. It was Julia Porcelli, another of the ardent spirits who joined the Worker movement in its early days and who made a noteworthy contribution to its development in the years before World War II.

Julia took the reporting job because she knew that some of the Worker people were going to be in the demonstration and she wanted to see them firsthand. "I was fascinated," said Julia, "with the people and the stories of how they lived and how they worked, the works of mercy, and . . . the meals they had so that the people at the *Catholic Worker* were very real."

Once the matter of getting a reporter had been settled, Sister Bernadette briefed the group on whom they might expect to see. Especially, the Cathedral High demonstrators should look for Peter Maurin, who could be recognized, Sister said, by his "broad shoulders and long arms" and his "magnificent head."

The next day, December 13, the students from Cathedral, carrying their school bags, assembled at 34th Street. There were students from other schools, too, and even some shoppers joined the group. In fact, so many people came that they could not just picket in front of the Mexican consulate. "We had to march all around 34th Street, 7th Avenue, Broadway," narrated Miss Porcelli. "Anyway it was a tremendous block that we had to circle completely." The marchers grew so numerous and the route so long that Julia, walking apprehensively in line, never knew when she passed the Mexican consulate. "We were so taken up with what we had to do and the courage it took to do this, so we marched up and down and little by little I could identify various Catholic Worker people. Then to keep our courage up we burst into song; you know this is a way of relieving tension." The song was "Father Lloyd's Catholic Action song," and, commented Miss Porcelli, "I never hear that song that I don't think of that picket line in 1934. And we sang it strong and brave and true."

Being the reporter, Julia felt she ought to concentrate more on identifying her Worker heroes than on the singing. "I saw Stanley [Vishnewski] and I recognized him because he was a young boy and they described him in the paper." When the line became less compact, she "got behind various people" looking for Dorothy. When she saw her, "I remember being disappointed in the way she looked, not so much her face, but the fact that she walked stooped over and she had sort of a cloth tweedish kind of coat, but it was very unstylish . . . very unattractive. I saw her face from profile and different views and she seemed very attractive." And as she watched Dorothy walk, Julia was struck by her "lovely stride."

Then the young reporter from Cathedral High got behind Maurin, "praying" that he would "just turn around and look a little bit pleasant." Finally, "he did turn around and he had this kind, friendly, fatherly, gentle look." Now feeling at ease, Julia told him that she wanted to talk to him for her report the next day. To her complete surprise, Peter asked, "What can you do?" "He explained that there was a store in Harlem . . . and that they had some children's classes," and that Julia could come and tell stories to the children.

It was several months before she went to the Harlem Worker house. Then, because she had trouble finding the address—2070 7th Avenue—it was late afternoon, almost dark, when she got there. "I remember coming into the store," narrated Miss Porcelli. "There was no electricity . . . and I don't think they had the kerosene lamp on." A man was sitting there, but rather than approach him or say anything, she decided she had better leave. She told herself that she ought "to get back and tell my mother where I was and what I'd been doing. I hadn't told her where I was going, just on a errand or something."

However, Julia mustered her courage and spoke to the man. It was Steve Hergenham, the German that Peter had met in Union Square. Later, Hergenham told Julia that he had "never seen anyone look so scared in his whole life." Julia thought that it was her fright "that brought out a great courtesy in him and a great gentleness that no one else seemed to bring out." He told Julia that he was holding classes for Negro children and that if she would come on Saturday morning, he would have a group there. She could tell them stories and read to them. "So that was that and I went home, gathered a few stories and returned the following Saturday morning."

Julia's story-telling was very successful, and on succeeding Saturdays a growing number of children came to the storefront. Sewing instruction was added to story-telling and "the girls brought their dolls and we made dolls' dresses and we had a lot of fun," even putting on "a little exhibit on the shelves." Hergenham was so impressed that he suggested Julia write her experiences for the *Worker*. So Julia wrote her story for "The Children's Corner."

Julia had not yet met Dorothy. One Saturday morning—it was March 3—Dorothy came to the Harlem storefront bringing Tamar and another young woman, Ade Bethune, with her. As it was Tamar's eighth birthday, Tamar and all the children would have a party for which Dorothy and Julia went to a store and got cookies and ice cream. After the party, Dorothy suggested to Julia that she come down to the Worker house and become a permanent member of the household. "All right," said Julia.

Why did she agree so readily? Because "as a child ... I didn't see many people living by faith, and I guess I was very hungry for things of the spirit and when I read the *Catholic Worker* I guess I felt, well, these were Catholic people, they were doing something for their neighbor. ... I instinctively felt, as a little old Italian lady told me down in Mott Street, God has all the grace but He wants you to use your hands, your feet, your time and your brain, and this is what Catholic Action is."

At first, Julia went occasionally to Fifteenth Street to help out during the day, because at night her mother wanted her home and accounted for. Her work, which she did because none of the boys would do it, was washing dishes. By this time, there were more young men there: Bill Callahan, Eddie Priest, Jim Montague, and Joe Zarella. Julia remembered that they all started growing beards and that they did not wash often. "They wanted to be free from the bourgeois things they had to do at home."

It was not until 1936 that Julia felt she could live at the Worker house without offending her mother's sense of propriety. She was twenty-two then, and she knew that "these were people I wanted to be with. There was unity, there was brotherhood, there was family, and I felt very strongly that they were my own family." Years later, Dorothy recalled the joyous excitement of those days, "that early zeal, that early romance, that early companionableness. How strongly they felt it. ... It is a permanent revolution, this Catholic Worker movement."

In March, 1935, the *Worker* moved to 144 Charles Street. The priests at Saint Veronica's parish "came across the house and helped us to secure it for less rent than we had been paying for our two stores on the other side of town. Now we had four floors, three of them for offices, meeting rooms, dining quarters, and the top floor for the House of Hospitality." The principal difficulty with the house was that it had never been wired for electricity, and for two months, illumination was provided by candles and kerosene lamps.

In the March issue of the *Worker,* Dorothy announced that a new Worker enterprise was in the making, and that with spring, the Catholic Worker was going to make a "heroic effort" in another direction. "We wish to open . . . a farm and school combined, where scholars can be workers and workers scholars. There are about a dozen who can move right in and start digging and making cold frames. We have no money for this venture. We are looking for a place of about a dozen acres, preferably on Staten Island."

This, the first of the Catholic Worker "agronomic universities," was conceived in the winter of 1935 when the cold and dreariness of winter made the initiation of such a project appear the height of appropriateness. But, like all of the Catholic Worker farm ventures, it was conceived and executed in such a slap-dash fashion that the wonder is that they lasted for more than a week. Dorothy knew nothing of farming, nor did any of the young people, although they were, of course, enthusiastic over the prospect of country living. Peter liked hard work and did more than his share, but he was no practical planner, and he was careful to let Dorothy and everyone else know that his role was to "enunciate the principles." Actually, the agrarian "commune" of 1935 was more successful than those that would, over the next thirty years, succeed it. But the success of the 1935 "garden commune," as it was called, was due to the youthful energy and common idealism of those who participated in the venture. It worked because it was not the "dozen" acres that Dorothy wanted, but one acre. Also, the rainfall that summer was ample.

Naturally, Dorothy had wanted their summer commune on Staten Island. Her cottage, which she apparently still owned and rented out, was there, and there, too, were her memories. Besides, she liked to ride on the Staten Island ferry. "Soon we rented a twelve-room house with a big attic in Huguenot, . . . right on the water." A wide porch ran all around the old-fashioned structure, which sat atop a little knoll that overlooked Raritan Bay. A thick wood stood on one side of the place and behind it was an almost limitless open space, which today is Wolfe Pond Park.

Steve Hergenham, as if he were writing an introduction to a "scholarly article" at the University of Berlin, stated the Worker objective in starting the garden commune: "to humanize large hordes of slum-dwellers . . . to restore to them their natural heritage—the gift and the opportunity to use their hands as well as their heads and hearts, their ingenuity and love to work to build, produce and create. A lop-sided money economy tends to rob them of the most sublime instincts; and it is the renascence of a rural economy, upon which we may hope to sink our foundation for a more rational and better social order."

Hergenham certainly did his part, lugging "hundreds of boxes of topsoil from the woods to enrich the carefully prepared beds."

Another who did his part, and more, was "a black-haired, black-eyed Jew" named Edelson. He "wandered into our office after he heard me speak at a meeting on the east side. He sat in the middle of the office declaiming the psalms in Hebrew and then sat down to supper with us. . . . Begging a nickel for the Staten Island ferry, he walked the distance from Fifteenth Street to the ferry and from the ferry to Huguenot." He "gave" his summer to the *Worker*, he said, "for the sake of communism, a Holy Communism, comradeship, cooperation, brotherhood, unity. . . . At times he declaimed mournfully how all the troubles of the world were his own fault, his failure. Wars had come about because of him, because of his sins, and he was another Cain who had killed his brother."

Dorothy "loved him, this Edelson, and it was one of the first tragedies" of the garden commune that one of the young men who accounted himself a Worker, but who did not stay long afterwards, "looked at him coldly calling him a madman." Eventually, this young Worker who professed efficiency "ran him off the place, frightening him by threatening to have him locked up. We have never seen him since."

Speakers came to the garden commune that summer to help Maurin "clarify" the thinking of the worker-scholars, some of whom preferred arguing under the shade of a tree rather than hoeing in the sun. Father Paul Hanley Furfey, sociologist from Catholic University, was a frequent visitor that summer, and there were professors from Columbia and other universities who came, exchanging a lecture for several days at the seashore, which in those depressed times was as good as one could do in the way of a summer vacation.

The young Worker who outdid herself was Julia Porcelli. Most of her work continued to be with children—the children to whom she had told stories at the Harlem house the previous winter.

Years later Dorothy wrote a tribute to Julia, who by then had become Julia Porcelli Moran. "Just this morning," wrote Dorothy, "I have been reading St. Teresa's autobiography in which she says, 'Let us then always endeavor to consider the virtues and good qualities which we perceive in others and to conceal their defects by the consideration of our own great sins. This is the kind of work which, though we cannot perform with perfection in a short time, yet we may gain great virtue thereby; and this consists in esteeming all others better than ourselves.' ✔ Perhaps Dorothy did esteem "all others" better than herself, but there was one, at least, she wanted to mention. She often thought "of the steady thoughtfulness of one young Italian girl who over the space of eight years took care of a growing family of orphans, bringing them clothes, extra food, presents for holidays," and who, otherwise, "worked hard enough, God knows, the rest of the year."

There was more picketing that summer. Some of the young men picketed the German consulate because of Nazi anti-Semitism, and then, when the German liner *Bremen* came in, they went to the docks to hand out literature protesting Nazi policies. With them was a pretty young girl from Milwaukee, Nina Polcyn. A student at Marquette University, she began reading the *Worker* at the urging of Father Franklin Kennedy, editor of the *Catholic Herald Citizen,* and her journalism professor, Jeremiah O'Sullivan. Nina went to Charles Street for a visit and was there for the *Bremen* affair. Years later, she recalled the riot that occurred when some communists, "who called themselves Catholic Workers," tore down the swastika from the ship. Some of the Worker people were arrested, including Dorothy, but Nina said she had been too timorous to get involved in the fray.

What Dorothy chose to remember of the occasion was Maurin's conduct. "I remember Peter when we picketed the German embassy down at the Battery, picking up the leaflets we were handing out which had been strewn around. He was obeying authority. He thought of authority and laws in relation to ... the common good." As to the picketing itself, he evidently approved of it, since he had picketed the Mexican consulate and the German consulate. His picketing of the Mexican consulate, however, may have been a deference to Dorothy. He never seems to have concerned himself at all about religious persecution in Mexico. "The great danger of the present day is Fascism," he said. It was a subject about which he talked much during these years.

In 1935, the circulation of the *Catholic Worker* made its greatest advance. "Our May Day circulation is 110,000," exulted the paper's headline in the May issue. That was the number printed, but whether or not all copies were circulated is another question. Bundles were sent off to schools and parishes—to anyone, in fact, for whom the Workers had an address and whose name, fancied or real, seemed to suggest potential readership. The paper, meanwhile, was taking on a better appearance. A young artist named Ade Bethune, another Cathedral High graduate, had begun to do drawings for the paper. Her work first appeared in the March, 1934 issue, with a picture of St. Joseph standing at a sawing table. Miss Bethune's art work would distinguish the paper for a decade.

Selling the paper on the streets accounted for some of the increase in circulation. This, in Dorothy's view, was a vital part of the Worker apostolate, something she emphasized throughout her life. "Yes," she noted some years later when it appeared that the early zeal of street-selling was flagging, "let us get out into Union Square, along Forty-second Street, in front of Madison Square Garden and distribute and sell the *Catholic Worker*. We have been doing that for many years, but we need to do much more of it. As the older ones get tired . . . let the younger students and workers take over the job of being fools for Christ." It was the man in the street, she said, who needed to be reached.

There was a mystique around a salesman of the *Worker* in the thirties: he or she was a front-line warrior, a person of ready wit and nimble feet. Running was sometimes necessary, for in the thirties, Worker salesmen were occasionally set upon by anti-Semites.

There was aggressive selling. Dorothy remembered one rainy night when she and some of her Worker friends were going to a meeting and there, standing in the downpour, was a seminarian selling the *Worker*, shouting "Read the *Catholic Worker*—the only thing that isn't all wet!" Big Dan Orr would follow communist salesmen who would shout, "Read the *Daily Worker!*" and Dan would respond, "Read the *Catholic Worker* daily!" Julia Porcelli recalled how they would stand half a block apart when they were trying to sell the *Worker*. "A person would hear you calling and then the second person they saw they would think about it and usually they bought from the third and vice-versa." Big Dan, though, liked to work alone. Forty-second Street was his beat.

The sense of community that came from selling the paper and feeding the poor was not unusual among those at Charles Street. Over the history of the Worker movement, there were occasions when concerted attempts to change its character were made by the people who were a part of it. In 1935, Tom Coddington made such an attempt. Apparently a person of a willful disposition, possessed of an invincible conviction that his point of view should prevail, he wanted to change the emphasis of the Worker movement from its primary objective of feeding and sheltering the poor to an organized and sociological approach to the plight of the poor. And he wanted Workers to have a more visible and active participation in social matters, such as the picketing of the Mexican consulate and the German ship *Bremen*. But more than this, he wanted organization in the Worker movement. He thought that there ought to be a paid, professional staff to handle matters and that the "unworthy" poor should have no claim on Worker hospitality.

There was much discussion about these issues, and for a while, the talk became so heated that Maurin thought "it would be better to walk out and leave the work to the dissenters rather than continue the argument." Peter, Dorothy said, "never ceased to reiterate that the way to reach the people was by the works of mercy carried on at a personal sacrifice. And he never ceased to hold forth against social worker schools, and techniques."

Part, and perhaps much, of the problem was Dorothy. Joe Zarella, in recalling this time, said that the very force of her personality had caused resentment in Coddington and the two or three individuals who supported him. Dorothy, said Zarella, was "dynamic" and "most attractive." But the agitators said that she was "domineering—never appointed anyone to have real authority."

It was true, though the authoritarian character of the Worker movement, while not set down in a "rule," was implicit in Dorothy's personality. Anyone who went to the Worker house as a part of its community understood it that way. And yet, over the years, there were many who went to the Worker house with visions of their own, only to find themselves in time running athwart Dorothy's principles. They were persons who frequently were themselves "wounded," each of whom had his or her own "truth." They would have preferred a mellower and milder Dorothy Day who could relax standards and give way to errant feelings. They would have had her less harsh and more "loving," one who could recognize that the "times" had their own laws and that these laws could supersede the "antiquated" laws of the Church.

But Dorothy had a "truth," too, and she did not think that her sense of the order and rightness of things was subject to the democratic process. She might have quoted Maurin: "I do not believe in majority rule. I do not believe in having meetings and elections. Then there would be confusion ... confounded with lobbying, electioneering and people divided into factions." As Dorothy thought about the matter, a community should be one of various authorities. "A baker would have charge of the bakery, the shoemaker of the shoes, the farmer of the fields, the carpenter of building."

But "what if the baker makes white bread? What if the carpenter refused to use the materials God sends in the way of logs or second-hand lumber, and will not work except with the best and most expensive, and according to government specifications?" Their authority then becomes invalid; "they are not educated to be leaders. The work of education comes first. . . . We must build up leaders. And the leaders must first of all change themselves." They must understand and live in conformity with the truths of spirit— of the Church. "And the job is so hard, so gigantic in this our day of chaos, that there is only one motive that can make it possible for us to live in hope—that motive, love of God. . . . And if we do not live in love we are dead indeed, and there is no life in us."

So Dorothy had been taught by Peter and, in her view, he was a truthful teacher; he truly saw how things were. Peter had said that the poor were first, whether they were "worthy" or "unworthy." That was her position. So the unworthy poor and the dirt and the poor organization remained, and the dissidents left. This kind of resolution of a problem, however, did not leave Dorothy exulting over the triumph of the truth over error. In her mind, someone had failed in setting a right example; someone had failed in teaching. "Meanwhile," she said, "we learn by our mistakes. We learn the hard way."

Dorothy was an authoritarian in her domain, but she accepted the authority of the Church, too much so, her liberal critics sometimes thought. This acceptance of authority was not only a personal disposition, it also was a principle governing the Worker movement. Obviously, a paper that departed from conventional middle-class affirmations as radically as did the *Catholic Worker,* prompted negative reaction in the form of critical letters. Some of these letters were directed to Dorothy and the *Worker,* but many also went to the office of the New York Catholic Archdiocese. The Chancery, unaccustomed to such mail, seemed unsure as to what action it should take. Finally, Monsignor Joseph A. Scanlan of the diocesan office "dropped in to pay us a call," Dorothy later wrote to a priest friend about the matter, "and said that he was asking the Cardinal [Patrick Hayes] to appoint a priest as our official spiritual adviser. . . . He thought that would be a good way to help us in our work. He further said that they would give the imprimatur if we did not think it would hinder us." Father Scanlan then asked Dorothy to suggest for the position a candidate whom she knew and who would be sympathetic with the work. So it was that Father Joseph McSorley, Dorothy's spiritual adviser, became the paper's nominal ecclesiastical censor. As a result, wrote Stanley Vishnewski, "whenever a problem arose at the *Catholic Worker* that had to do with faith or morals Dorothy would rush up to the Paulist Rectory at 59th Street and consult with Father McSorley."

McSorley was not an especially zealous overseer of what went into the *Worker.* "Indeed he seldom reads the paper," Dorothy wrote to a friend. "He was approved by the Cardinal as a spiritual director, that is all. But I am very sorry to say that again and again I go against his advice and use my own judgment. But we are on perfectly friendly terms, and he is the best confessor I have ever had. I would go to him with every personal problem and do exactly as he tells me. I obey of course. But he has never tried to direct the course of the paper in the confessional."

Occasionally, in the first decade of the *Worker's* history, Dorothy was summoned to the Chancery office, and initially it was Monsignor [later Cardinal] Francis McIntyre who saw her. She described her visits to Monsignor McIntyre in *Jubilee* magazine. "I would get a letter reading, 'Dear Dorothy, if you happen to be in the neighborhood of Fiftieth Street . . .' but I took care to go at once. Monsignor McIntyre would greet me in a most friendly fashion," and then he would summon an assistant who brought in a "big pile of letters" that were complaints he had received about the *Worker.* But "there was never any comment," only "a few friendly inquiries about the work." Later, during World War II, when Dorothy's pacifism caused an almost hysterical denunciation of her in some quarters, "Bishop McIntyre merely commented, . . . 'We never studied these things much in the seminary.'"

In 1934, the *Catholic Worker* was an explosive force in a universe which, to most middle-class Americans, seemed settled, and it is no wonder that many people, laymen and clergy, felt that Dorothy Day had been made mad by an excess of utopian romanticism or was a communist in disguise. "God give us patience," one priest wrote to her, to endure her insanity until "effective police action is taken against a publication like the *Catholic Worker* which boasts of and encourages the way of life of loafers, draft-dodgers, traitors to their country and sensational publicity-hungry psychotics."

But there were many priests and nuns who welcomed the *Catholic Worker* and the personality of Dorothy Day into their lives as heralds of a new time for the Church. One priest was the distinguished Benedictine liturgist, Virgil Michel. What Dorothy, Peter, and their friends were saying and doing was what Michel wanted to do in the liturgical movement. He worked, as Professor David O'Brien has written, to bring Catholics "back into participation in the liturgy" and make them recognize that "their responsibilities for the spiritual welfare of the Mystical Body were important steps in overcoming the strictly juridical view of the Church which had been dominant since the Reformation" and which "had reduced the laity to a passive role in Catholic life."

Father Virgil visited the *Worker* several times in 1934 and 1935. And, in September of this latter year, Dorothy, while visiting friends of the *Worker,* made a tour that took her to Cleveland, Chicago, St. Paul, and then to St. John's College, where Father Michel edited *Orate Fratres.* As Michel stoutly defended Dorothy and the *Worker* against its critics in that early era, Dorothy strongly approved of Michel's scholarly work.

"The fall months have been hard ones," Dorothy wrote in her journal, "but hardest of all for Mr. and Mrs. Johnson, who have had charge of the garden commune all summer and will be there all winter." Mary and Steve Johnson, she wrote, had had a difficult time during the summer, what with "their hosts of children, scores of young workers and students and all the visitors, over-running the place for weekends." But with the coming of fall, they had "even heavier responsibilities." In the summer, "we were dealing with healthy, normal young people. In the fall there was not only one but half a dozen sick, mentally and physically, suddenly on hand to be cared for." The garden commune had become a "household of sad afflicted creatures."

All of this meant an increase of care and work for the Johnsons.

"And then Joe Bennett came ... to die." Bennett had gone South with Father Harold Purcell to help with the building of Purcell's model community for blacks at Montgomery, Alabama. But "when he became critically ill, the priest with whom he was working brought him North and put him on Welfare Island. Joe got in touch with us and begged to be allowed to go down to the country."

He went to Huguenot, knowing that he was dying. "He did not want to die and he knew that only a miracle could save him. He prayed frantically, almost rebelliously, for a miracle." When Dorothy went to see him, he would moan, "How can God be good to let me suffer like this? He must heal me. I don't want to die."

Mrs. Johnson did her best. She nursed him with great tenderness, fixed special things for him to eat, and got a radio to put by his bed. "Outside the trees were turning red and gold. There was the sound of waves crashing on the beach in the fall storms. It was too unbearably beautiful, he cried." He could not leave it.

One day when only Mrs. Johnson was there, Bennett took a turn for the worse. He became delirious and began to beat his head against the radiator. Father McKenna, the Marist who had been so kind to Dorothy and Tamar in the fall of 1929, was sent for. He arranged to have Bennett put into a small private hospital nearby. Bennett died there a few days later.

Dorothy went to see him the morning of the day before he died. "He lay there semi-conscious, no longer suffering, no longer rebellious. He had received the last rites and once when he opened his eyes clearly for a moment, he said good-bye. I kissed him as I left."

After the funeral, Dorothy felt a great weight of guilt "because I was not there with him, because he was alone in the hospital, and not with his friends those last terrible moments when the soul is leaving the body. We must be alone when we die, that I know, but I do know too that I would like to have friends beside me to hold my hand, to make me feel the strength of their prayers, their strong happy prayers that would see where I could not see, the peace and light of the world to come."

But she had not been there and "Joe died alone, and he was the first one to help me that May Day we started the *Catholic Worker*. There will never a day pass but that I remember him in my prayers, and I pray he remembers us now. And I ask you who read this to pray that he has found refreshment, joy and peace."

For Dorothy, the year ended peacefully. With Christmas approaching, she went to Staten Island to bring Tamar to Charles Street for the holidays. Tamar, Dorothy had felt, would be much better off in the country with the Johnsons than in the city, where home life was nearly impossible. The ferry ride to the island was always a time of peace for Dorothy, and she took it as her moment of respite from the affairs of the Worker house. She wrote of her ride, of watching the gulls that "stood out white against the grey sky. They swept and glided, swooping down into the water now and then after a fish. Their cries and the sound of the water as the boat churned through it were the only sounds in the winter stillness." And then, when she reached the Johnson house, "there was the walk with Tamar, up the country road, past a thicket of birches with the blue-green twilight sky behind them." What was lovelier, she asked, than "the pure bare outline of trees in winter? I have always loved them and the heavy, shadowed sky beyond, tinged with purple."

On Christmas day, Dorothy and some others in the house took bundles of the *Worker* to the Municipal Lodging House at South Ferry, where twelve thousand men were being fed their Christmas dinner. Then they returned to Charles Street and their own dinner, provided by the Sisters and students of Cathedral High School. On Saturday afternoon, Dorothy indulged herself, as was her custom on Saturday afternoons, by listening to the Metropolitan Opera broadcast. The opera that afternoon was Wagner's *Götterdämmerung*, her favorite.

✥ 11

Spreading Personalism

"THE TROUBLE with Peter's teaching," Dorothy said on several occasions, was that it was "too simple." It was so simple that in his avoidance of abstruse theorizing and the use of technical jargon some people decided that he was a simpleton. One time—it was in the 1930s—Dorothy, or somebody, got Peter to appear on a radio program. What was his solution to the unemployment problem? It took Peter less than a half a minute, French accent and all, to give his answer: "Feed the hungry for Christ's sake, clothe the naked for Christ's sake, as the first Christians used to do, which made the pagans say about the Christians, 'See how they love one another.' "

In January, 1936, Dorothy and her fellow Workers had, for three years, been trying to hold this position. If her attachment to the poor had been a form of romantic extravagance, the romance would long since have died; if it had been a sign of a pathology in her own character, there would have been marks of it in her behavior. But in a kind of exegesis on Peter's personalist position, written out of her experience and thinking over the first years of the Worker movement, she affirmed this position as the only answer to the chaos into which the world seemed to be heading.

"Of course," she wrote in one of her manuscript reflections on Maurin, "as Pope Pius XI has pointed out, in times of crisis the state must intervene for the common good. In times of depression, in times of national catastrophe, the state had the duty to take care of the homeless, the poverty stricken. But even in those times, it is to be understood that all Christians, all men of goodwill, do their share first, in order to relieve the state of much of the burden. It is only after we have used all our own resources that we should call upon the state. It is only when our own insurance, our bank savings, our families, our own church can no longer care for us that we should look to the state."

Yes, she knew the argument of those who lived comfortably and who did not want to be bothered with the poor. A "natural pride, a 'praiseworthy' pride" that the worthy poor certainly possessed, so the comfortable would argue, made it much preferable that they receive their help from the state, rather than undergo the indignity of having to receive "charity" from individuals. After all, she knew the comfortable would say, we deserve exemption from bearing the burden of charity. "We have it coming to us. We pay taxes. It is our right." So forget feeding the hungry. "Away with it. Crucify it. Away with Charity. We will have none of it. We don't want to be the 'least of these,' Christ's children. We do not want to share His poverty. 'He had no place to lay his head. The birds of the air have their nests and the fox his hole, but the Son of Man has no place to lay His head.' We are not of His company. We do not know the Man. We deny Him, once, twice, thrice, and we have got the habit, and go on denying Him."

Dorothy enlarged on this synchronized recitation of middle-class impatience with Christ. "Surely Christ did not mean all that, and we are not to take Him literally. No, if anyone insults me, I'll let him have it. If anyone spits at me, I'll knock him down. If anyone encroaches on my rights, I will stick up for them. After all, it is my family, my home, my country. You cannot take these things literally. This is the time for the more militant virtues."

She continued on, observing that "one of our friends who was irked by our statements in the *Catholic Worker* on Caesarism and personalism, kept referring to Uncle Sam.... There was talk of farming communities, and jobs and land distribution ... and he kept saying staunchly, 'Uncle Sam will take care of it.'" And, "this attitude has been growing for some time now so steadily and imperceptibly that the state has taken over one function after another, in addition to the function of charity. 'We have no King but Caesar.'"

It was the brutal impersonality of the care of the poor by the state that inflamed Dorothy's sense of the inhumanity of it. Once she took Mary Sheean to a public clinic. Mary, who had remained at the Worker after having her baby, was ill with acute arthritis. As Dorothy observed, people sat around for hours waiting for some weary and petulant functionary to fill out forms. Among the questions asked were some quite personal ones, and Dorothy could see embarrassed petitioners shielding their answers with cupped hands so that others could not hear. "Sometimes the poor are called cases or clients," she wrote. "One social worker wanted to know what our caseload was."

"How long do you let your people stay?" another social worker wanted to know. "And our answer is 'since there are no jobs, we let them stay forever. They live with us, they die with us and we give them a Christian burial. We pray for them after they are dead. Once they are taken in, they become members of the family. Or rather they were always members of our family. They are our brothers and sisters in Christ.' "

Once she was called to the psychopathic ward at Bellevue Hospital "in order to get one of our women out. She had been attacked on the street, on her way home late one evening, and when she complained hysterically to a policeman, she was committed to the psychopathic ward. The police admitted evidences of such an attack; nevertheless she found herself in this mental ward for examination and was accused of having a persecution complex.

" 'What interest is it of yours?' the doctor asked me. 'She is not a relative. You have no responsibility in the matter. I should think you'd be glad the State is taking care of her.'

"But we had known her for some years. We felt capable of taking care of her until she was able to take care of herself. We assured him of this and told him moreover that she was our sister according to Christian teaching.

"The doctor looked at me sadly; 'Do you know that religious mania is the most dangerous kind?' "

And indeed Dorothy *did* know that "religious mania" was the "most dangerous kind." Some manias—building up portfolios of stocks, acquiring power to order the lives of others—cause no alarm, are not only accepted as legitimate means of achieving bourgeois goals but are loudly applauded in those most possessed by them. But to try to practice the love for others Christ enjoined on those who would follow *him*—*that* was dangerous. *That* was mad. "Yes," she said. "It is no easy thing to ask. It is no light burden to place on others, this burden of Christianity. But we are not the ones who place this burden on others. It is placed there by Christ who said, 'Take up your cross and follow Me.' And that cross is our brother. . . . It is easy to love one's friends, those who are naturally lovable, those from whom we receive delights of soul or body. But," she said, quoting Father Zossima in Dostoevsky's *The Brothers Karamazov,* " 'love in practice is a harsh and dreadful thing compared to love in dreams.' We have repeated it over and over. It is no new statement, no new attitude."

Dangerous or not, the mania spread. Houses of hospitality came to be started in other cities, largely because of Peter's essays in the *Worker.* The positions that Peter took and that Dorothy so passionately affirmed were absurd as the world went, but it was a noble absurdity that appealed to those who felt that what Peter was saying was true and that the world was mad. Bill Gauchat, who started a house of hospitality in Cleveland in 1936, said it best: "We were seeking something and there was nothing." Then one day Peter Maurin came to the Jesuit high school where Gauchat attended and gave a talk. "It was dynamite," Gauchat said. He knew then what he was going to do with his life. In Harrisburg a woman, Mary Frecon, "aflame with the desire for justice for the Negro," made a house in a slum that was "right in the shadow of the Capitol" into a hospitality center for her destitute neighbors. Houses were begun in Boston; Milwaukee; Pittsburgh; Detroit; Houma, Louisiana; Chicago; and San Francisco. By World War II there were thirty across the country. There was even one in England.

The founding of other houses of hospitality indicated an expanding interest in the Worker movement, and Dorothy, eager to give her personal witness to encourage its growth, began to travel about the country to give talks and to meet people. This traveling would go on for the rest of her years—or until she was too old to move. There were occasions when it provoked bitterness among some of the people in the New York Worker house, who would complain that Dorothy could leave the tension and poverty of the Worker house to enjoy the applause, good food, and clean beds that she found on the lecture circuit, but that they had to remain anchored to their tasks. Dorothy did find travel a respite from the frequently harsh life of the house, but she regarded the personal contact with others in the movement as necessary.

And she was right. She traveled for forty years, and the impact she had on the thousands to whom she spoke was incalculable. Her speaking was effective because it was completely without a calculated form and flourish. There were no warm-up humor, no notes, and no artful gestures. Looking a little frightened—as she was—she would make her points in a simple anecdotal form. But what she said was said so clearly, so richly, and so graphically that it transmitted directly the force of her person and the idea that animated her.

On February 1, 1936, she began a speaking and visiting tour that took her circling through the Midwest and upper South. Her appointment book for the year gives some idea where she visited. On February 10 it was Kansas City, "Ward High public meeting." The next day it was "Ward H.S. spoke twice." On the seventeenth and eighteenth she was in Lawrence, Kansas, and on the nineteenth, Memphis, Tennessee.

Her going to Memphis, though, was not to speak. The Southern Tenant Farmer Union, organized by some very brave Protestant ministers, had its headquarters there—such as they were: a bare room in an old building on Front Street. Dorothy knew of their work in trying to better the badly depressed conditions of the Arkansas sharecroppers—depressed although they worked the rich bottom land just west of the Mississippi—and she wanted these people to know that she, a Catholic, shared their concern to better the lives of these black tenant farmers. That the union was known to have communist support was all the more reason for her to be there.

So on the evening of the seventeenth she went to the room that the Union used as its headquarters, along with several others who were planning to go over into Arkansas early the next morning; there she slept on a cot.

In the March 7 issue of *America,* Dorothy told of her experience among the sharecroppers. "It was seventeen above zero when we started out this morning with a carload of flour, meal, lard, sugar, coffee, and soap. The car was so full in the back that Marie Pierce, the colored girl who is on the executive committee of the Southern Tenant Farmers Union, and I were crammed together warmly on the back seat."

The car rattled over the old Harahan Bridge that connected Memphis with Arkansas; then passing through the shoddy town of West Memphis, the driver headed south to Turrell. "We passed some Negroes with a sack of chickens over their shoulder on their way to sell them. . . . One of the evicted men told of trying to get relief. 'They told us to go out and kill rabbits,' he said, 'until March, and then the planters'd care for us. So they said. Hoover hogs, we used to call them rabbits. They ain't any now showing themselves. . . . When Roosevelt come in they said it was against the law to kill rabbits. Just ketch 'em, milk 'em, and leave 'em for the next fellow.' "

That afternoon they reached "the worst place of all, just outside Parkin, Arkansas. There drawn up along the road was a tent colony, which housed 108 people, four infants among them, and God knows how many children." Because of their union activity, all had been evicted from their shacks that here and there stood alone on the vast fields, sometimes without even a tree to shade them. Dorothy described their poverty: "They grow cotton but they dress in flour sacks. It's the richest land in the country but they aren't allowed to put in a garden or keep a pig. They can't go to school; every child that can works in the fields."

What did these union members want? "They wanted small farms of their own and some help from the government the first year to buy equipment and food until they get going. What the Union wants to do is to start Cooperative farms—of 2,400 acres compared to the planters' 60,000."

These objectives were certainly just, and Dorothy undoubtedly thought of St. Gertrude's remark, one that she liked to quote: "Property is proper to man." What did Dorothy do? In the April *Worker*, she told of her response to the poverty and misery she saw. "I sent a telegram to Mrs. Franklin D. Roosevelt. I told her what I had seen that day—108 people, amongst them 40 children, and four infants in arms, living in tents in the midst of snow and ice—cold and hungry. I told her of one old man who had died the night before. I told her the children were sick with colds. I drew a picture for her of the dumb and hopeless misery of these people and asked for help. I concluded, remember Christ's words, 'Inasmuch as ye have done it unto the least of these, you have done it unto Me.' "

And Mrs. Roosevelt? "To her credit," Dorothy wrote, "be it said that she responded immediately. She did not take my word for it, but got in touch with the Governor of the State at once." So the governor and his entourage drove to the road camp "and looked over the situation." Why, there was nothing wrong—just a bunch of "happy-go-lucky" people who refused to work.

This was what the governor gave out to the press, adding that all the trouble that he had been put to was the result of a "Catholic woman's report to Mrs. Roosevelt." The governor's statement was carried in the Memphis *Commercial Appeal* and was headed "Thriving on Perversion." It condemned outsiders "who came to criticize, saying that they were making fat salaries off the misery of the people."

So Dorothy was a busybody and a do-gooder, if not a "bleeding heart Liberal." The *Commercial Appeal's* reaction was as one might expect from that paper in those days, because it usually stood for Southern Bourbon traditionalism on all fronts. This, of course, included a view of blacks as a people set apart, and nowhere more apart than on the fields of the great planters of Arkansas. The trouble was that traditional white elitism sometimes trickled down to inflame the spirits of a class of whites about as bad off as the blacks. About three weeks after Dorothy had visited in the shack of some union members, a group of masked riders burst into the same house and killed one Willie Hurst, whose offense was that he had witnessed the killing of two union members by local white vigilantes.

Dorothy could only appeal to *Worker* readers to send every cent they could to the union. "I have seen the bare poverty of the union headquarters where three people are doing this work of fighting for the oppressed. They sleep in cots at the headquarters, they have neither heat nor telephone. . . . I spent a week with them and can vouch for their honesty. . . . We are in accord with their desire to start cooperative farming ventures, where diversified farming will feed the hungry."

When Dorothy got back to Memphis from the Arkansas fields, she telephoned Caroline Gordon. Caroline's husband, Allen Tate, taught at Southwestern at Memphis, and it was about this time that both were achieving recognition for their writing: Tate, the poet, and Gordon, the novelist. The first meeting between Dorothy and Caroline had been at Dorothy's beach cottage, when Caroline was visiting Malcolm and Peggy Cowley. Presumably, Dorothy had not seen her in the meantime; if so, they had not seen one another for at least six years. What Dorothy wanted was a bath, a clean bed, and some catching up on the news as to what was going on in the lives of their mutual acquaintances, most of whom, in one way or another, were involved in writing. But Caroline, with mock severity —although she meant it, too—told her that, because Dorothy was a communist and because she had experienced enough South-baiting from Dorothy's leftist friends, that Dorothy could not come. To which comment Dorothy "laughed heartily." She told Caroline that she had become a Catholic, and because Caroline was herself thinking along the same lines and would, in fact, shortly become a

Catholic, Dorothy spent the night and, it appears, the following day and night, too.

Dorothy's talking tour went on for another week, concluding on March 2 in Detroit, where Lou Murphy was starting a house of hospitality. Back at Charles Street in New York, talk was going on of another move. The Charles Street house was just not large enough. The "talk" had begun with a Miss Mary Lane, old, lame, and half blind. Miss Lane read the *Worker* and soon came to the conclusion that anyone who could write so passionately on the plight of the poor had to be a very holy person. One day Miss Lane went to the Charles Street house, perhaps to drop off some old clothes, as was her custom, and in a conversation with Dorothy she asked if she had "ecstasies and visions." Dorothy, startled, is said to have lapsed into the language of her college days: "Hell no; the only visions I have is of unpaid bills."

Mary Lane, who was good enough to believe that those who helped the poor were holy, was also good enough to help Dorothy get another location for the Worker house of hospitality. Miss Lane had a friend, Gertrude Burke, who, as part of her patrimony, owned two houses on Mott Street. The rear house had been built in 1860; the larger place, with its sidewalk storefront, was built later to accommodate the changing character of the area, as the residences of the well-to-do gave way to the requirements of an immigrant influx. When Miss Lane talked to Miss Burke about the needs of the Worker group for more space, Miss Burke suggested that they take the back residence, in return acting as landlords and rent collectors for those who lived in the front building. No, said Dorothy. Their business was not business, and so the matter was dropped. But the need for room became so pressing that Dorothy reopened the subject in a letter to Miss Burke. She was too late, Miss Burke said. The place had been given to some Catholic women who ran a cancer hospital for the poor of the Bronx. Well, thought Dorothy, she would importune these women. "Nothing ventured, nothing gained," as her mother would have said.

Her venture was successful. The women who ran the House of Calvary, as their hospital was called, said that Dorothy and her associates could use the rear house. With its sixteen rooms, there would be, at last, enough room. As the twenty rooms in the front house were vacated, Worker people began to move into them and soon both places were in full use.

The Catholic Worker was located at 115 Mott Street for fifteen

years. It, more than any other place, is associated with the movement in the days of its youthful strength, when the idealism and
sense of community of its young people were strongest and less
encumbered by the confusions in culture and belief that beset a
later generation.

It was Mott Street as a neighborhood that appealed to Dorothy.
In all the areas in which Catholic Workers lived over the course of
Dorothy's life, she wrote of none with such feeling as she showed
when she wrote of Mott Street and its life as she found it in 1936:

Mott Street, New York, is a mile long extending from Houston Street
down to Chatham Square. It is a curved street, very slightly and gently
curved. It turns into Chatham Square where the Bowery becomes Park
Row, and where East Broadway, New Bowery, The Bowery, Park Row,
Mott Street all run together. All of Chatham Square is dark and dank
under the elevated lines, for here the Second Avenue and Third Avenue
lines used to meet and part again. . . .

There are four streets that comprise "Little Italy"—Elizabeth, Mott,
Mulberry, and Baxter Streets. Mott Street is the most colorful of all. Beginning at the north end there is the old Cathedral, with a high-walled
graveyard around it and catacombs beneath it. Legend has it that the
builder of the tenement we live in stood on the steps of old St. Patrick's
and with a gun in his hand, held off the "Know Nothings" who were
rioting and attempting to wreck and burn the church. Here, thanks to the
churchyard, the sun pours down on the street and there are parades of
baby carriages and stout mothers backed against sunny walls, winter and
summer.

Farther south the street takes on the aspect of a canyon, and the buildings are six stories high and the street narrows so that little sun shines
here except in the middle of the day. But below Grand Street the push
carts begin, and these take from the drabness of the street, and the bright
fruits and vegetables light up the scene. Here are grapes, mushrooms,
yellow squash, tomatoes, bananas, beans and greens of all kinds; fish-
stands with whelks and live eels and snails. Here are cheese stores and
cheeses pressed into the shape of reindeer and pigs or just displayed in
twig baskets. They hang in skins, in raffia woven nets; they are white,
yellow and smoked, and the smoking takes place out in front of the curb-
stone, underneath barrels. There are spaghetti stores with all variety of
spaghetti, all shapes, all lengths and the wheat of which it is made comes
from all parts of the world and all families have their preference. There
are bakeries, and from down in the basements where there are ovens built
in, the warm delicious smell of fresh loaves steals out into the street to
mingle with the smell of pizzas. . . .

In their season there are vendors of roasted sweet potatoes, sweet corn, roast chick peas, and during fiestas, hot meat cakes and sausages. In the good weather one could live out of doors without ever carrying on any housekeeping inside. The fathers sit around tables playing cards, the mothers sit by the children's or grandchildren's carriages, knitting, crocheting, talking, shouting, laughing, crying, living out their lives under the open sky.

Dorothy notes in her appointment book that the move to Mott Street occurred on Saturday, April 18. A week later she described some of the circumstances of the move: "Little Felicia stood on the sidewalk as we moved . . . and surveyed us with a pleasant smile.

" 'Can we come into your office and to your meetings?' [she] wanted to know. Some young high school students stood around and read copies of the paper aloud and groups gathered and listened.

" 'Are the meetings free?' they asked.

"Dominick, who is eight, and several of his black-eyed friends were the active ones, insisting on helping us to move in, helping us to store things."

The moving was done in a "Model A" Ford truck that the Worker had bought in March. "There must have been twelve loads of furniture coming down from Charles Street on the old truck," Dorothy wrote. Several loads of things that could not be used immediately were stored in the basement of the front building. Two young men who would be closely associated with the Worker for the remainder of their lives stood in the basement and took books and odds and ends through the window as they were handed down to them. The two men were Charlie O'Rourke and Frank O'Donnell.

" 'There's a big rat like a kitten running around down here,' called Charlie O'Rourke calmly.

" 'We have lots of rats,' said Felicia. 'When they come out in the room, we jump on the bed while my father chases them with a broom.' "

The moving day, said Dorothy, "was a happy one." As the men loaded and unloaded the truck, women set up furniture in the old rear house, scrubbed floors, and put up curtains. "There is love and devotion going into . . . the house," Dorothy wrote. "Our benefactor is donating linoleum for the kitchen and dining room and curtains for the entire house and it will be a clean cheerful place."

At the same time the Mott Street move was in progress, Workers were involved in another venture, the establishment of Peter's "agronomic university," or farm commune, as Dorothy insisted he call it. Peter, as Dorothy wrote, "wanted to restore the communal aspect of Christianity. . . . He wanted farming centers where families could live and work together, communities of families where there could be a certain amount of common life." This statement of Dorothy's is, in a sense, the surface level view of what Maurin wanted—"to restore the communal aspects of Christianity." This objective, on the face of it, sounds innocuous—a group of religious zealots living in a farm community, assisting one another and letting the rest of the world go by.

But Maurin did not want to let the rest of the world go by; he was a revolutionary. He wanted to destroy the old world and build a new one where people would not be barbarized by just living in it, where they might more easily be good, where they could develop the most fundamental inclinations of their humanness. These inclinations were to be creative, not tenders of the machine; to be "scholars" in the sense that they understood how their daily lives related to the most fundamental questions of existence; and not to be zombielike lost souls who had been reduced to that status by the brainwashing imposed upon them by a highly complicated technical culture.

The heart of the problem was economic. The problem was that contemporary people worked for wages and were so bound by the wage system that they could not offer their work to their fellows as a gift. The logical end of a money economy was the ultimate reduction of existence to a price-tag accounting. An economy in which the wage was the ultimate criterion of value left nothing for human values. Money became the "truth" by which people lived, and this, in turn, opened the way for the development of a nonproductive class: those who lived by the manipulation of money, mainly through charging interest, and who, because of these practices, were able to exercise a lien on the work of others and condemn them to servile labor.

To restore dignity to work; to enable people to have vocations rather than "jobs"; to work for the common good, for the well-being of the community rather than for personal aggrandizement —these conditions were central to Peter's "economic" thinking. But the word *economic* suggested a fractionalization of the human impulse for creativity, and Peter saw work in a much larger vision than just the "economic" aspect of human existence. Work should arise naturally from the richness and gifts of the human personality. It should be a contribution to community, a movement toward freedom, and an expression of spirit and something that partook of the eternal.

There he opposed the increasing complexity of a technical culture that fostered an increasing specialization and repetitiveness in the performance of work. One of his phrased essays touched on this problem. "This complicated world is too complicated to be dealt with in an efficient manner by specialized technicians. Knowing more and more about less and less, specialized technicians do not know how to simplify a complicated world. We need fewer specialists and more encyclopedists, fewer masters of one trade and more jacks of all trades." The ideal machine, Maurin said, should be little more than an extension of the hand.

The "agronomic university," as Maurin called it, was the way to begin a cell-like action toward human reconstruction. Dorothy, whose spirit was claimed by the city, yet agreed with Maurin. The Workers should begin a farm commune.

The opportunity to get a farm came in the fall of 1935 when a reader of the *Worker*, retired schoolteacher Grace Branham, offered the Workers $1000 with which to buy a farm. In return, the Workers were to build Miss Branham a house on the farm and deed it to her with an acre of land. Dorothy says that she told Miss Branham that living in a Worker community would not ordinarily be a spiritually uplifting experience, that, in fact, things were not as they might appear to be from just reading the paper. It could be an unpleasant experience. But Miss Branham was not persuaded, and Dorothy ceased making her objections, feeling that she had given Miss Branham a truthful statement of what the latter might expect.

Search parties were launched in January. A car was borrowed from the generous Mrs. Porter Chandler, who probably clutched her rosary beads and invoked the intercession of the Virgin as she saw her car headed off on exploring expeditions loaded with Workers and with Dorothy, too, at times. The way Dorothy described their ventures, Mrs. Porter clearly had reason to seek the protection of heaven. "Every time the group ventured out, the rain began to pour, turned to sleet, caked the pavements and hindered our advance. The elements themselves seemed to conspire against our hunt. Every time we went out we skidded into snow banks, went off the road, narrowly escaped collisions, and barely saved the borrowed car from wreck."

In April they found their place, an old farm three miles out of Easton, Pennsylvania, on the top of a high hill—a "mountain," Dorothy called it. Dorothy described the farm as "thirty acres in extent, ten acres very poor woodland." It "had one old house, badly in need of repair, with five rooms and an attic." The outbuildings were all falling down, and the fields of twenty acres had long been untilled. The road to the farm, ascending from the highway below, was so rutted and steep that it was worth the poor car's transmission to attempt the ascent, but on April 15 ascend it did, bearing Dorothy and several more. That day Dorothy gave the owners $1000 and a note for the remaining $250 due. Several days later Jim Montague and five others took the loaded Ford truck and drove due west, taking the Holland tunnel under the Hudson, then through Newark, and out on Highway 22 across the rolling countryside of New Jersey to the Delaware River, and then only two miles to the farm. It was a seventy-five mile trip, and, because a bus traveled the route daily, passing right by the farm, the location seemed ideal.

The farm's "magnificent" view on all sides and accessibility to the New York Workers were all that recommended it. The few fruit trees were bowed with age and disease, and the land was worn out. Even so, the enterprise was launched in a glow of enthusiasm. Jim Montague, Eddie Priest, Bill Callahan, Cy Echele, and whoever else was handy began cleaning up and clearing the ground for an early summer garden. After a few days Dorothy appeared, bringing with her one of the women from the house. For several hours Dorothy planted onion seeds while the women tried to clean up the kitchen. That evening Dorothy and her companion cooked. Already, Dorothy wrote, "we have all the asparagus and rhubarb we can eat, dandelion and dockweed, mushrooms and milk." The milk came from Rosie, the Holstein, a gift from a Jewish family that read the *Worker*.

Supper done, "the boys all went out to mend a portion of the road where it comes up the hill, slanting perilously between fields. With the truck and plough they ploughed up one side, Eddie using a pick as supplementary help and Bill at work with the shovel." Then Cy Echele got the idea of "chaining a wide board behind the truck and all of them standing on it, balancing themselves with ropes, the truck pulling them along to level out the ploughed-up portion." Washing dishes in the kitchen, Dorothy was unaware of what was going on "until we heard loud yells of joy and triumph and went out to see the fun. The stunt worked pretty well, but in the course of the leveling one or more of the workers was always flung off into the field."

Thus it began. That summer they got some pigs, chickens, a goat, three ducks, and still another cow. They also got that summer, and the two summers following, more people than they had ever thought would come. Some eight years later Dorothy looked back to those first summers. "Because the farm is a permanent community, many of our basic problems show up there. Peter did not, most certainly, intend Houses of Hospitality on the land, yet many a time in the summer, the farm became a House of Hospitality, a children's camp, a worker's school. People come and stay for vacations and visits."

The basic problem to which Dorothy alludes was—as it always was in any Worker undertaking—the absence of a structure of authority. Writing about this period later, she discussed the problems that confronted them. The scarcity of food was the immediate problem, "but to raise the food it was necessary to work." Yet those who came to the farm from the city did not know how to work. They were "boss-minded and job-minded." They wanted to be ordered to perform their tasks. "The more people there were around, the less got done. Some cooked, washed dishes, carpentered, worked in the garden and tended the animals. But none worked hard enough. No one worked as I have seen sisters and brothers in monasteries work."

There was the problem of food. "One could of course live on bread and vegetables and oil or fat and wine. We had to rule out the latter at once because there were too many amongst us with a weakness, and St. Paul says to do without what causes your brother to stumble. So that brought us down to bread, fats, and vegetables. But most of us could not do without our tea and coffee. And the bread had to be a certain kind of bread and the cereal a certain kind of cereal."

They might have done without bread and eaten cornmeal mush. But most said that cornmeal mush, a dietary item eminently respectable in early days, "was fit only for chickens!" A family came to live on the farm and the mother made bread for all. "But there were those who could not eat it because it was not like store bread!" There were others who did not like fish; "they did not like liver and kidneys nor anything but the red meat of the animal."

When Maurin came to the farm, as must have been the case that first summer, he "inveighed against packaged foods and canned goods." "Produce what you eat and eat what you produce," was his continual cry. But, as Dorothy observed, the people who came to them, the poor, had no experience at all with eating food that they could grow, which, most certainly, was infinitely better for them from the standpoint of their health. Those at the farm would "take their pennies" down to Easton where they bought whiskey and packaged foods. It would take a long time, Dorothy thought, for people to overcome their addiction to money and its capacity to produce the immediate gratification of junk food.

One day a fight occurred over an egg. Usually there were enough eggs, bought from neighboring farmers for twenty-five cents a dozen, for each person to have one egg a day, which could be eaten at breakfast or lunch. An ex-soldier named Louis decided one morning that he would have his egg for lunch and put it aside. When he came in at lunch time, his egg was gone. Loud and angry talk, full of bitter accusations and recriminations, which was profane and obscene, was not an uncommon occurrence in Worker life. Louis was loud and angry, and carried on by the momentum of his words he hit the cook and knocked him down. "Peter was a witness to this fight," Dorothy wrote. "He has so complete a hatred of the use of force that he paled. Perhaps it was with wrath—'the righteous wrath with no undue desire of revenge' of which St. Thomas speaks. But Peter did have his revenge. 'Since there is not enough to go around,' he said, 'I'll do without both milk and eggs for the rest of the summer.'"

Still, as Dorothy noted, the bickering over the food did not cease. "This self-denial of Peter's led to another discussion which lasted all summer, a discussion as to whether justice came before charity, or after." As Dorothy saw it, "those who were holding the position that justice came first were the most avid to get their share of everything, and the last ones to practice self-denial. 'Justice comes first,' they always said firmly. And they are still saying it. . . . Which leads many to say, 'You see, your emphasis on freedom does not work. You need rules and regulations to enforce order.'"

Peter, though, was unyielding on the question of freedom. During the winter of 1938 or 1939 as Dorothy and Peter sat talking about the farm, Dorothy complained about a family that had settled there. The people talked much of poverty, but, said Dorothy, "I believe it is because they can't manage for themselves. They don't know how to run a house, and so they justify themselves by talking about poverty. But a room can be made beautiful with a few flowers, plants, a bookcase, curtains at clean windows." The family had not taken the initiative in improving the appearance of anything. "Look about," Dorothy said to Peter. He would see broken fences, junk lying around, and the road up to the farm was washed out and full of holes.

"But I will take those jobs," Peter said. "I will take the job this spring of straightening the place up, keeping things looking good. They will learn that way. And this year, instead of breaking rocks in the hot sun, I'm going down to the spring between the two farms and break that pile of rocks that is there. . . . I'll always have an extra hammer by my side, . . . and when anyone wants to help, I'll just hand him the hammer."

Dorothy, in one instance, wrote: "I remember one fellow, who used to sit out under the trees and watch Peter work. Peter always carried his point so far that he would never ask anyone to help him, or tell anyone to do a lot of work. . . . But Jim used to say, 'I'll work when I'm told to. I want someone to give me orders.' So he used to sit under the tree and do nothing all the day. I do not think he was very happy in this attitude. We used to blame it on his German mind. We could understand his point of view too, and he had the stubbornness to make his point, and go on sitting under a tree.

"But Peter never gave an order. He will sacrifice material success any day, in order to drive home his ideas in regard to personalism."

The summer of 1936 and those that followed until World War II, witnessed no settling in of Maurin's ideas to produce even a roughly functioning communal society. "Tied up as it is with our technique of the Works of Mercy," wrote Dorothy, "which forces us from Christian charity to accept all those who come to us for aid, it will never be strictly speaking a model for others to follow." The farm became a summer camp for those wishing to escape the heat and crowds of the city. Every summer it was "children again, invalids, unemployed, transients, and the many students and priests who came . . . to talk of these ideas of personalism, communitarianism, and . . . the solution to the problem of the unemployed."

Tents were set up for the men; the children and more men slept on pallets in the barns, and the women stayed in the house. The children were from Harlem, shepherded by Julia Porcelli, who the previous summer had taken care of them at Huguenot. Their presence at times made things somewhat uproarious. Some of the boys raided the grape arbor of a neighbor, who retaliated by giving the communitarians four puppies, as perpetually hungry and mischievous as the children. "Eleanor can tap dance like a professional, and her neatest trick is to tie tin cans to her feet and dance on them. The noise is very satisfying. Bernice is her big sister. She is ten and Eleanor is eight, and it was a great sight to see the motherly little girl scrubbing down her dusky sister Saturday night so that her delicious brown skin was all but veiled in soap-suds."

While the children played and ranged over the farm, the infirm sat beneath the trees, rolled and smoked their cigarettes, and wait-ed for the dinner bell to ring. In the afternoon, standing on a grassy knoll, Peter would conduct his teaching sessions. On many occasions priests came—getting out of the city, as it were—and they usually were involved in the discussions.

There were, of course, positive things about the "farm com-mune," as Dorothy preferred to call it. "It has done much for a number of people," she wrote. "Besides bringing to the attention of our readers and friends all over the country in most vivid fash-ion the ideas of farming as a way of life, as opposed to farming as an industry," it had "constantly heralded the land as a solution to the problem of the unemployed, which is the most pressing prob-lem of the day."

Some people did not work, but there were those who did: the young men who learned about farming and planted the fields, in the face of, as Dorothy put it, "working with few materials, with scant funds, with just what we can get our hands on from month to month." Yet crops and vegetables were produced and livestock maintained.

As for Dorothy, it might well have been that in the farm ven-ture she saw an opportunity to provide something better for Ta-mar. So many of Tamar's days in recent years had been spent at St. Patrick's boarding school on Staten Island. Tamar was a docile child who accepted her life with little protest, but it was becoming obvious to Dorothy that Tamar's interests were never going to be satisfied by what went on in the classroom. The little girl loved the outdoors and her animals, and she found life on the farm at Eas-ton a happy experience. Eventually—and it could have been in the summer of 1936—Dorothy was able to get Steve and Mary Johnson to make Easton their permanent home, with Tamar, as she had been on Staten Island, becoming their charge in the summertime.

As Dorothy's journal indicates, there were some unpleasant moments in Tamar's farm life: "Tonight ... [Tamar] had a nose bleed, a headache and a stomach ache, and although the latter probably came from eating green pears, as she confessed, still to think of the little time I have with her, being constantly on the go, having to leave her to the care of others, sending her away to school so that she can lead a regular life and not be subject to the moods and vagaries of the crowds of us! This is probably the cruellest hardship of all. She is happy, she does not feel torn constantly as I do. And then the doubt arises, probably she too feels that I am failing her, just as the crowd in Mott Street and the crowd here feel it. . . . Never before have I had such a complete sense of failure, of utter misery."

One wintery Saturday afternoon, Dorothy was sitting in her little "apartment" in the front building of Mott Street, "while the snow fell softly outside and the windows rattled in the wind." All was cozy and peaceful with the coal fire burning in the grate and the opera of the afternoon coming over the radio. But then the wind suddenly rose in volume, and "I began to think of my daughter, who had gone down to the farm for the weekend." As she sat, "so secure, storm warnings began to come over the radio, of increased snow, wind and ice in the highways." She took her worries to Peter, who allayed them.

" 'But it will make her sturdy,' he said, reassuringly. And he went on to quote D'Annunzio. At that point, two old street-walkers in the next room began having [an] ... argument and there was a terrific blare from the radio and I missed it [Peter's quotation]. I began to hear again when he was talking about trees. 'The wind is as good as the sun,' he was saying. 'The pine trees in the valley may be very beautiful to the eye with their widespread branches, but those on the mountainsides that have their roots imbedded in rocks, and have to be always stretching to reach the sun, and get much of the wind as a consequence—they are the ones that are useful and make good lumber.' "

Peter's remark probably had the consolatory effect intended for Dorothy: always meeting and overcoming the rigors that nature imposed on human life were good for the body and the spirit, too. Still, Dorothy, while not oversolicitous about Tamar, was not anxious to let her fend for herself. She sensed a vulnerability in Tamar —an almost desperate need for protection—and it was this that hurt Dorothy on those occasions when she was away from Tamar for any length of time.

The farm represented stability for Tamar and, despite the discordancy and confusion that occasionally turned the ideal community into something that was ugly, there were times, for Dorothy at least, when nature provided moments of such beauty that discord was muted. It was just after the move to the farm that Dorothy noted that "before bedtime, around nine, we all gather together, for the rosary and litany. Tonight there was a little breeze outside in the apple trees sighing around the house. The moon shone down on the hilltop, washing the fields in a soft glow. There was quiet and perfect peace and a happiness so deep and strong and thankful, that even our words of prayer seemed inadequate to express our joy. May St. Isidore, patron of farm workers, pray for us and praise God for us!"

When fall came, the tensions of the summer passed. Visitors returned home, and those "guests" who had thought in the spring that farm life was surely for them began to long for the city and soon were booking passage in the back of the Ford truck on one of its trips to Mott Street. "Maryfarm," as Dorothy named it, was at rest, and the glare of long afternoons when the sun had hung high for so long gave way to long shadows and evening peace. "Coming down at night from the city" Dorothy wrote, "the warm, sweet smell of the good earth enwraps one like a garment. There is the smell of rotting apples; of alfalfa in the barn; burning leaves; of wood fires in the house; of pickled green tomatoes and baked beans, than which there is no better smell, not even apple pies."

Dorothy reflected back on the summer. "From day to day we did not know . . . where the next money to pay bills was coming from, but trusting to our cooperators, our readers throughout the country, we went on with the work." The readers, as they always did, sent money. "Now all our bills are paid, and there is a renewed feeling of courage on the part of all those who are doing the work." Dorothy was grateful. It took so little to make her grateful. "This month of thanksgiving will indeed be one of gratitude to God. For health, for work to do, for the opportunities He had given us of service; we are deeply grateful, and it is a feeling that makes the heart swell with joy."

And what, after the summer had passed, with all of its talk about authority and personal responsibility, had been done about the schoolteacher, Grace Branham, who had given her $1000 to buy the farm and for which she was to have a house? There was progress. Steve Hergenham, the builder who had once built himself a house only to have it taken away because he could not pay taxes on it, began building the house for Miss Branham. It would take him two years to complete it, but when he did Miss Branham was deeded the house and her acre of land.

As for Hergenham, it was his last real job. Like Peter, he wanted to teach the young people, but generally he was disliked by them. With his heavy German accent he, as Dorothy said, "could never resist sneering at them for their inability to work. He criticized their lack of strength, their upbringing, the American way of life as well as their limitations." Finally, the undisciplined character of life on the farm so oppressed him that he left.

The Easton project was probably foremost among Dorothy's concerns through 1936, but there was Mott Street, too. As it always happened when the Workers moved to a new place, thinking that finally they had space enough, the space gave way to beds. As the summer progressed the Workers, with Gertrude Burke's permission, quickly took over the front building. Some back apartments there were taken over for women, and Julia Porcelli was put in charge of their care.

Later, because of crowding, the women were moved into a separate women's house on another street. "It was nicer and cleaner," Miss Porcelli recollected, "but it was away from the rest of the Catholic Worker and I didn't feel that I joined the Catholic Worker to be in charge of the women." The absence of a male presence, as she saw it, seemed to block certain main conduits in the flow of her personality, these "conduits" being the persons of Joe Zarella, Gerry Griffin, and Bill Callahan. Nonetheless, Julia did her best. "Our meals were cozy, we had a tablecloth and everyone would sign their name on it, and we had the rooms blessed, and some very interesting parties we had there. We'd have special parties on their feast days."

Dorothy had her own apartment in the front building, a luxury that she rarely enjoyed over the course of her Catholic Worker life. Taking her own apartment was not, however, self-indulgence. She was thinking of the need, for Tamar, to have a redoubt against the turmoil and tension of the house. But with Tamar at the farm most of the summer and Dorothy running between Mott Street and the farm, the apartment was in continual use for visitors. "Visitors always arrive unexpectedly with us," Dorothy wrote—"priests, seminarians, and college students." The visitor, as Dorothy admitted, ordinarily got little more consideration than the men and women who came in off the street. "We are apt to see only the beggar in him, or to treat him as the beggar is normally treated."

Visitors came and some of them, the more impressionable types, doubtless felt the impulse to turn and flee when they saw what they had gotten into. "People were shocked when they came down and found we were living in the slums," Julia Porcelli said. "Visitors would see the Catholic Worker from the outside instead of from the inside. They'd come and they'd see the simple diet, the rooms, the raggedy-looking people around—very unstylish—and they'd feel very sorry for us. We wore the clothes people sent in and we didn't have salaries, and people thought we were wonderful and we didn't feel wonderful." She herself was always hungry, Miss Porcelli said. "Whenever I got a little sad-looking Dorothy always said somebody should take me out and buy me a steak. If someone treated me for dinner that was the best thing, to get treated for dinner."

Some visitors came to talk with Peter. "I remember seeing Father [Bartholomew] Eustace," observed Miss Porcelli, "who later became Bishop, spend hours talking to Peter." This was in the summer of 1936. "It was very hot, and there was a space, a yard between the front building and the back building where Peter would sit and talk when it wasn't too noisy." Philosopher Jacques Maritain came again, as did Father Virgil Michel.

There was a Father Peter Fox, who later wrote articles on Catholic themes for the *New York Times*. Miss Porcelli thought he had gotten some of his ideas from Peter—such as "Catholic Charities should not be on Madison Avenue" and that "Catholic social workers should live in the parish" and "feed the spirit of the person who needed money for the rent or clothes for the children."

For all visitors, either those from off the street or those with carfare from uptown or out of town, who came to make a social call, there was a final acid test of their willingness to stay overnight with the poor. In his *Days of Action*, Stanley Vishnewski observed that "for a long time the test of a true Catholic Worker vocation was if one could put up with bedbugs. Some of the staff suffered a great deal from them and would wake up in the morning covered with bites." This "test," of course, also applied to visitors. For "a long time the odor of sanctity in the Catholic Worker was compounded of the fumes of kerosene [or Black Flag] and the peculiar misty odor exuded by the bedbug."

As Dorothy observed, the considerable increase in space that came with the Mott Street move was matched by a great increase in the number of "guests." This began in 1936 and went on through 1939, or until the war brought on that ideal state of "full employment." A breadline had begun on Mott Street. "We never planned to be running breadlines. We never planned to have so large a family staying with us. They just grew up around us. And it is not as though we could devote our whole attention to them, what with the paper, the correspondence, visitors, writings, etc." In 1937, there were days when the Worker was feeding a thousand men.

In the August, 1937 issue of the *Worker,* Dorothy wrote of the men that stood in front of the Mott Street house, waiting for coffee and bread. "Every morning . . . hundreds of men . . . come to us to be fed. They are the lame, the halt, the blind. Some are the unemployed, and some are the unemployable. From all over, men drift into New York for work or for food and while employment is picking up to some extent . . . New York will always have her street of the forgotten men. Too often the attitude is that these are the 'unworthy' poor. The attitude is 'You can't do anything with them, so why feed them?' which is an atheist attitude, since we must see Christ in each man who comes to us. Remember Lazarus who sat at the gate, nursing his sores! The modern social worker would wonder why he didn't go to the clinic to get fixed up and rehabilitated, but Our Lord only pointed the moral that the rich man at whose gate he sat did not feed him."

This description of the line probably sent frugal housewives to their coffee cans, priests and nuns to their purses, and the comfortable to their checkbooks to help out. Joe Zarella was the bookkeeper and financial manager at Mott Street, and there were times, it appears, when he was appalled at what he considered Dorothy's disregard of the canons of "sound" financial management. Where was the money going to come from? Bills were piling up, and so on.

Well might young Zarella have worried. When matters approached the point that the entire enterprise, Easton and Mott Street, would founder within days, someone would write out a petition and place it under the statue of St. Joseph. "We need money, St. Joseph! Make haste!" Once this lowly sweat-begrimed carpenter, the foster father of God, seemed to be taking the petitions too matter-of-factly. So, according to Julia Porcelli, who was Italian and had the gift to believe in such things, she, Dorothy, and some of the others took turns going over to the church to "picket" St. Joseph. Each one spent "perhaps an hour praying and begging for money. We were so behind with the butcher, the banker and everyone that we just didn't have a cent in the house."

"It was a peaceful and loving picketing," wrote Dorothy, "the crowd of us taking turns to go to the church and there in the presence of Christ our Leader, contemplate St. Joseph, that great friend of God, the Protector of His Church." Dorothy observed that the picketing was announced at the breakfast table, after which one of the young women sitting there looked startled and asked if she would be required to carry a sign.

Did the picketing work? Of course. Who could doubt it? Julia Porcelli told what happened. "I remember Gerry [Griffin] took this nap and he said, 'Don't wake me up until someone comes in with $100.' We went off and we ... were doing something—perhaps getting out the paper, perhaps just answering letters. Someone came in and wanted to see Gerry, or someone in charge, and didn't have too much to say. He was shown around, or given some papers, and he left an envelope. We put it on Gerry's desk. He came down and there was $100. I don't even know if we knew his [the donor's] name."

Such interventions came only in extreme circumstances. But even when things were normal, Workers lived from hand to mouth. Miss Porcelli remembered one time when she was asked to cook—"one of the few times I cooked at Mott Street and I was scared stiff—there was so little to make a meal, but we made a meal. Someone brought some beets in. Perhaps they had gotten them very cheaply or someone had given it to them—surplus foods or something—and they brought in a great big bunch of beets. That made a vegetable and someone brought in something else. Manna came from heaven. We often witnessed this at the Catholic Worker."

Usually, money came in daily. Dorothy explained: "The paper costs a cent a copy, or twenty-five cents a year. Many people send more. When our bills pile high, we send out an appeal, and usually this must be done twice a year, spring and fall; on St. Joseph's day in March and St. Francis's day in October. Always we got just enough to carry on. . . . Ask and you shall receive. That is, if the Lord wants you to have it. 'I have no need of your goods,' He has said, through the psalmist, and one of the ways we may know if it is God's will that we carry on this work is by the response to our appeals. If He wants the work done, He will send the means to do it."

And what of accountings, financial statements, audits, and the like? These, as Dorothy and Peter viewed them, represented the paraphernalia of the cult of money. Dorothy's guide in these matters was a moral logic. When people sent in money to feed the poor, it went to feed the poor. Those who lived and worked at the house of hospitality were clothed out of the same bins and fed at the same table as were those who came to them for help. The money Dorothy got from her speaking engagements and from the books that she wrote was used for Tamar.

So one fed the poor; one tried to begin the great work of giving an example of communal living; and one waged a "realistic" battle against the institutions that stood athwart the path that led to the achievement of a Christian humanism. These institutions, as she saw it, and as Maurin saw it, were the capitalistic system and the modern secular state, whether "democratic" or Marxist.

In the pre–World War II history of the Worker movement, Dorothy's assault on the "system" was principally a matter of supporting the attempts of labor to organize. This course, she recognized, was directly opposed to Maurin's idea. Unionism was a confrontational technique that had higher wages as the primary objective. Maurin wanted a cooperative society where work was a gift, not a commodity. But Dorothy, the radical, seemed to have found it difficult to give up the techniques of open confrontation, especially regarding capital. Perhaps there were times when she enjoyed the tension of battle. She could, of course, rationalize her position. "With our attitude toward the machine and the land, people wonder why we bother about unions. But things being as they are, the system as it is, steps must be taken. We are not angels and we cannot fly, we must take one step at a time. In order to better conditions for the workers, unions are necessary."

All of which sounds like a Marxist statement—the necessity of a little strife to achieve justice. But Dorothy also had another objective in mind. Pope Leo XIII had said that the workers had been lost to the Church. She would try to give the workers an example of someone who, bespeaking the Church, stood alongside them.

The first particular intervention in the cause of the worker occurred in 1933, and it was one on which Dorothy shortly fell on her face. In September, 1933, the *Catholic Worker,* on one of the few such occasions in its history, took a position on a particular aspect of federal policy. The *Worker* [Dorothy Day] professed to be "more and more enthusiastic" about Franklin Roosevelt's National Recovery Administration. It was "following the lines laid down by Pope Pius XI in his encyclical *Forty Years After.*" That was in September. In November the *Worker* saw the NRA as a type of "industrial fascism."

Well, what of it? Dorothy might well have said. Peter had changed her mind, and it was one of her first principles never to explain an inconsistency in principle. Her principle in the future would be to cease analyzing New Deal policies, or any other federal policy, except war.

The principle of unionism, as Dorothy saw it, was a clearer issue. In January, 1935, some of the Catholic Workers joined the picketers who were protesting the wage policy of the Orbach-Klein Department Store. "I remember the strike," Dorothy told Professor Rosemary Bannon years later. "There was a mass picket line on Fourteenth Street against the store and they [the police] would load up the police wagon with pickets and take them off. When we joined the picket lines, they stopped doing it. They [the Orbach-Klein employees] won the strike afterward, and had a victory rally in Union Square. I think it was a communist-influenced strike, because that was at the time when the Trade Union Unity League was still in existence."

A year later Dorothy and her paper supported the strikers of the Borden Milk Company over the closed shop issue. All "Catholic Borden employees" were asked to attend a meeting at the Worker house. If any came, or what they heard when they came, is not known. In any case, the Borden people were sufficiently concerned to buy an advertisement in the *Brooklyn Tablet* to set forth their side of the issue. The *Catholic Worker* was referred to in the ad as "a publication circularized among Catholics."

Again, Dorothy justified her active prounionism. "We do believe that they [the unions] are the only efficient weapons which workers have to defend their rights as individuals and Christians against a system which makes the Christ-life practically impossible for large numbers of workers. We believe that Catholic workers must use unions in their efforts to heed the exhortations of the Popes to 'de-proletarianize' the workers. (For we too are working toward a classless society.)"

If these "reasons" were not effective enough to convince readers, there was always the clincher: the communists knew how to "use" unions, why not Catholics?

Peter, one suspects, must have suffered silently over a phrase such as the unions' being "the only efficient weapons which workers have to defend their rights against a system which makes the Christ-life practically impossible." Dorothy had slipped again into the confrontational, name-calling mode. Further, as Peter certainly knew, there was nothing in the method or philosophy of unionism that would make living a "Christ-life" easier. If anything, the objectives of unionism, themselves so openly partaking of the spirit of the bourgeoisie, were themselves a major impediment to the "Christ-life."

But these were Depression days, and as many people saw the matter, it was a corrupt and greedy capitalist class that was responsible for the Depression and the suffering that went with it. And Dorothy was reluctant to give up her villains.

In July, 1936, she went to Pittsburgh to talk to Bishop Hugh C. Boyle about the "labor situation." "I got there just after supper on Monday night and we talked until ten about labor, about the social teachings of the church, about subsistence homesteads." She interviewed John L. Lewis about the same time, "prepared to like him, engrossed as he is in the ideal of an industrial democracy." Whether or not she liked him after she met him she never said.

The most direct and protracted of the Catholic Worker's—or, more precisely, Dorothy's—involvement in the affairs of organized labor was the seamen's strike. The "strike" was in part a struggle between the International Seamen's Union, an American Federation of Labor affiliate, and the National Maritime Union, an organization connected with the recently organized Congress of Industrial Organization. In Dorothy's view, the NMU came out of the tradition of the Industrial Workers of the World and this went a long way toward making it the correct bargaining agency for the seamen. On the other hand, the ISU had "become corrupt": its officials received big salaries and had "a company union mentality."

Ship crews organized in the NMU had been striking sporadically through 1936, and in January, 1937, the strike took on a determined character. The striking seamen, soon out of money, began showing up in the Worker food line. By January, 1937, their numbers became so large that Dorothy started another soup line at 181 Tenth Avenue, just around the corner from the headquarters of the striking seamen. "From the first day the place has thronged from 8 in the morning until midnight." This, of course, represented an extraordinary drain on the financial and physical resources of Dorothy, her young associates, and those loyal readers of the *Catholic Worker* who sent in their pittances. In the February issue of the *Worker,* Dorothy stated that she and her co-workers were $1200 in debt for food, "not to speak of $400 for the last month's printing bill and the same for this." They could "only beg from issue to issue of the paper, telling you, our readers, of our needs. You are doing this work—you are united with us in Christian solidarity."

The debts, as always, were paid, and that summer the strike ended. Dorothy was left with the question of what her and her friends' extraordinary effort had been worth. Had any of the men gone back to their ships with the conviction that the Church was their friend—a community in which they should take an active part? Certainly some of them who had spent their days at the Tenth Street store, drinking coffee and eating pumpernickel bread with cottage cheese piled on it, had also read some of the literature that dealt with the Church and the labor question.

Maybe some did, but in 1946, when Joe Curran, the head of the National Maritime Union, was testifying before the Dies Un-American Activities Committee on the support that his union had gotten from the communists back in the 1930s, Curran said, yes, the communists had been their friends because "there was no one else to help us." Curran's comment disturbed Dorothy, who remarked in the *Worker* that she thought the seamen would "long remember the gallon pots of coffee on the stove night and day."

Pots of coffee on the stove, if nothing else, were a part of the paraphernalia of the somewhat pious activism that marked the Worker participation in the seamen's strike. The memory of this episode remained more with the young Workers who participated in it than with anyone else. It was a memory of a heroic time, a confrontation with malign and reactionary forces, of physical danger, and of the strong sense of community that came from their extraordinary efforts. Yet, finally, so far as Maurin's idea was concerned, it was a moment of regression. It was a movement into the action of the world, of being lifted and swirled by time into one of its eddies. The main problem, after all, was not one of corrupt labor bosses and reactionary masters of capital. It was one of living so as to raise the human vision to a point of truth above time's capricious and endless farces.

But Dorothy was still groping and the year 1937 was one during which she would make herself into the Joan of Arc of the labor movement. Sometime in January, in the midst of the seamen's strike, she went to Flint, Michigan, to interview sit-down strikers in the General Motors Fisher Body plant. In the *Worker* she declared that the strike was "both legal and moral" and that "all the forces of capitalism are being mobilized" against it.

These were years of extensive traveling for Dorothy, so much so that from her appointment book it would appear that she spent more time on the road than she did at either the farm or the Mott Street house. Much of this travel was to fulfill speaking engagements. She had no "fee," but she took what was offered, and, what with the financial problems she and the Worker faced, speaking was important. Occasionally her fees, as she reckoned them, must have been large—upward of $100, as when on May 23 she spoke in Milwaukee to a Catholic Action conference at the invitation of Archbishop Samuel Stritch.

Speaking always unnerved her. Writing in her journal during this period, she commented on her feelings before the talk she was to give later that evening: "Tonight I have to speak . . . and I am so fatigued by a two weeks' speaking trip that I . . . [am] miserable about it. . . . It is only with the greatest effort that I speak. The idea depresses me for a day beforehand. I get physically sick from it." Practice did not make things easier for her. Thirty years later her journal would contain the same lament: "The exhausting, and even terrifying experience of *speaking* when it is easier to write—to close oneself in, behind a desk, in peace and quiet—not to be confronted and challenged for what you say."

After she had given her talk, did her tension dissipate? To the contrary, at least according to a "Bertha" whom she cites in her journal. "Bertha says I am gruff and indifferent to people (she means when I come off the platform or am meeting a mass of them at a time). . . . So I must learn to be more cordial to people and overcome that immense sense of weariness and even impatience when people, quite sincerely, tell me . . . how interested they are in my work. Mrs. Jordan told me I look at people as though they were going to steal five minutes of my time! It makes me unhappy to give such an impression. . . . I feel as tho I had failed. . . . I must do better, guard myself rigidly, control my fatigue, not mention it. But oh, it is so hard. I'll just have to work every day at it."

Dorothy must have been tired when she wrote this because the last two sentences sound like one of the pious utterances that Martha Finley's little Elsie Dinsmore was continually making; maybe Elsie's phrasing of her noble resolves crept into Dorothy's weary mind as Dorothy wrote her journal. After all, Dorothy, at the age of ten, had read *Elsie* and had wept along with her little heroine through the latter's failures in trying to be good. But a smiling, affable, and warm-handclasping Dorothy after a talk would never be. She was John Day's daughter and to be "gruff and indifferent to people" was a technique of survival.

She did have her quiet moments, though, and to have them was surely part of the reason for her traveling. Still again, her journal, this time written while riding the train to San Francisco, comments: "These hours on the train or bus are so precious—to be alone for a short while. It is a complete relaxation, a joy. I am a weak and faulty vessel to be freighted with so valuable a message as cargo."

In her *House of Hospitality,* published in 1938, Dorothy gives a full account of her traveling in the years 1937 and 1938. On February 17, 1937, she spoke to the Four Arts Club in Palm Beach, Florida. When she had finished, the president, presumably, said, " 'You know we never pay speakers.' " And another woman, with a tremor in her voice, said, " 'Miss Day, I hope you can convey to your readers and listeners that we would give our very souls to help the poor, if we saw any constructive way of doing it,' and still another told me, 'The workers come to my husband's mill and beg him with tears in their eyes to save them from unions. I hope you don't mind my saying so, but I think you are all wrong when it comes to unions.' "

Dorothy's sense of humor rarely encompassed situations in which she appeared as the victim, and in this instance she was bitter, so much so that she named the Four Arts Club in her *House of Hospitality.*

The trip could have produced another occasion for bitterness. She had Tamar with her, and her appointment book shows that she stayed in Miami for a week. Obviously, she had gone there to visit her mother, and, who knows, perhaps she even hoped for a reconciliation with her father. If she entertained any thoughts of finding a mellowed John Day, she was disappointed. In a long, newsy letter written to a relative in Chattanooga, Tennessee, Day comments on the passing of his sister Margaret, on his own misfortunes, and then on his children. This letter, as well as anything could, provides an insight into Day's character and, also, the sad and blind emptiness of his struggle with life. First, he comments on the funeral arrangements that he made for his sister Margaret. When he first learned that she had died,

I immediately got in touch with the undertakers at Chattanooga over the phone, and would have phoned you, but they could not tell me where you were. I phoned a second time and asked if she could be cremated and the ashes held for the disposal of her son, but there was no crematory nearer than Cincinnati. I had outgrown and forgotten the East Tennessee Fundamentalism and prejudices. I told them if they could get in touch with you that I would pay for whatever you advised. They wired back that you advised burial at Cleveland, and I wired money to cover the cost. Please advise me of all the horrible details.

I can remember, as a youngster, and after I was grown up, that I always had a real brotherly affection for Margaret. She grew up a spoiled and selfish brat, and while I no longer felt any affection for her, I would have gladly helped her any time I was able in a financial way. I got terribly broke in the panic after '29, and later understood that her boys were helping her, and have not heard from her in several years.

Then Day discusses his cousins, Clem and Kate, and his own family:

Mother Day and I have enjoyed seeing a lot of Clem and his family at Miami. They are really a nice family, although I kid Kate some about being a Georgia cracker Baptist, and telling her the only difference between a cracker Baptist and a cracker Methodist is that the Methodist can read and write. You mustn't think hard of me for what you would call my being sacrilegious. I think I made it clear to you when I last saw you, that while I respect and admire all religions, even the Catholics and Jews, it's all just a lot of Hooey for the ignorant, so far as I am concerned. I've arranged that when I shuffle off, which I may do at any old time now, that I shall be cremated at the least possible expense and without benefit of clergy....

I never have amounted to much as a success in the world, and have had a lot of hard luck and a little good luck at times. My best luck has been my family, for I have raised five and lost none, nor has there ever been any serious illness among any of us, except last year Della had a terrible siege just at this time of year. She was in the hospital with an infected hand for nearly three months. She lost one thumb and her case was considered a miracle, medically, because she didn't lose her arm. She is married to a Jew named Spier of a good southern family. The name is not Jewish and he does not look like a Jew, nor does any of the three kids show any looks of a Hebe, but they are smart little hellions, two boys and one girl, the youngest, which Mother says is the most perfect beauty of a kid she ever saw, but still a little hellion.

It seems obvious that John Day's favorite child was Donald. Donald was a journalist, the Baltic correspondent for the *Chicago Tribune*. Even so, he was "still the most unsophisticated East Tennessee kid of all of them. He's six foot two inches tall and weighs 240, married to an educated, high-class Russian, who has taught him a lot of languages, and who never had and never will have any children. Mother Day and Della have both been over there and spent several months with them, and Donald had her over here two years ago, and we thought she was really sweet." Still, said Day, he wished that Donald had "married that Baxter girl of Nashville."

His son, Sam Houston, was "one Day that probably will never be broke. He was pretty puny after he got back from the other side of the war, but he outlived it."

And John, Jr.? "He's had a bit of a rough road, which will do him a lot of good. He's the one that visited you with me. While living with his nut sister, Dorothy, he got married to a Spanish girl, daughter of an artist." John was "another newspaper nut, instead of being at some real business, but we'll hope he gets along."

And Dorothy? His comments were harsh:

Dorothy, the oldest girl, is the nut of the family. When she came out of the university she was a Communist. Now she's a Catholic crusader. She owns and runs a Catholic paper and skyhoots all over the country, delivering lectures. She has one girl in a Catholic school and is separated from her husband. You'll probably hear of her if you have any Catholic friends. She was in Miami last winter and lived out with Clem and Kate. I wouldn't have her around me.

Finally, Day tells of his own situation:

As for myself and the old woman: She's hale and hearty, and just got back to Miami yesterday, after spending the summer up here with the kids and me.... After I last saw you I made two wild goose chases to California and all I got was a bad attack of rheumatism, which I brought back to Florida the first of November and didn't get around again until along in January, and then not very good until the next summer. We had a big house then and fortunately Clem and Kate were there with us and she helped mother take care of the hellish invalid. By my rigid adherence to diet, I got rid of the rheumatic gout, but by that time I was out of a job and have been ever since. The first of last May, just after I had come to

New York, I had what I thought was a bad stomach attack, which came from too much food and too big a dinner. Lost thirty pounds in a week, and when I got hold of a real doctor, he found that my leaky heart had given out. . . .

This is a long letter to bore you with, but that's about all I have to say. After the *sickness* and all, I was in *mighty* bad financial shape when I got the bad news about Margaret's death. The undertaker asked for $115 which I wired this morning, and if it had been any more I'd have had to hock my watch, which is a shameful admission for a man of my age to make. I manage to keep going, pounding out an occasional story on this old type-writer. Got $750 from Saturday Evening Post for one published last May and expect to have another one with them soon.

Day's story, of course, was about horseracing. It was not much of a story, rather an interview with a legendary horse racing figure, an owner of a long line of track winners.

Somehow, John Day never lost his rural Southern sense of the special glory of the barber-shop rube. He closed his letter to Sally with "your cous*ing*" and then signed it "John Eye Day." "What a character," Sally must have said after she read the letter, and that is what he wanted her to say.

✿ 12

The Coming of the War

As A YOUNG socialist in her college days, Dorothy had been against war. Wars, so she and her comrades avowed, were organized by capitalists in the interest of increasing their profits. When she became a Catholic, she opposed war not because she still thought capitalists caused war, but because it was contrary to the teaching of Christ. "I just felt that it was simply not compatible with the gospel or the . . . idea of the brotherhood of man. I don't think you would change your brother or rectify great wrongs by the use of force. My absolute pacifism stems purely from the gospel teaching."

For most Catholics, such a position was almost unheard of. Historically, the relationship between the Church and bearing arms had been close. The medieval ideal of knightly valor appeared to have been that of the Church itself. Later, with the rise of the national state, there was the Thomistic doctrine of the "just war" to remove the pain of a suffering conscience for anyone who had scruples about killing in warfare.

Dorothy therefore had no strong Church tradition to back her. Neither could she rely on the support of an antiwar intellectual climate. After World War I there had been reaction against war by artists and some historians, but the air that people breathed still was laden with the spores of war—its legitimacy, its glamor, and even its necessity. By the mid 1930s there were unmistakable signs abroad that the disease of war threatened to fulminate. The *Catholic Worker* gave Dorothy's view: "We oppose . . . preparedness for war, a preparedness which is going on now on an unprecedented scale and which will undoubtedly lead to war." In another issue it emphasized that "the *Catholic Worker* is sincerely a *pacifist* paper. . . . The pacifist in the next war must be ready for martyrdom. We call

upon youth to prepare." All of which did not, apparently, upset
Worker readers. Many Americans by 1935 were convinced that they
had been "duped" by munitions-makers, bankers, and skillful British propaganda into entering World War I.

When the Spanish Civil War broke out in 1936, American Catholics found that conflict to be another matter. Most of the Catholic
press supported Franco, but the *Worker* declared itself neutral. In
the November, 1936, issue it said that "Catholics who look at Spain
and think Fascism is a good thing because Spanish Facists are fighting for the Church against Communist persecution should take
another look at recent events in Germany to see just how much
love the Catholic Church can expect."

The passionate arguments as to the identity of the authentic
villains in the civil war, Fascists or Loyalists, as Dorothy realized,
availed nothing. Both sides committed atrocities as both sides were
forced to desperate extremes. In October, 1938, Dorothy wrote an
editorial, "On the Use of Force," which placed her above the argument. She said that she realized that in the light of the conditions
existing in the world at that moment "it seems madness—to say as
we do—'we are opposed to the use of force as a means of settling
personal, national, or international disputes.'" Her position was
"truly" the "folly of the cross! But when we say 'Savior of the
world, save Russia,' [a phrase used in prayers in some churches] we
do not expect a glittering army to overcome the heresy. As long as
men trust to the use of force, only a superior, a more savage and
brutal force will overcome the enemy. We use his own weapons,
and we must make sure our own force is more savage, more bestial
than his own."

She continued: when "St. Peter drew the sword ... our Lord
rebuked him. They asked our Lord to prove His Divinity and come
down from the cross. But He suffered the 'failure' of the cross. His
apostles kept asking for a temporal kingdom. Even with Christ
Himself to guide and enlighten them, they did not see the primacy
of the spiritual. Only when the Holy Ghost descended on them did
they see." And now, she continued, "the whole world has turned to
the use of force.... Today the whole world is in the midst of a
revolution. We are living through it now—all of us."

As for Spain, she was "not praying for victory for Franco....
Nor are we praying for victory for the loyalists whose ... leaders
are trying to destroy religion. We are praying for the Spanish
people—all of them our brothers in Christ—all of them Temples

of the Holy Ghost, all of them members or potential members of the Mystical Body of Christ."

This editorial brought letters to Dorothy that were harsh beyond anything she had previously gotten. "If you cannot bring yourselves to sympathize with those Spaniards who, by the shedding of their own blood, are saving the spiritual heritage of future Spanish generations, and if you cannot be in tune with the immense majority of Catholics, the best and least you could do would be to keep your hands off a question about which you seem to know next to nothing."

So ran part of one letter. Another came from one of the Mott Street "guests": "Miss Day, since I do know you, Bill [Callahan] and our other associates, and since I do feel that the Catholic Worker does good work among . . . particular people . . . the fact remains that you are stubborn. . . . I know that hundreds of people have spoken to you in order to have you change certain ideals and conceptions of things concerning Catholic thought, yet you have never listened to anyone. You go only one straight narrow road, unassisted, unadvised, not listening to anything or anyone else. . . . You are known amongst the Bowery boys as a fool . . . [and] in true catholic-action circles of the modern type . . . you are not welcome, nor respected."

This Mott Street "guest," for the most part, had Dorothy well sized up. Others supported her position. One was Father Virgil Michel, who just weeks before his death wrote Dorothy to tell her that few things had given him "more comfort than your excellent article, 'On the Use of Force'. . . . Keep up the good work no matter what slanderous tongues may say. That is the way Christ himself did it." Another was Don Luigi Sturzo, the Italian priest who in the post–World War I era had opposed the rise of fascism and state socialism. Unacceptable to the Italian fascist government, he came to the United States to express his views. For the March, 1938, *Worker,* he wrote a piece on the Spanish war. "Is war sometimes necessary?" he asked. There were "those who believe in a 'holy' war in Spain to crush the 'Reds.' " They thought that war was necessary. "We do not. We do not believe in the necessity of any war, whether waged in the name of religion or in the name of the nation, in the name of right or in the name of fatherland. Was war sometimes the work of an inevitable fate? There are those who believe in the fatal inevitability of war. . . . We do not."

Father Sturzo was one of a number of Catholic intellectuals who resisted the attempts of a particular type of imperialistic mentality using the label "Catholic" to make the Spanish Civil War into a holy crusade. This type had for centuries had the vision of the faith made triumphant by what Dorothy called a "glittering army." The faithless would be ostracized, punished, even done away with until they could see their error, repent, and become baptized. Flags, anthems, and marching men were, of course, antithetical to the Cross. This conquering spirit was not only heretical, it was potentially murderous. It was this spirit, as national states began to emerge, that had weighed so heavily on the Moslems and, especially, on the Jews in Europe.

A strain of the contemporary anti-Semitism appeared in the Spanish war issue. Sometime in the course of that affair Jacques Maritain sent to Dorothy a statement called "A Frenchman's Thoughts on Affairs in Spain," which Maritain presumably had thought to publish and then decided not to. Anyway, he wanted Dorothy to see it. The substance of his statement was that the war in Spain was decidedly not a "holy war" and that introducing that fiction into the conflict "would create moral wounds and incurable animosities."

Maritain said that he was a convert to Catholicism and that "to the ministers of General Franco the word *convert* is a term of abuse, even of vilification, almost synonymous with *Jew* and *freemason.* This is a relic of those happy times when in Spain people were forced into baptism under pain of losing their citizenship. . . . I suppose the same ministers do not much like Saint Paul or Saint Augustine. . . . This is what a certain religious racism describes in curious jargon as being 'born Catholic.' "

As the affairs of American Catholics went, Peter Maurin's voice was small indeed, but he truly loved the Jews as the chosen people. In the late 1930s, Maurin set up a stall on the East Side, wishing nothing more than to discuss ideas with Jews who passed by. But few, if any, stopped to discourse, thinking, probably, that Peter was proselytizing. In the late 1930s and during the early war years, the *Worker* published a number of essays Peter wrote on the Jews under the theme, "Let's Save the Jews for Christ's Sake." One of many such essays declared, "The thought of the Church in every age has been that holiness is inherent in this exceptional, unique, and imperishable people which is protected by God, preserved as the apple of his eye in the midst of the destruction of so many peoples for the accomplishment of his ulterior designs." Maurin hoped that all Jews who so wished might be given free access to American hospitality.

Maurin seems to have thought that many Jews had adopted a disposition toward life that did not accord with their true destiny. As usual, his comment was brief and the illustration he used to make his point was concrete. "The Jewish *Daily Forward* looks forward and writes backward, and the reason it does not go forward is because it does not look backward, back to the prophets of Israel." His point, it appears, was that the *Daily Forward* affirmed state solutions rather than God's solutions to those perennial Jewish concerns of justice and community.

As for Dorothy, she was, in a social sense, practically Jewish. It was not just the years she had lived on the East Side. The people who were closest to her had been Jews: Rayna, Mike Gold, Lionel Moise, and then, during her years at the beach, Freda and Sasha Maruchess. Even after the beginning of the Catholic Worker movement she regularly visited Freda and Sasha. Over the years, as Dorothy grew in her spiritual life, that life took much of its nourishment from the Old Testament. The Psalms were her strong spiritual fare. Jailed in the late 1950s for her refusal to take shelter during an air raid warning, she commented in her notes how some of her fellow inmates longed for a "fix." Her morning "fix," she said, was her reading of the Psalms.

Like Peter, she thought of the Jews as a special people. "To be a Jew, singled out, a priestly people, unique—to be a Jew is something sacramental." On December 17, 1947, Dorothy, visiting at her sister Della's home, wrote in a note that she had just read a "booklet" by Father John Oesterreicher. "And now it is with great joy that I read ... another explanation of 'Salvation is from the Jews.' ... He quotes Msgr. Chas. Jourmet saying of the infant Church 'Never again on earth will the Church be so fervent, so loving, so pure as when she was wholly Jewish.' "

Dorothy's response to the plight of the Jews in Germany was to affirm Maurin's position. "Peter," Dorothy wrote in the *Worker,* "believes we should have more Jews than we do in this or any country. He calls them a bulwark against Nationalism.... Christians are followers of Christ. Because of this, says Peter, every time a Christian sees a Jew he should be reminded of Christ and love him for being of the race that Christ was part of."

In the United States, as World War II approached, anti-Semitism became a rampant disease, and one of its ugly signs could be discerned in *Social Justice,* the publication of Father Charles Coughlin, parish priest at Royal Oak, Michigan. The paper found the evils of the time in the workings of Roosevelt's New Deal and bankers, alike corrupted by some greedy international conspiratorial force that was taking from good, hard-working people their rightful due in the way of a job and fair wages. This malevolent force was in some instances capitalistic and in others communistic, but in all instances, the paper suggested, Jews were at the heart of what was going wrong with the world.

As the signs of the coming of another war became more obvious and frequent, *Social Justice* and Father Coughlin himself, in his Sunday afternoon national network radio talks, saw the "international conspiracy" behind that, too. By 1939 the Coughlin phenomenon, having taken on the character of a crusade, became the nucleus of a more extensive organization, the "Christian Front." Signaling the main turn of Coughlin's crusade from an economic populist to a predominantly anti-Semitic movement was *Social Justice's* serial publication, beginning August 18, 1938, of the "Protocols of Zion." The basic "big lie" in the way of anti-Semitic fakery, this fabricated "document" had been circulated in Europe for forty years with its purported revelation of plans made by the inner circle of Jewish strategists to take over the Western World and destroy its culture.

It was Bill Callahan who most directly and conspicuously denounced the increasing anti-Semitism abroad in the country, putting much of the blame for it on Father Coughlin. In his column in the *Worker* of May, 1939, "The Gadfly," Callahan chided Father Coughlin for the tactics of those who sold *Social Justice* and for his own responsibility in fueling the increasing anti-Semitism in the country: "We have stood in front of the House of God selling or distributing the *Catholic Worker,* and have been forced to listen to the loud, coarse gibes of your followers. . . . They stand about yelling 'Communists,' and have, on occasion, torn the papers from our hands and even struck us. Your followers are of that temper, Father." Callahan concluded with the statement that "if a real wave of anti-Semitism sweeps the United States, if in the future Jews are persecuted as they are in Europe, you, Father Coughlin, must be ready to assume a goodly part of the responsibility. Are you ready to do that?"

Callahan's criticism of Coughlin brought Callahan and the *Worker* an increase in the mail volume, much of it critical. "It surprised me greatly that you should take this stand when you know so well the conditions of this country," ran one letter. "Have you any idea what it means to have your parents, harassed with worry, driven to distraction, because they can't make ends meet and are sacrificing everything that they have worked hard for all their lives? Would you take the only champion we have from us? . . . Why shouldn't we know the truth about the Jewish situation as well as other current problems?"

The *Brooklyn Tablet* and its editor, Patrick Scanlan, were brought into the fray when Dorothy sent a letter to some New York papers and to the *New Republic* strongly criticizing Coughlin for his anti-Semitism and criticizing, too, Scanlan for his "pugnacious" defense of Coughlin. Scanlan wrote a letter to Dorothy's confessor and adviser for the paper, Father Joseph McSorley, about Dorothy's action. If he were "not mistaken," Scanlan wrote, "Canon Law prohibits Catholics writing for anti-Catholic publications without permission." Dorothy, said Scanlan in a second letter to McSorley, "should publicly apologize and endeavor to explain a position which is scandalous."

Ordinarily, apologies came from Dorothy only when she clearly recognized that her position was erroneous. In this instance her conscience was, as she saw it, completely clear.

Callahan's complaint about young Workers being set on by Christian Fronters was true. Julia Porcelli told of her experience selling the *Worker*. "I was almost arrested outside of St. Patrick's Church. I was selling the *Catholic Worker* up there and Christian Fronters (Father Coughlin's crew) . . . came out of the Church and grabbed the papers from me and were pulling me down the street and I was protesting, and picking them up [the papers] and guessed they were going to start on me. Then this policeman—he had been around—he came up and questioned me a number of times before this, and I told him I had permission from the pastor. He come around very slowly. I think he wanted them to get rid of me, but I held my ground and he sort of gently shoo'ed them away, and he was going to go and see the pastor and find out about it. He [the policeman] never came back to tell me to go away, but he looked like he thought I was a communist. I was real frightened at the moment."

In May, 1939, Dorothy and some acquaintances who were like-minded in their concern for the Jews formed the "Committee of Catholics to Fight Anti-Semitism." The purpose of the committee was "to oppose the dangerous aberration of anti-Semitism" and "to popularize genuine teaching among our Catholic people in all walks of life by means of leaflets, pamphlets, newsletters, radio broadcasts, educational programs, and a speakers' bureau." The committee, said its founders, "aims to reach primarily those who contrary to the teaching of Christianity and the principles of democracy are taking part, unfortunately, in spreading race hatred and minority hatreds in the United States." Some of the people named as the committee's organizers were Emmanual Chapman, a Jewish philosopher and professor who had added the Catholic faith to his Semitic heritage; novelist Margaret Culkin Banning; artist Jean Charlot; John Brophy, director of the C.I.O.; Baroness Catherine de Hueck; and a long list of priests and nuns. In Chicago John Cogley, the editor of the *Chicago Catholic Worker,* and two of Cogley's associates, Edward Marciniak and Marie Antoinette Roulet, organized the Chicago branch of the committee. Marciniak, former president of the Chicago Inter-Student Catholic Committee, became the president of the Chicago Committee. The immediate and principal work of the committee, as its initiators saw it, was to get out a paper to counteract the anti-Semitism of *Social Justice.* The first issue of the paper, principally Bill Callahan's work and called the *Voice,* appeared in July, 1939. It stated what the paper was about, listed its charter members, and put itself in direct opposition to *Social Justice.* Father James Gillis, editor of the *Catholic World* at the time, stated the case as the *Voice* saw it: "We may soon see . . . warfare between Jews and Gentiles in New York. God forbid! But unless the Jew baiters, some of them clerics, change their tune, blood will be upon their souls." During its life of over a year, the *Voice* printed statements of prominent Catholics who decried anti-Semitism, and featured editorials on the causes and manifestations of anti-Semitism in the United States at the time. The most interesting material in the paper described Christian Front meetings, written, one guesses, by Bill Callahan, who probably went to rallies and meetings incognito, perhaps even wearing a fake moustache and dark glasses. The *Voice* was published until the coming of World War II. By that time, overt anti-Semitism had been drowned in the tide of war.

On one occasion, though, the remarks of a prominent Jewish woman offended Dorothy. She had attended the luncheon of the National Conference of Christians and Jews given for "one hundred and eighteen American Writers." As she later talked of this meeting with Maurin, he suggested that she get the names of all who had attended and send them copies of the *Catholic Worker*. But Dorothy wondered what good it would do, since the paper was "Catholic," and then related an experience she had had at the luncheon. "One woman said at that luncheon that we would have to get rid of the Cross before there was a better attitude toward the Jew. She advised more aggressive attitudes and even knocking people about a bit. I suggested that this sounded like those who went around with a chip on their shoulder being 'militant' Catholics. And I remarked on the Negro, one-tenth of our population, not being represented (the luncheon was at Longchamps)."

Anyway, continued Dorothy, "I don't think she [the woman] liked to be compared to the militant Catholic." And, adding further injury to Dorothy's feelings, there was "President [Henry N., of Vassar] McCracken's report of the meeting [that] called hers [the woman who wanted to get rid of the Cross] the most significant contribution of the luncheon." The reason for the woman's remark, Dorothy supposed, was that she had been conditioned "early in life, through images and words suggestive of cruelty and ill-feeling," an emotion that had been "carried on from generation to generation." Such images, Dorothy thought, should be changed to "ideas of kindliness and good feeling" toward the elimination of intolerance. "Are those the popular thinkers, the key minds, the leaders of this generation?" she asked Peter. "And two college presidents at the meeting! I don't wonder Catholics keep themselves to themselves. No wonder they are a group within a group, almost a state within a state."

But Peter acted as though Dorothy's comment on the luncheon had not been made. "He went right on with his ideas. 'We must get all material from Paulding—he is literary editor of the *Commonweal* now—and he will give us more detailed stuff about the leading personalists in France. There is Mounier, editor of *Esprit,* whose *Personalist Manifesto* was translated by Virgil Michel. There is Davidson or Dennison—I cannot remember his name. He is an historian. There is Landberg, a psychologist, and Jacques Madaule, who ran for police chief in Paris.'" And Peter continued his thought.

These were the crises in the world, with which Dorothy would contend, and then there were those matters immediately at hand that touched her life. In January, 1939, her *From Union Square to Rome* was published by the Preservation of the Faith Press. It was advertised in the *Worker* as selling for $1.50 the copy. This was about the only time that she ever seemed to recommend the book to anyone. When in later years the book was introduced into a conversation of which she was a part, she would direct the subject to other matters, saying that she disliked the book because of its "journalistic title." She may have disliked it for other reasons. It was her "convert" book, ostensibly a statement to her brother John as to why she had left her radical life to become a Catholic. The book, like everything else Dorothy wrote, was autobiographical and is interesting because some of the things that are mentioned in *From Union Square to Rome* are omitted in her later "autobiography," as she called it, *The Long Loneliness*. The differences are not important, but they illustrate Dorothy's way of simply setting down and writing without much reference to what she had written previously.

The book was not widely reviewed. The *Catholic World* criticized it for "its rather niggardly measure of self-revelation," for being "uneven and highly emotional." The usual criticism of her writing was made—that it "rambles." The well-known syndicated columnist Westbrook Pegler criticized her for her "moral frowsiness" in her "distorted desire to be with the poor and the abandoned." He characterized her as, a former rough-and-tumble radical who became a Catholic.

There were approving letters. It was a "grand book," a priest wrote. A seminarian wrote to say that he was "fearful of becoming cold after ordination" and that at times "the temptations seemed . . . insurmountable." But reading Dorothy's book had been "the best thing I know to keep my feet on the ground and my head above the clouds."

Old John Monaghan, in prison as usual, wrote in to ask for a copy. He had heard of Dorothy's "From Times Square to Rome," and having been a "guest" at the Worker house he would like to read it. Could he keep it "long enough for several enemies of society to read?" If Dorothy had trepidations about loaning him the book, she should "forget, momentarily, that a con's guarantee is worthless." Monaghan hoped to be out and about sometime in the future and when that happened he would see everyone at Mott Street. "I liked you people and your style. . . . Peter was great. Perhaps I'll see him again some day."

Dorothy sent Monaghan a book. "Some day," if it ever came for Monaghan, was still a while away. In the June, 1941, issue of the

Worker, Julia Porcelli wrote of a prison visit she and Dorothy made to see Monaghan. And, imprisoned though he was, he kept his pen at work defending Dorothy from her detractors. One day, as he read the *Brooklyn Tablet,* he saw a letter to the editor from a "Mr. Moran." Mr. Moran, it seems, was most critical of Dorothy and the Worker movement, but whatever eloquence he had mustered in his denunciation of Dorothy could not equal Monaghan's statement of her virtues. "Mr. Moran, Hearken! Listen! Can't you hear the rumblings of a dream come true? The day has arrived and one of God's own . . . is giving her all. She and her fellow workers are building; trying to erect an edifice with the most difficult materials, and as usual the wreckers are nibbling at the weak spots, seeking to drive wedges under the structure. . . . Truly they [the Workers] are being fools for Christ's sake."

"Yes," continued Monaghan, "I know whereof I speak. I have enjoyed the hospitality of 115 Mott St. and the Easton farm. As I observed those people and their works . . . my silent prayer was: 'Dear God, send us thousands of Dorothys and Peters to show the workers of the country that once again we can hear "See those Christians, how they love one another." ' " From loving Christians, the old man's vision focused on Dorothy. "In my prison cell to-night, Mr. Moran, I am looking at pictures; pictures indelibly stamped in my mind—pictures of Miss Day at prayer, at the altar rail, talking to me, one of God's derelicts and a total stranger to her, and talking to the men in the bread line. At the same time I am looking at the final paragraph of your letter. God help you, Mr. Moran. But that is how the saint's crown of glory is formed, isn't it?"

Monaghan's letter somehow ended up in Dorothy's papers. Perhaps someone at the *Tablet* sent it over to her. Ordinarily, Dorothy would show strong negative feelings when she was called a saint. But Monaghan was different. It was his style. He was old-fashioned —his prose was full-blown. Besides, he was in prison.

In the midst of the accelerating crises of the world, there was one of those milestone events in Dorothy's own life, momentous in its overall proportion, but which appeared of such small importance when it occurred that she scarcely mentioned it.

In her journal for Tuesday, May 16, 1939, Dorothy wrote one line: "Met J. [John, her brother] at restaurant. Home at 11.30. Telephone call pop ill." Her entry for the next day was "Pop died this morning 7.30." On Thursday she noted that she had met her mother at the train. On Friday she entered one word: "Funeral." In the June, 1939, *Worker,* Dorothy said, "My father died last week. He was seventy years old, and worked right up to the day before he died. Mother said that if we had all been praying for the kind of death he wanted, it could not have been better. Which was a little consolation. We were all there at his funeral, two brothers, my sister, my mother, and I—all but Donald, who was in Finland at the time."

These remarks about her father's death sound as though she were hard put to dredge up some consoling sentiment to mark the occasion. Perhaps indeed there was little more to say. As John Day had written to his cousin in Tennessee a year and a half before, he knew that he was about to "shuffle off"—that it would be "any old time now"—and that when that happened he would be cremated. He wanted no clergy—no obsequies. And this was the way it was.

In the last years of his life, Day worked as an inspector for the New York State racing commission. His home, when he was in New York, was the Empire Hotel on Broadway at Sixty-Third Street. Grace, it seems, preferred Miami and came to New York only occasionally. Day lived alone in his last days, working at his job and otherwise still trying to write material that he could sell. When Dorothy heard that her father was ill that Tuesday morning, did she take the subway uptown to try to help him? She probably did not. Had she ever gone to the Empire Hotel to see him the last two years of her father's life? If she did, she did not mention it in her appointment book. But even if she had gone, as she bitterly recognized, she probably would have been ordered out. There was nothing in John Day that made for final reconciliations or a death-bed conversion. So when Dorothy wrote of death in the June, 1939, *Worker,* she wrote with much more feeling on that of Mr. Breen, the crotchety old man who lived at 115 Mott Street, who died the day after her father's funeral.

In the last years of her own life, Dorothy sometimes wrote of her father and of the good things she remembered about him in her childhood days. Perhaps then she began to understand him. On her frequent visits to Della in these years, one can be certain that they talked of their father many times, wondering at his strange behavior and pondering the reasons for it.

Few men die without leaving some mark or gesture that represents, finally, a sign of their hope. Although he had always carried a Bible, John Day wanted no preachers around him. For him there was one thing that testified to beauty and truth: a horse, charged with lean power, reaching for the finish line in the bright afternoon sun of a winter's day in Miami. So when he died his ashes were scattered over the Hialeah track in Miami, where he had been a steward and partner.

The summer of 1939! In Germany, Hitler, driven by some furious and maniacal sense of an impending ecstasy of community, decided to reduce Poland by war. On Mott Street, radios carried through open windows the music of Benny Goodman's band, giving out with "Don't Be That Way," and Tommy Dorsey's "The Dipsy Doodle." And hardly a day passed that one did not hear, at least twice, somebody's singing and playing "The Beer Barrel Polka."

For Dorothy, the music was little more than noise. Several months previous she had joined a group to have dinner with Raissa Maritain, the wife of the philosopher. Dorothy noted that Mrs. Maritain had "expressed a deep interest in the Negro in this country and the evening ended with a half hour visit to Harlem where we sat in the Savoy and watched the dancers and listened to swing music." A half hour of it was probably all that she could stand. Three or four hours of some solid Wagner would have been her fare.

Dorothy's life followed in its accustomed patterns. Usually she awakened early in the morning for her spiritual reading and personal prayers. This early routine was getting to be a necessary part of her life—her moment of confronting herself, of restoring herself to a right relationship to God. That part of the day she could be free from intrusions, for the understanding was abroad in the Worker house that one would have to have a most exceptional reason to violate her privacy. After her prayers and reading, she went to Mass.

On Saturday nights she went to confession, and many times after this rite she would feel relieved of whatever problem it was that had bothered her. But once, as she noted in her journal, her problem was not relieved. "Went to confession last night and communion this A.M. But feel a great sense of conflict, almost a beginning of the struggle all over again."

What conflict? It was likely the one that she referred to in some notes she made in 1946. "It took me a great many years not to wake up in the morning and reach out for human warmth near me." Then she added, "When will I learn to love all, men and women with an intense awareness of their beauty, their virtues . . . to see them as Christ sees them?" Another brief thought followed: "A sample of the love of God. Intense, of body and soul, yet pure. 'For thee my soul thirsteth, for thee my flesh longeth, O now exceedingly.' " Finally she wrote: "We are without sex, all of us when we say at each meal, 'Behold the handmaid of the Lord, be it done unto me according to thy word.' "

Love—the love of all and not an exclusive love, the love of God —was the point where all the questions of existence could be laid and there be answered. In the May, 1939, *Worker* she wrote one of her most remarkable spiritual reflections: "Hell Is Not to Love Any More." In its original form the phrase came from Dostoevsky's *Brothers Karamazov.* Stanley Vishnewski remembers Dorothy's once telling Gerry Griffin that "the only way he would ever understand the Catholic Worker was by reading Dostoevsky." "Fathers and teachers," says Dostoevsky's Father Zossima in a conversation with his fellow monks just before his death, "What is hell? I maintain that it is the suffering of being unable to love."

Dorothy gave her own statement of this theme: "God in his goodness has given the heart of man the capacity for human love, and it is good to compare this love between a betrothed man and woman and the love we are to bear each other. Love makes all things easy. When one loves, there is at that time a correlation between the spiritual and the material. Even the flesh itself is energized, the human spirit is made strong. All sacrifice, all suffering is easy for the sake of love." It was love, she continued, "which will solve all problems, family, national, international. This is the foundation stone of the Catholic Worker movement. It is on this that we build."

She did a full schedule of traveling and speaking that summer, but when hot weather came she stayed home, mainly at Staten Island, presumably in her old cottage, and at Easton. It was, it seems, just months after this that her cottage burned. How it happened, she never said, but Julia Porcelli suggests that it was set by people who objected to the Workers' taking black children to the Island during the summers.

In her journal for July 30, 1939, Dorothy says that "F." [Forster] was "transferring a lot in Princess Bay to Tamar, and we are going to build a camp there for children next year." This camp, called Our Lady Star of the Sea Camp, apparently caused the trouble. It was closed after 1941 because of objections to it by the Board of Health.

Dorothy and Tamar were on the Island on August 21, taking a vacation together. Dorothy needed one. She had been having "backaches, headaches" and "weakness" all summer. She wrote in her journal that evening that she was feeling better and that she and Tamar had "just finished some bread and butter and herring, and now it is about time for bed. We have been sleeping until 9 and 10 in the morning."

Startling news had come over the radio that evening. Germany and Russia had signed a nonaggression pact. She went next door to talk about it with her friends, Freda and Sasha Maruchess, because, as she mentioned in her journal, the news had caused their son Dick to be "much upset." Dick was now about eighteen years old and just right for the army. He had reason to be "upset," although he may have been disturbed at the unseemly spectacle of the Soviet Union, in which so many had invested their hopes, involved in a momentary affair of convenience with Germany.

The war came on Sunday, September 3, at 6 A.M. On the evening of September 23, Mott Street was alive with sound and action. The Italians were having a "festa," the feast of San Gennaro. Across the street from the Worker house, a dance was going on in a small park. A profusion of Japanese lanterns lighted the area, and a loudspeaker sent the recorded pulsations of swing music cascading up and down the street. Couples danced in the park and spilled into the street. In doorways little girls caught the beat and twirled one another around. "Mothers sat on benches and boxes along the street, and babies toddled up and down, narrowly escaping collision with passers-by." Dorothy and some of the people in the Worker house "sat there with them, enjoying the last days of summer weather. There was a bit of a chill in the air which made dancing enjoyable." The air was so clear "that the stars shone brightly. For a long while a brilliant half moon hung above the middle of the street down towards Canal Street. When I looked up later, I was surprised to see that it was passing behind the tall tenements, but the stars still shone with sparkling brilliance."

On the East Side, Dorothy noted, the feast of the Atonement was beginning for Orthodox Jews. As they sat, Kichi Harada, the Japanese woman who stayed at the Mott Street house, walked up. She had been over to the East Side and noticed that all of the stores were closed but in the synagogues there were lights. The doors of the synagogues were open, Kichi continued, so "I went upstairs and asked if strangers could come in. The man at the door told me I could go upstairs to the gallery and I went there and sat with all the women." Many of the women sitting there were weeping. "I never saw people so devoted," Kichi said.

One night in early December Dorothy lay in her bed, notebook on her lap, writing of her doings in the recent past. She had been to Della's that day, having walked with Tamar across town to the end of Eighth Avenue, where Della had picked them up. Mother Grace was there and Della's husband, Franklin, had played records for them. Della's family was growing: "Susie is sweet, Davie at movies, John at birthday party."

She was just as pleased to be in bed, though. The street was quiet. She could hear the "very clear" sound of the river boats, a "child crying, occasional auto horn, people talking."

When something bothered Dorothy, she would write it in her journal, because it almost invariably turned out that when she looked at her journal again what it was that had bothered her had gone. She had had to stay in bed the first part of the week with "cramped pains in the heart." Now she felt "much better, tho still some pain around heart, and headache."

Because she had odd, old-fashioned ideas about the meaning of symptoms, it is difficult to know what ailed her. She was now forty-two years old and beginning to suffer various and usually vague complaints. Her bed rests, too, may have been a device to avoid the continuous stream of people who for one reason or another wanted to see her. She was becoming well known, and many came to talk, to stay for several days, presuming that nothing could be better for Dorothy or suit her better than their presence—to take her out to dinner, to share with her their insights, and to demonstrate that they, too, could live with the abandoned for a few days. There were, of course, some people she genuinely welcomed. It was the flow of the mainly curious, always wanting to see her, that pressed on her time and good nature.

And always, there were tensions in the house—more than enough to produce "cramps around the heart." That early glow of community in the Worker house that included "guests" as well as those who came to help was all but extinguished by the caterwauling of people with broken minds and spirits. Much of it landed squarely on Dorothy. Her journal tells some of the story: "Michael first, then Cyril began tormenting me with demands for the impossible—Michael that we get him back in the seminary from which he was dismissed five years ago, and Cyril that I take him to Easton and give him a private room for his mind's health. He has recently been released from the Rockland State Hospital for the insane where he has been confined for trying to kill his brother." This "persecution" went on for weeks, Dorothy wrote. Michael "would come in and stand over me and with livid face, sweat rolling down his face, call down curses from heaven upon me, damning my soul to the lowest hell, for interfering, as he said, with his vocation. He was going to see to it, he protested, that I was going to be punished, and all who worked with me."

It got to the point where she was concerned about her life. "I was afraid, coming and going." It was bad enough to be pestered by two of them but then came Polly, "out of Manhattan State hospital [and she] . . . was very abusive."

Her journal of July 23, 1940, tells of conditions that had become almost desperate. "Today the telephone was turned off. Gas and electric next. No Mass. Ankle an excuse. It does get very badly swollen at night and pains. . . . Frank in, filled with grievances against Joe [Zarella] and me. I am so often shocked at the positive venom in the majority around me against . . . Joe. He is called a young punk, a stooge, a yes man and God knows what else. I probably don't hear the worst."

She probably did not hear "the worst." To those with inflamed minds and spirits, Zarella's balance, energy, and intelligence were an affront. His even-handed management of the house, wherever it touched any one of them, was seen as a calculated personal assault on a vital interest.

Matters were even worse at the farm, where factional feuding had on occasion broken into ugly scenes and where the blame for it all was usually placed on Dorothy. "Victor [Smith] says the conflict comes over the spiritual program. But the charges are mismanagement of funds, self glorification, domination, etc. God knows why the whole thing does not fall apart. The only indication (for me) of the will of God, can come thru the archbishop. Fr. Joachim is on my side, also Fr. McSorley, but they can be accused of not knowing the facts. . . . To be hated and scorned by one's very own—this is poverty. This then is perfect joy."

The state of things made her think of the war. "Already our houses . . . are like refugee centers. They are like camps set up in the midst of class war, or race war. We live from hand to mouth, as best we can, and there is never enough to go around, never enough warmth, never enough energy to keep clean."

As she thought of what she and Peter were trying to do, she

wondered at her "presumption." Even so, she said, "I have to go on. I pray for love that I may learn to love God, and I am surrounded by such human hatred and dislike that all natural love and companionship is taken from me." There was one thing more: she was not going to wallow in self-pity. "When these accusations begin to rain down on me, I can see all too clearly that though immediately and specifically not applicable, they are generally true, of the past if not the present."

There was another aspect of the matter on which she felt that she could be blamed. It was that of judging these people. It was "perhaps the greatest burden" that they had to bear, "the contempt, the judgment of others. 'If they would do this and this, they would get along better. If they would think this way, the way I think, if they did as I do, they would not have this mental breakdown.'" It was "everywhere. It is among those who work in the bureaus; it is in us who go to live with the poor. . . . If you say your rosary; if you keep better hours; stop drinking. . . . Oh yes, we have many plans to help the poor if we could only feed them, shelter them, clothe them . . . without assuming that we had all the answers."

It could have been these reflections that prompted Dorothy to send a circular letter to all of the Worker houses. It was an answer to those who were beginning to object to having the demented and the abandoned around the houses, an answer to those who wanted to throw them out. "We feel," she wrote, "and have always felt since the work started, that when we accepted a man in the group and gave him a bed, we were accepting him as one of a family, as a brother. It is so hard to remake men. It is not a matter of a few months or even a few years. On the one hand, we have to change the social order in order that men might lead decent Christian lives, and on the other, we must remake men to remake the social order. Order cannot be imposed from above." Changing things would take suffering and time. "But the more we suffer with it, the more we will learn. . . . Infinite patience, suffering, is needed. Think of Lazarus at the Gate. Read 'The Honest Thief' by Dostoevsky. There is a great lesson of love here." As for "getting rid of those who offend and taking in others, one may as well understand that the new batch will be exactly the same as the last. You cut off the head of the tyrant and two others spring up."

The tribulation that Dorothy experienced at Mott Street in

those first two years of the war in Europe was, as she observed, just a small part of the suffering that was going on in the world. "We are so much better off than the majority of sufferers in the world today, that it seems folly to talk of sacrifice." And after all of the suffering that she believed would come had occurred, "we will look back on our freedom and opportunity for personal initiative, and even to the means we have had, as rank luxury."

The assaults on her in this period were not just verbal. Once her person was invaded by body lice: "Every now and then I found an isolated one crawling on my suit, my dress, my underwear. Once at the beginning of my affliction I went to a tea ... for Jacques Maritain and some other exiles. George Shuster, president of Hunter College, was there and remarked on the tranquility of my appearance. And underneath my nerves were shuddering. We do not need hair shirts around Houses of Hospitality."

Meanwhile, there was the "other" war to involve her concern. Her attitude toward it was curious. The war was an object—something loathesome, an abomination, a thing so evil that to permit her passion to be even remotely aroused by it in the hope that a battle might be won, a nation might triumph, was to be stained by that evil. Never in the entire course of the conflict did she ever say or do anything to suggest that she felt one side or the other was right and should prevail. Her own disposition toward it is suggested by a note she wrote in her journal in the fall of 1940: "Turn off your radio, put away your daily paper. Read one review of events a week and spend time reading." For a while, at least, people will still "eat, sleep, love, worship, marry, have children, and, somehow, live in the midst of war, in the midst of anguish. The sun continues to shine, the leaves flaunt their vivid color, there is a serene warmth in the day and an invigorating cold at night."

In June, 1940, the "Peace Edition" of the *Worker* came out. An editorial, "Our Stand," was featured, and Dorothy's stand was the Sermon on the Mount. "For eight years we have been opposing the use of force—in the labor movement, in the class struggle, as well as in the struggles between countries. . . . But we consider that we have inherited the Beatitude and that our duty is clear." And if America were to be invaded? "We say again that we are opposed to all but the use of nonviolent means to resist such an invader."

Seen in the perspective of forty years, Dorothy's pacifist stand at this point was one of the significant events in contemporary religious history. In 1940 her absolute pacifism seemed a much too simplistic response to the problem of the various madnesses that the world then faced. A victorious war by the Allied nations would win more time for sanity and perhaps set the foundation on which could be made a major advance toward a more human world. Or so it seemed to those idealists who admitted war as the ultimate but necessary sacrifice that an otherwise peaceable people would have to make.

The "Our Stand" editorial caused a sizeable stir, especially when Dorothy followed it up with a ukase sent to all of the Worker houses. "We know that there are those who are members of 'Catholic Worker' groups throughout the country who do not stand with us in this issue. We have not been able to change their views through what we have written in the paper, or by letters, or by personal conversation. They wish still to be associated with us, to perform the corporal works of mercy. In some cases they will still distribute the paper. . . . In other cases, they will take it upon themselves to suppress the paper and hinder its circulation. In those cases, we feel it to be necessary that they disassociate themselves."

The immediate consequence of her pacifist proclamation was dissension in the houses and a drop in the circulation of the paper. From the Queen of Peace House of Hospitality in Sacramento, Arthur Ronz wrote Dorothy to say that if the *Worker* was going to be "as strong propacifist" as it had been, "I'm afraid a few would be enough. On the other hand, if . . . [it] returned to the essentials, that is, . . . [carried] news only about the in-season-out-of-season practice of voluntary poverty and the spiritual and corporal works of mercy—then we will take 500." Jane Marra from the Boston house wrote on December 1 to say that they in Boston "wanted to cancel another 1000 papers."

Letters opposing her position came in considerable volume. Some were abusive and some professed an inability to comprehend her lack of awareness as to what was going on in the world. On October 15, she got a letter from England. "The Atlantic is wide and maybe, it strikes me, you are not fully aware what is going on over here. . . . There are very few people in Britain that do not think war is horrible and that it is most of all horrible that a world that did not want to go to war has been driven to fighting." The English, said the letter writer, were fighting so "that there may once again be an order in Europe. . . . Do not think because we are involved in these things they are any less horrible to us than they are to you. ... If you have still the space in America to discuss whether a Christian can fight or not it is primarily because ... the Atlantic is wide and because the people of Britain and her allies are prepared to risk their own ... safety for the sake of their fellows, the men and women Nazism tortured and betrayed."

Dorothy could certainly understand the letter writer's position. More than once in the *Worker,* she showed her respect for the conscience of those who differed from her. One reaction to her announcement of pacifism, however, must have caused her some bewilderment, because the critic, Mike Gold, made his case against Dorothy out of some hazy impression of what he thought the "facts" ought to be. In his column in the Communist *Daily Worker,* "Change the World," Gold wrote "Some Comments on Loving Your Enemy," or the "War for Brotherhood," as he thought the war in Europe should be called.

He wanted to comment on something his "old friend Dorothy Day" had put out in "an earnest little paper, 'The Catholic Worker.'" Dorothy had announced that "her group is neutral and pacifist in this war against the Nazis. They refused to hate the Nazis and will work for 'peace.' I wonder what sort of peace they mean." In fact, said Gold, "I just can't ever believe the mystic who says he 'loves his enemy.' It is the most difficult of all tenets in Christian theology, and some of the noblest of human beings have spent unhappy lives trying to practice it. But who ever succeeded?"

There was this instance of Dorothy, for example. She had "always been an honest person, and has followed her own lights as truly and passionately as an honest person can in this twisted world." But, said Gold, "I would feel more respectful of her eternal pacifism if she had also been a pacifist during the Spanish war. Then she was on the side of Franco, however, and not a word of reproach for the fascist massacres of whole cities, of women and babies and the sick and the poor, with bombs and planes furnished by Mussolini and Hitler." Yes, Dorothy "has been more affected by the horrible politics of the fascists in the Catholic Church than she knows. ... Surely Christ was not a fascist."

Still, Dorothy's life followed its accustomed pattern. If the world had been scheduled to end in seven days, she would have spent those days with Tamar and in reading a good book. In March, 1940, she was reading N. K. Krupskaya's *Reminiscences of Lenin.* She noted that "most of the 2nd volume which I have just finished reading is about this struggle between philosophies. I finished the book last night." She had been reading the book in bed all day, "sick with a headache." That night when she went to sleep, she "dreamed of revolution and a poem, the last line of each stanza 'Be Kind, Cain!' It was almost in a tone of satire, directed at me." Someone "had said I was too kind to the Communists in my book [*From Union Square to Rome*], and the attitude taken by our opponents is that we do not realize what they are capable of. Indeed we do! Revolution, terror, mob-spirit, makes murderers. But still in spite of the poem, our stand has to be 'Love your enemies, overcome evil with good.'"

In September she noted that she had just finished Dostoevsky's *The Raw Youth*. She made a brief comment: "Many of the ideas of *The Possessed* and *The Brothers* [Karamazov] are in that early novel. Versiloff a more mature Stavrogin, Berdyaev said. I wish I had his [Berdyaev's] book on Dos[toevsky]. I have only a defective copy with 50 pages missing."

There were her hours and sometimes days with Tamar at Staten Island and at Easton. With Tamar now fifteen, her mother was beginning to cast about for a proper direction to her education. For several years Tamar had gone to St. Patrick's school for girls on Staten Island, but, as it turned out, she had little in the way of interest or aptitude for the standard liberal arts emphasis of a Catholic girls school. She was a quiet, self-effacing young woman who took her greatest pleasure in the animals on the farm at Easton and in the company of her mother.

During the year 1939-1940, Dorothy sent Tamar to Ade Bethune's home at Newport, Rhode Island, where Tamar would be instructed in handicrafts and the domestic arts. Miss Bethune, who had done the art work for the *Worker* over the early years of its publication, knew Tamar and was fond of her. The following year, Tamar went to a Catholic school for girls in Canada. This school, the *Ecole Menagere*, was a farm school for women. Dorothy sent Tamar there, one supposes, because she felt that her daughter needed to be more on her own. She felt, too, that Tamar should have some life apart from the Worker, both at Easton and at Mott Street.

Dorothy's New Year's resolution to "pay no attention to health of body but only that of soul" sounds like the old-fashioned pious intention that used to be included in New Year's resolutions, but in her case it was not empty piety. There was a singular, unremitting purposefulness in her spiritual pilgrimage and, curious as it is, in these years when the world was at war, she made her greatest spiritual gains—gains that gave her such a sense of the certainty of her course that in 1941 she would exclaim in her journal, "Help me, O my God, to write about these joys of the spiritual life."

The occasion for this clarification and heightening of her spiritual life was the Catholic Worker retreats, the first of which was in May, 1933. It occurred at the convent of Mary Reparatrix on Twenty-Eighth Street, which was just across the street from the "Little Church Around the Corner," where fashionable weddings were held. So situated, the convent, retreat house, and church were all enclosed by high buildings, and there was no garden in which she could walk. Her retreat was a private one in which she was left alone "to read retreats of bygone days which aimed to make you begin a retreat in a state of remorse, self-examination, penitence—I endured it for two days and could not wait to get away, to get out on the streets where I could breathe, walk freely, sense my freedom from restraint. I felt that I had been in jail, in solitary confinement." So she left, glad to be rid of the experience, and telling herself that "man is not made to live alone."

It was Dorothy's friend Sister Peter Claver who reintroduced her to the retreat. In 1938 she gave Dorothy a sheaf of retreat notes that she had acquired from her confessor, a Father Giri. The notes were from a retreat by Onesimus Lacouture, a Canadian Jesuit who in the early thirties developed a retreat form characterized by its rigor. Dorothy did not "find them at all appealing." She put them aside because she had a prejudice against Father Giri. She had once heard him "talking about the hypocrisy of the Protestant clergy and since I got my first religion from a Baptist or Methodist minister when I was seven and went to church with a little neighbor, I felt sorry he so maligned them. What could he know about it? It did not make for peace between Protestant and Catholic, so to speak."

But Sister Peter, who perhaps more than anyone understood Dorothy's spiritual need, felt that Dorothy should have a retreat, but more than that, she should have the particular retreat on which Father Giri's notes had been made. As it turned out, the process toward this objective was long and roundabout. Sometime in 1939 Sister Peter brought a Josephite priest to Mott Street, a Father Pacifique Roy. According to Dorothy's account in *The Long Loneliness*, as she and some of her Worker friends were sitting at the dining room table one morning Father Roy, just arriving, sat down and began to expound Gospel to them. He was another Peter in that he talked as long as there was anyone to listen. His "glowing" words held Dorothy "spellbound." God had become man so man could become God. There should be no lingering in "putting on Christ." Therefore the natural life should be just a subordinate incident in attaining the life of the spirit into which the person was initiated at baptism.

Dorothy was taken with the priest's simplicity and his single-purposed vocational aim of spreading the Gospel. "He preached the Gospel, the doctrine, he called it, to whoever would listen but if they did not respond he turned away and consoled himself with manual labor which was his 'attachment' and took up the doctrine with the next visitor he encountered." Many times when Father Roy went to another city he hitchhiked, and once, as Dorothy tells the story, when a car stopped, Father Roy found that his benefactor was a bishop.

In the latter part of 1939 and in 1940, Dorothy began to make occasional visits to Baltimore, where Father Roy was based, so as to attend some "days of recollection" that he was giving. They were "beautiful days," Dorothy says in *The Long Loneliness*. In her journal for June 19, 1940, she made some notes on Father Roy's conference for that day. "Charity is absolutely indispensable means. . . . Baptism of desire is love. Anyone who loves God belongs to the soul of the Church. . . . What is Christianity? . . . How much it asks. 'It is a terrible thing to fall into the hands of the living God.' Instead of fearing death which changes nothing we should fear life. Those who wish to enter heaven must be saints. Sanctity must be achieved in our lifetime. We are here for no other reason. . . . Heaven is not a place, a condition of soul—the vision of God, union with God. . . . Heaven does not occupy place. It can begin here." These phrases would have been dry fare for many, but for Dorothy they were succulent. Then she noted: "Invite Fr. Roy to visit us in August."

This, perhaps, was the genesis of her plan to have a Catholic Worker retreat at the Easton farm over the long weekend of Labor Day, 1940, modeled on those of Lacouture. To let Workers and friends of the Workers know what was expected of them, Dorothy wrote a pamphlet that was sent to all of the houses and that was subsequently printed in the *Catholic Worker*. All, she said, were "called to be Saints." One could not just drift through life. "We are either on the road to heaven or to hell. 'All the way to heaven is heaven, for He said I am the Way,' St. Catherine of Siena tells us. And likewise all the way to hell is hell. . . . It is so tremendous an idea that it is hard for people to see its implications. Our whole literature, our culture, is built in ethics, the choice between good and evil. The drama of the ages is on these themes. We are still living in the Old Testament, with commandments as to the natural law. We have not begun to live as good Jews, let alone as good Christians. . . . We are cannibals."

She noted that in all secular literature it had "been so difficult to portray the good man, the saint, that a Don Quixote is a fool; the Prince Myshkin is an epileptic, in order to arouse the sympathy of the reader, appalled by unrelieved sanctity." Those who truly believed should bestir themselves. "Too little has been stressed the idea that *all* are called. Too little attention has been placed on the idea of mass conversions. . . . There have been in these days mass conversions to nazism and fascism and communism"; why not, again, to God?

In the July-August, 1947, issue of the *Worker,* Dorothy described the gathering. From the Worker houses came old cars loaded with people and food. Of the thirty houses at the time, most sent representatives. "It was," wrote Dorothy, "the last great get-together the Catholic Workers had before we were separated by war, our workers dispersed to the far ends of the earth, in the service, in jails and conscientious objector camps, the houses closed." Altogether, there were five priests and over a hundred retreat participants.

Why did this retreat so deeply affect Dorothy? The mechanics and idea emphasis of Father Lacouture's retreat laid out a work and a contest for her that asked for an utmost performance. She did not want a tranquilizing piety, an "I'm OK—You're OK" approach to life. She wanted a hard contest, a war, and the Lacouture retreat gave her that. The "doctrine" that Father Roy talked about was an emphasis on those positions that made the Christian life different from ordinary life. A sharp distinction was made between the natural and the supernatural. In some of her retreat notes, Dorothy wrote it thus: "Supernatural actions bring with them a reward, an increase. Natural actions bring natural reward and end at the grave. We must try to amass more and more God in our hearts. 'Our hearts were made for thee, O Lord, and find no rest until they rest in thee,' " she added, quoting St. Augustine.

The character of the retreat is given in a letter Father Lacouture wrote to Sister Peter Claver about this time. If God were to bless the worker retreat, it should be made "as penitential as possible. Some think that the more freedom you leave to the retreatants, the more they come and so they let them talk a good part of the time and amuse them the rest of the time. That is pagan and not blest by God. . . . On the contrary, the more you ask that is contrary to nature the more people will come. For them the Holy Ghost will act more and draw them to the retreats and give them more light. . . . Exact absolute silence all day. Give them no recreation at all, and I am positive you will have more people coming."

Father Roy's retreat was only a taste, but it was a sweet taste. It was this retreat that Dorothy was probably recalling when she wrote in one of her random notes: "We were a little flock. We had broken bread together. Scripture became a love letter and retreat notes we took we kept rereading, going back to them to try to recapture that flow of rapturous assent to Truth." And in another note she added, "O the beauty of young people gathered together, on a retreat for instance, sitting under trees reading St. Augustine, St. Bernard, their missals, and their Bibles."

When the three days had passed, the people from the various houses all gathered together for "a social evening of talk and discussion. We found such unity amongst us all, that there seemed no reason for discussion. When we separated, it was with pain, we hated to leave each other, we loved each other more truly than ever before, and felt that sense of comradeship, that sense of Christian solidarity which will strengthen us for the work."

The retreat, with its simple Gospel emphasis, with its three days in which people were stripped of their words—words that many times were more apt to confuse and wound rather than clarify and heal—brought Dorothy and her friends as close to the peace of perfect community as one could ever come in life. It was thus that Dorothy described it as a "foretaste of heaven." And with the world at war she must have thought, how real is this community when compared with the lashing and hysteria of that false sense of community that occurs with war. She reflected on the young people at the retreat. They were truly leaders—John Doeble of the Baltimore house, for example, whose "quiet diffidence, most unassuming modesty," stood out "all the more" because of his bravery in providing hospitality to the most abandoned of the off-scourings of the Baltimore waterfront. Doeble was "a leader, yes undoubtedly, but what a contrast to the leaders of the day with their uniforms, their bombast, their display and their inhuman use of human lives."

After their final gathering, the various groups got into their heavily laden old automobiles and called out their final goodbyes. Then, with engines emitting a high whine that came from the first gear being used as a brake, they lurched down the sharp descent to the highway below. Most of them, and surely Dorothy more than any other, felt that the retreat was a never-to-be-experienced-again moment in the life of the Catholic Worker. The world was at war, and the pall of war was lowering over them. After that, as Dorothy said, they would be torn apart—not only by war but by the wash and flow of time.

The Easton retreat was the beginning of a series that went on, sporadically, for nearly a decade. At this point in her life the retreat was Dorothy's refreshment. The Bible, especially the Psalms and the Gospel, was for her so infinitely rich that its truth and beauty were a continuing delight to her, an elixir whose taste never dulled.

After the 1940 Easton retreat Father Roy, dissatisfied with his ability to do full justice to the Lacouture retreat, urged Dorothy to get in touch with Father John Hugo of the Diocese of Pittsburgh, a teacher at Mount Mercy College. This Dorothy did, and eventually a retreat for Worker groups was set up at Oakmont, Pennsylvania, for August 1941. Again, Dorothy sent out the word. "We do not need to insist on its [the retreat's] importance. No excuse, such as 'we have taken a wife,'—'we have bought a farm' 'we have a new yoke of oxen' is a valid one. It is no use worrying about what will happen to the houses, the farms, in our absence. If we depend on our own efforts, we are deluding ourselves. What we are aiming at is to bring men back to Christ, and it is presumption and effrontery and arrogance, if we try to do it without looking after ourselves first." Now was the time "to renew ourselves, to taste and see, that the Lord is sweet. . . . We are only anxious that you get the full benefit of the conferences and that Brother Ass does not revel before the week is out."

Because the draft was already taking some of the young men of the Worker houses and unsettling others, the Oakmont retreat was not the great gathering that the previous year's had been. For Dorothy, though, the 1941 retreat was the occasion of another step toward the spiritualization of her life. She later spoke of the six days of silence as heavenly manna.

Father Hugo, to her great satisfaction, presented the Gospels in the full meaning of their radical and uncompromising spirituality. As it turned out, Father Hugo became Dorothy's spiritual adviser, formally and informally, for most of her remaining life.

Both Father Lacouture and Father Hugo became controversial because their teachings were supposed to be "Jansenistic in tendency," meaning that they seemed to put nature in opposition to grace. The controversy became so heated that Father Hugo was "silenced," and Father Lacouture was sent to the Canadian wilds to instruct nomadic hunters. Articles on the controversy were written in learned theological journals, and Dorothy was "summoned to the New York Chancery and informed of the situation." It can be said that when the furor subsided no one was burned at the stake. In 1944 Father Hugo published his *Applied Christianity,* an amplification of Father Lacouture's retreat notes. His 1947 publication *The Sign of Contradiction* sought to respond to attacks on the retreat that appeared in the *Ecclesiastical Review.*

Dorothy was not bothered by the matter one way or another. She could see both sides of the question. She had read Martin Scheeben, "that great theologian, and my heart and mind give [such] ready assent to his glowing and beautiful words on the grandeur of the natural man, of natural virtues, of natural life, I could see how theologians would seize upon Father Roy's words to brand him a heretic." And she would not argue the point that Father Lacouture may not have been "much of a theologist as theologists go" and that he may not have stated his position with precisely the right words. As for Father Hugo's being silenced, it made her think of "that New Testament teaching, 'unless the seed fall into the ground and die, it remains alone, but when it dies it bears much fruit.'" This thought might have stood some elaboration, but what she meant, it appears, was that Father Hugo's work would have its good effect.

In her notes she expressed a personal point of view. Was a retreat supposed to "correct one's distortions of doctrine," or was its purpose to fill a spiritual need? Her need had been to confront Scripture in the spirit of a "rapturous assent to Truth," and the retreats had done that for her. "We were a little flock. We had broken bread together. Scripture became a love letter." It had been like "those first days of our conversions . . . those first days of the retreat which was a second conversion for so many—how filled with the keenest happiness they were for all of us. We were companions indeed, those of us who made the retreat."

Dorothy's rhapsodizing was more than vapor rising from a puffed emotion. There were Catholic Worker retreats for as long as anyone would attend them, and that would be for over a quarter of a century. For her, personally, the sweet taste of those early retreats and the one that she would make in July, 1943, never left her. She would talk of them for as long as she lived. Also, feeling for the retreat was expressed in a change in her person. Perhaps it was because she was mellowing—she was approaching forty-five— but she left off something about her that might be called brassiness. She stopped smoking; she stopped drinking, although what drinking she had done was scarcely more than having an occasional glass of the wine that her Italian neighbors had made. Her speech, which could turn salty at times, became more considered, and the salt seemed to have been washed out.

Particularly she got from Father Hugo's 1940 retreat a new sensitivity to what she took as the piercing truth of the Gospels. The words of Scripture struck a harmonic response with her open and receptive spirit. The Gospels seemed fresh and glowing. "Actually," she wrote in one of her handwritten notes, "I think to myself with a touch of bitterness, the ordinary man does not hear the word of God. The poor do not have the Gospel preached to them. Never have I heard it as I hear it now, each year in retreat, and with the sureness that it is indeed the Gospel. The average Catholic is baptized, instructed for his first holy communion, then confirmation, and then, Sunday after Sunday, the short Masses repeat themselves, with inadequate sermons, all the announcements, appeals for money. The shepherds are not feeding their sheep. But they themselves have not been fed. And the sad part is, the people are poor, and do not know they are poor. Poor, undernourished, even starving, as far as spiritual nourishment goes. The priest too. One has to make an attempt to know God before we can love him and serve him. Or try to know the Unknowable. The search goes on as long as we live."

It was hearing the Gospel anew that gave a new force to her character. It was a reinforced spirituality. And if there had ever been any questions about her course, they were gone now. She was on the track. Nothing could change her.

❧ 13
Rearing a Daughter

DOROTHY's appointment book states that on Sunday, December 7, 1941 (Pearl Harbor Day), she was in Elmira, New York, apparently giving a talk. Was she caught, even slightly, in the swirling cyclone of patriotic feeling that raised spirits to near-ecstatic heights of community feeling that Sunday evening? Not in the slightest. Nowhere—in journal or appointment notes—did she mention it. The next day she was back in New York City to spend the evening with her brother, John. Three days later she met Della for lunch and they spent the afternoon shopping. She did write to Tamar, in school in Canada, that she should not be overly disturbed over the war situation. "I hope you are not hearing all the scary rumors about air raids, etc. Our Mayor [Fiorello LaGuardia] just likes to run around like a chicken with his head off. We had two air raid warnings yesterday and afterward, when they had had big headlines to try to scare everyone, new editions of the paper came out and said they were practice." Anyway, Tamar would soon be home for her Christmas holiday. Dorothy said that she would go to Montreal on December 23 and meet Tamar at the bus station there so that they could ride back together on the train. If anything happened to prevent her meeting Tamar, she would "have a friend of mine in Montreal meet you and put you on the train."

Dorothy apparently met Tamar and brought her back to Mott Street, but Tamar's Christmas was not the happiest. She was sick with a sore throat and could not go to the farm. On January 6, she was put on the train to return to Montreal. Dorothy noted that Forster met them at the station. Otherwise, the only thing she found worth mentioning was that it was 10 degrees.

The next day the *Catholic Worker* came out. After Pearl Harbor the paper's 50,000 to 60,000 readers may have momentarily wondered about the position Dorothy would take on the matter. "We Continue Our Christian Pacifist Stand," read the headline. Then, wrote Dorothy, "We will bring the words of Christ who is with us always, even to the end of the world. 'Love your enemies, do good to those who hate you, and pray for those who persecute and calumniate you, so that you may be children of your Father in Heaven.'" Yes, the country was at war, she said, but "still we can repeat Christ's words each day, holding them close in our hearts, each month printing them in the paper. We are pacifists. Our manifesto is the Sermon on the Mount."

There were some people, she said, who were accusing her of having a "holier than thou" attitude in the stand she had taken on the war. No, she said, "we must all admit our guilt, our participation in the social order which has resulted in this monstrous crime of war." Dorothy concluded this part of her statement by recalling "a poor demented friend who came into the office to see us very often, beating his breast, quoting the penitential psalms in Hebrew, and saying that everything was his fault. Through all he had done and left undone, he had brought about the war, the revolution." Her "poor demented friend" was Edelson, the Jew, who used to visit the Workers when they were on Fifteenth Street and who worked with them in their garden commune. "His words," she said, "should be our cry, with every mouthful we eat." Her own prayer was "I am lower than all men, because I do not love enough. O God, take away my heart of stone and give me a heart of flesh."

Having stated her position with respect to the "holier than thou" charge, she wanted to deal with another characterization that had been made of her with respect to her pacifism. A "Catholic newspaper says it sympathizes with our sentimentality. This is a charge always leveled against pacifists. We are supposed to be afraid of the suffering, of the hardship of war."

Well, if she was soft and sentimental let those who made the charge come and live her life. Let them "come to live with the criminal, the unbalanced, the drunken, the degraded. . . . (It is not the decent poor, it is not the decent sinner who was the recipient of Christ's love.) Let them live with rats, with vermin, bedbugs, roaches, lice (I could describe the several kinds of body lice.) Let their flesh be mortified by cold, by dirt, by vermin, let their eyes be mortified by the sight of bodily excretions, diseased limbs, eyes, noses, mouths. Let their noses be mortified by the smells of sewage, decay, and rotten flesh. Yes, the smell of sweat, blood, and tears spoken of so blithely by Mr. Churchill, so widely and bravely quoted by comfortable people." There was also noise, "and some-times when one is tormented by vermin, dirt and smells, one is apt to forget the horror of noise, human . . . those ugly human noises, snorings, coughings, spittings, retchings, not to speak of the hid-eous sounds of argument, senseless or embittered or angered, the ugly notes of contempt, hatred, venom, malice—all of which can be conveyed in one symphony of hell to the tortured ear."

Dorothy's pacifism and the war caused a considerable reduction in the number of Worker houses around the country. She said in the January *Worker* that fifteen houses of hospitality had closed because of a lack of people to take care of them. Most of the men had been drafted. In the April issue, she wrote that "Mrs. Sheed [the wife of the publisher Frank Sheed] is quoted to have said that I have split the House of Hospitality movement from top to bottom by 'my' pacifism." The pacifist issue, aside from Dorothy, did pro-duce debate and divisions. Young John Cogley of the Chicago house, who in the years ahead would become editor of *Commonweal* and then the religion editor for the *New York Times,* sent Dorothy a note in the opening days of the war that gave his impression of the divisions in the houses. "The C.W. is gone. Now there are a group of pacifists defending their positions by calling attention to their good works and another group of die-hards like myself who leave gracelessly. Peace! Peace! And there is no peace. Give my love to all there who want it and to you, especially, goes the best from all who are left here."

So Cogley joined the army—which was all right in Dorothy's view so long as he had searched his conscience and had concluded it was the thing to do. Cogley's remark about "pacifists defending their positions by calling attention to their good works" probably did not sit well with her. Nor did his article in *Commonweal* some seventeen years later in which he discussed the pacifism of the *Catholic Worker.* "I have long found it hard to take the paper very seriously on this question because what it has had to say has usually struck me as simplistic, evasive, and even sentimental." There it was again! "Sentimental."

It was a slight wound, but even slight wounds festered with Dorothy a long, long time. An undated note fragment that Doro-thy appears to have written in the late 1950s may have been in response to Cogley's article. She was thinking about the "tragic future of pacifism" and observed that during the war some 80 percent of the young Workers had "betrayed it." Then she asked, "Is C. [Cogley] fragmentized?" She answered this question to herself: "He is." Then she wrote: "Catholic." What she meant by this is suggested by the comments that followed. "Just war theory dead. St. Thomas in trying to quiet consciences of Princes—is ruler justified in laying an ambush. Theologians go to incredible lengths to justify war. Acrobatics. . . . Hierarchy seems determined to follow state." So, it seems, if Cogley was "fragmentized" so were those who presumed to speak for the Church on the matter of war, including St. Thomas.

Dorothy's statement that 80 percent of the young Workers "betrayed" their pacifism was an accurate assessment. In 1941 she wrote that "we expected from our files, a rather large group of Catholic CO's." Rather than be assigned indiscriminately to the various conscientious objectors, Catholics formed themselves into the Association of Catholic Conscientious Objectors so as to be together in their own camps. And Dorothy, unwilling that the support for these camps should come from contributions of other religious groups, began to raise funds to finance them. Catholic camps were thus begun, but before the war ended they were closed, their internees who held to pacifist convictions being put to work in hospitals. Those who left the camps did so for various reasons. Some came to the conclusion that the war was just; others left for medical reasons. Gordon Zahn, the authority on the Catholic objector work camp experience during the war, remembered Arthur Sheehan, who later would write a biography of Maurin, as foremost among Workers who held to their pacifist convictions. There were, of course, other Catholic COs, but not from the Worker background.

Meanwhile at Mott Street the house had so few people to help with the work that Dorothy wondered "whether or not to make the paper an every other month affair." There was only Charlie O'Rourke to keep track of the mailing lists and Dave Mason to do the paper makeup. The house, too, was short-staffed. But that was not a problem since full wartime employment had reduced the line to a hundred or so men.

In one instance, the passion of war feeling invaded the house. One day Kichi Harada, the Japanese woman who had lost her job in the 1930s and who had become "one of the sad army of the homeless," as Dorothy described her, was subjected to another's seizure of shrill, patriotic excess. Miss Harada, who liked to cook, had planned a meal for the women in their own dining room. Just as she was placing all of the food on the kitchen table, another woman, standing by, began to loose a stream of vile abuse on the little Japanese. Reaching the crescendo of her hysterical outburst, she flung all the food "with a wide drunken sweep to the four corners of the kitchen floor." Dorothy, hearing the clamor, hurried into the kitchen. "It was," said Dorothy, "a moment for me of 'righteous rage.' " But, she added, "I've learned through long and painful experience that rage does not accomplish righteousness. So I persuaded the militant one to go up to bed and rest and I gathered up from the floor all of the food and laid it out in the plates for cooking."

That was only one incident. "Kichi was insulted many times during the war, even at our own table, and there were those who told her after the atom bomb that the Japs deserved everything they got."

Otherwise, the war appeared not to have greatly disturbed Dorothy's normal routine. Two days after Tamar left for Montreal, Dorothy wrote her a postcard. She said that she would try to send Tamar a card every day and that Tamar should likewise try to write her daily. "That is how Ade [Bethune] learned to write so well, writing to her mother every day. . . . Save these cards and I will not have to keep a diary this year." And Tamar, as usual, tried to do as her mother suggested. She did not write her mother every day, but she did save Dorothy's cards to her, and from them, over the next two years, one gets an account of Dorothy's activity as she recounted it to Tamar.

Because of the war and the effect that patriotic feelings might have on some of the houses, Dorothy, in the face of a bitterly cold January, decided to visit some of them and to do what she could to keep them open. In Pittsburgh Father Charles Owen Rice, the labor priest, met her and took her to the Pittsburgh Worker house. "Very cold, around zero," but the house was warm. "We came over the express highway last night, tunneling under two mountains. For 100 miles not a single stop. . . . There was snow on all the fields so it was very beautiful. . . . Don't forget your 15-minute visit [to the school chapel]." Four days later she was at Buffalo. "So many people to see, I get rushed around. Buffalo was wonderful—the House there is the House of Christ the Worker; and the chapel, the little Chapel of Divine Providence. Aside from Pittsburgh it is the only house with the Blessed Sacrament. . . . Joe and Marge have found an apartment."

The "Joe and Marge" were Joe Hughes, seaman, and Marge Crowe, a Catholic high school graduate who had gone to Mott Street in 1936 to help Dorothy with her letters and filing. Now they were planning to get married.

On January 15 Dorothy was back in New York to stay for a while. Her brief journal entries tell of her daily activity. Her days usually began with Mass but on Sunday, January 19, she stayed in bed all day. "Fluish. Read Mme. Maritain." This book—*We Have Been Friends Together,* Mrs. Maritain's story of her life—"delighted" Dorothy. "Madame Maritain is a Russian Jew, and throughout the book, in her love for wisdom she reminded me of my roommate at college, Rayna Prohme, of which I wrote in my book. . . . I have been so fascinated by this book that I carried it about for days and could not even loan it to anyone."

On January 23, as she told Tamar, she went to Della's and had "such a good sleep. . . . It is so good to wake up and see bare branches against the sky." On Saturday, the 29th, she informed Tamar that it was "very cold," that she was "wearing two coats and my feet are cold. Wish you would knit me some knee warmers." That night after confession she and Tina de Aragon, Tessa's sister, were going to see Tessa and John.

Dorothy concluded her card to Tamar on a note of annoyance. Tamar's cards were "full of short delarative sentences. . . . I'm sending you some of Ade's cards today so start printing your notes. You can get quite as much news on them if you don't race and scrawl." In her next card Dorothy said that she and Marge Crowe had "just finished making your candy which will be mailed tomorrow. Lent starts in two and one half weeks so you can't eat candy then. . . . But you do sound greedy, not offering any to others." Otherwise, Joe Zarella "goes out with Alice every day. It looks serious. For Joe I mean." Apparently it was serious for Alice, too.

So went Dorothy's days. In February she did no traveling. Steve Hergenham, Peter's German friend, was dying of cancer. In the January *Worker* she wrote of visiting him at Roosevelt Hospital and how Hergenham had told her that he had dreamed of "cold spring water, of sour milk clabber, just out of the cool cellar at Easton." Poor Steve, she may well have thought. How unspeakably sad it was—this vital, assured man that she had first known in 1934 when, reduced by depression, he had come to the apartment on

Fifteenth Street. Proud of his strength and his craft, he had built the house for Grace Branham on the farm at Easton. Then, when he could no longer stand the whining and malingering he saw around him, he left. Now he lay there on the hospital bed, his withered arms, once strong, resting on the white sheet that covered him, his sunken and fearful eyes looking over the edge of the brown paper bag into which he breathed as he acted out some absurd notion that the performance would ease his pain.

What was the answer to this—this vile thing that had produced this torture and this grotesque deformity of what a man could be? The spectacle dwarfed every issue of social reform and of the causes of nations. If a chance collocation of atoms or combination of chemicals could so degrade life and nullify it, then chance itself was God and nothing mattered. Hope, creativity, love, and beauty were illusions and all was madness. But if chance were not God, but something that finally was only a time-sustained mockery of God and illusion, if that wasted and flaccid flesh could be freed from the corruption of time and renewed with life of eternity—then the evil thing itself could have no triumph, but would itself die.

In the final accounting of Dorothy's life, her great power was that she believed. She believed in God and she believed, as she said, in the Creed, in the resurrection of the body. It was the force of this belief that over the years seemed increasingly to take over her person and that set her apart from others. It was of these things that Dorothy spoke to Hergenham.

In the February issue of the *Worker,* Dorothy wrote that "if you go down to Brooklyn Bridge, take a Madison Street bus, get off at Jackson Street and walk to the river, you find there St. Rose's Home for Incurable Cancer." In January Hergenham went to the St. Rose Home, and Dorothy and Peter Maurin made almost daily the trip that she described in the *Worker.* On February 3 Dorothy wrote to Tamar: "What cold! It is 5 above and this old home is terrific. Better outside than in. Tonight I went down to St. Rose's Cancer Home where Hergenham is now. Remember you visited it with . . . Stanley [Vishnewski]. Right on the river by our little park. I enjoyed the weather walking home, wearing Gerry's heavy overcoat." Her card to Tamar two days later said that Hergenham had been baptized at 5:30 that afternoon. "I am still quite stunned. Peter and I were godparents. He received 3 sacraments. Penance, baptism and extreme unction. Sunday he will receive communion.

It is very nice down by the river where he is. There are trees outside the window and birds in them so noisy it sounds like the bird house in the zoo. And always, boats going by." After the baptism she went to brother John's for supper. "Home by 12. Sleep by 2. Wasted my time reading trash."

The postals continued to Tamar, although Tamar may have winced when she got them because of Dorothy's harping upon her writing. "If you write smaller and are not in a hurry, your printing will be better. I should not boast. But I think of Ade's printing!" A week later: "When you do other things so well, you also must try to write better. The address is done neatly. Why not take your time and be more leisurely. That's your lecture for the day." Another: "Do write small and don't scrawl."

There were, of course, other matters for discussion. On February 4 Dorothy said that she was sorry Tamar was sick with "the cold. Why don't they put you to bed with hot lemonade?" The news was that Joe Zarella had "announced to me his engagement to Alice. They want to marry after Easter and live either at Fr. Hugo's house in Pittsburgh or on a retreat farm. Of course he may be drafted."

There was more romantic news on St. Valentine's day. Marge Crowe and Joe Hughes were married. "She is sending you a telegram or letter. I don't know which. . . . I made the wedding breakfast and Tina de Aragon was best girl." That afternoon Dorothy had "stopped at Forster's for tea and am dragging him out now. He gave me this new pen which I hope will not blot. He took your address, so maybe he will write. But he is as bad as you about letters." Like father, like daughter, Dorothy probably thought. She probably thought the same thing about most of Tamar's traits.

On February 21, Dorothy noted that it was "very cold. So two dresses, two sweaters necessary. . . . I'm each day for 7 a.m. Mass, and it is dark yet what with the new time. The morning star (is it?) shines at the foot of Bayard St. The sky is opalescent." As usual, she had visited Hergenham "who was most querulous because I was late." She wrote a card to Tamar the following week as she sat "in a beauty shop on 14th St. and 4th Avenue." She was "finally" getting her hair done for some speaking engagements. "There are 2 children and a dog running around this beauty parlor, which is very cheap. . . . If Gerry [Griffin] and Joe [Zarella] both get called up, you and I won't be able to go west."

In her card to Tamar on March 4, Dorothy told her that Hergenham had died the day before at six in the morning. March 4 was Tamar's sixteenth birthday, and Dorothy hoped that the presents she had sent had gotten there on time. Tamar should write and tell her about the birthday. She hoped that her daughter was "philosophical about such things by now. No use counting on anything in this uncertain life. I feel that you are practically grown now. Sixteen is a nice age."

Tamar's reaching sixteen probably gave Dorothy pause. At sixteen she herself had been at the University of Illinois, and she had certainly felt grown up, able to take care of herself. Tamar's life so far had been mostly a boarding school life with visits to her mother on weekends and during vacations. Even then, with Dorothy away so much of the time, she was cared for by Steve and Mary Johnson, who were provided with an apartment by the Mott Street house.

During the six months that Tamar had been at the school she told, in cards to her mother, what she was learning to do. "This week I have been setting up a loom and weaving." "This week I have been making the dress and knitting a yellow sweater. We will make hats later on. Have been spinning flax and it is hard at first." One day she learned to make "french mustard." All this Tamar liked. She also liked to walk through the woods and she liked to read. "Have been reading *Quentin Durward* all day and it's so good." Another card said that she had "finished *Villette* and I love it." She had three paperbacks on hand: *"Tale of Two Cities, Wuthering Heights,* and the *Swiss Family Robinson."*

But what now? In the Canadian school Tamar had been taught those things that a farm wife who lived in a primitive setting would have to know. Such training would be good for someone living on a farm like the Easton farm, but Dorothy hoped for something better for her daughter than a life like the few wives at Easton were leading. Anyway, she may have wondered, whom would she find there to marry? The prospects at the Easton farm seemed most unlikely. Or so she thought.

Still, Tamar liked the farm. She even had her own little house there. It was halfway down the hillside, built by old Mr. O'Connell, who had come to the farm from who knew where. He had built the little house with materials bought with money Tamar had saved. O'Connell had his cabin at the entrance of the farm on the main highway and, as Dorothy once had said of him, "he never missed a visitor. If they were shabby, he shouted at them, if well dressed, he was more suave. . . . And if anyone living on the farm had any skill, it was 'What jail did ye learn that in?' One man who became a Catholic after living with us for a year was greeted with taunts and jeers each time he passed the cabin door. 'Turncoat! Ye'd change yer faith for a bowl of soup!' He had locked all of the farm tools in his own cabin and guarded them with a shotgun." Later—it was in 1952, when Mr. O'Connell died at the age of eighty-four—the only thing Dorothy could think of to say about him was that "he was a terror."

On March 15, two weeks before Dorothy was to go to Montreal to bring Tamar home, her card to Tamar set the tone as to how things would be: "When you come home this time, let's go in for early hours and hard work. No moping around the way you did Christmas. If you're sick, you stay in bed. If well, you work. You are grown up now and must take responsibilities, which makes me very happy. We must help each other."

On the last day of March Dorothy was in Sainte Martine, the little village near Montreal where Tamar's school was located. The next day she wrote back to the Mott Street group that she and Tamar had stayed in a little French hotel the night before and then had gone to the convent for breakfast. "They served roast beef, fried potatoes, tomato juice, fried eggs, coffee, and cake! Tamar says that they always have huge breakfasts! ... A meeting tonight at the Pedagogical Institute. I dread it." The next day she had a visit with Karl Stern and his wife. Stern, a psychiatrist and refugee from Germany, had only recently converted to Catholicism. This was, apparently, Dorothy's first meeting with him. Their friendship would be lifelong.

Ten days later she noted that she was at the Easton farm and that Tamar was "all moved down" for the summer. With Tamar settled, she set forth the next day on a bus tour to the West Coast that would last for two months. Why did she set out on this trip at a time when the country was moving toward a crescendo of travel confusion? She explained in the *Worker:* "If it were not for the necessity of visiting our friends, our groups, our houses on the West Coast, I would not be here, but home at Maryhouse and Mott Street instead. I cannot say my work is specifically there." But "who knows when this traveling will stop for any of us. We all would like to settle. We all have a craving for stability, for permanence. And look at us, men and women, plucked up by work or war and settled someplace else than where we wish to be."

Her "work" was everywhere and if people, dislocated by war,

were to be subject to the pain of travel, then she could stand it as well as they. Her traveling brought to mind something Saint Teresa of Avila had said: " 'Life is but a night spent in an uncomfortable inn.' " And, continued Dorothy, "bus stations these days, crowded with soldiers, their wives and children, whole families on the move following the lure of jobs, are anything but comfortable. The bus is an inn itself, everyone sleeping on everyone else's shoulder, a mad confusion of feet and legs in the aisles."

She told of the discomfort of wartime bus travel in a card to Tamar written in a bus station. The place was thronged with people. "Every bus is late," she wrote. She spent "hours . . . in just sitting, waiting, reading. . . . I can't get half the things done I want to or see half the people, but in general the trip is successful. I'm very glad I came. It is really the last chance for the duration, as they are going to ration travel." She wrote to the group at Mott Street that she had wanted to write more frequently "but when you stop people take such possession of you. Not a moment to spare. And hard to think. We are supposed to be stopping for ten minutes and for 30 we have sat in the bus waiting to leave. Patience."

Still, she could read on the bus. "My library, as I travel, is made up of missal, Bible, short breviary, the life of Janet Erskine Stuart. . . . Whenever I read the Bible on the bus, someone asks me if I am a Seventh Day Adventist or a Jehovah's Witness."

Excerpts from the notebook in which she kept her brief travel diary gives an idea of what her days were like. April 26: "Stayed at Flagstaff last night. Arrived at 2 a.m. Mass at 8:30. Bus left [at] 11 for L.A.—2 a.m." April 27: "Mass at St. Bibiana's—L.A. Wrote editorial. Bus for San Diego at 1. Arrived at 5. Miss Kelly met me." On April 30 she was at "Julia's" and the next day she was "in bed all day with a headache." She visited a group of Redemptorist priests on May 5, and the next day at Santa Barbara she met with another group of priests. Following that she talked with a bishop who was "very friendly." She spent all of May 11 on the bus. "Babies in the lap. Odors. Gorgeous scenery thru Fresno, Stockton." On the thirteenth she had supper with "Minna," and the next day she stayed in bed, "seeing no one."

On May 17, at 6:30 a.m. she arrived at a "Japanese Camp." It was in California but where, she does not say. In the June *Worker* she said that she had seen "a bit of Germany on the West Coast. I saw some of the concentration camps where the Japanese men, women, and children are being held before they are resettled in the Owens Valley. . . . They are the first victims of war in this country, and if we did not cry out against this injustice done them, if we did not try to protest it, we would be failing in two of the works of mercy, which are to visit the prisoner and to ransom the captive."

She reached Seattle on May 21 and had an all-afternoon meeting with the people at the Seattle house of hospitality. In her "Day by Day" column in the June *Worker* she wrote of "sitting on the top of a hill, in a lovely garden outside of Our Lady of Lourdes Church, where we are having a 'day' [of recollection] beginning with a solemn high Mass at ten and ending with Benediction at three." She noted that in a field on the other side of the church, "within a few feet of me," was a large fish-shaped barrage balloon and that beneath it were tents for soldiers. "Over Bremerton, across the bay, the air is filled with barrage balloons, but hereabouts today they are all tethered in the fields looking like nothing else but grotesque idols, deities of the state, served by a uniformed priesthood who put their trust in all these works of their hands, to save them from the wrath of the Lord."

While she was in Seattle, she heard much talk of there being Japanese aircraft carriers in the sea between Seattle and Alaska and of an invasion or attack at hand. She did not believe it, but if it happened she would worry about it then. Her general impression, though, was that "no one seems to realize the war except as a gigantic adventure and a great prosperity suddenly descending upon us. There is more money than anyone has seen for a long time, and people are stocking up on clothes, electric iceboxes, stoves and other equipment that is still being sold, and the stores still seem to be pretty full." Looking "at the country and its people aside from the supernatural point of view, it is a discouraging sight. Practically every young man is affected, women are threatened with mobilization, and pagan attitudes prevail. . . . God help us all."

She returned home through Minneapolis, Milwaukee, and Chicago. The Worker houses in these places were in disarray, but she was trying to pick up the pieces and she seemed to have had good visits with friends. In Chicago, on June 3, she had dinner with Al Reser and Joe Diggles, and three days later she was in Milwaukee, visiting with Florence Weinfurter and Nina Polcyn.

It was June 10 at 11:30 p.m. when her bus, passing through Easton, let her off at the bottom of the hill by the farm. Tamar was there to meet her. Dorothy's log for the next day contained these brief observations: "Slept 9.45. Very hot. Many honors. More Heat. Miss Branham arrived. Tamar and Dave Hennessy."

"Tamar and Dave Hennessy"—a summer romance had begun to brew. Hennessy had come to the farm from Washington, D.C., some months previous. In Washington he had apparently been a roofer. He had read the *Worker* and having an interest in farm communities, he went to Easton. Dorothy apparently had not known him before, or if she had it was only slightly because his name does not appear in the *Worker* nor in her journals or notes.

Perhaps at first she was not overly concerned about the matter for she mentioned it no more that summer, at least not in her daily journal. Her summer was, as usual, one of much going and coming, but all of it in the city or between the city and Easton. It was, in a way, a summer of family and friends. Her note, "To Della's," occurs several times, along with "Della—lunch." Grace was in New York so there were frequent visits with her. Her mother seems to have had her own place at Minneola on Long Island, and Dorothy went there, or, if not there, to John's house.

Grace was now seventy-two years old and in poor health. On more than one occasion that summer she must have reflected on the unusual course of Dorothy's life, the worry and anguish that Dorothy had caused her and of how her daughter had changed so completely. Thank God those days were past. But it did not really surprise her. She had always been aware of the fact that Dorothy was "different."

On July 1 Dorothy had dinner one night with Sigrid Undset, and surely she saw Freda to talk of the experience, for it had been Freda that had urged Dorothy, almost vehemently, to read Undset's *Kristin Lavransdatter*. Dorothy had another interesting meeting. She and her mother had reminisced a lot about the early days of the family and Grace, thinking of when they had lived in Brooklyn, probably told Dorothy of the time that Mary Manley, the girl who had come to help the family, had taken little Dorothy to Mass with her. Somehow Dorothy located Miss Manley and they had spent an evening together.

At the Mott Street house, things were almost quiet. The line had all but evaporated. Reminiscing about this summer over thirty years later, Dorothy recalled that "Smokey Joe [Motyka] always boasted that he and I kept the CW going those war years. He was ignoring Dave Mason and Arthur Sheehan and Fr. Clarence

Duffy." Fr. Duffy, from Ireland, was technically responsible to his bishop there and therefore could not perform the functions of his priestly office outside of his home diocese. He had been in and around the Worker house since 1937.

Peter was there, too, but he seemed not to have been in the forefront of things as he had once been. Nearing seventy, he was tiring. Too, he had not shared Dorothy's preoccupation with the two concerns that had been uppermost in her life in the four years just past. Peter was a man of peace. Peace was so profoundly and integrally at the center of his vision that he did not have to particularize about it. Dorothy understood that. After Peter's death she wrote, of Peter and pacifism, that "Peter did not want to be *fragmented* by being labeled *pacifist* or *anarchist*. First of all we are Catholics, children of our holy Father Pius XII in this temporal order. First of all we are Catholics—then Americans, Germans, French, Russian, or Chinese. We are members of the Body of Christ or potential members. We are sons of God."

He was not a leading figure in the retreat movement, and it is easy to see why. The retreat philosophy, seeming to emphasize the primacy and even exclusivity of the spiritual over the natural or material, was not in line with Peter's ideas. He thought of the correlation of the two—of a personalist action that would redeem nature itself. Peter's work was his thought, and it therefore was his prayer. Besides, the retreats were too organized, and one was expected to be silent. How could he be silent when the world needed an instruction? But Dorothy had in no sense placed him on the shelf. To the contrary, she was thinking much of him and his ideas, for she was writing a biography of him.

All summer long Dorothy and Tamar had shuttled between Mott Street and Easton, although Tamar no doubt preferred the latter and likely wanted to stay there without interruption. She was, it seems, well on the way toward an "understanding" with David Hennessy. In fact, the signs were so obvious that Dorothy felt something had to be done. The thing to do was to get Tamar away from Easton and then hope that when winter came the haze of the summer's romance would clear and be forgotten. So it was arranged that Tamar would go again to Ade Bethune's at Newport, Rhode Island. On September 23, with David Hennessy, Stanley Vishnewski, and Joe Zarella there to see them off, Dorothy and Tamar got on the bus for Newport.

In the extended interview which Deane Mowrer held with Julia

Porcelli Moran in 1970, Miss Mowrer asked Mrs. Moran if she had known Tamar well in this period and Julia responded: "Well, as much as anyone could know Tamar. Tamar was very quiet and retiring and very shy."

Deane wanted to know what else she could say about Tamar.

"She was off at school a lot—boarding school here, boarding school there. She was up in Canada for about a year at the agricultural school. I remember a couple of times no one was around to sort of take care of her when she was living there and we went for a walk. She wanted to see the water and she was the kind of a child who didn't answer too much—was very quiet. We walked down to the piers and had a pleasant time."

Then Julia told of knowing Tamar at Ade Bethune's school at Newport. "I got to know her a little bit because she was an apprentice the same time I was. I got there prior to her coming. I believe they were hoping to get her away from this young man who was interested in her at the farm, and she was sent there to sort of cool off and forget about him. And meanwhile she was very happy and doing a certain amount of things: crafts, lettering, painting. We had folk dances there every week, and we had many young men coming, and Tamar was terribly shy, and I think she purposely would walk with a stoop to imitate her mother, although I'm sure there was nothing wrong with her back. I think she did this maybe in admiration."

Julia thought of some other things she remembered about Tamar that year. "She was very, very pretty, but I never saw her really fussing about how she looked." Julia thought that Tamar had gone out on her first date at Newport. "This young man was fascinated with Tamar, especially because her mother was an author, and a writer, various things. He was very interested, and I know she didn't want to have anything to do with him, she was nurturing this torch for this young man at Maryfarm." But "anyhow, I persuaded her to go on this date—I think to the movies. I think he took both of us—there may have been two boys—but we had a pleasant time and she opened up quite a bit. He was a very nice young man, and he took us for sodas afterward and she got to talking and dancing."

Tamar liked to dance, and she opened up that night. As Julia said, "she was being more a young girl with young people" rather than with "the varied group at the Catholic Worker." Was it the Catholic Worker, then, that repressed Tamar and drove her into her shell? It would be a facile conclusion to reach but probably not a correct one. Tamar was what she was—like her father. Dorothy noted in her journal when Tamar was three and the two of them lived on the beach that she thought of her daughter as "inarticulate and unresponsive." Tamar was as articulate and responsive as anyone else, but not to the same degree her mother was.

With Tamar at Ade's, Dorothy was free to travel. On October 17 she wrote Tamar from Bill and Dorothy Gauchat's Worker farm at Cleveland—the farm that Peter had been visiting during the summers. "Please, darling, try to learn everything you can while you are there; i.e., to keep busy every moment; to do everything Ade says; to remember your job. . . . If you do not make it out there—and Ade won't have anyone who won't learn—you will have to come to N.Y. and go to H.S. again and take shorthand and typing or go to textile high, or some such place."

A few days after Dorothy had returned to Mott Street she got a card from Dorothy Gauchat saying she had had a baby girl, Anita. The news was forwarded to Tamar. On December 3, Dorothy told Tamar that she had just been "over to Sam's [Day] place to see mother, who is in bed with high blood pressure." Grace had said that she wanted to go back to her place in Florida before the holiday traffic got bad. Dorothy would go with her. Three days before they left Dorothy wrote Tamar a frantic note: "Why don't you write? Surely you can put a few words on a postal every day just to let me know how you are. It is a matter of thoughtfulness and affection. . . . You really *must* write every day. I'll be very lonesome there [in Miami] over the holidays, just the two of us alone . . . and it will be hard to be away from you." Tamar's response was brief: "Why should I write. . . . I have nothing to say and my writing gets worse."

Two days before she left for Miami, Dorothy had breakfast with Forster to tell him all that was going on. In Miami she got a sugar ration card and did some baking. She rode a bicycle to church in the mornings, continued her writing of Peter's biography, and read. One Saturday afternoon she listened to the Texaco Company opera broadcast with Milton Cross as commentator. The opera was *Tannhauser*—what else? The following week she went shopping and sent presents to Newport. She bought a prayer book for Della. On Christmas Eve day she visited with her cousins on her father's side and then went to confession that evening.

In her card to Tamar on February 1, Dorothy said that her mother heard regularly from Della and Sam, but that she "gets no word of Donald and worries a lot." When the United States entered the war, Donald had been ordered home by his employer, the *Chicago Tribune*. As the *Tribune*'s Baltic correspondent, he had gone to Finland in the winter of 1939 to cover the Russian invasion of that country. From his Baltic experience and from what he saw in Finland he came to the conclusion that it was the Finns who were fighting the real menace to Western civilization—the Russians —so when his order came he asked for some time to think about it. But Russia now was an ally of the United States and the *Tribune* was in no position to indulge Day's conscience. He was peremptorily fired. In September, 1942, Grace got news that Donald had enlisted in the Finnish army. Now she had a son to worry about.

Having given Tamar the news of Donald, Dorothy told her daughter of her own doings: "I read, write, ride the bicycle, go to church, go to bed. The days move with no change, nothing to write about. I feel so settled, so rested—this has certainly been a godsend, a breathing space. And plenty of time to think. Do write soon—just those few lines a day are a joy to me."

In the January issue of the *Worker,* Dorothy told her readers that although Dave Mason had been picked up by the F.B.I. for draft evasion, the Mott Street house was still in good hands. Peter was back from the Gauchats' farm in Cleveland and with him were Arthur Sheehan, Jack Thornton, and Charlie O'Rourke. "God willing," she would be home in February, visiting "reader friends in the South" on the way back. She left Miami on February 12, taking the bus to Bradenton, a small resort town on Florida's west coast. She visited a friend who lived on Bradenton beach, going to Tampa the next day to see some Jesuits who were friends of the Worker. That night at nine o'clock she got on the bus, heading for Columbus, Georgia.

The ride to Georgia was for her another one of those deadening experiences of wartime bus-riding suffered by the millions who were unlucky enough to have to travel in those days. Dorothy described her trip in the March *Worker*. From Tampa she had traveled all night up the west coast of Florida to Tallahassee. "The bus was jammed, people standing in the aisles. Everyone in the armed forces going on leave and all those going to visit camps, like to travel all night to conserve some of their precious hours of leave." The bus pulled into the Tallahassee station at 5 a.m., with the thermometer at 14 degrees above zero. "I was chilled to the bone."

Inside the small station on Tennessee Street "every bit of floor space was taken by people sitting on their suitcases. The door opened and shut and let in blasts of cold wind. The pot-bellied stove roared, and when the doors were not open the atmosphere was stifling. Our waiting was a three-hour one and never did three hours drag so long. . . . Everyone in that bus station was in a stupor of fatigue. Hard to say a morning prayer in a place like that."

In Columbus she visited Holy Trinity, "the cradle of those two new religious orders founded by Father Judge, the Missionary Servants of the Most Holy Trinity." At Columbus she was indignant over the exploitation of blacks on the rural turpentine plantations. Her indignation was more than justified, but in the cities of the South that she saw, things appeared better. "I passed block after block of model housing for the Negro" for which "I, too, blessed President Roosevelt" In the rural sections "many a child" was named after the President, but "there are no houses in the rural sections."

From Columbus she went to Atlanta. She sent Tamar a picture postcard of a building. "Here is where I am now. Sister Peter Claver's sister started this mission and clinic and it has grown so they are now going to build a hospital next door. I do love that whole family of Sister Peter Claver's." It was "all most interesting, enlightening and encouraging, but I will be so happy to be near you again."

Making her way northward, Dorothy reached Newport on the morning of March 2 after an all-night trip. Tamar was there to meet her. She stayed through Tamar's seventeenth birthday and then, finally, went to Mott Street.

After Tamar's sixteenth birthday, Dorothy began signing her cards to Tamar as "Dorothy" and not "Mother." Likewise, Tamar began to address her as "Dorothy." This change was probably suggested, if not insisted on, by Dorothy herself. She may have thought that it would signify a more comradely and sisterly relationship between herself and her daughter and this, perhaps, would be a useful asset in dealing with the Tamar-David situation.

On April 27, however, Dorothy reverted to "mother" and lawgiver. She had written David about his courtship of Tamar, and David had returned unopened her letters with a note suggesting that "he was expecting me out to talk things over." Dorothy thought this "was very rude of him"; she could not go to Easton because Jack Thornton was being drafted and she was needed at the house. She would trust Tamar "not to write to Dave and to return his letters, if he writes any to you, unopened."

Dorothy was hurt but she was also fighting back. Tamar unquestionably was hurt, too, but she remained resolute on her course. At this point she and David were thinking of marriage and that prospect, as she probably viewed it, was the way to put her life and its consequences into her own hands rather than to let them remain in her mother's. If this was Tamar's thinking it was also Father Hugo's thinking, to whom Dorothy had written in her concern about the situation. Father Hugo said he was greatly concerned and would like to help. "But humanly, there is so little that one can do." To be sure, the conditions on which a marriage would be based seemed "unpropitious." But "there is no use opposing Tamar and Dave, as you have already found." He said he could understand Dorothy's wish that Tamar "start where you have ended," but Tamar would have to fashion her own destiny. And, "therefore if you forsee suffering for her, that is no bad thing by the divine standard of things." Suffering could destroy her, but it could also be the means of achieving sanctity.

Dorothy did accept the situation, but she insisted that Tamar not marry before she was eighteen, and Tamar, if not happy with this proviso, agreed to live with it.

Whatever the case, Dorothy's cards to Tamar became more cheerful. "It is a wonderful day," she wrote on May 6. Grace was coming back to New York and was going to see Della during the coming week. So Dorothy would have "a good complete family visit when I go up there." Two weeks later she asked Tamar to send her Raissa Maritain's *We Have Been Friends Together* "at once." One of Franklin Spier's friends, a Jew who had become a Catholic, wanted it. It was "easier going to Franklin's now, since he has a Catholic friend. . . . I do not have to bear the brunt alone. Della says 'who knows—we may all end up Catholics!' What a change! I told you Susie, Della and Franklin's daughter, is going to a Catholic school."

The following week Dorothy went to a play. Kenneth Burke and his wife, Lily, were there and Forster, too. "While the Burkes all talked about their academic educations I talked about yours. They were much impressed by your accomplishments." Dorothy had more bright chatter: "Last night a party at Sheed and Ward—many people not knowing each other. Peter enjoyed it—found

many friends. Maritain was there, very cordial—also Helene Iswolsky."

Miss Iswolsky, or "Helen," as most people came to call her, was
the daughter of the Russian Ambassador to France during World
War I. Because of the Russian Revolution, the family remained in
France. In the late 1920s, Helen had joined with Emmanuel
Mounier and his personalist circle. Because she was Russian, Nicolas Beryaev looked her up one day and invited her to join an infor-
mal discussion group that met in his apartment. It was in this
period that Miss Iswolsky became Catholic. During World War II,
when the Germans were approaching Paris, she managed to get on
one of the trains leaving Paris for southern France and from there
she reached the United States. A remarkable woman who embod-
ied the very best of the European cultural and intellectual tradition, she stayed in America for the remainder of her life. Dorothy
appreciated Miss Iswolsky for her noble character and for her intelligence. They became close friends and remained so until Miss
Iswolsky's death.

Otherwise, the days of summer went in their accustomed manner. There was more than the usual family visiting—hours spent
with Tamar, an occasional going to Sasha's restaurant to have
lunch. On Sunday, July 18, she took the train for Oakmont to
begin a week-long retreat given by Father Hugo and Father Louis
Farina. As she waited in the station, "I thought of Tamar and what
joy to do things for her, buy her presents, care for her."

The train, as usual, bore the signs of war. The coach was filled
with men in uniform, and it smelled strongly of tobacco smoke.
Somewhere along the line two families with six babies got on. One
of the women was pregnant. "I held one baby on my lap, a little
boy—babies at my feet, on my suitcase, one in corner by window. I
soon began to smell of baby." But "what a joy to be on the way to
a retreat."

The retreat was a deeply satisfying experience for her. If the
retreats of previous years had left her with a feeling of spiritual
exultation, this one deepened that experience. It was another forward step, a raising of her vision to a steadier and more assured
contemplation of God. The subject of the retreat, as she gave it in
her notes, was the "Four Great Truths": "the supernatural; the
Glory of God; the Supreme Dominion; [and the] Folly of the
Cross." The retreat, she wrote, "is to show us how to increase our

love for God. When we say we love God with our *whole* heart, soul, mind, and strength it means *whole*. We must love only God. . . . All the other loves I have I must use as samples of the love of God."

During the retreat, she took nearly 300 pages of notes. For the rest of her life, she kept thinking she would organize and make a book of them. But she never did. She could not find the time to organize this material or, for that matter, almost everything else she wrote.

This retreat led her to what she thought of as new levels of understanding of her relationship to God. One was an altered sense of the way in which God directed her. "I have always been so sure I was right, that I was being led by God—that is, in the main outlines of my life, that I confidently expected Him to show His will by external events. And I looked for some big happening, some unmistakable sign. I disregarded all of the little signs. I begin now to see them and with such clearness that I have to beg not to be shown too much, for fear I cannot bear it. I need strength to do what I have to do—strength and joy and peace and vision. Lord, that I may see! That prayer is certainly answered most overwhelmingly in this retreat."

She noted an interesting position with respect to Jesus' attitude toward traditional historical concerns. "Jesus was not class conscious." He never "objectivized" social evils or tried to "reform" social systems. "St. John is in prison by Herod. Does our Lord protest? Does he form a defense committee? Collect funds? Stir up public opinion? Try to get him out? He did not protest killing of him."

Jesus had no concern with nations or political systems. "He was in fact an appeaser. Did he denounce the Vichy men of the day, the publicans? Zacchaeus. Matthew. He did not try to free the 'oppressed' people of Israel. He did not protest the killing of Galileans in the Temple by the Roman soldiers. His kingdom was not of this world."

The Christian disposition, then, as she saw it, should not become politicized or socialized. It was, certainly, the work of the Christian to end injustice, but not to be assailing unjust systems. Injustice would be ended with the coming of the Kingdom. The Christian's work was to end the world—to end time and not to struggle with it.

She now wanted to live more certainly the life of love and to write about love. She did write about it—scraps here and there, written while riding on a bus or sitting in a station, whenever she found herself alone. One meditation on love, undated, was written on the tightly lined pages of a small 3- by 5-inch spiral notebook:

I should be afraid to write about love because I have seen the terrible things it can do to you, but I have set out upon the path and I cannot turn back now. Especially now when I begin to learn what it means, the height and the depth of it, the terror, the deep peace, the joy. No, there is nothing else worth writing about. What are all our lives about, what are we looking for, what do we want of each other? There is not one of us who has not gone thru the first stages of love and found them so enchanting that never in our lives can we go further. Always we want to stand in that first light, that first fullness of life and let it possess us utterly. And when love would take us on thru the darkness which is light-unutterable, we are blind and can go no further. We hold back. We clutch at our memory, our own understanding of love and refuse to be taught.

But we had better look out! There are two dangers. We either fall into a snare of pleasure—sink into the immanence of love or we presume, we fly too high—and in our confusion get lost in the transcendence of love. . . . We pray for love. We get it, and it comes in strange forms and ways, and we are likely to pass it by in pride or find ourselves grasping phantoms.

There is no end to the folly of love. We had better not presume to ask for love. God may take us at our word. We will not know what is happening to us. If only we did not struggle. If only we did not make a move. We throw our own perverse wills into the balance and there are strange results in this search for love. You see it everywhere, on Broadway and 42nd St. Love, sex, pleasure, tenderness, fellowship, light, warmth, satiety—it is all so bound up together even on that low level. Or you might go still lower and find it in the teen-age gangs, the neighborhood clubs, the brothels, the lust for money, to get women, to get love.

It is sad—it is horrible, but it is not to be despised. Should we hate and judge our brothers—we who also want love? Even in the perversity, so openly spoken of today, there too is the search for love. When we search for love in creatures, when we turn from God to creatures instead of seeking God *thru* creatures, then all is perversity. There is not natural love, or unnatural love, not human sin, or inhuman sin, as people try to flatter themselves. "Me, I'm just human! I'm not a pervert."

We are all a perverse and stiffnecked generation. Oh, if God would only compel us to lie quiet, to know that underneath are the everlasting arms.

In the retreat she saw more clearly the necessity of aiming for sainthood. "We are put here to become saints. Every life should be dedicated to Him. . . . God has invited us to a union with himself. We must combat the idea that only a few are called to sanctity." There was a need now for "greater saints . . . than ever before." Never had people been so victimized by external forces that would turn them from truth. "Never has the world been so organized, press, radio, education, recreation, to turn minds away from Christ. St. Paul was converted when he had murder on his mind. We are all called to be saints. God expects something from each one of us that no one else can do. If we don't, it will not be done."

During the war years it seems that at times Dorothy was avoiding the Worker, fleeing to Della's, to John's, visiting Sister Peter Claver, and taking frequent trips, some of which kept her away for months. She could justify her course, but was it the right one? She was not sure. "The world is too much with me in the Catholic Worker. The world is suffering and dying. I am not suffering and dying in the CW; I am writing and talking about it." And this was "why as soon as possible I will try to organize days of recollection— primarily for myself. I will not be able to stand the impact of the world otherwise. Primarily for myself. But that will mean others— how many, who can tell?" After that there would be more retreats. "We can do nothing today without saints, big ones and little ones. The only weapons we will develop will be those of prayer and penance." Then the world would leave her and her friends alone. The world would say: "After all, they are not doing anything. Just a bunch of smug fools praying. We will not be as tormented by its scorn as we are by the praise of the world for works of mercy, houses of hospitality, and farming communes." To the depths of her soul, she was tired of being in the stream of things, sought out, praised by an increasing number of people who saw her as the sign of a new life in the Catholic Church.

She would think about taking a leave from the Worker and from her traveling. In the meanwhile, though, there had been other matters with which to be concerned. The increasing slaughter of the Jews in Europe troubled her deeply, and in the summer of 1943, in a *Worker* editorial, she said some attempt should be made at a negotiated peace in order to save those Jews who were still alive. The May issue featured a talk made by Jessie Wallace Hughan, secretary of the War Resisters' League. "If we persist in our present war aim of unconditional surrender . . . we shall be signing the death sentence of the remnant of Jews still alive. If, on the contrary, we demand the release of all Jews from the ghettos of occupied Europe and work for a peace without victory ... there is a chance of saving the Jews."

In the June *Worker,* Dorothy told of a meeting at which she had spoken a month previous, where "a member of the audience arose to protest defense of Jews and to state emphatically that she did not believe the stories of atrocities told. She made a long speech, and at its close she was applauded by several hundred present. Against such astounding unbelief the mind was stunned. And yet we of America and England who read and believe, do nothing to oppose the restrictions against immigration of Jews, their seeking sanctuary in this country."

Years after the war, when Dorothy was once asked how she justified her pacifism in view of the slaughter of the Jews, she replied that winning the war had not saved many Jews.

There were her own immediate worries. Around the first of July she noted in her journal: "Yesterday I felt on the verge of tears, tormented by thoughts of Easton and Tamar." At Easton families had begun to settle on the farm. The head of one family, claiming for himself preeminence within the affairs of his own household, seemed to wish to extend his domain over others at the farm. After all, the family was the basic institution, ordained by God, so should he and his household not be subserved by the rest? Or so his argument seemed to be.

As for Tamar, there was that perennial question, where should she attend school next? Particularly for the next academic year? On July 6, Dorothy wrote to Tamar to discuss the matter. After she had completed the retreat, Dorothy said, she would go to Mott Street to get out the August issue of the paper and then she would go to Upton, Massachusetts, to get Tamar, who would be at the Catholic Worker farm there. "Mother is looking forward to seeing you, also Della, and we'll have some picnics and swim together." Then they would visit an agricultural school, Farmingdale, on Long Island. "I must say after prayer and fasting ... I'm all in favor of the idea if they will take you with what credits you have." But Tamar should make up her own mind.

Dorothy knew that Ade thought Tamar should complete high school, but Dorothy was against it. When Dorothy made up her mind about something, there was little point in trying to change it by recourse to a higher and finer logic. She already had the answer and, determined to have her way, she could strike out wildly. She did so now. Tamar should not go to high school because "my two brothers went one year to high school and were practically illiterate when they launched themselves into the world. Now one [Sam Day] is the editor of the *Journal American* here and the other [Donald Day] speaks four languages and has been a foreign correspondent for twenty years. This high school business is the bunk."

But, said Dorothy, "it is up to you." Tamar could even stay at Ade's another year if she chose. "I know that they [Ade and her mother] both love you dearly and feel that they have a great deal to offer, as they no doubt have. . . . If you don't want to settle anything until after we see each other, let it go at that. Perhaps that will be better. Much love, darling." And then, "Dorothy."

In her next letter Dorothy returned to the agricultural school idea. "I'm sending you the farm school catalogue with various parts of it underlined. . . . With the training you have so far had, I'm sure you could register for this fall, or next if you so wish. If you waited until the following fall, you would have to go to high school up there, and to me the idea is not so good. Remember that it was quite a wrench to me to take you out of high school so for you to go back and take a good deal of unnecessary work in order to get some of the necessary seems foolish." The only career Dorothy could see her daughter fitting herself for was farming, "whether on one of the farming communes or on a farm where you are working and earning a salary." In fact, "earning a salary" for a while might not be a bad idea. "I do firmly believe that young women should have a dowry and a hope chest, and be prepared to help their husbands as much as possible."

So Tamar would go to Farmingdale. And that, when all the factors were balanced, did make more sense than anything else, especially because Tamar would undoubtedly get married as soon after she reached eighteen as a wedding could be arranged. But there was another reason, perhaps, why Dorothy wanted her daughter at Farmingdale. As she had said in her notes on the retreat, she wanted to get away from the Worker for a while, to pray, to read, and to think things through. Near the agricultural school was an abandoned orphanage, owned by some Dominican sisters from Germany. If Tamar were at Farmingdale and Dorothy could get a room in the empty orphanage, then she could be with Tamar for a longer period of time than she had ever been before. It may have even entered her mind that Tamar wanted to be married just to have some stability in her life. Perhaps now, Dorothy may have thought, she could, by staying closer to Tamar, enable her to weigh better the advisability of her prospective marriage.

She announced in the September *Worker* her intention of leaving her active life for a while. "For the last few years I've been thinking a great deal of putting aside the responsibility of the Catholic Worker . . . but every time that idea came to me I put it aside as a temptation. It was during my retreat this summer that the conviction came to me that I should take this step." After one of the conferences at the retreat "when I was kneeling before a statue of the Blessed Mother . . . suddenly I began to think of how beautifully hidden and quiet a life was hers." The *Worker* readers could thus understand Dorothy's desire to withdraw from the scene, and because Providence had something to do with this desire they could only agree with her. Or so Dorothy seemed to suggest.

In her papers, Dorothy left an account of her time away. She had initially planned to take a year off, "from all active work, all responsibility." She had wanted to put herself under complete obedience to a spiritual director, Father Hugo, "but I didn't." Seemingly some of the things that he would have her do she either could not or would not. She was leaving her work, but she could not leave her mother, Tamar, and some of her friends. "My mother is getting older, and she was not too well and my daughter was at that crucial age . . . when she needed my support, advice, my just being there, near at hand, available, not tugged at by many other people at all times so that she could never get a word in edgewise with me."

Dorothy started the year in September by going to the Grail, "a school for the apostolate for young girls" at Loveland, Ohio. There she and Tamar stayed as guests for a month. In October they went to Farmingdale to the State School of Applied Agriculture. Tamar was put in a boarding house and Dorothy went to the convent. "I took no money from the Catholic Worker, so I could not afford to board there. . . . I begged the use of an abandoned school room where cooking had been taught. Here amidst the sinks and gas stoves, half of which had been dismantled and stored in the corner of the room, I made my home for 6 months. It was a large room with French windows looking down a leaf-strewn path to the convent and chapel." She cooked her own meals there on a gas burner and bought the food with money she got by book reviewing and writing some articles.

"It was a hard six months," Dorothy said. Tamar, with her roommate, would come over every afternoon for a cup of hot chocolate, but on the whole she was too engrossed in her work to

do anything more than visit with her mother. On Friday afternoons Dorothy would walk to the village and there take a train to
Minneola to see her mother. Otherwise, for "most of the week
those seven long days I was alone. I got up at 6.30 for a seven
o'clock Mass. The sisters, of course, were already in chapel for
their meditation and morning prayers. Then after a solitary breakfast, the only meal I enjoyed during the day, I returned to the
chapel for another two hours' of praying and meditative reading."
Sometimes "I prayed with joy and delight. Other times each bead
of my rosary was heavy as lead, my steps dragged, my lips were
numb. I felt a dead weight. I could do nothing but make an act of
will and sit or kneel, and sigh in an agony of boredom." When, the
following March, she ended this more or less solitary retreat, she
"came to the conclusion . . . that such a hermit's life for a woman
was impossible. Man is not meant to live alone. . . . To cook for
one's self, to eat by one's self, to sew, wash, clean for one's self is a
sterile joy. Community, whether of the family, or convent, or
boarding house, is absolutely necessary."

Dorothy wrote this account of her "leave" in 1951, and it was
obvious that she thought of it in terms of publication. Actually,
during the six months of her "leave," she lived something far short
of the life of a hermit. There was visiting to and fro with Tamar.
As she said, she visited her mother on weekends. As she did not
say, she visited others during this period. At the end of the first
month, she spent a weekend with Della. She had just had her forty-
sixth birthday and so the weekend took on a mildly festive character, what with going to a picture show and visiting Freda and
Sasha.

Two weekends later she was back at Della's, for Franklin was
having his tonsils out that weekend and Della needed Dorothy's
support. On Sunday, while Della was at the hospital, John and
Tessa came to Della's and visited with Dorothy. The next day she
called David Hennessy, apparently asking him to meet her for a
talk. After their talk she met Peter Maurin for Mass at St. Andrew's
Church, and then they went to lunch. Dorothy did not get back to
Farmingdale until December 1, having been away for nearly a
week.

And so it went for the next four months. Once she got a letter
from Father Hugo suggesting that there be "more silence and solitude" in her days, but that seemed impossible. Dorothy's daily log
notes more conferences with David Hennessy, conferences with

Dorothy and Della, 1940s. Franklin
Spier, courtesy Susanna Miyake.

Dorothy's parents with their grandchildren. Courtesy John Spier.

Dorothy with her grandchildren, ca. 1960. Courtesy Dorothy
Day–Catholic Worker Collection, Marquette University.

A. J. Muste and Dorothy at draft card burning, November 1965. Ben Fernandez, courtesy Tom Cornell.

With Cesar Chavez and Coretta Scott King, Cathedral of St. John the Divine, New York, 1973. Courtesy NC News Service.

Arrested with United Farm Workers in Fresno, 1973. Courtesy Religious News Service.

With Bill Moyers, 1972. Courtesy WNET-TV.

At Tivoli. Bob Fitch, courtesy Black Star.

Courtesy *The Milwaukee Journal.*

Forster, trips to town, letter writing and, as usual, the frequent note, "To Della's."

March 4 was Tamar's eighteenth birthday and she was now free to marry, according to Dorothy's terms. Tamar apparently lost no time in pressing for an immediate resolution to that matter. It was likely the next evening, when Dorothy, Tamar, and David had dinner together, that Dorothy accepted finally the fact that Tamar was to be married and soon. That night she said that she got no sleep at all "what with thinking of T. and D. and their immediate marriage."

On April 1 Dorothy resumed her journal keeping. It was a sign that her attempt at putting aside the world was about to end. Her writing for the past six months had been "spasmodic." She had written some new chapters for her book on Peter and five drafts for articles. She had gotten "quite out of the habit of diary keeping but since my spiritual adviser counsels against writing for some months save for meditations I shall try to be more regular about this and write some every day, whether just to keep track of events or to write 'reflections' as I am so fond of doing." So she would begin with the events of that day, which was a "typical one. Arose at 5.45. Mass at 6.30. Breakfast 7.30. Reading Van Zeller's Isaiah and poring over maps of the Assyrian Empire until 8.30. Dishwashing. Listened to the news. I have just resumed this vice this last month in my worry over my brother in Helsinki [Donald] and Gerry [Griffin] . . . and God only knows where . . . others of our crowd are."

She had gone to the chapel "to practice in my use of the weapons of the spirit for an hour and a half. It is too hard. I accomplish nothing, I tell myself everyday. Like St. Teresa I hold on to a book so as not to be utterly bare before Him. My mind like an idiot wanders, converses, debates, argues, founders. If I get in 15 minutes of honest-to-God praying I'm doing well. It is an act of will being there, knowing I'll have to keep up this struggle thru life and yet proceeding 'at the pace of a hen.' "

The chapel was hot, and Dorothy was irritated with "a Sister who makes the stations at least four times while I am there, round and round the chapel. I beat my breast for judging my neighbor in my thoughts." Then the previous night there had been the "Sister Nurse" who was "walking rapidly up and down the walk between the bldgs with one of the old Sisters who had lost her mind. 'Three times today she has run away from me,' she said to me thru the window. 'I am trying to tire her out. She is a bad girl.' And tucking her patient's hand in her arm, she hurried her up and down the paths, their habits flying in the March wind. I love the Sisters, all of them, they work hard, they pray, they keep going from day to day and keep faith alive in the world."

When she returned to her room from the chapel, she found Tamar there. "She is calm and peaceful, finishing up her term exams. . . . She is marrying someone who accepts poverty, manual labor, loves country life and literature."

This, of course, was the end of Dorothy's stay in Farmingdale. She had, unquestionably, sought solitude for prayer and thought. But she had tried to combine this with her concern for Tamar, and Tamar, as she well knew, was her first concern. One might suppose that it was the matter of Tamar in the first place that brought her to the idea of a sabbatical from the Worker. And if, in her terms, she had anticipated a happy consequence on that score it certainly did not turn out that way. She had done what in conscience she felt she ought to do; she had failed, so the only thing to do was to go with the grain of things. On March 25 she took Tamar to John and Tessa's where Tessa's mother, Mrs. d'Aragon, measured Tamar for the wedding dress that she was to make.

The next afternoon Dorothy, back at Mott Street, felt a "sad" and "blank" grayness of mind. In the afternoon she went to the library just to sit and read.

Tamar and David were married on April 19 at eight o'clock in the morning in St. Bernard's Church at Easton. Afterward, there was a wedding breakfast at the farm, cooked by John Filliger, one-time seaman, now the head of the farm work. On her way to the church Tamar was filled with misgivings over the possibility of Peter's using the wedding breakfast as an occasion to make his "points." He did, too, or tried to, until Dorothy quieted him. A year later, on Tamar's nineteenth birthday, Dorothy wrote of the poverty with which Tamar was introduced to marriage. Tamar and David were going to live in an old shack on the farm and "their honeymoon was taken up with using sulfur candles, kerosene" and whatever weapons they could bring to bear against the bedbugs they found in the house. "On her wedding even she planted a rose bush. There was neither mirror nor bath to prepare her for her wedding. She bathed in a pail the night before, and never did see how lovely she looked in her wedding dress, made by Mrs. d'Aragon."

Several years later she wrote one of her "meditations" on married love, and her thoughts had a particular reference to Tamar. "If we crave human love, if women in their vanity can only love themselves if others love them, and suffer as they grow older in their desire for love; if it is love of which we dream from our childhood on, it is most generally the love of man and woman we are thinking of. It is the libido, the force in us all."

When a son or daughter left his or her father and mother for the one he or she loved, "they are one flesh. It is a love of union. I thought of this when my daughter, who was young and shy, turned resolutely to the man she loved and was so ready to go to the ends of the earth, to leave me to whom she had been so close, only child that she was. I remember warning her one time as we walked down Mott Street and she was holding close to my arm, clinging to me as she often did, that she must learn to be self-reliant, to depend on herself, to learn to stand alone. I probably hurt her by so saying. We are always hurting those we love."

Later, she thought of the advice she had given Tamar and decided that it had not been good advice. "Man is not made to stand alone. That also is a Bible saying. It made me both happy and unhappy to see my only one go to another and cling to him and put him before all others, even if it meant never seeing me again. It did not mean that of course. Fortunately we have never needed to be separated very far or very long." Tamar was married, and Dorothy would accept that fact and do the best she could.

✿ 14

The Middle Years

BECAUSE Peter Maurin's room at Mott Street was on the first floor of the rear building, its single window looking out on the wall of the adjoining building, two or three feet away, it remained dark late into the day. Peter did not mind, for he usually slept until ten in the morning. When he got up he would go to St. Andrew Church on Duane Street, near City Hall, and sit in the church for an hour or more before the noonday Mass, just thinking. One day in January, 1944, Dorothy met Peter at the church, and after Mass they walked along the Bowery to the Eclipse Restaurant, where he usually had his breakfast. The Eclipse was simply a large room with dingy, scarred walls painted dark green. "On the walls were half a dozen cracked mirrors, some of them completely broken in half, and on the fragments painted with chalk, food was advertised." That day the Eclipse was featuring "Pig ears, spaghetti, bread and tea, 15." Lamb stew was twenty cents. Peter ordered lamb stew, but Dorothy thought she would have the special, the egg and mush. After taking Dorothy's order, the waiter shook his head and countermanded it. "Lamb stew," he said. "So I ordered it too. It was hot and good. There were a few pieces of potato and carrot, plenty of meat and plenty of grease. The grease made it hearty."

They talked about labor leaders. Maurin said that Philip Murray, president of the C.I.O., had "made a very important analysis of unemployment." But, despite wartime full employment, Peter thought things were getting worse. Workers had "become just as acquisitive as the Chambers of Commerce." The acquisitive spirit would take over the world. "People are preoccupied about this world. . . . If we were more preoccupied about the next world, maybe it would solve the problems of this world, too."

Peter's talk was in fragments. He was too busy eating. In his old age he seemed to be "always hungry." Dorothy wondered if it was because he was "remembering lean years in France," when as a "family of twenty-three or so" there was "never . . . enough to go around." Old age had begun to claim Peter. It had been apparent for over a year. Dorothy recalled that when she had returned from her three-month West Coast trip in the spring of 1942, she had found him confused. "His face was drawn and gray, his voice slow, he could not remember proper names." Dorothy took him to a doctor, "a friend of mine, a German. . . . She had spent a year in one of Hitler's concentration camps for refusing to sterilize epileptic children." She did the usual examination and questioned Peter about his symptoms. His answers were brief, so Dorothy speculated to the physician as to the cause of Peter's trouble. "I told her about the visitors who kept him up until two to three every night in a hot, stuffy room, dinning into his ears their insane ramblings." Over a period of months, some of the demented at Mott Street had been regularly descending on Peter, subjecting him to hours of listening to the festerings of their diseased minds.

When Dorothy suggested that this could be the cause of Peter's problem, he turned and looked at her "pleadingly. 'But they are driven from pillar to post. None will listen to them. I was trying to find out what they are trying to say.'" Peter's "only admission," Dorothy said, "was that they kept him from thinking. And to Peter, the thinker, who walked the street pondering human problems, who sat by the hour meditating in church, who valued his long hours of quiet as he did his hours of conversation, to be kept from thinking must have been torture."

Thinking of Peter, Dorothy then thought of Dostoevsky's Prince Myshkin, who, like Maurin, "is described as entirely passive, [who] willingly accepts suffering, is easily put upon, answers offense by begging forgiveness, and exaggerates the good in others while constantly overlooking evil." Dostoevsky, she said, described this "submissiveness" as "the most fearful force that can exist in the world."

Peter did not recover. He was becoming senile. "I can no longer think," he said, so he ceased talking. In her journal for the winter of 1945, Dorothy noted that "he sits by the fire, a continual source of irritation to Fr. [Duffy]. 'Peter loves the stove,' he will say." But Peter never answered. "He never justifies himself. His silence is perfect." And then Dorothy thought of herself: "I have the same faults. . . . I criticize, I justify. . . . My particular examen every day is on holy silence."

Dorothy told of a time when Peter was lost. "For three days we searched the streets of the Bowery, the hospitals, for him. For three days and nights we listened for his slow step on the stair, the sound of his cough or the door opening. He had wandered out for a little walk, and had gotten lost. And we wondered with a dreadful constriction of the heart, whether this was the way Peter Maurin was going to end. Was he, the poor man, going to wander out on the streets and disappear, lost and forgotten, perhaps put as dead storage in a vast mental hospital such as we have in New York state, where fifteen thousand inmates sit around in wards all day every day of the year—many of them just because they have this loss of memory? And, we would never find him?"

But he came back, "panting a little from exhaustion," but smiling nonetheless. "This place is very hard to find," he said.

One cold night during the winter of 1946, a young physician who practiced in Easton asked his wife to ride along with him to make an after-hours house call in the country. Years later, his wife, Mrs. Geraldine Nicholas, wrote of that event. "If I remember correctly, it was close to 11 o'clock. We drove down Route 611 along the Delaware and turned off sharply to the right and up a dirt road which was very steep and bumpy. We parked in what seemed like a field." Dr. Nicholas got out "and made his way on foot to a building. It was very dark so I could not follow where he went. About half an hour later he returned and opened the car door and held it open a while . . . he looked toward the sky. He said very quietly, 'What . . . a man, what a joy to serve him.' He got into the car and kept exclaiming" about this "beautiful" old man, "all wrapped in coats and covers almost like carpets sitting up straight on a stool. . . . I remember my husband mentioning the 'beautiful man' several times the next day. He just couldn't get over the fact that the woman in the cottage insisted on paying him." The man, of course, was Maurin.

The decline of Peter was, for Dorothy, the falling away of a certain prospect in life and the beginning of another. Maurin had provided her with a vision of a human destiny that had come from a logic and knowledge of things infinitely larger than anything she had known before. Out of that vision had come her vocation, and Maurin, the worthy teacher, had given that vocation great strength by his own saintliness. The retreats, as she said, simply underlined what Maurin had taught her. Her vocation was confirmed.

The prospect, where the work of her vocation was concerned, rested on a diminished but substantial base. It was diminished, of course, because of the war. Half of the houses of hospitality had closed, and others were struggling. One of the most active Worker houses had been the one in Boston, run principally by Jane Marra. In the latter part of 1945, a rebellion broke out against her management by the others who worked there. A new head was selected, and Miss Marra was deposed. The situation was so irregular and rancorous that the Boston Archdiocese withdrew its support from the house and so did Dorothy. She even went to the remarkable length of dissolving the house. To Jane Marra's "successor," she wrote that the house was "officially disbanded." What money the house had should be turned over to the Archbishop. Furthermore, in "this issue" of the *Catholic Worker,* February, 1946, "I am calling attention to the fact that there is now no house in Boston, no work, nor group. The only thing that will be there will be the selling of the paper."

So Dorothy had wiped out a house. She could do something like that and would do more of it in the future. No one dared challenge her. On the other hand, she did work to sustain other houses. Beginning in the spring of 1946, she did a lot of traveling to evaluate the situation in the houses and to encourage Workers there to take a new heart in what they were doing, to understand that they were in the very front line in the struggle against those forces that would cast humankind in that final refuse heap of nothingness. She wanted "to emphasize our fellowship in the work." She wanted "to gather together the group in the house . . . and talk to them about what the whole work is, their part in it; that they are truly playing a part in it though perhaps they do not see it. The men who cook, wash dishes, scrub, clean, launder, ministering to others, are part of a movement—to try to convey to them the glimpse of the 'whole.' They see only part. We all see thru a glass darkly. . . . Our joy in the work increases with our vision of the whole. . . . Workers must be scholars and scholars workers, as Peter says."

She was greatly aggrieved when she interpreted something that John Cogley had written as seeming to suggest that the Worker movement was a thing "in the dim and distant past." He wrote of the "mushroom growth" of the movement that had occurred in the

1930s, but he seemed to say all that was over. It assuredly was not over, Dorothy said. There were yet eleven houses "still trying to work out a theory of love . . . so that the revolution of love instead of that of hate may come about. And nobody could deny but what the problem now was greater than it ever had been."

Then Don Gallagher, who had started the St. Louis house, had written an article in "the Historical Review printed by St. Louis University." Gallagher, she said, had spoken "of the C.W. as something in the past." Well, rejoined Dorothy, the movement to her was "still one of the most important in the country today" because it pointed to the problem of the poor, a problem that had been met only with words. There had been "too much tackling of the problem from above. There are too few who will consider themselves servants, who will give up their lives to serve others, who will sow the things of this world." There had been "too much talk of raising up of leaders, and too little of the raising up of servants." In fact, there had been "just too much talk, and too little being what we are talking about."

As for Peter Maurin's not being an "original thinker, he never claimed. . . to be an original thinker but called himself an agitator, an integrator, a maker of a synthesis, and above all, he called for a synthesis to be made by others."

Later, Dorothy confided to her journal that she had gotten a letter from Cogley saying that her attitude had "hurt him." In fact, he was "in a state." But, she said, she would "try to say nothing about it. Writing is hard." She let it pass. "The less said, the sooner forgotten," she might have said, thinking of one of her mother's aphorisms. But she had nót let pass Cogley's correct appraisal of the situation, nor had she let pass Gallagher's comments, which certainly had been made in good conscience. But Dorothy was thin-skinned; and she could not overlook or really forgive what she took to be any mark of defection from the way she saw things. She could recognize Peter's total submissiveness as a mark of saintliness, but she did not have that spirit nor could she develop it. In her inability to accept gracefully a course which a communist would have labeled "deviationist," she was, again, like her father. In old age she would learn to take even this, but not before the pathway of her life was crowded with people whose sensibilities had been bruised by her harshness. Over a long and close association, she could sometimes be difficult to deal with.

Cogley and Gallagher were looking at the Worker movement, as Dorothy said, "as something in the past," and to them, as to some other young people who had lived before the war and then through it, what had happened before 1939 seemed remote. Even so, for some young men, whose lives had been altered by the war, the Worker had been the last worthwhile life they had known, a life they would like to resume where they had left off. In the July–August *Worker* of 1945, Dorothy wrote of those who had returned. "Even [Dwight] Larrowe, former head of the Catholic conscientious objectors, who changed his position (God knows why—we don't) ... is back from Germany.... Martie Rooney, of the Rochester group ... visited us on his way home. He had spent the last year in a German prison camp."

Jack English, out of his Roumanian prison camp, "stayed a week with us and helped clean house." As English mopped floors, or whatever he did, he probably talked to Dorothy about what he wanted to do with his life. Many people, sick of death and destruction, felt, in those months just after the war, a disposition to put their lives to some creative use. Such was Jack English's feeling and he, like others who had read Thomas Merton's *The Seven Storey Mountain,* thought about taking up the religious life. In 1951 he entered the Trappists.

John Thornton, of the Easton farm, had just been sentenced to four years in prison for refusing conscription. His wife and two children would, for a while at least, remain at the farm. And the fate of Thornton's wife would be the fate of a good many other wives whose husbands' antiwar, anticonscription conscience led them to prison. The sacrifices made by these women and their children would be difficult to reckon.

The war's end found prospects as changed for the *Catholic Worker* as for the members of the movement. In May, 1945, Dorothy told how the paper was doing: "We have at the present a single-subscriber list of 23,000 and what we call the bundle file (orders of two to a thousand) go out to 27,500 more. Back in 1938 ... we printed 190,000 copies of our anniversary issue and thanks to the thirty Houses of Hospitality over the country, and widespread circulation in many schools and colleges, we had a regular run of 160,000 copies a month. Since the war, and our pacifist stand, our circulation has dropped to 50,500." Now, she said, the paper had a "tried and true" body of readers.

Across the river in Brooklyn, a priest connected with the *Tablet* gave the *Tablet*'s readers an "outside opinion" of the *Worker.* It was "published by a group who are doing a great deal of good. Their work is with the poor and needy. Dorothy Day is a convert who went the whole way and then some—she may be called an extremist—zealous to a fault. She has exemplified self-sacrifice to the letter—made herself poor for the poor and that sort of thing. She and her group are radical in the sense that whoever does not go along with their ideas isn't really living Catholicism as it should be lived."

Circumscribed by the war, as *Worker* circulation was, the paper did have something like 50,000 enthusiastic readers, and their number would rise again in the following two decades. The *Worker* of the postwar years was a much better paper than it had been in the 1930s. It was well written, largely by women. Doris Ann Doran wrote on the desolation in Europe, Irene Naughton on the relationship between economics and community, Ade Bethune on arts and crafts, and Julia Porcelli on discrimination against blacks. Shortly, though, men were writing again. John Cogley wrote reviews of books and movies, and Gordon Zahn, who had been a C.O. at the Rosewood Training School for the mentally retarded, produced exceptional articles on mentally retarded children. An ex-bomber crewman, Tony Aratari, wrote pieces on literary themes. Aratari recognized the brilliant mind and spirit of the French Jewish mystic Simone Weil, and brought her to the attention of *Worker* readers in the February, 1951 issue. Then there were Bob Ludlow and Tom Sullivan. Ludlow wrote weighty pronouncements on the relationship of the Worker idea to the pathology he saw in the life around him. Apparently his pieces were too heavy for some, but his writing was intelligent, and touched on real issues.

Sullivan was brilliant, too, as the chronicler of the doings at the Mott Street house. He brought into the consciousness of the readers the sights, smells, and sounds of the Mott Street dining hall, and he could appreciate the bizarre humor in situations that sometimes could be almost grotesque. And to complement these literary talents with an extraordinary artististic talent came a Cologne-born Quaker, Fritz Eichenberg, whose woodcuts in the years following would give a striking character to the *Worker*.

But the principal reason for the *Worker's* postwar ascendancy was Dorothy herself. In the August, 1944, issue, after her "year off," she said that she had "taken over the paper and the work again" and "am once more the mother of a very large family." Because she had never actually dropped the paper, her taking it over was not news. It had always been that way. From the first issue until the last years of her life, when she no longer had the strength to do so, she was the *Worker*'s editor, censor, and principal news writer.

The paper also served as her diary. In the February, 1946, issue, she began calling her column, "On Pilgrimage," explaining that "We should always be thinking of ourselves as pilgrims anyway." Her column by itself is a work of considerable literary significance. In it she gave a continuing account of the movement and action of her own life, her daughter, her grandchildren, her travels, and the books she read—all measured by the spiritual dimension in which she saw things. In "On Pilgrimage" she was the personable, chatty, and frequently eloquent Dorothy who ingratiated herself into the consciousness of *Worker* readers as she did with those who knew her face-to-face. In print she was as she was in real life—devoid of artificiality and affectation to such an extent that readers felt that they had a friend, a confidante, to whom they could talk and tell everything without being misunderstood and labeled.

And readers talked to her in their letters. Some were pathetic. "I am writing this letter from Bellevue Hospital psychiatric ward," ran one. "I had gone to see the landlord about a certain matter. While I was standing in the front office one of the men . . . made derogatory remarks about tenants. . . . He poured out his emotional filth at me. . . . I fought in an unorthodox way. My method was that I made announcements in the street informing the public of how they had treat me. . . . I was placing this as a moral issue in the hands of the public. . . . Some people gathered." She concluded: "I shall not eat . . . until they set me free. I was born free. . . . I need help. Please help me. . . . Please help me."

A woman wrote to tell of her loneliness. "Until the first Friday of Our Lady Month of May, I had a very good husband . . . and now he's gone, I'm scared to death of the future. . . . Now here I am writing you all about my troubles as if you haven't enough of your own to worry you." A letter from a Methodist pastor in a rural area declared that "the arrival of the *Catholic Worker* is always like a visit from a friend who moves with freedom and fearless abandon to follow the direction of Christ. . . . If we truly seek to follow Christ we will want to work with all people in hope of persuading them to know Him too." The pastor enclosed a dollar bill "with which to keep us in . . . touch with your work."

Over the years thousands of letters like these accumulated in cardboard boxes under the tables in Worker houses. Of course, not all were from people who were troubled or ill. And no person wrote Dorothy so many letters of unabashed praise and over such a long period of time as did a distinguished member of the American Academic community. Read Bain was a professor of sociology at Miami University, and when he began writing letters to Dorothy in the early 1950s, he had nearly a quarter of a century of teaching behind him. He had served as the president of the American Sociological Association and for four years had been editor of the *American Sociological Review*. In 1950 he became the editor of another journal, the *Humanist*.

His first letter to Dorothy was written in 1952, and after that he continued to write, every year or so, for the next two decades. Bain was a humanist in the age of science. If there was a God, it was some kind of evolutionary persistence, some final principle of predictability in human behavior. But to him Dorothy was something beyond anything that could be covered by his sociological laws and jargon. For more than twenty years, he wrote letters to her, one at least every year and sometimes more frequently. In his first letter, dated October 13, 1952, he said, "you are on the right track" because she had struck "at the economic inequalities and cruel denial of life values" that had "grown up in modern capitalism." It was this fact that had been "the source of vitality in the communist movement—a crazy, cruel system that lovers of fellow man must abhor." Bain could see that she was "trying to bring man back to the basic truths of early Christianity—lost for a thousand years." The "thing you see clearly . . . is that human love is the essence. Simplicity, kindliness, fairness, generosity, reverence for the spontaneous need for freedom and brotherly love—these are man's best hope."

Over the years Bain became even more enthusiastic about Dorothy. "I still say she is headed for sainthood," he wrote seven years and many letters later. "If I were Pope I'd canonize her tomorrow. Certainly she is more intelligent, literate, and literarily gifted than 90 percent of the saints. She writes like an angel." Then, shifting form his third-person analysis, he addressed Dorothy directly: "When I read your Pilgrimage thru the world, the Christian myth becomes almost believable. Maybe I . . . will become a Catholic in my old age. I strongly doubt it, but I can admire you . . . yes, I suppose I can love you, though I never could do the things, or believe the things, you do."

Once Bain got a reply from Dorothy, who ordinarily did not respond to "fan" mail. Whatever else she said to him she must have said that he should not praise her as he did. But Bain was not squelched. "There is every reason why I should write you, even though I never got a scratch of a pen from you. My reason is that I am so grateful to know that there are people like you and your Group in the world. . . . So I shall keep your letter and hand it down to my grandsons."

The letters continued. One of the last ones, undated but apparently written in the early 1970s, had "answered" in Dorothy's handwriting on the top of the first page. Bain on one point had not changed his mind. "As the years go by, I am more and more certain that you will eventually become a Saint. . . . you will be sainted because you are a gift to God and a servant par excellence. . . . If I were a praying man, I would say a special prayer for you and your vocation every night. As it is, a day seldom passes without my thinking of you and your work—and being thankful that the crazy human race can produce some people like you and your fellow workers." But on another point he had changed. Once he had said to Dorothy that he thought that "science can save us." But no longer. "Sometimes when I think of you and this dying world, I weep like Jeremiah," he said.

Dorothy could write Bain a letter once every five years and that was enough. But letters from Bellevue Hospital, a sick bed, or a prison required an answer. In the April, 1941 issue of *Preservation of the Faith,* there is an article by her, "The Apostolate of Writing," in which she discussed her work of letter writing. "I wake up with letters to answer and I go to bed with letters to answer. When I go out on a speaking trip, I take a bundle of letters with me and even on a social call, bring a few of the longer letters we have received to read on the subway and meditate on the answers to be given." Many of the letters, she said, "demand thought and prayer, so that an hour in the presence of the Blessed Sacrament is necessary before presuming to answer some of them." Dorothy's letters to the "lonely" people, one must assume, are mostly lost. But one has survived and it is probably characteristic of those she wrote to these anonymous people. It was sympathetic and to the point, without the inclusion of the usual anodyne of slippery pieties. "We all want someone to lean on," she began, "and we all feel alone and we all rebel against freedom and responsibility. We always will. But we just have to take it." The only remedy, she said, was prayer, "and usually we will put off that and look for someone to lean on and give us comfort. We might as well make up our minds that we are not going to find it. We may think we find it, but such support crumbles under us." As for "controlling" the lives of others, it was hard enough to control oneself "without trying to control others. I always feel that we should expect everything from people—'they are a little less than the angels'—and then on the other hand, be surprised or disappointed about nothing, remembering 'they are but dust.'" In short, "you can depend on nobody but God and yourself."

The Worker idea was made up of concentric circles in which the dynamism moved outward from the personalist center. In the paper, Dorothy's column was her personalist center, but the paper as a whole in this postwar period put much emphasis on Worker economic and political "positions." Over the years Dorothy's position on economic and political matters has been described as "anarchism." That was all right, she told Professor Rosemary Bannon, but those who so described her should understand that "our concept of anarchism is a religious one and it stems from the life of Jesus on earth who came to serve rather than to be served and who never coerced. There was no question of force. They [the apostles] went away sorrowing because they could not take what He had to say."

If Dorothy had been pressed for a more definitive statement of her position, she might have quoted a note she made on Martin Buber's "Hasidic Axioms," which she had read. "According to Buber, constructive socialism 'becomes possible only thru the formation of small voluntary groups . . . who not merely share the means of production, or the forces of labor, but who, as human beings, enter into a direct relationship with one another and live a life of genuine fraternity. Such a socialism would have to resist any mechanization of living. The association of such groups would have to resist the dictates of an organized center, accumulation of power, and a political superstructure. The focus of such groups, or cells, is not a political but a religious motivation.'"

This was Dorothy's position entirely. "It is our firm belief," she said, that "we need to decentralize. . . . We need to be getting into regional groups or communities so that the local community would deal with the problems of that community or that region." She thought a "study needs to be made of the village communes of China, new ways of governing a country—like Tanzania." These were countries "that are the opposite of our particular capitalist, affluent society."

She was critical of the "system," which had, as she saw it, debased the concept of work. The "priests and laity" alike have lost their concept of work, they have lost a philosophy of labor, as Peter Maurin has always said. The attempt of publicists of the system to romanticize the laborer's role as a machine server was a grotesquerie. As easily could "one sanctify a saloon, a house of ill fame. When one gives one's self up to one's work, when one ceases to think and becomes a machine himself, the devil enters in. We cannot lose ourselves in our work without grave danger. . . . As soon as one becomes 'beside one's self,' as soon as we lose ourselves, as soon as we give ourselves up to anything, whether it is sex, or drink, or work at the machine, there is the danger of the devil entering in." In much of what went as "work" in the contemporary economic process, the person "is 'spent.' He is emptied. He is emasculated. We can no more bless it, 'sanctify it,' than the priest can bless the scrap iron which he sprinkles with holy water in the churchyard before it sets off to kill Japanese or Germans. . . . And yet, that is what the clergy are doing when they accept this system, this *industrial* capitalism."

"Distributism" was a term much used in the *Catholic Worker* during this period. This, as David O'Brien has written, was an "extreme rejection of capitalism" that had developed in England "where the distributists, Hilaire Belloc, G. K. Chesterton, and Father Vincent McNabb, advocated the rejection of machine technology and urban civilization in favor of a frank return to a peasant, handicraft society." Dorothy did not want to return to a "peasant" society. She wanted all that modern science and technology could provide if it could be made compatible with a work that was creative and humanizing. "There is nothing wrong about cars," she said. "In fact they are a joy and a delight." She had a "love for cars." But if cars could be made only by dehumanizing the worker, then cars would have to be made by another system.

But Dorothy did not want to be labeled just a "distributist," a "socialist," an "anarchist," or anything else. She was a personalist and a Christian and that, as she saw it, was label enough for any human situation. But, she said in a fit of agitation, "speaking of Anarchism . . . I wish people would not be so afraid of words." She, like Peter, wanted people to think. "I wish people would study more the early principles on which our country was founded. I wish they would really read and study and discuss as the Russian Jews do on the East Side in the public squares and in the cafeterias, not to speak of the way the communists do in their worker's schools and cell meetings and caucuses."

What did she think about participating in the political process? "I have never registered, nor voted," she once noted. "It was a matter of principle, yes, and also because I did not know any candidates, and also because of discouragement with the prevailing political system. Yet we are to rebuild society within the shell of the old, to use the I.W.W. jargon."

Part of the changing prospect for the Worker movement after the war was a termination of the Easton farm experiment. Maryfarm had begun as a farming commune "but we must confess our failure. Farming communes are not possible without interior discipline, without a philosophy of labor," she wrote in the November, 1944, *Worker*. So she would make the farm into a retreat center and would herself take charge of the venture "to try to build here this training center for Catholic Workers, for apostles, for followers of our Lord." She asked Father Hugo to be the chaplain in residence, the retreat master, but he declined. "I have been definitely forbidden to give any retreats," he wrote. The first retreat began on September 10, 1944. "From now on," wrote Dorothy "every other month or two," there would be a six-day retreat, "during which there will be silence, work on the land, and prayer." Matters seemed to have begun auspiciously. Father Roy was there "laboring as a priest, electrician, plumber, and carpenter." There were three Grail girls, "sent out as shock troops," and they were "making the barn habitable for our winter retreats."

Retreats were held through the summer of 1946. On November 15, Dorothy noted in her journal that "the priest to give the retreat showed up with a heavy smell of liquor on his breath. Perhaps he had a cold. 'The ways of the Lord are unscrupulous.' " But it was not the priest with booze on his breath that caused Dorothy to give up the farm. It was, she noted in her journal, "the story of the Smiths, the Thorntons, the Toblers . . . who all but wrecked the retreat house. They, like us, were undoubtedly trying to grow in the love of God and the love of each other. But it took them along strange paths and caused a break-up of our establishment, a separation between the families and the retreat house. . . . It was primarily a struggle for power, for authority to 'legislate' in regard to the farm and its disposition."

Another person, an acquaintance of Dorothy's, visited the farm for a retreat and was upset by what to her seemed to be blatant improprieties on the part of one family head. "What business has a married man with a family consoling another man's wife?" she asked. What did he mean by "(1) taking her to town, (2) by just going up and talking to her of an evening, (3) by consenting to plans of leaving his wife and taking another woman to visit her husband?" Also, she was concerned with the utter disrespect and disregard for authority among Catholic Workers. But why was she telling Dorothy all this? She probably would not be disturbed because she was "a little Bohemian and probably won't agree with me."

The problems there were such that Dorothy had unburdened herself to Abbot Frederic M. Dunne of the Trappist monastery at Gethsemani. Abbot Dunne did not know what to advise. "Those matters at the Farm about which you write are truly almost of a nature as to make one wonder if the evil spirit has not a hand in the whole affair. If they profess to lead others to a nobler mode of living, surely they would not conduct themselves in the manner you write about, unless they are sadly under the spell of some illusion. Let your charity embrace these evildoers in your prayers."

Charity, yes—but Dorothy had had enough of the turmoil, and she took advice that Peter had given: when situations became intolerable, when rival groups contested for power and property, give them everything and withdraw. When such became the case at Maryfarm at Easton, that was what she did.

There were also changes within her family after the war. Mother Grace died on October 24, 1945. When Dorothy's father had died, she briefly noted the event in the *Worker*. In the November *Worker*, she wrote of her mother's death at length. "It made me happy that I could be with my mother the last few weeks of her life, and for the last ten days at her bedside daily and hourly. Sometimes I thought to myself that it was like being present at a birth, to sit by a dying person and see their intentness on what is happening to them. It almost seems that one is absorbed in a struggle, a fearful, grim, physical struggle, to breathe, to swallow, to live." And so, Dorothy said, she kept thinking to herself "how necessary it is for one of their loved ones to be beside them, to pray for them, to offer up prayers for them unceasingly." Grace knew she was dying, and occasionally she and Dorothy talked about it. "I told her that we could no more imagine the life beyond the grave than a blind man could imagine colors, and how we could go just so far in our reasoned belief, and that our knowledge was like a bridge which came to an end, so that it did not reach the other shore."

The night Grace died, Dorothy and John were in the room. Dorothy had been trying to get her to eat some custard. But Grace said that she was tired, that she wanted to sleep, and bade John kiss her goodnight. Dorothy sat by the bed, holding her hand. And then "she just turned her head and sighed. That was her last breath, that little sigh; and her hand was warm in mine for a long time after."

To be with her mother when she died was something for which Dorothy "had prayed so constantly; for years I had offered up that prayer. And God granted it quite literally." One of the good consequences of her "sabbatical" from the Worker, as she later remarked, was that she, in her weekly visits to her mother at Minneola, had come back to her parents, having left them in her youth. Of course, she never "left" her mother. One suspects in her feeling for the ultimate resolution of the longing to love, that in her desire to be with her mother at death she was also with her father. This kind of mystical reordering of persons and things was a gift that Dorothy abundantly possessed.

On March 29, 1946, she sat on the front porch of the Hennessy cabin at Easton. It was a "perfect spring day. . . . A blue haze hangs over the valley below me, the cherry and pear trees below . . . where I write are about to burst into bloom. Here on the porch, two leaping baby goats are a great distraction." She thought of William Cobbett's book, *American Gardener,* "a very rare book which deserves reprinting" and stated Cobbett's idea of "how necessary it is for families who wish to settle on the land to learn gardening and small husbandry and some craft. We should be thinking in terms of village economy instead of farm economy. There is such a need for shoemakers, carpenters, stone masons, gardeners, etc." Likely she was thinking of the lack of a development of this kind of economy among the families at Easton.

But why worry? She had a granddaughter, Rebecca. "Tamar and I go out walking with her in the evening. What joy." In fact, there was new life all around her. "The hen has four black chicks. The cow has a white calf. The angora has a tiny kid called Mouse. Whitey, a kid called Susie."

But as Dorothy recognized, what Tamar and David needed to

do was to begin a life of their own, to have land of their own, away from the quarreling and distractions that had become part of family life at Easton.

Forster Batterham was ordinarily not a writer of letters, but on February 27, 1947, he wrote one to Dorothy. Tamar had written him, he said, "saying that they wanted to buy a farm somewhere and asked about the lot on Staten Island as a source of revenue. I investigated and find it can be sold to the people in the building across the street for $750 cash. I will add an additional $250 and send her $1000 for the down payment. The balance can be financed locally thru the bank. . . . I am writing this to you as it was your wish to have Tamar use the lot and you are probably familiar with their plans. Let me know what you wish me to do."

What Forster suggested was apparently done, and sometime late in the year of 1947, the Hennessys moved into an old, vacant farmhouse at Berkeley Springs, Virginia. How they chose the farm is not clear, but it was likely through people who knew of it, who lived in the area, and who had had some contact with the Worker. The house, as Dorothy described it, had "eight rooms . . . a porch front, side and back, a good tin roof." The out-buildings consisted of "a shed, pigpen, chicken house, smokehouse, an old cannery from which the machinery has been removed, and which is used now to house goats: the four does, one buck and two kids." There were "fifty-five acres of hilly woodland, and twenty acres of fields." The owners were asking $2500 for it, and the Hennessys were in the process of buying it. The landscape was beautiful, the house was capacious and charming in its old age and no doubt, so they all thought, it could be "fixed up," after the basic items of running water and electricity were added. For the moment they could make do with kerosene lamps, the pitcher pump on the back porch, and an outhouse. In this healthful environment, the family would wax and, at least, be fed. Besides, Hennessy, who had a taste for books and book-trading, would develop his mail-order business in books and perhaps provide the family with funds. Or so they thought.

Hennessy did start something called "The Distributist Bookstall," and there were some orders but, predictably enough, it drained the meager resources that the family had. As for the good life on the farm, it had its moments, but for the Hennessys it was poverty and unremitting work. Just to exist seemed a struggle. Hennessy by temperament seemed to have been suited more for the congenial life of a professorial chair, endowed for the life of a twenty-year research project, than for farming. And Tamar, no driver herself, did all that she could, what with her continuing pregnancies.

Here indeed was a struggling family, ill-equipped by natural endowments and by simply not having the fundamental resources to set an example in the cause of agrarian self-sufficiency. Perhaps it was Dorothy's urging that led them to it, but, even so, Tamar and David wanted to do it too. For Hennessy, it was a vision, but beyond his reach; for Tamar, the life suited her as well as any could.

In the first fifty pages of her small book, *On Pilgrimage,* published as "Catholic Worker Books" in December, 1948, Dorothy wrote of her four-month stay at the Hennessys beginning in January, 1948. The book, like most of Dorothy's work, includes parts of her "On Pilgrimage" column and parts from her journal.

There she explains why she left "the work," as she was fond of calling it, for such a long time. She said, it was "taking care of your own, children and grandchildren" that, "in a way," was "taking care of yourself. There was also the sacrament of duty as Father McSorley calls it." She knew she was needed at Mott Street, "writing letters, seeing visitors, speaking about the work while others do it," but "one can become a veritable Mrs. Jellyby [a Dickens character] looking after the world and neglecting one's own who are struggling with poverty and hard work and leading, as such families with small children do these days, ascetic lives." Also, Tamar was expecting.

When Dorothy got there the temperature was 14 degrees below zero, and she wrote her first observations by candlelight while she lay in bed. At her foot was a hot-water bottle, the bottle being a pint-sized whiskey bottle. That day she could not get her borrowed car started to make the twelve-mile trip to the village. "We need kerosene for the lamps and for the small portable heater. Five gallons for eight-five cents. Candles thirty-five cents a dozen. We do not read late as we are too tired, David with constant woodchopping, water-fetching, etc."

The days passed. "Breakfast of sausage, hotcakes, apples, and coffee. Dishes, water heating for clothes, breadbaking." For lunch, "bread and cheese." There were stewed tomatoes for supper. "For meat we have a side of bacon which will last us the winter. We have just finished some sausage friends gave us. Once a month we have chicken. Once every few weeks we buy liver." Still, "everything tastes delicious, and best of all is the smell of fresh baked bread in the house."

Because Tamar and David were up at night with the children, Dorothy got up at seven and built the fire in the kitchen and main room. Sometimes, when they could start the car, she drove Tamar to the village for shopping and a visit to the doctor. Dr. Tobias had an office in a store just off the square, and one afternoon when Dorothy, Tamar, and the children got there the office already had twelve people in it. All, as Dorothy noted, were poor and shabbily dressed. The doctor was "a tired, youngish man, full of common sense. He gave calcium pills to Tamar, some cough medicine for the children, and said to wait. He charged $35 for the delivery. The hospital bill would be $4 a day for the mother and $1 for the child."

On February 16, Dorothy noted, "still no baby." Tamar had gone far beyond the time the doctor had predicted, but, mused Dorothy, such things happened. She remembered the doctor telling her that she was two months pregnant when she knew that it was five months. "One of the strangest cases I ever heard of," she wrote, "was of a young woman in Margaret Sanger's birth control headquarters (planned parenthood, they call it now), who confessed one day, to the girl at the desk next to her, that she was going to have a baby the very next day! There was a great hullabaloo in the office." No doubt there was. "How have I failed you?" a shaken Mrs. Sanger must have asked her young employee.

With childtending, firebuilding, dishwashing, and cooking, Dorothy's devotional life was compressed. In the bitter cold she said her prayers in bed, "brief, half-conscious, and the planning, the considering, the figuring of ways of 'making ends meet,' goes on. Until I catch myself and turn to God again."

Eric was born on February 20, and christened on March 7. "Father Ignatius performed the baptism whereby Eric was made a son of God and heir of heaven." All the day before, Dorothy and Tamar had cooked. A ham had been sent to them, and Tamar made lemon pies and baked a cake. Dorothy made the baptismal robe from pieces of linen she had bought at Woolworth's. She had "embroidered it around the edges with little red crosses and on one side a large red cross, and on the other a blue shell and below it flowing water and another little fish."

Dorothy left the Hennessys at the end of March. She had not been happy at the prospects of departure. Every day during Holy

Week she had driven the twelve miles to Mass in Berkeley Springs, and then, before starting back, she would stop in a little restaurant for a cup of coffee. "There was a juke box of course in the coffee shop (one cannot get away from them), and every morning that same song blared forth. 'Now is the time that we must say good-bye.'" It "irritated" her but moved her too. She did not want to go back to Mott Street. But "there was no excuse to stay."

After Dorothy left, the financial pressure momentarily eased for the Hennessys. On June 2, Tamar wrote to her mother. "The check arrived yesterday. Thank you for sending it. We should be able to get the home in condition now." Tamar's spirits soared. "You should see how beautiful the walnut tree is next to the house. It is all cleared, and we plan a seat and a swing for the children. With the house covered and a fence around, the place will be gorgeous." The check to which Tamar referred could have been the proceeds from the sale of the Staten Island land that Forster had given her. In any case, the amount was small indeed when compared with the needs of a growing family, and life for the Hennessys at Berkeley Springs soon became precarious again. Dorothy, from what she earned from speaking and writing, sent the Hennessys all that she could. "We are thinking of buying . . . coal with the money you sent," Tamar wrote. "The children are getting over their colds." Della had sent the family three "beautiful chairs," and Forster had sent a quilt, a baby mattress, scissors, and a radio. "The radio stations get mixed up so we are trying to put up more aerial." Later, the family got a car, but it was anything but a joy. Tamar wrote to her mother that the garage had been able to fix the bumpers, but not the doors. The "body is too rotten." They had "charged for fixing the wiper but I can't work it. I will take the car back anyway for new points. It uses too much gas, backfires, won't go up hills."

Oh, to have a decent car just once, Tamar probably thought many times in her life, for it was she who did the driving and not David. It was in the car that poverty was unmasked: worn kingpins and shimmying wheels; thin tires; clouds of gray smoke trailing from the exhaust and a leaking radiator plugged with Octagon soap on the outside and oatmeal on the inside. Tamar must have known all about these things, and Dorothy, too, for that matter. In June, after she had returned from her visit to the Hennessys, Dorothy was given a 1932 Chevrolet. It took seventy-five dollars worth of work to get it running, but it did run—and with a commanding voice. The car "sounded either like a Mack truck or an aeroplane but I trust after we get the muffler fixed (there are a few large holes mended with tin cans) we will have a little more holy silence." Nonetheless, Dorothy was "much pleased with the car."

When Dorothy arrived at Mott Street with the car and began to tell Tom Sullivan about it, he interrupted her. She had just acquired another one, Tom explained. It was a 1924 Columbia, donated to the Worker. The year 1924 was the last one for the Columbia line, a light car made in Detroit that sold for less than $1000. Its claim to technological distinction was its "thermostatically controlled radiator louvres." Dorothy made no mention of this, but did say that the car "was in much better shape" than the Chevrolet. "To think of it" she exclaimed, "a car for the farm and a car to pick up stuff around New York. The men in the office talk of exchanging the two for a truck, but I am dead set against it. These will get us there."

As a successful beggar, Dorothy had few equals. Her appeals for cars, or financial help, either through the regularly issued written appeals for the ordinary expenses of running the Worker house, or her requests for help with some extraordinary expense, were so guileless, so full of the sweetness and goodness of putting a morsel of food into the mouth of a representative of the "unworthy poor, that one could not but help." "When I read your article . . . in the Oct. *Catholic Worker,* I regretted I had no means to help," ran one letter. "Later, thru God's Goodness I was reminded of a little account in the bank, left for some years from a little church society for which I was Sec. Treas. The enclosed check is for the full amount, and I am sending it in memory of the good pastor who fostered the devotion to the Sacred Heart as an alms for the peace and repose of his soul and all poor souls."

And so it went: the many small donations that came from those who were themselves almost impoverished. Dorothy well knew these people and she was determined, in her own poverty, to be faithful to the trust they had in her. "A car for the farm," Dorothy had said. Yes, there was a new Catholic Worker farm, five miles out of Newburgh, New York, and sixty miles from Mott Street. This acquisition, one suspects, was in Dorothy's mind even as she was signing away the Easton farm. In her abbreviated diary notes she says that on January 7, 1947, she was at "Fr. Fiorentino's, 186 Morris Place. Chancery; cold and rain." On January 10 she was off to Detroit to be at the wedding of Justine L'Esperance and Lou

Murphy, Detroit Workers who were to be married the next day. On January 31 she noted that she went to Newburgh with Jack English . . . lunch on train. Walked over farm; beautiful day."

That afternoon they went into Newburgh, saw a lawyer, signed a note for what seems to have been $6000 and paid $2000 down. The $2000 had come from the Father Fiorentino that Dorothy had visited. Dorothy had no doubt spoken of the Easton retreats and how good it would be to carry on the retreat tradition. But they needed a rural setting, an old farm somewhere would do—just the thing, in fact. Father Fiorentino wrote a check. On February 11, the deal was closed.

The Newburgh "Maryfarm" was more of a farm than the Easton place. Maryfarm at Easton, high above the Delaware River and the town of Easton, had a beautiful view, but mountaintops do not ordinarily make good farms. The Newburgh Maryfarm, close to the Hudson River, was on level land. In front of the farm ran country road 7K, which ran from the Hudson to intersect Highway 17. Caroline Gordon, who visited Newburgh in the course of its Catholic Worker life, used the farm as one of the settings in her novel, *The Malefactors.* Later, she said that she liked it the best of all. There was a large old stone farmhouse, three large and very old Norway pines in the front yard, and an orchard walk along which some of the Workers had placed the Stations of the Cross. There were outbuildings in stages of disrepair.

The first function of the Newburgh farm was that of a retreat house, and summer retreats were held there until the farm was sold in 1955. "The beauty of the young people gathered together on a retreat," Dorothy rhapsodized in the summer of 1954. Young people, "sitting under trees reading St. Augustine, St. Bernard, their missals and their Bibles. Newman [Cardinal John Henry] said the first need of a university in Greece was a grove of trees. Here at Maryfarm we wander between hedges of wild cherry making the stations, or . . . under the great and ancient oaks or sit under the maples and the pines watching the traffic, which has all the fascination of movement, a flowing stream." As she wrote she noticed that "one of the girls has a flute which she goes off and plays. . . . There is the beauty of all the seasons on this land, on these farms which have been made beautiful and fruitful by hard work, the hard work of saints and sinners, and all the inbetweens."

There was more of it, noted as she sat under a tree. "It is very hot. There is a hot wind. The birds are vocal, there are clothes, sheets, towels flapping on the line. Occasionally the cawing of a crow. Now John F. [Filliger] is changing the cow to another part of the field and hammering in the stake which holds her. . . . He loves his animals and they are well cared for." John Filliger, the onetime seaman, was a steady worker. He knew what he was doing. By the end of the first summer, Dorothy noted that it had been "a tremendous summer on the farm, . . . producing broccoli, rutabagas, potatoes, corn in such abundance that . . . loads are brought in [to Mott Street] to help feed the breadline and all of us at St. Joseph's House of Hospitality."

The first year was so successful that as the second began, Dorothy seemed to have felt it necessary to make it clear that there would be no reintroduction of a situation that had caused the collapse of the Easton farm. "Where the whole problem comes down to the issue of the family and the farm, and who shall have control of the retreat house and the land, the emphasis [in the instance of families] is more on one's own personal future, than on the work itself. . . . This problem has come up from the time we began and started with the marriages of F. [Frank] O'Donnell and D. [Dorothy] Weston. There has been a long history of these discussions in the time of J. [Jim] Montague's marriage." The same was true of Eddie Priest and Bill Callahan. John Mella's marriage "and short residence at the farm brought the problem out very strongly."

There had, in fact, been a long history of this problem of families and their interests versus the primary objective of the Worker, which was to feed the poor. She mentioned other names that had been a part of the problem and included the "Hennessys." "In all of these cases there were the same problems: "who was to have control, where the authority lay, what money was coming to them, and always the family pointed out that . . . [it] came first, that the family was the unity of society."

No, said Dorothy. The primary concern of the Worker was the poor. "I think most of the families that have been involved realize this after they have gotten out of the work; they have recognized that in taking a wife and bringing forth children their status in the lay apostolate has changed, that their first obligation has to be to take care of their own and not to ask others to support them, no matter how hard they might have to work, but to go out and to earn the cash that ought to enable them to live as a private unit. One of the things we have always pointed out was that because all of us did not have bacon and eggs and grapefruit for breakfast, we were able to feed so many on the bread line." So "people should marry with the understanding that they are going to get a job to support their own families to the greatest extent possible. . . . I do not think they should start building [houses], marry, or settle at Newburgh."

Finally, said Dorothy, "we can never get away from the fact that we are supported by the money of people living in the world, so we cannot be too self-satisfied about having left the world and industry or industrial capitalism. There is many a work we can do, even to the working in factories because of necessity, because we do not have crafts by which we can support ourselves."

To whom was Dorothy speaking? She does not say. But the message was clear: if you marry within the framework of the Catholic Worker, then you had better leave because your primary obligation is to your family.

In the July–August issue of the *Catholic Worker,* the main news was that the retreats were "going on apace." Generally, Dorothy continued to relish those insights into the life of the spirit that retreats gave her. "After I make a retreat," she wrote in the summer of 1948, "I carry around my notes in a little 5-cent notebook I carry in my purse and read them over on the subway, while waiting for a telephone message, at odd moments during the day, and it is wonderful how sweet they are to the heart. They sound like commonplaces but they have a distilled sweetness like a drop of precious ointment."

Moreover, the geometry of the spiritual life enabled Dorothy to put one subject into the focus of her understanding. The subject, sex, continued to undergo, after the war, a major separation from the idea of spirit, treated increasingly as a datum. It was this process that made Dorothy critical of the Kinsey Report when it was published. In her book *On Pilgrimage,* she said she was "certainly not going to read the Kinsey report," and she explained why she was not. She said that at the age of seventeen, when she lived in the psychology professor's home at the University of Illinois, she had found Havelock Ellis's *Sexual Pathology* among his books and had read it. At the time she knew about sex, and talked about it from the time she was six years old, and beyond any rational process of her own, she had accepted the traditional sense of this subject as a force of such volcanic proportions that even to permit it to move into an "objective" framework for discussion was taboo. Reading

Ellis seemed to have reinforced that feeling in her. Here was this volcanic force running wild. "I felt it then in its most hideous form, and there was no beauty in it, no love, but it was like the uncoiling of a dank and ugly serpent in my breast. These may be extreme ways of expressing myself but I am sure that all times there has been this consciousness of evil is us all. Evil as a negation, as an absence of good, as a blackness, a glimpse of hell 'where everlasting horror dwelleth, and no order is.' "

The trouble with the Kinsey report and all of the other efforts to objectify and quantify sex was that it tended to break down those ordering restraints that history, in tradition, had placed around the subject. Its potential for proliferation into the aberrant, into the demonic, had been loosed. The conscience, the censor that transmitted the ordering signals of tradition into a personal consciousness, had been blunted and defaced. "In physical depression, after illness, or after physical excess," conscience had always left its "feelings of guilt." She wondered "why the very testimony of guilt in us all is not a witness against such a book as Kinsey's." The trouble with the book was that "it makes people cease to regard themselves as the least of all, as the guiltiest of all, as the saints say we should, and instead we say, 'I'm as good as he is,' or 'he is as bad as I am, in fact, much worse.' And we compare ourselves with others instead of with God; horizontally, instead of vertically. Christ said, 'Be ye therefore perfect, as your Heavenly Father is.' "

But everything today was measured against what other people were doing, and this "doing" was moving into the racing tide of a downward plunge. In some notes she made during this Newburgh retreat period, she observed that "what was most daring to believe and live by a generation ago is now a commonplace." The pollution of those ordering values respecting sex, so far as most of the young were concerned, was "in the air they breathe." She remembered the days back before World War I when "a friend" [Dorothy herself, no doubt] was told "seriously her health would be endangered if she did not get rid of some of her inhibitions—in other words succumb to the advances of one or another of them. That was the talk of the intellectuals in those days. Now this present day there is M., a former nun of a contemplative order, who after 7 years or so in the convent is out these past 5 years . . . earning a living. She is working right now in a government loft at a power machine mending army and navy clothes. Her companions are . . . the poor from our neighborhood. And they are talking the same way. They discuss their weekend amours with a horrifying frankness. They live for their gluttony and their lust. And they assure her she will have a nervous breakdown if she does not live in the same way. One generation the intellectuals, the next generation the poor, the workers."

So it was that in contemporary times "we look for happiness in sex, for pleasure, for ease, for fulfillment," as she observed in another journal entry, "And we lose it or spoil it in two ways: first by not accepting it all as from God, as a sample of God's love; as a foretaste of a new heaven and a new earth; by seeking such happiness as an end in itself. And second, by frittering away our taste for true happiness. If we eat always between meals, we have no taste for the banquet. If we listen all day to cheap claptrap on the radio, we have no taste for the symphony. Our ears, our taste is dulled." And, certainly, "in these days when all the senses are indulged and catered to, there is a living on the surface, a surface excitement, a titillation, which never goes below to the great depths of passion." Everyone was being affected by it. This debasement of sex had become an aspect of culture. "Music is savage, stirring the blood, movements of the dance are provocative, dress is immodest, pictures are suggestive."

Finally, this objectification of sex was opening its potential for moving into those pits of darkness she had felt after reading Havelock Ellis. "When sex became cheap and on the surface, there was an ever-widening and increasingly frantic pursuit of excitement, of titillation. When sex is so used, it takes on the quality of the demonic. . . . Aldous Huxley has given us a glimpse of this hell in 'After Many a Summer Dies the Swan,' showing the sexual instinct running riot like cancer cells through the body, degenerating into sadism and torture and unspeakable violence." Dorothy said she knew that she was speaking "in extreme terms. But long before I was a Catholic" she had felt this attitude. And now, in her late forties, the retreats were confirming this attitude. There could never be any final satisfaction for the appetite of the senses. "The eye was not satisfied with seeing nor the ear with hearing. All things physical brought with them the sense of saity. As one of the early fathers said, 'The more you have of physical food, the less you want it, the more of spiritual, the more you want it.' Only 'to taste . . . the Lord is sweet.' "

But none could accuse Dorothy of rejecting sex. She could quote Father Hugo at length on why churchmen of past times had resorted so frequently to sexual imagery to describe the ecstasy of union with God. Sex had its ecstatic moment, but it was only a moment—the moment of completion, or union with another, where, finally, rest and peace overcame passion. For a moment, time ended. Sex, in its right order, was a foretaste of heaven. "It is in sex-love that people catch glimpses of harmony and peace unutterable," she wrote. "That is why . . . unfulfilled marriage is a tragedy to be dealt with by physicians and psychiatrists. If the act, which is called by St. Paul 'the marriage debt,' is not paid generously and to the full, people are warped."

But being "warped" most assuredly did not come just from the absence of sex. People were "warped" only when sex was noncreative and put solely to the end of sense indulgence and aside from its God-ended purposefulness. "The prevention of conception when the act which one is performing is for the purpose of fusing the two lives more closely and so enrich them that another life springs forth—the aborting of a life conceived, these sins are great frustrations in the natural and spiritual order."

Of course there was self-denial and "suffering" in preserving the passion and purity of sex. But such suffering was nothing when God was the end. It was "as little noted as the tearing aside of the virginal veil or the budding forth of a new life." Although sex was nothing but a "gross material reality," directed toward God it was something "in which the soul can . . . exult. 'With desire have I desired to eat the Pasch,' Christ said."

Then Dorothy asked how it was that she was so "presumptuous in writing of so high and lofty a thing." It was "because I am not now suffering that I can write, but it is also because I have suffered in the past that I can write. I write to comfort others as I have been comforted." And write she did, not just to those who might read her book *On Pilgrimage,* or her retreat notes. In one instance, at least, in her later life, she wrote of her own experience, her own suffering, to a young woman who was close to the Worker movement. The woman had had an abortion and, seemingly, was close to the edge of despair. Dorothy wrote to the woman of her own experience, trying to comfort her "as I have been comforted."

For most, Dorothy recognized, it was in "this dear flesh" that love was ratified. She was probably quoting someone when she observed in one of her notes that it was "characteristic of the Son of Man to will that cure should come from contact with his flesh. During his life it was the exception when he healed from a distance. 'He, laying his hands on them, healed them.' Not a word about merits. They came to him. That was enough." And in April, 1948, she wrote this meditation on love: "Spring, sap rising, weather raw but something in the air—growth. Fall mild and beautiful, spring restless. Resurrection of the body, remember last end, but thy youth shall be restored as the eagle's. Love, desire for love. We are made for love, at 50 or at 80. Whole and entire. A child's love. Embrace, a man's head on one's breast." She would be the Bride of Christ and sing as the Bride sang in "The Song of Songs": "Let Him kiss me with the kisses of His mouth. Your love is more delightful than wine; delicate is the fragrance of Your perfume, Your name is an oil poured out, and that is why the maidens love You. . . . We shall praise your love above wine; how right it is to love You."

Reaching that nuptial bed was to suffer and to struggle, and during the Newburgh retreats the theme of constancy is frequently emphasized in her notes; "Perseverance is the greatest of all virtues . . . the less we apply ourselves, [the] colder we become, [the] harder for us to receive. Religion is not just thinking—it is love. We shall be pierced. . . . Constant effort necessary. No standing still. Either getting better or worse. Intention easy." In her retreat notes of August, 1952, she observed that "When a man says he has done enough, he has already perished. Movement necessary—forward or backward. No vacation in spiritual life."

Buoyed as she may have been with these reflections, she found the retreats themselves sometimes difficult to bear. Her nerves were sometimes frayed, and when they were, small grotesqueries in the behavior of others lacerated her. "This morning between conferences I wept, partly for joy, partly for the misery of life, partly in self-pity at being so overwhelmed, partly thru fatigue and nerves." Why was she so overwrought? "For instance. During the second conference one of the 'friends of the family' came in, stood in the back, sat down, got up, sat down again. Again at rosary, the chapel was crowded, so he together with half a dozen others, knelt in the convergence room, and he chose a huge overstuffed chair to kneel before, and bending over it, buried his face in the depths of the upholstery. It was a heavy August day. There was sensuality in the gesture, pathology even." On another occasion Dorothy passed a note to the person sitting beside her. "What is the matter with . . . girl sitting next to Arthur Lacey? Is she having a breakdown or something? Has she acted this way before?"

Some retreats bored her to the point of collapse: "Meanwhile I listen as tho fixed to the Cross, aching, stiffening, while Elias travels from Carmel to Sinai, fleeing, while Matthew jumps up from his tax table (the kind Jesus overturned, perhaps) and prepared a banquet, a farewell to his past life, a feast for Jesus, an invitation accepted. And Peter fished, and jumped into the sea from the constraint of the boat, and Zacchaeus climbed the tree!" It was all too much physical activity for her, even though they were "gestures of spiritual impulses."

There were other annoyances, "obstacles in the way." There was one priest's "voice and inflections, dramatics." The best retreat masters had been "Fr. Roy, Fr. Farina, Hugo, Meeman—these men are natural, sincere, earnest, intense. Much easier to listen to." Once during a prayer meditation she began to dwell on what to her at the moment was a major grievance—the way people took her books. "My mind . . . goes to the volume of letters which they [Sacco and Vanzetti] wrote from jail. . . . I had found it being used as a door stop, wedged under a door to hold it open—all battered by wind and rain! And my St. John of the Cross left out under an apple tree, too—rainsoaked! And my Halgren's catechism, stolen. I know by whom because he thought I was aspiring to be poor, must be kept poor. My autographed Maritain, Eric Gill!"

One retreat, in September, 1953, emphasized respect for others, to see the Christ in others, "especially those in authority, as David saw it in Saul even when Saul kept trying to kill him. Even as Uriah did when he must have known the gossip of the Court." These sentiments flowed on for another half page, and then Dorothy abruptly ceased, commenting to herself: "I'm afraid I have not kept this spirit of respect toward Senator McCarthy."

One day at Newburgh her journal contained a curious entry: "All day in a state of unrest, feeling how M. [Lionel Moise] 'had women hypnotized,'" as she recalled someone saying. And that was all she said, or ever would say about Lionel Moise in her journal. What prompted this "state of unrest"? Moise had died two weeks previous, and it is likely she had just heard of it, by some unknown means. In any case her "unrest" seemed to have carried over in a hypercritical, almost catty, mood that fell on Caroline Gordon, who was there at the time for several retreat days. "Caroline ... came during the 7.30 conference and she stopped up to have bread and milk. (My bread is beginning to be very good.) She wears a dress like a bathing suit, short, backless. And she brings a lovely statue of the Virgin and Child. Earlier in the week she brought a friend, non-Catholic, 'a nymphomaniac,' she said blithely, who started at once to flirt with Bud and John. When Father saw her in dungarees [the "nymphomaniac"] he came to tell her she could not go to the chapel that way. She did not want to go at all." Caroline's dress, revealing a high curve of bosom, also provoked critical comment from the priest. Turning to Dorothy, he quoted an old alcoholic priest he had once known: "If they bare their bosoms at the communion rail, I'll take out my handkerchief and cover them."

The day Caroline Gordon left, Dorothy had to go to Mott Street to attend to some business, but she returned that night at 9:30. At Newburgh she found the "mist hanging like veils around the mountains. Cool—black." The house was crowded, "every bed taken, even hot attics. . . . Tables are set for 36 inside." She was immediately presented with a list of problems. The kitchen stove was not working—"holes in pipes—needs cleaning—replacing—need bread pans—rusted and worn out." There was a whole section of screen rusted out on the front porch, a screen missing in one window in the chapel. So there were "many flies." Furthermore, with so many people at the farm the outhouses were inadequate to the traffic, and bathing facilities were too limited.

The next morning, August 20, Dorothy "slept thru Fr. F.'s Mass and Compline" and "felt much better." Father "F." was Reverend John Faley, a craggy-faced, white-haired man who had once been an alcoholic of such proportions that he had been reduced to Bowery life. In his late fifties, and now a teetotaler, he had come to Newburgh, apparently at Dorothy's invitation, to serve as a chaplain. He was no Mass-at-the-dining-room-table kind of priest, performing the rite in a flowered shirt and dungarees. In fact he avoided the dining room table for any use, having his meals brought to him in his room. He was a rigid, severe man to whom retreatants, generally, were not warmly drawn. But Dorothy respected him. When she made ready to leave for Mott Street later in the morning of the day that she slept through his Mass, she went to his room to tell him goodbye. But "he kept me until 12, giving me a conference, and a very good one, on life, death, [and] resurrection." She noted that "he can confess priests now who come here—a great joy to him."

The priests who went to Newburgh or to Mott Street were usually men in some sort of trouble. They were psychotic, or alcoholic, or in some kind of rebellion against Church authority—usually all of these things. They went to the Worker because they probably felt safe and because, as many seemed to have thought, they could reconstruct their lives there. They were a disruptive factor in whatever house they stayed and a drain on Dorothy. "Fr. Cordes, Fr. K., and their drink!" she wrote. "I worry that I do not give them enough attention, and yet each one would absorb you completely—your time and energy, if you would let them. And now Fr. Wenceslas. Persecuted, he thinks. . . . He writes bitter, sarcastic letters to Bob, inviting him to psychoanalyze him."

And they kept coming. "Fr. Walls and niece arrived bearing popcorn, in a Cadillac. I told him due to . . . Fr. Kiely's last outbreak, and our crowded condition, I would no longer try to handle problems such as him which I was not able to cope with—that it would be spiritual presumption. Then Fr. Elias showed up quite the worse for wear after a wet Christmas in town."

Alcohol, which in its kindliest visage could brighten the glow of community and dissipate those shadows that darken the large questions of existence, could also be a raging fire that destroyed community and laid bare the reality of hell. In the Catholic Worker house, alcohol was a rampaging demon, a destroyer, and Dorothy's detestation of it was near absolute.

There was, of course, another form of clerical instability that began to show itself in the Worker movement after the war. It was the priest who wanted out. One, reading about the Newburgh farm, thought it would be just the place for him. Would there be room, he wrote Dorothy, "for another priest in your movement?" Oh yes, to be sure, and of course, he had "given this matter much thought." If she thought his "Franciscanism" was "an obstacle to my acceptance, please say so. This formality can be taken care of." He had, in fact, "been considering secularization. . . . I feel that the formal vow of obedience, in my present circumstances, does not allow me to see Christ in the poor, in the workers, in the sick, in the needy . . ." and so on. Dorothy would hear a lot more of this kind of chirping in the years ahead, but it never sounded to her as anything but discordant. A matter of conscience? She agreed that conscience was first but, as she saw it, when a commitment was made to the good, whatever the vocation, a large part of achieving that good was in fulfilling the commitment, whatever the suffering. Her response to this particular importunity is not known, but she probably advised its author to serve the poor, sick, and needy where he was.

Surrounded as she was with human frailty, she was surely given the "hard contest" that she wanted. But the hard contest was not hers alone. Over the history of the Worker movement there were, and are, others of the same spirit. One, Larry Heaney, died in March, 1949. Heaney and his wife, Ruth Ann, had been for a while on the Easton farm, but Heaney wanted to make his own effort, to be free of that bitter contentiousness that existed among the families at the Easton farm, which, in the long run, seemed to have come from their own inability to provide for themselves. So the Heaneys and the Marty Paul family had started the Holy Family farm at Rhineland, Missouri. The rigors of that life, seemingly, had used all of Heaney's strength, and he died of a lung abscess.

Dorothy went to Heaney's funeral, and after staying several days with the family she started back to New York, stopping off at the Gauchats' farm in Avon, Ohio. She had gone to bed and was asleep when the telephone rang. Maurin had died. It was Sunday, May 15. That morning he had been dressed and helped to the chapel for Mass. In the afternoon he had been taken out of doors and seated in a chair in the sun where he could watch the cars passing along the highway. That night, at eleven, Hans Tunnessen heard Peter coughing in his room, and a sound of distress in that cough made Hans investigate. Peter was dying, so Father Faley was summoned. As he and some others in the house prayed that God would give Peter a safe passage, Maurin passed. He was buried from the Salesian Transfiguration Church on Mott Street in St. John's Cemetery, Queens, in a plot donated by Dominican Father Pierre Conway. The suit that covered him had been gotten from the clothes bin.

Whether passing cars or sitting in the sun brought any ease to Peter's pain those last years of his life, no one could tell because he remained silent. He was incontinent; he had to be fed, dressed, and undressed, but he did not become querulous. Dorothy wrote in the *Catholic Worker* just after his death that "if he had been a babbler, he would have been a babbler to the end." The fact was, she said, that "he had been stripped of all—he had stripped himself throughout life." The one thing he had had was his mind, "the one thing, perhaps, he took delight in. He could no longer think. He could no longer discuss."

Confused and dumb as he was, he went to Mass. "Mass, Peter'" someone would say, and he would struggle to his feet and be led to the chapel. Constancy, the most important of virtues, she probably thought. After Peter's funeral, she went back to the Heaney farm in Missouri to help Ruth Ann. She was there for a month.

❧ 15

Back to Staten Island

THE *Catholic Worker* began the year 1949 with something of a flourish. It was one of those spectacles that pique the interest of observers of the Catholic scene who particularly enjoy a confrontation between the flock and the shepherd. In this instance the flock was Dorothy Day and her friends. The shepherd was Cardinal J. Spellman, archbishop of the Diocese of New York, who, on being named to that position in 1938 following the death of Cardinal Patrick Hayes, had been pledged the "loyalty and devotion" of the *Catholic Worker*.

Sometimes, though, loyalty could be stretched beyond the limits of a tolerant conscience, and this, as Dorothy saw the matter, was the case when the gravediggers of Calvary Cemetery, Local 293 of the International Food, Tobacco and Agricultural Workers Union, went on strike against their employers, the trustees of St. Patrick's Cathedral, principal among whom was Cardinal Spellman. In the course of the strike, which went on for over a month, Cardinal Spellman was quoted as saying that it was communist-inspired, that he was "proud and happy to be a strikebreaker," and that his resistance to the strike was "the most important thing that I have done in my ten years in New York." Whether or not Cardinal Spellman actually said these things is another matter. The fact was that he did refuse to negotiate with the cemetery workers for as long as they were in a union that was a C.I.O. affiliate, and that he eventually broke the strike. In the latter weeks of the affair, some of the cemetery workers began showing up at the Mott Street house, seeking assistance. Hearing their story and considering their plight, Dorothy decided that "the strike was justified," and the Catholic Workers joined the picketers at the cemetery.

This squaring off with the Cardinal was not a situation in which

Dorothy felt heroic or noble. As she saw it, the strike "could have been headed off in the very beginning. The trustees could have shown the books to the workers if justice was on their side, proven in black and white that they were incapable of paying what the strikers asked." Well, she said in the April *Worker,* it was "all yesterday's news now, those strikers who had to drop their life insurance because they couldn't meet payments." The "terrible significance" of the strike was that "here in our at present peaceful New York, a Cardinal, ill-advised, exercised so overwhelming a show of force against a handful of poor working men. It was a temptation of the devil to that most awful of all wars, the war between the clergy and the laity."

Some Catholics, of course, saw Dorothy's action as little short of defying God himself, and wondered when she would be struck down for giving "a public example of disobedience toward him." But Spellman seemed not to have noticed, and years later Julia Porcelli observed that his well-disposed attitude toward the Catholic Worker was "one of the most glorious things" in his history. "I think this will get him in heaven if nothing else will. . . . He allowed us to live. He allowed us to exist. . . . He was always very pleasant even when we criticized him during the cemetery strike." Julia was a generous and good soul, and Italian, reared in the tradition of not questioning church authority. And she was grateful that Cardinal Spellman had let the Worker live. But he could hardly have done otherwise. Dorothy, after all, had not denied the Faith.

The summer passed more tranquilly. Dorothy made several short speaking and visiting tours, and otherwise, for the most part, went from city to farm and back again. One morning she returned to Mott Street from Newburgh and went to her room to catch up on her journal. She was in a heavy mood. It was "one of those hot days. . . . The city seems more than usually oppressive, with its noise and sleeplessness and tensions. The house is full of visitors, and all day long seminarians and priests are dropping in. The children are vociferous in the playground across the street, and the young men roam the streets all night. The hot sun pours down, the pavements burn the feet, the congestion of people is unbelievable."

She was bothered by the preenings of two of the women of the house. One was putting up her hair in curl papers every night. Another had taken to wearing a bow in her hair and making eyes at the men. What had gotten into them? Dorothy knew very well what had gotten into them. But this was not the worst of it. Another woman was "very drunk," and Dorothy had "tried to persuade her to go home—she agreed but wanted to kiss me." The thought made Dorothy shudder. Not only was it a woman who wanted to kiss her but "a horrible lustful woman" who had a "toothless wet mouth." It was most depressing "to see that ugliness of passion."

To have to put up unremittingly with such reminders of fallen human nature was unfair. She said so in the *Worker*. Why should those at Mott Street "bear so large a burden?" Why should they have to "face long lines of hungry, sick, and aged people in the morning and evening? It could well have been distributed through the parishes, the parish halls, the parish properties, the parish societies; and if the old societies are too stodgy to take care of these new needs in a changing world, then new societies . . . should be formed. Why should a priest in Brooklyn call us at ten o'clock at night to ask us to take in a girl who would probably shudder at the sight of Mott Street at that hour? Where are the parish groups for emergencies? The State would be able to organize them in a war, famine, or flood. Why not the parishes?"

In May she went to Berkeley Springs, overcome with a compulsion to see Tamar and the children. She, Dave Mason, and Helen Crow started at 8:15 in the morning from Thirty-Fourth Street and First Avenue, and it was still light when they got to the Hennessys. They had had trouble with a tire: "it was shot . . . so brought two winter retreads for $25.50." She spent $5 for gas and oil and had a good trip "aside from a fearful storm and no windshield wiper. One storm after another thru the mountains and lightning and thunder and the rain in sheets." There was "no window in one side of the car, and it leaked under the windshield on our feet. I just kept going, electric storms make me too nervous." They had their lunch in the car: "liverwurst and whole wheat bread. . . . For desert, bananas."

At Tamar's everything was tranquil. On May 22 Dorothy sat beneath a pear tree writing her journal. "Becky, just five, runs around driving stakes for an imaginary goat, Eric and Susie cracking black walnuts with a hammer. They play with real tools. Dave M. [Mason] is trying to fix rear seat of the car. Sunny and windy. Today bread making, washing, and a visit to the brook.

"Split pea soup for dinner. Some of Tamar's bacon for breakfast. It is so beautiful that I cannot even think, only breathe and bask in the sun. The baby Nicky sleeps and wakes, laughs and sings all day. The children eat well, sleep well, and entertain each other all day." And Tamar looked wonderful—"weighs 135 lbs. I weigh 180—a disgrace—partly my age and also I should not eat fats. Down here we have been having milk, cream, butter, and cheese— truly a luxurious diet."

Two days later she and her friends drove back to Mott Street, again through rain. She felt good about the Hennessys, a feeling that was sustained by a letter from Tamar in June. A bricklayer was going to fix the chimney and build a wall around the spring, and the garden was flourishing. "Good seeds make all the difference," Dorothy noted and then concluded her journal by saying that she would not meddle. "It is far better to let them work things out for themselves."

She went to Berkeley Springs twice more during the summer. She was becoming increasingly attached to her grandchildren, hav- ing said once in the *Worker* that she wanted to love every child as she loved them. Seeing them, however, was not the only reason she was making these trips to Berkeley Springs. With Tamar now in her fourth pregnancy, there was, in the background of Dorothy's feelings, always the dull ache of worry over the Hennessys' desper- ate struggle to survive. She could go on with her writing and her work, but at times something would bring Tamar and her hard life abruptly to mind. Then Dorothy would be seized with a great im- pulse to visit her daughter so as to throw her own strength into the battle.

On September 9 she noted that she had written to Tamar "about staying on" in Virginia. She did not note *what* she wrote— whether or not she wanted the family to remain where they were. In all likelihood, she told them to choose a course by which they could provide for themselves at a level that would afford some graciousness for their lives. She may have suggested that they leave the farm and that David get a job. Whatever she suggested, she must have said it in the blunt, direct manner she used when she thought that the air needed clearing.

When she got a reply, it was from David. Her letter had upset them and he had asked that Tamar not answer it. Anyway, things were going all right. He had interviewed for a job at a bookstore and would know something soon. If he did not get the job, he and the family would move into a tenant house on a neighboring farm.

A month later he wrote to Dorothy to say that she need not visit them. Tamar was well, and the baby showed no signs of coming just then.

The baby came on December 19, and hours later Tamar wrote to her mother: "It's a 9 lb. boy and came so fast Mrs. Slade didn't arrive in time. She has taken ever so much better care of me compared to hospitals. Della sent a box, and I am about to write her a card."

"What I have learned," noted Dorothy as she prepared to comment on matters at Berkeley Springs after receiving Tamar's letter. She had learned that when she was troubled about the family, to "turn away completely from it to God. Sin is turning from God to creatures, and too much absorption in the sins and sorrows of the world" came from "turning from God." Besides, she wanted to live by the example that was set by the saints, and "it was the duty of a saint to be happy."

Thus consoled, she set out on one of her transcontinental tours. She took it in easy stages, presumably relishing the bus riding and the station stops where she could have a cup of coffee and eat a doughnut without having to make conversation with anyone. On December 22 she stopped for the night with the Gauchats in Cleveland. On Friday, the twenty-third, she arrived in Chicago in time for the funeral of one of the Chicago Workers, John Bowers. That afternoon she visited with Jesuit Martin Carrabine, a priest close to the Chicago Worker group, and with some of the people who had come to the funeral, most of whom, in previous years, had been with the Chicago Worker. Jim O'Gara was there, along with Tom Sullivan, John Mella, and Gerry Griffin. That evening she went to the Cogleys for dinner and a bed. The bed was scarcely used. At eleven P.M. she was taken to the home of Milton Mayer of the *Progressive* magazine. There, "among other people I met Saul Alinsky.... We talked about Kropotkin and his ideas of anarchosyndicalism, which are much like the guilds of the Middle Ages." The topic was heavy but safe. One wonders what was in the minds of Mayer and Alinsky, liberal reformers, as they talked to this orthodox Catholic. For them, no doubt, the radical credentials of the Catholic Church, as Dorothy probably emphasized, were beyond anything they could grasp. Whatever they thought they could not but have been impressed with her intelligence, the force and dignity of her person, and the passion for social justice that animated her, as it animated them.

The next morning, Saturday, she took the 10:30 bus for St. Louis and "froze all day." She visited Monsignor Hellriegel's parish in Saint Louis, and that night, Christmas eve, she went to midnight Mass and heard it sung by Monsignor Hellriegel's famous children's choir. At 2:15 A.M. Christmas morning, she sat at the parish kitchen table catching up on her journey notes. The Mass, she said, was "unutterably beautiful."

The next day she stopped over in Tulsa to see Monsignor Hillenbrand, who was dying of cancer. At the hospital she found him "in great pain," so her visit was brief. Next was Amarillo, to accept the overnight hospitality of a Dominican who had a mission on the outskirts of town where there were "the tiny houses of the Negro population with never a tree or bush to break the monotony." At the mission school there, the nuns taught 150 children. Dorothy stopped over because "Father offers hospitality to any Catholic Worker wayfarers who may happen by." She got to Phoenix on Friday night, December 30, and was met at the station by Ammon Hennacy.

So far as Dorothy was concerned, Hennacy was little more than an acquaintance. She had first met him in 1938, when he was among some people that heard her speak at Marquette University. After that he saw Dorothy when she visited Milwaukee, and from time to time he wrote to her. The subject of his letters was Hennacy: Hennacy, single-handedly, almost, standing at the front line against the forces that oppressed humankind. This was a childish boasting, in a way, but he never "grew up," as some would observe. The remarkable thing about him was the extent to which he would, time after time and throughout the course of his life, forego ease and comfort in order to press his crusade against the accretion of woe that, in his view, had been heaped on the world by selfishness. When others turned away, Hennacy was there to fast, march, and picket for as long as his flesh would sustain him. And his flesh seemed invincible. No, he never "grew up," because he carried the exuberance and freshness of youth with him into old age. The romance of doing heroic battle against the forces of darkness never left him.

It would, according to conventional lore, be appropriate to depict him as having been born of Irish immigrant parents in a city slum, where the family all but succumbed to poverty. His name was Irish, but his antecedents had lived in America for enough generations to obliterate marks of the old country heritage. The Hennacys owned a farm near Negley, Ohio, and were Baptists. Ammon was born there on July 24, 1893, and enjoyed a happy and wholesome youth. He was bright and energetic, and he was very sentimental. The only war of which he seemed ever to have approved was the Civil War. It was a disposition that scarcely could have been else. At the top of a hill behind his house was a pine tree, planted the day that Lincoln was shot. A picture of John Brown hung in the parlor, and when he was five a young girl of the neighborhood taught him to play a one-finger piano rendition of a Civil War song. It was about camp fires, shot and shell, and a dream of "my own Bluebell." When Hennacy played the piece, he wept because he had not been in the war.

A sharp-witted extrovert, his quick tongue usually dominated any confrontational situation and so he became a salesman. In 1913 he went to Cleveland to sell, door-to-door, a new product called "cornflakes." He was so persuasive, or the cornflakes such a hot item, that he made $8 his first day out. But making sales was not all he wanted. He read a lot, and Jack London and Upton Sinclair most impressed him. Marshaling his resources, he entered Hiram College that fall. The next summer, while selling cornflakes in Portage, Wisconsin, a willowy young woman named Zona Gale, author of *Miss Lulu Bett,* answered Hennacy's knock. Hennacy sold his cornflakes, but she sold him on the idea of transferring to the University of Wisconsin for his sophomore year. His interests included another willowy young woman, the daughter of a socialist state senator, but she was unmoved by Hennacy's romantic salesmanship. Otherwise, he enlarged his awareness of the radical ideas fermenting in the world. He spent his third year in college at Ohio State. After that, straitened circumstances at home required that he give up college.

When the United States entered the war, Hennacy not only refused conscription, but began a covert campaign of resistance to it. Arrested, he was sentenced, on July 3, 1917, to two years in the federal penitentiary in Atlanta. After serving a year, he was discovered by prison officials to have been subverting prison discipline by calling on his fellow prisoners to boycott what he called the "rotten" fish that was served on Friday evening. Or so Hennacy told it. Anyway, he was put in solitary confinement, a condition that he endured for seven-and-a-half months. During this period he read the Bible and pondered his plight. In solitary, he was converted. He was converted from a belief in force as the means of overthrowing the "system," to a belief in personalist action as the way to redeem the world. "Hate piled on hate" only brought more "hate and revenge." He would turn to the nonviolence of Jesus and try to return good for evil. His conversion meant little else to him in terms of a system of belief or worship. It was a change in tactic, almost, although he had never been a violent man. He was released from prison on March 20, 1919. On the following Christmas Eve, he and Selma Nelms, the daughter of the socialist sheriff of Milwaukee, agreed to "live together for as long as we loved each other —for the Revolution." For five years Ammon and Selma roamed: a job here, a job there, one of which was selling Fuller brushes. Tiring of their vagabondage, they finally settled in Waukesha, Wisconsin. Hennacy got a job with a dairy and began building a house. It was, when finished, a cozy nest, and Selma, in the time that they were there, bore two daughters. But Hennacy, the eternal activist, imprudently organized a strike of dairy workers in 1931 in the midst of the Depression and was fired.

Having to give up their home, they moved into Milwaukee, some twenty miles east, and Ammon became a social worker. In 1937 he began associating with the Milwaukee Catholic Workers and this, of course, led to his meeting Dorothy. And that was all there was to it. But Ammon was impressed with Dorothy to a degree that he began writing her letters, telling her of his view of things. Here was a person, he sensed, whose radicalism was more ordered and more deeply rooted than his own. Dorothy's control and strength was a stirring force with him.

Then came World War II. Selma, wanting some kind of an ordered life and an opportunity for her musically talented daughters, left Milwaukee with the two girls and left Ammon. Of what account was the Revolution now, Selma may have thought, when that ideal was simply a catch-all for a particular type of personal vanity that was exercised at the expense of the two lives that had been given into Ammon's and her care? No wonder she wearied of the effort and in her hurt turned to a religion that separated Ammon from her bed, or so Ammon charged. Later, Ammon would tell Dorothy that Selma was the one woman he truly loved, but then he said that there had been no time in his life but what he was, or thought he was, in love with some woman.

Now, on December 19, 1949, Dorothy stopped to visit this man. She stayed in Phoenix two days, journeying about, with Ammon in tow, to see people that she knew, that she wanted to talk with and to encourage. She left on Sunday night, January 1, and, just as Ammon had been at the bus station to greet her he was there to see

her off. When she left, he felt that a fresh inspiration had come
into his life. No doubt Dorothy encouraged him in his writing and
no doubt, too, she encouraged him to think of coming to Mott
Street to amplify his "One-Man Revolution" and to write his memoirs. Yes, that would be his life, Ammon thought. He "did not have
to have physical contact with any woman: I had work to do." So
there would be no more repining for Selma and the felicities of the
married state. It would be off to New York for a new life.

Dorothy's thoughts on leaving Phoenix soon turned to another
matter. "At 2 A.M.," she wrote in her journal, "the bus broke down
20 miles out of Yuma in the desert just over the Mexican border. It
was cold, the bus was crowded with sailors trying to get back on
duty." She was moved to note that "Sailors in peacetime are something else from sailors in wartime, I must say." She did not enlarge
on this "difference," saying only that they stayed on the bus "till
light, and then an unsavory character at a desert shack with an
ancient auburn-haired wife made us coffee which was wonderful."
A little while later a relief bus from San Diego, 200 miles away,
picked them up and took them back to that city.

Where Dorothy was concerned, the situation at San Diego was
not auspicious. She asked that she might see the bishop there, Bud-
dy, but he refused to see her. Not only that but he would not allow
the nuns at Our Lady of Peace to hear her speak. "Probably our
pacifism," Dorothy thought. But all was not lost. "Dear Monsignor
Forrestal gave me a check for $75, just what the sisters would have
given to make up for it, and we had a good visit." Monsignor
Forrestal also gave Dorothy a book on spiritual life—"a great
present."

"Tomorrow I must see Archbishop McIntyre," she wrote on
January 9. This was the Father Francis McIntyre who, at the time
she was becoming a Catholic, had tried to help her straighten out
her marital problems and with whom she later carried on a running correspondence as to what to do about the vagrant priests
who were showing up at the Worker. He was "most touchingly
cordial," Dorothy wrote. "People love him here. They say he is
humble and holy, and that is the way I have always felt about him."
Still, Dorothy did not "understand the archbishop and his friendliness to me" when, at the same time, he "expressed hostility toward
those who are working for justice. He acts as tho he thought I were
holding people down instead of trying to stir them up." The bishop's hostility, Dorothy knew, had been directed toward a young
Catholic, Dan Marshall, who had been instrumental in challenging

California's law banning interracial marriage. The bishop, according to Dorothy, had "reprimanded" Marshall, "doing it as a citizen" and not as a churchman. "As though he could," Dorothy noted.

Bishop MacIntyre wanted to know how things were going back in New York, especially with respect to the fortunes of Father Clarence Duffy. They had not been going well, as Dorothy had written in the December, 1949, *Worker*. Father Duffy had fallen out of favor with the New York hierarchy. Yes, he was headstrong and cantankerous, Dorothy said, but he was a priest "who was speaking of very real problems," of "war and peace, of unemployment and housing, of race prejudice, and of the need of all men to work together." So Father Duffy was suffering because of those who governed the Church. Then Dorothy cited the German priest Romano Guardini as saying "that the Church was the Cross and one could not separate Christ from his Cross. He said, too, that we must learn to live in a state of permanent dissatisfaction and impatience with the Church. We have to suffer and hang our heads at all the accusations made against us." Then Dorothy added her own emphasis to Guardini's reflection. "We are all guilty, we all make up the Body of Christ. And we must suffer with bitterness, the Little Flower said, if need be, and without courage, and that is what makes the suffering especially keen." Like Father Duffy, she said, we all must suffer. Still, where she was concerned, "we recognize and accept the authority of the Church as we do that of Christ himself." Not to accept that authority was to cast oneself adrift, to be sooner or later impaled on some snag or shattered in the wrenching and tossing of the flow.

She returned to New York to face a pressing matter. Sometime during the preceding fall, she, Father Faley, John Filliger, and some of the others had begun to talk of selling the Newburgh farm. There were reasons: it was too far from the city; it was too noisy because of the highway in front and a nearby military airport where jets continually took off and landed. But more than this, life at Maryfarm had settled into a kind of stagnation and had begun to curdle. There was much quarreling and drinking. There had been a fight. And when things got to that point—as they usually did on a Worker farm—Dorothy could think of nothing except to move and begin again. The matter now pressing was that she had found an old farm on Staten Island and she had to make up her mind whether or not she should try to buy it and if she did how she would pay for it.

The death-rattle at Maryfarm was one part of it. The other part was that the Staten Island place was just ten blocks from the beach, and from the location of her old cottage—all places familiar and dear to her.

Although she badly wanted the farm, she had no money to make a down payment. So she got a $1000 advance from Harper Brothers on a book she was writing and, on the strength of a hope that the Newburgh farm shortly could be sold, she paid the thousand to the owner of the farm. On March 20, she noted that there was "no sale yet, and we hope St. Joseph will send us a message today." She was at Newburgh, probably thinking that by her presence she might expedite a sale that was pending. It was a mild spring day, "sun, birds, no wind," although there was "still snow and ice on the north slopes here." This kind of day ordinarily would put her in a lyrical mood, but not today. The continual planning, scheming, and politicking in which she was involved in order to get the Staten Island place depressed her. She thought of "Mauriac's women in the *Desert of Love* and *The Enemy*." They were "terrifying." They bespoke the "evil force in us."

Three days later, her mood was sunnier. "Dear God, I thank Thee," she noted. "The farm is sold—to Charlie who runs the fruitstand across the road." The next morning, "a beautiful and cold day," she took the 10 A.M. bus to the city. When she got to Mott Street, an old friend was there to greet her. It was Mike Gold and his wife, having "just gotten in from France and Italy." It had been fifteen years since she had last seen him and now he had two sons; the oldest, ten years old, was named Nickolai, "after Lenin."

Seeing Mike could very well have evoked a mood of reminiscing when she wrote her journal that evening, but if such existed she did not mention it. Her journal was to record spiritual reflections and the events of the day. That day at Mass there had been a man "so foul in smell that the congregation had to stay on one side of the church." Then that afternoon two men from St. Francis Church had visited "and they were the kind like California George, talking constantly of miracles, confraternities, dangling with crucifixes, difficult but their minds set on the honor and glory of God." Well, she thought, "if I ever go off on the head, I hope to go in that way, haunting churches, saying beads, etc. A happy way to be."

She had gone to the city to see if, on the strength of the note she would get from the purchaser of the Newburgh farm, she could borrow the money to pay for the Staten Island place. The man at the bank was dubious. What income did Dorothy have? What was the legal personhood of the Catholic Worker? To explain that St. Joseph would take care of the financial exigencies was not an acceptable way of dealing with banks.

She was back where she had started. Then, a week later, another crisis developed. One of the men at Mott Street, who was going through the morning mail, came running to her room to tell her that the owners of the Mott Street house were going to sell it and that they would have to be out by July 1. So in the May *Worker* Dorothy announced that she and her friends were going to have to find another place and that this would require her raising $25,000. She was putting the readers of the *Worker* on notice that they could contribute.

Raising such an amount over a period of two months without a professional fund-raiser, without a campaign featuring pledge cards, advertising, and a corps of workers being subjected to a daily motivation session, seemed a remote goal. But Dorothy needed no apparatus to raise money. There were many people, some of means and some who lived close to poverty, who felt so certain of the truth of Dorothy and her work that they felt it a privilege to give her what they could. And Dorothy had a rare and extraordinary talent for making people feel her gratitude for their help. On June 3, she noted in her journal: "We have $25,000." She further noted that, unfortunately, she needed $10,000 more with which to pay the bills so "I must take to reading Mother Cabrini again to get in the mood for asking. Our Father's business in N.Y. seems to demand a fortune."

It certainly seemed so. And the inevitable consequence of this "business" was that Dorothy and the Workers were becoming landowners. The question was, where would it end? In this instance it ended with the purchase of a large house at 221 Chrystie Street, which even had marks of gentility, with its iron grilling over the porch and an iron fence enclosing a large front yard. It even had bathrooms and hot water.

The Workers stayed on at Mott Street until August, and to Dorothy her last days seemed interminable. The place seemed to have lost its life and it oppressed her. She saw it as "vermin-ridden, cold, damp and drafty in winter and dirty and noisy all summer, with cries of children, gossiping women, quarreling neighbors, jukeboxes, blocked traffic, grinding garbage trucks, [and] factory machinery." When she climbed the steps to her fifth-floor room, she was glad that it was for the last time. After all, she had already passed the half-century mark in the years of her life and her breath did not come as easily as it used to.

There was, of course, the other business of the Staten Island farm. In March, when it appeared that she would not be able to get it, she appeared to accept the situation. Her friend, Eileen Egan, had suggested "that where [Newburgh farm] a saint [Peter Maurin] had lived and died" should be considered a sacred place. It was even good, Dorothy told herself, that her "will" had been frustrated.

Maybe so, but she still wanted to move to Staten Island, and she was not resigned to losing the $1000 she had put down on it. The crisis came one morning while she was at Mass, she told *Worker* readers. "Like the importunate widow, I asked for a sign from the Lord. . . . I kept saying to myself, 'if I don't hear something by eleven o'clock this morning, I am going to drop the whole idea.' It was a promise to the Lord." Sure enough, before the clock struck eleven (if she had a clock) "a friend had called and offered to loan me several thousand dollars." The friend was Madeline Krider, and although Dorothy had already received $1000 from her for the house, she was able to get $2000 more for the farm. Later, the loan was made into a gift. "I had my sign."

On April 5, Dorothy noted that "Jane said the mortgage had gone thru, and the bank called to tell her." This development had been made possible by creating a trusteeship to hold the properties of the Catholic Worker. This arrangement not only made the loan possible, it enabled Dorothy, through the rest of her life, to absolve herself personally of any property-holding that would require her to pay federal taxes. The closing occurred sometime in July, and on the last day of August Dorothy moved to the new Peter Maurin Farm. In the September *Worker* she told how the summer's property acquisitions had come about. "I have often said that Peter Maurin had so compelling a way with him, had so great a moral force, that if he had asked me to get up in the middle of Madison Square Garden to speak, I would have obeyed. . . . I feel that my behavior this past month, this compulsion that was on me to go on with the purchase of the Staten Island farm regardless of the fact that we had just finished purchasing a $30,000 headquarters on Chrystie Street, was due to Peter."

So Peter was to blame! Still agitating, it seems, but having, in his immortal life, broadened his concerns to include real estate. Perhaps some readers of the *Worker* wondered a bit, but then decided that Dorothy had given the facts as she saw them. And no doubt she had.

The Staten Island acquisition brought a felicity into her life that she had once had and had surely missed. It was the Staten Island ferry ride. One day during the summer as she was riding over to the Island she wrote of her feelings and thoughts in a notebook. "The trip is so beautiful. The sky and water is so lovely, in all its moods that I often find myself just thinking, and thinking 'to the point' on what has been going on down below the surface of my mind." Just then she was looking at the Statue of Liberty and she thought of John Cogley "and his taking his children to see the Statue of Liberty and his profound concern with affairs of the community, city, state and federal gov. And I went on to think how little we have down at the CW to clarify our *Positions,* especially man's duty to the City." Perhaps she was thinking of all the services that not only the Worker but also she had received from the city. And what had she and her friends done for the city in return? They had taken care of the poor, but had that been enough? She was, it seems, thinking of the question of taxation, something that had been introduced by the Worker's new status as property holders. This was a matter about which she rarely talked, possibly because there were no clear-cut lines she could draw. She generally was able to manage her personal affairs and those of the Worker so that she paid no taxes. With the federal government's involvement in military matters, she felt a moral obligation to pay no taxes. Where the city was concerned, the case was different.

She had, of course, other concerns during 1950. Her mother's sister, "Aunt Jennie," had a stroke on April 22, and Dorothy spent a lot of time at the hospital with her, feeling, one surmises, that she was reaffirming those family "roots" that for some years she appeared to have disdained. Her Aunt Alice also spent a lot of time at the hospital, and she told Dorothy stories about her mother's family, and her grandfather, Napoleon Bonaparte Satterlee, who had gone to the Civil War at the age of eighteen and had died in 1879 of the wound he had gotten in the war. But Aunt Jennie recovered and lived some years more.

In April, Bill Duffy died at Mott Street. Red Miller had found him dead on the floor one morning. "We called the priest, and the police. He lay there on the floor completely stiff and rigid—one arm half up as tho frozen in one position just as he started to move. His face was like wax and his blood had come from his nose and dried on his upper lip and chin." Bill, with the Worker for some years, had been in charge of the hot water heater in the basement "which was jocularly called Duffy's tavern." Nightly, he and his friends would gather there and drink until the discordancies of the world were muted and all that they could hear was one harmonic chord. Dorothy noted the response to Bill's death. "Fred, the German cook, with a thoughtful decency swept out the yard. . . . Everyone came in as usual and in the awed hush . . . sneaked in and relished much the extra meal they had filched before the breadline started at one-thirty."

One June afternoon Dorothy had a visitor whom she had known in a bygone time. It was Christine Ell, the Village restaurateur of three decades past, who, like Dorothy during the winter of 1918, had been one of Jimmy Wallace's patrons in the dim back room of his Golden Swan saloon. Christine, with lithe body and long, muscular legs, had been the "available woman"—available to listen to the woeful recitations of would-be poets and artists and available, too, on occasion for that particular consolation that she could provide for men. Now she was approaching old age. Why she had come, Dorothy did not say, but perhaps the business was so trivial and perhaps so pathetic that Dorothy did not want to mention it for fear of dishonoring the past. It is not inconceivable that Christine came for help with a particular problem: getting Social Security, getting something—desperately seeking something secure and final before she died.

Several days later Dorothy had another visitor, Sister Peter Claver. She had just returned from a pilgrimage to Rome. "She told me of the Pope's Mass, Lourdes, where she left part of her heart. It was she who first gave me the retreat notes of Fr. Lacouture, introduced me to Father Roy, and he in turn to Fr. Hugo." All of which reminded her that she should begin writing her book on the retreat. What should she call it? She could only think of three subtitles: "Childhood. Life of Nature. The Unwilling Celibate."

Dorothy noted one exciting Friday night meeting at the Mott Street house. Carol Jackson, one of the editors of *Integrity*, spoke. It was on "the problem . . . of science, psychology, and the whole field of human knowledge and man's capacity to extend his field, bring order out of chaos." By an exclusive concentration in these areas, said Miss Jackson, scholarship was not bringing order into society but "chaos." The meeting was "tumultous," Dorothy said. She added that Fritz Eichenberg and John Cogley were there, but whether or not they contributed to the tumult she did not say.

On Saturday night, June 17, Dorothy noted that she and Tony Aratari had gone to Helen Iswolsky's apartment to meet the well-known French Jesuit intellectual, Jean Danielou. She found him "very vigorous, alive. . . . His book *Salvation of the Nations* only one translated. Speaks English well but with some difficulty." Other distinguished clerics were there, "Fr. Lynch, editor of *Thought* . . . Fr. Oesterreicher." Father Oesterreicher "seemed hostile—he said he needed to exorcise us for our bad thoughts. He is infuriated by our pacifism. Fr. D. [Danielou] said he recognized need of nonviolent resistance, but also of violent." All right, thought Dorothy, "she could be violent by destroying armaments, machines to make them."

One night in July someone suggested that they make a long walk as a kind of pilgrimage. So at 11:15 they started out for the Our Lady of Mount Carmel Church on 115 Street and First Avenue. They got there at 1:30 A.M. and had to wait nearly three hours for Mass. The walk exhausted Dorothy, and when she got home at 6 A.M. she went to bed and slept for eight hours. A walk of nearly five miles was getting to be too much for her. She complained several times that summer of having difficulty breathing.

She had other symptoms that summer. At Thanksgiving she mentioned having had "miserable rheumatic pains" and "hot flashes" all summer long. She assumed, she said, that she was beginning her "change in life," although as she later noted her menstrual cycles continued until she was fifty-four years old. In mid-September she noted that "Last Sunday Tessa took me to her doctor and he said I had a tumor." This pronouncement seemed not to have disturbed her at all because for two weeks she traveled about giving talks, even going to Ithaca to speak to the Cornell Newman Club. Nonetheless, she had been having tests in a city clinic and on September 29 she observed that "I go to the clinic again Wed. to get a final verdict as to operation." Days later she wrote that "I got news on feast of St. Francis no operation needed."

When she heard that she needed no operation, she took a long walk. It was a cold, gray day on the Island. She went over to the beach where her cottage had been. The water was rough and surged far up the shore. She went to Great Kills to see an old barge at the foot of Wyman Street and then she went to South Beach.

She did not say so, but the walk could well have been an occasion of a communion with the past. Passing Woodrow Road, where Peggy and Malcolm had once lived, brought Peggy to mind. How her life had changed—how much time had swept away! Peggy and Malcolm had been divorced and then, on July 31, 1931, Peggy had gone to Mexico, where she had fallen in with an old acquaintance of hers and Dorothy's, the poet Hart Crane. Crane was homosexual; nonetheless, he had found Peggy an interesting, even exciting, companion. They became inseparable and Peggy, completely understanding and most helpful, had introduced him to the delights of heterosexual love. Then tragedy: returning home on a ship Crane had one night either fallen or jumped overboard. Then Peggy married a "Doc" Feyling and had lived in Washington, but Feyling died—from drink, someone said. She had married again, this last time to Howard Conklin. They had been living in Atlanta.

And what of Freda and Sasha? Both were old and ill and no longer lived on the Island. Several times in her journal in the late 1940s Dorothy had mentioned Sasha's being ill. Once she had visited him on the Island and had sat with him on the beach one evening. They had talked of those years back in the twenties when they had been neighbors.

These were the quiet days of fall, when the trees glowed with rich colors. "Sunny and bright and very hot with that beautiful autumn stillness," Dorothy wrote. "Crickets, an occasional rooster, a car going by now and then, these disturb the stillness only to make me appreciate it more." When she got up at seven in the morning, the sun streamed on the trees outside her window. She said her prayers facing it.

What had been her problem? She did not say, but having had a long history, since 1920, of gynecological problems one supposes that these in turn brought on the prolapsed rectum for which she would later have surgery. For the moment, though, she was all right.

One day in early October, Father John Schutz said the first Mass at Peter Maurin Farm. Hans Tunnesen had built the altar, and "Michael" had varnished it. "The altar stone was one from the Philadelphia house, on which ... Fr. Pacifique Roy had offered Mass." The Maryknollers furnished the chalice, and a Monsignor Corrigan gave them a tabernacle. The prie dieu was from the Marists, and Ade Bethune made the vestments. (Dorothy, who liked occasionally to flash a French title, referred to Ade in this instance as "Mde. de Bethune.")

It was after this Mass, or one several days later, that Dorothy, in her meditation after Mass, thought about "Peter's silence with others." Was this not, absolutely, the way that she should treat the criticism she so frequently got from members of the house—that she was imperious, that she was harsh? She knew she was, and while this criticism hurt she would nonetheless try to remain silent. Then she thought of Peter and "that difficult issue of the common good," especially as it applied to the family. "For instance, a family who wishes to put away an epileptic child for the common good of the family. Or put an old person in a home because others will have more peace and quiet." And she remembered Peter's response: "It was the high priest who said, better one should die— shall we put Jesus to death?"

One day a priest brought twelve boys over from Jersey City to spend the day. They were black, and Dorothy was disturbed at their lack of response to the day's activities. "What faith required to work with them. Also they need more attention."

On the Saturday after Thanksgiving she went to the opera, *The Flying Dutchman.* She met Forster there and commented that he "did not mention his health once." She added that she "had been writing about him in my book" *[The Long Loneliness].* Several nights later she went to *La Traviata* on the invitation of a woman friend. Dorothy's comment was that *La Traviata* reminded her of *Tann-hauser*—"hell is too much pleasure." Her friend, hearing of Dorothy's ailments, expatiated on "the virtues of molasses, sunflower seed, and vinegar." Days later, Dorothy heard Mendelsohn's violin concerto on WQXR and this swept her away. "It lifts the heart!" she exclaimed.

On December 4 she went to Pittsburgh for a brief retreat. "It rained on the way down the glare of lights on the black pavements was hard on the eyes." But it was "like getting home" to get to the retreat house at Oakmont, the first time she had been there since 1944. She noted that she went to confession to Father Farina "and felt much consoled with his help." After her days at Oakmont she went to Loveland, to the Grail, the center for training women for the lay apostolate. The Grail farm was "so beautiful, . . . the fields and hills all white, the . . . river rushing on thru the valley below and the cars on the bridge above. Sheep, goats, rabbits, chickens—

a warm cozy farm.... Pumps for water, outside toilets, wood stoves, bare, scrubbed and beautiful." It was all beautiful—"a beautiful sung Mass" and the evening vespers. Dorothy spent one day in bed, "resting and reading Scheeben, *Glories of Grace*." It was "tremendous," another "lifting of the heart."

On Christmas Eve she was at the Hennessys. "Tamar and I trimmed the tree and set out the toys. The children went to bed at six, like angels."

⚜ 16
The Circle Begins to Close

IN MARCH, 1950, Dorothy noted that she had been to a morning Mass with Ammon Hennacy. The next month there was another note: "Put Ammon on bus 12:30 last night." There were other such journal entries of Ammon's comings and goings, but it was not until 1952 that he came to stay. He had finally decided to "major" in "feeding bums," as he put it. "Feeding bums," though, was never truly his style. There was something self-effacing about it. Hennacy was not self-effacing. He was a front-line fighter, always ready to go "over the top" when the bugle sounded, or when he thought he heard it sound. What his cause was, he never defined in a logical way. Whatever it was, it had to be against authority—usually the state, but also the Church. He liked to call himself an anarchist, and that, finally, was what he was. Anything else got in Hennacy's way. He stayed with the Worker for eight years, a colorful figure who wrote colorful pieces in the *Worker* of his joustings with evil—his fasts, his picketing, his leafleting, and his confrontations with tax collectors, wherein Hennacy always had the last word. Hennacy was colorful, slim, and vigorous with flashing eyes, an almost hatchet face, and wiry, steel-gray hair that he wore long until he came to Chrystie Street. When he came to live there, Dorothy decreed that he have it cut. No man was Hennacy's master, but a woman was, and it was Dorothy. He probably came to the Worker because he had fallen in love with her.

Why he loved her as he did—that is, a valentine, red-rose love —is a question beyond answering, but he did. The flame burned for six years and was witnessed to by valentines and red roses (one each day) and letters to Dorothy when he was off picketing and fasting. Writing to Dorothy on August 1, 1951, he said that he wished that he had known Dorothy in the twenties but, even so, "each of us had to learn a lot the hard way and I think we could easily have 20 years more now of good spade work to do together. We each have no illusions about sex so we can put our minds to our work. (I am not getting theoretical either, for right now I would like to embrace you and kiss you)."

Ammon's passion appears to have reached an almost overflow point throughout 1953 when off on one picketing venture or another he wrote to Dorothy sometimes twice a day. His letter of January 13 contained a quotation from Father Divine, the well-known black cult figure of the 1930s and 1940s: "'Love, it is wonderful!'" Then he fell into the mood of love's dire prophecy. "As we agreed that evening . . . we are close to each other no matter the arrangement of time, space, or death—and the time may come when one of us or both are locked up for years and can never get a word to the other." When that came to pass, they would have to live on memories. Hennacy concluded with a schoolboy's confession: "When I'm away from you, I get very brave about all the things I want to say to you—then when I see you I get bashful . . . and all of my thoughts about you are holy ones."

To be sure, his thoughts when he was around Dorothy of necessity were "holy," but that was not the ideal situation from his point of view. Still, he accepted it. "There has been nothing of sex in my love for you. I have been trying, as you said, to make my love for you make me love others more, and I am, at least in my thoughts, not a meanie toward anyone." In a letter of December 8, his feelings overflowed. Ethereal love was enough. It was enough that they could be "One in Spirit where time and space are nonexistent. . . . I thank God for you daily. I love you! I love you!"

It was all quite sophomoric, and Hennacy's "loving from afar" attitude toward Dorothy seems, by today's indulgent standards, altogether quaint. Even so, however juvenile and archaic Hennacy's words, imagery, and the sentiment itself, that Dorothy could evoke such a feeling in him says something of his innocence and idealism at this time in his life. It is a pity that it could not have been sustained for the rest of his days.

And what of Dorothy? Her feelings at the onset of Hennacy's burgeoning love are expressed in a prayer-meditation she wrote during a fifteen-minute conference break on a retreat at the Newburgh farm on August 18, 1952. Her lines were addressed to "Dear God," and she went on to say that she wanted "to be very direct, and say to you, I believe you are a personal God and hear me when I speak, even my trivial petty speech. I will tell you personally over and over I love you, I adore you, I worship you. Make me mean it in my life. Make me show it by my choices." What she wanted, directly and precisely, was "for Ammon": "that you give him light to come with humility to the baptism font, to be confirmed a perfect Christian. How much he would learn to bring strength and comfort to others, to turn from the world and turn to you." She was "very hopeless and pessimistic about asking this, so forgive this too, in me, my unbelief, my lack of faith." And she knew that God could understand her feeling. "I am so surrounded by the poor in interior and exterior goods, they are so gaunt, I can see their faults clearly. So I don't expect too much from them." She wanted someone in the movement who would have great strength, and at the moment she wanted "with a great longing that Ammon become a Catholic, and I ask this now, here on the eve of the feast of your mother's immaculate heart, so soften his heart and convert him now."

Still, "not as I will but as You will, be it done. I am quite content, tho it makes me feel low at times, to see so many failures in our work. A humiliation too, for all of us, to see one outside the Sacraments, without their help, doing the things we should be doing." Yet whatever happened, she would "continue to love Ammon and have faith in him, and look up to him, and count on him, whether or not he ever becomes a Catholic. And I won't say anything to him about it because I want you to do all the work."

This prayer tells how Dorothy felt toward Ammon and what she would have of him. She would "love" him as Christ had enjoined his followers to "love one another." But how good it would be to have another Joan of Arc for the faith, this time Ammon, who would do the heroic and glittering things that would lift her work out of the slough of continuing failure and "humiliation too" that was always besetting it. On November 17, 1952, her prayer was answered. Father Marion Casey, who had given the August retreat at the Newburgh farm, baptized Ammon at Hutchinson, Minnesota. Dorothy was his godmother and Robert Ludlow, his godfather. Ammon began to wear a Joan of Arc medal.

Some time later, Dorothy wrote another of her reflections on love, and this one seems to have been in the way of a particular reference to Hennacy's love for her. It was, finally, the love of God he felt, for "Enough men have been in love with me, even as an older woman, for me to know the purity of that love." It was "the purity of that love . . . and the truth and beauty I write about in the Christian life that they love, not an aging body. I mention this to show again the hunger in men's hearts for love and for truth." But there was always the danger, "the slant given by the scar of original sin, so that one needs to be guarded in loving. . . . In any physical expression of that love, this body of ours at whatever age is treacherous."

During his years at the Chrystie Street house, Hennacy was the *Catholic Worker's* most colorful and energetic salesman. He liked to go sell the paper across the street from St. Patrick's and sometimes, in his column, he would tell merry tales of his confrontation with the policeman in the area and of some of the people who came out of the church and said he was a communist. The paper, after World War II, was increasingly concerned over the issue of nuclear armaments, and its pacifism became its most vocal position. To this Hennacy added his own accounts of his fastings and picketings. Each year, on the anniversary of the dropping of the bomb on Hiroshima, Hennacy and some of the younger Workers, principally Bob Steed, would fast and picket the Federal Building for as many days as years had elapsed since the bomb had been dropped. He referred to himself in the *Worker* as a "Christian Anarchist" and made much of his refusal to pay taxes. He would even write to the Internal Revenue Office when he thought a new tax man was on his case to state explicitly his position so that no one would have any doubts about it. He did all this with such flair, if not bombast, that people were irritated. Even Father Hugo, whose "The Immorality of Conscription" had been twice published in the *Worker*, was upset. On November 17, 1955, he wrote to say that he was "concerned by the direction the paper has been taking . . . since Ammon became a definite member of your staff." He was at first "puzzled, then disturbed" by discussions of "Catholic anarchism." Father Hugo said that he was sorry to have to write as he did, but "in departing from the truth, you depart also from genuine love."

For her part, Dorothy would have nothing to do with the anarchist label, saying once that she would leave that for Ammon. If she had to be designated as something beyond Christian and Catholic, she would prefer "personalist" or "distributist." Because Ammon had been writing for the paper through the 1940s, it may

have been that as the 1950s began some people, in good conscience, had been led to think of the *Catholic Worker* as reflecting an
"anarchist" point of view. And the words "Catholic" and "anarchist" were incompatible.

Whatever the case, on March 3, 1951, Dorothy was asked if she
could drop by the New York Chancery office; there Monsignor
Edward Gaffney "told me we would have to cease publication or
change our name." This was the ultimate blow on top of some
others she had gotten that day. The owner of the Staten Island
farm called "and wants payment. . . . (Mae Bellucci paid it)." Four
of the women in the house had been drunk for two weeks, and one
of the men had been put in jail for ten days. And "I," wrote Dorothy, "have flu and a headache and infected eye." After reciting her
woes, she could not "think of any other immediate troubles right
now except not being able to work on *The Long Loneliness*," the
autobiography she was doing for Harper. Furthermore, the Chancery's notice brought no helpful reaction from the paper's staff. A
new man, Mike Harrington, "urges me to fortitude and the fighting against obscurantism in the Church." Another "comes out with
hopeful suggestions about adding a box to the paper 'published
without ecclesiastical approval.'"

Several days later Dorothy gave her response to Monsignor
Gaffney's request in a letter to him. "First of all I wish to assure
you of our love and respectful obedience to the Church, and our
gratitude to this Archdiocese, which has so often and so generously
defended us from many who attack us." And, "because we do not
wish to take advantage of such kindness, nor count on the official
protection which the name Catholic brings us," she had said to
Cardinal Spellman that "we would change the name rather than
cease publication." But, continued Dorothy, "you very rightly advised me to talk matters over with the staff here and let you know
the results of our conference."

The results were that "None of course wishes to change the
name. All feel that the *Catholic Worker* has been in existence for
eighteen years . . . under that name, and that this is no time to
change it so late in the day." Why, wrote Dorothy, "I am sure none
thinks the Catholic War Veterans (who also use the name Catholic)
represent the point of view of the Archdiocese any more than they
think the *Catholic Worker* does." Nonetheless, "We are all ready to
receive respectfully and give practical heed and application to all
scientific, scholarly criticism and correction of mistakes; to all disci-

plinary directions as to . . . wrongdoing, and to all theological or spiritual censures of theological or spiritual errors." But "we cannot simply cease the publication of a review which has been built up, with its worldwide circulation of 63,000 over the last 18 years. This would be a grave scandal to our readers and would put into the hands of our enemies, the enemies of the Church, a formidable weapon."

On the other hand, "I will admit that I personally am at fault in not being more careful an editor and censor. It is my job as publisher and editor, and it has always, I know, been expected of me at the Chancery office. I confess that I have not given sufficient time to the matter of the paper, being occupied with so many other cares."

But "regardless as to whether or not I am at fault, I and my associates have spent years . . . working . . . for a new society within the shell of the old, a communitarian society as opposed to the capitalist; the cooperative order as opposed to the corporative state." As to the *Worker's* opposition to capitalism, "it is no new thing. . . . The Vatican paper warned us recently of regarding Americanism or Communism as the only two alternatives." And they were not anarchists, as people used that term. "No one by now can consider us as anything but pacifist in our techniques of changing the social order. It is hard to see why our criticism of capitalism and labor unions should have aroused such protest." But it doubtless was "the way in which it was said." So she would "try to be less dogmatic, more persuasive, less irritating, more winning."

She would try to do better, but she and her associates would not cease publication, nor would they, at that point, change the name of the paper. The final disposition of the matter now lay with Monsignor Gaffney, and he chose to do nothing. What could he do, anyway, he probably wondered. When had the *Catholic Worker* ever gone contrary to Church doctrine? When had the *Catholic Worker* done else but raise up and magnify the Church? It never had, in any instance. So the notion of censuring Dorothy and her friends was silly and pointless. Monsignor Gaffney was doubtless responding to letters and calls that came to the Chancery office complaining about the *Worker* and its views. Yet, as Dorothy said on several occasions, if Cardinal Spellman had ordered her to stop the publication of the *Catholic Worker* she would have obeyed. This comment, cited by journalists down through the years, was something that produced wonderment in enlightened circles.

Before she sent her letter to Monsignor Gaffney, Dorothy showed it to Mike Harrington and Bob Ludlow. "No one liked it," Dorothy commented in her journal. Presumably, the tone of her letter had been too submissive. But Dorothy was not disturbed. She "read Berdyaev" that day. She had met Della at noon, who was "in town to see the psychiatrist. She and I lunched at a cheap place." Dorothy did not expand on why Della was seeing a psychiatrist. Psychiatry was something for which she ordinarily had little use. Her remedy for most ailments could be found in the proper herbs brewed into a tea. As for emotional distress, that was a matter that went with life, and its cure in any case lay in the spirit, not in tinkering with a person's psychic components.

In the June, 1951, *Worker,* Dorothy published a criticism of the paper that was contained in a personal letter to her. It was from E. I. Watkins, the English writer. Watkins admired Dorothy and the *Worker,* but the paper lacked "a sense of proportion. You protest and rightly protest against crimes committed by the American Government. . . . But you go on to suggest that all governments are equally sinful. . . . You rightly denounce in this number of the *Worker* the judicial murder of seven negroes. But what of the Communists' massacre in Greece 1946-49 of 46,985 men, women, and children?"

Watkins had made a point and Dorothy, recognizing its worth, published this letter. When she answered it, she apparently invited him to the farm, for later that year he spent several days there. And yet, whatever the criticism he had made of the paper, or whatever the rather vacuous and defensive criticism made by the Chancery office, the fact was that the *Catholic Worker* was a distinctive paper in Catholic journalism, standing apart from the others for its radical gospel message, its intellectual depth, and Dorothy's effective writing.

On January 19, 1952, Harper brought out Dorothy's *The Long Loneliness.* Having a book published provides an author with a few sunny days, and it did for her. "Good reviews. *Newsweek, NY Times,* and *Herald Tribune,*" she noted. In the February *Worker,* Tom Sullivan wrote of "a man sporting a beret and a beard" who was "rushing about interviewing people for a profile on Dorothy Day to appear in the *New Yorker.*" Sullivan dreaded "to think of the rough time the *New Yorker* might give one if they are so inclined," but his dread, if it was real, was unfounded. Dwight McDonald's "Profile" on Dorothy appeared in the *New Yorker* on October 4, the first of a two-part sketch. It was Dorothy's first introduction to a general segment of the educated public, and McDonald explained her with unusual insight. In preparing his profile, McDonald wrote to Max Eastman for whatever recollections he might have of Dorothy, but Eastman professed to have none and referred McDonald to Floyd Dell. What Dell said is not known, but McDonald's letter moved him to get a copy of *The Long Loneliness,* his impressions of which he wrote to a friend. Dorothy had written "with nostalgic enthusiasm about the end of bumming around and sitting up all night in saloons that used to bore me to death when I felt able to endure it. She writes very interestingly about her free love Anarchist marriage, or whatever it should be called, and her baby." Then Dell recalled the review that Dorothy had written of his *Janet March* in the *Liberator* back in 1923. It had been, in his view, a good review. "Aside from the praise, which is always very satisfying to the author," Dorothy had seen the point, "unnoticed, I believe, by everyone else who ever wrote a review of the book."

On July 1 Dorothy had lunch with someone from the Harper office who would talk with her about the sale of her book. She noted that evening that it had "only sold 9500 copies" and that the royalties were "always less than one figured on." In this instance, less the $1000 she had gotten as an advance, they amounted to $1600. It had already been disbursed. "Tamar got $500. $500 for P.M. farm. $400 to repay Mae Bellucci, who gave $200 to Willock and $200 to Tom."

The $200 that Mae Bellucci had given to Edward Willock could hardly have been put to a more worthwhile cause. Willock, one of the editors of *Integrity,* was an artist and writer of considerable talent. Still a young man, and with a large family, he was suffering from a type of uncontrollable blood pressure that was killing him. He would live ten more years, pain-racked and poverty-stricken.

Over the following decade, *The Long Loneliness* brought Dorothy $1000 more in royalties and some recognition. Eugene Exman, a Harper editor, liked the book, and that fall he invited Dorothy to a two-day gathering of select literary figures for a kind of literary retreat to discuss "the philosophical basis for a religious faith." Whether or not Dorothy went is not clear. Another person who liked the book was young Tom Cornell, recently graduated from college and now footloose. He "happened to pick up a copy ... from a friend who had been quite unimpressed by it." Cornell was so impressed that in the spring of 1953 he went to Chrystie Street to help out with the work.

The Long Loneliness was Dorothy's second autobiographical statement. It was, understandably, a more mature work than her *From Union Square to Rome*, which was a convert book, heavy with apologetic matter. *The Long Loneliness* was autobiographical, too, but rather than explaining her position in terms of standard apologetics, she brought her life to the focus of its meaning in the thought and person of Peter Maurin. It is this perspective, and Dorothy's talent for writing, that makes *The Long Loneliness* a book whose reputation will be enriched, rather than destroyed, by time.

The publication of *The Long Loneliness* made Dorothy think again of working on a book about Maurin. The publishing house of Devin-Adair had rejected her manuscript on Maurin in 1946 on the grounds that it was a series of anecdotes unbound by a central idea. Now she would turn again and try to do better. "Thinking of the Peter book. Phrased or not phrased? My writing about him—explaining him." But "when—oh, when is there time to write? The art of human contacts. The discipline of writing, of work. It will get done." But even then she was thinking of a book on St. Therese of Lisieux.

Why did she want to write a book about St. Therese? Because she was the saint of "the little way," who had said that sanctity was not always a matter of heroic fastings, of spectacular deeds and great miracles performed. It was fidelity and constancy in bringing the love of God into the routine affairs of daily life. "The popes have repeated this after her. What she could do, everyone could do. She kept repeating this. Her sisters said the same thing." Dorothy knew of no other "who says this: this is the way for everyone."

How had Dorothy arrived at a "conviction" of the truth of "the little way"? Because "I see around me sin, suffering, and unutterable destitution. There is misery, materialism, degradation, ugliness on every side. All I see some days is sin. The problem is gigantic. Throughout the world there is homelessness, famine, fear, and war and the threat of war. We live in a time of gigantic evil. It is hopeless to think of combating it by any other means than that of sanctity. To think of overcoming such evil by material means, by alleviations, by changes in the social order only—all this is utterly hopeless."

Dorothy thought about this project for several years, broaching the subject to Exman at Harpers. In the course of their discussions, Exman suggested that she go to France "to gather material" on the saint's life. But Dorothy demurred. Why, she did not say, but one supposed that more than the affairs of the Worker, the continuing

struggles of the Hennessys to live with their growing family preoccupied her time and thoughts to the point that she did not want to
be separated from them for such a distance for any length of time.
But Exman persisted, bringing up the subject again in a letter on
April 19, 1956. "You write at your best when you write directly
from the soil of your daily experience. . . . You should revise the
work with Mr. Shaw's help on the very soil of France." Harper
Brothers, he said, "will make it financially possible."

It was tempting, no doubt—the author's dream of being set up
in some rustic center in Europe to research the great book fermenting in the mind of the would-be author! Dorothy did not go.

In July, 1950, David Hennessy got word that he had been given
a job in Westminster, Maryland, with a bookstore. Two weeks later
he wrote to say that he had rented a house there—eight rooms, in
the country, and twenty minutes from work. Dorothy was "delighted" with this development, and in August she went to Berkeley
Springs for the last time, to help the family move. But the job, for
whatever reason, did not work out, and in March the Hennessys
decided that they would be better off at Staten Island. Hennessy
could get a job there. So sometime during the summer—perhaps
late summer—they moved to Staten Island, and until Hennessy
could find a job and a house they lived at Peter Maurin Farm. That
occurred just before Christmas. In the February, 1952, issue of the
Worker, Dorothy told of the Hennessys' new abode. They lived at
201 Winant Avenue, Rossville, and were "cozy indeed in a four-
room house, all seven of them, almost too warm even when the
thermometer is down to 10." The little house was in bad shape, "so
there is a lot of work to do to make the place presentable," but
when "David can close in a room in the attic, and get his books
together again, he will reopen his Distributist Book Stall. As it is, he
is taking orders for Gill, Belloc, Chesterton, Cobbett, Fr. McNabb,
and other distributists."

So ended the hope that Dorothy had had that the family could
survive on the land, apart from the Worker community and her
help. In the end, the Berkeley Springs situation had become impossible. The family had been reduced to such destitution that to
Tamar a survival under any circumstances seemed utterly hopeless. The Hennessys, with David working in a factory, lived at Rossville for four years, and for Dorothy it was a time of a growing
attachment to her grandchildren. "Tamar, the children, and I are
sitting on the beach," she wrote one June afternoon in 1953. "The

tide still high but going out. The children wading and digging. Mary stands in the water watching the waves come in until she is dizzy and staggers back almost falling. Susie . . . goes in too deep, and Eric and Mary follow. It is misty today, the sun hazy, and you cannot see the Jersey shore." Since leaving Berkeley Springs, the Hennessys had had another child, Mary, born in July, 1951. Now Tamar was in the advanced stages of her sixth pregnancy, marking time, in fact, for the pains to begin. They began in the dawn hours of August 9. "I was sleeping well," recalled Dorothy, "when Betty Lou burst into the room to say, 'Tamar is having her baby—David wants you to come right over.' I was dressed in a moment and Betty Lou too. . . . It was beautiful driving thru the dawn, and we were so happy to be getting there on time." The baby was "little Margaret, born at 8:30 p.m."

Dorothy invariably greeted the arrival of her grandchildren with joy and in her notes, at least, seemed not overly stricken when the persistently fruitful Tamar would inform her that another was on the way. Once a priest, though, offended her mortally with a saturnine rejoinder when Dorothy told him of the onset of Tamar's fourth pregnancy. It was Father Fiorentino, who had generously contributed to the purchase of the Newburgh farm. His rejoinder was, "not much control there." "Having heard this from other Jansenist Catholics, I could control myself to a certain extent," said Dorothy, "but for a priest to say such things. . . . Do you know the facts of life, I wanted to say. Instead I said meekly, 'Once a year may produce such a result.' That's right, he said. The trouble is . . . he says the first thing that comes into his head and reconsiders it afterward."

This was recorded in Dorothy's notes in July, 1949. The comment was taken from her notebook and put in the *Worker* for the following month, possibly for Father Fiorentino's edification. When Father Fiorentino visited Newburgh in August, 1952, Dorothy commented on his presence and again included his "not much self-control there" remark. Then twenty-four years later, when Dorothy was seventy-five years old, she wrote in the December, 1972 *Worker:* "Once a monsignor, a generous donor to the CW, on hearing of one of our dear and poverty-stricken friends about to have her sixth child said, 'Not much self-control there.'"

As it has been previously observed, Dorothy's wounds bled a long time, and there were many occasions after concluding her journal at night that the pages were soaked with blood from the slights and abuses she had received that day and in past days. Except for Della and a few close friends, it was to her journal that such matters were confided.

In her public character, she appeared fearless and aggressive—always ready to do battle whatever the cost in wounds. Some of her controversial actions, the air-raid drill resistance, especially, came more from Hennacy than her own disposition. The decade of the 1950s, though, with the anticommunist theme taking on the character of a major national issue, was a time in which Dorothy's sense of the right proportion of things was so affronted that on several occasions she moved into the front line of the fray. As some of her more robust critics saw it, her actions labeled her as being "soft" on communism to the point of suggesting a mental aberration, and if they spoke from the position where the bourgeois Catholic stood, she was in outright heresy.

From the Catholic standpoint, the issue was brought into focus by a Vatican decree of excommunication against communists. The decree had two parts: the first part forbade actions that gave direct or indirect support to antireligious doctrine even if those who supported those doctrines were not avowed communists. The second part dealt with those who, in belief and practice, affirmed the materialistic basis of existence. Shortly after the decree was published, a priest on the staff at St. Patrick's ventured to interpret the decree for the faithful. The presence of Cardinal Spellman sitting there on the altar seemed to add the note of official ratification.

It was, according to the newspaper clipping that someone at the Worker house had clipped, a frothy declamation. The decree had "turned the clock to midnight on the masquerade party," had "unmasked the fifth columnist, the fellow traveler," and so forth. "The toying parlor pink must show his true color." As the more florid phrases had been underlined in red by someone at the Worker house, it seems likely that the feeling was that the sermon had been aimed at them.

Dorothy ignored it, and well she might have, because no part of it, except by someone suffering an advanced case of simple-mindedness, could have applied it to either her words or actions. The personalist position of Peter Maurin and Dorothy Day, as they had applied it to the conditions of life in the twentieth century, was the most fundamental and clear-cut anticommunist idea and program that had been defined by an American Catholic voice. Dorothy knew that she was not of the company, as the priest at St. Patrick's had defined it, of "religious centaurs, . . . collaborators, equivocators, appeasers, temporizers, straddlers," nor of any of the other categories that he had named in his sermon. She was untroubled in conscience, nor did the words from St. Patrick's, so far as she was concerned, ever do more than reverberate through the vaulted heights of the cathedral and then die.

But she was troubled by what she considered to be the injustice suffered by communists at the hands of anticommunist enthusiasts. From time to time the *Worker* protested the arrest of communists under the Smith Act, especially the conviction and imprisonment, in 1949, of eleven communists. On March 10, 1952, she spoke, along with some others, at Carnegie Hall against the Smith Act. "Why?" she asked in her journal the next night. "To oppose repressive laws. . . . With two lawyers about to go to jail and a splendid Negro woman who risks her life in working for her race in South Carolina. All communists, unfortunately." Others who had spoken with her were "Fowler Harper of Yale, Mr. Fairchild of NYU, I. F. Stone, Corliss Lamont. Who knows what they are?" She had written her speech and had made her position clear "so was not afraid" of any reaction.

But of course there was reaction. Columnist Joseph A. Brieg in his "As Matters Stand," asked if "Dorothy Day's heart" bled "only for the poor" that she saw "in her houses of hospitality. Do the Christian martyrdoms, the blasphemies, the sacrileges, the horrible lies, leave her cold? Doesn't she know that it was precisely such Communist fronts [The National Council of the Arts, Sciences and Professions] as the one she addressed which confused the people and opened the way for the tortures and the Godhaters in Europe and Asia?"

Columnist Brieg's words were on the passionate side, but Dorothy's friend, Karl Stern, while more dispassionate, was still critical. "I do not agree with you on your stand in the question of the Communist trial in the last C.W. I think that I can realize that you have never lived under a dictatorship and also somehow you still identify Communism today with the work of a Carl Liebknecht, a Rosa Luxemburg . . . and a Henri Barbusse. But believe me, several of my friends who were Communists and were in Russia, told me that people who have not lived under Hitler (as we have) cannot imagine that inferno of cynicism, cruelty, etc. The face of

Communism has changed entirely. I watched that from first-hand exposure in Germany in the early thirties. And although I also hate the Red-baiting of the Catholic press, and although I have nothing against those chaps being granted bail, I still feel that our society has a right to defend itself."

To which Dorothy may have agreed. One day as she sat in church, she noted that "as often as I am away from the issue of Communism I am forced back to it." She was aware of a "seething revolt of human beings" in the world, "away from poverty and degradation, and toward recognition of their dignity as men, their human freedom, the satisfaction of their economic needs, [men] that are truly free to exercise their freedom." Communism appeared to many to "back them." The present time, she said, was "a sad day for us when there are so few Catholic leaders, so few Catholics who will risk job security and their life's blood for their brothers." Her meditation was "being written in Church where I am so often stimulated by the life-giving sacrament to coordinate love of brother with the struggle going on." That the "revolt" going on in the world would be successful only when its end was the love of God was a truth "very clear to me." But this was what she could continue to affirm with all of her strength even though "I will be accused once again of being weak in the head" or, at best, "big-hearted." But when one thinks in terms of the heart one thinks of love, "and the love of the Sacred Heart, whose month this is. Christ in His Humanity. That is what the Sacred Heart devotion means, and June is the month set aside for that great feast."

On Friday, June 19, 1953, the international ramifications of the communist question settled out, for Dorothy and millions more throughout the world, into a moment of black eclipse, a blacking out of the light that gave life its savor. At sundown that day Julius and Ethel Rosenberg were executed at Sing Sing for providing the Soviets with highly classified atomic information. At the beginning of the week set for their execution, Dorothy had written to Cardinal Spellman asking that he join his voice with the Pope's, who had asked that the Rosenbergs' lives be spared. What rejoinder, if any, Cardinal Spellman made is not known. That Friday evening, as the time set for the execution approached, Dorothy found it "unbearable to think of these young parents being put to death, notwithstanding the protests of the world." But think, she did, and at eight o'clock, the time of their execution, she was putting her grandson Nicky into the bathtub at Tamar's house, "knowing that Ethel

Rosenberg must have been thinking with all the yearning of her heart of her own soon-to-be-orphaned children." "Feeling close to their humanity," she prayed that fear would be taken from them. She noted that the rabbi who followed them to the execution chamber was reading Psalms, the "same Psalms Cardinal Spellman reads every week as he reads his breviary."

Did the Rosenbergs love God? she asked. "Who can hear the Word of God without loving the Word? Who can work for what they conceive of as justice, as brotherhood, without loving God and brother. If they were spies for Russia, they were doing what we also do in other countries, playing a part in international politics and diplomacy, but they indeed were serving a philosophy, a religion, and how mixed up religion can become." It was the same among those who affirmed Christianity. "What confusion we have gotten into when Christian prelates sprinkle holy water on scrap metal, to be used for obliteration bombing, and name bombers for the Holy Innocents, for Our Lady of Mercy."

Several weeks after the execution, Dorothy had a dream of Peter. The sense of his presence had filled her "with such love and affection. But the dream was terrible. It was that he was about to be electrocuted like the Rosenbergs, and that after elaborate preparations—he was all geared up in an iron harness, and witnesses' chairs had all been prepared like for our Friday night meetings—there was then a release. He was not to be executed at all. I had been clinging to him, with fear, too, lest by this close contact with his harness, I too should be killed. Afterward I was with someone I did not know, sitting by the river, trying to find a place to be alone with him." If Dorothy thought that this dream meant anything, she did not say.

The 1950s were years of a rupture in the process of time, when the flow of things, as erratic as it had become in the twentieth century, suddenly ended. The bedstream suddenly dried. There was no past. Time was given over to a new force, the splitting atom. Thrown as it was, as a pawn into the increasingly polarized politics of nations, the atom bomb became a threat to existence itself. Who, possessing the ability to view the development in a balanced way, could conclude other than that the managers of human affairs had gone totally insane? The *Catholic Worker* had, since the dropping of the bomb on Hiroshima, tried frequently to show the proportions of this madness and awaken consciences to oppose it. Now in 1955 New York City had air raid drills, making it a violation of the law not to take cover when the alarm was given. As for Ammon Hennacy, New York had given him the opportunity of going to jail again. After all, it had been over thirty-five years since he had been behind bars. "Ammon ... frankly says he wants to be a martyr," Dorothy noted. As for her own feelings, "we must take up our cross and follow our Master, and perhaps jail would put another compulsion on us, if being more truly poor." Her own last incarceration had been twenty-five years in the past, and while she could objectively recall its pain, she no longer could feel it.

So just before 2 P.M. on June 15, "we went to the park and sat down on the benches there, and when the sirens began their warning we continued to sit. At 2:05, a number of elaborately uniformed men with much brass, stars and ribbons of past battles hung upon their blue auxiliary police outfits, marched upon us and told us to move. When we refused, they announced we were under arrest, and the police van was driven up inside the park." Thereupon all were put into the van and taken to the "bull pen" outside the courtroom. Finally, at 11:30 that night they were called into the courtroom, and the police attendant began calling out their names. Many names he mispronounced, and when he got to Hennacy he called him "Hennaky." This so relieved the tension of the huddled defendants that they began to laugh audibly.

"What's all the stir about?" demanded Judge Louis Kaplan, and Judith Malina, an actress, spoke up "in a very clear voice, 'We are hungry. We are light headed.'" As Dorothy observed, Judith was dressed "rather dramatically, all in white, with a long white scarf with her black hair falling down around her shoulders." Judith was acting.

"Approach the bench," said Judge Kaplan. Miss Malina, still acting, did so. "She admits she is always acting," said Dorothy. "That is her profession."

Had she ever been in a mental institution? Judge Kaplan asked. She "pertly" replied, "No, have you?" This "made the judge go into a rage. . . . He lost his temper completely, shouted, and demanded that she be taken to Bellevue for observation."

Miss Malina then cried out her protest, and her husband, an actor, too, began to cry out with her. Both, screaming, were led from the courtroom. Ammon, it appeared, had been upstaged.

Their case came up on December 22. The seven Worker people, among whom was a young girl named Pat Rusk, just come to the Worker, made their statements as to why they had disobeyed the law. Trying to take cover from the atom bomb was an ultimate insanity. If there were survivors, would they then begin to plan some new and unexplored depth of the madness into which they could further plunge, or would they, as the Workers were now doing, begin to turn away from the abyss? If it was the latter, then how much better the turning begin now. Judge Hyman Bushel listened, found them guilty, and suspended their sentence.

The alarms and the arrests went on for the next five years. In the raid alarm scheduled for April 17, 1959, Dorothy, Ammon, and those others who represented the Catholic Worker in the non-compliance action were joined by Deane Mowrer. Miss Mowrer was a woman of cultural taste and education who had once been a college teacher of English. Having undergone a critical assessment of the directions in which her life might go, she decided that the Catholic Worker was the kind of apostolate that she wanted. Some-time in the mid 1950s she had introduced the subject to Dorothy. Dorothy wrote to Deane on April 5, 1959, of her feelings on the approaching demonstration: "I must say my stomach turns upside down at the thought. However we will be having the prayers of many to sustain us. Pope John says that no one is so abandoned as the prisoner. We will be truly poor as far as we can be. Of course they may be tired of us and not even arrest us. But I have a feeling that the CD [Civil Defense] people love all that publicity, the very thing we cringe from."

They were arrested, and as had become the custom, it was "Officer O'Hearn" who did the arresting. They were sentenced to the usual thirty days in prison, with five off for good behavior, yet Dorothy may have been right: the authorities were getting "tired" of the Workers and their courtroom statements. After having served ten days, they were taken back to the courtroom. Dorothy made a brief note of what happened: "Judge Noonan—very pleasant. Suspended sentence. He has Blessed Mother on his desk." So far as Dorothy was concerned, the experience had not been bad at all. "I had a perfectly happy time in jail," Dorothy wrote in the May *Worker*.

This *Worker* "happy time" pronouncement may have been in part for the public. In her journal, she wrote of her dismay at the extent of the sexual perversion she had seen among the inmates. "How to write about this subject?" she asked herself. "Shall we call it particular friendships? [to] use that term used by writers of religious treatises too delicate for so heavily evil a subject. St. Paul said,

'Let these things be not so much as mentioned among you.' But wars, slave labor camps, concentration of those of one sex together have led to a return of black paganism, a playing around, perhaps innocently at first, perhaps with a hunger for affection, for life, with dark forces."

Later, she said to Professor Rosemary Bannon that it was "almost impossible to describe these dark forces, the lesbian attitude, the girls' affection toward each other and their attitude toward men, and their attitude toward life and children. One girl said, 'I want to have children so I suppose I will have to go ahead and have a man—get married.'" It was all "utterly horrifying, hideous —and yet through it all you felt a sense of how injured they were."

This was her attitude toward homosexuality in the prison. What about those "injured" at the house of hospitality? Stanley Vishnewski, in his history of his life at the Worker, says that homosexuality was a continuing concern in the Worker houses and was something with which Dorothy could not contend. If active "particular friendships" developed, the "friends" sooner or later left the house. On the other hand, she was not so narrow-minded that she made critical judgments on the basis of the disposition alone. It was only when an affair became obvious that she took action.

As Dorothy thought of the overall picture of the resistance actions that were going on over the country at the time she, Ammon, and her friends were going to jail, it did not seem to her that they had done anything particularly noble. Annually they went to City Hall Park, sat on a bench while the sirens sounded, and were then put in jail for a while. They were not scourged, beaten, or shot at. They knew that they were as safe as they would be if they were at home. And for their demonstrations they got a lot of approving publicity. Too much, Dorothy thought. The struggle then going on which, in her view, revealed true heroism and a true faithfulness to the principles of nonviolent action was the struggle that blacks like Martin Luther King, Jr., and black people in Montgomery, Alabama, were making against segregation. The emergence of King as a leader impressed on her the need "to find leaders, loyal to a cause," leaders worthy of "esteem" and "respect," to "whom one can be loyal." She believed that King's doctrine of nonviolence was an expression of love, not of fear, because "love casts out fear." But this led to the counterproposition that violence, too, could cast out fear. "While men fight, they are not afraid. The fear is before and after. They know that as long as they can fight back the hate will strengthen them to overcome fear." Therefore she did not believe "people can fight with *love*, with *charity*. Fighting is an expression of a denial of freedom, not a working for it. To fight for freedom is only forging new chains for man, exchanging old chains for new. God wants men to be free, to love him and serve him in free choice. The whole doctrine of freedom explains, to my satisfaction at least, the mystery of iniquity, the problem of evil in the world."

" 'We have not yet resisted unto blood,' " she concluded, quoting Hebrews 12:4, but were Catholics, the body of the Church, doing anything? "Oh yes—I know the scandal of the church—how much they could do, how much more they could do. But the personalist, libertarian says not what *they* do but I, what can I do?"

Whatever the public acts of resistance in which Dorothy participated, she never did it as just Dorothy Day. As she said once, quoting St. Teresa of Avila, she did it as "a daughter of the Church." It was as "a daughter of the Church" that she went to Americus, Georgia, in April, 1957. There, Clarence Jordan, a Baptist minister, had started a communitarian farm where the guiding ideals on the issues of race and war were the same as those of the Catholic Workers. During much of 1956, the Koinonia community had sustained periods of siege from some people in the area who were aggrieved over the community's denunciation of the traditional canons of segregation and the interracial character of its own life. Perhaps Dorothy thought that at Koinonia she would have the opportunity to "resist unto blood," and she almost did. On the night of Holy Saturday, the day before Easter, she sat in a station wagon under an old live oak tree at the gate to the farm. Some time after the deep quiet of night had settled, she heard a car speeding her way along the highway. Fearfully, she huddled down on the car seat—a well-advised defensive action, for as the car passed a shotgun blast was directed at the station wagon. Pellets hit the car but none hit Dorothy.

One wonders why she sat there that night. She was a most unlikely sentry. Guns, speeding cars, and mobs terrified her. Furthermore, a floodlit car, standing at the gate of the farm, was an invitation to late-night roisterers to take their shotgun off the rack in their pick-up truck and fire a blast for white supremacy. But the farm's roadside produce stand had been bombed before, and the thought probably was that a car standing guard there might prevent another attack. Unquestionably, Dorothy not only volunteered for the duty but insisted on it.

Her action struck some, though, as rather theatrical. In Sally Fitzgerald's *The Habit of Being* [Farrar, Straus, & Giroux, 1979, p. 218], there is a letter from Flannery O'Connor to "A." Flannery relates that "D.D. had been to Koinonia and had been shot at. All my thoughts on this subject are ugly and uncharitable—such as: that's a mighty long way to come to get shot at, etc. I admire her very much. I still think of the story about the Tennessee hillbilly who picked up his gun and said, 'I'm going to Texas to fight fuh muh rights.' "

Before Dorothy returned to Chrystie Street, she stopped off at Conyers, Georgia, to see Jack English, four years on his way toward becoming a Trappist monk. She took an almost proprietarian attitude toward his budding vocation, and if occasionally he was beset with doubts, Dorothy would hasten to shore up his resolution. In her letters to English, she would affirm her conviction that he did have a vocation, that he could withstand the temptations of flesh, palate, and worldly ease, but then if there was any serious doubt in his mind she would give a sulfurous description of life at the Worker house and of the trials to which she was subject.

On the last day of the year, 1953, she wrote to English, saying that "I have such utter faith in you, Jack, that you are bearing a tremendous burden of temptation for us all, that you are sacrificing for us all. It is as though you are lightening our load so that we can endure here in the world. You surely have a vocation, I know it, and you never could have remained this long, you never could love it as you do."

There English was, sitting in his cell, with his life so serenely ordered to thought and prayer, and here she was with Slim "right now on the top steps just outside the open window," doing what he always did, "talking to himself from morning to night." When "I suggested that he have clinic care, he said that he would never leave" and if he were taken away "he would make this place look like the evacuation of France and worse." All this was going on at the moment. Yesterday had been worse. "I had to drive the station wagon down, for it smelled of vomit and human excrement from people sleeping in it at night. We spent the day scrubbing out the thing at the farm." So, Jack, she concluded, "just contrast that with your life down there."

Eight months later English was still at Conyers and Dorothy was still exhorting him to stay: "Do hold on, from day to day, we need you there so. You are holding us up in ways you do not know of.

You with your flounderings are preventing others from falling. What a strength there is in going on just from hour to hour, day to day. You don't know anything about it, what is generated by that suffering. Of course you have to suffer—to attain love. You may be just within grasp of something and turn back. It's like marriage, this going to orders. So many turn back, so many keep starting in again. Marriage, failure, divorce, remarriage, and so on. What do they ever learn of love?"

It was, perhaps, Dorothy's many letters to English, urging fortitude and persistence, that kept him on at Conyers. In the March, 1959 *Worker,* she wrote "The Story of Jack English's First Mass." He had been the first editor of the *Catholic Worker* to be ordained a priest. She had known him "since he was a boy in college, the John Carroll University in Cleveland, and he was one of the first to start a house of hospitality." Then came the war and "Jack was in it. . . . Somehow or other Jack missed out on the sadness and bitterness that struck other Catholic Workers when there were great arguments about war, 'just wars' . . . all of which discussions split up our houses and groups around the country." Or maybe there had been so much discussion because "John Cogley was the most articulate of them, heading the house of hospitality in Chicago . . . and editing a fine paper, the *Chicago Catholic Worker.*" In any case, Jack was in uniform in no time "and of all things a gunner on a bomber and on his way to England." Dorothy recalled that in London Jack had run into "an old Communist friend of mine, . . . Charles Ashleigh, who had been one of the hundreds of the I.W.W.'s arrested in Chicago during the First World War."

Then Jack had been shot down over the Ploesti oil fields and after that had always been "maddeningly casual about his war and prison experiences—all we knew was that he had an injury to his spine and many wounds which kept him in the hospital for a year after he came home." Dorothy believed that Charlie O'Rourke, "God rest him," had been the reason for Jack's staying in New York. "Anyway, Tom Sullivan from the Chicago house returned from the South Pacific at that time, and he and Charles and Jack were cronies, and there they were, with Bob Ludlow and Joe Zarella and Gerry Griffin and Jack Thornton and a whole house full of young people."

Dorothy thought of all this as Father Charles, as he was now called and as Dorothy would thereafter call him, said his first Mass. Also at the Mass Dorothy prayed for Charles Ashleigh, "wondering if he were alive or dead, but knowing just the same that those potent spiritual weapons of Father Charles would be reaching out to him ... farther than any intercontinental ballistic missle."

In a letter to English on April 5, 1956, Dorothy asked him if he knew that she had been "convicted of being a slum landlord ... and fined $250 for operating a firetrap?" Oh, there had been "all kinds of suffering. But the unjust judge started a wave of publicity and sympathy, and we were sent enough money to put in a sprinkler system and are in the midst of other changes."

The "firetrap" charge had come from a fire in the house one early morning in April, 1953. A burning cigarette had ignited a lounge, and the house had been filled with smoke to the point that one of the men living there had died, although he was already in an advanced stage of emphysema. This had been one incident that had brought the Worker house to the attention of city authorities who dealt with housing standards. Another had occurred in October, 1955, when Dorothy had been summoned to the city Workman's Compensation Board to answer questions about what wages were being paid to Workers at the Chrystie Street house. Dorothy poured out her woe in the October, 1955, *Worker*. The judge "was aggressive—acting as tho I were an exploiter of labor." Was the Catholic Worker a charitable agency? The judge decided that it was not; it was a private enterprise organized for profit. Did the Workers have a license? Did they have a license to solicit funds, etc? Dorothy tried to answer in composed and thought-through phrases, but the judge hurried on. She had "better consult a lawyer" or she would find herself "in a great deal of trouble."

Dorothy got a lawyer, Dorothy Tully, and went to court one morning in the following February. Dorothy wrote the day's events in her journal that night. At court "there was no opportunity given to speak. . . . It was 'no charity to house people in a fire trap.' " The judge "ordered an immediate vacate notice. I had no money to pay my fine so they gave me notice to pay by Friday. I thought it over carefully and then in the hall notified Miss Tully I was going to jail." Miss Tully had said, no, wait and see what she could do to "get a delay in executing the order to vacate."

That afternoon a *New York Times* reporter called Dorothy, but he called her about another matter. Was it true that "we had refused Ford Foundation money and why?" Dorothy answered his question. "I told him of the recommendation of Milton Mayer to apply for the money, and of our own emphasis on personal responsibility and dislike of organization and grants for this type of work. I went on to tell him how I had been fined this morning and our imminent eviction. He came right down to see us, telephoned Judge Nickols and the housing commission, with the result that we are to go back up to court tomorrow morning."

At court the next morning, the judge almost beamed. There was new evidence, he said. There would be no fine, but the Workers would have to install a sprinkler system and otherwise fireproof the building.

Whereupon the press, the radio (the Dave Garroway "Strike-it-Rich" program and the John Daly program) told the people of New York and the world of the struggles of a valiant woman to feed the poor and the insensitivity of a heartless bureacracy to her efforts. When the money that poured in was added up, it came to $40,100, more than enough to do everything that had to be done. As Dorothy noted in her journal on March 3, "help came from an old cellmate, the leader of the suffragists, Lucy Burns, from army, navy, chaplains, from people on old age pensions, from Italy, Calif., etc." It was such a deluge that she felt unclean about it, as if her integrity had been violated.

This feeling did not persist. One night, late in February, she closed her day with "now it is raining—it is 11 P.M. and having had a bath I feel relaxed. Listening to Rigoletto on WQXR." There was also a dinner to look forward to on February 28, dinner at "the Sallamagundy Club" with Della and Franklin.

The fireproofing at Chrystie Street represented an investment of short duration. In March, 1958, the Workers got a notice from the city that they would have to be out of their house by August 27. The New York City Transit Authority was extending a subway line, and the house was to be demolished. "We are hunting daily for a new place," Dorothy wrote in the April *Worker*. As for her, she "would rather live in an Italian neighborhood where there is such basic Catholicism that the ancient virtue of hospitality is understood." On Mott Street, the Italian families "took care of their own. The old and senile were not put away in institutions but were cared for by the younger generation."

In October the Workers rented an old loft at 39 Spring Street. It was a large barnlike place that had been used by a theatrical group and then a ballet troupe. It was rented on the assumption that it was large enough so that the men in the line would not have to stand outside. Although this was true, the place had no living or sleeping quarters, and the deficit had to be made up by renting rooms in the area.

The Spring Street place turned out to be so unsuitable for use as a house of hospitality that the Workers stayed there only two years. Dorothy did not like it: she had to climb several flights of steps to get to her apartment, which so exhausted her that sometimes she had to stop and rest. The undertaker next door did not like having a house of hospitality next to his place, and he frequently complained that "Bowery men were loitering in doorways, drinking, smashing bottles, urinating, molesting women and children . . . horrifying and frightening his customers, the relatives who came to 'wake' their dear ones at his undertaking parlor." Another complainant, a Miss Black, "trembled all over as she talked to me." Seemingly, war was declared. "We have been plagued by broken glass and garbage strewed in our doorway. All our windows have been broken across the front of the house, a firecracker has been thrown at Ammon by children who called him an old stew bum and—blasphemy—the face of Christ our Brother, painted by Mr. Dewett of the Ave Maria shop, on tin and nailed on our door has been defaced by vandals."

Spring Street had its moments, though. One was narrated in a letter to Dorothy, written in January, 1960. It spoke of internal dissension in the house and how it was handled. The problem was "Stuart's seemingly affectation and insidious mannerisms he displayed when with . . . us." So "us" concluded that Stuart was "insensitive to our feelings." The problem had been resolved that morning, happily, and now "the office has a healthy atmosphere"; in fact, "things are rather friendly, human and purposeful." But not until stern action had been taken. "I found it necessary—with Aristotelian moderation—to slap Stuart once during our meeting" and "with God's grace and the natural wisdom we received from this encounter, I am sure that the office and the CW will now be a family, in the true meaning of that term."

Would that all of their problems could be solved with such philosophical precision, Dorothy may have thought. One day she witnessed a scene that struck her as so banal as to be obscene, and she described it in her journal that night. "Marilyn had a visitor who took her to the rodeo and then played popular music to her while he bounded up and down on his seat and stuck his neck back and forth like a turtle. Later he chased her around the house like a wolf."

In March, 1959, Dorothy and Bob Steed, a young man from Memphis who had been in and out of the Trappists and then had become one of the managers at the Worker during this Spring

Street period, went to the New York municipal building to get a check for "$27,000 of money due on the house on Chrystie Street." With the check in hand they met their lawyer, Dorothy Tully, and had a cup of coffee. It was a day for relaxing. That afternoon Dorothy went with Ammon to the American Theater to see a Soviet movie about the World Youth Festival. "Then to Della's. We found her sick with a temperature of 102. She caught cold in the snow the other night." That was not the only time she had an unsatisfactory visit with her sister. Several months later she noted: "To Della's for supper where I was not much wanted since they had David [Spier]. He has such hard work—is very thin."

And what was done with the $27,000? She thought about building their own house of hospitality but gave up the idea. There was, of course, the mortgage on the Peter Maurin Farm to be paid off and presumably that was done. Also in the meantime Dorothy had decided that she needed another beach house—or that the Workers needed a beach house. She found one, less than a mile from the location of her original cottage. She made a list of people to whom she would write for a contribution. Whether or not this was the action that resulted in the Worker acquisition of the two beach cottages in which Dorothy spent many days of the last several years of her life is not clear. Presumably, it was. The term "cottage," however, would be giving the two structures a grace they did not possess. They were rudimentary shacks made in part from driftwood. Nonetheless, they were on the beach.

Dorothy's list of people to whom she planned to write for a contribution included Clare Booth Luce, who was to be asked for $100, and "Mrs. Longworth," who would be asked for an unspecified amount. How Alice Roosevelt Longworth got on the list is an interesting story. In January, 1957, Paulina Sturm, thirty-one years old, died suddenly, from what no one was certain, but presumably it was heart failure. The requiem Mass was held in Georgetown, and Dorothy and some of the people from Chrystie Street were there. Mrs. Sturm was Mrs. Longworth's daughter and thus Theodore Roosevelt's granddaughter. A Catholic convert, she had read Dorothy's *The Long Loneliness* and had written Dorothy to tell her how much she liked the book and to urge her to continue to write. With her letter Mrs. Sturm included "a large gift."

"Then Ammon sent her his book also [*The Autobiography of a Unique American Rebel*], and that summer (it was 1952) Mrs. Sturm came to visit the Workers at Chrystie Street." Dorothy, telling the story in the *Worker* of February, 1957, said that Ammon "met her at the station, and with his usual overflowing friendliness, took her everywhere with him, introducing her to the street corners where he sold papers.... Her little daughter had gone to a summer camp, so Paulina stayed with us for six weeks, and when we were arrested the first time for our disobedience, and our bail was fixed at $1000 each by Judge Kaplan, she paid my bail."

Did Dorothy write to Mrs. Longworth and, if so, did Mrs. Longworth contribute? There is no record on the matter, and likely Dorothy did not write. A letter of solicitation would have been inappropriate and Dorothy, perhaps after thinking about it, recognized that fact.

So she may have used a part of her $27,000 to pay off what she owed on the two beach places. Whatever it was, it could not have been much, and she still had money left. Four months after getting the check from the city she noted that there was still $25,000 in the bank and that she and some others had been talking about what to do with it. If she was a beggar, she could also be a donor. The decision as to where some of the money would go was as follows: "Little Sisters $500 for fare to take vows. Si Yamamoto a down payment for house.... Garden tractor for John with equipment." Otherwise, the two beach cottages would be winterized. The Staten Island farmhouse would be repaired and provided with gas heat, and what was left was to buy a house rather than build.

The $27,000 was only a half payment on the Chrystie Street house. Later the Workers got the remainder, plus $3,579.39 in interest. In the September, 1960, *Worker* Dorothy said she was returning the city's interest payment because she was opposed to moneylending at interest. All the Church Councils had "forbade it." It was a gesture; she was "making a point," as Peter had done. The concept of interest, she truly believed, was profoundly at odds with Peter's idea of work performed as a gift, as wholly of itself being creative and central to the idea of a Christian humanism. Interest was, finally, the driving energy of bourgeoisity, an instrument of human fragmentation rather than of community.

Of course, some *Worker* readers were upset by her action. How much of the money that she had received in donations had come from interest? How could she trace every dollar to its source to be certain it did not carry the taint of interest? Dorothy was not perturbed. She had made a point.

In May, 1958, the *Worker* had its twenty-fifth anniversary. Dorothy wrote some of her thoughts in the May *Worker*. "Yes," she said, twenty-five years ago "we thought we were embarking on a career in journalism, the few of us who worked that first year getting out the paper, but like true revolutionary movements, we attracted all the cranks, the reformers, the theorists, the fools for Christ, who wander like wandering monks of St. Benedict's day. Some who came to us were holy, some had not even begun to learn to 'keep the commandments.' In fact, to this very day, common sense in religion is rare, and we are too often trying to be heroic instead of just ordinarily good and kind." She concluded with a prayer: "God be thanked for the work He had given us to do. And may he continue it another twenty-five years!" Where Dorothy was concerned, He almost did.

The staff of the *Catholic Worker* had undergone another evolution. Bob Ludlow had gone, feeling that with all his insights and writing ability that the Worker movement was no longer his life. Tom Sullivan had gone, to lead his own life but always remaining a Worker at heart and staying in touch with Dorothy. Mike Harrington was no longer there, presumably because he did not believe that the human search found its end in the Church but in some form of social organization. And others, too, like others before them, went their own ways to fashion their own lives in work and marriage.

The *Catholic Worker* was still Dorothy's paper, and in the November issue of 1958 she asked, "What kind of man is he going to be, this new Pope? What kind of man has he been, this former Angelo Giuseppi Roncalli, who is now seventy-seven years old?" She had a feeling about him, and quoted a question he had asked, "Why should the resources of human genius and the riches of the people turn more often to preparing arms—pernicious instruments of death and destruction—than to increasing the welfare of all classes of citizens and particularly the poor?" This Father Roncalli had then answered his own question when he said that "there are grave and intricate difficulties in the way, but they must be overcome, even if by force."

What did that mean? "What did the pope mean by 'even if by force?' " "I find no difficulty in understanding it," said Dorothy. "Heaven must be taken by violence, and working for a better order here in this world means a terrible struggle." Yes, continued Dorothy, "we must set ourselves with all the force we possess, against war, and the making of instruments of war, and our means are prayer and fasting, and the nonpayment of federal income tax which goes for war. We pray the Holy Father has a long life, and a forceful one."

There were more personal things in her life during these last years of the 1950s, foremost of which was Tamar and the grandchildren. When Dorothy thought of her grandchildren, she had to think big—in terms of numbers, anyway. By the end of 1960 there were eight of them, Martha having been born in July, 1960, and Hilaire Peter in August, 1959. Dorothy now had eight grandchildren, and she was grateful for them all. "I had a good talk with her about children," she wrote of a young married woman she knew who was debating the issue of whether or not to have children. That Dorothy did not say what she said to her young friend was in character, for overall, she did not talk or write much about birth control—or abortion, either. But when she did it was to affirm fully the position of the Church on these matters. Why she did not discuss the subjects more than she did is fairly obvious. The affirmation of her life was not made in the role of the reformed sinner whose stock in trade was to dwell on past sins. One night, during November, 1958, she had a dream. John Stanley, one of the men of the Worker house, remarkable for the brilliance and passionate intensity with which he confronted his own existential dilemmas, "came to me and asked if I felt *shame* for my past, and I said no. I must look up those words, *remorse, contrition.*"

What she meant, presumably, was that like the penitent in the confessional she felt contrition for her past. As the penitent was required to do, she had said that she would amend her life. And that, one may say, is what she had struggled to do after she left the confessional on the day of her baptism. She amended her life by affirming life. She affirmed it completely, not just the right of conscious, decision-making life to exist, but life as it partook of the mystery of creation. It was all sacred, and its beauty could be sustained only in love.

But what of that great paradox—that seeming contradiction between the "good" of time and that of eternity? To not willfully thwart the mystery of creation; cherish life in all of its development, even to the mystery itself. Then would not the world and the nature she loved be despoiled by an antlike explosion of the world's population where the few, with their sense-sated lives protected by their investment portfolios and armaments, live their short lives of self-indulgence while the masses suffered? That was the vision of the bourgeois and of time, and according to these two dispositions toward life it was a likely vision. But a new and kindlier world, the Peter Maurin kind of world, would transcend that vision and cause it to fade. Whatever the circumstances, death was the end of life, and investments and armaments piled to the sky could do nothing about it. But love had its own life, which could end time and its paradoxes. All life, all creation, was good, and no part of it could be denied in the interest of a more comfortable life. She opposed war and struggled against poverty, but she also spent herself as well. Dorothy could give her life fighting war and working for a just social order, but she could also spend it for Tamar and her grandchildren.

"And now I am again with my daughter who has just had her eighth child," Dorothy wrote in the *Worker* in September, 1959. "Her home is a mile away from Peter Maurin Farm, so we are back and forth every day. I sleep in a little attic room facing north to the Jersey shore a mile away where factory after factory takes the place of the peace and apple orchards which used to be just across [the bay]."

Perhaps it was the proximity of their place to the Peter Maurin Farm and the industrialization and consequent pollution of the land around them that made the Hennessys think of moving again. "They want real country, not Staten Island," Dorothy explained. And so they began a search that ended in their buying an old farm near Perkinsville, Vermont. In September, 1957, Dorothy drove Tamar and the children to Perkinsville to begin their life in their new home. David Hennessy drove a truck loaded with household possessions. She wrote of this trip in the October *Worker,* and what with the mild September weather, the new baby, and the excitement of moving to a new place, it was a happy time for all of them. The house had twelve large rooms and was situated on twenty acres of land with woods, a stream, and land for garden and livestock. As it turned out, after September, 1957, the Perkinsville farm was the permanent home for the family.

Perkinsville, as had been the case with Berkeley Springs, was a full day's drive from New York, but in the decade ahead Dorothy would drive it many times. She went there because she wanted to be with her grandchildren, but more than that, she had a continuing concern about Tamar and the welfare of the family. Things were better in Vermont than they had been in West Virginia, but still the rearing of eight children was a struggle that at times went beyond Tamar's strength. After the move to Vermont, David Hennessy suffered a deterioration in health that finally removed him as a factor in providing for the family. The job was Tamar's—and Dorothy's. Dorothy, as was her custom, contributed out of her personal earnings. It was not much. "I don't know what this statement means," Tamar wrote to her mother after receiving a Harper royalty check for $17.13. What Tamar was confused about is not clear. It was evident enough, though, that the royalties on *The Long Loneliness* had about played out.

In most instances, Dorothy's frequent and sometimes extended visits to Perkinsville were not an unwelcomed chore for her. When she was at Tamar's, she would occasionally complain of tensions and noise that so many children were bound to produce, but usually she was quite happy to be with the family. In April, 1958, she noted that the night she had come "Sue fried the chicken . . . for supper and she also helps with the barn. . . . The girls both look lovely as they set off to school. Becky irons all her clothes and mends them too, and her room is beautifully tidy. Sue and Mary who share a room keep their place neat, and beds are made before they go to school. . . . I used to think Eric worked too hard, carrying coal and ashes, etc. He is certainly a boy to be depended on. All the children are a happiness."

There were other compensations. She could walk with the children to the top of the hill in the evening and get a magnificent view of the countryside. She could have her evening to herself for reading and writing. "Reading *Nickolas Nickleby*," she wrote in November, 1958. "What a help Dickens is in time of trouble. Tamar disconsolate. Hilaire adorable but cries at night so she [Tamar] misses sleep. They are all so good. Not whiney. . . . We cut up pig for lard. . . . Picked mushrooms in the woods."

She may, or may not, have been at Tamar's when she noted several other books she read during this period. "Last night I sat up . . . reading *Lolita*, a truly terrible tale, a horrible picture of American life, a vicious tale, reminding me of *Letters from the Underworld*." She read *Marjorie Morningstar* and labeled it "trash." In February, 1959, she read Thomas Merton's *The Seven Storey Mountain*.

She thought that in the latter part of the book he had "plunged himself so deeply in religion that his view of the world and its problems is superficial and scornful." It was a view with which at this time Merton would have completely agreed.

As for her own book writing, she got a letter from Eugene Exman at Harpers saying that he could not print her biography of St. Therese. Dorothy noted Exman's reasons: "The intellectual Catholic readers were against it. Just another book ... etc." But Exman offered an alternative: "He offered to help in getting it out under our imprint, and advancing us money to publish it. So we could sell it for $1.50 when they would have to charge $5.00. So it is better for us." Therese was published in 1961 by Fides. It was brief and straightforward, and, as everyone had said who had read the manuscript before it was published, it was undistinguished. As Dorothy herself said in one of her letters to Jack English, "I'm a diarist—a journalist, not a biographer."

Dorothy was a diarist indeed—books, journals, notes, and monthly columns in the *Catholic Worker*—all about herself and people around her. But when it came to someone else's taking up her story, she quavered, agonized, and resisted. In 1956, Harcourt Brace published Caroline Gordon's *The Malefactors*. In her book Miss Gordon had used Dorothy and Peter Maurin as models for one of the plot segments of the novel. The setting for this segment was a farm to which people came for religious retreats. This, obviously, was Newburgh. The principal character of this part of the novel was a large woman of rare spirituality and presence, but who had had a murky past. And this, obviously, was Dorothy, as it was obvious that the mute and shattered man who had seeded a vision in the mind of this woman was Peter Maurin.

It was presumably in 1955 that Miss Gordon, or Harcourt Brace, sent the manuscript of the novel to Sue Brown to read and comment on. This was the Sue Brown who, as Sue Light, had known Dorothy during her Village days. In reading the manuscript, Mrs. Brown came across an episode in which the saintly woman had, in her less-than-saintly younger years, staged a black Mass in Greenwich Village. Whereupon Mrs. Brown sent the manuscript to Dorothy and Dorothy, according to Mrs. Brown, "remonstrated with Caroline" by writing her a letter. "I remember the letter," added Mrs. Brown. No doubt she did. Then Mrs. Brown went on to explain that there had been a black Mass "staged by this Greenwich Village group" but that "Dorothy had absolutely nothing in any way to do with it," and that Caroline Gordon had been wrong to associate Dorothy with it.

So the black Mass part of *The Malefactors* was excised, and on January 30, 1956, Dorothy wrote a letter to one of the editors at Harcourt Brace. "Thank you for the revised page proof that you sent last week. Taking out the reference to the Black Mass does a great deal to remove the offense, of course, though the alchemical experiment with 'consecrated wine obtained from some friendly priest' is to my mind so fantastic as to be unbelievable." She could see, Dorothy continued, "that the idea of the 'precious blood' and the idea of Horne's perversion, his desire for blood, are so inextricably tied up that those references cannot be tampered with." Dorothy could see "what Caroline is trying to do, and [I] respect her desire to show the profound aspect of the Church in reference to the most loathesome of sins" (the practice of homosexuality).

Still, Dorothy was not happy. "I had really thought that fiction writers did not need to be so photographic. Peter Maurin, presented as he is, in all his darkness, with no contrast of the light of his earlier days, also hurts. But it is all too late now. I only wish Caroline had shown me the book, when she had the opportunity last winter, or this summer."

Finally, Dorothy wanted one thing clear. She "would not dream of taking any kind of 'action.' It should not need to be stated."

The book came out in February, and Della showed Dorothy the review that appeared in the *New York Times Review of Books*. "I do not feel injured," Dorothy wailed, "but guilty and doing penance."

Flannery O'Connor, who knew Caroline Gordon well and thought highly of her technical skill, stated her view of the affair in a letter to William Sessions on July 22, 1956. Flannery cited Jacques Maritain as saying that he did not think Miss Gordon had been "unkind or superficial" to Dorothy and Peter, and "the Lord knows that was far from her intention. I don't know anybody who has a greater respect for Dorothy Day. In any case, it's as a novel that the thing has to stand or fall" (*Letters of Flannery O'Connor*, pp. 166-167).

"Doing penance" was shortly in store for Dorothy again. In February, 1958, she got a telephone call. It was Sue Jenkins with more glad tidings. Agnes Boulton O'Neill was writing a book about Village days and her life with Eugene O'Neill. The following afternoon Mrs. Jenkins brought the manuscript for Dorothy to read. Three days after Sue Jenkin's visit, and after Dorothy had had time to look at the manuscript, Agnes herself called. Apparently everything was amicable. "She is sweet, stayed for supper," wrote Dorothy that evening. Likely they talked about the "old days," but only about the light things in their lives then—of which there were few.

The book, *A Part of a Long Story*, was published in September. "Tom brought us Agnes B.['s] book. How people love gossip," said Dorothy, obviously in a self-righteous mood. Nonetheless, her feeling that her person was violated in some very grievous way when others wrote about her was a lifelong one. To bear it was "expiation," she wrote. She was "St. Francis with [a] chicken around his neck." The image was apt. St. Francis wore the dead fowl strung around his neck as a sign of his gluttony. Dorothy's gluttony had been in writing about herself. St. Francis had his roast chicken, and she was being written about. "I should rejoice," she concluded.

It may be said, too, that Dorothy's abhorrence of being written about was not matched by a firm indisposition on her part to write about others. Less than two months after Agnes Boulton's visit, Dorothy decided that she would write about her own days and nights with Eugene O'Neill. On the evening of April 22 she and Louise Spier (Della's sister-in-law) had gone to the Gate Theater to see *The Brothers Karamazov*. When Dorothy got home, she observed in her journal that it was "time to write an article about that period —4 mos. of my life, 40 years ago." There were "so many books written about Gene—and that winter figures in them too, and so many articles—Malcolm's among them." But what did Cowley know about her "capacities as Gene's 'philosopher'" or her alcoholic capacity, for that matter? "Nothing. He was a student at Harvard that winter," she said.

She wrote a few pages that summer and the following winter on O'Neill, her "Told in Context" piece, the main point of which was her aggrieved response to Cowley's statement in his *Exile's Return* concerning her drinking capacity. Dorothy's journal notes that summer indicate, though, that O'Neill was on her mind. One night in June she wrote of an acquaintance who "told me today of living next door to Gene O'Neill in New London, Conn., and she was 7 yrs. older." Gene's mother "lovely, a convert. The father big, devout Irishman. Often had actors there, sometimes whole company.

Every Sat. night he'd line them up to find out who were Catholics to send them to Mass next day. He wanted Gene to be a priest. James [Jamie O'Neill] was always a roughneck." A week later, Professor Murray Hartman from Long Island University gave the Friday night talk at the Worker house. O'Neill was his subject. There was also a note that she had made in May, 1956: "At Mass this morning prayed for the dead. Gene O'Neill and his black despair and tragic death—a lack of trust which would almost make him refuse to believe if he were faced with the Beatific vision."

In the later part of the 1950s there were signs that the circle of her life was beginning to close. Her physical stamina, once prodigious, was beginning to wane. She tired easily and "when I am tired," she noted, "I complain about everything. . . . I should keep a pebble in my mouth for silence." She complained occasionally of feeling stifled and "breathless." Once, when she went to the blood center to give blood for someone she knew, she was told that she had high blood pressure. "Also they said I had just enough for myself. Strange thing to say." On another occasion, "they said I had high blood pressure at the hospital where I offered my blood." Well, she knew what to do for that. "I am taking garlic tablets." One day she woke up feeling "dizzy and vague." She spent the day in bed reading "old diaries trying to figure out all that happened the last eight years. So much and yet so much remains the same. What different? With me, I am now past 60. . . . I feel strong but somewhat stiffened up." She had cramps in her legs and leg pains. During the time that she was in prison in 1957, the "doctors in jail had told me my heart was enlarged, irregular, etc.," so after she was released she went to see a "Dr. . . . on 79 St.," who found "everything normal." That was what Dorothy had expected he would find, because Dorothy had decided "at the time that they [the prison doctors] were trying to find some excuse to pardon me, to be rid of me."

The circle had begun to close, as so often happens, with the reappearance of people who had once been a part of her life. It was not just that Agnes Boulton had visited her and that there had been these latter-year reflections on Eugene O'Neill. Once she got word that Romany Marie wanted to see her—the Romany Marie who had been the proprietor of the restaurant where Louis Holladay had died and where, likely, there had been meetings with Lionel Moise. If Dorothy ever saw Romany Marie she did not say, but she probably did see her. Then sometime in 1952 Peggy returned to Staten Island. Her husband, "Doc" Feyling, had died in 1950, from too much drink, it was said. Peggy had then married Howard Conklin. In 1952 Peggy and Howard found themselves a place on Staten Island near Peter Maurin Farm, and Dorothy and Peggy resumed their friendship.

Then Forster, who, because of Tamar, had never been completely out of Dorothy's life, came back into it, bringing with him his burden of personal tragedy. In 1929, after Dorothy had made her exit from his life, Forster entered into another common-law marriage. The woman's name was Nanette, and now, after thirty years of life with Forster, she was dying of cancer. "My heart is wrung for them," Dorothy wrote on the evening of October 22, 1959. Then she commented on Forster's seeming helplessness in the face of the situation, how he had turned so completely to Dorothy and to his sister, Lily, for help and solace. "One would think he is taking up where he left off with me, or rather that I had always been with him, as Lily has," Dorothy noted, adding that she wondered at "how much presumption there is in my attitude of trying to be with Nanette, giving in to F.'s clinging attitude." Dorothy might have been more precise had she altered her phrasing somewhat. Rather than "where he left off with me" she might have said, "where I left off with him." As for the "presumption" in her moving in as one of the inner circle of the family to take care of Nanette, it may have been not so much that as it was discharging an obligation to Forster.

Nanette had had an operation in September. After that Forster took her to their Staten Island cottage, which was in the general area of Peter Maurin Farm. The fall days passed. Dorothy awakened at 6:30 and spent her usual hour of prayer and reading before going to Forster's for breakfast. "Usually they have everything ready, but it is company they want and the radio and newscasts plus my presence [that] begins their day." In the mornings, when Nanette could sleep, Dorothy wrote letters. One day she got seventeen written and "then we shopped, Nanette buying corduroy pants for F."

It had been Forster's sister Lily, Kenneth Burke's first wife, who had brought Dorothy and Forster together in the first place, and now Dorothy was seeing much of Lily. With her customary strong sisterly concern for Forster, she, like Dorothy, was spending much time at his cottage in this period, and the friendship they had forty years earlier was renewed. "She is writing a book," wrote Dorothy, "and is terribly interested in it. About interracial problems. She is wonderfully alive. . . . Working still for the Jefferson Library on 15th St. The only Marxist library in the country."

Once Lily, who usually spent the nights with Nanette, went to Peter Maurin Farm to sleep there. It was rainy and cold; she could not sleep on Forster's porch. "We talked a long time," Dorothy noted. The talk was "of religion and death."

The first days of fall, as they always did, touched her with a quiet somnolence. One afternoon, late, she sat in front of the recently acquired beach house "so calm and sunny, air full of crickets, an occasional cry of gulls." The tide was rushing in, and the summer growth of grass was high around the house. Stanley Vishnewski had just been there for two days, making a private retreat. But now it was "very solitary," and Dorothy thought with a pang how she missed her grandchildren. Well, she thought, "I must remember how engrossed they are in their own life and how happy. I must 'desire to be forgotten,' desire 'to be neglected,' the one thing needful. Seek ye first the kingdom. There is no end to that."

Putting the things that concerned her into a relationship with those basic lines that directly flowed to God could keep her days on their course, but where Tamar and the grandchildren were concerned it was sometimes difficult. One October night while she was staying at the beach cottage she could not get to sleep. She worked, read, and said the rosary while "looking out the window at the heavy swells crashing on the shore." It was 4 A.M. before she got to sleep and 7 A.M. when she awoke. Whether she should go then to see Tamar or wait until Nanette's travail had ended was the question she kept turning over in her mind. It was resolved by her spending several days with the Hennessys.

Nanette lived through the year, but on January 7 it was apparent that she was close to the end. It was the first day that she kept to her bed, "too weak to move," Dorothy noted. "Jean [Walsh] and I stayed with her. We said the rosary together, and at eleven, Lucille [a visitor, apparently] baptized her. She [Nanette] had said many times she was sorry for sin, had asked God's mercy, had kissed the infant of the Little Sisters, had venerated the relic of the Little Flower." Dorothy got to bed at four in the morning. Four hours later Nanette died. Dorothy recorded some of her last remarks. "The cross was not as bad as this, she said. . . . People in concentration camps suffered like this, she said, showing her arms." Lily came at eleven, and she, Forster, and Dorothy went to the funeral parlor. "He wanted cremation. 'It is finished, this is the end. I want no praying over her,'" Dorothy quoted Forster as saying. "He referred to our praying some of the office of the dead before we washed her, or rather, they washed her."

The next day, Saturday, Dorothy went to Father Faley's funeral. He had died, of cancer, two days before Nanette's death. "Death is a lonely affair," Dorothy reflected, but the nuns at St. Vincent's hospital "could do no more." After Father Faley's funeral Dorothy went "to confession to Fr. Gartland where he said I should read the 2 encyclicals *Mediator Dei* and on the Mystical Body." Then to a "good supper of hamburger, salad, soup, and a mousse of whites of eggs, made by Ann Marie."

✢ 17

The Travail of the Sixties

ONE MORNING—it was January 12, 1960—Dorothy, after her morning prayers, felt too tired to get up. She had had a restless night, "a dream of Siamese twins, male and female, somehow married, and how to avoid the revulsion that such close association brings." She realized that her weariness and the pressures that worked on her had permitted the desolate sea of the grotesque, the cesspool of existence, to cast up this image. "Only prayer helps keep a balance," she noted as she lay in bed, trying to shake the spell of the dream.

She was visiting the Hennessys, and, as she noted, "Tamar is pregnant again." The situation there was not good. Tamar was tired, as she had every reason to be, and David, now forty-six years old, was increasingly incapacitated by what in general terms was called a nervous disorder. He still wanted a life with books, but at his age the achievement of that goal, as he probably realized, was increasingly beyond his reach.

Dorothy stayed at the Hennessys for three days, helping Tamar bail out the kitchen sink and the laundry tubs because the drains were frozen. She observed that Tamar had been working at her spinning wheel, "the old-fashioned farm-house wool wheel at which one stands, drawing out the thread and turning the wheel by hand." It had "all its parts," was "well balanced and spins beautifully fine thread. . . . Tamar has her hand-woven curtains at living room and bedroom windows, two hand-woven blankets, the wool for which she dyed herself, linen towels, linen tablecloth, and various other pieces of cloth put away for future use." What was the point of these hours put in on spinning and weaving when Tamar might have been going to P.T.A. meetings and the like? "What it does is to restore the sacramental aspect of things. One gets a feeling and a knowledge of materials, of God's creation. . . . And to plant a bed of flax is to see a most heavenly blue mass of flowers."

On Sunday morning, January 17, back in New York, she was on a CBS radio program, "Lamp at My Feet." Then to Della's for a "quiet dinner." That afternoon she boarded a bus, heading for the Sandstone penitentiary in Minnesota. Ammon Hennacy was to be released in a few days, after having served his time for climbing over a fence at an Omaha missile base to distribute pacifist leaflets to the base personnel. Having greeted Ammon and celebrated his release with a festive meal, she went to Fargo, North Dakota, where she was to speak at a meeting at Father Marion Casey's parish hall. On January 8, she arrived in Chicago, met by Nina Polcyn.

Dorothy stayed in Chicago for nearly a week, meeting with the people of the Chicago Worker house and visiting with Nina and Florence Weinfurter. One day Nina drove her down Cottage Grove Avenue to Thirty-Seventh Street, where the Day family had lived when they arrived in Chicago after the San Francisco earthquake. The old flat still had its room "with one window looking out to the lake where my sister and I used to draw pictures, and write stories and dress our dolls." Dorothy wrote of this visit in the March *Worker*, saying that she was glad that the building had survived and that she would like to have gone up to see the old back porch and the kitchen where she and Della had "spent so many happy hours."

She continued her travels on to the West Coast, visiting friends of the Worker and giving talks as she went. When she got to Seattle on February 26, her niece, Sue Spier, and Sue's husband, Mike, were there to meet her. Two days later at Mass, Dorothy said that she had "prayed for her and Mike most especially. I love her as my own—my only sister's only daughter. So close to me. She is a good teacher . . . and a good helpmate to Mike."

On March 4 she spoke to a group of students from Washington University. The meeting was held on a houseboat, and several who listened seemed to have thought that Dorothy was all wet. They "proclaimed themselves atheists before [the] meeting started," and one "most talkative young man . . . as I was leaving, stood up and began to read from some underground publication." Nonetheless, the meeting "was good."

Several nights later she was on the train traveling south to Berkeley. "I saw Mt. Shasta for an hour as we rode over some plateau. White and luminous." Having visited her nephew, John Spier, in Berkeley, a week later she took a bus to Fresno "to see Betty and Pepe who had been saved by a miracle by Our Lady of Guadalupe." Because of polio Pepe had been in an iron lung, "and Betty vowed she would walk barefoot with the child to the shrine from her home if he were cured. Which she did. The first 5 miles were as tho she walked on glass. The last ten easier." Pepe had been cured.

At the end of June, as the time approached for the arrival of Tamar's baby, Stanley Vishnewski brought the six oldest of the Hennessy children to Peter Maurin Farm for Dorothy to care for. The next day Dorothy brought an old rowboat for $35 so that the children might have something to do out of the house and away from the front porch. A noisy debate arose over what the boat should be called. Jimmy Hughes, Marge Hughes's son, wanted to call it the "Admiral Day"; Dorothy, wishing to divest herself of part of the burden of keeping the children from harm, urged "Guardian Angel." So "Admiral Day's Guardian Angel," it became. Through the days that followed the Hennessy boys spent hours in the boat fishing. No one drowned, surely protected, as Dorothy viewed it, by the active company of guardian angels summoned to assist her.

One evening things got out of hand, and Dorothy had what she called a "set to" with the children. "It cleared the air," she noted, and no doubt it did because she could certainly make things clear. But apparently someone at the farm, thinking her not very up-to-date with her old-fashioned discipline, gave her several books on child psychology. She did not say what she did with them, but the discipline problem would have to have been dire indeed for her to have resorted to the counselings of a psychology text.

Tamar's baby, born on July 9, was a girl, and Dorothy immediately began arrangements to take the children back to Perkinsville. The next day, Della met them at the train station to see them off. At Perkinsville Dorothy found the house in a state of confusion so she enlisted the help of a neighbor, Myrtle Baker, who not only did the washing but also changed all the beds. For her part, Dorothy cared for the children, did housework, and drove daily to Springfield to visit Tamar in the hospital. One morning she awoke discovering that she had a sore ankle from operating the clutch on

Tamar's 1949 Willys. The car was ailing in most of its parts—bad tires, a proneness to convulsive shimmying—and an oil hog. Dorothy noted that she spent $55 to have new kingpins put in. But she liked to drive, and she observed that if she "ever had a good car" she would "be on the road always." One afternoon she took David Hennessy, increasingly incapacitated by his nervous disorder, to see a psychologist. He should learn to drive, the psychologist told him. But David increasingly was removed from the center of things and shortly had to leave the family.

The newest Hennessy, Catherine Ann, was baptized on July 17, and with that rite having been performed, Dorothy felt she could take a day for the spiritual revitalization she felt she needed. She went to a monastery—she did not say where—for a day of recollection. She tried to think through the problems she faced. "What to do?" she asked herself. "What is primary?" To do what Jesus had commanded, she wrote to herself: "to love God with our whole heart, mind, and strength." She resolved not to try to understand why God had permitted matters to take the course they had, "not to think it out, or reason it out, but to assent. . . . All we have to believe is in God who created us and Son who redeemed us."

Regarding David, he had, one supposes, taken on a role and a task that was utterly beyond his capacity to give substance. This much is clear: Dorothy, who had had strong reservations about Tamar's marriage to David, did all that she could to sustain it. What troubled her, though, as one gathers from her notes, was the feeling that she herself, by the force of her own personality, had been responsible for some of his suffering. One finds many times in her notes her prayerful wish that she could be less dominating.

She returned to Spring Street still very tired. "Feeling oppressed and low physically. . . . Feeling very poorly. . . . Heat and noise in town." There was bad news from Perkinsville: the beams in the Hennessy barn had cracked from an overweight of hay, and the chimney was falling down. Then she got "two letters from Della telling me not to come up." Her feelings were hurt. The letters were "rather offensive to pride."

Having reminded herself that she "should not worry" about taking care of Tamar's roof and chimney, she still was forced to conclude that "the ceilings will fall" if she did nothing, so during the first week of August she returned to Perkinsville. "I am praying that my Therese [Dorothy's book] will pay the costs." She decided that she would pray to the parents of St. Therese. They most certainly would understand the concern that she as a mother felt for her daughter. In the meantime she would borrow $300 from Catholic Worker funds.

During the first days of her visit she felt contented, occupied, as she was, with the daily chores of "washing, cleaning, cooking, putting food away for the winter." It was "all on the side of life." But after a week of it she was in a depressed mood again. She fancied that the older girls resented her presence. It had been "a mistake to give so much time here this summer. I've quite outworn my welcome. . . . I will be glad to be gone." Her feelings had been hurt again. But three days later she was "sad to go. My heart is so tied up with them all. I worry about Becky—I worry about anyone who is not happy—on the way to being happy."

Two weeks later, though, after some speaking engagements and a retreat, she was back at Tamar's "to find her new chimney up and half the roof done and the workmen half crazy with the children." Tamar was "very happy with it all." On Labor Day she was finally back at Spring Street. One morning, late in September, Ammon brought her the morning mail, and in it were two checks for talks she had given, one from the New School for Social Research and the other from Muhlenberg College. So she "returned [$]300 to CW of money borrowed for Tamar."

During this period Dorothy experienced a recurring dream, "a dream so rich and pervasive that it remains with me for a few days and it is my real life, and my ordinary life but a dream." The dream began with an experience of a burgeoning springtime. "The air is full of sweet smells and the ears rejoice in the sound of birds; the eyes—all the senses are delighted. Everything springs up overnight all around." And in the midst of this lush abundance of sense delectation she "suddenly" found herself "with a child—it must have been mine, since I was nursing it but the child was not real to me. I did not have joy in it until I suddenly realized I had another baby too, a little colored child to nurse, and I thought 'how wonderful, to be a foster mother to a colored baby—to give it my milk even though I do not seem to have too much!' In my dream I was conscious of my aged breasts—but somehow they had milk for both, and I woke with a sweet joy—that particular tender warm peace one feels when nursing a baby."

The happiness from the dream "stayed with me thru a few days, so that I wanted to write it down, not to lose it." What did it mean? This question "began to haunt me. My breasts were lean; I remembered to have felt them, as I had seen my daughter do, to see at which breast my own baby had nursed last. I began to fret— was such a dream a sign of my presumption? Was I an empty cistern, trying to refresh others? Was it self-aggrandizement, this generosity? Was I neglecting to help others?" She did not know. But the dream, which at first had filled her with a warm and tender feeling, now began to trouble her.

When she was at the farm that summer, she saw much of Peggy. "Peggy came at noon. Spent afternoon," she noted. "I had intended to drive her home but battery died on Chevrolet. She left carrying food, money, basket, rocks—looking very frail. . . . She has a lump in her breast. And ah me—having finished an article on Hart Crane, she is doing one on me. And yet how little she knows of my life."

It is doubtful that Peggy ever wrote the article about Dorothy. And Dorothy was right. What had Peggy ever known of that search for spirit that had driven Dorothy, even in those early years? As for Peggy, her days of wine and roses were over. On April 24, 1963, she wrote a pathetic note to Dorothy: "We were evicted, with Howard [Conklin] carted back to the hospital and everything else thrown in the street, except the two cats." Howard did not live long after this, and Peggy, after his death, became a member of Dorothy's extensive Worker household.

Christmas, 1960, at Peter Maurin Farm was a pleasant time for Dorothy. On Christmas Eve afternoon, Larry Evers came "walking up icy Bloomingdale Road with all his clown paraphernalia." After all had gone to the eight o'clock Christmas morning Mass, Evers "put on his show, . . . bird noises, shell game, Punch and Judy, etc. He also had a bird and a mouse, and he left with a kitten and homemade bread, some money."

Helen Iswolsky, who had come to visit, remarked to Dorothy that Evers's performance "was like a medieval player arriving on a holiday." Helen brought news of Jacques Maritain: "He is now in Princeton, to sell the house in which he, his wife and sister in law who was also his secretary lived for so many years. Within the last year both have died, and she says he wrote her, sending a picture of Raissa on her deathbed, and told her he was going back to France to spend his remaining days with the Little Brothers of Jesus at their Toulouse center."

Dorothy was very fond of Helen. She "always brings us such beauty, such loftiness of thought about life and man. . . . I had just been reading about Herzen and Proudhon and the influence of the latter. I had wanted to talk to her about Herzen but with so many people it was hard."

One evening, just after Dorothy had gotten back from another visit to Tamar's, Ammon Hennacy and one of the young women of the house, Mary Lathrop, came to Dorothy's room to tell her that they wanted to be married. "Talked till two," Dorothy noted. There was a lot to talk about. Mary Lathrop, some forty years younger than the sixty-nine-year-old Ammon, had been with the Worker for a year or so, having come there out of a strong sense of wanting, somewhere, to work at something that partook of a religious commitment. Through hard work and her willingness to do what she could to add some graciousness to daily life, she soon won Dorothy's affectionate approval. Dorothy spoke of her in her notes as "a dear," but also once described Mary's pulling the beard of one of the men of the house—a man who "had not appeared from his room since."

It was, of course, to be expected that this active blond girl should be persuaded by the super-salesman Hennacy to engage with him in the street apostolate of selling the *Catholic Worker*. It was the agreeable togetherness of this work that, for Hennacy at least, brought thoughts of a more permanent union. As for Mary, her position on the subject may have been more the result of Hennacy's irresistible salesmanship than anything else.

That the special ardor Hennacy once held for her had cooled, was all right with Dorothy; in fact it may have given her relief. What bothered her about the prospects of a marriage between Ammon and Mary was the question of whether Ammon, as the Church viewed it, was free to marry. Even more, Dorothy was troubled that, while a conformation to the standards of the Church was important to Mary, it seemed unimportant to Hennacy. In fact, his convert ardor had quickly become tempered by the set of his personality. Assaults on authority figures had long produced the real coin of his life, and he was not disposed to deprive himself of the satisfaction this activity brought to his person after he was baptized. He continued to see society in terms of those who perpetrated absolute evil and those who were the doers of good. His saints were Eugene V. Debs, Sacco and Vanzetti, Alexander Berkman, and Warren K. Billings, the latter having served thirty years in prison—unjustly, many said—for the San Francisco Preparedness Day bombing in 1915. "I talked to Ammon about not judging others," Dorothy wrote. But "he doesn't see it. . . . Black is black and white—white." She was critical of his "declining to study Church history" and his "protesting Mariology." She observed that he expected "no change in the Church." If only, she thought, he would read the "lives of heroes of the Church." But he was "on the natural level."

Some of his talk around the house annoyed her. He and some others, she wrote to a friend in 1960, had been going around the Worker house using words like "Homo and Lesbian to such an extent that I forbade their use . . . while I was there." Ammon, she continued, had said that "I am afraid of sex," that he had gone so far as to say that "I hated it. He says if things are true we must not be afraid to talk about it among ourselves. Which is nonsense. The less we talk of these things the better. . . . I am afraid I know too much of sin from personal experience to feel romantically inclined in talking about it."

Once Dorothy got a letter from a person she knew who had heard Ammon give a talk. As this friend had listened to Ammon she had "suddenly felt an actual repulsion to the vulgarity of Ammon, to his language, to his self-love, to his sarcastic . . . comments about his wife deserting him, and to his thoughtless pronouncements (to make people laugh) such as that Tolstoy's wife was, of course, bitchy—he no doubt identified himself with T. at least in this respect. . . . Part of it was due to my anger at myself for bringing such disappointment upon me when I should have known better than to expect anybody but Ammon to be [first?] with Ammon."

Dorothy, likely thinking that her correspondent had said things that Ammon needed to hear, showed him the letter. She immediately regretted it. "I felt that it was cruelty on my part. . . . I must take him as he is."

But Ammon had his admirers. Some of the young people at the Worker house enjoyed the irreverent barbs he launched at priest and church. They liked to be with him when he sold the *Worker,* to hear him give back, with good humor and wit, far more than he took when he was baited by someone who took offense at the *Worker.* And who could ever say that he did not perform up to the measure of his words? Where in the world was there another old man like this—marching to New London, Connecticut, to picket the launching of the atomic submarine *Polaris,* where he twitted the communists for opening their meeting by singing the *Star-*

Spangled Banner; climbing the fence of missile bases to pass out pacifist leaflets; and fasting forty days as a penance for the dropping of the bomb on Hiroshima. And he was never so happy, so vivacious, and so persuasive as when he was in the company of a pretty girl. He was real theater, and wherever the sweeping beam of the spotlight passed near him he hurried to be in its center. But beneath the drama there was a person driven toward a vision of humankind freed from its chains. The trouble was that "the chains" so frequently took on a human visage.

On January 2, 1961, Ammon left New York and the Worker to begin a new life at Salt Lake City. He left because whatever the sense of mission he felt that he might live out as a Catholic Worker with Dorothy had been lost. He liked the West, and he went there hoping that Mary would go too and that they would be married. Mary did go, but not to marry Ammon. In the excitement of selling the paper on the streets of New York, his persuasive power had all but overcome her doubts, but in Salt Lake City the doubts returned. Homesick, she left.

The business had disturbed Dorothy. When Ammon first came to the Worker she had hoped that he would become its knight, that he would brighten its life and give it a new force—give strength to its spirit. But he had become a scoffer. "We will always have scoffers in our midst," she wrote to a friend, but Ammon had been one "to an extreme degree." And, she thought, he had made scoffers of others. Some of their scoffing had touched her. They felt that "I am ultra-pious, afraid of sex, priest-ridden, etc." She had just gotten "a terrible letter from John Stanley, bitter, full of hatred, of priests most especially. He says he is writing me another in much greater detail, and I doubt if I will be able to read it. . . . Now he is a follower of Ammon. 'They know not of what spirit they are,' despising others as they do."

In February, Ammon wrote Dorothy to tell her that he would continue to write for the paper, that she could call him "our Salt Lake City correspondent." On September 3 she noted that "Ammon this month says if we do not print his stuff on Mary, not to print it at all. So for the first time he will not be in." She added that she "should send him Camus quote." The quotation, as she wrote it in her journal, was, "I have always drawn my hope from the idea of fecundity. Like many men today I am tired of criticism, of disparagement, of spitefulness—of nihilism. . . . It is essential to condemn what must be condemned, but swiftly and firmly. On the other hand, one should praise at length what still deserves to be praised."

Back in August of the previous year, while on her retreat, Dorothy made her customary notes. "I have offered for Fidel and Raoul Castro that they do not forsake their faith but communicate frequently, if not daily, and that the spirit of bitterness leave their heart. The spirit of violence and retaliation. I do believe they are on the side of the poor, and against exploitation and are working for worker." Pieces appeared in the *Catholic Worker* through the following year, written principally by two enthusiasts of the Cuban revolution, Dave Dellinger and William Worthy, correspondent for the Baltimore *Afro-American*. Neither Worthy nor Dellinger informed their writing with any sense of the order and rightness of things as Peter Maurin, for example, might have seen them, and many *Worker* readers were struck by what they saw as a lopsided and misleading view of the Cuban revolution. In the July-August, 1961 edition, Dorothy wrote her own statement, "About Cuba." She acknowledged that the *Catholic Worker* stood with the poor, and that by standing there "we are often finding ourselves on the side of the persecutors of the Church." This was "a tragic fact." She noted that Catholics were spending "billions of dollars in buildings, plants, as they have come to be called, including Church, school, convent and rectory" as compared to the relatively small amount that was spent "on the family, on youth." Her defense of Castro was that he was, after all, a Catholic, and cited his supposed statement that he was not persecuting the Church but was punishing bad Catholics.

It was a lame justification of Castro and brought her more outraged letters. There were some, though, who said that they agreed with her position and applauded her for her courage. During the summer of 1962, she got several letters from a Mario Gonzalez in Havana. In April he wrote to Dorothy, hoping that she could do something to prevent another invasion of Cuba like the Bay of Pigs affair of just a year previous. His ideas on the matter suggest a hazy awareness of the realities that obtained not only at the Worker house but in Christendom: "Could Ammon Hennacy persuade the American bishops to come to Cuba on a journey of reconciliation to show the Church is really interested in uniting all Christians under one banner of humility and love?" Why did not "the new, healthy pope [John XXIII] come to Cuba and put a stop to the silence that supports these aggressions to the people of Cuba? Can some of you ask him to make all Cuban and American Catholics give up hatred?" And "what would Dorothy Day do if you were the Pope?"

In another letter Gonzalez said that he was not "anti-anything." But he would not like bishops and cardinals "until they teach me a lesson in humility, not by washing my feet but by turning their palaces into hospitals, schools, and houses of hospitality.... I simply do not understand why the Vatican has not ordered them to do so. Nothing could be more effective to recapture the spirit of Christian humility, which has been lost in the splendor of pomp and circumstance. Only humility can save the shipwreck before an ocean of guilt devours them for doing what they know to be utterly wrong."

Well, Dorothy may have thought, Gonzalez had certainly misread Hennacy if he thought Ammon would lead a delegation of bishops to Cuba, but then Gonzalez had that radical idealism that was so close to Christ's truth. If only others like him would cease pointing their fingers at bishops and cardinals, and affirm the Church rather than criticizing it continually out of their bitterness and despair!

In the September, 1962, issue of the *Worker* Dorothy told readers that she would herself go to Cuba and "take our readers with me." She knew that some readers might not care for the trip. Some of the previous editors of the *Worker,* Bob Ludlow in particular, "have accused us of giving up our pacifism. What nonsense.... We are against capital punishment, whether it takes place in our own country or in Russia or Cuba. We are against mass imprisonments." She went to find "concordances," to see for herself how things were. She got her papers to visit Cuba from the Czechoslovakian embassy and embarked on an old Spanish ship making its last voyage before retirement.

Seeking "concordances," Dorothy seemed to have found few with communist officialdom. She heard Castro speak and otherwise took the guided tours to which visiting foreigners were treated. Because of travel prescriptions, she returned home through Mexico writing, on October 11, to Deane Mowrer back at the Worker house, now at 175 Chrystie Street, to describe her visit. The heat in Cuba, "95° every day and night," was "terrible." But already she was "looking forward to starting home, stopping along the way to speak and earn back what I have spent. Tell Stanley [Vishnewski] that if there are any speaking engagements in my mail, which he can open, to send them on to me." But she was glad that she had gone. "You cannot imagine how the Cuban Catholics to whom I spoke welcomed our message. I felt greatly reassured that I had done the right thing to come."

So there had been concordances, at least with some Cuban Catholics. But she had not been able to see her earnest correspondent Mario Gonzalez, "I felt heartbroken that I did not find him in Havana. All my friends were working every day until seven at night so there was no one actually to help me get around." Sometime later she got a letter from a Catholic couple she had met in Havana, who reported that they had met and talked with Gonzalez. "We talked about you, the mail situation and anarchism. He gave me the impression of being a talented and honest person." As regards the mail, the couple had "not received a single copy of *Cross Currents, Jubilee,* or any other periodical, except the C.W." They had "had a conversation ... with the Postmaster trying to clarify things. He told me that there is no censorship on religious literature of the type I described to him, but that according to international agreements, any material detrimental to the dignity of the functionaries or the people of the country, may be confiscated."

The "pilgrimage" to Cuba, in regard to Castro and his revolution, seemingly produced no lingering sweet odor of problems resolved or understandings reached. Perhaps Dorothy had gone there hoping somehow to meet with Castro, to exercise her persuasive force on him in the interest of a larger tolerance of religion in Cuba. But no such thing happened, or could have happened, for that matter. Perhaps she had acted on some presumed "intuition" she had that something might happen, a "feeling" she had about Castro that made him assume slightly heroic proportions in her mind. After all, she said, he had done "something" about the wretched social conditions in Cuba.

The problem that Dorothy never fully addressed, at least publicly in the *Worker,* was the problem of freedom. Socialist revolutions with their flags, rallies, marching men and women, and their martyrs, too, were great cyclonic forces driven by the energy of idealism, which fed on a vision of freedom, a freedom from all the dehumanizing consequences of exploitation and greed. But such were the harsh effects on the person of an impatient and angry dismantling of heaven so as to have a paradise on earth that only a more pervasive tyranny was produced. "No, Miss Day," Eugenie Batista wrote to Dorothy, "he [Castro] has imposed on the whole Cuban people a more abject type of slavery than any class or part of the people in Cuba may have suffered before."

In the *Worker's* Cuban articles, some of which Dorothy herself wrote, and in her journey to Cuba, Dorothy did show what to many seemed an excessive enthusiasm for Castro personally and for his revolution. But in the ultimate resolution of the question of where she stood on the question of communism, it would be far astray of the truth to say that she was given to woolheadedness. She no doubt knew the character of Dostoevsky's Grand Inquisitor too well to not understand the nature of that great problem that increasingly was separating humankind into two irreconcilable positions on the issue of where lay a true freedom. The Inquisitor had said that people were sheep who would follow anyone who gave them bread. So he would give them bread, games, and "innocent dances," and when their flesh played out and could no longer sustain the spirit that it animated, the spirit too would die. But Christ, who sat mute through the Inquisitor's learned classroom lecture on the nature of objective reality, offered no infallible formulas for the improvement of the human situation. The destiny of the person was in eternity, not in time, and to bind humankind to time was to deny to it the most fundamental requirement for appreciating its true end: its freedom.

That Dorothy understood the Inquisitorial proposition as an annulment of the most fundamental requirement of a true humanism can not be doubted. Her retreat notes indicate clearly that she understood the problem. Still, as a Catholic, she categorically opposed confrontational tactics where communists were concerned. The Christian community should become so confident and secure in its own truth that it would wage the only war that in the end it could not lose—that war in which its only arms would be the "weapons of the spirit," those weapons that Dorothy believed were invincible. It was out of this conviction that she went to Cuba.

In the July-August, 1964, issue of a publication called *American Dialog*, she wrote an article, "The Papacy and World Peace," in which she declared that "there are many areas on which Catholics and Communists can work together." She made her case for "cooperation" by citing a paragraph from John XXIII's *Pacem in Terris*, published, she said, "one year ago to the day in which this is written." In the encyclical, John had said that Christians might work with nonbelievers "for the attainment of some practical end, which was formerly deemed inopportune or unproductive" but which "in the future" might be "considered opportune and useful." Such cooperation, the Pope added, must "always" be "in accordance with the principles of the natural law, with the social doctrine of the

Church and with the direction of ecclesiastical authority." Working together, however, toward final objectives was impossible. The path of the believer led toward eternity, and that of the communist was bound to time. There was, finally, her conviction of the truth of a phrase that Peter Maurin had used: "Christianity has a communism of its own."

As for her "personal attitude toward Communists," Dorothy said she had "too many past memories of associations with them not to love them dearly." She explained that her first rosary had been given to her "by a communist, and my first statue of the Blessed Virgin also. Both women said I was always dropping into Church and so chose such gifts for me on the occasion of Christmas." But then Dorothy was not one to let the matter of faith stand between her and the warmth of friendship.

In April, 1963, she was off on another pilgrimage—this time to the Vatican. She explained in the *Worker* that she was going "to the representative of the Christ on earth to present ourselves as though a first fruits of his great encyclical *Pacem in Terris,* to thank him, to pledge ourselves to work for peace, and ask too, a more radical condemnation of the instruments of modern warfare."

The trip to Rome was, for the most part, a tourist's visit. She may have seen the Pope, but she did not speak with him, or with anyone in the higher levels of curial officialdom. The most significant time of her trip was when "Fr. Urban, Trappist, ... offered the Holy Sacrifice of the Mass on the anniversary of Peter Maurin's death in a chapel to Our Lady in the crypt close to the tomb of St. Peter under the altar in the great Basilica of St. Peter." After the Mass "I prayed at the tombs of Pius II, Pius XI and Benedict XV, the pacifist pope, as he has been called." Then she went down "into the most recent excavations."

In October she went to England to give one of the main talks at an English Catholic conference. On the afternoon of October 18, "we went with two young English Catholic Workers to Highgate Cemetery, thru Hamstead Heath, where we visited Karl Marx's grave, which stands out because it has a huge bronze or iron bust of him." Standing at Marx's grave, Dorothy noted the names on the markers in the Marx plot: "Jenny von Westphalen, beloved wife of Karl Marx," and daughter Eleanor. She jotted down her impressions of the scene on a fifteen-cent memo book she had brought with her: "birds singing—mist—crucifix opposite—Cross behind." She observed that there were fresh red roses on Marx's grave. In a letter to Della, Dorothy said that she and her friends had said a prayer for Marx and that she had "remembered his wife Jenny especially." As she left the cemetery, she said she passed the place where Herbert Spencer's ashes had been deposited. No doubt she recalled her youthful attempts to read Spencer's ponderosities on evolution, and she might well have thought that Marx and Spencer had one thing in common besides being interred in the same cemetery. Their tedium as writers was unmatched by any other two people she knew about.

She gave her main talk at Spode House, some hundred miles north of London in Staffordshire. According to Eileen Egan, who arranged the trip for Dorothy, Dorothy "answered questions on voluntary poverty, on draft resistance, on civil rights and on refusal to take shelter in civil defense practice as well as on the pacifism of the movement." She got a glowing review in the English *Catholic Herald*. "She says what needs to be said, and nothing more. She practices voluntary poverty in words, as well as in goods. . . . Something of early Christianity, you feel, is still with us, and like early Christianity, one of its strengths is its indifference to the organs of power in society, its nonparticipation in war and politics and civil defense. 'What can you expect,' she says, 'except suffering?' "

Although she got home in time for her sixty-fifth birthday, the occasion went unremarked in her journals. She probably spent the day with the Spiers and then went to 175 Chrystie Street to deal with the problems that always accumulated in her absence.

On December 16 she rode the ferry over to the Island and did what she usually did on the ferry. She noted what she saw and felt, as if by the written word she could extract a moment of beauty from time and place it in eternity, there to be a pledge to her own immortality. "A beautiful white Israeli ship going by . . . white seagulls coasting, a freighter going out, a ferry coming in, and we too, on a ferry, marking time, waiting the passage of this traffic of the sea, to get out into the cold bay where a wind . . . makes pathways in the choppy sea."

The ferry ride's moment of peace was likely supported by a feeling of self-satisfaction. Harper & Row had just brought out her *Loaves and Fishes,* a kind of further narration of life in the Worker house in the fashion of her *House of Hospitality* that Sheed and Ward had published in 1936. It had been a while in the writing—a writing that was touched by some slight author-editor turbulence.

"If you are willing to follow Mr. Sammis's editorial guidance," Eugene Exman had written to Dorothy on January 18, 1962, "I think the next step would be for him to come to see you and talk over the best possible procedure for you doing what still needs to be done. He is prepared to work with you insofar as you would like his help."

But Dorothy ruffled up at what she felt was a too-close editorial supervision. Exman was upset. "The word from Mr. Sammis has always been that everything was going fine, that you were very cooperative and understanding, and that he was sure you would approve of his last lot of corrections and revisions. Before I leave the office today, I will have a conference with Mel Arnold who has been supervising Sammis's work, and tell him to hold up the ms. til you and I can have a talk.... You must be satisfied with the book." Dorothy was apparently satisfied. Writing to Deane Mowrer later, she said that she had "won a victory at Harpers. But I must spend the weekend correcting Mr. Sammis's corrections." Dorothy probably told herself that she had "won a victory," but it is more likely that the final score favored Mr. Sammis, who probably had much to do to straighten out a text written in spare moments.

A review in the London *Tablet* made a comment about the book that others had made about her autobiographical writing. "It is anecdotal and patchy and conceals for reasons of humility or charity many of the things one longs to know." The reviewer did not say what he longed to know, but if it was self-revelation he wanted, his longing would have been unsatisfied for a long time.

"I spent Christmas at the farm," she wrote in the January, 1964, *Worker*, "and we had just enough visitors to make things festive. The chapel is beautiful, we have some snow and some bitter weather, and now it is like spring out, and ... people are grumbling about pneumonia weather, and the fact of winter ... just beginning.... So I shall overcome doldrums by getting under the covers early at night and reading Jane Austen."

So all was comfy and cozy—the happy news that Dorothy knew readers like to hear at times. But, gentle reader, just wait a moment, Dorothy seemed to say, because I have an important announcement which I shall drop casually upon you as I snuggle under the covers with my book. The Workers were going to move to a "new place ... up the Hudson.... We have sold the Peter Maurin Farm ... [and] have made a down payment on a new place where there are three buildings, one large enough for a year-round use for our entire family. We will have at last a Folk School (like Highlander Folk School), a place for study and discussion."

The news, at least to *Worker* readers, was unexpected because there had been little prior discussion of a move. And the reason for the move, as Dorothy explained it, was not one that had suddenly arisen. The problem was the increase in taxes occasioned by "the building of the new bridge [Verrazano] over the Narrows, thus starting a real estate dealer's field day. . . . Knowing that we would receive over $100,000 for a property for which we paid $16,000, I began to look for a place where we would have room not only for our farm family but for your courses and retreats in the summer."

But the immediate reason for the sale was, as she confided to Eileen Egan, that the Workers needed "a place like Spode House. . . . It should be large enough to house people for a whole weekend or for several days. It should be a place . . . far enough from the city so that people would not be tripping back and forth."

There was also money available for the purchase. Dorothy's antipathy toward money-granting foundations did not include all of them, for a year previous she received a donation from one. "Please accept our enclosed check in the amount of $5,000. We know that you will make wise use of this gift in your holy work. We desire that this gift remain anonymous." So the money was probably accepted. At least there was no record of its having been refused.

To have a good thought meant to act. She began to search the *New York Times* real estate ads and soon found what she was looking for. The ad described "a property on the Hudson, twenty-five acres, with three large buildings, one completely furnished and habitable." In previous years it had served as a "resort, school, . . . army headquarters, boys' camp, [and] orphanage." In addition to the main furnished building there was a second large old structure, majestically overlooking the Hudson, originally the home of General de Peyster. A third, set apart another hundred yards from the main building and the de Peyster home, was a structure that may have served as a staff headquarters home. "We are in the village of Tivoli, in the township of Red Hook, just north of Bard College and the Christian Brothers at Barrytown," noted Dorothy.

Forthwith, the Tivoli place was bought. Ninety miles north of New York on the east bank of the Hudson, it was not only commodious, it was a place of much beauty. One reached it by taking the main street through the village of Tivoli and following its eastward half-mile descent to the banks of the Hudson. Then, turning right onto a rutted and pot-holed road, one ascended through a grove of trees to emerge at the rear of the de Peyster place. Between this old edifice and the main building was a broad lawn, overlooking the Hudson some forty feet below at the foot of the steep bluff that edged the lawn. From this lawn one got a sweeping view of the river, of the boats and barges that labored upstream, and of the irregular dark mass of the Catskill Mountains on the other side.

And what of Dorothy's ferry ride and the memories that made the Staten Island farm seem in a particular way to be the place for her? She said she was sad at leaving the Island, but then she may well have thought, had it not been up and down the Hudson that her own grandfather, the whaler, had sailed a century before?

During the 1960s the Tivoli farm had a social stability that Worker houses previously had not had. The stability was due possibly to its distance from the city, but it came also from the settled character of a core of people who lived there. The once-peripatetic Arthur Lacy gave up his wandering to perform various useful offices—getting the mail, showing an active solicitude over the welfare of guests who came to visit, and, in his way, performing the services of a resident chaplain in the way of leading in community prayer. John Filliger, as usual, did the gardening, withdrawing in the evening to his own remote part of the house to have a few beers with comrades. Hans Tunnesen did the cooking, while German George, suffering from cancer, doggedly continued to set the table for the twenty to over a hundred people. The number depended on the season of the year, because Tivoli was extremely popular as a summer vacation center. Alice Lawrence, always pleasant and accommodating, took care of the linens. And Irish Arthur Sullivan, who must have been related to the redoubtable John L., took care of trying situations.

There was a community of intellectuals. Deane Mowrer began regularly contributing to the *Worker* her "A Farm with a View," and while she could not herself see the view, her sensitivity to the sounds of nature around her were so true in their faithful description that one might imagine that it was Thoreau he was reading. Marty Corbin, alive to current ideas, edited the *Worker*. Artistically talented Rita Corbin did Catholic Worker Christmas cards each year, as well as other assignments. The Tivoli place had a succession of notable visitors that gave it an atmosphere of culture and learning. Helen Iswolsky came frequently and at times made her home there. Karl and Wiebe Stern were frequent visitors. Stern brought his violin and Mozart music, happy to leave his role as psychiatrist back at the hospital.

No one would tag Stanley Vishnewski with the label of "intellectual"—in any case Stanley would not long have tolerated such a label. Living out thirty years with the Worker, he was a leavening presence at the Tivoli house where his sagacity, his robust humor, and his essential human decency softened what for newcomers might have been a harsh introduction to Worker life. Peggy Scherer, later to become one of the managers of the New York house, remarked that when she first went with the Catholic Worker at Tivoli, Stanley allayed her anxieties by his calm manner, taking time to talk to her and making little of difficult situations with his sometimes outlandish humor.

And there was Peggy, spending her remaining years quietly and with all of the contentment she could muster, facing, as she did, the increasing diminishments of age. She would appear in the dining hall early in the morning, a robe drawn snugly around her still graceful figure, and go to the little side bar near the kitchen door where one could make a cup of coffee and toast a piece of bread. Then she would go to a table, light a cigarette, and begin to read whatever paperback it was in which she was currently engrossed. But she liked to talk, too, and if anyone was around who was interested in the earlier years of her life she could tell lively stories of life in Paris in the early twenties when she was there with Malcolm Cowley.

Of Dorothy's dreams about what could be accomplished by locating anew, the Tivoli place came closest to fulfillment, at least for a while it seemed so. The peace conferences held there during the 1960s and into the 1970s vitalized its life. For Dorothy, closing out seven decades of life, the note of peace was appropriate, not only where her own lifelong conviction was concerned, but for the world, too, for the cloud of war in Vietnam was again settling its weight of woe on the world.

The organization called PAX was initially an English Catholic peace group. The American PAX was started in 1962 by a group that included Howard Everngam and James H. Forest, with Dorothy Day, Thomas Merton, Philip Scharper, among others, as its sponsors. Forest, described by John Deedy ["Behind the Catholic

Peace Fellowship," *U.S. Catholic,* August, 1968] as an "interesting fellow," was born in Salt Lake City and enlisted in the Navy at seventeen. In 1960 he became a Catholic, a move that was synonymous with his conviction that the state had no right at all to demand that he kill another fellow human. A young man of this conviction inevitably would go to the Catholic Worker. That Everngam was the first chairman, as Eileen Egan saw it, was particularly fitting because Everngam, who made harpsichords, was a craftsman like Eric Gill, who had been a chairman of the English PAX.

The American PAX lasted a decade, during which time it published a quarterly called *Peace,* the contents of which contained talks given at the PAX conferences. In 1972 PAX became PAX Christi, a name change that delighted Dorothy because, as she said, it was Christ who was the life of true peace.

Beginning in 1964, the PAX Tivoli Conference was held during the last weekend of July, an event repeated annually through the remainder of the decade and into the 1970s. Eileen Egan, herself dedicated to the PAX ideal and a principal organizer of these conferences, has given, in her manuscript, "Tivoli Daying," a lively description of a time whose passing she viewed with sadness. "Two hundred people came to Tivoli from as far west as California, some hitch-hiking from long distances for the 1966 PAX Conference on 'Peace Beyond Vatican II.'" Gordon Zahn talked at that conference, as did Thomas Stonier, the biologist, who talked on "The Forbidden War." In the 1969 Conference, the theme was "Training for Nonviolence: The Gandhian Experience and Today's Problems." Dorothy spoke at this meeting, as did Marty Corbin.

There were, of course, many others who spoke, the transcript of whose remarks is recorded in *Peace* magazine. But it was not just speaking that provided substances for the conferences. Miss Egan writes that "Mary Lou Williams, the renowned jazz pianist, played her own compositions and led us in her mass in honor of Martin Luther King. Karl Stern played the violin and was delighted when a flautist was able to join him in a number of Mozart compositions." There were poetry readings and films. "Howard Everngam, besides showing his own footage of every peace demonstration held in New York City, showed a broad selection of films relating to peace and war."

There was dancing when "a guitar-playing Sister, Peg Hunkeler, struck up 'The Lord of the Dance' immediately after a peace liturgy under the fir trees." The episode took on the proportions of a frontier revival meeting when the "whole group linked hands and began dancing on the lawn, turning in ever-widening circles until the lawn was a mass of moving people." Miss Egan relates that even Dr. Stern was caught up in the dancing circle—an activity that sounds incongruous for one whose artistic communion was with Mozart. In any case, no one fell off the bluff.

There were, Miss Egan says, "many priests" at the conferences who "dressed in T-shirts and loud shorts." Eileen thought that this was all right "since I saw their dress as a way of presenting themselves in another role." But Dorothy disagreed. "Someone might need to talk to a priest to get advice or consolation," she said. "Many of the people around here are troubled. As it is, we don't know that those young men in the plaid shorts are priests until they are leaving us."

Ultimately, though, it was Dorothy who gave a savor to the conferences. With her "always with us, we seemed to achieve a heightened sense of community and commitment to peace."

In September, 1965, during the last session of the Vatican Council, Dorothy and Eileen Egan went to Rome as part of a PAX effort to have the Council issue a strong peace statement that would include the support of conscientious objection, the validation of Gospel nonviolence, and the banning of nuclear weapons. Their mission was that of peace lobbyists, of whom two of the Catholic Worker PAX disposition, Jim Douglass and Gordon Zahn, were already there. Writing back to the Worker house on September 17, Dorothy said that on the previous Tuesday, the fourteenth, she had attended the opening Mass of the Council session and that evening, after having dinner with Bishop John Wright of Pittsburgh and Douglass, had then watched the penitential procession of the bishops through the streets of Rome.

Her own penitential offering for the success of the Council was for her, at least, more rigorous. On October 1, at a convent near the catacombs of Saint Priscilla, she began a ten-day fast with nineteen other women. In her "On Pilgrimage" column in the November *Worker* she told of her ten days: "Each day we followed a schedule. There was Mass at 7:15 and then prayer together. From 9 to 12 we kept to our rooms in silence, reading, writing or praying. During the day we divided up our time in the chapel so that throughout the day and night there was always one of us keeping vigil." At noon they all went to the garden, where they read together. Their reading included "a book by Martin Luther King." In the afternoon they heard talks by priests, and at six a French doctor came in to see how everyone was doing.

"As for me," Dorothy wrote, "I did not suffer at all from the hunger or headache or nausea which usually accompanies the first few days of a fast, but I had offered my fast in part for the victims of famine all over the world, and it seemed to me that I had very special pains. They were certainly of a kind I have never had before, and they seemed to pierce to the very marrow of my bones when I lay down at night." When she thought of the people of the world who were starving, her fast, she concluded, "was a small offering of sacrifice, a widow's mite, a few loaves and fishes. May we try harder to do more in the future."

Otherwise, as she complained in a letter to a friend, "every moment of my day from the time I get up is taken, and I don't even have time to take a bath, which one has to do at the railroad station. Just washbowl baths in cold water ever since I was here." What did she do during the day? At noon she and others got a briefing on the actions of the Council—"then lunch with priests and bishops until 2:30 and then a panel discussion on the latest that has taken place on the floor, which sounds much like a CW round table discussion, with questions coming from the floor on such things as to where is Heaven and is there a personal devil—such questions being brought up by skeptical newsmen because of such allusions in speeches. They miss all the intellectual content."

One afternoon she was invited by Cardinal Leo Suenens to a discussion that was to honor Frank Duff, an Irishman who had started the Legion of Mary. Everyone had to introduce himself, Dorothy continued in her letter, "and when I said Catholic Worker the whole place applauded." The meeting was "in a great villa looking like something out of Hollywood or La Dolce Vita, overlooking all Rome, on top of a high hill with a view of the Alban hills all around." Dorothy was asked to say something, so "it gave me a chance to talk of the dignity of the human person which Schema 13 stresses so much, and also to talk about our witness for peace coming from the level of the marketplace and the street corner through demonstrations. Afterward Cardinal Suenens came to me and thanked me. But, oh dear, now I hear someone coming in this Notre Dame Center to grab me and I will keep on going all day, here and there, seeing people, walking, walking, walking.... I am emulating Betsy Trotwood in David Copperfield!"

And oh yes, Dorothy concluded, the people at the Worker were to understand, as per the cable she had recently sent, that they were not to demonstrate "with the Los Angeles group or any other" during Pope Paul VI's visit to the United Nations in New York. She had heard that one of the young Workers had said that she would "try to provide a place for Father Du Bay and his crowd." William Du Bay, at the time, was trying to organize "The American Federation of Priests" and otherwise loudly vocalizing his differences with Cardinal McIntyre. The priest union idea, however, was not anything that George Meaney, president of the AFL-CIO, would touch, nor would Dorothy Day, who probably thought that Du Bay was out of his mind. "I am afraid the editor of *Ramparts* [magazine] is egging him on," continued Dorothy. "Are we expected to have an empty house of hospitality to give him? Or throw out the poor we have?"

Dorothy returned to New York to confront a tragedy within her own household. At 5:20 A.M. on the morning of November 8 Roger La Porte doused himself with gasoline in front of the United Nations building and then lighted it. Hours later he died in a hospital. He had set himself ablaze because he believed that by his own death he might fire the conscience of the world in opposition to the war, and such was his idealism that he was willing to die by fire for this end.

La Porte had for several weeks been in the habit of dropping by the Chrystie Street house in the late afternoon to help set the table for the evening meal. And on the way to the hospital in the ambulance he had said, "I am a Catholic Worker." Therefore, his death was ascribed to some noxious strain of fanaticism that Dorothy Day and the Catholic Worker had engendered in him. Thomas Merton wrote to Dorothy to say that something was wrong when an idea moved a person, even in the spirit of the highest idealism, to take his own life. John Leo, writing in the *National Catholic Reporter,* said that the Catholic Worker movement had "never been well-grounded intellectually" and was "traditionally intolerant of distinctions which are not its own." He hoped that the Worker's "sort of built-in rejection of complexity" had not been operative in La Porte's death.

Dorothy was deeply hurt by these reactions. Had she not made the affirmation of life the first reason for her own existence? Leo's comment about the Worker's having "never been well-grounded intellectually" made for bitterness. Was she a fool? Had Peter Maurin been a fool? As for her influencing La Porte, she had not known him.

That she felt ill-used by her critics is indicated by a journal note she made some two years after La Porte's death. When he had died, "and I was interviewed by radio and television, as to CW responsibility; when I even had to be rescued from bodily attack at a meeting at N.Y. Univ. Catholic Center, for my so-called responsibility, I felt a hostility on the part of the young people around me, Roger's peers in age and education and background. 'She did not know him, she was not his friend,' they seemed to be thinking. 'What right has she to speak?' "

Well, Dorothy thought to herself, "I speak because I am listened to, I write because I am read. I am asked, so I must give what I have to give. . . . Let these young ones too write what they have to give, let them share their richness and abundance. They were his companions."

Reacting two years after the event, and in particular to the students of New York University, was not a response that most people would have given. But Dorothy desensitized herself with a glacial slowness to what she felt were injustices done her, and when she singled out what could have been an imagined hostility of the students, she was using them as a catch-all for every other criticism she had gotten. In some far-fetched way, nonetheless conceivable, her citing students as the offenders may have reflected a grievance that she had against youth as she saw its character in her own household. The youth of the 1960s—armored by penicillin and vitamins against the intercessions of the tragic early deaths that had given to past times a disposition to affirm the reality of eternity—discovered a just-created world. The past and all it signified, all its ties to eternity, now lay a moldering ruin. A new day had come that made all of the past seem as night, and its dawn was aglow with spangled light, rich color, and capricious motion. The new instrument of beatitude was not suffering but sense, and the prevailing philosophy was, in the phrase of the new age, "if it feels good, do it."

This new disposition appeared among some of the young people of the early 1960s who came to the Chrystie Street house. They had come to rid the world of the dark cloud that rolled in from the past and threatened their life and world—the cloud of war. They came—most of them at least—because they were Catholic and because at the Worker house they might deal strong blows at the war in Vietnam, representing as it did to them, the ancient misery of humankind that had to be ended to make real their new world dream. They were idealists, but most of them, in one way or another, were adrift. The Church and the old world had little to say to them. They lived in their rooms and apartments around the Chrystie Street house and made up their own standards.

In 1962 there were young people living in Worker house apartments whose standards were so at variance with traditional morality that Dorothy, in one of her moments of a towering righteous anger, threw them all out. So awesome was her performance that it was thereafter referred to around the Worker house as "the Dorothy Day stomp." Dorothy explained her action in a letter to the mother of one of the girls who had been tossed out. The girl had been "one of the crowd in a CW apartment renting for $21 dollars a month. She was part of a group that reversed all standards, turning night into day, clinging together, a dozen of them, to the extent that they all began sharing apartments, girls and men." Then when "Charles Butterworth and Ed Forand spoke to them about this, there was indignant talk about our infringing upon their freedom. I insisted that we no longer pay the rent of the apartments they were using, nor eat with us, as certainly people do not support the Catholic Worker to support a group of young ones who live from hand to mouth. . . . There were as many as a dozen sleeping in her little two-room place, and then finally the landlord padlocked the place and they went over the West Side, I understand, which I take it means some loft in the Village. A few of them are quite promiscuous, and Jim Forest, who also sided with them, left us."

But the "worst thing that happened was the publication of a twelve-page . . . 'literary magazine' edited by Ed Sanders, which had an obscene title, 'F . . . You!' and [contained] poetry which was pornographic." Sometimes, Dorothy continued, she did not "wonder [that] the communists wipe out the so-called intellectuals and Lenin had to write to Rosa Luxembourg of the bourgeois morality of the young. This whole crowd goes to extremes in sex and drugs and then flatter themselves they are at least not perverts. . . . Also it is a complete rebellion against authority, natural and supernatural, even against the body and its needs, its natural functions of child bearing. It can only be a hatred of sex that leads them to talk as they do and be so explicit about the sex function and the sex organs, as instruments of pleasure. . . . This is not reverence for life. . . . It is a great denial, and is more resembling Nihilism than the revolution which they think they are furthering."

Ed Sanders's "literary magazine" carried his statement of the affair. "Several staff members of the Catholic Worker were stomped off the Worker set as a result of publishing in *Fuck You,* a Magazine of the Arts, or as a result of continued association with its editor[;] the head stomper at the CW has succumbed to the Jansenist dialectic and flicked 4 people off the set there. This outburst of Calvinistic directives seems to us not in the spirit of anarchy, nonviolence, and the view of Christ in every man. However, we understand the need of the grand old lady of pacifism for a closed metaphysical system where there are no disturbances, such as *Fuck You,* a Magazine of the Arts. Therefore in future issues of this magazine we shall refrain from any mention of the Catholic Worker to save Miss Day from any more metaphysical distress."

Dorothy's "distress," metaphysical or otherwise, could not be relieved by omitting her name and cause from Mr. Sanders's "Arts" venture. The drink of gall that was being forced on her now in her old age in increasing amounts was the disposition of the young people around the Worker to single out the Church as one of the main anachronisms from past times that inhibited the free flow of their new universe toward its golden destiny. The Catholic Worker was, before it could make even one small tentative step into the world of affairs, Catholic. It was not a sign to be worn, turned this way and that to reflect whatever glancing beam of position or opinion that came from the roilings of time. She, more than most, understood the intensity, the idealism, and passion of youth, and how the flesh so insistently clamored for its own place in the excitement of making a new world. But a satisfied flesh, if there could ever be such a thing, was not the end of existence. The end of existence was God, the community of eternity, and not the brief communion of togetherness that came from a soggy joint being passed from one to another.

In general, though, the young Workers did not want to give up their Catholicism. For many who had gone to parochial schools and Catholic colleges, it was something that could not be easily discarded. After all, they *were* the Church, as they told themselves, and it was a large part of their cause to make it anew also.

It was, it appears, an aspect of this difference of viewpoint between Dorothy and some of the young Workers that led to the formation of the Catholic Peace Fellowship. The PAX association, as Jim Forest said, was too much of a "superparochial thing." The young people wanted to take direct and even heroic action against the war in Vietnam. PAX weekends and the petitioning of bishops was not enough.

The beginnings of the Catholic Peace Fellowship were, according to Jim Forest, in the contents of a letter that John Heidbrink, secretary for the Fellowship of Reconciliation, sent to Forest and Anne Taillefer in 1961. Heidbrink's letter "suggested that perhaps the time was approaching when the Fellowship of Reconciliation [a European interfaith peace organization] might serve as a midwife to a Catholic group specifically concerned with peace, conscientious objection, interfaith activity and dialogue with radical nonbelievers." So, Forest continued, "by 1963 it became clear that something else was needed. With that awareness, the CPF began to fall together around the encouragement of John Heidbrink, Fr. Phil Berrigan, Marty Corbin . . . and I agreed to serve as co-chairman. . . . We were particularly concerned about Catholic COs."

During the 1960s the Catholic Peace Fellowship inspired the resistance of many thousands of young Catholics to the war in Vietnam and their determined conscientious objection to the draft. Many of them were sent to prison. The heroes of this resistance were the priest brothers Dan and Phil Berrigan, and Workers such as Tom Cornell, Bob Gilliam, David Miller, and Mike Cullen. All were involved in dramatic public demonstrations of defiance of the federal conscription law and the apparatus that had been constructed to enforce it. All served prison terms—more than one, in the case of the Berrigans.

The Berrigan brothers gave the movement its drama and the intensity of feeling. Dan Berrigan especially was the spirit center of the movement. Not only did he provide drama to what they were all doing, but he was the counselor, the comforter, and even the provider for some of the younger ones. In their sometimes desperate financial exigencies, "Dan," as they called him, was there with a check. Sometimes he lifted their spirits with gourmet dinners that he cooked in his apartment. "Oh, to have one of your stuffed flank steaks!" Jim Forest wrote from the Waupun, Wisconsin, prison where he, as one of the "Milwaukee Fourteen," was serving time. He got "no wild rice with mushrooms" there, "no Four Roses."

Their togetherness was exciting and uplifting. It was "impossible," Forest said in another letter to Berrigan, "to be so sad with so much love breaking out. And your talk on Saturday was good to hear. I never tire of you or the Beatles or Joan Baez!" They closed their letters to one another with "Love and Peace," and provided dramatic emphasis to their statements by using words like *incredible* and *terribly*. If something was true, it was true "very definitely."

And who can say that in the long run they did not give a needed example of opposition to war at a time when wars could no longer be glorious (if they ever had been) or solve anything (if they had ever solved anything). And in the long run, and this not counting their jail experiences, did they not suffer for their example by lives constricted to a mold, having to live lives constrained by the path on which they had set themselves and which they later found impossible to leave?

That Dorothy gloried in the example of their resistance there is no doubt. A willingness to go to prison for a worthy conviction was, as she saw it, a noble disposition. But it seems that as she grew older, she more and more recognized the value of "the little way," and especially of the value of steadfastness to one's commitment when that commitment had been registered to uphold the order of Heaven. And she thought she saw among some of the CPF membership a disposition to take Heaven's order into their own hands. The particular circumstance that brought her to seize the issue by the scruff of the neck and to take a stand was the general awareness that Jim Forest, having found his first marriage a mistake, was on a new adventure of romantic involvement.

Having thought "about this for weeks and wondering what to do," Dorothy decided that she had to make her position clear. So, after prayerful deliberation, she wrote Forest a letter: "First, when God asks great things of us, great sacrifices, He intends to do great things with us[;] though they will seem small, they will be most important. Who knows the power of the spirit. God's grace is more powerful than all the nuclear weapons that could possibly be accumulated. Second, when we are asked to show our love for God, our desire for Him, when He asks us as Jesus asked Peter, 'Lovest thou me?' we have to give proof of it. 'Lovest thou me more than these, more than any human companionship, more than any human love?' It is not filth and ugliness, drugs and drink and perversion he is asking us to prefer him to. He is asking us to prefer him to all beauty and loveliness. To all other love. He is giving us a chance to prove our faith, our hope, our charity."

Dorothy continued, getting into the substance of the matter

and, as usual, not mincing her words. The people of the peace movement had "done great things ... and you dishonor them by setting yourself to be something you are not, which you have rejected, a Catholic, Catholicism. What's more you certainly dishonor the Church in their eyes, and vindicate in them the anti-Catholicism which I have always sensed there. To them it must seem that laymen are so weak and despised (so little is expected of them by their spiritual directors, their priests), that no heroic action, no self-renunciation is expected of them. It must seem to the Protestant that sex itself is dishonored, regarded as a physical necessity like food. . . . 'Oh yes, he can sin, go to confession Saturday night, and continue to go to the sacraments,' meanwhile hoping he can continue as he is, hoping to have his cake and eat it too." Of course, she knew "that among you young people confession seems to have been thrown out as a useless sacrament, and I have seen young people going to communion with the permission of the 'underground' priests while they continue their living together, not bothering about marriage either in courts or in church." To her, Dorothy said, sex was "important, not just a plaything, a pleasure. By our sexuality we are co-creators in a most real sense. Here we are as pacifists, seemingly on the side of life, and so many in the peace movement denying life."

She had said what she wanted to say except for one thing. "I am afraid that I must ask you to take my name from your stationery as one of the sponsors [of the Catholic Peace Fellowship]. I hate saying this, but I do not think that while you are the head of the CPF it can be considered a Catholic Peace Fellowship."

Having written the letter, Dorothy had Stanley copy it and then gave it to Marty Corbin for him to read. "Marty disapproved," Dorothy wrote in her journal. "He talks of primacy of conscience, even erroneous conscience. I do not think it applies here."

That settled the matter where she was concerned. As for Forest, he responded by saying that he could not agree with Dorothy that he had left the Church, "though I understand your thinking and admit that you may well be right." But he wondered if the conditions of being a Catholic could be "defined as precisely as you suggest." Conceivably in the hope of shoring up his position and to reassure himself, he sent off copies of Dorothy's letter to several priests whom he knew, two of whom were Thomas Merton and Dan Berrigan. The "problem," as Merton saw it, was "terribly difficult." He "immediately" was reminded of his own "attempt to resign when Roger [La Porte] burned himself. . . . At that time I think Dorothy was quite angry with me. Yet I think the problem of what others interpret as suicide is on a par with the problem of what others interpret as 'immorality.' ... I think I take a much more flexible view of it than Dorothy does, though I am no 'underground priest.' In other words I am much more prepared to concede that before God you are perhaps doing no real moral wrong. But as I say, God alone knows that." Finally, though, Merton said that he did "agree with her that quite apart from the question of sin, it would be better for the head of the Catholic Peace Fellowship to have made the kind of sacrifice she speaks of, and that a lot of us have to make in one way or another." And, "if in the end it were possible for you to consider the thing in terms of sacrifice, this of course would be ideal and admirable. I do not urge this on you, certainly not as an obligation. I only say that in the abstract, and in terms of Catholic tradition and the lives of the saints, this is theoretically 'the best.' " Merton said that he knew that a lot of what was constituted the traditional position of the Church was "very much under fire today from people whom I cannot dismiss as morally irresponsible." His own monastic vocation, for example, was "constantly being called into question on these grounds, and if I hold on to it, which I certainly do, it is no longer on the grounds that it is 'best' but on more existential grounds: 'it may be absurd, I may not understand it, it may look like madness in the eyes of all these cats, but it happens to be what I am called to, and this is what I am going to do.' " Merton's letter was honest and thoughtful. People were living in a new and strange time that made the order of the old seem pointless. He had made a commitment; he would try to keep it. That was his point.

Berrigan responded directly to Dorothy. Yes, he could "qualify in fact, as what you call an 'underground' priest." He did not so designate himself out of some romantic feeling for the term, because it was "not easy to stand apart from any official policies of the Church and of his Jesuit Order" when he "deeply loved" both. "But stand I do. And I am strengthened by the reflection that you too have been, in the noblest sense, an 'underground' Catholic during most of your life." And now, could Dorothy "having brought one revolution to pass, forbid others to carry forward the next wave?" As far as Forest's marriage commitment was concerned, he had little doubt "after witnessing the suffering of so many victims, that in this aspect at least, we have departed from the spirit and compassion of Christ."

That Forest had sent her letter out to become the subject of disquisitions in moral theology annoyed Dorothy. Needless to say, nothing changed her position. But on the other hand she carried no burden of personal grievance against Forest. A year after writing the much-discussed letter to him she wrote to him again. And Forest, who bore no grudges, wrote to Father Berrigan of his pleasure at having heard from her. "Just a few days ago we received a letter from her which came across like the first flower of spring." He was especially glad to get the letter because Dorothy had become "more mother to my conscience than any other woman." Her letter had been "utterly unexpected." Dorothy wrote again, six years later. She was in Detroit to see Lou Murphy, who was in the hospital with tuberculosis, and while she was there something moved her to write Forest. She wanted, before Easter came, "to apologize for my critical attitudes and to promise to amend my life—or attempt to by 'mortifying my critical faculties.' I don't remember ever hearing you criticize people."

The matter was closed. Jim Forest was an intelligent, well-disposed person, an effective writer whose vision was peace and who had made personal sacrifices for it way beyond the measure of what most people were willing to give. He certainly was due her goodwill.

Still, for her the 1960s had been full of signs of something vital having gone out of the world—a glue that had held things together no longer worked. And there was the war in Vietnam, a grotesque torture that depressed the spirits of all and seemed to her to accentuate the discordant and even the grotesque in a world apparently becoming meaningless. On May 11, 1969, she wrote to Della from St. Cloud, Minnesota, where she was visiting several Catholic Worker families. She found that that singular effluence of the 1960s, the "hippies," were more numerous there than in New York. "They are marrying young—17 and 18, and taking to the woods up by the Canadian border and building houses for themselves—becoming pioneers again. It's as tho they were determined to live—to get out of the war atmosphere they have lived in all their lives—a new generation entirely." A new generation of pioneers, yes, but Dorothy found them "maddening." Hippies, in her view, were the offscourings of middle-class affluence who affirmed nothing except the principle of reducing every principle to the absurd. In view of all the horror in Vietnam, Dorothy could imagine that "the soldiers would like to come back and kill these flower-power, loving people" who had "not known suffering." What more properly would be in order for them was "prayer and penance" and "fasting."

But Della should not be irritated with her outburst, Dorothy said in her letter. "I know how little leisure you have. How nursing [her husband, Franklin] when you are not well yourself is a desperately hard existence. I just had to chat a little with you on paper." It was only, Dorothy explained, that she was "sick of war—writing about it" when she wanted to write about creative and God-ended things. But there were young people who, God knew, were doing heroic things. Mike Cullen of Casa Maria in Milwaukee had prayed and fasted heroically. And within the week, Dorothy told Della, Mike and his thirteen associates, Jim Forest included, were to go on trial for burning draft records in Milwaukee.

Dorothy had her personal stake in the Vietnam War. Her grandson, Eric Hennessy, was in the Rangers and had been in active combat. Drafted in 1967, he was now, in December, 1969, about to return home. A week before Christmas Dorothy drove to Perkinsville to be there to greet him, getting there at 3:30 one afternoon, "just in time to pick up Katie, Hilaire, Martha and Maggie who were walking the last four miles home because 'they were tired of the noisy school bus.'" Two days before Christmas it began to snow and continued to fall over the next week until forty-eight inches had accumulated. "There was sliding down the hills on some kind of contraption and a great running in and out for dry clothes, and soon all the registers were steaming with socks, mittens, caps and scarves. . . . Before I left I think there were seventeen young people there coming and going, rushing in and out, filling up on peanut butter and honey sandwiches." Sometimes all of them would come into the house to listen to the record player, "which one or the other of them would occasionally turn up to its loudest. I guess I had a complete course in rock this vacation, but began to wonder, my bedroom being right off the living room, about brain damage."

The snow and the waiting continued, and it was not until nine o'clock in the morning, the day after Christmas, that the telephone rang. All ran to answer it, but Hilaire got there first. It was Eric, home at last.

Then Dorothy spoke of family, a "family where, as in all families, there are grave differences of opinion." The difference, for Dorothy at least, was surely the gravest. Tamar and the children had ceased practicing their religion, finding nothing there that seemed to have any meaning for their lives. Yet, Dorothy continued, and she was obviously alluding to this new circumstance of Tamar's life, she and the family were "yet united and happy. . . . There is always an unspoken agreement, just as there was in my family of three brothers and a sister, parents and in-laws, not to dispute, not to argue, but to find points of agreement and concordances. . . . Not to judge, but to pray to understand."

Dorothy did try to understand, but sometimes when she thought of her daughter and grandchildren a great feeling of frustration and remorse would overcome her. "I have buried Tamar," she once said to a person close to her. In a letter to Tamar several months before her Christmas visit, she told Tamar of her love for her. "You alone do not make demands on me but welcome me when I come and do not reproach me. You do not know how grateful I am for that. You are a real comfort to me always."

✦ 18
The Pilgrimage Ends

SUDDENLY, almost, it must have seemed to Dorothy, that many of the people with whom she had shared so much her life were dying. More and more, her "On Pilgrimage" column in the paper was taken up with notices of the death of people she had known. Mike Gold died in May, 1967, and she wrote of her early years in New York and of her association with him, how "great things were happening in the world." Then she wrote of the Russian revolution, and how she and Mike saw it: "It liberated people, the ancient lowly, the burden bearers, the poor, the destitute, and opened up to them a new life." The two of them had longed to take part in the suffering that was then occurring in the world because it was all a prelude to a "victorious resurrection" in society. "I thought in those terms then," Dorothy said.

On December 11, 1968, she received a telegram from the Kentucky Trappists telling her of the death of Thomas Merton. A correspondence between Merton and Dorothy had begun during the 1950s, and then, in the 1960s, he had written several antiwar articles for the *Worker*. It was in this latter decade that some of the younger war protesters who associated themselves with the Worker urged Merton to leave the monastery and join them on the active front of protest—where it counted—they said. These importunities fell on Merton at a time when he was troubled as to the course his religious life ought to take, and at least in one instance he had written to Dorothy, tentatively suggesting the possibility of his working as a missionary priest with American Indians. But Dorothy strongly urged him to remain where he was, and weeks before his death he had written to her to say that she need not worry as to his future course: "I honestly realize that my function now is not to try to be a voice in the peace movement. . . . It is more and more clear to me that if I pretended to keep up with politics here and tried to utter profound judgments from my solitude I would be deceiving myself and perhaps others."

On January 6, 1970, Dorothy wrote in her journal that she had gotten many presents in the mail, including money for bills. There was even a surplus on hand so she made some benefactions of her own: $500 went to the "Farm Workers Credit Union in Delano; $2000 was sent to Karl Meyer "for co-op house in Chicago"; and "$50 to Ammon." The "$50" was in addition to the $75 a month that the Catholic Worker regularly sent Hennacy.

Nine days later she was in Kansas City, visiting some Loretto Sisters and the *National Catholic Reporter*. Early in the morning she got a telephone call from Joan Thomas in Salt Lake City. Joan Thomas was Ammon Hennacy's wife, and her news was that Ammon had died the day before. He had been picketing and fasting, protesting the impending execution by the State of Utah of two young men, and as he walked up a hill he had had a heart attack.

What happened to Hennacy after he left New York in 1961 was told in 1968 with the publication of a new edition of his autobiography. He had added a chapter, "I Leave the Catholic Church," and at the top of the first page of this new chapter be placed a picture, "My Second Wife; Artist and Painter, Joan Thomas." He had left the Church because he had found that "any increase in spiritual emphasis that I have gained has been in spite of and not because of attendance at Mass and taking Communion." So he did not think it was "worthwhile" to call himself a Catholic. Furthermore, as a Christian anarchist he had "no business belonging to such a reactionary organization." He did not believe in original sin, indulgences, the infallibility of the Pope, or obedience to any church official if it is "against my conscience. . . . Of course I do not believe in confessing to a priest." His "real conversion," he said, had been made back in 1918-1919 when he was in solitary in the Atlanta federal prison.

Dorothy was right. Hennacy had solemnly affirmed the Church in his baptism but then had never taken the time to understand what it was he had affirmed. He was too busy waging his "one-man revolution." As for his "conversion" in solitary, whatever it was, it had not done much to blur his separation of society into the two great camps of good and evil: Hennacy against the "bastards." He had gone to Salt Lake City an embittered man—old and lonely, and with some feeling of clearing the wastes of New York City from his system by breathing the clear air of the West. One also feels that he may have gone there because, where the Church was concerned, his "we against they" outlook was greatly simplified. He could do battle against the local bishop with a good spirit. The issue was simple.

What was at the heart of this undercurrent of hostility toward the Church? Who knows? But maybe it had something to do with his loneliness and grief when he lost Selma and his daughters. He wanted to recapture something he had lost before his time ran out. He wanted a woman in his life again and his hope that something like that could be worked out with Dorothy, even a "spiritual" relationship, had not worked out at all. In 1965 he married Joan Thomas, and although he was old and she was young, the marriage, as he saw it, seemed to have been worth what price he had to pay. In his last years, he clutched at what was left to him in the way of the companionship and even excitement of having a woman, and especially a young woman, with him again.

When Dorothy heard of Ammon's death, she was, apparently, at the office of The *National Catholic Reporter* talking to Bob Hoyt, its editor. She broke short her visit and took a 10:30 A.M. plane to Salt Lake City, reaching there at 4:30 in the afternoon. She recorded in her journal the remainder of the events of that day: "No one at the airport—Joan distraught. I took a cab away out high above downtown section and went to an address given me. No one home. Kept cab waiting. Got address of mortuary . . . and went away from the beautiful background of snowy mtns., down town again. The bill $5.50. There was a quiet group there. Carmen and Sharon [the Hennacy girls] arrived with their husbands, and Selma Hennacy." That evening Dorothy went to the wake and then, before going to her room at the YWCA, had dinner with Joan Thomas. The funeral was at 8:30 the next morning.

Dorothy recorded the remainder of the story in her journal. "Msgr. Macdongall from the Cathedral telephoned me a few days later and told me Fr. Winteret, the chaplain of Holy Cross hospital, had talked often with Ammon during his week in the hospital and had had a long talk with him the night before his death. I did not ask and he did not volunteer what they talked about." Later, "both Msgr. MacDongall and Fr. Winteret . . . called me . . . to tell me A. had received the last rites of the Church while he was still alive." But Hennacy had not requested the rite; it was performed while he was apparently unconscious.

All of which did not trouble Dorothy at all. "Ammon had spent a lifetime upholding the sacredness of life, opposing all wars," and that would save him.

After the funeral Ammon's body was cremated and, as he had wished, his ashes were scattered over the graves of the Chicago Haymarket anarchists.

Dorothy wrote of Ammon's death in the February *Worker*. It was "hard to do," she said in her journal, "his attitude toward religion and the institution of the Church." But she felt that she "had to be truthful and face up to what always hurt me in Ammon—his deep distrust of the Church as being on the side of the State—and his contempt for priests." In the *Worker* Dorothy said that she had to "admit that Ammon was a great one to judge when it came to priests and bishops, and his words were coarse on many an occasion, so that it hurt me to hear him, loving the Church as I do. But there's that love-hate business in all of us, and Ammon wanted so much to see priests and bishops and popes stand out strong and courageous against the sin and the horrors and the cruelty of the powers of this world." But "we cannot judge him, knowing so well his own strong and courageous will to fight the corruption of the world around him."

Joan Thomas wrote her statement in the *Worker*. "Outside of God, Ammon was my best friend, and he said I was his. . . . Part of the secret of this Friendship was that we did not try to infringe upon each other's individual identities or destinies. We all know that Ammon's destiny was—to be—yes—the one-man revolution for this century." Yes, "we were legally married," but marriage "is an inward-growing and crippling thing. Marriage can never compare to Friendship, which reaches outward to the ends of the world and the universe like the arms of the cross."

Whatever the relationship was called, "marriage" or "Friendship," it seemed to have muted some of the discordancies in Hennacy's life in his last years.

After Hennacy's funeral Dorothy went to Tallahassee, Florida, to visit a friend. While there, she spoke to several classes at Florida State University, and it was apparent that the speaking came with a considerable effort. In going to a classroom, she walked very slowly. It was because of arthritis in her knees, she said. But she had trouble getting her breath, and talking exhausted her. Back in New York she stayed long enough to get out the paper and then went to Detroit. Lou Murphy, of the Detroit Catholic Worker, met her. Hours later, a young woman, a nurse, thought Dorothy needed immediate attention, and persuaded her to go to a hospital for an examination. When the examination was completed, the physician told her what he had found and Dorothy wrote his words in her journal that night: "This is a case of heart failure," which startling words meant that water in my lungs, hardening of arteries, enlarged heart, and so on were responsible for the pains in my chest and shortness of breath, which makes me sit gasping for 5 minutes after I walk a block or have to hurry *or* am oppressed by haste, urgency, etc."

Fifteen years previous a prison physician, after the air-raid sentencings, had told her that she had high blood pressure and an enlarged heart but she had attributed his diagnosis to his "wanting to get rid of me." This time she believed what was told her. "I say to myself . . . 'Lord, I want to do your will. If you do not want this [a new venture she was about to undertake], please prevent it.' I used to add, 'even if it takes a Mack truck.' But I've quit saying that since I do believe God takes you at your word." Putting herself out of harm's way where a Mack truck was concerned, she went on to ask herself, "does God mean, by my at present troubles or rather illness, . . . I should give up the projected trip around the world, to Australia and back, projected and to be paid for by Australian priests, and the Central American one [a priest she does not identify]? I am afraid it does mean just this."

Well, God could wait. All she had to do, as she told Della in a letter from Detroit, was to take "3 digitalis tablets and one to help get rid of water. From now I'll take one of each, daily." She had been "persuaded by the young nurse staying with us to get these tests because she said all I needed was a daily pill to keep that water out of the lungs." Anyway, she felt "very virtuous at having gotten all this over with. Dr. Breydert and Dr. Yanovsky have been after me for years to have these tests." And all she needed was a couple of pills daily. What a relief! She could take her trip. God's recommendation had been a little premature.

Dorothy, with Eileen Egan as her traveling companion, took her trip late that summer, traveling to Australia, India, and Africa. She wrote full and thoughtful accounts of her journey in the *Worker*. She was in England when she heard of the death of Peggy. Ill with cancer, Peggy told Dorothy before Dorothy left that she was close to death, that death had taken more time in reaching her than she had expected or wanted. With Dorothy's frequent traveling, and with the always pressing business of dealing with household affairs when she was at Tivoli, Dorothy and Peggy had not had an especially close association during Peggy's Tivoli years. It was the comradeship of their youth that bound them, and neither, one suspects, wanted to spend time in reminiscing about those days, which for Dorothy, particularly, were not pleasant to recall. Yet Dorothy always liked Peggy and was solicitous about her welfare. "It is wonderful," she wrote in her journal "how young and old . . . turn to Peggy, who is always calm, equable, unjudging. 'She has something,' Kay Lynch says, speaking of the way men are attracted to her. Her continued enjoyment of life, for instance, as epitomized by the bottle [of wine] by her bedside. Her enjoyment in books and flowers and nature. She is a Colette. But she prays too. I love to have her join in 'Pour forth, we beseech thee, O Lord, Thy grace into our hearts.'"

In 1968 Peggy had become a Catholic, instructed by Jack English, or Father Charles, as he was called in religious life. Then one Sunday in May she was baptized by a visiting Redemptorist priest, Father Hickey. The baptism was an occasion for a kind of reunion of those who had been close to Peggy in the early years. Malcolm Cowley with his wife drove over from Sherman, Connecticut, and brought Sue Brown with him. Over the years, following their divorce, Cowley had remembered Peggy and done what he could to help her. Now, as Peggy's life seemed to be closing, he could do no more than to express his gratitude to Dorothy for the way in which she had cared for Peggy. She had been kind to Peggy beyond the normal requirements of friendship, Cowley said.

Why had Peggy become a Catholic? "Because she had wanted a place in which to be buried," Cowley cited Dorothy as having said to him—a consideration that probably figured into Peggy's calculations, because there were already people from the Tivoli house being buried in the Tivoli cemetery plot up on Highway 90 that had been given to the Workers. Maybe so, but there was more to it than that. "We used to say the Angelus before lunch and dinner," Dorothy wrote one evening in her journal, a prayer that ended with the words, "Pour forth we beseech thee, O Lord, thy grace into our hearts so that we to whom the message of the Incarnation was brought by an angel, may by His passion and Cross be brought to the glory of his resurrection.'" Peggy joined with the others in asking this blessing, and once Dorothy asked her afterward if she "really" knew what she was asking for when she prayed for a share in Christ's "Passion and Cross." And Peggy had responded "stout-ly," "I do mean it."

And then Dorothy mused to herself over having used the word *stoutly* as a description of Peggy's speech, because "she is a tiny wisp of a thing." But, said Dorothy, "I like that forthright, determined-sounding, old-fashioned word." And Peggy, Dorothy continued, was showing that she had indeed meant it. "Now she sits in a wheelchair or lies in her bed surrounded by cats, plants, flowers, books, candy, wine or whiskey and is a picture of contentment. In and out of the hospital she never utters a complaint, or a word of criticism of others. She accepted the faith which Fr. Jack English instructed her in a few years ago."

Dorothy had written her reflection on Peggy the evening of the day she got her news in Detroit of the nature of her physical problems. Six weeks later she got a letter from Father Jack English, now back at the Trappist monastery in Conyers. English had himself certainly been burdened with a weighty share of the Cross. The wounds he had gotten in the Ploesti oil field raid never completely healed, and he was often pain-racked. Pain and an already existing tendency toward alcohol had combined to make the latter years of his life into a succession of despairing plunges into alcoholic depths. Because of this he had separated himself from the monastery, eventually going to the Tivoli farm. But the problem had continued there and, as he told Dorothy in his letter, there had been "one half hour a few months ago, when, with seventy sleeping tablets and a bottle of scotch on hand, I debated ending everything." But "God's hand reached out in the form of a person, Peggy, it was, who stopped me. So here I am back at Conyers, as though I had never left and yet somehow, radically changed. We begin a retreat this evening."

"Father Jack," apparently after writing Dorothy, wrote to Deane Mowrer to tell her that she, as a person, and the way in which she had dealt with her blindness, had been "a great strengthening factor in my life." And this too had been "Peg's work the last years since she came into the Church. I did not 'confront' her, as Dorothy said in her column. After there was a deep common bond of human love established, when I came to the realization that she did in truth believe, then I cautiously asked why she had never made the obvious move and she said 'No one ever asked me.'"

In the summer of 1971, Dorothy was on the go again—this time to Russia. Corliss Lamont, the wealthy publicizer of a humanistic philosophy based on science and not religion, offered to sponsor Dorothy, along with some others, on a trip to Russia. Dorothy accepted, and Nina Polcyn went with her as her companion. Dorothy found the trip immensely interesting but had no thought to seek out "concordances" among Soviet officialdom. She was too tired for that. She was not too tired, though, to attend a conference of Soviet authors and tell them of the high estimation in which she held Alexander Solzhenitsyn. This, of course, did not make for a "concordance."

As Dorothy's life moved into the 1970s it was apparent that she was physically failing—not that there was any dramatic alteration in her condition—only that she had begun to lose weight and that the slightest exertion tired her. On November 4, 1971, she wrote to Sister Peter Claver, saying that in four days she would be seventy-three years old. "Do pray for me," she said. "God has been good." A month later she wrote to Father Dan Berrigan and said that she had been "really down and out" for several months with what her doctor called "a chronic cough and a mild 'heart failure.'" Her heart condition was not as bad as it sounded, she said. After a rest she would be all right. Anyway, she wanted "to live to 95 like W. E. B. du Bois."

She did have her rejuvenated moments, and when they came she traveled. Her last major adventure came in August, 1973, when she went to the San Joaquin Valley in California to join Caesar Chavez's United Farm Workers in its demonstration against the Teamsters Union. In her support of Chavez and the Mexican itinerant workers, she, along with a thousand-or-so others, was arrested and briefly jailed. "If it weren't a prison, it would be a nice place to rest," she commented. All over the United States newspapers carried a picture of her, just before she was taken off to jail, looking haggard and seated on a portable chair. She was becoming an object of attention from the press—her age and her years of struggle against "power and principalities."

No, she did not want to be put on a perch from which position she might look over the scene and comment on how much progress the world had made in her lifetime—to say how, no doubt, things were improving every day and when her time came she could say that she "was leaving a world better than she found it." In fact, the state of the things dismayed her. The accelerated rate in the change of everything seemed a disturbing intrusion into a world that once had had some order. Everywhere she saw the old environment being remodeled to accommodate the new—shopping malls, superhighways, new institutional structures, and a new jargon-filled language—all justified in the name of progress, of keeping up with some new force in the thrust of life. Where would anything be left for memory—those objects and dispositions toward life that stood in their antiquity as a sign of eternity?

Dorothy's critical view of things can be accounted for to some extent by her health. The "pills" that she thought would set life aright no doubt kept her going, but her energy reserve was thin. During the winters, she developed congestions and coughs that kept her in bed for weeks at a time. To conserve her energy and to have a better air to breathe, she spent the winter of 1975 in one of the two cottages on the beach at Staten Island that the Workers owned. She lived alone, although Marge Hughes and her son, Johnny, were immediately at hand in the next cottage. Marge had been with the Worker almost from the beginning and her devotion to Dorothy, after annoyances and misunderstandings had faded to their proper proportion, was unqualified. Periodically, someone came to the Island from the First Street house to bring the mail and the news; other than that, she had no contact with the world except for her telephone. And the telephone was used almost exclusively for conversations with Tamar, Della, and Forster. The calls from Forster pleased her. "Once someone has taken a part of your life," she would say, "that part always belongs to that person."

That summer she went back to Tivoli and, increasingly, she found things to dismay her. Although the place had natural beauty, it was not Grand Hotel. It was a Catholic Worker house, and more and more, the young people who came there found the community in the particular dispositions of their own condition rather than in Peter Maurin's "common unity." Physically, the place showed it. It had a dilapidated and frowzy appearance, the more painful to witness because of the sad desolation that had befallen the noble de Peyster mansion, still grand and proudly erect, but that was increasingly called on to surrender its last claim to graciousness in favor of the immediate need for a roof over the heads for young wanderers. Frequently, whoever would unroll his or her sleeping bag in the old place would be taken with its spaciousness and the magnificent prospect of the Hudson it provided, and would resolve to stay a while. Plastic would be nailed over the doorway, and posters depicting the undulant posturings of favorite rock band leaders would cover the walls.

There was, to be sure, a sense of community among these youthful inhabitants. It was a sense that had its roots in their apartness, their apartness from the conventions of the past and from the older people who lived in the main house—the ones who prayed before meals and said Vespers in the evenings. The community of these mansion-dwellers was the community of the present, where togetherness came from the joint that was passed among them, its haze masking the face of time the destroyer, altering it into a graceful companion where the old beams above them were freed of the weight of tradition and the breath of the person next to them was no longer foul but sweet.

That fall Dorothy wrote to Sister Peter Claver, and her message was glum. "Here at the farm we have had two priests who have now departed. (Least said, soonest mended, my dear mother used to say.) They were loved by the young people, much hard labor was accomplished, but there has been a great falling away of devotions of any kind—including daily Mass." In fact, on Sunday, of the seventy people at the farm "only a scant half dozen get to Mass at the parish and our own Vespers and Compline daily." When a priest did come to the house for a Sunday Mass, "they all go and receive too. (Catholic and non-Catholic—children unprepared and adults unshriven). I'm considered an ancient old fogey, and the more praise given me by the press—by those who do not know me—the more the young edge away from me." And to add "another grotesque and horrible misery descending on me—two of the . . . women associated with our movement have come to me to proclaim themselves lesbians. Scripture—St. Paul's writings—no attention is paid to that. It is all 'women's lib.' And I am just not 'with it' any more, and you can imagine the kind of desolation I feel."

"So," she concluded, "I should really stay here and suffer." There was one thing that was positive. "We do have a gem of a chapel and permission for the Blessed Sacrament. What an immense consolation. And also I have to learn daily over and over not to judge. But how not to?"

She did not make particular judgments but she continued to write notes on the subject of the "rebellion" of youth and why they "leave the Church now."

For one thing, they were uninstructed. "They have never been taught the motive which Father Roy so stressed, the supernatural motive which makes each act in life full of meaning, nourishment, growth." Their service to the Church was given in a "grudging" way. There was "no joy in it, no obedience, since it was compelled, as they throw off their chains, as they think and 'all is permitted.' . . . Satisfied flesh, in youth, satisfies conscience." Even so, "they continue to receive the Host, if the Mass pleases them, if they have 'felt it,' made contact with others. . . . In our group of young ones, they find love in each other, somewhat in the poor, those of them who serve the line for instance. But only those they *see* around them. They give up confession but receive. They 'feel' they are right so they are right." Meanwhile, "they despise the old, who have made such a mess of the world, and with the old—the ancient Church itself. They want 'to rebuild the Church in the shell of the old,' as one of them said."

As for sex, "I must say the new morality is depressing," Dorothy wrote to Sister Peter Claver. "How much sorrow is being laid up for these young ones." She should know about that, she seemed to be saying. Again, she noted her thoughts on the subject. "Sex is in its pleasure, its joy, its 'well-being'—the image thruout the Old Testament of the beatific vision. The nearest we come to God." Because God was Creator the experience of sex should be Godlike—itself creative. "When man takes to himself the right to use sex as pleasure alone, cutting it away from its creative aspect, by artificial birth control, by perverse practices, he is denying 'The absolute Supremacy of the Creative Deity.'" He was then giving himself over to simple lust "under which woman is victim and suffers most of all," and for whom abortion became the ultimate tragedy. "Birth control, abortion, free love—all in the name of love."

Having affirmed these positions, she, far more than most, recognized the relationship between their ideal application and the social order. Her understanding of this relationship was stated in a talk that Father Vincent McNabb had made in London in 1924. At least she had preserved the script of the talk and had underlined in red Father McNabb's principal point. He believed that the spread of "neo-malthusian birth control" was due "mainly . . . [to] the present urban and industrial civilization." It was "probably true" that "this civilization with its wage basis, and therefore money basis, cannot give the normal family wage to the wage-earner of the normal family." "Which meant that many of our people are faced with the alternative of the heroic virtue of conjugal abstinence or sinful neo-malthusian birth control." Therefore, concluded Father McNabb, "we clergy . . . must do more than we are . . . doing to change this urban industrialized civilization." Dorothy could have added that the problem, as Father McNabb had defined it, was also related to the problems of divorce and abortion.

She was upset by the increasing use of explicit sexual language, especially when it was used as an instrument of derision in public demonstrations. "I have myself been at enough demonstrations [and] marches of protest these past few years to know that in all of them were groups carrying inflammatory slogans on their signs" and how there could always be heard "the shouting of four-letter words which by now have lost all their meaning. I myself cringe before such words because of the contempt and hatred they express and involving the perversion of the act of creation. To use such a word is to drag the sacred and the beautiful into the mire." It was "hard to talk about these things," she wrote. "What I am trying to say is that the use of the word coarsely or humorously applied to the sexual act is calculated to enrage. There can even be said to be an element of the demonic about it."

Dorothy's critical reflections on those who had broken with all tradition and had given themselves over to "the cult of youth" came from a first-hand experience with them at the Tivoli farm. And because the place was Catholic Worker, it attracted the most desolated of souls in whom the revolt from tradition manifested itself in a kind of pagan culture in which sex was prominent. In a time when a greatly increasing number of the young had been lost to all the love, security, and order that came from a stable family structure, they picked up the crumbs of sense stimulation wherever they could be found. And God, always dying, could for a brief spasm be brought to life in the orgasm.

Dorothy's reflections were not just the vaporings of old age. She herself had learned a lesson and seen a truth. How sad, she thought, it was that youth could not also see, that it should suffer as she had suffered. There was, though, one thing that lifted her spirits, she told Sister Peter Claver. "I can be happy over that jewel of faithfulness in the slum, St. Joseph's house. But sad indeed is the spiritual misery of Tivoli, which is set in the most beautiful surroundings."

Back when Dorothy had become a Catholic, there was much about the life of the Church that she did not understand. Nonetheless, she totally accepted the principle that in affirming the Church she was affirming Christ and that the work of her life was to know the mind of the Church and to conform to it insofar as she was humanly capable. For years she had been going to Mass, practically on a daily basis, and then suddenly those things to which she had become accustomed at Mass and which had consoled her, were changed. Once she wrote down some of the things that bothered her. "Everything said or written is challenged, new meanings and insights are sought and found in the counsels of poverty, chastity, and obedience; there is a new morality and a new theology. Old customs are being tossed aside as meaningless or offensive to others." Certain prayers of the Mass, "old and beautiful" had been dropped, and "the saints to whom the people addressed themselves in their loneliness and sorrow have been moved to the back of the church when they have not been moved down to the basement."

Worse, "now even the prayer, the Hail Mary, has been left out of the listing of Catholic prayers from the new Dutch catechism, so we are told in our diocesan paper." And this, she obviously thought, was going too far. "God was our father, so I could approach Him, daring to say 'Our Father.' But it was reading of Jesus Christ in the New Testament that made me want to put off the old man and put on Christ, as St. Paul said. And who had given me our Lord but the Virgin Mary? It was easy to pray to her, repetitious tho it might seem. Saying the rosary as I did so often, I felt that I was praying with the people of God, who held on to the physical act of the rosary as to a lifeline. What if there was repetition and the mind wandered? It could always be drawn back through remembering the mysteries, the joyful, the sorrowful, and the glorious. (I never think of the Visitation to Elizabeth without thinking of some pregnant woman who needs our prayers.) In fact, I never think of the rosary itself as a whole without thinking of Father [Louis] Farina's talks to married couples, the joyful mysteries reflecting not only the honeymoon aspect of human love but the joys of the marriage, then the sorrowful mysteries which are a part of every life and finally the glorious, achieved through fidelity and perseverance."

She had "said rosaries on picket lines and in prisons, in sickness and in health." As for "its repetitious aspect, I always think of Sister Madeleva's poem—God speaking to the soul who wonders whether He is not wearied by our repetitions: 'Doth it not irk me that upon the beach the tides monotonous run? Shall I not teach the sea some newer speech?' "

These, as she said, were her "gripes." And perhaps she was being querulous. The changes, she thought, were part of the pain that went with the beginning of a new life for the Church. "The turbulence in the Church today is a result of a newfound, newly realized emphasis on the liberty of Christ, and the realization too that we have scarcely begun to be Christian, to deserve the name Christian." And there was one change that she approved of wholly. "Let me say at once that to me the tremendous thing is the worship of God in the vernacular, in the speech of the people."

Nonetheless, "I am afraid I am a traditionalist," she wrote in the *Worker*. She did not like to see the Mass offered with a large coffee cup as a chalice. She supposed that she was "romantic too, since I loved the Arthur legend as a child and reverenced the Holy Grail and the search for it." She could not imagine that the Holy Grail was, after all, something in which people had had their morning coffee.

In the December, 1972 issue of the *Worker*, Dorothy's "On Pilgrimage" column took the form of a letter to Father Dan Berrigan. Part of it was a criticism of those religious orders "up and down on both sides of the Hudson River" that owned "thousands of acres of land, cultivated, landscaped, but not growing food for the hungry or founding villages for the families or schools for children." But the point that she seemed to want to make was a clear statement to her readers as well as to Father Berrigan on where she stood on some of the issues of the time that involved the traditional teaching of the Church. She had in mind "divorce, birth control, abortion" and she would accept no watering down of the teaching of the Church on any of these subjects. "The teaching of Christ, the Word, must be upheld. Held up though one that it is completely beyond us—out of our reach, impossible to follow. I believe Christ is our Truth and is with us always." And even if one fell short, the effort to fulfill Christ's truth should continue. "Forgiveness is always there. He is a kind and loving judge. And so are 99 percent of the priests in the confessional. The verdict is always 'not guilty,' even though our 'firm resolve with the help of His grace to confess our sins, do penance and amend our lives' may seem a hopeless proposition." And she did "believe that the priest is empowered to forgive sins."

One morning, when she was at First Street, she lay abed to make some notes. Someone brought in the mail, and in it was a letter from a person who had once been close to the Worker movement but who now seemed to despise the Church. The letter was "a stab in the heart—the bitterness, hatred of the Church poured out and to think that this venom has been piling in him—this poison he is spewing out, from some terrible wound. It is appalling when to me my faith, my feeling that the Church is Christ on earth, is my joy, my delight, my solace."

It is enough to say that during these last years of her life there were others, some of whom, she had felt, would do great things for the Worker movement and for the Faith but who had left. "Sick of the Church, sick of religion," she seemed to hear at every hand. "The Desert Fathers themselves complained of it and called it *acedia,* defined in the dictionary as spiritual sloth and indifference. And the remedy for that, according to spiritual writers is faithfulness to the means to overcome it, recitation of the Psalms each day, prayer and solitude, and by these means arriving or hoping to achieve a state of well-being."

Needless to say, she was upset over the exodus of priests and nuns from their religious life. Once, in the late 1960s after Charles Davis had announced his departure from the priesthood, Bob Hoyt of the *National Catholic Reporter,* telephoned Dorothy to get her reaction. "I told him I could not make any statement. How can one intrude into the personal lives of others, this most interior life of faith and love, of the heaven and hell that are within us?" Several days after she had given her statement to Hoyt, she wrote in her journal that "it gets so that when I see a priest without his collar staying with us I wonder whether he is on his way out of the Church."

When, as occasionally happened, she got a letter from priests or nuns who were tired of their lives, of their vocations, and suggested that they might find their real work at the New York house, she immediately discouraged the thought. "Dear Sister," she wrote. "I can only greet your letter with the greatest of sorrow. The older I get the more I feel that faithfulness and perseverance are the greatest of virtues—accepting the sense of failure we all must have in our work, in the work of others around us, since Christ was the world's greatest failure." Joining the Workers, she continued, would solve nothing. "I can only say that within a very short time after you do that you will be most disillusioned with us (whether we deserve it or not is not the question)," would then set about to find something else. "You will then wander from one to another, it is the usual pattern, and how little peace there is in this."

The calm center of Dorothy's life in these years was in her relationship with Della, and her greatest pleasure, it appears, was to withdraw from the affairs of the house and write her sister a letter. On April 5, 1972, Dorothy said that she was in hiding in her upstairs room at Tivoli. "Sometimes I stay upstairs for lunch and supper ... but always get down for Compline." It was a cold and windy day and she doubted that she would go to the First Street house. "O dear! ... Too many people, and I am up and down, feeling better really, but the sight of mail to do drags me down. But it's fun writing you. . .. I'm reading *War and Peace,* from beginning to end, first time since the old Huguenot, S.I. days."

That summer she spent much of her time at the Worker Staten Island beach cottage, and a letter from there to Della told of more reading. "Last night I read *A Once and Future King* by White in paperback. The best book I've read for a long time. It is the story of the youth of King Arthur. *The Crystal Cave* by Mary Stewart which I found so fascinating is about the youth of Merlin. In the White book Merlin is an old man, a tutor to Arthur. Both books have the charm of the *Idylls of the King*. . . . Do read both." How she loved to read! Dorothy exclaimed. Books "take me back to the joys of youth those afternoons in Lincoln Park when I felt Scott's *Lady of the Lake* come to life in that beautiful park. Remember?"

So much of the closeness of her association now with Della was in remembering. Winter came. "Snow, snow, snow!" Dorothy wrote. Did Della remember "the time that you and Forster and I walked to the Huguenot Station thru heavy snow—you were on your way that day to Florida." Della had been reading Floyd Dell's *Moon Calf*. Would Della please save it for her, Dorothy asked. "I'd like to read it again."

One morning at Tivoli she woke up "with gloom pressing down" on her. The reason for her cloudy state was that she had to give a talk at the Red Hook Methodist Church that evening.

She had said her morning prayers and then, to distract herself, she began to read Martin Luther King's *Strength to Love,* a collection of sermons. "They warmed my cold heart," she wrote. To distract herself further, she went on to note that when she was fourteen she had read Wesley's sermons, "which I picked up in a second-hand bookstore on North Clark Street in Chicago." Thinking of the reading she had done as a child she recalled other books. Her Aunt Jenny, her "only Catholic relative," had sent her "Sherlock Holmes and Rider Haggard." Then there had been the Frank Merriwell, Jack Karaway, and Tom Playfair books. "Tom Playfair went to a school run by priests and could speak Latin! I was in my first year in high school and had started to study Latin and was fascinated by the pursuit of wisdom."

Then there was Elsie Dinsmore, and "how in the following of principle (she would not perform on Sunday on the piano for her godless father's guests) she all but lost her life. Her passionately loved father had punished her by making her sit on a high piano stool on a hot humid day until she fainted and falling off struck her head. 'If the wound had been one inch nearer, I would have lost my darling,' the repentant and converted father cried.' "

Dorothy's account of Elsie's travail at the piano stool was a little loose, but essentially correct. What crossed Dorothy's mind as she wrote her Elsie account was how frequently "this fervent love between father and daughter" had been "criticized in discussions of children's books as approaching the incestuous." But, said Dorothy, she had found "nothing unhealthy" about it. "I can imagine children starved for love becoming obsessed by the desire for it. In our quiet reserved home we were sure of the solid affection of our mother and father, tho he was reserved and shy with us."

The inclusion of her father among the subjects discussed in her morning reverie on childhood reading may have been circumstantial, but Dorothy had a way of saying things quite matter-of-factly that had a more than passing significance—even when she was presumably saying these things to herself. However much John Day may have come up in family discussions, this was one of the first times that she had referred to him in her notes and journals. As memories of the past became increasingly a part of her daily nourishment, the admission of her father into them was significant.

She began to think more of her brother Donald, now also dead; of the rift between him and the family and how, as she thought about it, they might have somehow helped him more. After his "resignation" from the Chicago *Tribune,* just as World War II began, Donald had become a passionate partisan of the Finns in their war against Russia. In 1944, when it seemed that Russia would overrun Finland, the Finns advised him to go to Germany and so he, with his Russian wife, Edit, went to Berlin. There, in the latter months of the war, Donald became a part of the German war propaganda effort by making appeals over the Berlin radio for a do-or-die resistance to the Soviets. When the war ended, he and his wife were in Bavaria, and there he was arrested by the Americans on charges coming from his having made the Berlin broadcasts. Imprisoned for a brief period, he still remained suspect, and was prohibited from returning to America. He and his wife lived in Bad Tolz, southern Bavaria, until the latter part of 1953, at which time he was given permission to go to Finland.

Donald's letters home, usually written to Della, suggest an uncomprehending attitude on his part as to why he had almost become a pariah, not only to the government but to his own family. Apparently Della had written him an accusatory and reproachful letter, suggesting that anti-Semitism had been his sin. Responding, Donald said that the letter had shocked Edit and himself and that it had left him with a "sense of helplessness." He denied that he was or had been anti-Semitic. He denied that he had given comfort to the Germans. "We came to Germany as refugees and only after the Finns told me to leave as quickly as possible." In Germany "I spoke against Bolshevism, not against the Jews, and I shall always fight them [the Communists] as long as I live. The Nazis were bad enough, but the communists are worse."

In the 1960s Donald began to write to Dorothy and she, presumably, to him. His letters were affectionate and usually contained folk remedies for Dorothy's rheumatism and other ailments. His last letter to Dorothy was on August 3, 1966. He was still full of forebodings about communism: "I shudder at the thought of what our dark future will bring." He closed his letter affectionately: "Edit and I send our warm love to you with sincere wishes for health for yourself and success for your work." Then he added a postscript: "I just read this letter to Edit, and she reminded me to ask God's blessing on you and yours and to tell you that neither of us have ever forgotten the help you gave us when we lived in real poverty in Bad Tolz. Thanks again, Dearest." Donald died of a heart attack on September 30.

Although the past loomed larger in her thoughts, she had by no means withdrawn from the world around her. There were even pleasant moments—traveling, of course. A friend, having been somewhat prodded by her into the gesture, gave her a Datsun, and she drove, with some degree of imprecision, to the towns around Tivoli and sometimes to Ossining to see Della. Back in Tivoli after one visit, she said that she had arrived on schedule. The visit had been restful, Dorothy said, and that she always felt like "writing you a real note of gratitude for the way you are always trying to take care of me when I come up. I go away refreshed, rested, *nourished*. A relief to be away from the youth group and health foods. I do love a healthy soup, a comforting meal."

In October, 1973, Dorothy wrote to Sister Peter Claver to tell her that Forster was "very sick" and in the hospital. For several years Forster had been undergoing operations for an intestinal cancer—excisions and resections. "I visit [him] every few days," Dorothy said. "He is so glad to see me!" Several weeks later she wrote to Father Dan Berrigan that her "dear daughter's father has had 6 operations . . . and is feeling low. He likes to see me hobble in and out with a cane. I am so happy he hangs on to me." But his appreciation for her presence was "only when he is sick."

One night when she was at the hospital there were several people in the room that she and Forster had known back in the 1920s. In the course of the conversation, one turned to Dorothy and remarked that it was too bad that she had not married Eugene O'Neill. Later, Dorothy passed the comment on to friends, acting as if this observation had been the height of ridiculousness. But maybe it pleased her, too.

Then, from Della, in the form of a note, she got another reference to those days. Della was "on the way to doctor with F. [Franklin] again, so no time for a real letter." But she had seen on television a "life of Hart Crane . . . and all our old friends . . . last night. Sue Jenkins—Malcolm, Peggy, etc. Very interesting."

But all was not reminiscing in this interchange of letters between Dorothy and Della. In her letter of June 16, 1973, to Della, Dorothy said that she was going to be at Tivoli the first week of July while "Ruth Collins, our real estate agent (manager of our property) is looking for an old hotel in our neighborhood for old women put out of hospitals to actually live in the streets." She added that she had "been asked by the diocese to do this, and that is what is filling my summer. We already have $35,000 toward it, given for that purpose."

So a search had begun for a new women's house and sometime in the process the Trappist community of Rochester, New York, gave $100,000 toward the project. As a result of this gift, and some others too, the Workers acquired in late 1973 an old music school on Third Street, a block away from the First Street Saint Joseph House. Dorothy told of the acquisition in the March-April, 1974, *Worker*. The house had been bought and paid for, but many changes would have to be made in the place and that would take much time. In the meanwhile, "What shall we name it?" She thought it should be called Maryhouse, because "the flesh of Jesus is the flesh of Mary." How great the dignity of woman, how large a part she has played in the redemption of the world."

It was, however, not until the spring of 1975 that contracts were let for the remodeling of the structure and not until a year later that it was ready for general use.

The year 1975 must certainly have registered with Dorothy the realization that her pilgrimage was in its closing days. People were dying with whom she had for years had an association. Bill Gauchat, who back in the 1930s had begun the Cleveland house and who, with his wife, Dorothy, had at last been able to build a hospital-home for children who had been battered or born with gross birth defects, died after a long struggle with cancer. Dorothy, nearly overcome with her own frailty, insisted on going to the funeral. Little Julia Porcelli, who back in the 1930s had worked with Peter Maurin at the Harlem house, died that year, leaving her husband, Philip Moran, and their children. Then Karl Stern, ill and grief-oppressed over the loss of his son and wife, died; as did Arthur Sheehan, "one of our editors," Dorothy wrote in the *Worker*, "the only one of us who had the diligence and the perseverance to research and write the biography of Peter Maurin, our founder."

Perhaps it was as a gesture to a meaningful part of her past that led her in July, 1976, to make one last retreat with Father Hugo in Pittsburgh. As she left the church after the Mass that completed the retreat, she paused to say goodbye to Father Hugo, and then asked him to give the homily at her funeral.

After the retreat, she went back to Tivoli to prepare herself for a major ordeal. She was to give one of the principal talks at the Catholic Eucharistic Congress to be held in Philadelphia in August. The prospect so upset her that she was in a depression for days before the time that she was to speak. She was filled with dread, she told a friend. It was as if she were confronted with a black pit with no way around it.

Nonetheless, she was at Philadelphia on the afternoon of August 6, a city then filled with alarms over "Legionnaire's disease." Seventy-nine years old, this would be her last major speaking appearance, and most of the people at the Congress sensed this. Her looks seemed to confirm what they felt. She was very frail. Her eyes, with their unusual slant, were large and luminous in a face where pale, translucent skin clung to the outlines of the bone structure beneath it. Her white hair was, as usual, braided and wound around her head.

She was supposed to speak on "Women in the Church," but, characteristically, she ignored the subject and dwelled on those things that were on her mind. She spoke of the love of God and of the necessity of taking that love into all creation. She told of her own experience of the awakening of that love. "My conversion began ... at a time when the material world began to speak in my heart of the love of God." It had been as Saint Augustine had written, "What is it that I love when I love Thee?" And he had answered his question by listing all of the beauties of creation that delighted his senses. That had been her experience, she said.

She talked of the Church, saying that her love and gratitude to it had increased with the years. "She taught me the crowning love of the life of the Spirit." And then, referring to the previous day's ceremonies at the Congress which had honored the military, she said that the Church had also taught her that "before we bring our gifts of service, or gratitude, to the altar—if your brother have anything against us, we must hesitate to approach the altar to receive the Eucharist. " 'Unless you do penance, you shall all perish,' " she quoted.

She reminded her audience that it was August 6, the day on which the atomic bomb had been dropped on Hiroshima. So great had become the contempt for life in the twentieth century that this holocaust was only one of many. After World War I, itself a holocaust, there were the Armenians, "all but forgotten now, and the holocaust of the Jews, God's chosen people. When He came to earth as Man, He chose them. And He told us, all men are brothers, and that it was His will that all men be saved, Japanese, Jew, Armenian." God "gave us life, and the Eucharist to sustain our life. But we have given the world instruments of death of inconceivable magnitude."

The talk was short but she had made her plea for peace. Worn out, she returned to Tivoli. On Labor Day night, at the First Street house, she had a heart attack. Eileen Egan says that the next day Dorothy was supposed to go to the wedding of her godchild, Dorothy Corbin, and that she, Eileen, and Dr. Marion Moses had argued that night, after the traditional Friday night house meeting, that she should not go to Tivoli the next day. Dorothy replied: "She is my godchild. I've got to be at her wedding." But during the night she began to have trouble breathing, and Dr. Moses was called back and Dorothy was taken to Beth Israel Hospital.

The result of the attack was that more of her strength was taken and, increasingly, her time was spent in bed. By the following May she was still unable to resume anything like a normal life. She wrote to a friend that she could only write one or two letters a day, and then it had to be "early in the morning after reading my Psalms while I still have the strength God has given me thru good sleep. I cannot tell you the state of nervous exhaustion I've been thru. It's been like a constant trembling of my nerves, a need for solitude and no responsibility, and I have been taking it for so long, bearing so much, I feel like an utter failure." But, she said, she was "beginning to recover from the miserable state of depression."

"Utter failure" though she may have felt herself to be, these were the years when honors came pouring in on her. Some she accepted; some she did not. And whether she did or did not seemed to depend on her mood. Most, she turned down, probably because the honoring institution wanted her to be present for the ceremony and she was just too weary to travel, to sit through the speeches, and to meet people. One honor no doubt delighted her. On her eightieth birthday, a black limousine drove up in front of the First Street house and Cardinal Terence Cooke got out to give personally to Dorothy a birthday greeting from Pope Paul.

At Marquette University, the occasion was recognized with a two-day recognition of her life and work, which began with a Mass in Marquette's Gesu Church. A number of people with historic ties with the Worker movement came: Nina Polcyn Moore, Florence Wienfurter, Marge Hughes, and Sister Peter Claver. But it was Stanley Vishnewski, showing his slides of Dorothy's life and telling funny stories about how difficult it was to live in a house with a saint, that gave the occasion a leaven of warmth and lightness.

When Stanley referred to Dorothy as a saint, he was not doing it out of an affected piety. He had been with the Worker for over forty years and if anyone had had the opportunity to take the full measure of Dorothy's spirit it was he. Behind his humor, his quips and funny stories, Vishnewski was a person whose soul craved an answer. Why?—the whole thing? One morning he stood in the dining room of the house at Tivoli and made his statement. If Dorothy Day's whole life had been a charade, if what she had suffered for—and he knew something of what she had had to suffer—if it had all been false, a drama of escapism, then life was not worth living for anyone. "There is no hope for any of us."

The press, of course, was eager to canonize Dorothy but she would have none of it. She knew what kind of a saint the reporters had in mind—the woman who fed the poor and stood up to comic figures like church cardinals, judges, and city officials. But Dorothy would have none of it. The object of her life had not been something that would make a story suitable for a television drama. Her passion had been for God.

After 1976 Dorothy virtually withdrew from the affairs of the world of the Worker movement. Her lot, as she knew, was to await death. Content to spend as much time as she could in the company of her daughter and grandchildren, she remained in her room at Maryhouse, coming downstairs only for the evening Mass that was said at the house. In her room, which overlooked Third Street, she could look out onto the dismal prospect of a narrow street, shadowed by five-story buildings, shoulder to shoulder, whose unkempt and desolate appearance suggested that they, like the people who passed before them, felt that their existence mattered not at all. In front of these buildings, parked cars at the curbs were jammed against one another. One structure, ugly with shattered windows and an aspect of grotesque garishness, was fronted by motorcycles —powerful, brutish machines with signs and symbols that proclaimed their owners' defiance of civilized norms. The building was the home of the Hell's Angels, a motorcycle gang about whose doings fearful stories were told.

It was in this part of New York that Dorothy had spent a half-century of her life, where just blocks away she had lived in 1917 as the acting editor of the *Masses* and where in that cold winter of 1918 she had whiled away the nights with Eugene O'Neill and the young radicals and artists of the Village. A few blocks to the west and south was New York's Lower East Side, the home of the Jews. She had never left them. Mott Street was two blocks away, the street of the Italians. She remembered sitting on the front steps of the Mott Street house, watching them celebrate the feast of San Gennaro. Perhaps she remembered that night soon after the war had begun, the cool clear air and the half moon shining brightly over Mott Street.

In this time, when she was confined to her room, she wrote of the things that impressed themselves on her mind and they were published in the *Catholic Worker.* Many of her thoughts were of the past, of her father and mother, and of the closeness of the family when they had lived in Chicago. On Saturday afternoons she listened to the opera. She still preferred Wagner, "pagan though he is." But she also liked Verdi and Puccini.

In the October-November *Worker* of 1978, she said that on Sunday, October 22, she had "watched the inauguration of Karol Cardinal Wojtyla of Poland, the 264th Pope.... I sat at the TV set from the early hours until it was time for our Sunday Mass here at Maryhouse." One morning, some months later, Frank Donovan, "that jewel of faithfulness," brought her a copy of *Granma,* a Cuban newspaper. With obvious pleasure she noted that it featured "in a box on the front page, the message of Pope John Paul II to Fidel Castro, blessing Cuba, a communist country as the Pope flew over Cuba on his way back to Rome from Mexico." She thought of the new pope as had St. Catherine of Siena, who "used to write of the Holy Father, calling him 'Our dear sweet Christ on earth.'"

In some ways, Dorothy's "On Pilgrimage" columns became a litany of death. In the May 1980 *Worker* she wrote of Della's death. It was not an anguished farewell. She recalled the happy times that she and her sister had had together and recalled, too, their differences. Della had been a convinced disciple of Margaret Sanger on the issue of birth control and, years later, she would "exhort me ... not to urge, as a Catholic, Tamar, my daughter, to have so many children." So, wrote Dorothy, "I got up firmly and walked out of the house, whereupon she ran after me weeping, saying 'Don't leave me, don't leave me. We just won't talk about it again.'"

After Della it was Stanley. He died of a heart attack at Maryhouse on November 14. It was said that his last words were, "it must have been that Catholic Worker soup I had." But Dorothy was, herself, so close to the edge of eternity that she could write little about Stanley. Robert Ellsberg, Daniel Ellsberg's son, a talented young man who had been helping out at Maryhouse, wrote Stanley's story for the *National Catholic Reporter.*

In the summer of 1980, Sister Peter Claver wrote to Frank Donovan, to ask if she and Father Hugo might visit Dorothy. Donovan discouraged it, saying that Dorothy "hasn't felt up to seeing anyone for several weeks. Her cardiac reserve (as the doctors put it) is very slight, and any extra exertion or excitement, even brief visits, uses it up rapidly and leaves her drained and feeling ill for days afterward."

Sister Peter Claver was not a person to be put off when her mind was set on something, and on November 8, Dorothy's eighty-third birthday, she set out from Philadelphia for Maryhouse. There, Donovan greeted her cordially but told her that Dorothy had said that morning that she did not want to see anyone, that she would take the telephone off the hook, listen to the opera that afternoon, and try to get downstairs that evening for Mass. But, said Donovan, he would tell Dorothy that Sister was there. Dorothy could make the decision about seeing her.

Of course Dorothy would see her, so Sister went up the stairs to Dorothy's room. She "was sitting in the dark corner" looking "thin and frail but her welcome was warm and loving; her face radiated her familiar smile." For a few moments they reminisced about the retreat that Dorothy had taken with Father Hugo back in the days of World War II. Pointing to some flowers on the table, Dorothy said that she was still sowing. Then "holding hands, we said the Our Father together; we embraced one another. I kissed her and made the Sign of the Cross on her forehead."

Dorothy died on November 29, just as night began to soften the harshness of the poverty and ugliness of Third Street. Her daughter, Tamar, was in the room with her. There was no struggle. The last of the energy that sustained her life had been used.

The funeral was on December 2 at the Nativity Catholic Church, a half block away from Maryhouse. An hour before the service, scheduled for eleven o'clock in the morning, people began to assemble in the street. Some were curious onlookers, the hollow-eyed and stumbling people who roam the streets of lower New York, but others were drawn there by some sense of the propriety of paying their last respects to the woman who had clothed and fed them. There were American Indians, Mexican workers, blacks, and Puerto Ricans. There were people in eccentric dress, apostles of causes who had felt a great power and truth in Dorothy's life. And there were reporters and television cameracrews, moving around in the crowd, looking for people who had known Dorothy and asking them to say something about her, hoping that it would be the kind of thing that would be dramatic in print. But most who came were friends Dorothy had made over the years.

At the appointed time, a procession of these friends and fellow Workers came down the sidewalk. At the head of it Dorothy's grandchildren carried the pine box that held her body. Tamar, Forster, and her brother John followed. At the church door, Cardinal Terence Cooke met the body to bless it. As the procession stopped for this rite, a demented person pushed his way through the crowd and bending low over the coffin peered at it intently. No one interfered, because, as even the funeral directors understood it was in such as this man that Dorothy had seen the face of God.

After the funeral Mass, her body was taken to Richmond, Staten Island, and buried in a cemetery that was only a short distance from the scene of her conversion.

What was her legacy? It was nothing material, for the New York archdiocese felt it appropriate to pay for the opening of her grave. Her legacy was vision—a vision of ending time with its evil nightmares by bringing Christ back on Earth.

Index

DATE DUE

GAYLORD   #3522PI   Printed in USA